REBECCA WEST: A CELEBRATION

REBECCA WEST: A CELEBRATION

Selected from her writings
by her publishers
with her help

CRITICAL INTRODUCTION
BY
SAMUEL HYNES

THE VIKING PRESS · NEW YORK

First published in 1977 by The Viking Press
625 Madison Avenue, New York, N.Y. 10022

Published simultaneously in Canada by
Penguin Books Canada Limited

Library of Congress Cataloging in Publication Data

West, Rebecca, pseud.
  Rebecca West: a celebration

  Bibliography: p.
  Includes index.
  I. Title.

PR6045.E8A6   1976   828'.9'1209   76–21281

ISBN 0–670–59061–4

ACKNOWLEDGMENT is made to Yale University Press for material from *The Court and The Castle* by Rebecca West © 1957 by Yale University Press, Inc.

"A Grave and Reverend Book" originally appeared in *Harper's Magazine*. "Parthenope," "Mr. Setty and Mr. Hume," and "Greenhouse With Cyclamens" (under the title of "Extraordinary Exiles") originally appeared in *The New Yorker*. "The Salt of the Earth" originally appeared in *The Woman's Home Companion*. Portions of *Black Lamb and Grey Falcon* originally appeared in the *Atlantic Monthly*. Portions of *The Meaning of Treason* and *The New Meaning of Treason* originally appeared in *The New Yorker, Esquire,* and *Harper's Magazine*. Other acknowledgments of sources appear in the Bibliography, pp. 761–766.

Printed in the United States of America
Set in Linotype Juliana

Contents

CONTENTS

IV. LITERARY CRITICISM

V. LATER FICTION

VI. HISTORY AND TRAVEL

CONTENTS

APPENDIX

Introduction

IN COMMUNION WITH REALITY

by Samuel Hynes

"There have as yet been very few women thinkers and artists," Rebecca West wrote in 1931; "that is to say, women who have not adopted masculine values as the basis of their work." She could think of only six: Madame de la Fayette, Madame de Sévigné, Jane Austen, Colette, Willa Cather, Virginia Woolf. Not many women have appeared in the years since then that one would want to add to Dame Rebecca's list, for the terms she set are severe: to be both a thinker and an artist, and to escape the limitations and distortions that follow when a gifted woman adapts her talents to the world of men.

The point that Dame Rebecca was making was not that woman artists should be explicitly and exclusively feminine, but rather that they should be free to realize their gifts without considering the roles that social definitions of gender impose. Thus in an essay on Clemence Dane she distinguished between a novelist who is female, and a woman novelist, of which she took Miss Dane to be an example—

which is to say that she has not allowed herself to be merely a mirror in which to reflect life; before treating her material she has treated herself. She has created herself in the form in which the man-governed modern world, so far as it can be ascertained from its art, thinks woman ought to be created. In other words, she moulds herself in the likeness of the heroine of standard fiction.

(This was written in 1928, before Germaine Greer was born.) For Dame Rebecca, the ideal creative condition for a woman is to be beyond roles—to be a mirror of reality itself. Virginia Woolf was saying much the same thing, at the same time, in A Room of One's Own, when she described the "androgynous mind," and offered as a definition that "it is resonant and porous; that it transmits emotion without impediment; that it is naturally creative, incandescent and undivided."

ix

Whether one takes Dame Rebecca's definition or Virgina Woolf's one must conclude that the greatest living example of a woman who has achieved that state, who has been both a thinker and an artist, and who has managed over some sixty years to express a spacious sense of reality, is Rebecca West. Indeed, one might propose that her achievement is not to be located in this book or in that one, but in the whole—that her books combine to make one created work of art, the mind of Rebecca West. There is support for this view in the fact that the name by which she is known is itself a persona taken from a work of art. When a writer chooses another name for his writing self, he is doing more than inventing a pseudonym: he is naming, and in a sense creating, his imaginative identity. Hence George Orwell—a commonplace Christian name and an English river—together name the plain-speaking Englishman that Eric Blair chose to be in his work. And Rebecca West is another such: the brilliant and rebellious Ibsen heroine is chosen to replace Cicily Fairfield (a name that in itself seems almost too good an example of English gentility). To choose that name was to claim the ideas and the radical posture of Ibsen, and particularly his ideas about women, as one's own public identity. The choice suggests an exceptional woman, willing her life to be an example of woman's situation.

One must feel some discomfort in the fact that an appreciation of so considerable a talent as Dame Rebecca's should start, inevitably, with the problems arising from her sex. In the case of some other woman writers this might be avoidable; but Dame Rebecca has made the subject a continuing theme of her work and of her life. There is scarcely a book of hers that does not have in it a feminist character (often thrust in anyhow, simply to make a speech against corsets), or a feminist idea. And her own career as a successful professional writer has demonstrated both the problem of being a woman artist, and the solution to it.

In the years before the First World War, when Rebecca West was a young girl in London, making a place in journalism, she was an active Suffragist, and her early work shows the feminist spirit of that time very clearly. Her first book, *Henry James* (1916), is at its best when it deals with James' female characters: Daisy Miller, Claire de Cintré, Isabel Archer, Nanda Brookenham: all those cherished Jamesian sensibilities are treated severely, irreverently, and wittily. James had refused, she concludes, "to dramatize in his imagination anything concerning women save their failures and successes as sexual beings." One is at first astonished that James, of all writers, should be convicted of being just another insensitive male, as though he were Hemingway or Norman Mailer, but the case is well and cleverly made. It is surely the first book that could be called feminist literary criticism.

Dame Rebecca's second book, the delicate and beautiful *The Return of the Soldier* (1918), is feminist in another way. It is a rare kind of book, a woman's war novel, in which the madness and destruction of man's war are refracted in the crystal of a woman's enclosed, private life. From it emerges the antithesis that continues throughout Dame Rebecca's work, between the will-to-die, which is male and creates poverty, war, and the ruin of civilizations, and the will-to-live, which is female, and bears and nourishes. *The Return of the Soldier* is a small masterpiece; but it is more nearly a "woman's novel," in the sense that *Pointed Roofs* and *Mrs Dalloway* are woman's novels, than anything else Dame Rebecca wrote, and one can understand why she chose not to continue in this manner, after such a bright beginning. For it comes too close to being *merely* a woman's novel, and so confirming the notions about women that exist in a man-governed modern world. Perhaps one might say that, though it was feminist, it was not androgynous enough.

Those first two books anticipate the later work in other ways than by their feminism: the critical book is witty, stylish, and full of self-assurance and high spirits; the novel holds implicit in it Dame Rebecca's mature sense of the world and human values. The world of the novel is a difficult one for sensitive persons to survive in: it is full of pain and suffering, frustration and betrayal, it will not adapt itself to human needs. In that world the greatest human value is realism— to know things as they are. At the end of the novel the heroine thinks:

There is a draught that we must drink or not be fully human . . . I knew that one must know the truth. I knew quite well that when one is adult one must raise to one's lips the wine of the truth, heedless that it is not sweet like milk but draws the mouth with its strength, and celebrate communion with reality, or else walk forever queer and small like a dwarf.

Communion with reality is a large ambition, and one that must lead a woman away from her private world, to politics and art and history, to law and religion and crime. It is the course that Dame Rebecca has followed, extending and deepening her account of reality until few modern writers can match her range, or her steady moral seriousness.

In the books of the following decade or so, one can see Dame Rebecca reaching out toward larger subjects. In the 1920s there were two novels, both now forgotten: *The Judge* (1922), a long, melo-dramatic story of sex, guilt, and power, interesting for the autobio-graphical beginning in Edinburgh, and for remarks about the nature of man-woman relations, but imaginatively lifeless; and *Harriet Hume* (1929), subtitled "A London Fantasy," written, Dame Rebecca said, to find out why she loved London. Neither melodrama nor fantasy was the right form for Dame Rebecca's mind to expand in, and these are her least successful novels.

Two critical books of the same period—*The Strange Necessity* (1928) and *Ending in Earnest* (1931)—are collections of essays and reviews that indicate the growth of Dame Rebecca's reputation as a journalist. Each book contains one extended essay, and both of these are important to an account of the development of her thought. In *The Strange Necessity* the title essay addresses questions that are to recur in her work, questions as central to her thought as questions of gender: "Why does art matter?" she asks, "And why does it matter so much? What is this strange necessity?" The answer derives from her view of man as divided between the will to live and the will to die: art is necessary because it sustains life.

The essay is interesting for the strength and subtlety of its argu-ment, but it is perhaps most interesting for the shape that the argu-ment takes. It begins like an essay by Virginia Woolf, mixing an account of a stroll in the city with thoughts about literature, making it all seem informal and easy, and consciously charming, and very womanly. But it moves on to a level of intellectual toughness and knowledge where Virginia Woolf could never have followed, drawing upon psychology and physiology, and making skilful use of Pavlov's *Conditioned Reflexes*. It is as though Dame Rebecca were acting out her liberation from the stereotypes of her sex, and showing us how a free mind might play upon ideas.

Her conviction of the moral necessity of art also underlies Dame Rebecca's elegiac essay on D. H. Lawrence in *Ending in Earnest*. It is not surprising that she should admire Lawrence, for he was a writer much like herself—a moralist, a preacher against death, an artist who could not confine his imagination within conventional literary forms. "One will rejoice," she wrote, "that our age produced one artist who had the earnestness of the patristic writers, who like them could know no peace till he had discovered what made men lust after death." She might have been writing about herself.

By 1930, Dame Rebecca's version of reality was virtually complete in its broad outlines. Her world was a dualist world, in which good and evil, life and death battle eternally, an uncertain world, where man wanders unsupported and unknowing. His enemy is within him: the will-to-die that hates life, the need to be cruel and to suffer. His hope is in his capacity for knowledge, for communion with reality, and for the imperishable order of art. Out of art, reason, and tradition man might construct the Just City; but that goal is obstructed by the spirit that denies.

That understanding of the world is clear, but it had not yet found imaginative expression. The literary forms Dame Rebecca worked in were still those of the woman novelist—the novel and the literary essay; and in the novel she was still hunting for a personal voice. One has no sense of increasing skill and assurance in the fiction she wrote during the 1930s, neither in the stories of *The Harsh Voice* (1935) nor in the novel *The Thinking Reed* (1936). The two books are different in manner from each other, and from the earlier fiction, and the differences suggest uncertainty, and nervous experiment. One might well have concluded in 1936 that Dame Rebecca was not a novelist and would never be one.

But three years earlier she had taken a step that was to free her from restraining literary convention: she had agreed to write a short life of Saint Augustine. The assignment was an odd one for a literary journalist to take on, but it was a wise one: it led Dame Rebecca to history, religion and psychology and it engaged her mind with a great mind and a body of thought that touched her own deeply, and shaped her thinking for the rest of her career.

Dame Rebecca's Augustine is an archetype of modern man, both in his psychological nature and in his political situation. Psychologically he is introspective and life-denying, disgusted by physical existence— and especially by sex—guilty, and convinced of the need to expiate his guilt by suffering. Politically, he is civilized man, possessed of a tradition and a culture but uncertain of its present value and threatened by anti-culture, the barbarian at the gate. His importance is that he made himself an archetype by imposing his nature upon the doctrine of the Church, and thus creating Western man in his own image; he gave his authority to man's desire for guilt and punishment, for cruelty and suffering. For Dame Rebecca, we are all the heirs of

xiii

Augustine's problems: "Every phrase I read of his," she later wrote, "sounds in my ears like the sentence of my doom and the doom of my age."

One aspect of that doom has to do with art. Augustine's true vocation, in Dame Rebecca's view, was for imaginative writing; he denied that vocation, and, though he made an art of his denial in the *Confessions*, he bequeathed to posterity a complex of life-denying and art-denying ideas that still determine the content of our literature and our attitudes toward it. Dame Rebecca seizes this opportunity for further speculations on the psychology of art, and on art's friends and enemies. The argument follows closely from "The Strange Necessity," and one can see Dame Rebecca extending her command of reality by taking her theory and fleshing it with details drawn from the history of religion. The process is like that of a landscape painter, who has his scene sketched, and is now filling the canvas, building and adding details, but not altering the form. By writing the life of Augustine, in the terms she had chosen, Dame Rebecca had clarified and particularized her vision. She was ready to write her masterpiece.

And what an odd masterpiece *Black Lamb and Grey Falcon* is! Superficially it is a travel book about a trip to the Balkans in 1937. But it includes so much more, is at once so comprehensive and so personal, that it has no genre, unless one invents one, calling it an epic testament, and placing it with the other great literary oddities of that odd genre—with Robert Burton's *Anatomy of Melancholy*, T. E. Lawrence's *Seven Pillars of Wisdom*, James Agee's *Let Us Now Praise Famous Men*. It is a narrative of a journey, and a long meditation on the patterns of Western history; it is a book of Balkan portraits, and a theory of the relations between East and West in Europe; and it is a book about its own time, a moving response to the contemporary political, moral and spiritual condition of Europe. Dame Rebecca's intention, she wrote, was "to put on paper what a typical Englishwoman felt and thought in the late nineteen-thirties when, already convinced of the inevitability of the second Anglo-German war, she had been able to follow the dark waters of that event back to its source."

The sources are in fact many: the Roman Empire and its decline, Augustine, Napoleon, and behind them all man's divided nature, living and creative, but in love with cruelty and death. It is a dark book for a dark time. The barbarians are at the gate again, and in the past—as the book shows us—barbarism has triumphed, because men have willed it so. "If human beings were to continue to be what they are," Dame Rebecca sombrely concludes, "to act as they have acted in the phases of history covered by this book, then it would be good for all of us to die." But she is not without hope, and the principal source of hope, as in her earlier work, is in art: "Art gives us hope that history may change its spots and man become honourable."

The book itself is that—a major example of the art that gives us hope. In its pages are combined all the gifts that earlier Dame Rebecca had distributed among many books: the vivid characterizations and descriptions; the powerful analyses of history and politics; the wit; the passages of meditative and lyric beauty. In "The Strange Necessity" Dame Rebecca quoted approvingly a remark by George Santayana that one might start with any work of art or natural object and infer the whole universe; *Black Lamb and Grey Falcon* starts with a visit to a minor Balkan state and ends by giving order and meaning to past and present, to religion, art, morals and politics, to the people of the Balkans and their troubled land. It is an extraordinary achievement.

The historical importance of *Black Lamb* is, or should be, very great, for it is a supreme effort, by a mind at the height of its powers, to understand the catastrophe of the Second World War as it came on; it stands at the end of the 1930s like a massive baroque cenotaph. The importance for Dame Rebecca is also great and obvious: in this one book she cast aside entirely the restrictions of "woman writer" and revealed the true range of her mind. It is, in its majestic scale, an answer to the notion that the proper scale of a woman's imagination should be a "little bit (two inches wide) of Ivory."

Rebecca West's greatest period of creativity began with *Black Lamb*, and one can see now how the books that follow depend on it and derive from it. The two books of trials, *The Meaning of Treason* (1949) and *A Train of Powder* (1955), relate to *Black Lamb* in two ways: they extend Dame Rebecca's "world" into the realm of law, and they complete her meditation on the meaning of modern history. Law must obviously be a crucial concept to one who sees the world divided between civilization and barbarism, for law is the wall that men build against disorder. Treason is a wilful breaching of that wall, and fascism is a denial that a wall can exist, and so of course Dame Rebecca would be fascinated by the case of Lord Haw-Haw, and the judgement at Nuremberg, and would see those trials as political tragedies. Her accounts of the trials are, in a sense, journalism, but they are journalism raised to a high level of art and thought, with the richness of understanding that makes *Black Lamb* a great book. Character and setting are created with extraordinary vividness, action and dialogue are as convincing as in a novel. Yet they are scrupulously factual, and because they are factual (as *Black Lamb* also is), they perform an important moral function.

Dame Rebecca writes: it is the presentation of the facts that matters:

The facts that, put together, are the face of the age . . . for if people do not have the face of the age set clear before them they begin to imagine it; and fantasy, if it is not disciplined by the intellect and kept in faith with reality by the instinct of art, dwells among the wishes and fears of childhood, and so sees life either as simply answering any prayer or as endlessly emitting nightmare monsters from a womb-like cave.

The face of the age in these cases is the face of a traitor, a Nazi, a murderer, a lynch-mob. But one must confront that face for the sake of reality, and once more it is art that comes to our aid. Dame Rebecca's art takes us beyond the facts, to the questions they raise: what in men leads them to betray their fellows? What are the foundations of stability and chaos in human societies? What defences can men build against the strain of evil in themselves? These are moral questions, and those three "factual" books—*Black Lamb* and the two books of trials—are moral books; but they are also artful and imaginative. Here Dame Rebecca has found her true form, in which art and fact meet, and keep faith with reality.

Of Dame Rebecca's three most recent books, two are novels, one an ambitious critical study. *The Fountain Overflows* (1957) is about the condition of childhood, as *Black Lamb* is about the condition of Serbs and Croats—that is, childhood is a metaphor for a view of the world. The particular childhood here is very like Dame Rebecca's own, and the book has considerable biographical interest. But as a novel it is flawed by the insistent, intruding intelligence of the author, turning recollection into ideas about music or about childhood itself, or, sometimes, dealing with fictional parents and siblings in what seems a personal, resentful way. It is, in short, not fully realized as fiction, and, though one reads it with pleasure at the author's bright company, it will not quite do as a novel.

The Fountain Overflows seems, in retrospect, a regression, back from the large authority of the previous studies to the restraints of the earlier fiction. The book that followed it, *The Court and the*

Castle, recovers that authority. It is her most considerable work of criticism, a brilliant, expansive, stimulating, eccentric book. One can get at its curious nature best, perhaps, by glossing the subtitle: "A Study of the Inter-actions of Political and Religious Ideas in Imaginative Literature."* One knows, of course, that Dame Rebecca began her journalistic career as a political writer, and that she has always had an acute political sense; that quality is everywhere evident in her best books. It is also apparent that her sense of the nature of man and his world is a religious one. But how do these sets of ideas interact? To a religious mind, man's moral state is a constant, but political ideologies are transient; politics therefore ought to follow from religion, and to take pragmatic rather than ideological forms. In Dame Rebecca's case this certainly seems to be true. Her religion, as it appears in her books, is mainly a concern with the existence of evil; given the reality of evil, ideas about the uses of power and about the structures of society follow, but they do not coalesce in a political system. She has, one might say, political wisdom but not a political ideology. Given the persistence of evil, it is appropriate that her study of the interactions of political and religious ideas should begin with Augustine and end with Kafka; for they share an eternal problem.

It is difficult to define in a word the peculiar note of authority that Rebecca West's criticism has, but perhaps the best term is episcopal: she writes like a fourth-century African bishop, praising the righteous, condemning heretics, explaining doctrine, confident always of the rightness of her judgements and of their firm moral bases. She is easy with terms like Manichaean and Pelagian, and can use them as metaphors for literary situations; and the language is significant, for in her world heresies do exist, and they matter. A woman admirer of Dame Rebecca once described her, wryly, as a "female Patriarch," and that phrase does indeed describe her critical posture.

The Birds Fall Down (1966) is her last novel, and her finest; indeed it is excellent enough to bear comparison with the great political novels, with *The Possessed* and *Under Western Eyes.* Like those novels, it is concerned with the international political spasm that began in nineteenth-century Russia and spread across Europe; or, rather, it is concerned with the victims of that spasm. For there is not much political theory in the novel, only the deeply imagined thoughts

*The British subtitle. The American, which preceded it, was "Some Treatments of a Recurrent Theme."

and actions of persons caught in the stress of political motives: a young girl, an old Russian count, an anarchist, a double agent. It is Dame Rebecca's most completely imagined novel, perhaps because it is the one that is farthest from the particulars of her own experience. It alone should assure her of a place in the history of English fiction.

In *Black Lamb* Dame Rebecca records—or perhaps invents—an interview with a girl in Vienna, a university student who has come seeking material for a thesis on Dame Rebecca's works. The girl is lumpishly, Germanically pedantic, and Dame Rebecca winces at the prospect of becoming her dissertation:

I explained that I was a writer wholly unsuitable for her purpose . . . that I had never used my writing to make a continuous disclosure of my own personality to others, but to discover for my own edification what I knew about various subjects which I found to be important to me. . . .

Her work, she concludes, "could not fuse to make a picture of a writer, since the interstices were too wide."

This is an acute observation, and it remains true: Dame Rebecca's work has not fused in the minds of critics, and she has no secure literary status—the interstices between her books, between *Black Lamb* and *The Return of the Soldier*, between *The Meaning of Treason* and *Saint Augustine*, are too wide; she is too difficult to define. Surprisingly, she does not seem even to have gained a following among the partisans of women's liberation, though one would think that in the True Church of Women she well deserves a Lady Chapel. Perhaps she would have fared better if she had continued as she began, as a novelist who also wrote essays. *The Return of the Soldier, Harriet Hume*, and *Letter to a Grandfather* prove that she could do the Virginia Woolf manner well enough to win a place among woman novelists of sensibility. But what she told the Viennese girl is obviously true: she wrote for another reason, to discover what she knew. In the end it is the inquiring mind that we know, and not the personality, or the sensibility. Or the gender, for to discover what she knows, a woman must stretch beyond woman's matters. That fine, strong androgynous mind that we meet in her books is her achievement; knowing it, we could not wish that her work were anything except what it is.

PUBLISHERS' NOTE

The introduction above is a slightly shortened version of an article
first published, unsigned, in *The Times Literary Supplement* (London)
for December 21, 1973. Grateful acknowledgement is made to the
editor of the TLS for permission to reprint it here.

The contents of this *Celebration* had already been discussed with
Dame Rebecca by the publishers in some detail. As to the complete
books or articles, and independent portions of books, she generously
accepted their choices, whether her own preferences or not, while
adding two or three others of her own. She also allowed all of these
to be left untouched, scrupulously resisting afterthoughts.

In the few incomplete selections, however, she patiently adjusted
the original text herself, sometimes adding or subtracting passages
and correcting phrases that could be misleading out of context.
Thus in "The Strange Necessity", in "Greenhouse with Cyclamens I
[1946]" (from *A Train of Powder*), and especially in the long selections from *Black Lamb and Grey Falcon*, her own later imprint
appears here. Only a few explanatory footnotes [in brackets] were
supplied by the publishers to cover some omissions. All substantive
omissions are indicated by small marks [◇] in the text.

My personal thanks are offered to three international conspirators
who gave far more than ordinary helpfulness in preparing this
Celebration: Catharine Carver and Gwenda David in England and
Peter G. Snyder in America; and also to Alan Maclean of Macmillans,
Dame Rebecca's current London publisher, who contributed the title
and generous encouragement.

A brief factual biography and a bibliography of Rebecca West's
published books, with studies of her work by others, precede the index
of titles, names and places in the appendix beginning on page 759.

MARSHALL A. BEST
Senior Consulting Editor
The Viking Press

I. EARLIER FICTION

The Return of the Soldier (1918)

The Salt of the Earth (1934)
From The Harsh Voice: Four Short Novels

FROM The Modern "Rake's Progress" (1934)

FROM The Thinking Reed (1936)

The Return of the Soldier

"Ah, don't begin to fuss!" wailed Kitty; "if a woman began to worry in these days because her husband hadn't written to her for a fortnight——! Besides, if he'd been anywhere interesting, anywhere where the fighting was really hot, he'd have found some way of telling me instead of just leaving it as 'Somewhere in France.' He'll be all right."

We were sitting in the nursery. I had not meant to enter it again after the child's death, but I had come suddenly on Kitty as she slipped the key into the lock and had lingered to look in at the high room, so full of whiteness and clear colours, so unendurably gay and familiar, which is kept in all respects as though there were still a child in the house. It was the first lavish day of spring, and the sunlight was pouring through the tall arched windows and the flowered curtains so brightly that in the old days a fat fist would certainly have been raised to point out the new translucent glories of the rosebuds; it was lying in great pools on the blue cork floor and the soft rugs, patterned with strange beasts; and it threw dancing beams, that should have been gravely watched for hours, on the white paint and the blue distempered walls. It fell on the rocking-horse which had been Chris' idea of an appropriate present for his year-old son and showed what a fine fellow he was and how tremendously dappled; it picked out Mary and her little lamb on the chintz ottoman. And along the mantelpiece, under the loved print of the snarling tiger, in attitudes that were at once angular and relaxed—as though they were ready for play at their master's pleasure but found it hard to keep from drowsing in this warm weather—sat the Teddy Bear and the chimpanzee and the woolly white dog and the black cat with the eyes that roll. Everything was there, except Oliver. I turned away so that I might not spy on Kitty revisiting her dead.

But she called after me:

"Come here, Jenny. I'm going to dry my hair."

And when I looked again I saw that her golden hair was all about her shoulders and that she wore over her frock a little silken jacket trimmed with rosebuds. She looked so like a girl on a magazine cover that one expected to find a large "7d." somewhere attached to her person. She had taken Nanny's big basket-chair from its place by the high chair and was pushing it over to the middle window.

"I always come in here when Emery has washed my hair; it's the sunniest room in the house. I wish Chris wouldn't have it kept as a nursery when there's no chance——"

She sat down, swept her hair over the back of the chair into the sunlight, and held out to me her tortoise-shell hairbrush.

"Give it a brush now and then like a good soul. But be careful. Tortoise snaps so."

I took the brush and turned to the window, leaning my forehead against the glass and staring unobservantly at the view. You probably know the beauty of that view; for when Chris rebuilt Baldry Court after his marriage, he handed it over to architects who had not so much the wild eye of the artist as the knowing wink of the manicurist, and between them they massaged the dear old place into matter for innumerable photographs in the illustrated papers.

The house lies on the crest of Harrow-weald, and from its windows the eye drops to miles of emerald pastureland lying wet and brilliant under a westward line of sleek hills blue with distance and distant woods, while nearer it ranges the suave decorum of the lawn and the Lebanon cedar whose branches are like darkness made palpable, and the minatory gauntnesses of the topmost pines in the wood that breaks downward, its bare boughs a close texture of browns and purples, from the pond on the hill's edge.

That day its beauty was an affront to me, because like most Englishwomen of my time I was wishing for the return of a soldier. Disregarding the national interest and everything except the keen prehensile gesture of our hearts towards him, I wanted to snatch my cousin Christopher from the wars and seal him in this green pleasantness his wife and I now looked upon. Of late I had had bad dreams about him. By night I saw Chris running across the brown rottenness of No Man's Land, starting back here because he trod upon a hand, not even looking there because of the awfulness of an unburied head, and not till my dream was packed full of horror did I see him pitch forward on his knees as he reached safety—if it was that. For on the war-films I have seen men slip down as softly from the trench parapet, and none but the grimmer philosophers would say that they had

4

reached safety by their fall. And when I escaped into wakefulness it was only to lie stiff and think of stories I had heard in the boyish voice, that rings indomitable yet has most of its gay notes flattened, of the modern subaltern.

"We were all of us in a barn one night, and a shell came along. My pal sang out, '*Help me, old man, I've got no legs!*' and I had to answer, '*I can't, old man, I've got no hands!*' "

Well, such are the dreams of Englishwomen today; I could not complain. But I wished for the return of our soldier.

So I said: "I wish we could hear from Chris. It is a fortnight since he wrote."

And then it was that Kitty wailed, "Ah, don't begin to fuss," and bent over her image in her hand-mirror as one might bend for refreshment over scented flowers.

I tried to build about me such a little globe of ease as always ensphered her, and thought of all that remained good in our lives though Chris had gone. My eye followed the mellow brick of the garden wall through the trees, and I reflected that by the contriving of these gardens that lay, well-kept as a woman's hand, on the south side of the hill, Kitty and I had proved ourselves worthy of the past generation that had set the old house on this sunny ledge, overhanging and overhung by beauty. And we had done much for the new house.

I could send my mind creeping from room to room like a purring cat, rubbing itself against all the brittle beautiful things that we had either recovered from antiquity or dug from the obscure pits of modern craftsmanship, basking in the colour that glowed from all our solemnly chosen fabrics with such pure intensity that it seemed to shed warmth like sunshine. Even now, when spending seemed a little disgraceful, I could think of that beauty with nothing but pride. I was sure that we were preserved from the reproach of luxury because we had made a fine place for Chris, our little part of the world that was, so far as surfaces could make it so, good enough for his amazing goodness.

Here we had nourished that surpassing amiability which was so habitual that one took it as one of his physical characteristics, and regarded any lapse into bad temper as a calamity startling as the breaking of a leg. Here we had made happiness inevitable for him. I could shut my eyes and think of innumerable proofs of how well we had succeeded, for there never was so visibly contented a man: the way he lingered with us in the mornings while the car throbbed at the door, delighting just in whatever way the weather looked in the familiar frame of things, how our rooms burned with many-coloured brightness on the darkest winter day, how not the fieriest summertime could consume the cool wet leafy places of our garden; the way that in the midst of entertaining a great company he would smile secretly to us, as though he knew we would not cease in our task of refreshing him; and all that he did on the morning just a year ago, when he went to the front. . . .

First he had sat in the morning-room and talked and stared out on the lawn that already had the desolation of an empty stage although he had not yet gone; then broke off suddenly and went about the house, looking into many rooms. He went to the stables and looked at the horses and had the dogs brought out; he refrained from touching them or speaking to them, as though he felt himself already infected with the squalor of war and did not want to contaminate their bright physical well-being. Then he went to the edge of the wood and stood staring down into the clumps of dark-leaved rhododendra and the yellow tangle of last year's bracken and the cold winter black of the trees. (From this very window I had spied on him.) Then he moved broodingly back to the house to be with his wife until the moment of his going, when I stood with her on the steps to see him motor off to Waterloo.

He kissed us both; as he bent over me I noticed once again how his hair was of two colours, brown and gold. Then he got into the car, put on his Tommy air, and said, "So long! I'll write you from Berlin!" and as he spoke his head dropped back and he set a hard stare on the over-arching house. That meant, I knew, that he loved the life he had lived with us and desired to carry with him to the dreary place of death and dirt the completest picture of everything about his home, on which his mind could brush when things were at their worst, as a man might finger an amulet through his shirt. This house, this life with us, was the core of his heart.

"If he could come back!" I said. "He was so happy here."

And Kitty answered: "He could not have been happier."

It was important that he should have been happy, for, you see, he was not like other men. When we had played together as children in that wood he had always shown great faith in the imminence of the improbable. He thought that the birch tree would really stir and shrink and quicken into an enchanted princess, that he really was a

Red Indian and that his disguise would suddenly fall from him at the right sundown, that at any moment a tiger might lift red fangs through the bracken; and he expected these things with a stronger motion of the imagination than the ordinary child's make-believe. And from a thousand intimations, from his occasional clear fixity of gaze on good things as though they were about to dissolve into better, from the passionate anticipation with which he went to new countries or met new people, I was aware that this faith had persisted into his adult life.

He had exchanged his expectation of becoming a Red Indian for the equally wistful aspiration of becoming completely reconciled to life. It was his hopeless hope that some time he would have an experience that would act on his life like alchemy, turning to gold all the dark metals of events, and from that revelation he would go on his way rich with an inextinguishable joy.

There had been, of course, no chance of his ever getting it. Literally there wasn't room to swing a revelation in his crowded life. First of all, at his father's death, he had been obliged to take over a business that was weighted by the needs of a mob of female relatives who were all useless either in the old way with antimacassars or in the new way with golf clubs.

Then Kitty had come along and picked up his conception of normal expenditure and carelessly stretched it as a woman stretches a new glove on her hand. Then there had been the difficult task of learning to live after the death of his little son. It had lain on us, as the responsibility that gave us dignity, to compensate him for his lack of free adventure by arranging him a gracious life. But now, just because our performance had been so brilliantly adequate, how dreary was the empty stage. . . .

We were not, perhaps, specially contemptible women, because nothing could ever really become a part of our life until it had been referred to Chris's attention. I remember thinking, as the parlourmaid came in with a card on the tray, how little it mattered who had called and what flag of prettiness she flew, since there was no chance that Chris would come in and stand over her, his fairness red in the fire-light, and show her that detached attention, such as an unmusical man pays to good music, which men of anchored affections give to attractive women.

Kitty read from the card, " 'Mrs William Grey, Mariposa, Lady-smith Road, Wealdstone.' I don't know anybody in Wealdstone."

That is the name of the red suburban stain which fouls the fields three miles nearer London than Harrow-weald. One cannot now protect one's environment as one could in the old days. "Do I know her, Ward? Has she been here before?"

"Oh, no, ma'am." The parlourmaid smiled superciliously. "She said she had news for you." From her tone one could deduce an over-confidential explanation made by a shabby visitor while using the door mat almost too zealously.

Kitty pondered and said, "I'll come down." As the girl went she took up the amber hairpins from her lap and began swathing her hair about her head. "Last year's fashion," she commented; "but I fancy it'll do for a person with that sort of address." She stood up and threw her little silk dressing-jacket over the rocking-horse. "I'm seeing her because she may need something, and I specially want to be kind to people while Chris is away. One wants to deserve well of Heaven."

For a minute she was aloof in radiance, but as we linked arms and went out into the corridor she became more mortal with a pout.

"The people that come breaking into one's nice quiet day," she moaned reproachfully, and as we came to the head of the broad staircase she leaned over the white balustrade to peer down on the hall, and squeezed my arm. "Look!" she whispered.

Just beneath us, on one of Kitty's chintz armchairs, sat a middle-aged woman. She wore a yellowish raincoat and a black hat with plumes whose sticky straw had but lately been renovated by something out of a little bottle bought at the chemist's. She had rolled her black thread gloves into a ball on her lap, so that she could turn her grey alpaca skirt well above her muddy boots and adjust its brush-braid with a seamed red hand which looked even more horrible when she presently raised it to touch the glistening flowers of the pink azalea that stood on a table beside her.

Kitty shivered and muttered, "Let's get this over," and ran down the stairs. On the last step she paused and said with a conscientious sweetness, "Mrs Grey?"

"Yes," answered the visitor.

She lifted to Kitty a sallow and relaxed face whose expression gave me a sharp, pitying pang of prepossession in her favour; it was beautiful that so plain a woman should so ardently rejoice in another's loveliness.

"Are you Mrs Baldry?" she asked, almost as if she were glad about it, and stood up.

The bones of her cheap stays clicked as she moved. Well, she was not so bad. Her body was long and round and shapely and with a noble squareness of the shoulders; her fair hair curled diffidently about a good brow; her grey eyes, though they were remote, as if anything worth looking at in her life had kept a long way off, were full of tenderness; and though she was slender there was something about her of the wholesome endearing heaviness of the draught-ox or the big trusted dog. Yet she was bad enough. She was repulsively furred with neglect and poverty, as even a good glove that has dropped down behind a bed in a hotel and has lain undisturbed for a day or two is repulsive when the chambermaid retrieves it from the dust and fluff.

She flung at us as we sat down:

"My general is sister to your second housemaid."

It left us at a loss. "You've come about a reference?"

"Oh, no. I've had Gladys two years now, and I've always found her a very good girl. I want no reference." With her finger-nail she followed the burst seam of the dark pigskin purse that slid about on her shiny alpaca lap. "But girls talk, you know. You mustn't blame them. . . ."

She seemed to be caught in a thicket of embarrassment, and sat staring up at the azalea.

Kitty said, with the hardness of a woman who sees before her the curse of women's lives, a domestic row, that she took no interest in servants' gossip.

"Oh, it isn't"—her eyes brimmed as though we had been unkind— "servants' gossip that I wanted to talk about. I only mentioned Gladys"—she continued to trace the burst seam of her purse— "because that's how I heard you didn't know."

"What don't I know?"

Her head dropped a little.

"About Mr Baldry. Forgive me, I don't know his rank."

"Captain Baldry," supplied Kitty wonderingly. "What is it that I don't know about him?"

She looked far away from us, to the open door and its view of dark pines and pale March sunshine, and appeared to swallow something.

"Why, that he's hurt," she gently said.

"Wounded, you mean?" asked Kitty.

Her rusty plumes oscillated as she moved her mild face about with an air of perplexity.

9

"Yes," she said, "he's wounded."

Kitty's bright eyes met mine and we obeyed that mysterious human impulse to smile triumphantly at the spectacle of a fellow-creature occupied in baseness. For this news was not true. It could not possibly be true. The War Office would have wired to us immediately if Chris had been wounded. This was such a fraud as one sees recorded in the papers that meticulously record squalor, in paragraphs headed "Heartless Fraud on Soldier's Wife."

Presently she would say that she had gone to some expense to come here with her news, and that she was poor, and at the first generous look on our faces there would come some tale of trouble that would disgust the imagination by pictures of yellow wood furniture that a landlord oddly desired to seize and a pallid child with bandages round its throat.

I turned away my eyes and tried to be inattentive. Yet there was something about the physical quality of the woman, unlovely though she was, which preserved the occasion from utter baseness. I felt sure that had it not been for the tyrannous emptiness of that evil, shiny, pigskin purse that jerked about on her trembling knees, the poor driven creature would have chosen ways of candour and gentleness. It was, strangely enough, only when I looked at Kitty and marked how her brightly coloured prettiness arched over this plain criminal, as though she were a splendid bird of prey and this her sluggish insect food, that I felt the moment degrading.

She was, I felt, being a little too clever over it.

"How is he wounded?" she asked.

The caller traced a pattern on the carpet with her blunt toe.

"I don't know how to put it ... He's not exactly wounded. ... A shell burst. ..."

"Concussion?" suggested Kitty.

She answered with an odd glibness and humility, as though tendering us a term she had long brooded over without arriving at comprehension, and hoping that our superior intelligences would make something of it. "Shell-shock." Our faces did not illumine so she dragged on lamely. "Anyway, he's not well." Again she played with her purse. Her face was visibly damp.

"Not well? Is he dangerously ill?"

"Oh, no!" She was too kind to harrow us. "Not dangerously ill."

Kitty brutally permitted a silence to fall. Our caller could not bear it, and broke it in a voice that nervousness had turned to a funny diffident croak.

"He's in the Queen Mary Hospital at Boulogne." We did not speak, and she began to flush and wriggle on her seat, and stooped forward to fumble under the legs of her chair for her umbrella. The sight of its green seams and unveracious tortoise-shell handle disgusted Kitty into speech.

"How do you know all this?"

Our visitor met her eyes. This was evidently a moment for which she had steeled herself, and she rose to it with a catch of her breath.

"A man who used to be a clerk along with my husband is in Mr Baldry's regiment." Her voice croaked even more piteously and her eyes begged, "Leave it at that! Leave it at that! If you only knew——"

"And what regiment is that?" pursued Kitty.

The poor sallow face shone with sweat.

"I never thought to ask!" she said.

"Well, your friend's name...."

Mrs Grey moved on her seat so suddenly and violently that the pigskin purse fell from her lap and lay at my feet. I supposed that she cast it from her purposely because its emptiness had brought her to this humiliation, and that the scene would close presently in a few quiet tears.

I hoped that Kitty would let her go without scaring her too much with words and would not mind if I gave her a little money. There was no doubt in my mind but that this queer ugly episode, in which this woman butted like a clumsy animal at a gate she was not intelligent enough to open, would dissolve and be replaced by some more pleasing composition in which we would take our proper parts; in which, that is, she should turn from our rightness ashamed.

Yet she cried, "But Chris is ill!"

It took a second for the compact insolence of the moment to penetrate: the amazing impertinence of the use of his name, the accusation of callousness she brought against us, whose passion for Chris was our point of honour, because we would not shriek at her false news, the impudently bright indignant gaze she flung at us, the lift of her voice that pretended she could not understand our coolness and irrelevance.

I pushed the purse away from me with my toe and hated her as the rich hate the poor, as insect things that will struggle out of the crannies which are their decent home, and introduce ugliness to the light of day. And Kitty said, in a voice shaken with pitilessness:

"You are impertinent. I know exactly what you are doing. You have read in the *Harrow Observer* or somewhere that my husband is at the front, and you come to tell this story because you think that you will get some money. I've read of such cases in the papers. You forget that if anything has happened to my husband the War Office would have told me. You should think yourself very lucky that I don't hand you over to the police." She shrilled a little before she came to the end. "Please go!"

"Kitty!" I breathed.

I was so ashamed that such a scene should spring from Chris' peril at the front that I wanted to go out into the garden and sit by the pond until the poor thing had removed her deplorable umbrella, her unpardonable raincoat, her poor frustrated fraud. But Mrs Grey, who had begun, childishly and deliberately, "It's *you* who are being . . ." and had desisted, simply because she realized that there were no harsh notes on her lyre and that she could not strike these chords that others found so easy, had fixed me with a certain wet, clear, patient gaze. It is the gift of animals and those of peasant stock. From the least regarded, from an old horse nosing over a gate or a drab in a workhouse ward, it wrings the heart. From this woman . . . I said checkingly, "Kitty!" and reconciled her in an undertone, "(There's some mistake. Got the name wrong, perhaps.)" "Please tell us all about it, Mrs Grey."

Mrs Grey began a forward movement like a curtsey. She was grovelling after that purse. When she rose her face was pink from stooping and her dignity swam uncertainly in a sea of half-shed tears. She said:

"I'm sorry I've upset you. But when you know a thing like that it isn't in flesh and blood to keep it from his wife. I am a married woman myself and I know. I knew Mr Baldry fifteen years ago." Her voice freely confessed that she had taken a liberty. "Quite a friend of the family he was." She had added that touch to soften the crude surprisingness of her announcement. It hardly did. "We lost sight of each other. It's fifteen years since we last met. I had never seen or heard of him, nor thought to do again till I got this a week ago."

She undid the purse and took out a telegram. I knew suddenly that all she said was true; for that was why her hands had clasped that purse.

12

"He isn't well! He isn't well!" she said pleadingly. "He's lost his memory, and thinks—thinks he still knows me."

She passed the telegram to Kitty, who read it and laid it on her knee.

"See," said Mrs Grey, "it's addressed to Margaret Allington, my maiden name, and I've been married these ten years. And it was sent to my old home, Monkey Island at Bray. Father kept the inn there. It's fifteen years since we left it. I never should have got this telegram if me and my husband hadn't been down there a little while back and told the folks who keep it now who I was."

Kitty folded up the telegram and said in a little voice:

"This is a likely story."

Again her grey eyes brimmed. People are rude to one, she visibly said, but surely not nice people like this. She simply continued to sit.

Kitty cried out, as though arguing:

"There's nothing about shell-shock in this wire."

She melted into a trembling shyness.

"There was a letter too."

Kitty held out her hand.

She gasped. "Oh, no! I couldn't do that."

"I must have it," said Kitty.

The caller's eyes grew great, she rose and dived clumsily for her umbrella, which had again slipped under the chair. "I can't," she cried, and scurried to the open door like a pelted dog. She would have run down the steps at once had not some tender thought arrested her. She turned to me trustfully and stammered, "He is at that hospital I said," as if, since I had dealt her no direct blow, I might be able to salve the news she brought from the general wreck of manners. And then Kitty's stiff pallor struck to her heart, and she cried comfortingly across the distance, "But I tell you I haven't seen him for fifteen years." She faced about, pushed down her hat on her head, and ran down the steps on to the gravel. "They won't understand," we heard her sob.

For a long time we watched her as she went along the drive, her yellowish raincoat looking sick and bright in the sharp sunshine, her black plumes nodding like the pines above, her cheap boots making her walk on her heels; a spreading stain on the fabric of our life. When she was quite hidden by the dark clump of rhododendra at the corner Kitty turned and went to the fire-place. She laid her arms against the oak mantelpiece and cooled her face against her arms.

13

When at last I followed her she said,

"Do you believe her?"

I started. I had forgotten that we had ever disbelieved her.

"Yes."

"What can it mean?" She dropped her arms and stared at me imploringly. "Think, think of something it can mean which isn't detestable!"

"It's all a mystery," I said; and added mildly, because nobody has ever been cross with Kitty, "You didn't help to clear it up."

"Oh, I know you think I was rude," she petulantly moaned, "but you're so slow, you don't see what it means. Either it means that he's mad, our Chris, our splendid sane Chris, all broken and queer, not knowing us .... I can't bear to think of that. It can't be true. But if he isn't ... Jenny, there was nothing in that telegram to show he'd lost his memory. It was just affection—a name that might have been a pet name—things that it was a little common to put in a telegram. It's queer he should have written such a message, queer that he shouldn't have told me about knowing her, queer that he ever should have known such a woman. It shows there are bits of him we don't know. Things may be awfully wrong. It's all such a breach of trust. I resent it."

I was appalled by this stiff dignified gesture that seemed to be plucking Chris' soul from his body. She was hurt, of course. But there are ways pain should not show itself. . . .

"But Chris is ill," I said.

She stared at me. "You're saying what she said."

Indeed there seemed no better words than those Mrs Grey had used. I repeated, "But he is ill."

She laid her face against her arms again, "What does that matter?" she said. "If he could send that telegram, he. . . ." She paused, breathed deeply, and went on with the sick delight the unhappy sometimes find in ungraciousness. "If he could send that telegram he isn't ours any longer."

2

I was sorry, the next morning, that the post comes too late at Harrow-weald to be brought up with the morning tea and waits for one at the breakfast table; for under Kitty's fixed gaze I had to open a letter which bore the Boulogne postmark and was addressed in the writing of Frank Baldry, Chris' cousin, who is in the Church.

"Dear Jenny," it began, "I am sorry to have to tell you that poor Chris has been disabled. He has had shell-shock and although not physically wounded is in a very strange state indeed. I got a wire from him on Thursday saying he was in hospital about a mile from Boulogne and that he wanted to see me. The telegram had not been sent direct to me, but to Ollenshaws, although I left the Ollenshaws curacy for Pentmouth nearly fifteen years ago. Sumpter is still there, luckily, and forwarded it on at once. I started that evening and looked hard for you and Kitty on the boat, naturally expecting to see you. But, as you now know you were not there. I found the hospital in a girls' school which had been taken over by the Red Cross. The Red Cross is everywhere here.

"I found Chris in a nice room with a southern exposure with three other officers, who seemed very decent. He was better than I had expected but did not look quite himself. For one thing he was oddly boisterous in his greeting. He seemed glad to see me, and told me he could remember nothing about his concussion, but that he wanted to get back to Harrow-weald. He said things about the wood and the upper pond that seemed sentimental but not so much out of the way. He wanted to know if the daffies were out yet, and when he would be allowed to travel, because he felt that he would get well at once if only he could get home. And then he was silent for a minute as though he was holding something back. When he did begin to let out what he was holding back I was amazed. I will try and set it down as far as possible in the order in which it occurs. He informed me—with just the boyish manner he might have used fifteen years ago— that he was in love with a girl called Margaret Allington, who is the daughter of the man who keeps the inn on Monkey Island at Bray on the Thames. I gasped, 'How long has this been going on?' He laughed at my surprise, and said, 'Ever since I went down to stay with Uncle Ambrose at Dorney after I'd got my degree.' Fifteen years ago! I was still staring at him, unable to believe this bare-faced admission of a deception carried on for years, when he went on to say that though he had wired to her and she had wired a message in return, she hadn't said anything about coming over to see him. 'Now,' he said quite coolly, 'I know old Allington's had a bad season—oh, I'm quite well up in the innkeeping business these days!—and I think it may quite possibly be a lack of funds that is keeping her away.

15

I've lost my chequebook somewhere in the scrim and so I wonder if you'd send her some money. Or better still, for she's a shy country thing, you might fetch her.'

"I stared. 'Chris,' I said, 'I know the war is making some of us very lax, and nobody could be more broadminded than I am. But there are limits. And when it comes to asking me to go over to England and fetch a woman. . . .' He interrupted me with a sneer that we parsons are inveterately eighteenth-century and have our minds perpetually inflamed by visions of squires' sons seducing country wenches, and declared that he meant to marry this Margaret Allington. 'Oh, indeed,' I said. 'And may I ask what Kitty says to this arrangement?' 'Who the devil is Kitty?' he asked blankly. 'Kitty is your wife,' I said quietly, but firmly. He sat up and exclaimed, 'I haven't got a wife! Has some woman been turning up with a cock-and-bull story of being my wife? Because it's the damnedest lie!'

"I determined to settle the matter by sharp common-sense handling. 'Chris,' I said, 'you have evidently lost your memory. You were married to Kitty Ellis at St George's, Hanover Square, on the third, or it may have been the fourth'—you know my wretched memory for dates—'of February in 1906.' He turned very pale and asked what year this was. '1916,' I told him. He fell back in a fainting condition. The nurse came and said I had done it all right this time, so she at least seemed to have known that he required a rude awakening, although the doctor (a very nice man, Winchester and New) told me he had known nothing of Chris' delusions.

"An hour later I was called back into the room. Chris was looking at himself in a hand mirror, which he threw on the floor as I entered. 'You are right,' he said. 'I'm not twenty-one, but thirty-six.' He said he felt lonely and afraid, and that I must bring Margaret Allington to him at once or he would die. Suddenly he stopped raving and asked, 'Is Father all right?' I prayed for guidance and answered, 'Your father passed away twelve years ago.' He said, 'Good God, can't you say he *died*?' and he turned over and lay with his back to me. I have never before seen a strong man weep and it is indeed a terrible sight. He moaned a lot and began to call for this Margaret. Then he turned over again and said 'Now tell us all about this Kitty that I've married.' I told him she was a beautiful little woman and mentioned that she had a charming and cultivated soprano voice. He said very fractiously, 'I don't like little women and I hate everybody, male or female, who sings. O God, I don't like this Kitty. Take her away.'

16

And then he began to rave again about this woman. He said that his body and soul were consumed with desire for her and that he would never rest until he once more held her in his arms. I had no suspicion that Chris had this side to his nature and it was almost a relief when he fainted again.

"I have seen him since and it is evening. But I have had a long talk with the doctor, who says that he has satisfied himself that Chris is suffering from a loss of memory extending over a period of fifteen years. He says that though of course it will be an occasion of great trial to us all he thinks that in view of Chris' expressed longing for Harrow-weald he ought to be taken home, and advises me to make all arrangements for bringing him back some time next week. I hope I shall be upheld in this difficult enterprise.

"In the meantime I leave it to you to prepare Kitty for this terrible shock. How to do that you will know better than I. I wish she could be spared the experience, but since he is coming back and is certain to betray his real forgetfulness of her—for I am convinced there is no shamming in the business, there is a real gap in his memory—she must of course be made to understand. I hope she may have strength in the time of trial that lies before her and if I can be of any help to her no one will be more glad than I to render it. Tell me if I can run over now or any time either to talk to her or to help, so far as I can help, with him. You know how much I have always cared for dear old Chris. Yours ever, FRANK."

Over my shoulder Kitty muttered, "And he always pretended he liked my singing...." And then gripped my arm and cried in a possessive fury. "Bring him home! Bring him home!"

And so, a week later, they brought Chris home.

From breakfast-time that day the house was pervaded with a day-before-the-funeral feeling: although all duties arising from the occasion had been performed one could settle to nothing else. Chris was expected at one, but there then came a telegram to say he was delayed till the late afternoon. So Kitty, whose beauty was as changed in grief from its ordinary seeming as a rose in moonlight is different from a rose by day, took me down after lunch to the greenhouses and had a snappishly competent conversation about the year's vegetables with Pipe the gardener. After she had said many such horticulturally scandalous things as "I know Queen Mary's prolific, but she isn't sweet," she tugged at my hand and we went back to the house and found a great piece of the afternoon still on our hands. So Kitty went

17

into the drawing-room and filled the house with the desolate merriment of an inattentively played pianola while I sat in the hall and wrote letters and noticed how sad dance music has sounded ever since the war began. And then she started a savage raid of domestic efficiency and made the housemaids cry because the brass handles of the tallboys were not bright enough and because there was only a ten to one instead of a hundred to one risk of breaking a leg on the parquet. After that she had tea, and hated the soda-cake. She was a little shrunk thing, huddled in the arm-chair farthest from the light, when at last the big car came nosing up the drive through the dusk.

We stood up. Through the thudding of the engines came the sound of Chris' great male voice, that always had in it a note like the baying of a big dog. *"Thanks, I can manage by myself. . . ."* I heard, amazed, his step ring strong upon the stone, for I had felt his absence as a kind of death from which he would emerge ghostlike impalpable. And then he stood in the doorway, the gloom blurring his outlines like fur, the faint clear candlelight catching the fair down on his face. He did not see me, in my dark dress, nor huddled Kitty, and with the sleepy smile of one who returns to a dear familiar place to rest, he walked into the hall and laid down his stick and his khaki cap beside the candlestick on the oak table. With both his hands he felt the old wood and stood humming happily through his teeth.

I cried out, because I had seen that his hair was of three colours now—brown and gold and silver.

With a quick turn of the head he found me out in the shadows, "Hullo, Jenny!" he said, and gripped my hands.

"Oh, Chris, I am so glad," I stuttered, and then could say no more for shame that I was thirty-five instead of twenty. For his eyes had hardened in the midst of his welcome as though he had trusted that I at least would have been no party to this conspiracy to deny that he was young, and he said: "I've dropped Frank in town. My temper's of the convalescent type." He might as well have said, "I've dropped Frank, who has grown old, like you. . . ."

"Chris," I went on, "it's so wonderful to have you safe. . . ."

"Safe," he repeated. He sighed very deeply and continued to hold my hands. There was a rustle in the shadows, and he dropped my hands.

The face that looked out of the dimness to him was very white; her upper lip was lifted over her teeth in a distressed grimace. And it was immediately as plain as though he had shouted it that this sad mask meant nothing to him. He knew, not because memory had given him

18

any insight into her heart but because there is an instinctive kind-liness in him which makes him wise about all suffering, that it would hurt her if he asked if this was his wife, but his body involuntarily began a gesture of inquiry before he realized that that too would hurt her and he checked it half-way. So, through a silence, he stood before her slightly bent, as though he had been maimed.

"I am your wife." There was a weak, wailing anger behind the words.

"Kitty," he said, softly and kindly. He looked round for some graciousness to make the scene less wounding, and stooped to kiss her. But he could not. The thought of another woman made him unable to breathe, sent the blood running under his skin.

With a toss, like a child saying, "Well, if you don't want to, I'm sure I wouldn't for the world!" Kitty withdrew from the suspended caress. He watched her retreat into the shadows, as though she were a symbol of this new life by which he was baffled and oppressed, until the darkness outside became filled with the sound like the surf which we always hear at Harrow-weald on angry evenings, and his eyes became distant and his lips smiled. "Up here . . . in this old place . . . how one hears the pines. . . ."

She cried out from the other end of the room, as though she were speaking with someone behind a shut door. "I've ordered dinner at seven. I thought you'd probably have missed a meal or two. Or would want to go to bed early." She said it very smartly, with her head on one side like a bird, as if she was pleading that he would find her very clever about ordering dinner and thinking of his comfort.

"Good," he said. "I'd better dress now, hadn't I?" He looked up the staircase and would have gone up had I not held him back. For the little room in the south wing with the fishing-rods and the old books went in the rebuilding, absorbed by the black and white magnificence that is Kitty's bedroom.

"Oh, I'll take you up!" Kitty rang out efficiently. She pulled at his coat sleeve, so they started level on the lowest step. But as they went up the sense of his separateness beat her back; she lifted her arms as though she struggled through a fog, and fell behind. When he reached the top she was standing half-way down the stairs, her hands clasped under her chin. But he did not see her. He was looking along the corridor and saying, "This house is different." If the soul has to stay in his coffin till the lead is struck asunder, in its captivity it speaks with such a voice.

19

She braced herself with a gallant laugh. "How you've forgotten," she cried, and ran up to him, rattling her keys and looking grave with housewifery, and I was left alone with the dusk and the familiar things. The dusk flowed in wet and cool from the garden as if to put out the fire of confusion lit on our hearthstone, and the furniture, very visible through the soft evening opacity with the observant brightness of old well-polished wood, seemed terribly aware. Strangeness had come into the house and everything was appalled by it, even time. For the moments dragged. It seemed to me, half an hour later, that I had been standing for an infinite period in the drawing-room, remembering that in the old days the blinds had never been drawn in this room because old Mrs Baldry had liked to see the night gathering like a pool in the valley while the day lingered as a white streak above the farthest hills; and perceiving in pain that the heavy blue blinds, which shroud the nine windows because a lost Zeppelin sometimes clanks like a skeleton across the sky above us, would make his home seem even more like prison.

I began to say what was in my mind to Kitty when she came in, but she moved past me, remote in preoccupation, and I was silent when I saw that she was dressed in all respects like a bride. The gown she wore on her wedding-day ten years ago had been cut and embroidered as this white satin was, her hair had been coiled low on her neck as it was now. Around her throat were her pearls, and her longer chain of diamonds dropped, looking cruelly bright, to her white small breasts; because she held some needle-work to her bosom I saw that her right hand was stiff with rings and her left hand bare save for her wedding-ring. She dropped her load of flannel on a work-table and sat down, spreading out her skirts, in an arm-chair by the fire. With her lower lip thrust out, as if she were considering a menu, she lowered her head and looked down on herself. She frowned to see that the highlights on the satin shone scarlet from the fire, that her flesh glowed like a rose, and she changed her seat for a high-backed chair beneath the furthest candle sconce. There were green curtains close by, and now the lights on her satin gown were green like cleft ice. She looked cold as moonlight, as virginity, but precious; the falling candlelight struck her hair to bright, pure gold. So she waited for him.

There came suddenly a thud at the door. We heard Chris swear and stumble to his feet, while one of the servants spoke helpfully. Kitty knitted her brows, for she hates gracelessenss and a failure of physical adjustment is the worst indignity she can conceive. "He's fallen down those three steps from the hall," I whispered. "They're new. . . ." She did not listen, because she was controlling her face into harmony with the appearance of serene virginity upon which his eyes would light when he entered the room.

His fall had ruffled him and made him look very large and red, and he breathed hard like an animal pursued into a strange place by night, and to his hot consciousness of his disorder the sight of Kitty, her face and hands and bosom shining like the snow, her gown enfolding her and her gold hair crowning her with radiance and the white fire of jewels giving a passion to the spectacle, was a deep refreshment. She sat still for a time, so that he might feel this well. Then raised her ringed hand to her necklaces.

"It seems so strange that you should not remember me," she said. "You gave me all these."

He answered kindly. "I am glad I did that. You look very beautiful in them." But as he spoke his gaze shifted to the shadows in the corners of the room. He was thinking of another woman, of another beauty.

Kitty put up her hands as if to defend her jewels.

In that silence dinner was announced, and we went into the dining-room. It is the fashion at Baldry Court to use no electric light save when there is work to be done or a great company to be entertained, and to eat and talk by the mild clarity of many candles. That night it was a kindly fashion, for we sat about the table with our faces veiled in shadow and seemed to listen in quiet contentment to the talk of our man who had come back to us. Yet all through the meal I was near to weeping because whenever he thought himself unobserved he looked at the things that were familiar to him. Dipping his head he would glance sideways at the old oak panelling; and nearer things he fingered as though sight were not intimate enough a contact, his hand caressed the arm of his chair, because he remembered the black gleam of it, stole out and touched the recollected salt-cellar. It was his furtiveness that was heartrending; it was as though he were an outcast and we who loved him stout policemen. Was Baldry Court so sleek a place that the unhappy felt offenders there? Then we had all been living wickedly and he too. As his fingers glided here and there he talked bravely about noncommittal things; to what ponies we had been strapped when at the age of five we were introduced to the hunting-field; how we had teased to be allowed to keep swans in the pond above the wood, and how the yellow bills of our intended pets had sent us shrieking homewards; and all the dear life that makes the bland English countryside so secretly adventurous. "Funny thing," he said. "All the time I was at Boulogne I wanted to see a kingfisher. That blue, scudding down a stream. Or a heron's flight round a willow. . . ." He checked himself suddenly; his head fell forward on his chest. "You have no herons here, of course," he said drearily, and fingered the arm of his chair again. Then raised his head again, brisk with another subject. "Do they still have trouble with foxes at Steppy End?"

Kitty shook her head. "I don't know. . . ."

"Griffiths will know," Chris said cheerily and swung round on his seat to ask the butler, and found him osseous where Griffiths was rotund, dark where Griffiths had been merrily mottled, strange, where Griffiths had been a part of home, a condition of life. He sat back in his chair as though his heart had stopped.

When the butler who is not Griffiths had left the room he spoke gruffly.

"Stupid of me, I know. But where is Griffiths?"

"Dead seven years ago," said Kitty, her eyes on her plate.

He sighed deeply in a shuddering horror. "I'm sorry. He was a good man."

I cleared my throat. "There are new people here, Chris, but they love you as the old ones did."

He forced himself to smile at us both, to a gay response, "As if I didn't know that tonight!"

But he did not know it. Even to me he would give no trust, because it was Jenny the girl who had been his friend and not Jenny the woman. All the inhabitants of this new tract of time were his enemies, all its circumstances his prison bars. There was suspicion in his gesture with which, when we were back in the drawing-room, he picked up the flannel from the work-table.

"Whose is this?" he said curiously; his mother had been a hard riding woman, not apt with her needle.

"Clothes for one of the cottagers," answered Kitty breathlessly. "We—we've a lot of responsibilities, you and I. With all the land you've bought there's ever so many people to look after. . . ."

He moved his shoulders uneasily, as if under a yoke, and after he had drunk his coffee pulled up one of the blinds and went out to pace the flagged walk under the windows. Kitty huddled carelessly by the

22

fire, her hands over her face, unheeding that by its red glow she looked not so virginal and bridelike, so I think she was too distracted even to plan. I went to the piano. Through this evening of sentences cut short because their completed meaning was always sorrow, of normal life dissolved to tears, the chords of Beethoven sounded serenely.

"So like you, Jenny," said Kitty suddenly, "to play Beethoven when it's the war that's caused all this. I could have told that you would have chosen to play German music, this night of all nights."

So I began a sarabande by Purcell, a jolly thing that makes one see a plump, sound woman dancing on a sanded floor in some old inn with casks of good ale all about her and a world of sunshine and May lanes without. As I played I wondered if things like this happened when Purcell wrote such music, empty of everything except laughter and simple greeds and satisfactions and at the worst the wail of unrequited love. Why had modern life brought forth these horrors that make the old tragedies seem no more than nursery shows? Perhaps it is that adventurous men have too greatly changed the outward world which is life's engenderment. There are towns now, and even the trees and flowers are not as they were; the crocuses on the lawn, whose blades showed white in the wide beam let out by the window Chris had opened, should have pierced turf on Mediterranean cliffs; the golden larch beyond should have cast its long shadows on little yellow men as they crossed a Chinese plain. And the sky also is different. Behind Chris' head, as he halted at the open window, a searchlight turned all ways in the night like a sword brandished among the stars.

"Kitty."

"Yes, Chris." She was sweet and obedient and alert.

"I know my conduct must seem to you perversely insulting." Behind him the searchlight wheeled while he gripped the sides of the window. "But if I do not see Margaret Allington I shall die."

She raised her hands to her jewels and pressed the cool globes of her pearls into her flesh. "She lives near here," she said easily. "I will send the car down for her tomorrow. You shall see as much of her as you like."

His arms fell to his side. "Thank you," he muttered. "You're all being so kind——" he disengaged himself into the darkness.

I was amazed at Kitty's beautiful act and more amazed to find that it had made her face ugly. Her eyes snapped as they met mine.

"That dowd!" she said, keeping her voice low so that he might not hear it as he passed to and fro before the window. "That dowd!"

This sudden abandonment of beauty and amiability means so much in our Kitty, whose law of life is grace, that I went over and kissed her, "Dear, you're taking things all the wrong way," I said. "Chris is ill——"

"He's well enough to remember her all right," she replied unanswerably.

Her silver shoe tapped the floor, she pinched her lips for some moments. "After all, I suppose I can sit down to it. Other women do. Teddy Rex keeps a Gaiety girl and Mrs Rex has to grin and bear it."

She shrugged in answer to my silence. "What else is it, do you think? It means that Chris is a man like other men. But I did think that bad women were pretty. I suppose he's had so much to do with pretty ones that a plain one's a change. . . ."

"Kitty! Kitty! how can you?" But her little pink mouth went on manufacturing malice. "This is all a blind," she said at the end of an unpardonable sentence. "He's pretending. . . ." I was past speech then, who had felt his agony all the evening like a wound in my own body, and I did not care what I did to stop her. I gripped her small shoulders with my large hands and shook her till her jewels rattled and she scratched my fingers and gasped for breath. But I did not mind so long as she was silent.

Chris spoke from the darkness. "Jenny!"

I let her go. He came in and stood over us, running his hand through his hair unhappily. "Let's all be decent to each other," he said heavily. "It's all such a muddle and it's so rotten for all of us. . . ."

Kitty shook herself neat and stood up. "Why don't you say, 'Jenny, you mustn't be rude to visitors?' It's how you feel, I know." She gathered up her needle-work. "I'm going to bed. It's been a horrid night."

She spoke so pathetically, like a child who hasn't enjoyed a party as much as it had thought it would, that both of us felt a stir of tenderness towards her as she left the room. We smiled sadly at each other as we sat down by the fire, and I perceived that, perhaps because I was flushed and looked younger, he felt more intimate with me than he had yet done since his return. Indeed in the warm friendly silence that followed he was like a patient when tiring visitors have gone and he is left alone with his trusted nurse; smiled under drooped lids and then paid me the high compliment of disregard. His limbs relaxed, he sank back into his chair. I watched him vigilantly and was ready at that moment when thought intruded into his drowsings and his face began to twitch.

"You can't remember her at all?" I asked.

"Oh, yes," he said, without raising his eyelids. "In a sense. I know how she bows when you meet her in the street, how she dresses when she goes to church. I know her as one knows a woman staying in the same hotel. Just like that."

"It's a pity you can't remember Kitty. All that a wife should be she's been to you."

He sat forward, warming his palms at the blaze and hunching his shoulders as though there was a draught. His silence compelled me to look at him and I found his eyes on me, cold and incredulous and frightened. "Jenny, is this true?"

"That Kitty's been a good wife?"

"That Kitty is my wife. That I am old. That—" he waved a hand at the altered room—"all this."

"It is all true. She is your wife and this place is changed—and it's better and jollier in all sorts of ways, believe me—and fifteen years have passed. Why, Chris, can't you see that I have grown old?" My vanity could hardly endure his slow stare but I kept my fingers clasped on my lap. "You see?"

He turned away with an assenting mutter. But I saw that deep down in him, not to be moved by any material proof, his spirit was incredulous.

"Tell me what seems real to you," I begged. "Chris, be a pal —I'll never tell——"

"Mmm," he said. His elbows were on his knees, and his hands stroked his thick tarnished hair; I could not see his face, but I knew that his skin was red and that his grey eyes were wet and bright. Then suddenly he lifted his chin and laughed, like a happy swimmer breaking through a wave that has swept him far inshore. He glowed with a radiance that illuminated the moment till my blood tingled and I began to run my hands together and laugh too. "Why, Monkey Island's real. But you don't know old Monkey. Let me tell you——"

I have lived so long with the story which he told me that I cannot now remember his shy phrases. But this is how I have visualized his meeting with love on his secret island. I think it is the truth.

25

THE RETURN OF THE SOLDIER

From Uncle Ambrose's gates one took the field-path across the
meadow where Whiston's cows are put to graze and got through the
second stile, the one between the two big alders, into a long straight
road that ran, very tedious in the trough of hot air that is the Thames
valley, across the flat lands to Bray. After a mile or so there branched
from it a private road which followed a line of noble poplars that led
to the pretentiously simple porch of a *cottage ornée* called "The
Hut." One passed that and went on to a group of outbuildings which
gave, as it seemed impossible that bricks and wood and plaster should
give, an impression that they were knock-kneed. There was a shed
that let in the rain through its mossy tiles and sported a board
"Garage"; there was a glass-house containing a pinched and sulky
vine; there was a hasty collection of planks set askew over an agricultural machine of some sort; there were three barrels of concrete and
an empty and rusting aviary. "Margaret's father," said Chris, "had
bought them at sales." Past these marched the poplars and lifted their
strong yet tremulous silver spires on each side of the gravel slope
which went down to the ferry; between two of them—he described it
meticulously as though it were of immense significance—there stood
a white hawthorn. In front were the dark green glassy waters of an
unvisited backwater; and beyond them a bright lawn set with many
walnut trees and a few great chestnuts, well-lit with their candles,
and to the left of that a low white house with a green dome rising in
its middle and a veranda whose roof of hammered iron had gone
verdigris colour with age and the Thames weather. This was the
Monkey Island Inn. The third Duke of Marlborough had built it for a
"folly," and perching there with nothing but a line of walnut trees
and a fringe of lawn between it and the fast full shining Thames
it had a grace and silliness that belonged to the eighteenth century.

Well, one sounded the bell that rung on a post, and presently
Margaret in a white dress would come out of the porch and would
walk to the stone steps down to the river. Invariably, as she passed the
walnut tree that overhung the path, she would pick a leaf and crush
it and sniff the sweet scent; and as she came near the steps she would
shade her eyes and peer across the water. "She is a little near-sighted;
you can't imagine how sweet it makes her look." (I did not say that

I had seen her, for indeed this Margaret I had never seen.) A sudden serene gravity would show that she had seen one, and she would get into the four-foot punt that was used as a ferry and bring it over very slowly, with rather stiff movements of her long arms, to exactly the right place. When she had got the punt up on the gravel her serious brow would relax and she would smile at one and shake hands and say something friendly, like, "Father thought you'd be over this afternoon, it being so fine, so he's saved some ducks' eggs for tea." And then one took the pole from her and brought her back to the island, though probably one did not mount the steps to the lawn for quite a long time. It was so good to sit in the punt by the landing-stage while Margaret dabbled her hands in the black waters and forgot her shyness as one talked. "She's such good company. She's got an accurate mind that would have made her a good engineer, but when she picks up facts she kind of gives them a motherly hug. She's charity and love itself." (Again, I did not say that I had seen her.) If people drifted in to tea one had to talk to her while she cut the bread and butter and the sandwiches in the kitchen, but in this year of floods few visitors cared to try the hard rowing below Bray Lock. So usually one sat down there in the boat, talking with a sense of leisure, as though one had all the rest of one's life in which to carry on this conversation, and noticing how the reflected ripple of the water made a bright vibrant mark upon her throat and other effects of the scene upon her beauty; until the afternoon grew drowsy and she said, "Father will be wanting his tea." And they would go up and find old Allington, in white ducks, standing in the fringe of long grasses and cow-parsley on the other edge of the island, looking to his poultry or his rabbits. He was a little man with a tuft of copper-coloured hair rising from the middle of his forehead like a clown's curl, who shook hands hard and explained very soon that he was a rough diamond. Then they all had tea under the walnut tree where the canary's cage was hanging, and the ducks' eggs would be brought out, and Mr Allington would talk much Thameside gossip: how the lock-keeper at Teddington had had his back broken by a swan, mad as swans are in May, and how they would lose their licence at the Dovetail Arms if they were not careful, and how the man who kept the inn by Surly Hall was like to die, because after he had been cursing his daughter for two days for having run away with a soldier from Windsor Barracks, he had suddenly seen her white face in a clump of rushes in the river just under the hole in the garden fence.

Margaret would sit quiet, round-eyed at the world's ways, and shy because of Chris.

So they would sit on that bright lawn until the day was dyed with evening blue, and Mr Allington was more and more often obliged to leap into the punt to chase his ducks, who had startd on a trip to Bray Lock, or to crawl into the undergrowth after rabbits similarly demoralized by the dusk. And then Chris would say he had to go, and they would stand in a communing silence while the hearty voice of Mr Allington shouted from midstream or under the alder-boughs a disregarded invitation to stay and have a bit of supper. In the liquefaction of colours which happens on a summer evening, when the green grass seemed like a precious fluid poured out on the earth and dripping over to the river, and the chestnut candles were no longer proud flowers, but just wet white lights in the humid mass of the tree, when the brown earth seemed just a little denser than the water, Margaret also participated. Chris explained this part of his story stumblingly, but I too have watched people I loved in the dusk and I know what he meant. As she sat in the punt while he ferried himself across it was no longer visible that her fair hair curled diffi-dently and that its rather wandering parting was a little on one side; that her straight brows, which were a little darker than her hair, were nearly always contracted in a frown of conscientious specula-tion; that her mouth and chin were noble yet delicate as flowers; that her shoulders were slightly hunched because her young body, like a lily stem, found it difficult to manage its own tallness. She was then just a girl in white who lifted a white face or drooped a dull gold head. And as that she was nearer to him than at any other time. That he loved her, in this twilight which obscured all the physical details which he adored, seemed to him a guarantee that theirs was a changeless love which would persist if she were old or maimed or dis-figured. He stood beside the crazy post where the bell hung and watched the white figure take the punt over the black waters, mount the grey steps and assume their greyness, become a green shade in the green darkness of the foliage-darkened lawn, and he exulted in that guarantee.

How long this went on he had forgotten; but it continued for some time before there came the end of his life, the last day he could remember. I was barred out of that day. His lips told me of its physical appearances, while from his wet, bright eyes and his flushed skin, his beautiful signs of a noble excitement, I tried to derive the

THE RETURN OF THE SOLDIER

real story. It seemed that the day when he bicycled over to Monkey Island, happy because Uncle Ambrose had gone up to town and he could stay to supper with the Allingtons, was the most glorious day the year had yet brought. The whole world seemed melting into light. Cumulus clouds floated very high, like lumps of white light against a deep, glowing sky, and dropped dazzling reflections on the beaming Thames. The trees moved not like timber shocked by wind, but floatingly, like weeds at the bottom of a well of sunshine. When Margaret came out of the porch and paused, as she always did, to crush and smell the walnut leaf and shade her eyes with her hand, her white dress shone like silver.

She brought the punt across and said very primly, "Dad will be disappointed, he's gone up to town on business," and answered gravely, "That is very kind of you," when he took the punt-pole from her and said laughingly, "Never mind, I'll come and see you all the same." (I could see them as Chris spoke, so young and pale and solemn, with the intense light spilling all around them.) That afternoon they did not sit in the punt by the landing-stage, but wandered about the island and played with the rabbits and looked at the ducks, and were inordinately silent. For a long time they stood in the fringe of rough grass on the other side of the island and Margaret breathed contentedly that the Thames was so beautiful. Past the spit of sand at the far end of the island, where a great swan swanked to the empty reach that it would protect its mate against all comers, the river opened to a silver breadth between flat meadows stretching back to far rows of pin-thick black poplars, until it wound away to Windsor behind a line of high trees whose heads were bronze with unopened buds and whose flanks were hidden by a hedge of copper-beech and crimson and white hawthorn. Chris said he would take her down to Dorney Lock in the skiff, and she got in very silently and obediently, but as soon as they were out in midstream she developed a sense of duty and said she could not leave the inn with just that boy. And then she went into the kitchen and, sucking in her lower lip for shyness, very conscientiously cut piles of bread and butter in case some visitors came to tea. Just when Chris was convincing her of the impossibility of any visitors arriving they came; a fat woman in a luscious pink blouse and an old chap who had been rowing in a tweed waistcoat. Chris went out, though Margaret laughed and trembled and begged him not to, and waited on them. It should have been a great lark but suddenly he hated them, and when they offered him a

29

tip for pushing the boat off he snarled absurdly and ran back, miraculously relieved, to the bar-parlour.

Still Margaret would not leave the island. "Supposing," she said, "that Mr Learoyd comes for his Bass." But she consented to walk with him to the wild part of the island, where poplars and alders and willows grew round a clearing in which white willow herb and purple figwort and here and there a potato flower, last ailing consequence of one of Mr Allington's least successful enterprises, fought down to the fringe of iris on the river's lip. In this gentle jungle was a rustic seat, relic of a reckless aspiration on the part of Mr Allington to make this a pleasure garden, and on it they sat until a pale moon appeared above the green cornfield on the other side of the river, "Not six yet," he said, taking out his watch. "Not six yet," she repeated. Words between them seemed to bear a significance apart from their meaning. Then a heron flapped gigantic in front of the moon and swung in wide circles round the willow tree before them. "Oh, look!" she cried. He seized the hand she flung upwards and gathered her into his arms. They were so for long while the great bird's wings beat above them.

Afterwards she pulled at his hand. She wanted to go back across the lawn and walk round the inn, which looked mournful as unlit houses do by dusk. They passed beside the green and white stucco barrier of the veranda and stood on the three-cornered lawn that shelved high over the stream at the island's end, regarding the river, which was now something more wonderful than water, because it had taken to its bosom the rose and amber glories of the sunset smouldering behind the elms and Bray church-tower. Birds sat on the telegraph wires that span the river there as the black notes sit on a stave of music. Then she went to the window of the parlour and rested her cheek against the glass, looking in. The little room was sad with twilight, and there was nothing to be seen but Margaret's sewing-machine on the table and the enlarged photograph of Margaret's mother over the mantelpiece, and the views of Tintern Abbey framed in red plush, and on the floor, the marigold pattern making itself felt through the dusk, Mr Allington's carpet slippers. "Think of me sitting in there," she whispered, "not knowing you loved me." Then they went into the bar and drank milk, while she walked about fingering familiar things with an absurd expression of exaltation, as though that day she was fond of everything, even the handles of the beer engine.

When there had descended on them a night as brilliant as the day, he drew her out into the darkness, which was sweet with the scent of walnut leaves, and they went across the lawn, bending beneath the chestnut boughs, not to the wild part of the island, but to a circle of smooth turf divided from it by a railing of wrought iron. On this stood a small Greek temple, looking very lovely in the moonlight. He had never brought Margaret here before because Mr Allington had once told him, spatulate forefinger at his nose, that it had been built by the Dook for his excesses, and it was in the quality of his love for her that he could not bear to think of her in connection with anything base. But tonight there was nothing anywhere but beauty. He lifted her in his arms and carried her within the columns and made her stand in a niche above the altar. A strong stream of moonlight rushed upon her there; by its light he could not tell if her hair was white as silver or yellow as gold, and again he was filled with exultation because he knew that it would not have mattered if it had been white. His love was changeless. Lifting her down from the niche, he told her so. And as he spoke her warm body melted to nothingness in his arms. The columns that had stood so hard and black against the quivering tide of moonlight and starlight tottered and dissolved. He was lying in a hateful world where barbed-wire entanglements showed impish knots against a livid sky full of booming noise and splashes of fire and wails for water, and the stretcher bearers were hurting his back intolerably.

Chris fell to blowing out the candles, and I, perhaps because the egotistical part of me was looking for something to say that would make him feel me devoted and intimate, could not speak.

Suddenly he desisted, stared at a candle flame, and said: "If you had seen the way she rested her cheek against the glass and looked into the little room, you'd understand that I can't say, 'Yes, Kitty's my wife, and Margaret somehow just nothing at all.'"

"Of course you can't," I murmured.

We gripped hands, and he brought down on our conversation the finality of darkness.

4

Next morning it appeared that the chauffeur had to take the Rolls-Royce up to town to get a part replaced, and Margaret could not be brought from Wealdstone till the afternoon. It fell to me to fetch her. "At least," Kitty had said, "I might be spared that." Before I started

I went to the pond on the hill's edge. It is a place where autumn lives half the year, for even when the spring lights tongues of green fire in the undergrowth and the valley shows sunlit between the tree trunks, here the pond is fringed with yellow bracken and tinged bramble, and the water flows amber over last winter's leaves. Through this brown gloom, darkened now by a surly sky, Chris was taking the skiff, standing in the stern and using his oar like a gondolier. He had come down here soon after breakfast, driven from the house by the strangeness of all but the outer walls, and discontented with the ground because everywhere but this wet intractable spot bore the marks of Kitty's genius. After lunch there had been another attempt to settle down, but, with a grim glare at a knot of late Christmas roses bright in a copse that fifteen years ago had been dark, he went back to the russet-eaved boat-house and this play with the skiff. It was a boy's sport, and it was dreadful to see him turn a middle-aged face as he brought the boat inshore.

"I'm just going down to fetch Margaret," I said.

He thanked me for it.

"But, Chris, I must tell you. I've seen Margaret. She came up here, so kind and gentle, to tell us you were wounded. She's the greatest dear in the world. But she's not as you think of her. She's old, Chris. She isn't beautiful any more. She's drearily married. She's seamed and scored and ravaged by squalid circumstances. You can't love her when you see her."

"Didn't I tell you last night," he said, "that that doesn't matter?" He dipped his oar to a stroke that sent him far away from me. "Bring her soon. I shall wait for her down here."

Wealdstone is not, in its way, a bad place; it lies in the lap of open country and at the end of every street rise the green hill of Harrow and the spires of Harrow School. But all the streets are long and red and freely articulated with railway arches, and factories spoil the skyline with red angular chimneys, and in front of the shops stand little women with backs ridged by cheap stays, who tapped their upper lips with their forefingers and made other feeble, doubtful gestures as though they wanted to buy something and knew that if they did they would have to starve some other appetite. When we asked them the way they turned to us faces sour with thrift. It was a town of people who could not do as they liked. And here Margaret lived, in a long road of red brick boxes, flecked here and there with the pink blur of almond blossom, which debouched on a flat field where green grass rose up rank through clay mould blackened by coal dust from the railway line and the adjacent goods yard. Mariposa, which was the last house in the road, did not even have an almond tree. In her front garden, which seemed to be imperfectly reclaimed from the greasy field, yellow crocus and some sodden squills just winked, and the back, where a man was handling a spade without mastery, presented the austere appearance of an allotment. And not only did Margaret live in this place; she belonged to it. When she opened the door she gazed at me with watering eyes and in perplexity stroked her disordered hair with a floury hand. Her face was sallow with heat, and beads of perspiration glittered in the deep dragging line between her nostrils and the corners of her mouth.

She said, "He's home?"

I nodded.

She pulled me inside and slammed the door. "Is he well?"

"Quite," I answered.

Her tense stare relaxed. She rubbed her hands on her overall and said, "You'll excuse me. It's the girl's day out. If you'll step into the parlour. . . ."

So in her parlour I sat and told her how it was with Chris and how greatly he desired to see her. And as I spoke of his longing I turned my eyes away from her, because she was sitting on a sofa, upholstered in velveteen of a sickish green, which was so low that her knees stuck up in front of her and she had to clasp them with her seamed floury hands; and I could see that the skin of her face was damp. And then my voice failed me as I looked round the room, because I saw just what Margaret had seen that evening fifteen years ago when she had laid her cheek to the parlour window at Monkey Island. There was the enlarged photograph of Margaret's mother over the mantelpiece; on the walls were the view of Tintern Abbey, framed in red plush; between the rickety legs of the china cupboard was the sewing-machine and tucked into the corner between my chair and the fender were a pair of carpet slippers. All her life long Margaret, who in her time had partaken of the inalienable dignity of a requited love, had lived with men who wore carpet slippers in the house. I turned my eyes away again and this time looked down the garden at the figure that was not so much digging as exhibiting his incapacity to deal with a spade. He was sneezing very frequently, and his sneezes made the unbuckled straps at the back of his waistcoat wag violently. I supposed him to be Mr William Grey.

I had finished the statement of our sad case; and I saw that though she had not moved, clasping her knees in a set hideous attitude, the tears were rolling down her cheeks, "Oh, don't! Oh, don't!" I exclaimed, standing up. Her tear-stained immobility touched the heart. "He's not so bad—he'll get quite well. . . ."

"I know, I know," she said miserably. "I don't believe that anything bad would be allowed to happen to Chris for long. And I'm sure," she said kindly, "you're looking after him beautifully. But when a thing you had thought had ended fifteen years ago starts all over again, and you're very tired. . . ." She drew one of those dreadful hands across her tears, her damp skin, her rough, bagging overall. "I'm hot. I've been baking. You can't get a girl nowadays that understands the baking." Her gaze became remote and tender, she said in a manner that was at once argumentative and narrative, as though she were telling the whole story to a neighbour over the garden wall, "I suppose I ought to say that he isn't right in his head and I'm married—but oh!" she cried, and I felt as though after much fumbling with damp matches and many doubts as to whether there was any oil in the wick I had lit the lamp at last, "I want to see him so! It's wrong—I know it's wrong, but I am so glad Chris wants to see me too!"

"You'll do him good!" I found myself raising my voice to the pitch she had suddenly attained as though to keep her at it. "Come now!"

She dipped suddenly to compassion. "But the young lady?" she asked timidly. "She was upset last time I went. I've often wondered if I did right in going. Even if Chris has forgotten her," she gave out with an air of exposition, "he'll want to do what's right. He couldn't bear to hurt her."

"That's true," I said. "You do know our Chris. He watches her out of the corner of his eye, even when he's feeling at his worst, to see she isn't wincing. But she sent me here today."

"Oh!" cried Margaret, glowing. "She must have a lovely nature!"

I lost suddenly the thread of the conversation. I could not talk about Kitty. She appeared to me at that moment a faceless figure with flounces, just as most of the servants at Baldry Court appear to me as faceless figures with caps and aprons. There were only two real people in the world, Chris and this woman whose personality was sounding through her squalor like a beautiful voice singing in a darkened room, and I was absorbed in a mental vision of them. You know how the saints and the prophets are depicted in the steel engravings in old

Bibles; so they were standing, in flowing white robes, on rocks against a pitch black sky, a strong light beating on their eyes upturned in ecstasy, and their hands outstretched to receive the spiritual blessing of which the fierce rays were an emanation. Into that rapt silence I desired to break, and I whispered irrelevantly, "Oh, nothing, nothing is too good for Chris," while I said to myself, "if she were really like that, solemn and beatified," and my eyes returned to look despairingly on her ugliness. But she was really like that. She had responded to my irrelevant murmur of adoration by just such a solemn and beatified appearance as I had imagined. Her grave eyes were upturned, those terrible hands lay palm upwards on her knees as though to receive the love of which her radiance was an emanation. And then, at a sound in the kitchen, she snatched my exaltation from me by suddenly turning dull, "I think that's Mr Grey come in from his gardening. You'll excuse me. . . ."

Through the open door I heard a voice saying in a way which suggested that its production involved much agitation of a prominent Adam's apple, "Well, dear, seeing you had a friend I thought I'd better slip up and change my gardening trousers." I do not know what she said to him, but her voice was soft and comforting and occasionally girlish and interrupted by laughter, and I perceived from its sound that with characteristic gravity she had accepted it as her mission to keep loveliness and excitement alive in his life. "An old friend of mine has been wounded," was the only phrase I heard, but when she drew him out into the garden under the window she had evidently explained the situation away, for he listened docilely as she said, "I've made some rock-cakes for your tea. And if I'm late for supper there's a dish of macaroni cheese you must put in the oven and a tin of tomatoes to eat with it. And there's a little rhubarb and shape." She told them off on her fingers, and then whisked him round and buckled the wagging straps at the back of his waistcoat. He was a lank man with curly grey hairs growing from every place where it is inadvisable that hairs should grow, from the inside of his ears, from his nostrils, on the back of his hands; but he looked pleased when she touched him and said in a devoted way, "Very well, dear. Don't worry about me. I'll trot along after tea and have a game of draughts with Mr Podds." She answered, "Yes, dear. And now get on with those cabbages. You're going to keep me in lovely cabbages just as you did last year, won't you, darling?" She linked arms with him and took him back to his digging.

35

When she came back into the parlour again she was wearing that yellowish raincoat, that hat whose hearse plumes nodded over its sticky straw, that grey alpaca skirt. I first defensively clutched my hands. It would have been such agony to the finger tips to touch any part of her apparel. And then I thought of Chris, to whom a second before I had hoped to bring a serene comforter. I perceived clearly that that ecstatic woman lifting her eyes and her hands to the benediction of love was Margaret as she existed in eternity; but this was Margaret as she existed in time, as the fifteen years between Monkey Island and this damp day in Ladysmith Road had irreparably made her. Well, I had promised to bring her to him.

She said, "I'm ready," and against that simple view of her condition I had no argument. But when she paused by the painted drain pipe in the hall and peered under contracted brows for that unveracious tortoise-shell handle, I said hastily, "Oh, don't trouble about an umbrella."

"I'll maybe need it walking home," she pondered.

"But the car will bring you back."

"Oh, that will be lovely!" She laughed nervously, looking very plain. "Do you know, I know the way we're coming together is terrible, but I can't think of a meeting with Chris as anything but a kind of treat. I've got a sort of party feeling now!"

As she held the gate open for me she looked back at the house. "It is a horrid little house, isn't it?" she asked. She evidently desired sanction for a long suppressed discontent.

"It isn't very nice," I agreed.

"They put cows sometimes into the field at the back," she went on, as if conscientiously counting her blessings. "I like that. But otherwise it isn't much."

"But it's got a very pretty name," I said, laying my hand on the raised metal letters that spelt "Mariposa" across the gate.

"Ah, isn't it!" she exclaimed, with the smile of the inveterate romanticist. "It's Spanish, you know, for butterfly."

Once we were in the automobile she became a little sullen with shyness because she felt herself so big and clumsy, her clothes so coarse against the fine upholstery, the silver vase of Christmas roses, and all the deliberate delicacy of Kitty's car. She was afraid of the chauffeur, as the poor are always afraid of menservants, and ducked her head when he got out to start the car. To recall her to ease and beauty I told her that though Chris had told me all about their

36

meeting he knew nothing of their parting, and that I wished very much to hear what had happened. And in a deep, embarrassed voice she began to tell me about Monkey Island. It was strange that both Chris and she spoke of it as though it were not a place, but a magic state which largely explained the actions performed in it. Strange too that both of them should describe meticulously the one white hawthorn that stood among the poplars by the ferryside; I suppose that a thing that one has looked at with somebody one loves acquires for ever after a special significance. She said that her father had gone there when she was fourteen. After Mrs Allington had been taken away by a swift and painful death the cheer of his Windsor hostelry had become intolerable to the man. He regarded the whole world as her grave; and the tipsy sergeants in scarlet and the carter crying for a pint of four-half, and the horses dipping their mild noses to the trough in the courtyard, all seemed to be defiling it by their happy, silly appetites. So they went to Monkey Island, whose utter difference was a healing, and settled down happily in its green silence. All the summer was lovely; quiet kind people, schoolmasters who fished, men who wrote books, married couples who still loved solitude, used to come and stay in the bright little inn. And all the winter was lovely too; her temperament could see an adventure in taking up the carpets because the Thames was coming into the coffee-room. That was the tale of her life for four years. With her head on one side, and an air of judging this question by the light of experience, she pronounced that she had then been happy.

Then, one April afternoon, Chris landed at the island, and by the first clean quick movement of tying up his boat made her his slave. I could imagine that it would be so. He was so wonderful when he was young; he possessed in great measure the loveliness of young men, which is like the loveliness of the spry foal or the sapling, but in him it was vexed into a serious and moving beauty by the inhabiting soul. When the sunlight lay on him, discerning the gold hairs on his brown head, or when he was subject to any other physical pleasure there was always reserve in his response to it; from his eyes, which though grey were somehow dark with speculation, one perceived that he was distracted by participation in some spiritual drama. To see him was to desire intimacy with him so that one might intervene between this body which was formed for happiness, and this soul which cherished so deep a faith in tragedy. . . . Well, she gave Chris ducks' eggs for tea. "No one ever had ducks' eggs like father did.

37

It was his way of feeding them. It didn't pay, of course, but they *were* good." Before the afternoon was out he had snared them all with the silken net of his fine manners; he had talked to father about his poultry and walked about the runs, and then as on many succeeding days he had laid his charm at the girl's feet. "But I thought he must be someone royal, and when he kept on coming I thought it must be for the ducks' eggs." Then her damp, dull skin flushed suddenly to a warm glory, and she began to stammer.

"I know all about that," I said quickly. I was more afraid that I should feel envy or any base passion in the presence of this woman than I have ever been of anything in my life. "I want to hear how you came to part."

"Oh," she cried. "It was the silliest quarrel. We had known how we felt for just a week. Such a week. Lovely weather we had, and father had noticed nothing. I didn't want him to, because I thought father might want the marriage soon and think any delay a slight on me, and I knew we would have to wait. Eh, I can remember saying to myself, 'Perhaps five years,' trying to make it as bad as I could so that if we could marry sooner it would be a lovely surprise." She repeated it with soft irony. "Perhaps five years!"

"Well, then, on Thursday afternoon I'd gone on the backwater with Bert Wells, nephew to Mr Wells who keeps the inn at Surly Hall. I was laughing out loud because he did row so funny. He's a town chap, and he was handling those oars for all the world as though they were teaspoons. The old dinghy just sat on the water like a hen on its chicks and didn't move, and he so sure of himself! I just sat and laughed and laughed. Then all of a sudden—*clang-clang!* the bell at the ferry. And there was Chris, standing up there under the poplars, his brows straight and black and not a smile on him. I felt very bad. We picked him up in the dinghy and took him across, and still he didn't smile. He and I got on the island and Bert, who saw there was something wrong, said, 'Well, I'll toddle off.' And there I was on the lawn with Chris, and he angry and somehow miles away. I remember him saying, 'Here I am, coming to say good-bye because I must go away tonight, and I find you larking with that bounder,' and I said, 'Oh, Chris! I've known Bert all my life, through him coming to his uncle for the holidays and we weren't larking. It was only that he couldn't row.' And he went on talking and then it struck me he wasn't trusting me as he would trust a girl of his own class, and I told him so, and he went on being cruel. Oh, don't make

me remember the things we said to each other! It doesn't help. . . .
At last I said something awful and he said, 'Very well, I agree. I'll
go,' and he walked over to where the boy was chopping wood and got
him to take him over in the punt. As he passed me he turned away
his face. Well, that's all."

I had got the key at last. There had been a spring at Baldry Court
fifteen years ago which was desolate for all that there was beautiful
weather. Chris had lingered with Uncle Ambrose in his Thameside
rectory as he had never lingered before, and old Mr Baldry was filling
the house with a sense of hot, apoplectic misery. All day he was up in
town at the office and without explanation he had discontinued his
noontide habit of ringing up his wife. All night he used to sit in the
library looking over his papers and ledgers; the housemaids often
found him in the morning asleep across his desk, very red, yet looking
dead. The men he brought home to dinner treated him with a kindness and consideration which was not the tribute that that victorious
and trumpeting personality was accustomed to exact; in the course of
conversation with them he dropped braggartly cheerful hints of impending ruin, which it would have been humiliating to address to us
directly. At last there came one morning when he said to Mrs Baldry
across the breakfast table, "I've sent for Chris. If the boy's worth his
salt . . ." It was an appalling admission, like the groan of an old ship
as her timbers shiver, from a man who doubted the capacity of his son
as fathers always doubt the capacity of the children of their old age.
It was that evening, as I went down to see the new baby at the lodge,
that I met Chris coming up the drive. Through the blue twilight his
white face had a drowned look. I remember it well because my
surprise that he passed me without seeing me had made me perceive
for the first time that he had never seen me at all save in the most
cursory fashion; on the eye of his mind, I realized thenceforward,
I had hardly impinged. That night he talked till late with his father
and in the morning he had started for Mexico, to keep the mines
going through the revolution, to keep the firm's head above water and
Baldry Court sleek and hospitable, to keep everything bright and
splendid save only his youth, which after that was dulled by care.

Something of this I told Margaret, to which she answered, "Oh, I
know all that," and she went on with her story. On Sunday, three
days after their quarrel, Mr Allington was found dead in his bed.
"I wanted Chris so badly, but he never came, he never wrote," and
she fell into a lethargic disposition to sit all day and watch the

Thames flow by, from which she was hardly roused by finding that her father had left her nothing save an income of twenty pounds a year in unrealizable stock. She negotiated the transfer of the lease of the inn to a publican and, after exacting a promise from the new hostess that she would forward all letters that might come, embarked upon an increasingly unfortunate career as a mother's help. First she fell into the hands of a noble Irish family in reduced circumstances named Murphy, whose conduct in running away and leaving her in a Brighton hotel with her wages and her board unpaid, still distressed and perplexed her. "Why did they do it?" she asked. "I liked them so. The baby was a darling and Mrs Murphy had such a nice way of speaking. But it almost makes one think evil of people when they do a thing like that." After two years of less sensational but still uneasy adventures, she had come upon a large and needy family called Watson who lived at Chiswick, and almost immediately Mr William Grey, who was Mrs Watson's brother, had begun a courtship that sounded to me as though it had consisted of an incessant whining up at her protection instinct. "Mr Grey," she said softly, as though stating his chief claim to affection, "has never been very successful." And still no letter ever came.

So, five years after she left Monkey Island, she married Mr William Grey. Soon after their marriage he lost his job and was for some time out of work; later he developed a weak chest that needed constant attention. "But it all helped to pass the time," she said cheerfully and without irony. So it happened that it was not for many years that she had the chance of revisiting Monkey Island. At first there was no money and later there was the necessity of seeking the healthful breezes of Brighton or Bognor or Southend, which were the places in which Mr Grey's chest oddly elected to thrive. And when those obstacles were removed she was lethargic; and also she had heard that the inn was not being managed as it ought to be, and she could not have borne to see the green home of her youth defiled. But then there had come a time when she had been very much upset; she glared a little wildly at me as she said this, as if she would faint if I asked her any questions. And then she had suddenly become obsessed with a desire to see Monkey Island once more.

"Well, when we got to the ferry Mr Grey says, 'But mercy, Margaret, there's water all round it!' and I said, 'But, William, that's just it!'" They found that the island was clean and decorous again, for it had but recently changed hands. "Father and daughter the new people are, just like me and dad, and Mr Taylor's something of dad's cut, too, but he comes from the North. But Miss Taylor's much handsomer than I ever was; a really big woman she is, and such lovely golden hair. They were very kind when they heard who I was; gave us duck and green peas for lunch and I did think of dad. They were nothing like as good as his ducks, but then I expect they paid. And then Miss Taylor took William out to look at the garden. I could see he didn't like it, for he's always shy with a showy woman, and I was going after them when Mr Taylor said, 'Here, stop a minute, I've got something here that may interest you. Just come in here,' and he led me to the roller desk in the office. Out of a drawer he took twelve letters addressed to me in Chris' handwriting.

"He was a kind man. He put me into a chair and called Miss Taylor in and told her to keep William out in the garden as long as possible. At last I said, 'But Mrs Hitchcock did say she'd send my letters on.' And he said, 'But Mrs Hitchcock hadn't been three weeks before she bolted with a bookie from Bray. And after that Hitchcock mixed his drinks and got careless.' The Taylors had found these stuffed into the desk when they came."

"And what was in them?"

"For a long time I did not read them. I thought it was against my duty as a wife. But when I got that telegram saying he was wounded I went upstairs and read those letters. Oh, those letters. . . ."

She bowed her head and wept.

As the car swung through the gates of Baldry Court she sat up and dried her eyes. She looked out at the strip of turf, so bright that one would think it wet, and lit here and there with snowdrops and scillas and crocuses, that runs between the drive and the tangle of silver birch and bramble and fern. There is no æsthetic reason for that border; the common outside looks lovelier where it fringes the road with dark gorse and rough amber grasses. Its use is purely philosophic; it proclaims that here we estimate only controlled beauty, that the wild will not have its way within our gates, that it must be made delicate and decorated into felicity. Surely she must see that this was no place for beauty that has been not mellowed but lacerated by time, that no one accustomed to live here could help wincing at such external dinginess as hers. . . . But instead she said, "It's a big place. How poor Chris must have worked to keep it up." The pity of this woman was like a flaming sword. No one had ever before pitied Chris for the magnificence of Baldry Court. It had been our pretence that

41

by wearing costly clothes and organizing a costly life we had been the servants of his desire. But she revealed the truth that although he did indeed desire a magnificent house, it was a house not built with hands.

But that she was wise, that the angels would of a certainty be on her side, did not make her any the less physically offensive to our atmosphere. All my doubts as to the wisdom of my expedition revived in the little time we had to spend in the hall waiting for the tea which I had ordered in the hope that it might help Margaret to compose her distressed face. She hovered with her back to the oak table, fumbling with her thread gloves, winking her tear-red eyes, tapping with her foot on the carpet, throwing her weight from one leg to the other, and constantly contrasted her appearance with the new acquisition of Kitty's decorative genius which stood so close behind her on the table that I was afraid it might be upset by one of her spasmodic movements. This was a shallow black bowl in the centre of which crouched on hands and knees a white naked nymph, her small head intently drooped to the white flowers that floated on the black waters all around her. Beside the pure black of the bowl her rusty plumes looked horrible; beside that white nymph, eternally innocent of all but the contemplation of beauty, her opaque skin and her suffering were offensive; beside its air of being the coolly conceived and leisurely executed production of a hand and brain lifted by their rare quality to the service of the not absolutely necessary, her appearance of having but for the moment ceased to cope with a vexed and needy environment struck one as a cancerous blot on the fair world. Perhaps it was absurd to pay attention to this indictment of a woman by a potter's toy, but that toy happened to be also a little image of Chris' conception of women. Exquisite we were according to our equipment; unflushed by appetite or passion, even noble passion; our small heads bent intently on the white flowers of luxury floating on the black waters of life; and he had known none other than us. With such a mental habit a man could not help but wince at Margaret. I drank my tea very slowly because I previsioned what must happen in the next five minutes. Down there by the pond he would turn at the sound of those heavy boots on the path, and with one glance he would assess the age of her, the rubbed surface of her, the torn fine texture, and he would show to her squalid mask just such a blank face as he had shown Kitty the night before. Although I have a gift for self-pity I knew her case would then be worse than mine; for it would be worse to see, as she would see, the ardour in his eyes give place to kindliness than never to have seen ardour there. He would hesitate, she would make one of her harried gestures and trail away with that wet patient look which was her special line. He would go back to his boyish sport with the skiff; I hoped the brown waters would not seem too kind. She would go back to Mariposa, sit on her bed, and read those letters. . . .

"And now," she said brightly, as I put down my cup, "may I see Chris?" She had not a doubt of the enterprise.

I took her into the drawing-room and opened one of the French windows. "Go past the cedars to the pool," I told her. "He is rowing there."

"That is nice," she said. "He always looks so lovely in a boat."

I called after her, trying to hint the possibility of a panic breakdown to their meeting, "You'll find he's altered. . . ."

She cried gleefully, "Oh, I shall know him."

As I went upstairs I became conscious that I was near to a bodily collapse; I suppose that the truth is that I was physically so jealous of Margaret that it was making me ill. But suddenly, just like a tired person dropping a weight they know is precious but that they cannot carry for another moment, my mind refused to consider the situation any longer and turned to the perception of material things. I leant over the banisters and looked down at the fineness of the hall: the deliberate figure of the nymph in her circle of black water, the clear pink and white of Kitty's chintz, the limpid surface of the oak, the gay reflected colours in the panelled walls. I said to myself, "If everything else goes there is always this to fall back on," and I went on, pleased that I was wearing delicate stuffs and that I had a smooth skin, pleased that the walls of the corridor were so soft a twilight blue, pleased that through a far-off open door came a stream of light that made the carpet blaze its stronger blue. And when I saw that it was the nursery door that was open, and that in Nanny's big chair at the window Kitty sat, I did not care about the peaked face she lifted, its fairness palely gilt by the March sunlight, nor the tremendous implications of the fact that she had come to the dead child's nursery though she had not washed her hair. I said sternly, because she had forgotten that we lived in the impregnable fortress of a gracious life, "Oh, Kitty, that poor battered thing outside."

She stared so grimly out into the garden that my eyes followed her stare.

It was one of those draggled days, so common at the end of March, when a garden looks at its worst. The wind that was rolling up to check a show of sunshine had taken away the cedar's dignity of solid shade, had set the black firs beating their arms together and had filled the sky with glaring grey clouds that dimmed the brilliance of the crocus. It was to give gardens a point on days such as these, when the planned climax of this flower bed and that stately tree goes for nothing, that the old gardeners raised statues in their lawns and walks, large things with a subject, mossy Tritons or nymphs with an urn, that held the eye. Even so in this unrestful garden one's eye lay on the figure in the yellow raincoat that was standing in the middle of the lawn.

How her near presence had been known by Chris I do not understand, but there he was, running across the lawn as night after night I had seen him in my dreams running across No Man's Land. I knew that so he would close his eyes as he ran; I knew that so he would pitch on his knees when he reached safety. I assumed that at Margaret's feet lay safety, even before I saw her arms brace him under the armpits with a gesture that was not passionate, but rather the movement of one carrying a wounded man from under fire. But even when she had raised his head to the level of her lips, the central issue was not decided. I covered my eyes and said aloud, "In a minute he will see her face, her hands." But although it was a long time before I looked again they were still clinging breast to breast. It was as though her embrace fed him, he looked so strong as he broke away. They stood with clasped hands, looking at one another (they looked straight, they looked delightedly!), and then as if resuming a conversation tiresomely interrupted by some social obligation, drew together again and passed under the tossing branches of the cedar to the wood beyond. I reflected, while Kitty wept, how entirely right Chris had been in his assertion that to lovers innumerable things do not matter.

5

After the automobile had taken Margaret away Chris came to us as we sat in the drawing-room and, after standing for a while in the glow of the fire, hesitantly said, "I want to tell you that I know it is all right. Margaret has explained to me."

Kitty crumpled her sewing into a white ball. "You mean, I suppose, that you know I'm your wife. I'm pleased that you describe
that as knowing 'it's all right,' and grateful that you have accepted
it at last on Margaret's authority. This is an occasion that would make
any wife proud." Her irony was as faintly acrid as a caraway seed,
and never afterwards did she reach even that low pitch of violence,
for from that mild forward droop of the head with which he received
the mental lunge she realized suddenly that this was no pretence and
that something as impassable as death lay between them. Thereafter
his proceedings evoked no comment but suffering. There was nothing
to say when all day, save for those hours of the afternoon which
Margaret spent with him, he sat like a blind man waiting for his
darkness to lift. There was nothing to say when he did not seem to
see our flowers, yet kept till they rotted on the stalk the daffodils
which Margaret brought from the garden that looked like an allotment. So Kitty lay about like a broken doll, face downward on a sofa
with one limp arm dangling to the floor, or protruding stiff feet in
fantastic slippers from the end of her curtained bed; and I tried to
make my permanent wear that mood which had mitigated the end
of my journey with Margaret, a mood of intense perception in which
my strained mind settled on every vivid object that came under my
eyes and tried to identify myself with its brightness and its lack of
human passion. This does not mean that I passed my day in a state of
joyous appreciation; it means that many times in the lanes of Harrow-
weald I have stood for long looking up at the fine tracery of bare
boughs against the hard, high spring sky while the cold wind rushed
through my skirts and chilled me to the bone, because I was afraid
that when I moved my body and my attention I might begin to think.
Indeed grief is not the clear melancholy the young believe it. It is like
a siege in a tropical city. The skin dries and the throat parches as
though one were living in the heat of the desert; water and wine taste
warm in the mouth and food is of the substance of the sand; one
snarls at one's company; thoughts prick one through sleep like
mosquitoes. . . .

A week after my journey to Wealdstone I went to Kitty to ask her
to come for a walk with me and found her stretched on her pillows,
holding a review of her underclothing. She refused bitterly and added,
"Be back early. Remember Dr Gilbert Anderson is coming at half-past
four. He's our last hope. And tell that woman she must see him.
He says he wants to see everybody concerned," and continued to look

45

wanly at the frail luminous silks her maid brought her, as a specu-
lator who had cornered the article for which there had been no
demand might look at his damnably numerous, damnably unprofitable
freights. So I went out alone into a soft day, with the dispelled winter
lurking above in high dark clouds under which there ran quick fresh
currents of air, and broken shafts of insistent sunshine that spread a
grey clarity of light in which every colour showed sharp and strong.
On the breast that Harrow-weald turns to the south they had set a
lambing-yard, whose pale lavender hurdles and gold strewn straw
and orange drinking-trough were new gay notes on the opaque winter
green of the slope, and the apprehensive bleatings of the ewes wound
about the hill like a river of sound as they were driven up a lane
hidden by the hedge. The lines of bare elms darkening the plains
below made it seem as though the tide of winter had fallen and left
this promontory bare and sparkling in the spring. I liked it so much
that I opened the gate and went and sat down on a tree that had been
torn up by the roots in the great gale last year, but had not yet
resigned itself to death and was bravely decking itself with purple
elm-flowers. That pleased me too, and I wished I had someone with
me to enjoy this artless little show of the new year. I had not really
wanted Kitty; the companions I needed were Chris and Margaret.
Chris would have talked as he loved to do when he looked at leisure
on a broad valley, about ideas which he had to exclude from his
ordinary hours lest they should break the power of business over his
mind, and Margaret would have gravely watched the argument from
the shadow of her broad hat to see that it kept true, like a housewife
watching a saucepan of milk lest it should boil over. They were
naturally my friends, these gentle speculative people. Then suddenly
I was stunned with jealousy. It was not their love for one another
that caused me such agony at that moment; it was the thought of the
things their eyes had rested upon together. I imagined that white
hawthorn among the poplars by the ferry on which they had looked
fifteen years ago at Monkey Island, and it was more than I could bear.
I thought how even now they might be exclaiming at the green
smoke of the first buds on the brown undergrowth round the pond,
and at that I slid off the tree-trunk and began walking very quickly
down the hill. The red cows drank from the pond cupped by the
willow roots, a raw-boned stallion danced clumsily because warmth
was running through the ground. I found a stream in the fields and
followed it till it became a shining dyke embanked with glowing

green and gold mosses in the midst of woods; and the sight of those things was no sort of joy, because my vision was solitary. I wanted to end my desperation by leaping from a height, and I climbed on a knoll and flung myself face downwards on the dead leaves below.

I was now utterly cut off from Chris. Before, when I looked at him I knew an instant ease in the sight of the short golden down on his cheeks, the ridge of bronze flesh above his thick fair eyebrows. But now I was too busy reassuring him by showing a steady, undistorted profile crowned by a neat proud sweep of hair instead of the tear-darkened mask he always feared, ever to have enough vitality left over to enjoy his presence. I spoke in a calm voice full from the chest quite unfluted with agony; I read *Country Life* with ponderous interest; I kept my hands, which I desired to wring, in doeskin gloves for most of the day; I played with the dogs a great deal and wore my thickest tweeds; I pretended that the slight heaviness of my features is a correct indication of my temperament. The only occasion when I could safely let the sense of him saturate me as it used was when I met Margaret in the hall as she came or went. She was very different now; she had a little smile in her eyes as though she were listening to a familiar air played far away, her awkwardness seemed indecision as to whether she should walk or dance to that distant music, her shabbiness was no more repulsive than the untidiness of a child who had been so eager to get to the party that it has not let its nurse fasten its frock. Always she extended a hand in an unbuttoned black thread glove and said, "It's another fine day again," or diffidently, as Kitty continued to withhold her presence, "I hope Mrs Baldry is keeping well." Then as our hands touched he was with us, invoked by our common adoration; I felt his rough male texture and saw the clear warmth of his brown and gold colouring. I thought of him with the passion of exile. To Margaret it was a call, and she moved past me to the garden, holding her hands in front of her as though she bore invisible gifts, and pausing on the step of the French window to smile to herself, as if in her heart she turned over the precious thought, "He is here. This garden holds him." My moment, my small sole subsistence, ended in a feeling of jealousy as ugly and unmental as sickness. This was the saddest spring.

Nothing could mitigate the harshness of our rejection. You may think we were attaching an altogether fictitious importance to what was merely the delusion of a madman. But every minute of the day, particularly at those trying times when he strolled about the house and grounds with the doctors, smiling courteously, but without joy, and answering their questions with the crisp politeness of a man shaking off an inquisitive commercial traveller in a hotel smoking-room, it became plain that if madness means liability to wild error about the world, Chris was not mad. It was our peculiar shame that he had rejected us when he had attained to something saner than sanity. His very loss of memory was a triumph over the limitations of language which prevent the mass of men from making explicit statements about their spiritual relationships. If he had said to Kitty and me, "I do not know you," we would have gaped; if he had expanded his meaning and said, "You are nothing to me; my heart is separate from your hearts," we would have wept at an unkindness he had not intended. But by the blankness of those eyes which saw me only as a disregarded playmate and Kitty not at all save as a stranger who had somehow become a decorative presence in his home and the orderer of his meals he let us know completely where we were. Even though I lay weeping at it on the dead leaves I was sensible of the bitter rapture that attends the discovery of any truth. I felt, indeed, a cold intellectual pride in his refusal to remember his prosperous maturity and his determined dwelling in the time of his first love, for it showed him so much saner than the rest of us, who take life as it comes, loaded with the inessential and the irritating. I was even willing to admit that this choice of what was to him reality out of all the appearances so copiously presented by the world, this adroit recovery of the dropped pearl of beauty, was the act of genius I had always expected from him. But that did not make less agonizing this exclusion from his life.

I could not think clearly about it. I suppose that the subject of our tragedy, written in spiritual terms, was that in Kitty he had turned from the type of woman that makes the body conqueror of the soul and in me from the type that mediates between the soul and the body and makes them run even and unhasty like a well-matched pair of carriage horses, and had given himself to a woman whose bleak habit it was to champion the soul against the body. But I saw it just as a fantastic act of cruelty that I could only think of as a conjunction of calamitous images. I think of it happening somewhere behind the front, at the end of a straight road that runs by a line of ragged poplars between mud flats made steel-bright with floods pitted by the soft slow rain. There, past a church that lacks its tower, stand a score of houses, each hideous with patches of bare bricks that show like

48

sores through the ripped-off plaster and uncovered rafters which stick out like broken bones. There are people still living here. A slut sits at the door of a filthy cottage, counting some dirty linen and waving her bare arms at some passing soldiers. And at another house there is a general store with strings of orange onions and bunches of herbs hanging from the roof, a brown gloom rich with garlic and humming with the flies that live all the year round in French village shops, a black cat rubbing her sleekness against the lintel. It is in there that Chris is standing, facing across the counter an old man in a blue blouse, with a scar running white into the grey thickets of his beard, an old man with a smile at once lewd and benevolent, repulsive with dirt and yet magnificent by reason of the Olympian structure of his body. I think he is the soul of the universe, equally cognizant and disregardful of every living thing, to whom I am no more dear than the bare-armed slut at the neighbouring door. And Chris is leaning on the counter, his eyes glazed. (This is his spirit; his body lies out there in the drizzle at the other end of the road.) He is look-ing down on two crystal balls that the old man's foul strong hands have rolled across to him. In one he sees Margaret; not in her raincoat and her nodding plumes but as she is transfigured in the light of eternity. Long he looks there; then drops a glance to the other, just long enough to see that in its depths Kitty and I walk in bright dresses through our glowing gardens. We had suffered no trans-figuration, for we are as we are and there is nothing more to us. The whole truth about us lies in our material seeming. He sighs a deep sigh of delight and puts out his hand to the ball where Margaret shines. His sleeve catches the other one and sends it down to crash in a thousand pieces on the floor. The old man's smile continues to be lewd and benevolent, he is still not more interested in me than in the bare-armed slut; and Chris is wholly enclosed in his intentness on his chosen crystal. No one weeps for this shattering of our world. . . .

I stirred on the dead leaves as though I had really heard the breaking of the globe and cried out, "Gilbert Anderson, Gilbert Anderson must cure him." Heaven knows that I had no reason for faith in any doctor, for during the past week so many of them, sleek as seals with their neatly brushed hair and their frock-coats, had stood round Chris and looked at him with the consequenceless deliberation of a plumber. Their most successful enterprise had been his futile hypnotism. He had submitted to it as a good-natured man submits to being blindfolded at a children's party and under its influence had recovered his memory and his middle-aged personality, had talked of Kitty with the humorous tenderness of the English husband and had looked possessively about him. But as his mind came out of the control he exposed their lie that they were dealing with a mere breakdown of the normal process by pushing away this knowledge and turning to them the blank wall, all the blanker because it was unconscious, of his resolution not to know. I had accepted that it would always be so. But at that moment I had so great a need to throw off my mood of despair, so insupportably loaded with all the fantastic images to which my fevered mind transmuted the facts of our tragedy, that I filled myself with a gasping, urgent faith in this new doctor. I jumped up and pushed through the brambles to the hedge that divided the preserves in which I was trespassing from our own woods, breathless because I had let it go past four and I had still to find Chris and Margaret for the doctor's visit at the half-hour.

There had been a hardening of the light during the afternoon that made the dear familiar woods rich and sinister and, to the eye, tropical. The jewel-bright buds on the soot-black boughs, and the blue valley distances, smudged here and there with the pink enamel of villa roofs and seen between the black and white intricacies of the birch-trunks and the luminous grey pillars of the beeches, hurt my wet eyes as might beauty blazing under an equatorial sun. There was a tropical sense of danger too, for I walked as apprehensively as though a snake coiled under every leaf, because I feared to come on them when he was speaking to her without looking at her, or thinking in silence while he played with her hand. Embraces do not matter; they merely indicate the will to love and may as well be followed by defeat as victory. But disregard means that now there needs to be no straining of the eyes, no stretching forth of the hands, no pressing of the lips, because theirs is such a union that they are no longer conscious of the division of their flesh. I know it must be so; a lonely life gives one opportunities of thinking these things out. I could not have borne to see signs of how he had achieved this intimacy with the woman whom a sudden widening of the downward vista showed as she leant her bent back, ridged by those cheap stays, against a birch that some special skill of the forester had made wonderful for its straight slenderness. Against the clear colours of the bright bare wood her yellow raincoat made a muddy patch, and as a dead bough dropped near her she made a squalid dodging movement like a hen. She was not so much a person as an implication of dreary poverty, like an open door in a mean house that lets out the smell of cooking cabbage and the screams of children. Doubtlessly he sat somewhere close to her, lumpishly content. I thought distractedly how necessary it was that Gilbert Anderson should cure him, and tried to shout to her but found my throat full of sobs. So I broke my way down through the fern and bramble and stood level with them, though still divided by some yards of broken ground.

It was not utter dullness not to have anticipated the beauty that I saw. No one could have told. . . . They had taken the mackintosh rug out of the dinghy and spread it on this little space of clear grass, I think so that they could look at a scattering of early primroses in a pool of white anemones at an oak-tree's foot. She had run her dreadful hands over the rug so that it lay quite smooth and comfortable under him when at last he felt drowsy and turned on his side to sleep. He lay there in the confiding relaxation of a sleeping child, his hands unclenched and his head thrown back so that the bare throat showed defencelessly. Now he was asleep and his face undarkened by thought one saw how very fair he really was. And she, her mournfully vigilant face pinkened by the cold river of air sent by the advancing evening through the screen of rusted gold bracken was sitting beside him, just watching.

I have often seen people grouped like that on the common outside our gates, on Bank Holidays. Most often the man has a handkerchief to shelter him from the sun and the woman squats beside him and peers through the undergrowth to see that the children come to no harm as they play. It has sometimes seemed to me that there was a significance about it. You know when one goes into the damp odorous coolness of a church in a Catholic country and sees the kneeling worshippers, their bodies bent stiffly and reluctantly and yet with abandonment as though to represent the inevitable bending of the will to a purpose outside the individual, or when under any sky one sees a mother with her child in her arms, something turns in one's heart like a sword and one says to oneself, "If humanity forgets these attitudes there is an end to the world." But people like me, who are not artists, are never sure about people they don't know. So it was not until now, when it happened to my friends, when it was my dear Chris and my dear Margaret who sat thus englobed in peace as in a crystal sphere, that I knew that it was the most significant as it was the loveliest attitude in the world. It means that the woman has gathered the soul of the man into her

51

soul and is keeping it warm in love and peace so that his body can rest quiet for a little time. That is a great thing for a woman to do. I know there are things at least as great for those women whose independent spirits can ride fearlessly and with interest outside the home park of their personal relationships, but independence is not the occupation of most of us. What we desire is greatness such as this which had given sleep to the beloved. I had known that he was having bad nights at Baldry Court, in that new room with the jade-green painted walls and the lapis lazuli fireplace, which he had found with surprise to be his instead of the remembered little room with the fishing-rods. But I had not been able to do anything about it.

It was not fair that by the exercise of a generosity which seemed as fortuitous a possession as a beautiful voice a woman should be able to do such wonderful things for a man. For sleep was the least of her gifts to him. What she had done in leading him into this quiet magic circle out of our life, out of the splendid house which was not so much a house as a vast piece of space partitioned off from the universe and decorated partly for beauty and partly to make our privacy more insolent, out of the garden where the flowers took thought as to how they should grow and the wood made formal as a pillared aisle by forestry, may be judged from my anguish in being left there alone. Indeed she had been generous to us all, for at her touch our lives had at last fallen into a pattern; she was the sober thread whose inter-weaving with our scattered magnificences had somehow achieved the design that otherwise would not appear. Perhaps even her dinginess was part of her generosity, for in order to fit into the pattern one sometimes has to forgo something of one's individual beauty. That is why women like us do not wear such obviously lovely dresses as cocottes, but clothe themselves in garments that by their slight neglect of the possibilities of beauty declare that there are such things as thrift and restraint and care for the future. And so I could believe of Margaret that her determined dwelling in places where there was not enough of anything, her continued exposure of herself to the grime of squalid living, was unconsciously deliberate. The deep internal thing that had guided Chris to forgetfulness had guided her to poverty so that when the time came for her meeting with her lover there should be not one intimation of the beauty of suave flesh to distract him from the message of her soul. I looked upward at this supreme act of sacrifice and glowed at her private gift to me. My sleep, though short, was now dreamless. No more did I see his body rotting into union with that brown texture of corruption which is No Man's Land, no more did I see him slipping softly down the parapet into the trench, no more did I hear voices talking in a void: "*Help me, old man, I've got no legs. . . .*"—"*I can't, old man, I've got no hands. . . .*" They could not take him back to the Army as he was. Only that morning as I went through the library he had raised an appalled face from the pages of a history of the war. "Jenny, it can't be true—that they did *that*—to Belgium? Those funny, quiet, stingy people. . . ." And his soldierly knowledge was as deeply buried as this memory of that awful August. While her spell endured they could not send him back into the hell of war. This wonderful kind woman held his body as safely as she held his soul.

I was so grateful that I was forced to go and sit down on the rug beside her. It was an intrusion, but I wanted to be near her. She did not look surprised when she turned to me her puckered brows, but smiled through the ugly fringe of vagrant hairs the weather had plucked from under the hard rim of her hat. It was part of her loveliness that even if she did not understand an act she could accept it.

Presently she leant over to me across his body and whispered, "He's not cold. I put the overcoat on him as soon as he was fairly off. I've just felt his hands and they're as warm as toast." If I had whispered like that I would have wakened him.

Soon he stirred, groped for her hand and lay with his cheek against its rough palm. He was awake by then but liked to lie so.

In a little she shook her hand away and said, "Get up and run along to the house and have some hot tea. You'll catch your death lying out here."

He caught her hand again. It was evident that for some reason the moment was charged with ecstasy for them both.

It seemed as though there were a softer air in this small clearing than anywhere else in the world. I stood up with my back against a birch and said negligently, knowing now that nothing could really threaten them, "There is a doctor coming at half-past four who wants to see you both." It cast no shadow on their serenity. He smiled upward, still lying on his back, and hailed me, "Hallo, Jenny." But she made him get up and help her fold the rug. "It's not right to keep a doctor waiting in these times," she declared, "so overworked they are, poor men, since the war. . . ." As I led the way up through the woods to the house I heard her prove her point by an illustrative anecdote about something that had happened down her road. I heard,

53

too, their footsteps come to a halt for a space. I think her grey eyes had looked at him so sweetly that he had been constrained to take her in his arms.

6

I felt—I remember it with the little perk of self-approbation with which one remembers any sort of accurate premonition even if its fulfilment meant disaster—a cold hand close round my heart as we turned the corner of the house and came on Dr Gilbert Anderson. I was startled, to begin with, by his unmedical appearance. He was a little man with winking blue eyes, a flushed and crumpled forehead, a little grey moustache that gave him the profile of an amiable cat, and a lively taste in spotted ties, and he lacked that appetiteless look which is affected by distinguished practitioners. He was at once more comical and more suggestive of power than any other doctor I had ever seen, and this difference was emphasized by his unexpected occupation. A tennis ball which he had discovered somewhere had roused his sporting instincts, and he was trying at what range it was possible to kick it between two large stones which he had placed close together in front of the steps up to the house. It was his chubby absorption in this amusement which accounted for his first gape of embarrassment. "Nobody about in there—we professional men get so little fresh air——" he said bluffly, and blew his nose in a very large handkerchief, from whose folds he emerged with perfect self-possession. "You," he said to Chris, with a naïve adoption of the detective tone, "are the patient." He rolled his blue eye on me, took a good look, and as he realized I did not matter shook off the unnecessary impression like a dog coming out of water. He faced Margaret as though she were the nurse in charge of the case and gave her a brisk little nod. "You're Mrs Grey. I shall want to talk to you later. Meantime—this man. I'll come back." He indicated by a windmill gesture that we should go into the house and swung off with Chris.

She obeyed; that sort of woman always does what the doctor orders. But I delayed for a moment to stare after this singular specialist, to side-track my foreboding by pronouncing him a bounder, to wish, as my foreboding persisted, that like a servant I could give notice because there was "always something happening in the house." Then, as the obedient figure at the top of the stairs was plainly shivering under its shoddy clothes in the rising wind that was polishing the end of the afternoon to brightness, I hastened to lead her into the hall. We stood about uneasily in its gloaming. As usual the shining old panelling seemed aware of all that was going on and conscious that it was older and better than the people who owned it; the white nymph drooped over the black waters of the bowl and reminded one how nice, how neat and nice, life used to be; the chintz sang the vulgar old English country-house song. Margaret looked round her and said, in a voice slightly flattened by the despondency which she evidently shared with me, "It is nice to have everything ready that people can want, and everything in its place. I used to do it at Monkey Island Inn. It was not grand like this, of course, but our visitors always came back a second time." Abstractedly and yet with joy she fingered the fine work of the table leg.

There was a noise above us like the fluttering of doves. Kitty was coming downstairs in a white serge dress against which her hands were rosy; a woman with such lovely little hands never needed to wear flowers. By her kind of physical discipline she had reduced her grief to no more than a slight darkening under the eyes, and for this moment she was glowing. I knew it was because she was going to meet a new man and anticipated the kindling of admiration in his eyes, and I smiled, contrasting her probable prefiguring of Dr Anderson with the amiable rotundity we had just encountered. Not that it would have made any difference if she had seen him. Beautiful women of her type lose, in this matter of admiration alone, their otherwise tremendous sense of class distinction; they are obscurely aware that it is their civilizing mission to flash the jewel of their beauty before all men, so that they shall desire it and work to get the wealth to buy it, and thus be seduced by a present appetite to a tilling of the earth that serves the future. There is, you know, really room for all of us; we each have our peculiar use.

"The doctor's talking to Chris outside," I said.

"Ah," breathed Kitty. I found, though the occasion was a little grim, some entertainment in the two women's faces, so mutually intent, so differently fair, the one a polished surface that reflected light, like a mirror hung opposite a window, the other a lamp grimed by the smoke of careless use but still giving out radiance from its burning oil. Margaret was smiling wonderingly up at this prettiness; but Kitty seemed to be doing some brainwork.

"How do you do, Mrs Grey?" she said suddenly, shaking out her cordiality as one shakes out a fan. "It's very kind of you to come. Won't you go upstairs and take off your things?"

"No, thank you," answered Margaret shyly. "I shall have to go away so soon."

"Ah, do!" begged Kitty prettily.

It was, of course, that she did not want Margaret to meet the specialist in those awful clothes, but I did not darken the situation by explaining that this disaster had already happened. Instead I turned to Margaret an expression which conveyed that this was an act of hospitality the refusal of which we would find wounding, and to that she yielded as I knew she would. She followed me upstairs and along the corridors very slowly, like a child paddling in a summer sea; she enjoyed the feeling of the thick carpet underfoot, she looked lingeringly at the pictures on the wall, occasionally she put a finger to touch a vase as if by that she made its preciousness more her own. Her spirit, I could see, was as deeply concerned about Chris as was mine, but she had such faith in life that she retained serenity enough to enjoy what beauty she came across during her period of waiting. Even her enjoyment was indirectly generous; when she came into my room the backward flinging of her head and her deep "Oh!" recalled to me what I had long forgotten, how fine were its proportions, how clever the grooved arch above the window, how like the evening sky my blue curtains. . . .

"And the lovely things you have on your dressing-table," she commented. "You must have very good taste." The charity, that changed my riches to a merit! As I helped her to take off her raincoat, and reflected that Kitty would not be pleased when she saw that the removal of the garment disclosed a purple blouse of stuff called moirette that servants use for petticoats, she exclaimed softly Kitty's praises. "I know I shouldn't make personal remarks, but Mrs Baldry is lovely. She has three circles round her neck. I've only two." It was a touching betrayal that she possessed that intimate knowledge of her own person which comes to women who have been loved. I could not for the life of me have told you how many circles there were round my neck. Plainly discontented with herself in the midst of all this fineness she said diffidently, "Please, I would like to do my hair," so I pulled the arm-chair up to the dressing-table and leant on its back while she, sitting shyly on its very edge, unpinned her two long braids, so thick, so dull.

"You've lovely hair," I said.

56

"I used to have nice hair," she mourned, "but these last few years I've let myself go." She made half-hearted attempts to smooth the straggling tendrils on her temples, but presently laid down her brush and clicked her tongue against her teeth. "Tchk! I hope that man's not worrying Chris. . . ."

There was no reassurance ready, so I went to the other side of the room to put her hat down on a chair, and stayed for a moment to pat its plumes and wonder if nothing could be done with it. But it was, as surgeons say, an inoperable case. So I just gloomed at it and wished I had not let this doctor interpose his plumpness between Chris and Margaret, who since that afternoon seemed to me as not only a woman whom it was good to love, but as a patron saint must appear to a Catholic, as an intercessory being whose kindliness could be daunted only by some special and incredibly malicious decision of the Supreme Force. I was standing with eyes closed and my hands abstractedly stroking the hat which was the emblem of her martyrdom, and I was thinking of her in a way that was a prayer to her, when I heard her sharp cry. That she should cry out sharply, whose essence was a patient silence . . . I turned very quickly.

She was standing up, and in her hand she held the photograph of Oliver that stands on my dressing-table. It is his last photograph, the one taken just a week before he died.

"Who is this?"

"The only child Chris ever had. He died five years ago."

"Five years ago?"

Why did it matter so?

"Yes."

"He died five years ago, my Dick." Her eyes grew great. "How old was he?"

"Just two."

"My Dick was two. . . ." We both were breathing hard. "Why did he die?"

"We never knew. He was the loveliest boy, but delicate from his birth. At the end he just faded away, with the merest cold."

"So did my Dick. A chill. We thought he would be up and about the next day, and he just——"

Her awful gesture of regret was suddenly paralysed. She seemed to be fighting her way to a discovery.

"It's—it's as if," she stammered, "they each had half a life. . . ."

I felt the usual instinct to treat her as though she were ill, because it was evident that she was sustained by a mystic interpretation of life. But she had already taught me something, so I stood aside while she fell on her knees, and wondered why she did not look at the child's photograph, but pressed it to her bosom as though to staunch a wound. I thought, as I have often thought before, that the childless have the greatest joy in children, for to us they are just slips of immaturity lovelier than the flowers and with a power over the heart, but to mothers they are fleshy cables binding one down to such profundities of feeling as the awful agony that now possessed her. For although I knew I would have accepted it with rapture, because it was the result of intimacy with Chris, its awfulness appalled me. Not only did it make my body hurt with sympathy, it shook the ground beneath my feet. For that her serenity, which a moment before had seemed as steady as the earth and as all-enveloping as the sky, should be so utterly dispelled made me aware that I had of late been underestimating the cruelty of the order of things. Lovers are frustrated; children are not begotten that should have had the loveliest life, the pale usurpers of their birth die young. Such a world will not suffer magic circles to endure.

The parlourmaid knocked at the door. "Mrs Baldry and Dr Anderson are waiting in the drawing-room, ma'am."

Margaret reassumed her majesty, and put her white face close to the glass as she pinned up her braids. "I knew there was a something," she moaned, and set the hairpins all awry. She said nothing more; but the slow gesture with which, as we were about to leave the room, she laid her hand across the child's photograph, somehow convinced me that we were not to be victorious.

When we went into the drawing-room we found Dr Anderson, plump and expository, balancing himself on the balls of his feet on the hearthrug and enjoying the caress of the fire on his calves, while Kitty, showing against the dark frame of her oak chair like a white rosebud that was still too innocent to bloom, listened with that slight reservation of the attention customary in beautiful women.

"A complete case of amnesia," he was saying, as Margaret, white-lipped yet less shy than I had ever seen her, went to a seat by the window and I sank down on the sofa. "His unconscious self is refusing to let him resume his relations with his normal life, and so we get this loss of memory."

"I've always said," declared Kitty, with an air of good sense, "that if he would make an effort. . . ."

"Effort!" He jerked his round head about. "The mental life that can be controlled by effort isn't the mental life that matters. You've been stuffed up when you were young with talk about a thing called self-control—a sort of barmaid of the soul that says, 'Time's up, gentlemen,' and 'Here, you've had enough.' There's no such thing. There's a deep self in one, the essential self, that has its wishes. And if those wishes are suppressed by the superficial self—the self that makes, as you say, efforts and usually makes them with the sole idea of putting up a good show before the neighbours—it takes its revenge. Into the house of conduct erected by the superficial self it sends an obsession. Which doesn't, owing to a twist that the superficial self, which isn't candid, gives it, seem to bear any relation to the suppressed wish. A man who really wants to leave his wife develops a hatred for pickled cabbage which may find vent in performances that lead straight to the asylum. But that's all technical!" he finished bluffly. "My business to understand it, not yours. The point is, Mr Baldry's obsession is that he can't remember the latter years of his life. Well—" his winking blue eyes drew us all into a community we hardly felt—"what's the suppressed wish of which it's the manifestation?"

"He wished for nothing," said Kitty. "He was fond of us, and he had a lot of money."

"Ah, but he did!" countered the doctor gleefully. He seemed to be enjoying it all. "Quite obviously he has forgotten his life here because he is discontented with it. What clearer proof could you need than the fact you were just telling me when these ladies came in—that the reason the War Office didn't wire to you when he was wounded was that he had forgotten to register his address? Don't you see what that means?"

"Forgetfulness," shrugged Kitty, "he isn't businesslike." She had always nourished a doubt as to whether Chris was really, as she put it, practical; his income and his international reputation weighed as nothing against his so evident inability to pick up pieces at sales.

"One forgets only those things that one wants to forget. It's our business to find out why he wanted to forget this life."

"He can remember quite well when he is hypnotized," she said obstructively. She had quite ceased to glow.

"Oh, hypnotism's a silly trick. It releases the memory of a dissociated personality which can't be related—not possibly in such an obstinate case as this—to the waking personality. I'll do it by talking

59

to him. Getting him to tell his dreams." He beamed at the prospect. "But you—it would be such a help if you could give me any clue to this discontent."

"I tell you," said Kitty, "he was not discontented till he went mad."

He caught at last the glint of her rising temper. "Ah," he said, "madness is an indictment not of the people one lives with, only of the high gods! If there was anything it's evident that it was not your fault——" A smile sugared it, and knowing that where he had to flatter his dissecting hand had not an easy task he turned to me, whose general appearance suggests that flattery is not part of my daily diet. "You, Miss Baldry, you've known him longest...."

"Nothing and everything was wrong," I said at last. "I've always felt it...." A sharp movement of Kitty's body confirmed my deep, old suspicion that she hated me.

He went back further than I thought he would. "His relations with his father and mother, now?"

"His father was old when he was born, and always was a little jealous of him. His mother was not his sort. She wanted a stupid son, who would have been satisfied with shooting."

He laid down a remark very softly, like a hunter setting a snare. "He turned, then, to sex with a peculiar need."

It was Margaret who spoke, shuffling her feet under her chair.

"Yes, he was always very dependent." We gaped at her, who said this of our splendid Chris, and I saw that she was not as she had been. There was a directness of speech, a straight stare, that was for her a frenzy. "Doctor," she said, her mild voice roughened, "what's the use of talking? You can't cure him." She caught her lower lip with her teeth and fought back from the brink of tears. "Make him happy, I mean. All you can do is to make him ordinary."

"I grant you that's all I do," he said. It queerly seemed as though he was experiencing the relief one feels on meeting an intellectual equal. "It's my profession to bring people from various outlying districts of the mind to the normal. There seems to be a general feeling it's the place where they ought to be. Sometimes I don't see the urgency myself."

She continued without joy. "I know how you could bring him back. A memory so strong that it would recall everything else— in spite of his discontent."

The little man had lost in a moment his glib assurance, his

knowingness about the pathways of the soul. "Well, I'm willing to learn."

"Remind him of the boy," said Margaret.

The doctor ceased suddenly to balance on the balls of his feet. "What boy?"

"They had a boy."

He looked at Kitty. "You told me nothing of this!"

"I didn't think it mattered," she answered, and shivered and looked cold as she always did at the memory of her unique contact with death. "He died five years ago."

He dropped his head back, stared at the cornice, and said with the soft malignity of a clever person dealing with the slow-witted, "These subtle discontents are often the most difficult to deal with." Sharply he turned to Margaret. "How would you remind him?"

"Take him something the boy wore, some toy they used to play with."

Their eyes met wisely. "It would have to be you that did it."

Her face assented.

Kitty said, "I don't understand. Why does it matter so much?" She repeated it twice before she broke the silence that Margaret's wisdom had brought down on us. Then Dr Anderson, rattling the keys in his trouser pockets and swelling red and perturbed, answered, "I don't know why. But it does."

Kitty's voice soared in satisfaction. "Oh! Then it's very simple. Mrs Grey can do it now. Jenny, take Mrs Grey up to the nursery. There are lots of things up there."

Margaret made no movement, but continued to sit with her heavy boots resting on the edge of their soles. Dr Anderson searched Kitty's face, exclaimed "Oh, well!" and flung himself into an arm-chair so suddenly that the springs spoke.

Margaret smiled at that and turned to me, "Yes, take me to the nursery, please." Yet as I walked beside her up the stairs I knew this compliance was not the indication of any melting of this new steely sternness. The very breathing that I heard as I knelt beside her at the nursery door and fitted the key in the lock, seemed to come from a different and a harsher body than had been hers before. I did not wonder that she was feeling bleak, since in a few moments she was to go out and say the words that would end all her happiness, that would destroy all the gifts her generosity had so difficultly amassed. Well, that is the kind of thing one has to do in this life.

61

But hardly had the door opened and disclosed the empty sunny spaces swimming with motes before her old sweetness flowered again. She moved forward slowly, tremulous and responsive and pleased, as though the room's loveliness was a gift to her; she stretched out her hands to the clear sapphire walls and the bright fresco of birds and animals with a young delight. So, I thought, might a bride go about the home her husband had secretly prepared for her. Yet when she reached the hearth and stood with her hands behind her on the fire-guard, looking about her at all the exquisite devices of our nursery to rivet health and amusement on our reluctant little visitor, it was so apparent that she was a mother that I could not imagine how it was that I had not always known it. It has sometimes happened that painters who have kept close enough to earth to see a heavenly vision have made pictures of the Assumption of the Blessed Virgin, which do indeed show women who could bring God into the world by the passion of their motherhood. "Let there be life," their suspended bodies seem to cry out to the universe about them, and the very clouds under their feet change to cherubim. As Margaret stood there, her hands pressed palm to palm beneath her chin, and a blind smile on her face, she looked even so.

"Oh, the fine room!" she cried. "But where's his cot?"

"It isn't here. This is the day nursery. The night nursery we didn't keep. It's just a bedroom now."

Her eyes shone at the thought of the cockered childhood this had been. "'I couldn't afford to have two nurseries. It makes all the difference to the wee things." She hung above me for a little as I opened the ottoman and rummaged among Oliver's clothes. "Ah, the lovely little frocks! Did she make them? Ah, well, she'd hardly have the time, with this great house to see to. But I don't care much for baby frocks. The babies themselves are none the happier for them. It's all for show." She went over to the rocking-horse and gave a ghostly child a ride. For long she hummed a tuneless song into the sunshine and retreated far away into some maternal dream. "He was too young for this," she said. "His daddy must have given him it. I knew it. Men always give them presents above their age. They're in such a hurry for them to grow up. We like them to take their time, the loves. But where's his engine? Didn't he love puffer-trains? Of course, he never saw them. You're so far from the railway station. What a pity! He'd have loved them so. Dick was so happy when I stopped his pram on the railway bridge on my way back from the shops, and he could sit up and see the puffers going by." Her distress that Oliver had missed this humble pleasure darkened her for a minute. "Why did he die! You didn't overtax his brain? He wasn't taught his letters too soon?"

"Oh, no," I said. I couldn't find the clothes I wanted. "The only thing that taxed his little brain were the prayers his Scotch nurse taught him, and he didn't bother much over them. He would say 'Jesus, tender leopard,' instead of 'Jesus, tender shepherd,' as though he liked it better that way. . . ."

"Did you ever! The things they say! He'd a Scotch nurse. They say they're very good. I've read in the papers the Queen of Spain has one." She had gone back to the hearth again and was playing with the toys on the mantelpiece. It was odd that she showed no interest in my search for the most memorable garment; a vivacity which played above her tear-wet strength, like a ball of St Jacob's fire on the mast of a stout ship, made me realize she still was strange. "The toys he had! His nurse didn't let him have them all at once. She held him up and said, 'Baby, you must choose!' and he said. 'Teddy—please—Nanny!' and wagged his head at every word."

I had laid my hand on them at last. I wished, in the strangest way, that I hadn't. Yet of course it had to be. "That's just what he did do."

As she felt the fine kid skin of the clockwork dog her face began to twitch. "I thought perhaps my baby had left me because I had so little to give him. But if a baby could leave all this——." She cried flatly, as though constant repetition in the night had made it as instinctive a reaction to suffering as a moan. "I want a child! I want a child!" Her arms invoked the life that had been squandered in this room. "It's all gone so wrong!" she fretted, and her voice dropped to a solemn whisper. "They each had only half a life. . . ."

I had to steady her. She could not go to Chris and shock him, not only by her news, but also by her agony. I rose and took her the things I had found in the ottoman and the toy cupboard. "I think these are the best things to take. This is one of the blue jerseys he used to wear. This is the red ball he and his father used to play with on the lawn."

Her hard hunger for the child that was not melted into a tenderness for the child that had been. She looked broodingly at what I carried, then laid a kind hand on my arm. "You've chosen the very things he will remember. Oh, you poor girl. . . ."

I found that from her I could accept even pity.

She nursed the jersey and the ball, changed them from arm to arm and held them to her face. "I think I know the kind of boy he was. A man from the first." She kissed them, folded up the jersey and neatly set the ball upon it on the ottoman, and regarded them with tears. "There, put them back. That's all I wanted them for. All I came up here for."

I stared.

"To get near Chris' boy," she moaned. "You thought I meant to take them out to Chris?" She wrung her hands, her weak voice quavered at the sternness of her resolution. "How can I?"

I grasped her hands. "Why should you bring him back?" I said.

I might have known there was deliverance in her yet.

Her slow mind gathered speed.

"Either I never should have come," she pleaded, "or you should let him be." She was arguing not with me, but with the whole hostile reasonable world. "Mind you, I wasn't sure if I ought to come the second time, seeing we both were married and that. I prayed and read the Bible, but I couldn't get any help. You don't notice how little there is in the Bible really till you go to it for help. But I've lived a hard life and I've always done my best for William, and I know nothing in the world matters so much as happiness. If anybody's happy you ought to let them be. So I came again. Let him be. If you knew how happy he was just pottering round the garden. Men do love a garden. He could just go on. It can go on so easily." (But there was a shade of doubt in her voice; she was pleading not only with me but with fate.) "You wouldn't let them take him away to the asylum. You wouldn't stop me coming. The other one might, but you'd see she didn't. Oh, do just let him be. . . .

"Put it like this," She made such explanatory gestures as I have seen cabmen make over their saucers of tea round a shelter. "If my boy had been a cripple—he wasn't; he had the loveliest limbs—and the doctors had said to me, 'We'll straighten your boy's legs for you, but he'll be in pain all the rest of his life,' I'd not have let them touch him. . . .

"I seemed to have to tell them that I knew a way. I suppose it would have been sly to sit there and not tell them. I told them anyhow. But oh! I can't do it. Go out and put an end to the poor love's happiness! After the time he's had, the war and all. And then he'll have to go back there! I can't! I can't!"

I felt an ecstatic sense of ease. Everything was going to be right. Chris was to live in the interminable enjoyment of his youth and love. There was to be a finality about his happiness which usually belongs only to loss and calamity; he was to be as happy as a ring cast into the sea is lost, as a man whose coffin has lain for centuries beneath the sod is dead. Yet Margaret continued to say, and irritated me by the implication that the matter was settled, "I oughtn't to do it, ought I?"

"Of course not! Of course not!" I cried heartily, but the attention died in her eyes. She stared over my shoulder at the open door, where Kitty stood.

The poise of her head had lost its pride, the shadows under her eyes were black like the marks of blows, and all her loveliness was diverted to the expression of grief. She held in her arms her Chinese sleeve dog, a once prized pet that had fallen from favour and now was only to be met whining upward for a little love at every passer in the corridors, and it sprawled leaf-brown across her white frock, wriggling for joy at the unaccustomed embrace. That she should at last have stooped to lift the lonely little dog was a sign of her deep unhappiness. Why she had come up I do not know, nor why her face puckered with tears as she looked in on us. It was not that she had the slightest intimation of our decision, for she could not have conceived that we could follow any course but that which was obviously to her advantage. It was simply that she hated to see this strange ugly woman moving about among her things. She swallowed her tears and passed on, to drift like her dog about the corridors.

Now, why did Kitty, who was the falsest thing on earth, who was in tune with every kind of falsity, by merely suffering somehow remind us of reality? Why did her tears reveal to me what I had learned long ago, but had forgotten in my frenzied love, that there is a draught that we must drink or not be fully human? I knew that one must know the truth. I knew quite well that when one is adult one must raise to one's lips the wine of the truth, heedless that it is not sweet like milk but draws the mouth with its strength, and celebrate communion with reality, or else walk for ever queer and small like a dwarf. Thirst for this sacrament had made Chris strike away the cup of lies about life that Kitty's white hands held to him, and turn to Margaret with this vast trustful gesture of his loss of memory. And helped by me to safeguard the dignity of the beloved, so that neither God in his skies nor the boy peering through the hedge should find in all time one possibility for contempt, and had handed him the trivial toy of happiness. We had been utterly negligent of his future, blasphemously careless of the divine essential of his soul. For if we left him in his magic circle there would come a time when his delusion turned to a senile idiocy; when his joy at the sight of Margaret disgusted the flesh, because his smiling mouth was slack with age; when one's eyes no longer followed him caressingly as he went down to look for the first primroses in the wood, but flitted here and there defensively to see that nobody was noticing the doddering old man. Gamekeepers would chat kindly with him and tap their foreheads as he passed through the copse, callers would be tactful and dangle bright talk before him. He who was as a flag flying from our tower would become a queer-shaped patch of eccentricity on the countryside, the stately music of his being would become a witless piping in the bushes. He would not be quite a man.

I did not know how I could pierce Margaret's simplicity with this last cruel subtlety, and turned to her stammering. But she said, "Give me the jersey and the ball."

The rebellion had gone from her eyes and they were again the seat of all gentle wisdom.

"The truth's the truth," she said, "and he must know it."

I looked up at her, gasping yet not truly amazed, for I had always known she could not leave her throne of righteousness for long, and she repeated, "The truth's the truth," smiling sadly at the strange order of this earth.

We kissed, not as women, but as lovers do; I think we each embraced that part of Chris the other had absorbed by her love. She took the jersey and the ball and clasped them as though they were a child. When she got to the door she stopped and leaned against the lintel. Her head fell back, her eyes closed, her mouth was contorted as though she swallowed bitter drink.

I lay face downwards on the ottoman and presently heard her poor boots go creaking down the corridors. Through the feeling of doom that filled the room as tangibly as a scent I stretched out to the thought of Chris. In the deep daze of devotion which followed recollection of the fair down on his cheek, the skin burnt brown to the rim of his grey eyes, the harsh and diffident masculinity of him, I found comfort in remembering that there was a physical gallantry about him which would still, even when the worst had happened, leap sometimes to the joy of life. Always, to the very end, when the sun shone

66

on his face or his horse took his fences well, he would screw up his eyes and smile that little stiff-lipped smile. I nursed a feeble glow at that. "We must ride a lot," I planned. And then Kitty's heels tapped on the polished floor and her skirts swished as she sat down in the arm-chair, and I was distressed by the sense, more tiresome than a flickering light, of someone fretting.

She said, "I wish she would hurry up. She's got to do it sooner or later."

My spirit was asleep in horror. Out there Margaret was breaking his heart and hers, using words like a hammer, looking wise, doing it so well.

"Aren't they coming back?" asked Kitty. "I wish you'd look."

There was nothing in the garden. Only a column of birds swimming across the lake of green light that lay before the sunset.

A long time after Kitty spoke once more. "Jenny, do look again."

There had fallen a twilight which was a wistfulness of the earth. Under the cedar boughs I dimly saw a figure mothering something in her arms. Almost had she dissolved into the shadows; in another moment the night would have her. With his back turned on this fading happiness Chris walked across the lawn. He was looking up under his brows at the overarching house as though it were a hated place to which, against all his hopes, business had forced him to return. He stepped aside to avoid a patch of brightness cast by a lighted window on the grass; lights in our house were worse than darkness, affection worse than hate elsewhere. He wore a dreadful decent smile; I knew how his voice would resolutely lift in greeting us. He walked not loose-limbed like a boy, as he had done that very afternoon, but with the soldier's hard tread upon the heel. It recalled to me that, bad as we were, we were yet not the worst circumstance of his return. When we had lifted the yoke of our embraces from his shoulders he would go back to that flooded trench in Flanders under that sky more full of flying death than clouds, to that No Man's Land where bullets fall like rain on the rotting faces of the dead. . . .

"Jenny, aren't they there?"

"They're both there."

"Is he coming back?"

"He's coming back."

"Jenny, Jenny! How does he look?"

67

"Oh. . . ." How could I say it? "Every inch a soldier."

She crept behind me to the window, peered over my shoulder and saw.

I heard her suck her breath with satisfaction. "He's cured!" she whispered slowly. "He's cured!"

The Salt of the Earth

From The Harsh Voice: Four Short Novels

Alice Pemberton had not expected to enjoy the motor drive home, since because of it, the previous afternoon, she had received a bitter hurt. She had gone into the drawing-room to tell her mother that one of the young men who had been coming in for tennis so much of late, was very pleased indeed to give her a lift to Camelheath. With her invariable consideration she had been careful to mention the proposal nonchalantly, though she knew she would enjoy the drive through the spring countryside, and would find the society of the obviously admiring young man just such a gratification as a woman of forty needs from time to time. There could be no getting away from the fact that this meant her leaving her mother two days earlier than had been planned, and she was never one to take family duties lightly. But before she could well get the sentence out of her mouth there had flashed into her mother's eyes a look which nobody in the world could mistake for anything but an expression of intense, almost hilarious relief.

"It ought to be lovely for you!" Mrs Anglesey had exclaimed. "You'll go through the New Forest, I expect. It'll be at its best with all the trees coming out."

"Very well, mother dear," Alice had said quietly, and had gone out of the dark drawing-room into the sunlit garden. Though she was reassured by the sight of the young man in white flannels, plainly eager to hear her decision, she could hardly still the trembling of her upper lip.

"Not, my dear, that I shan't be terribly sorry to lose you!" her mother had called after her, but a second too late, a semitone too high pitched.

That night she lay awake for quite a long time wondering why it was that her mother had always had such a curious attitude to her. It was not that she did not care for her. Alice knew that quite well.

When she had had diphtheria as a girl at school, when she had been operated on for appendicitis, the extremely passionate quality of her mother's anguish and relief had been as recognizable as the brilliance of lightning. Nevertheless she could not help seeing that in the ordinary intercourse of life Mrs Anglesey felt her as a burden. She had sometimes suspected that her mother had hurried on her marriage to Jimmy not only because, as she had so often said at the time, long engagements dragged young romance past its proper time or ripening, but because she wanted her out of the house; and she had had to do more than suspect, she had often to record in black and white on the pages of her diary, that when her mother came to stay with her her visits were apt to be far briefer than those she paid to Madge or Leo.

"Of course there may be some reason for it," Alice pondered, determined to be broad-minded and generous. "I am the eldest of the three, I was born very soon after she married. Perhaps I came too soon, before she was reconciled to giving up all her pleasures for her babies, and she may have felt a grudge against me that she has never lived down."

But she could not help thinking that her mother ought to have lived it down if she had any sense of gratitude. For neither Madge nor Leo had done anything like as much for their mother as she had, and she had been willing to make even greater sacrifices, had they been accepted. Though she and Jimmy had loved each other so much, she had been quite willing to face a long engagement, simply because she hated to imagine what home would be like without her. Since her father's death she had done what she could to replace his influence. She had kept Madge and Leo from getting out of hand as fatherless children notoriously do, she had tried to prevent her mother from giving away to that strain of fecklessness and untidiness which her most fervent admirers had to admit existed alongside her charm and vividness. Well, all that hadn't been appreciated. Alice remembered, and it was as if a pin had stuck into her, how Mrs Anglesey had grown gay and gayer as the wedding-day approached, and at the actual ceremony had shone with a radiance quite unlike the melancholy conventionally ascribed to the bride's mother. She rolled over in bed, rubbing her face angrily against the sheets.

Anyway, even if her mother had not valued her properly then, she ought to have learned to do so, in the last few years of her age and mellowness. Hadn't she noticed what her daughter had done for her during this visit? Alice had put out of doors the horrible gipsyish old dressing-gowny tea gowns her mother had loved to shuffle in for the evenings, and had bought her some nice old-lady dresses from quite a good shop, in the proper colours, dove-grey and dark brown. She had gone over the housekeeping books and saved pounds by changing several of the shops, and had put an end to the custom by which cook had brought in the menu-book last thing at night and launched out into what proved simply to be shockingly familiar gossip. One can't get on those terms with one's servants. She had hired a car, too, and taken her mother round calling on all the nice people with whom she had lost touch, and when her mother had insisted on calling on the Duchess, and had settled down to chat as if they were two old cronies, she had been firm and just taken her home, for it does not do to presume on one's acquaintance with people like that. It had all been a lot of trouble, too, particularly when she was still feeling so weak. But it had all gone for nothing. And so, too, she suspected, had all she had done for Madge and Leo. They hardly ever seemed to realize any of her kindnesses to them, and sometimes they were quite rude. And Leo's wife, Evie, was almost worse.

But perhaps this was the price she had to pay for her perfect marriage. At least Jimmy adored her. "My dear husband!" she sighed, and presently went off to sleep, but not, as it appeared, to rest. For there began to hover about her a terror which she had met before in her sleep, and she stood helpless while it circled closer and closer, unable to move hand or foot, able only to shriek. Able to shriek, it appeared, not only in her dream, for she opened her eyes and found her mother leaning over her and trying to shake her, although she herself was shaking so that there was very little strength in her hands.

"Oh, mother darling!" said Alice. "These wretched nightmares! I wish I didn't have them so often!"

Mrs Anglesey sat back, still shaking, her grey hair wild about her.

"Oh, my poor little girl," she gasped. "My poor little girl! What can it be that frightens you so?"

The immediate preludes to the motor drive, therefore, were not auspicious. Alice had a headache when she woke in the morning, and on the young man's arrival her mother proved uncommonly tiresome. She insisted on getting up to say good-bye to her daughter, and when she presented herself on the front lawn Alice realized that a ruby velveteen morning gown adorned with moulting marabout of a fawn shade that owed more to time than to the dyer, had somehow got back from the dustbin to which she thought she had sent it. The young man was very nice about it, even affecting interest when Mrs Anglesey insisted on telling him the story of the time when she met Edward the Seventh at Monte Carlo; and he dissembled what must have been his emotions when, after he had started his engine, a shriek from her made him stop again.

"Alice! Have you remembered to send them a telegram to say you're coming?"

"No. I don't want to. It'll be a lovely surprise for Jimmy. And I like walking in on servants unexpectedly. It does them good."

The engine birred again. There was another shriek.

". . . and Alice!"

"Oh, mother dear!"

"Be sure you look in the kitchen for the copper pan. It's no use your laughing, my dear, it might be that—" she had her arm over the side of the car and they had to let her go on talking—"you know, Mr—Mr?—Mr Acland, is it?—my daughter came here for a little sea air after she's been terribly ill, and my doctor says that though he didn't see her during one of the attacks he thinks it sounds like irritant poisoning. Anything gastric he says wouldn't have been cured so soon. And we can't account for it any way except that I say it is one of the copper pans I gave her for her wedding that they've forgotten to have re-coppered. That's dreadfully dangerous, you know. The Duchess' sister Jane died of it somewhere abroad. So I tell Alice she must look most carefully when she gets home. Oh, my dear Mr Acland, you don't know how ill she was, yellow as a guinea, and such vomiting and diarrhoea. . . ."

These are not words one wants shouted to the winds as one drives off, looking one's best, beside a young man of twenty-three who believes one to be very nearly his contemporary, for a journey through the springtime. But the day went very well indeed. They got out of the town very soon and cut up through pine woods to the heathy hills, presently turning and looking their last on the Channel, where immense pillars of light and darkness marched and counter-marched on a beaten silver floor against a backcloth of distant storm. Not long after they were in the New Forest, where the new grass blades were springing up like green fire through the dark, tough matting of heather, and in the same plantations the black ashes affirmed it was still winter, the elms went no further than to show a few purple flowers, the oaks made their recurring confusion between spring and autumn and were ablaze with red young leaves, and the birches and hawthorns were comfortably emerald.

Up there, as the morning got along, they had their lunch, sitting by a stream that reflected a bank of primroses. Mr Acland told Alice many things. Helping in his father's factory seemed rather grim after Oxford. It was terribly hard work, and no chance of success, only the hope of staving off failure. Life was awfully difficult just now, particularly if you were young. When, for example, was he likely to be able to afford to marry? And he would like to marry. Not that he knew anybody at the moment that he wanted to marry. There had been somebody ... but that had proved to be a mistake. He supposed he wasn't quite like other people, but he wanted something more than mere prettiness. He wanted ideas ... broadmindedness ... sympathy.

He kept his eyes on Alice as he spoke, and that was very natural, for she was very nearly a perfect specimen of her type, and time had done almost nothing to spoil her. A touch of silver gave her golden hair a peculiar etherealized burnish, and the oval of her chin was still firm. She had neither crowsfeet nor lines round her mouth, perhaps because she habitually wore an expression of childlike wonder, which kept her blue-grey eyes wide open and her lips parted. She did in actual fact look under thirty, and what was more than that, she looked benevolent, candid, trustworthy, all in terms of grace. Her acts of kindness, her own resolutions of honesty, her Spartan guardianship of secrets, would all, one felt confident, be transacted so that the whole of life would take a more romantic form for ever more. It was no wonder that Mr Acland felt the liveliest satisfaction at her appearance.

His own, however, did not satisfy her nearly so well. She realized this when, speaking as earnestly as he had done, and encouraging him to seek for the perfect mate by relating her own story, she fixed her eyes on his face. Proudly yet modestly she described how she had lived all her life in Camelheath, and admitted that many people might pity her for this, since it would be idle to deny that it was quite the dullest town that could be found within fifty miles of London, but she claimed that nobody in the world could have lived a richer and fuller life than she had, thanks to the circumstance that when she was nineteen the leading solicitor in the town had sent for his nephew to come and be his junior partner, and that the boy had immediately fallen in love with her. "We have been married nineteen years, and we are as much in love as ever," she said. The sound of her own words made Jimmy's face appear before her, and she realized with an almost shuddering intensity how much she would rather be looking at him than at Mr Acland. This was no vague, sentimental preference. There was some particular feature in Jimmy's face that gave her deep and delicious pleasure; yet she could not think what it was. Academically, she acknowledged, Mr Acland's broad-browed fairness was more likely to earn points than Jimmy's retiring, quickly-smiling darkness, but that was irrelevant to the intense joy he gave her by this quality which, just for the moment, though she would have liked to tell the boy about it, she could not name.

After she had told her story they got back into the car, feeling very warm and intimate but a little solemn and silent; and about half-past three they stopped in front of the Georgian house at Camelheath which was her home.

"It's a very pretty house," said Mr Acland.

"We've done a great deal to it," said Alice.

She rang. Though she always carried a key she hardly ever used it, for she liked to keep Ethel on the alert about door-opening; and this technique had evidently paid, for Ethel confronted them before a minute had passed.

"Why, it's the mistress! And looking so well, too! Why, I never did expect to see you looking so well, ever again, mum! Well, the master will be pleased. . . ."

Cook, who had been waddling upstairs when the door opened, leaned over the banisters and joined in.

"Well, mum, it's no need to ask if you're feeling better! I didn't never see anybody so far gone come right up again! You're the proper picture of health, now, you are, mum. . . ."

She beamed at them while they ran on, regretting that Mr Pemberton wouldn't be able to run over from his office that very minute, because old Mr Bates up at Stickyback Farm had died three days ago, and he had had to go to his funeral this afternoon, assuring her that Mr Pemberton had missed her ever so, that when Ethel had taken him up his blacks for him to change into after lunch he had said, "Well, thank goodness, we'll be having your mistress with us very soon." Of course the servants adored her. Well, so they might. She knew she had an almost perfect manner with subordinates, and she really took trouble over training them and thinking out devices for ridding them of their little faults. She would never need to part with her servants, if it was not for the curious vein of madness running through all women of that class, which invariably came out sooner or later in some wild attack of causeless rage. Well, there was some ground for hoping that these two were superior to the rest of their kind. Cook had been with her eighteen months, Ethel nearly three years. Perhaps at last all her kindly efforts were going to be given their reward.

Graciously smiling, she dismissed them and took Mr Acland into the drawing room. But he would not stay for tea. He had to admit, with some nervous laughter and blushes, that his home was not quite in the direction he had led her to suppose: that, in fact, he had made quite a preposterous detour to drop her at Camelheath, and that he would have to keep quite good time for the rest of his drive to get back for dinner.

"But it's been wonderful to see where you live," he said, looking round with admiration. Alice was leaning on the Adam mantelpiece, her brilliant fairness and her quiet, good beige suit harmonizing with the pale golden marble. On the fine Chippendale furniture, polished till amber light seemed to well up from the depths of the wood, were bowls of daffodils and early tulips; and between the mellow green brocade curtains a garden tidy to the last leaf showed spring flowers against the definite fine-grained darkness of hoed earth, a quaintly planned rose-garden here and there ruddy with new shoots, and orchard boughs rising frosted with blossom above black yew hedges.

"It's lovely, of course. But can you find people fit to be your friends in this little town?"

"I don't ask for very much, you know," said Alice bravely, "and I'm the centre of quite a little world here. Do you see that house over the fields, standing among the elms? My sister, Mrs Walter Fletcher, lives there."

"It looks as if it was a lovely house, too."

"It might be. But poor Madge is a funny girl. She isn't a very good manager." She paused and sighed. "Then, as you drive out of town, you'll pass a big modern villa just by a fork in the road. That's where my little brother lives. At least he isn't little at all now, in fact he's the local doctor, as our father was before him. But I always think of him as my little brother. I had so much to do with him as a baby, you see, and then I haven't been able to see so much of him in later years. He made a marriage that from some points of view hasn't been a success." She looked into the distance for a minute and then said simply. "You know, I used to mind terribly not having any children.

75

But I realize that if I had I wouldn't have been able to do a whole lot of things for others that badly needed doing."

"I'm sure that's true," said Mr Acland gravely, "there aren't enough people like you to go round."

Soon after that he went. Alice was quite glad, for it would have been an anti-climax for him to have stayed any longer now that they had established this peculiarly deep and reticent sympathy. She walked out with him through the front garden, pausing sometimes to show him her collection of old-fashioned English herbs. "They have such lovely names," she said, "rosemary . . . thyme . . . musk . . . herb-of-grace . . . and dear old lavender. They give one the feeling of an age I believe I would have liked better than this horrid, hustling present day."

When they said good-bye he held her hand a minute longer than was necessary. "I wish you'd promise me not to do too many things for other people," he said. "I expect that's how you got ill."

"I'll try and be more sensible," she smiled.

As soon as she got back to the house she started on a tour of inspection. There was a pile of visiting-cards on the tray on the hall table—odd how many people had called while she was away—and lifted them to see if there was much dust underneath. But there was none there, nor anywhere in the drawing-room, nor in the dining-room, nor in the little library. Everywhere the flowers were fresh, and the water in the vases had been changed that morning, the ash trays had been emptied and polished, and the oak floors shone like brown glass. She went upstairs, running her hand along the fluting of the banisters.When she reached the landing she paused and examined her fingers, but they were still pink and clean.

There was nothing wrong in her bedroom, either. The billows of glazed chintz, biscuit-coloured and sprigged with rosebuds, had evidently just been put up again after a visit to the cleaner's. The silver toilet set on the dressing-table caught the afternoon sun with its brightness; and on the top of the tall-boy the pot-pourri bowl of blue and white porcelain shone with the proper clean milky radiance. She felt a great relief at getting back to her own house, so airy and light and spacious, so austerely empty of anything that was not carefully chosen and fine and mellow, after her mother's cluttered rooms. But she did not linger any longer, though this was perhaps her favourite room in the house, but opened the door into her husband's dressing-room. Perhaps Ethel had let herself be careless there.

76

Everything was all right there, too, however. There were too many books on the table beside the bed; its Sheraton legs quivered under the strain if one added the weight of a finger tip. She took an armful and put them back on the shelves on the wall, marvelling at the kind of book her quiet Jimmy liked to read: crude, violent tales about tramps, sailors before the mast, trappers of wild animals. But there was nothing else in the room that she could have wished different. The brushes and combs lay in front of his swinging mirror, gleaming and symmetrical; even the sock and handkerchief drawer was in perfect order; and the photograph frames along the mantelpiece almost gave her what she wanted, for it seemed impossible that Ethel could have got them quite as bright as this without neglecting some of her other duties. But as she turned away, her eye was caught by something about the largest photograph, the one standing in the middle of the mantelpiece, which showed her as a bride looking with wide eyes and parted lips over her sheaf of lilies. There was a hair running half across it, under the glass. She took up the frame and slipped out the photograph and then paused in surprise. There was no hair on the glass; but the photograph had been torn almost in two.

"Ethel!" she said angrily, and stretched her hand towards the bell. But she perceived that this damage must have been done long ago. Somebody had tried their best to repair it by pasting the torn edges to a piece of paper beneath, and had made a very neat job of it. It had only become visible now because the paste had shrunk and hardened with age and the torn edges were gaping again. One of Ethel's predecessors must have done it during the frenzies of spring cleaning. "It must have been Lilian Hall," thought Alice bitterly. She could remember the names of all her many hated servants. What a pack they were! One could not trust any of them. She peered eagerly into her husband's wardrobe, for she knew that her careful supervision of his valeting had given him such confidence that he never looked at his clothes or shoes. But the suits hung sleekly pressed and completely buttoned from the hangers, and down at the bottom black shoes looked inky, brown shoes glowed with their cornelian tints.

When she saw the grey tweeds she felt a little startled, for he always wore them at the office, until she remembered he had had to change to go to a funeral. The sight of his everyday suit brought him vividly before her, with his dark, thoroughly pleasant but not excessive good looks, his slouch that seemed not so much slackness as a modest retreat from notice, the curious thrilling sense of expectation which, in spite of his quietness, he still gave her after their nineteen years of marriage. She put out her hand and stroked the suit affection-ately, and then paused, puzzled because she had felt through the tweed something hard of an odd shape. It was lying along the bottom of his right hand inside breast pocket, and when she fished it out she saw that it was a cylindrical tube of very thick glass fitted with a screw-top, and two-thirds full of white powder.

"Why is Jimmy carrying medicine about with him? Can he be imagining he's ill again?" She wondered not for the first time, why she should be the only perfectly normal person, who never said she was ill except when she was ill, in a family of hypochondriacs. Then her heart contracted. "Perhaps he really is ill!" She remembered what her mother had suggested, that there might be a faulty cooking vessel in the kitchen which was tainting the food with mineral poison, and she hoped that poor Jimmy had not been keeping from her the news that he had had an attack like hers. To see what the medicine might be, she put her finger in the white powder, and sucked it; but though the haunting bitterness of its taste reminded her of something, she could not put a name to it. But she recognized the container. Old Dr Godstone, who had looked after the local practice during the period after her father had died and before her brother had been ready to take it over, had used these funny glass containers for some of his drugs. How like Jimmy to go on using something made up by that silly old man, which had probably lost whatever virtues it ever had through the lapse of time, instead of going along to Leo and having something really up to date made up! What would Jimmy do without her?

She went down the stairs humming with satisfaction and looked down on the top of Ethel's head in the hall, as she bent over her mistress' suitcase. Then it flashed over her why the house was so tidy. Mrs Anglesey had rung up after all and warned them she was coming back. That had happened once before, shortly after Ethel had first come to her. She had come back and found the house a whirl-wind of plate-powder and blacking-brushes with the girl's attempts to catch up with her neglected work. What a talking-to she had given her! The silly girl had cried her eyes out, and would probably have left if her mother hadn't been so ill. Of course she had greatly improved since then, and no doubt she had allowed less to fall in arrears this time, but only some such warning would account for the exquisite order she had found everywhere.

"Ethel!" she called, in a coolly humorous tone.

The girl's sleek head cocked up. "Yes, mum."

"The house is beautifully tidy."

"I'm so glad you found it right, mum."

"So tidy," said Alice, who had got down to the hall and was standing with her head lowered so that she could look searchingly into Ethel's doe eyes, while a whimsical little smile played round her lips, "that I was wondering if Mrs Anglesey hadn't telephoned this morning to warn you I was coming back."

The girl grew pale and caught her breath for a second, then banged the suitcase down on the floor. "No, she didn't," she said. "The house has been this way all the time you've been away, and would have stayed so if you'd been away twice as long. And if you don't believe me you can call up the Post Office and see if there's been any but local calls put through here all day."

"Oh, very well, very well," said Alice, "but such things have been known to happen, haven't they, before now?"

The girl's eyes blazed. She picked up the suitcase and went up the stairs with it. As she went by her resentment was as tangible as a hot wind.

"What tempers they all have!" thought Alice. "And how tiresome it is just when I've got home! I wonder if anyone realizes just how much it costs me to run this house in self-restraint and patience." She sighed as it occurred to her that her own household was only one of her responsibilities, and looked at her wrist-watch. It was improbable that Jimmy would be in before five, she might just as well go over and see how Madge and Leo were getting on, and what new problems she would have to cope with in their households. "Ah, if I only keep my health!" she said, looking at herself very gravely in the glass over the hall table. It often struck her that there was something terrifying in the way the happiness of so many people, Jimmy, Madge, Walter, and their two children, Leo, Evie, and their four, all depended on her physically fragile self.

She liked the little walk across the fields to Madge's house; every corner of the district was dear to her, for she was one of those people who feel that they live in the nicest house in the nicest town in the nicest county of the nicest country. But she was not so happy when she was inside Madge's garden. If it looked as wild as this in the spring, what would it be like in autumn? She knew Walter had turned off one of the gardeners, but it shouldn't have been necessary to do that, considering his income, if only Madge had been a better manager. It was really impossible to guess what she did with all her money. And if one did have to turn away a gardener, surely one tried to repair the damage by taking on as much of his work as possible. But she wasn't in the least surprised to find Madge lying on the sofa in the drawing-room, wearing an invalidish kind of tea-gown that suggested she had been sticking in the house all day. She looked a very bad pasty colour. It was really dreadful, the way she was letting herself go.

But she jumped up and kissed her sister with quite a show of animation. "Why, Alice, how marvellous you look! But I thought you weren't coming back till Friday?"

"That's what I had planned, but a young man gave me a lift in his car," answered Alice. "We had such a lovely drive across the New Forest. It's been the most glorious day. Haven't you been out at all, dear?"

"As it happens, I haven't."

"My dear, you ought to make some effort to get over this tendency to lie about. It isn't good for you. You're a most dreadful colour. . . ."

"Am I?" asked Madge, with a curious, distressed urgency. She sat up on her cushions and stared at herself in a mirror on the other side of the room.

"Yes, you are," said Alice, "most earthy and unwholesome. And it's all because you don't take enough exercise. Look at me!" she laid a finger against her perfect cheek. "I'm out in all weathers. Really, dear, you must be careful. You know you're five years younger than me, and you look at least five years older."

"I dare say you're right," said Madge listlessly. "But you, dear? Are you quite better? You haven't had any more of those terrible attacks?"

"Not a trace of them. Mother's doctor thought they might have come from some pan in the kitchen that we hadn't had re-coppered. I'm going to look. I certainly hadn't a suspicion of a recurrence while I was away. But I did have another of those awful nightmares, you know. I suppose it's all the worry that weighs down on me."

"What worry?" asked Madge, rather petulantly.

Alice smiled to herself, but the smile was a little sad. Didn't Madge really know even how much of her happiness she owed to her sister's readiness to take on what most people would have pushed away as unnecessary worries? How Alice worked over her when she was a girl, always saying to her just as they went into the ballroom, "Now do hold yourself properly and try to hide those dreadful elbows," and keeping near her to see that she was behaving properly and saying the right things to her partners, and on the way home telling her all the things she had done wrong! And then, since Madge's marriage to Walter, Alice had been on hand day in, day out, always ready to point out faults in her housekeeping, to explain just why her parties had not been successful, to suggest where she was going wrong in bringing up her children. There was no use pretending it had always been an easy task. Madge had a childish intolerance of criticism, she sometimes became quite rude.

"Well, Madge," Alice began quietly, but Madge was asking, "How did you leave mother?"

"Oh, mother's all right," said Alice indulgently. "It's funny how she's quite happy muddling along."

"I don't see that she does much muddling," said Madge. "She knows how she likes to live, and she lives that way."

"Oh, my dear!" exclaimed Alice. "I call it a terrible muddle. Just think what I found her doing . . ." But Madge cut in quickly, "Here are the children coming in from their walk, and please, please, don't encourage Betty!"

"My dear, I think you're so wrong about Betty," Alice started to explain, but the children were with them. Little Godfrey ran straight to his mother; there was really something very morbid and effeminate about the way he always clung to her, and he ought to have been told to be polite and run and kiss his aunt instead of staring at her with great vacant eyes. But Betty went at once to Alice, who held out her arms. The child had a touch of her own brilliant fairness and neatness and decision, which was urgently needed in this dingy, feckless household. It was really very strange, the way that Madge did not seem to appreciate having such an attractive little girl. She supposed that it was just such an unreasonable aversion, probably springing from some odd pre-natal cause, as her own mother felt towards her. Every now and then she gave Betty a little smile, to show that there was a special understanding between them; but really she regretted having done it before long, for the poor child began to make confidences to her, which seemed to exasperate Madge. When Betty said that she had been sure her aunt would get better, because she had prayed for her every night, Madge had been visibly annoyed; and when Betty carried on the conversation along these lines to the point

81

of describing a lecture on Indian missions that had been given at their local school and expressing a hope that she herself might become a missionary some day, Madge called sharply, "Annie, Annie!"

The nursemaid hurried in from the hall.

"Take the children straight up to the nursery," Madge told her, and leaned back on the cushions with her eyes shut until the din of protest had died, and she was alone with her sister again. "I asked you not to encourage Betty," she said. "I really don't see why you should come here and make my family talk the idiom of very old volumes of *The Quiver*."

"My dear, I never heard such nonsense," Alice objected. "If modern ideas have come to such a pass that a little girl of ten can't show a nice healthy interest in religion. . . ."

"Betty's interest in religion isn't nice or healthy," said Madge. "It's sheer priggishness and exhibitionism."

"If you used shorter words and didn't try to be so scientific, and looked after your children in an old-fashioned way, it might be better. Must you have that untidy girl from the village as a nursemaid? I refused to let her come in and help Ethel last winter, she's so slatternly."

"We know she's not ideal. But we can't afford anyone better."

"But my dear, why can't you? Your money seems just to run through your fingers. It isn't fair to Walter, and it's simply cruel to the children. They ought to have a nice, well-trained woman to look after them and teach them pretty manners."

She waited for any defence that might be forthcoming, but Madge had fallen into one of her sulky silences. "Well," said Alice at last, "you're a funny set, you new-fashioned mothers, I must say. Goodness knows what I shall find when I get to Leo's."

"Oh, are you going to Leo's?" said Madge. "I'll go down the avenue with you if you like." She was on her feet at once and moving towards the door, while Alice thought in amazement, "Why, I believe she's trying to get me out of the house, and I haven't been here for much more than half an hour! How queer and . . . petty!"

But she tried to conceal her feelings as they walked under the trees to the high road. "Nobody can say I am tactless," she thought, as she passed by the patches of rough grass and weeds without pointing them out to her sister. "And I'm not saying anything about how absurd it is that she should be wearing those trailing things that she has to hold up round her when she gets a breath of fresh air, instead of being out and about in sensible country clothes. I'll just give her a word about pulling herself together when we part." But when they came to the gate she forgot, for Madge let her skirts fall and put both her arms round her giving her a hug as if they were children again.

"Dear Alice, I'm so glad you are better," she said, and stood with her head on one side for a minute admiring her. "I love to see you looking so young and pretty. It was horrid when you were ill. You ought always to be well and happy."

"You're crushing my coat," said Alice; but she was pleased. "I think she is really grateful, though she's so odd and ungracious," she said to herself as she hurried along to Leo's house. "Well, it's encouraging."

She received no such encouragement when she arrived there. The front door was open, and when she passed into the hall she saw Colin, the eldest boy, walking up the staircase in the undisciplined manner of the bookish young, taking an immense time to mount from step to step because he had his nose deep in an open book.

"Colin!" she called.

He turned round, but did not answer the greeting. For a minute he stared blankly at her, his black forelock falling over his brows— heaven knew why Evie let her children go about with their hair that length—and his mouth stupidly open. Then a look of consternation spread over his face, he slammed the open book, and without saying a word rushed upstairs two steps at a time.

"Well, of all the manners!" breathed Alice. She heard her brother's short dry, tired cough from the surgery, further down the passage, and made a step in that direction. "Leo really ought to be told," she thought furiously. But just then her sister-in-law came to the top of the stairs. She stared down on Alice incredulously, turned and whispered, "Hush!" as if she were quelling a tumult in the shadows behind her, and then ran downstairs saying, "Well, Alice, this is a surprise! We thought you weren't to be with us till Friday!"

How hopelessly odd she was, how neurotic and unstable, the very last person to be a doctor's wife. She was trembling and breathless as if she had had a severe shock instead of merely receiving a visit from a sister-in-law. It was no wonder the children were such unattractive little savages.

"A young man gave me a lift in his motor car," said Alice, trying to pass things off lightly, "and I thought I'd come along and see how you all were. How are you, Evie? That's right. And Leo? No symptoms, I hope?"

"None," said Evie, "absolutely none." She said everything with such odd over-emphasis that it really made one feel uncomfortable.

"Can I see him?" said Alice, moving towards the surgery.

"No, you can't," said Evie, stepping between her and the surgery door. "He's out. He's gone to Cadeford for a consultation."

There was a minute's silence.

"Has he, Evie?" asked Alice, raising her eyebrows and smiling.

Again there came the sound of Leo's high, dry, tired cough.

"I'll come some other day," said Alice, turning to the front door, "when I'm not in the way."

Evie put out a weak, shaking hand. "It's only that he's so busy...."

"Oh, my dear, I understand," said Alice, "It's a wife's duty to protect her husband. And anyway you of all people must know by this time that I'm not one of those people that bear grudges."

With a frank smile she held out her hand and after Evie had gripped and released it she let it rest for a minute on a half-inch of gaping seam in the other's jumper. "I wish you'd let me send you my little sewing-woman one day. Let me ring up and find out what day would be convenient. It would be a real pleasure if you'd let me treat you to that. I always think one feels much calmer and happier when one's really neat and tidy."

She found herself walking back to her house at a swinging pace. "I mustn't be angry with her," she kept on telling herself. "I know there's nothing the matter with the woman but jealousy, and it's a shame that Leo's children should be brought up as ill-mannered little gutter-snipes, but I must remember that she can't help being what she is. It's only by chance that I was born what I am instead of like her." When a turn of the road brought her house in sight tears of relief stood in her eyes. There, in her beautiful, orderly spacious rooms, she could shut out all these awful people who loved quarrelling and unkindness. Already the afternoon sun was low over the fields, and it would soon be time to turn on the lights. She liked to think of that, because it had occurred to her once, when she had driven home later and seen from far off the rosy glow of her curtained windows, how fortunate, how right it was that her house could send brightness shining out into the dark, but that the dark could not come into her house and dim the brightness. In one's own home one was safe. She would take off her suit the minute she got in and put on a soft, lacy dressing-gown, and put eau-de-cologne on her forehead, and lie down on the couch in her bedroom till Jimmy came.

But when she got home she was waylaid by the cook. "Might I speak to you, mum?"

She followed her into the big, clean, airy blue-and-white kitchen. "Well?" she said, looking round. "I'm sure you've nothing to grumble about in your kitchen, Cook! It's really a picture. Everything you could possibly want. . . ."

"Yes, indeed, mum," said Cook. "But I was going to tell you we'd forgotten to say Mr Robert Norman's coming to dinner with the master, and I wanted to ask you if I should cook something special for you, or if you'd have what they do."

"What are you giving them?"

"Artichoke soup, cod, saddle of mutton, and apple dumpling, and welsh rarebit."

"Oh, Cook," said Alice, "what a dreadful dinner! So dull and so heavy! After all the trouble I've taken working out menus with you, you really shouldn't give the master dinners like that because you think I'm going to be out of the way."

"I wouldn't do no such thing," answered Cook, with her colour rising. "The master's eaten full as dainty every night you been away as when you was here. But Mr Robert Norman likes to eat when he eats, and it was for him the master ordered this very dinner. I ain't nothing to do with it, 'cept cook it best I can."

"I can't think he really wanted this awful dinner," said Alice. "Are you sure you haven't made a mistake? Such things have been known to happen, you know, Cook. We're none of us perfect. Do you remember when just after you came you sent up a rice pudding at a dinner party when I ordered ice pudding? That was funny. Fortunately they were all very nice about it. Oh, don't be offended, Cook. We all make mistakes sometimes."

"We do, mum," said Cook. "And shall I cook you anything separate?"

"Well, I certainly won't be able to eat much of this terrible meal," smiled Alice. "But I'll try to get along on the cod and some of the apples out of the dumpling. And then before I go to bed I'll have my usual glass of hot chocolate malted milk."

"I've got a new brand of that for you," said Cook, " 'The Devon

Dairymaid,' instead of Harrison & Cooper's. The man at the stores told me he had it, and I ordered a small tin to try."

"Oh, Cook, why did you do that? Haven't you a tin of the old sort left?"

"No, mum. It was all finished when you left. But it was twice you complained that the old kind tasted bitter."

"Yes, but I've tried this new kind when I was staying with Mrs Anglesey, and it's horrid. It's just as dark as the other, but it has hardly any chocolate flavour, and you know I can only get down the malted milk if I don't taste it. I do think it's a pity you did that without asking me."

"Well, I'll get a tin of the old in the morning."

"Yes, but there's the new tin wasted, and every penny counts nowadays. And there's tonight. I'll have to do without one of the very few things I enjoy. But send it up just the same. Now do remember not to do this sort of thing. The times when you should show initiative you never do, giving people the same dreadful dinners I've taught you not to do, and then you go and make a perfectly unnecessary purchase like this. It's heartbreaking, Cook." She repeated, "Yes, it's simply heartbreaking," but Cook made no answer, so she moved towards the door, but was plucked back by a recollection.

"Oh, by the way, Cook, are you sure that there's none of the copper pans that need re-coppering?"

"Quite sure, mum. We had the man to look at them only a few months ago. And anyway I'm cooking more and more in the fireproof and the aluminium."

"That can't be it, then. You know, Mrs Anglesey's doctor thought that my attacks might have been not gastric at all, but due to irritant poisoning. And the only way we could think that I could have been poisoned was through some of the copper vessels having worn out. I can't think of any other way, can you, Cook?"

"No, mum, I can't. If you was a lady with a nagging tongue, always finding fault with everything, and making trouble where there's only kindness meant, then I suppose we might all be wanting to drop poison in your food. But you aren't like that, are you, mum?"

Alice's heart nearly stopped. Cook's face was bland, but her tone was unmistakably insolent. What was the reason for this madness that afflicted one and all of the servant class?

"We'd better talk about this tomorrow, Cook," she said quietly, and left the kitchen. She supposed that they would both be going

86

now, Ethel as well as Cook. How could they be so causelessly mal-evolent as to do this when she had just come home? The tears were rising in her eyes and she was going blindly towards the staircase when she heard an exclamation, and turned to see that the front door had opened and Jimmy was standing on the step outside, paralysed with amazement in the act of pulling off his gloves.

She ran to him and stretched her arms up his tallness. "Yes, I'm back two whole days too early! But a nice young man gave me a lift in his car!" Under her lips his face felt worn and cold; but clients' funerals were always trying, "Oh, my dear, I'm so much better!"

"I'm glad of that," said Jimmy. "I'm very glad of that."

"And, oh, I'm so pleased you've come in!" she cried. "It's been so horrid ever since I got back. Madge was horrid to me except for a little bit at the end, and Evie was horrid, and Colin was a hateful little beast, and Ethel was horrid, and now Cook's been horrid. Why does nobody but me want to be happy and live in peace?"

Jimmy put his arm round her shoulder and led her into the house, looking down on her tenderly as one might on a crippled child. "Poor little Alice," he said, "Poor little Alice."

II

Ethel had lit the log-fire in the drawing-room, and it spat at them playfully while they crouched on the rug, Jimmy stretching out one hand to the warmth while Alice rubbed the other.

"It'll be a glorious blaze in a minute," said Alice, "and just as well, for you're simply icy, my darling. Was it too dreadful at the funeral?"

"No, not really," said Jimmy. "It wasn't too cold, or too harrow-ing, even. They'd all been expecting the old chap to go for ages so nobody felt it as a great shock."

"I like the younger son best, I hope he stays on at the farm, he's an awfully nice boy. Oh, Jimmy, the young man who brought me home was so nice. And it was miles out of his way really. He's coming to see us some day, you will like him. He was so sweet and patient with mother, too. Just think, she would not let us get off this morning until she'd told him the whole of that interminable story about how she met King Edward at Monte Carlo."

"But perhaps he liked hearing it."

"Oh, my dear, who could? Who cares about such things nowadays.

87

Besides, it's rather vulgar, I always think. But, darling, I do appreciate the way you turn a blind eye to my family's failings. I know perfectly well they're awful. . . ."

"But, Alice, I don't think your family's awful."

"You chivalrous darling, you know it is. Anyway Madge and Evie were pretty awful this afternoon, I can tell you."

"What did they do?"

"Oh, Madge was lying on the sofa looking horribly pasty and unwholesome. She hadn't put her foot outside the house all day. I can't understand why she's letting herself go. And then she's so silly about Betty. Just because the child's got a natural leaning to religion. . . ."

"But, Alice, it's Madge's foot and Madge's house. If she doesn't want to put one outside the other, surely it's her business. And surely Betty's her child and her business too?"

"But, Jimmy dear, Madge is my sister. You haven't any family feeling. You don't understand that I can't watch my sister doing everything wrong and let her do it."

"Why not? She's thirty-five, darling. Time she learned to save her own soul."

"Nonsense, dear. You'd never have any civilization at all if you didn't have the people who knew best teaching all the others what to do."

"Oh, Alice, dear!"

"Well, it's true, darling. And that's why I won't give up going to Leo's house, however rude that woman is. Do you know what she did this evening? She looked me straight in the face and told me that Leo was out, when I could hear him coughing in the surgery! Did you ever hear of a wife being so jealous of her husband's sister? But I'm not going to give up. I've got a duty to that household. I must see the children get some sort of upbringing. That Colin's a perfect little savage."

Jimmy had got up and was standing above her, lighting his pipe. "Alice, Colin belongs to Leo and Evie, not to you."

"But, darling, you don't understand! If they can't look after him properly then I must do what I can," she answered absently. She loved the look of his face, lit red by the flame.

He sat down in the armchair and beckoned her to come and sit on his knee. "Alice, I wish you'd promise me something. It would really do a lot to make me happy. Will you do it?"

"I'll do anything for you, darling."

"Then promise me to leave Madge and Walter, and Leo and Evie alone for a bit. Don't visit them unless they ask you. Don't try to manage their affairs."

Alice stood up. "Jimmy, how absurd you are!" she exclaimed. "I've never heard you say anything so silly before! Anyone would think I was tactless or interfering."

"That's what I want you to promise."

She stared at him with eyes made immense by tears. "Jimmy, you don't think I'm tactless and interfering, do you? Because I couldn't bear to think you so completely misunderstood my character! As for being tactless, that is absurd, because if there is one good quality that I've got, it's tact. I've always been able to handle people without hurting their feelings. And as for interfering, I simply loathe it. But after all Madge and Leo are my sister and brother, and the trouble is that since they were babies they've depended on me for everything, and they'd never get anywhere if I didn't push them." She suddenly dropped on her knees and looked up into his face with an expression of panic. "They don't think I'm tactless and interfering, do they? Because I couldn't bear that, it would be so ungrateful of them! And you know I've thought of them, all my life long, far more than I've thought of myself."

Sobs began to shake her, "Oh, you poor child!" said Jimmy, and drew her close to him. "I know you have. But people are funny after they've grown up and married and got children. They like to be left alone."

"But they couldn't think that," said Alice, the tears running down her cheeks, "unless they'd stopped loving me."

"My dear, I'm sure they haven't. But I want you to make that promise all the same. Just humour them. Just let them be silly. To save your nerves."

"I'd rather do what was right than save my nerves."

"To please me, then," said Jimmy. He took her by the shoulders and smiled into her eyes, his dark, secret smile. "I might beat you if you didn't," he told her gravely.

He always made her laugh when he said that. "Silly!" she giggled, and he crushed her suddenly in his arms. "I promise!" she whispered in his ear, and disentangled herself just as Ethel brought in tea. "But all the same," she said, to cover her embarrassment because she knew her hair was rumpled, "I think they're preposterous if they are offended."

For tea there was a whole jarful of strawberry jam, which neither of them liked very much, and only a little cherry jam, which they both liked so well that the household supply rarely lasted thus late into the spring. It might have been thought there was enough of this for two, but she knew how thick he liked to pile it on his buttered toast, so she gave it all to him, and took the precaution of spreading it for him and putting it on his plate, so that he had no chance to be unselfish. Then, when the tea had been cleared away, she went and sat on his knee again and they were both silent, looking into the blazing wood.

"Lovely your hair is," he said at last. "You're a lovely child, and capable of being noble, even about cherry jam."

She leaned further back, putting her face close to his. "Yet you haven't kissed me properly yet," she said.

"Haven't I?"

"No. You let me kiss you in the hall. But you haven't kissed me."

He murmured something under his breath and bent his lips towards her. But she twisted out of his grasp.

"Why did you say that under your breath?"

"What did I say?"

"You know perfectly well what you said. You said, 'Forgive me.' Why should I forgive you? Oh, Jimmy, what have you been doing?"

"Nothing. I didn't mean anything. They were just words that passed through my mind. Something I've been reading."

"Jimmy, really? Is that really true? You haven't been unfaithful to me?"

He shook his head. "No. I couldn't have done that, even if I'd wanted to. I've thought of you continually nearly all the time you've been away. No husband ever was haunted more steadily by the presence of his absent wife."

Her storm of suspicion weakened. "Is that true?" she asked piteously. "Are you sure? But then what did you want me to forgive you for?"

"I wanted you to forgive me for being me," he said, "and having to be what I am, and do what I have done." A smile passed over his lips. "Just as you might ask me to forgive you for being you."

She laughed happily at the idea, and settled down in his arms again, to receive his embrace. After his mouth had left hers she nodded her head wisely. "Yes, you love me. But how tired you are."

He muttered, lying quite relaxed, his head against her breast. "Yes, that's just it. I love you. But I'm so tired that I don't know what to do ... I don't know how to carry on. ..."

"My poor darling, there's nothing worrying you in your business, is there?"

"Nothing." She could hardly hear his voice, he was evidently just dropping off to sleep.

"Well, everything else will be all right now I'm home."

"I hope so ... I hope so ..." She saw his hand drowsily groping for the table beside the chair, to touch wood.

They sat thus, with the twilight deepening on them to darkness, the firelight showing redder and more comforting. Sometimes they sighed in contentment, sometimes one or the other began to murmur a phrase of endearment, but did not finish it, sometimes they slept. Then all of a sudden, the room was flooded with light and Ethel was saying, "It's seven o'clock, and time you were dressing because Mr Norman do come early and no mistake. And I'd like you to have a look at the table, mum, to see if you think I did it right."

She spoke with the benignity of conscious pride, which they understood when they stood in the dining-room and saw the shining glory she had made.

"I put the tall daffies at the corner," Ethel told them expansively. "Nobody else done a table that way, that I ever see, but it gives you the good of them without you having to crane your necks to see who you're eating opposite. And I put the little dwarf daffies in the middle.

"My word, you've made a lovely thing of it, Ethel," said Jimmy. "The flowers aren't so many that the table looks crowded, but it's a grand show."

Alice said, "Wait a minute," moved a fork a little to the left, leaned over and shifted the linen centrepiece under the dwarf daffodils a fraction of an inch, then moved back and surveyed the table with great satisfaction. "Yes, that's very nice."

Jimmy sighed, very deeply. He seemed to be terribly overtired.

Ethel, blossoming under the warmth of praise, continued, "There's so many daffodils out now that even old Wray can't be stingy about bringing them up to the house, though he'd do anything to keep all his flowers to hisself in the garden."

Alice said stiffly, "Well, Ethel, we've all of us so many faults that I don't think it becomes any of us to make fun of others."

There was a minute's silence, before Ethel swung round and went out of the room. "I say, I don't think you need have said that," said Jimmy. "She didn't mean to be ill-natured. She just said it as you or I might have said it." He had dropped into a chair and looked very white and lined.

"Nonsense, darling," said Alice, "you can't have servants talking against each other. But, oh, Jimmy, you do look tired. I wish this old man wasn't coming."

"Oh, I like old Norman. We get on awfully well together. He's been in a lot while you've been away. The nurse who looks after his imbecile child isn't well, and Mrs Norman has to take charge in the evenings a good deal. So he's been glad to come along and have something to eat, and play a bit of two-handed bridge."

"Funny darlings you must have been together," said Alice. "Let's go and dress."

It was quite a successful dinner, Alice thought. She put on the new turquoise dress she had bought when she was staying with her mother, and the old man's eyes had brightened when he saw her. He was a gentleman farmer, the wealthiest and most important of his kind in the district, and there was some seignorial dignity about him, as well as the ashes of romantic charm, for, till he had been sobered by the tragic issue of his marriage, he had been a famous beau and blood. Even now that he was silver-haired, he made every woman he spoke to feel a little better-looking than she really was, and Alice found herself glowing as she entertained him, and forgetting to be sorry that she and Jimmy were not alone. But Mr Norman seemed to tire very soon. His frosty grey eyes stopped sparkling and grew heavy, he talked less and less, and though they had started bridge he rose and left at twenty minutes to ten.

"What a handsome old thing he is, in his weather-beaten way," said Alice, when Jimmy came back from seeing him out. "But does he always leave so early?"

Jimmy went over to the fire and kicked a log down with his heel. "No, I've known him stay quite late."

"I expect that dreadful heavy dinner made him sleepy," said Alice. "I was sure when I heard what you'd ordered that it was a mistake."

Jimmy sat down in an armchair, and stared into the fire. "No, I don't think it was the dinner. But I think it was a pity you tried to teach him those new Culbertson rules. He's an old man, and he'd probably been out on horseback, since eight o'clock this morning, and he just wanted to fiddle round with the cards a bit."

"Oh, my dear, he can't have found that a strain! And anyway, what's the use of doing anything if you don't do it well? Still I probably was wrong. But you forget, when you've been away, what clods the best of these people are."

"Yes, clods," said Jimmy, "without brains, without feelings, without sensitiveness. I think it was a pity too that you told him he ought to take his child to that brain surgeon at Geneva. "

"Well, why shouldn't I? He's a wonderful man. Mother knows somebody who told her about the most marvellous cure. . . ."

"I dare say," said Jimmy, "but you see Norman and his wife took the child there six years ago, and it wasn't any good."

"But why didn't he tell me so? What an extraordinary thing of him to do, to let me go on talking about it and never say a thing!"

"I expect he likes so little hearing the child talked about that when people start he just lets them say what they have to say and finish, and doesn't prolong it by getting up an argument."

"Well, if he feels like that even when people are trying to help him, I can't help it," said Alice, "but I must say I'm disappointed to think the old man's so ungracious."

"And I think it was a pity, too," said Jimmy, "that you told him so much of the ways you've reformed me since we were married, the way I naturally forget everything and lose everything unless you look after me. You see, he's thinking of handing over all his business to me, because he isn't satisfied with the firm of solicitors at Rosford that have handled his affairs up till now. The old partners are too old, and the young partners are too young, and he thinks I'm about right."

"Well, my dear, nothing I said can have made much difference. He can't have taken it as seriously as all that. And I did say I'd got you over all those things."

"Oh, I don't think he thought I really do lose and forget things more than most people," said Jimmy, "but I think he thought that a man whose wife talked about him like that couldn't be very good stuff."

"What a funny, old-fashioned point of view!" laughed Alice. "But I wish you'd dropped me a hint of all this. I might have said a few things that would just have turned the scales."

"I know. I was afraid of that," said Jimmy. "I think he might not have liked having his mind made up for him."

"If he's such a hopeless old crotchet as that," said Alice, "I wonder you want to have anything to do with him."

93

"Well, for one thing, I really do want some new business," said Jimmy. "It's odd how people don't come to me. It's almost as if one or other of us were unpopular in the county. And for another thing, I'm fond of old Norman, and I'd like him to feel confidence in me for his own sake. It's worrying for an old man to have a wife thirty years younger than himself, with a big estate and the responsibility of the child, and not feel that he's put some reliable person to look after her. I wanted to do that for him."

"Well, my dear, it's certain to come all right," said Alice. "We must just have him to dinner again, and I shall be specially nice to him. Are you coming to bed now, dear?"

"No, dear," said Jimmy, "not at once. I want to stay down here for five minutes and think something out."

He looked so boyish and pathetic, as he lay back in the chair with his long legs stretching out in front of him and his dark hair rumpled, and his perplexed eyes staring into the fire, that she had to bend over and kiss him as she passed. "Poor little boy!" she murmured in his ear. "You're sure you've got no special business worries? You will tell me if you have, won't you? If you've got into a muddle, it's quite likely I shall be able to think of some way out."

"Thank you, dear," said Jimmy, "there's nothing special. It's only that I'm living under a strain, and I've got to make up my mind to bear that strain."

"But what strain, darling?"

"Oh, just these difficult times, these difficult times."

She kissed the top of his head. "Poor little overwrought fellow!" she crooned, then straightened herself. "Don't be too long coming up to bed."

She enjoyed undressing in her own lovely room after having been away so long. Humming to herself she kicked off her satin shoes and peeled off her stockings, and stood on the rug in front of the fire, digging her bare toes into the clean, smooth, clipped lamb's pelt, as she cast her several skins of silk. She liked the mountainous softness of her bed, with its fluffy apricot blankets and honey-coloured taffeta quilt, and the secret, sacred look the hangings gave the shadowed pillows, and the rosy, lacy nightgown they had spread out for her. In her mind's eye she saw her gaunt, voluble, wild-haired mother pacing her utilitarian room where there was a mahogany bed and a a big round table with a reading lamp and many books on it, and she shuddered. "Will I ever get old?" she thought, "and stop matching my lovely room? I suppose I will some day, and quite soon too, for I am not young. It will be awful. But Jimmy will be nice to me, he will somehow spare me the worst of it. He always tries to spare me things, he is always kind. I thought he was a little fault-finding this evening, but that was only because he was tired. Oh, I am a lucky woman, I ought to be very kind to other people out of gratitude." Grave with this reflection she went into the bathroom, and as she lay in the warm waters a way she could be kind occurred to her. It was such a good plan that she longed to work it out at once, and a pricking urge to activity swept through her body, so that she had to jump out of the bath almost at once and rub herself with hot towels. Then she heard Jimmy go into the bedroom, and she flung on her dressing-gown and hurried in to tell him the news.

"Jimmy," she said, sitting down on the long stool in front of the dressing-table and brushing her hair with long, vigorous strokes, because her inspiration had filled her with vigour. "I've had an idea."

He had opened the dressing-room door, but he turned. "Well, it suits you, darling," he said, and came and stood by her, smiling as he watched her glowing face in the mirror, the flash of her arm as she passed the brush to and fro, and the changing lights in her hair.

"Listen," she explained, "I've been thinking over Madge. She can't go on as she's doing. I can't stand by and see my sister turning into a dowdy, middle-aged frump years before her time. Darling, do you realize she's a whole five years younger than I am? I must do something about it, and tomorrow morning I will. I'm going straight to Walter, and I'm going to suggest that he send Madge for a month to that wonderful sanatorium near Dresden where they did Mrs Lennox so much good. It's just what she wants. They give you massage and baths, and above all they won't let you be soft. They get you out of bed at seven o'clock and make you do exercises in the pinewoods in a bathing dress, no matter how cold it is. She'll come back a different person. And while she's away I'll take on Betty and Godfrey—I am sure I could bring out Betty quite a lot, they don't understand her— and maybe I could look into the housekeeping books and see where the waste is, why there's always this air of pinching and scraping where there's ample money. Don't you think it's a grand idea?"

Jimmy sat down beside her on the stool. He took the hairbrush from her and laid it down on the dressing-table, then gripped both her hands with his. "Alice," he said. "Have you forgotten the promise you gave me this evening, in front of the fire? Didn't you give me your word you wouldn't interfere with Madge and Walter, or Leo and Evie any more?"

"But heavens alive, this isn't interference!"

"My darling, what else is it?"

"Oh, it may be interference, strictly speaking, but you must admit that sometimes one just has to interfere. If Madge fell down in the road and there was a car coming along, surely you'd let me drag her out of the way?"

"Alice, won't you stop doing this thing if I tell you I'd rather you didn't?"

"No, I don't think I will. I hate the way you've suddenly started objecting to everything I do that's kind. And anyway I don't think it would be fair to Madge not to do it."

"Then," said Jimmy, "I'll have to tell you a whole lot of things that we all rather wanted to keep from you." He got up and walked to the fire and stood on the hearth, looking down on her intently. "Alice, you're all wrong about Madge and Walter. If you went to Walter tomorrow and told him that Madge ought to go to a sanatorium in Dresden, it would be monstrously cruel of you. Because he couldn't afford it."

"But darling, it wouldn't cost much more than a hundred pounds."

"Walter hasn't got a hundred pounds."

"What do you mean, Jimmy? You must be mad. You know perfectly well they've at least three thousand pounds a year."

"They had, Alice. They haven't now. We live in bad times, and the worst of it is we've come straight to them out of times that were too good. About six years ago, when prices were rocketing, Walter sold out all his safe stuff, his gilt-edged, and bought things like steel and oil. They aren't worth a tenth of what they were. I tell you Walter hasn't got a hundred pounds. He owes quite a number of hundred pounds to the banks and the income-tax people."

"But, Jimmy, Walter must have been atrociously reckless. I do think when he had a wife and children he ought to have been more careful. I do think someone ought to speak to him. . . ."

"Anyone who spoke to him would be a meddling fool that likes to kick a man when he's down. The whole world did what he did. It seemed the only sensible thing to do at the time. I'm sorry, Alice, but there isn't a single way of looking at the situation which affords one the slightest justification for feeling superior to Walter."

"Well, goodness knows, one wouldn't want that. Oh, I am sorry for them. But I do hope Madge is doing everything she can. . . ."

"She's doing marvels. I've been over all the books. There isn't a woman living who could have been pluckier and more sensible. Madge is all right."

"I'm glad. Dear little Madge. But what I don't understand is why they didn't tell me? It seems a little cold and inconsiderate, when they know how fond I am of them. I can't help feeling just a weeny bit hurt. . . ."

"They're hurt themselves, Alice. Walter's a proud man, and he cares for his family. He wanted to give them the best of everything, and leave them to carry on the life his stock have always lived, in the house where they've been for a couple of centuries. Now he can't give them anything but the bare necessities, they may not be able to go on living in that house. They're struggling nobly, but they may be beaten yet. While they're struggling they don't want anyone to talk to them about the tragedy, to suggest that if they had acted differently it needn't have happened, that they aren't taking it as sensibly as they might, that this and that little treat they give themselves when they're at breaking-point is an unjustifiable extravagance. That would just put the lid on their torture."

"Yes, but I obviously wouldn't be that someone. I only would have tried to help. Well, I am sorry!" She sighed and took up her hairbrush again.

Jimmy came back and sat beside her. He put his arm round her body, and kissed her ear, and she rested her cheek against his. He whispered to her and she said, "What, darling?" but then recoiled from him with annoyance, exclaiming. "No, of course I won't speak about it to them! I wouldn't care to, since they haven't chosen to tell me themselves."

"That's a good girl," said Jimmy.

Alice went on brushing her hair, and presently she smiled at the dark face she saw smiling at her in the mirror. "Aren't we lucky to have no worries?" she said. "Really, we couldn't be more at peace with ourselves and the world. But I suppose that's partly our own doing. We might have had lots of worries if we'd given way to them. I think I shall say something to Madge, you know. That's what she's doing, giving way to her troubles. Just because Walter's lost some money and she has to be careful, she needn't lie about on sofas looking dowdy and listless—Jimmy, Jimmy, what are you doing? Let go my wrist!"

"Alice, won't you please take it from me that there isn't any necessity to say anything at all to Madge, that she's one of the finest women who ever lived, and that she doesn't need any advice at all?"

"No, I can't take it from you, because I can see with my own eyes, and—Jimmy, you're hurting!"

He got up and went back to his place on the hearth-rug, and looked down on her again with that queer, intent look.

"Jimmy, what's the matter with you? Your eyes are blazing! And you haven't said you're sorry!"

He did not seem to hear. "Alice," he said, "have you ever read a fairy story where the princess lived in a beautiful palace, with a beautiful garden, and was warned by her fairy godmother that she could enjoy all this happiness for ever only if she didn't pick one particular flower, or eat one particular fruit? If she ignores that prohibition, she loses the whole thing. Out palace, out garden, out princess. It's quite an important story. You'll even find it in the Bible. And you sometimes find it coming true in real life."

"Jimmy, what are you talking about?"

"The point is that the fairy godmother's perfectly right, though there's no reason on the surface to show that she is. When the princess picks that flower or eats that fruit, the whole thing really does fall to pieces. If I ask you to take me as a fairy godmother, and ask you not to speak to Madge about being listless, will you remember and grant me this favour? Do it, do it, darling. Let's pretend we're people in a fairy-tale."

Alice turned her back on him and stared into the mirror, and presently saw him reflected just behind her. "Well," she began, but he said, "No. You needn't make any promise or half-promise. I can see from your face that you'd speak to Madge, if I went down on my knees, if the heavens opened. You couldn't possibly give up such a good opportunity of ordering somebody about, of making them feel inferior to you, of making their destiny seem so that if it worked out well they'd have to thank you for it, and not themselves."

"Jimmy!"

"Now listen. Madge doesn't lie on sofas and look dowdy because she's a sloven. She does it because she's ill. So ill that it's an effort for her to walk, to put on her clothes."

"Jimmy, you're dreaming! Madge has always made a fuss about little ailments, but she's as strong as a horse."

"Alice, Leo arranged for her to see a specialist six months ago. and I sneaked up to town to go with them. He said there wasn't any doubt. She's got pernicious anaemia."

"Oh, my dear, I know all about that. There's a wonderful new treatment for pernicious anaemia. I'll soon see to it that . . ."

"Alice, there isn't anything you can see to. There is a wonderful new treatment for pernicious anaemia, which cures everybody except two or three people out of every hundred. And the trouble is that Madge seems to be one of those two or three people. She's persevering with the treatment, and the tide may turn at any moment, but up till now she's been getting worse and worse. Do you understand? She's very, very ill."

Alice stood up. Her hairbrush slipped from her hand to the floor. "Oh, poor little Madge! My poor little Madge!" she whispered.

Jimmy gathered her into her arms. "I knew you'd feel pretty bad when you heard that," he said. "I've always known you really cared for her a lot. Cry if you want to, dear."

But she swallowed her tears and drew away from him briskly, saying, "But we ought to do something! What can we do for her?"

"Heavens alive, why should we have to do anything? Why must you always try to be omnipotent, and shove things about? Tragic things happen sometimes that we just have to submit to. We can't do anything in this particular case except stand by and be sorry for little Madge, and hope that the tide will turn, and give her as many presents and treats as we can. And above all we mustn't ever talk of it again. We mustn't even think of it, in case it shows in our talk, because Walter doesn't know."

"Walter doesn't know! But that's absurd. He ought to be told."

"Dear, he's having a hard struggle. Madge doesn't want him to be worried by knowing that she's dangerously ill. Particularly when the danger might pass and he'd have had the worry all for nothing. Besides, it's Madge's husband, and it's Madge's secret, and it's for Madge to decide whether he shall be told."

"But, really, Jimmy, I think you're wrong. Walter ought to be told. It's only fair to him. You know how irritable he is. I've often heard him say things to her lately that he wouldn't have said if he'd known how ill she was."

"Alice, I think I'll kill you if you don't promise not to tell Walter."

99

"Jimmy! What a queer, exaggerated thing to say! What's the matter with you tonight, Jimmy? I've never known you like this."

"Stop staring into that mirror. Put down that hairbrush. Turn round and look at me."

She wriggled round on the stool, her lip quivering. "It was your face I was looking at in the mirror, Jimmy."

"Listen," he said, "because I'm going to tell you the truth. . . ."

"Don't tell me anything tonight. I'm tired and you're tired. . . ."

"I'm going to tell you the truth about yourself, and I'm going to do it now, because it may be too late tomorrow. Alice, you're the salt of the earth. In all the twenty years I've known you I've never seen you fail once in honesty or courage or generosity. You wouldn't tell a lie if you were to gain a million pounds by it. You'd hold your hand in the fire to save a person or a principle you valued. You'd give away your last crust to anyone you felt as kin. I know perfectly well that now you've learned Madge is hard up you'll cover her with presents, even if it means you have to go without things yourself. And besides that, you've got a kind of touching, childish quality—a kind of—a kind of . . ."

"Jimmy, what's the matter with you? Why, you're almost crying! What's the . . . ?"

"Well, we'll leave that. The point is that nobody likes having salt rubbed into their wounds, even if it is the salt of the earth."

He bent over her like a boxer, peering at a recumbent adversary to see how his blow had told; but her blue gaze returned his steadily. "I'm afraid I'm not clever enough for all this," she said. "I haven't the vaguest notion of what you're driving at."

"I'm trying to tell you that you hurt people. You hurt them continually and intolerably. You find out everybody's vulnerable point and you shoot arrows at it, sharp, venomed arrows. They stick, and from time to time you give them a twist."

"Jimmy. . . ."

"I know why you want to talk to Walter. You'll point out to him that he's been sharp to Madge several times lately, and that she's probably a dying woman. That'll harrow him. It'll add remorse to the agony he'll be filled with by the dread of losing her. It'll turn a simple, honourable grief to something shameful and humiliating. But it'll do worse than that. Walter's a man who lives on his temper. He can't find his way in action unless he lets himself go. When something happens he's quite incapable of thinking it out quietly. He has

100

to swear and storm and stamp about, and at the end of all the fuss some definite plan has crystallized in his mind, and he can get on with it. Madge doesn't care when he snaps at her, she knows perfectly well that at the bottom of his heart he hasn't a thought except for her and the children. But if you pretend to him that what he did in temper was of deadly importance, then you break his mainspring. He'll go about cowed and broken, he won't be able to stand up to life. That's the worst of you, Alice. You find out what people live by, and you kill it."

Alice said gravely, "Jimmy, I don't understand this. Are you telling me that Madge and Walter have been talking against me? I've sometimes thought Madge wasn't quite loyal."

"Oh, stop talking nonsense."

"But you're being rude!"

"No loyalty can live near you. You are disloyalty itself. Of course we talk against you behind your back. We have to protect ourselves. You're out to kill your nearest and dearest. No, sit still. I've got a whole lot more to tell you. Do you want to know the real reason why you aren't welcome in Leo's house? You think it's because Evie's jealous of you. That is the most utter rubbish. The trouble about Evie, if there is any trouble about Evie, is that she's over-trained. She's had every instinctive naughtiness like jealousy educated out of her. If she thought your brother was fonder of you than of her she'd set her teeth and invite you to lunch, tea, and dinner, at her house for every day in the week. But she knows that Leo can't bear you. Oh, he loves you, as we all do, because we know that apart from this devilish cruelty you're an angel, and because you've got this queer power of seeming a pitiful child that one can't help loving. But you frighten Leo. You see, he came back from the war after he'd been gassed, and forgot it. He felt splendid, and he married Evie, and they had four children. Then he had to remember he'd been gassed. He had that attack of pneumonia, and that slow recovery. And every day when he was getting better you went and saw him, and you sat and looked at him with those round eyes and asked, with an air of prudence and helpfulness that meant damn-all, 'But what are you going to do, Leo, if you have a breakdown and have to give up your practice?'"

"Well," said Alice, "if a sister can't express her concern when her only brother's ill, I really don't know what we're coming to."

"Darling, don't you see what you were doing? You were up to your murderous tricks again. You were killing the thing by which

101

he lived. He knows his number's up. He knows that one winter's day he'll get pneumonia, and then he'll die. And he doesn't want to die. He doesn't want to leave Evie. He adores her wit and her carelessness and her funny offhand way of treating everything as if it were a joke. People do, you know. Leo and Evie have a lot more friends than we have, you know. He doesn't want to leave his children either. And especially he doesn't want to leave Evie and the children deadly hard-up as he knows he will. So the only way he can get on from day to day is to forget that he's ill and going to die. But every time you come near him you remind him of it. 'How's the cough today?' you say, 'Oh, Leo, you ought to be careful.' My God, if you knew how often Evie's telephoned me, 'He's feeling low today, for God's sake keep her away....'"

"Jimmy," said Alice, "are you admitting to me that behind my back you've entered into a conspiracy against me with that woman?"

"But don't you understand that I'm telling you something real and true that you've got to listen to? This is something that you've done and mustn't go on doing. You've tortured Leo. Don't you realize that's why the eldest boy hates you so? Colin adores his father and he knows that every time you go to the house you leave him fit to cut his throat with depression. Naturally he gets black in the face when he sees you. But you're wrong when you hate him just as you're wrong when you like that abominable little pest Betty. She's becoming practically what they call a problem child. Just about her age children often start imitating some particular person in their surroundings, and somewhere in Betty's surroundings she seems to have found somebody who is an aggressive prig and public nuisance, who spends the whole of her forcible personality in proving everybody else her inferior. I can't think who it can be, of course. But anyway, she's almost driving the family mad. Will you try and realize in future when you try to stir up trouble against Colin that you do it because the boy comes between you and somebody you're trying to hurt, and when you encourage Betty it's because you scent she's going to be as cruel as yourself?"

Alice turned round on the stool and began to brush her hair again. "You're simply being rude," she said icily. "I think you'd better sleep in the dressing-room tonight."

"Oh, for God's sake listen to me and try to understand! Don't you realize that there's something wrong in this household and that we've got to alter it? Hasn't it struck you as odd that we've got no friends?

People come here to formal dinner-parties and they ask us back, but they keep at arm's length. They're afraid of us. They're afraid of you. Look how you got old Norman on the hip tonight. Look how we can't keep our servants. And look how your own mother had to pack up and leave the town where she was born because she couldn't bear your tongue. . . ."

"Oh, Jimmy, Jimmy, you mustn't say that!"

"It's true. You couldn't bear to admit her qualities, that she was brilliant and erratic and a marvellous story-teller. You built up a pretence that she was silly and untidy and garrulous. Didn't you tell me today what a shame it was that she'd made the young man who brought you here listen to the story of how she met Edward VII at Monte Carlo? Well, you're no fool. You ought to see that that's one of the funniest stories in the world, that she tells it superbly, and that the whelp, whoever he was, was damn lucky to have the chance of hearing it. But you don't see that because you want to make her out senile and worthless. Well, she knew that perfectly. She went to Madge and Leo crying and said that she hated leaving them, but that you made her feel she ought to be either in her coffin or in a home for the aged. . . ."

"Stop, Jimmy, stop! I know that's true!" She was crying now, with the deep, painful, interminable sobs of a child, with their overtone of rebellion against wrong.

"Oh, my poor little girl, don't cry!" He had taken her into his arms, he was pulling out his big handkerchief. "You don't know how I've hated saying all this."

"But it's true about mother. I know that it's true about mother. She was so horrid to me."

"Horrid to you? But she was crazy with anxiety when—when you were ill, and she wrote again and again saying how much she wanted you to come down and have your convalescence with her. Don't think she doesn't love you. We all love you—only . . ."

"No. No. She doesn't love me. She was horrid to me last night. I did everything I could to be nice to her, I helped her in all sorts of little ways. But when I told her that I was going home two days earlier than I had meant, she was glad. She gave an awful look of relief that I'll never forget." She rubbed her weeping face against his coat-collar, but raised it to accuse him with miserable puzzled eyes. "Of course mother's always been horrid about me underneath, and of course we haven't any friends. People have always loved being nasty

103

to me all my life. The girls at school gave me a most horrible time. And I've always minded it so because I do so like people to like me." Sobs choked her. "That young man—who brought me home in his car—he liked me."

"I'm glad of that," said Jimmy. "Poor little Alice, I'm glad of that."

For a minute her memory blotted out this hot room full of quarrelling, and built round her the fresh morning on the moors, with its background of sooty branches and sharp green buds, its music of birds singing high in blue, shower-washed spaces, its foreground of forget-me-nots bending all one way under a glassy grey current. She remembered how gravely the boy's eyes had rested on her face, how gravely he had said good-bye. Then her face was contorted with a fresh spasm of weeping. "People are always so nice to me at first," she murmured, "but afterwards when I get to know them something hateful happens to them and they turn round and are cruel to me. But what I can't understand is why quite suddenly you've taken sides with them against me."

He gently pushed her away from him and took her face between his hands. "Alice, is that really all that I've been saying has meant to you? Haven't I made you feel the slightest suspicion that maybe you do things to people which they think horrid?"

"You've been talking a terrible lot of nonsense," said Alice. "What's the use of pretending that a dreadful boy like Colin, who sticks out his underlip when he sees you and looks awful and hasn't any manners, is a nice child, and that a charming little girl like Betty, who's always polite and clean and well-behaved, is for some obscure reason a little horror? And as for the rest, I think I understand only too well, thank you. For one thing it's perfectly plain that you've been listening to Evie. She's apparently made some wonderful story out of the simple fact that, being fond of my only brother, I've guessed that there's something wrong with his health, and shown a very natural anxiety. And as for Madge, I can see she's been disloyal. But sisters often are, and I never thought poor Madge was perfect, and I won't let it make a bit of difference. What worries me is that you should have listened to all these people when they were being spiteful about me."

"But, Alice, hasn't what I've said made any difference to you at all? Don't you feel that you've been doing some things that maybe, after what you've heard, you'd better stop doing?"

"No, I don't," said Alice. "It seems to me that what you've been attacking me about, thanks to all this nonsense you've been listening to, is just what you have to do when you're one of a family. I can't suddenly pretend that I haven't got any relations. Why, they'd be the first to be hurt. If I stopped going round to Evie's and helping her to clear up the messes she's always getting into, there'd be no end to her complaints."

"Sometimes," said Jimmy, "you don't strike me as a grown-up, wicked person at all. You strike me as a child who for some extraordinary reason wants to be punished, and who goes on behaving worse and worse so that she'll compel somebody or other to punish her. Do you really mean to go on just the same?"

"Yes, I think so. If there's anything particularly you object to, I might . . ."

"Do you mean, for instance, to speak to Walter about Madge?"

She sat down on the stool again, and stretched behind her for the hairbrush with an enchanting gesture. "As a matter of fact, I do."

"Alice!"

"You see, I must." She squared her jaw and looked like an exquisitely beautiful, tear-stained little bulldog.

"Why?"

"I happen to know something about Walter that makes it necessary."

"What's that?"

"Walter hasn't always been the husband to Madge that he ought to be."

"You mean he's been unfaithful to her? Ah, that little blonde slut at Cadeford."

"And he'd better be warned that this is no time for that sort of thing."

Jimmy whistled. "You could have a whole lot of fun out of that, couldn't you?" he said. "You might even get poor Walter into such a state of dither that he confessed everything to Madge, and that would kill her outright. She doesn't understand that sort of thing, God bless her. Really, this is a find of yours, Alice. With your peculiar gift there's no end to what you might be able to make of it."

He slid to the floor at her feet so suddenly, and in so limp a heap that she thought he had fainted, and was about to scream when he gripped her kness, laid his head on her lap, and spoke softly, "Alice, remember what I said to you. About the unreasonable requests in the fairy-tale, and how the threats came true. That if the flower was eaten, the fruit plucked, the castle falls to pieces. I'm going to make another of those unreasonable requests."

"My dear, I'm tired. This is my first night home, and I'd hoped for something rather different. What is it?"

He raised his head and his eyes implored her. "Let me sell the business. Let's sell this house. Let's go abroad. Let's stop bothering about Madge and Walter, and Leo and Evie, and just be ourselves. We wouldn't be rich, but with what father left me, we'd have enough for comfort. Please, Alice. Please."

"Jimmy, I can't fathom you tonight. Do you really mean this?"

"I mean it more seriously than I've ever meant anything in my life."

"You seriously mean that for no reason you want us to sell all our beautiful things and give up my family and my friends, and wander about as if we'd done something awful and had to live abroad? Jimmy, I really think you're mad."

His head dropped back in her lap. It felt as heavy as a lump of lead, as if he were asleep. Then he looked up, and she saw with a kind of faint disgust, for she hated emotional displays in men, that the tears were thick on his lashes. "Forgive me, Alice," he said. "I think I've been mad, too, all evening. I've said cruel things to you, and they were useless as well as cruel. However, that's all over. You're a wonderful woman, Alice. You've got me right back where I was before you went away. As I was during your illness and before it. Perfectly sane." He jumped lightly to his feet and gave her a loud, almost a smacking kiss on the cheek. "Well, I'll go and undress now. The time's over for talk."

"I'm glad you're sensible again," she said, "and if I've irritated you by sticking to my point about Walter, do forgive me. But, you see, I am so fond of Madge."

"And just how fond I am of Madge," he answered, "is one of the things that you will probably never know."

The dressing-room door closed softly behind him. She sighed with relief that the scene was over, and went on with her hair, putting down her brush and using her comb. But she had to admit that she felt shattered by this curious breakdown of Jimmy's, this appearance of frenzy and unreason in a character that had seemed till now wholly free from them. When a coal fell from the fire, she started; and when behind the swaying red taffeta curtains there was a tap on one of the windows, she swung round and said aloud, "What's that?" and again there opened around her an image of a lost paradise, of foregone security and peace, the sense of that blue cold noon on the clean heath. Then she remembered that the ivy had not yet been pruned this year, and that its dark arms often stretched as far as the window-panes, and she turned about again. But she felt uneasy and tearful, and was glad when Jimmy came in again, slim and well-made in the dark blue silk dressing-gown she had given him for Christmas, which he would wear only seldom, because he said it was too dandified for ordinary occasions.

He came and stood beside her, and she stopped combing her hair while she studied his reflection, and she uttered a faint exclamation of dismay.

"Anything the matter?" said Jimmy.

"No. Only when I was in the New Forest with that young man this morning, I looked at him and thought he was very good-looking, but that he hadn't something in his face which you have, and which I specially love. . . ."

"Yes?"

"And now I see what it is. It's your mouth."

"Well?"

"And yet your mouth's cruel. Your lips are full, but you hold them them so that they're thin—it's a cruel mouth."

"Is it?" He bent down close to the glass. "It may be. It's hard to tell about oneself. I think I hate it when I have to be cruel, but maybe I don't. Probably one never gets into a position when one's forced to do something unless one really wants to do it."

"Jimmy . . ." she threw her comb down on the dressing-table. "I wish you wouldn't go on being so horrible and hateful and queer. I know I seem not to have any nerves, but I have, really. I'm frightened of lots of things. I have those nightmares, you know."

"What are your nightmares about?" he asked. "You've never told me what they actually were about."

"Why, I am standing in a room—now I come to think of it, it's this room—and something awful comes nearer and nearer to me, circling round me, drawing in on me, and I know that in the end it's going to destroy me utterly."

"And you can't stop it?"

"No. The funny thing is—now, that's something else I never remembered before after I'd woken up—I could perfectly well stop this awful horror coming at me. Only for some reason I can't. I have to go on doing the very thing that brings it nearer."

Jimmy turned away from the mirror. "God, what a life this," he said, "full of presciences that don't do us any good, full of self-consciousness that tortures us by telling us just what sort of hole we're in but never how to get out of it. It's nothing to cling on to, really."

"Jimmy, you're being odd again," she said. "Please don't. I can't stand it, my first night home." There ran before her mind's eye pictures of everything which had happened to her during this day which had risen so early to its peak, which was falling, in spite of all she could do, to such a dark, perplexing decline, and the memory of her first, slow, satisfied inspection of her home made her exclaim: "Oh, Jimmy, I found two things in our room that interested me."

He was at one of the windows now, staring out into the night between the red curtains, but now he strolled back to her. "What were they?"

"Well, you know that big photograph of me in my wedding dress? Just think, it's been torn nearly the whole way across!"

"No!"

"Yes, really. Whoever did it tried to cover it up by gumming the edges together, but now the gum's got old and it's cracked, and the tear shows again. I thought at first it was a hair under the glass. It must have been that dreadfully clumsy housemaid we once had called Lilian Hall."

"I wonder if it was."

"It would be Lilian, she ruined everything she touched. Then the other thing was the tube of white powder in your pocket."

"You found that too?"

"Yes. What is it?"

He dug down into his dressing-gown pocket and showed it to her on the palm of his hand.

"Yes, that's the thing," she said. "It looks like one of old Dr Godstone's phials."

"That's just what it is," he said. "Once in his dispensary I picked it up, years ago, and he told me what it was. Then long after when he died and I was going through his effects I saw it and remembered the name on the label, and I slipped it in my pocket, though I never thought I'd need it then. Yet I suppose I must have known I would, really, or I would never have taken it."

"Well, there's no label on it now. What's it for?" said Alice.

"It's just something that sends people to sleep."

"But if you want anything of that sort, why don't you go down to Leo and get him to give you whatever's most thoroughly up to date? You know what old Dr Godstone was. This is probably something that was used in the Ark."

"Oh, don't be too harsh on the old man. There's nothing wrong with this. It works quite right if you give it in the right dose. If you give too little it's no good; and if you give too much that's bad, too. But if you give the right dose, there's no more trouble."

"Well, I suppose that's all right, provided you know the right dose."

"I do now," he said. He sighed deeply and stood for a second or two rolling it backwards and forwards on his palm, as though he would not be sorry to drop it; but he kept his eyes on it all the time. "I only found that out ten days ago. Saturday before last I felt restless all the morning. . . ."

"Oh, darling, I ought never to have left you," said Alice, "but I wrote you every Monday, Wednesday, and Friday, so you must have had a letter from me that morning."

"I had," said Jimmy. "Well, in the afternoon I got out the car and drove right across England to Bathwick. I'd never been there before in my life, I don't know anybody there. When I found myself driving past the Public Library I stopped and walked in, just as if I was a good Bathwick ratepayer, and consulted a book on drugs. And I got the proper dose."

"Well, it seems a casual way of taking medicine," said Alice, "but I suppose you'll be careful. Come in, Ethel."

But it was Cook who came in with a glass and a steaming jug on a tray. She put it down on the dressing-table with a clatter, and her body was solid as masonry with grimness.

"Seeing as how there was unpleasantness about the new brand of chocolate," she said, ignoring Alice's absent smile, "I came up myself to explain that this is the old brand which I got through sending my sister's girl special down to the stores."

"Good gracious, is Minnie back from her place in London? I'm afraid they'll never keep her anywhere, you know, she's so untidy. . . ."

"She's home on her holidays, while the family's gone to Italy," said Cook with quiet triumph and shut the door with a bang.

"What's all that about?" asked Jimmy. He was still rolling the phial of powder backwards and forwards across his palm, and looking at it as if it were a jewel.

"Oh, a fuss about nothing. She's a rude woman, and she'll have to go. It's only that she bought another brand of chocolate malted milk," said Alice, filling her glass from the jug, "and I like this. The sort she got was mawkish stuff, I could taste the malted milk through the chocolate, and I hate that. This is very strong, you can't taste anything but the chocolate."

"So if you hadn't made a row with Cook, you'd be drinking something with a milder flavour tonight?" said Jimmy. "By God, that's funny."

"Why?" asked Alice, and raised the glass to her lips. But she set it down again, because Jimmy was holding up his finger and jerking his head towards the door. "What's the matter?"

"Why has Cook gone down the passage to the spare rooms instead of going upstairs to her bedroom?"

"Has she?"

"Yes, I heard her."

"What an extraordinary thing. But these women," she tip-toed to the door, opened it softly, and stood for a minute on the darkened landing, peering down the passage and listening. But she heard nothing save the creaks and stirrings that are the voice of an old house at night, and presently she heard Cook's ponderous tread across the ceiling above her. She went back into the bedroom and said, "Jimmy, you're dreaming," and sat down at her dressing-table and drank her chocolate.

Jimmy did not answer her, and she turned and looked at him over the rim of her glass. He was standing on the rug in front of the fire, his hands shoved so deeply into the pockets of his dressing-gown that his shoulders were hunched up, and his tallness looked rangy and wolfish. He was watching her with eyes that stared like a fever patient's, and his teeth pulled in his lower lip and let it go, again and again, as if he were enduring agony.

"But you look so ill," she said, and set down her glass.

"Drink up that chocolate!" he told her, and she obeyed, then turned to him, her brows knit in annoyance, her lips parted, waiting for an explanation. But he said nothing, only came towards her and took the empty glass out of her hand with so curt a movement that she cried out in protest. It was a movement of a quality utterly unexpected in him, quite unlike any gestures she had ever seen him make throughout all the years they had been together. So might a burglar have snatched a ring from her finger. She stared at his back as he hurried out of the room, and put her hands to her head, trying to puzzle it out, when she heard the bathroom taps running.

"But what are you doing?" she asked as he came in with the clean glass in his hand and put it down, on the tray beside her, and poured into it what chocolate was left in the jug, "What are you doing?" she repeated, as he poured the chocolate back again out of the glass into the jug. Her own voice sounded far away in her ears, but his voice sounded further away as he answered, "Just taking precautions that probably won't be successful, but I really don't care much about that."

She wanted to ask him to repeat what he had said, and say it more intelligibly, but then she thought she would rather tell him that she felt very ill. Sweat had come out on her forehead, snakes seemed to be sliding through her bowels, she wished she could either sit in a chair with a back to it or lie down, she was afraid she was going to slip down on the floor. She found it, however, difficult to speak. But Jimmy had seen for himself what was happening. She felt his hands slip under her armpits, and knew that he was carrying her over to the bed. With a great effort, for her lids were now very heavy, she opened her eyes and tried to see his face, and though everything shimmered glassy and wavered about her, she was sure that he was looking sorry for her, and as he laid her down and drew the blankets over her, she caught the words, heard indistinctly as through the surf of a tremendous sea, "Poor little Alice." She rolled over, cooling her damp forehead against the fresh linen pillow-slip, and moaning, because she knew that it meant something, if she could but collect her wits and think what it was, that now the taste of chocolate had gone, her mouth was full of a haunting bitterness. But she was too tired, she could only mutter that she wanted some water.

FROM The Modern "Rake's Progress"

THE RAKE IS THROWN OUT OF
HIS HOTEL

You know how it is when they pull down a house in London, how the loosestrife springs up as soon as the sunshine can fall on the earth, purple in flower-time, silver in seed-time. They will have to beat a path through a gentle purple jungle, these visitors from the next civilization, perhaps from another star, who come for a holiday trip to see the broken arches, the domes sliced like cut cake with daylight, the shells of houses where the red hare couches, which once were London. But they will think it well worth while, for the insight it gives them into our augustan age. They will walk about oh-ing and ah-ing, while their eyes forge a past perfection for the ruins, imagining that when they were whole they were right. "Look," the professor of archæology who is their guide will say, "this was the 'Magnificent,' one of the superb edifices they called hotels. Oh, what precious marbles! Oh, what breadth of design! Men were masters then, and no mistake!" They will brood as they walk through the halls, and sink into nostalgia for the past. For it will be pretty, with all those flowers and ruins, and they will be male and female; and it adds something to a day's outing, if one can feel a little wistful towards evening. "How nobly," they will mourn, "life must have been lived in such a setting! That was indeed an age of power. Would we could learn the formula! Tell us, professor, what did they do in these proud palaces they called hotels?" "We don't quite know," the professor will say. "They seem to have been places of amusement. But they must have been more than that, or they would not have spent quite so much money on them. And there are traces in pictures of fertility rites." (That would be the cabaret.) So they will stand in the gentle purple jungle, rolling their eyes at the splendid broken spans, at the vaults where the eyries are; and they will not dream that anybody ever frequented these halls less dignified than a statesman come to draw up a sapient treaty. Not for one minute would they ever think of our poor George as now we see him. When he had to leave

his house he came to the Hotel Magnificent, because they all knew
him there. Often and often he had taken part in the ritual that is
performed all day long and far into the night in the cells of this
vast honey-comb of masonry. A man of one order feels a material
desire: to bathe in warm, scented waters, to change into clean clothes,
to eat the roe of a fish from a Russian river, to drink a wine made
of grapes grown in a certain blessed Burgundian acre. A man of
another order gets him what he wants and then stands waiting,
bending his head. Then the man of the first order takes money from
his pocket and the man of the second order murmurs, "*Thankyousir . . . thankyousir . . . thankyousir. . . .*" George has had it said to
him a hundred times at the "Magnificent," and he has had other
unction applied to his self-esteem there, too. Many women have
looked at him at once abjectly and imperatively, as if they would sue
him for restitution of the *droit de seigneur*, did he not show himself as libertine as rich men ought to be for the wheels to go round.
Many men have slapped him on the back and called him "Good Old
George," and stood him one drink and been stood two by him, and
told him what staunch friends he would find them to the grave. So
George establishes himself in the "Magnificent" as in a second
home, and goes out to look for work. But he finds none. Persons into
whose business he proposes to introduce himself look panic-stricken
as if it had been proposed that they should engage the Spirit of
Chaos as a managing director, however great an appreciation they
may have expressed for him in the past. The word goes round.
Nobody will see him, everybody he calls upon is always out. When
he gets back to the "Magnificent" there is silence. Nobody murmurs,
"*Thankyousir . . . thankyousir . . . thankyousir . . .*" for he has no
more money to take from his pockets. He sees approaching a day
when he will have to leave, but he is incredulous that it will ever
arrive. A young man knows that he has not always been as he is,
but was once a child; yet he cannot believe that some day he will
change again, and be old. Even so George knows he was once poor,
but cannot believe that when he became rich he did not become
immutably so, eternally a member of the class that pays and is
thanked. But the day advances coldly on his incredulity, and is here.
George is borne out through the hall, losing his dignity in a sudden
realization that life is even more difficult than he had suspected. He
had believed that men belonged to either of those orders, the men
that paid and the men that murmur, "*Thankyousir . . . thankyousir*

. . . *thankyousir.* . . ." But what happens if one belongs to neither?
Nothing tells him in the blank eyes of the women that once offered
him the most intimate kinds of felicity or the men that used to call
him "Good Old George." The Hotel Magnificent will perhaps be not
a less agreeable place when its arches are broken, its domes sliced by
the sky, its courtyards choked with loosestrife, purple in flower-time,
silver in seed-time.

FROM The Thinking Reed*

"Man is but a reed, the most feeble thing in nature; but he is a thinking reed. The entire universe need not arm itself to crush him. A vapour, a drop of water, suffices to kill him. But if the universe were to crush him, man would still be more noble than that which killed him, because he knows that he dies and the advantage which the universe has over him; the universe knows nothing of this."

—PASCAL'S PENSÉES

I

The knocking on the door did not wake Isabelle because she had started up from sleep very early that morning. This was a new thing. Until about a fortnight before, she had slept for nine hours every night, no matter when she might have gone to bed. She needed the rest, for she was still young, she was two years younger than the century, she was just twenty-six; and though her white skin never flushed, and her fine small features were as calmly gay as if she were a statue that had been carved looking like that, she was in motion all her waking hours. She was beautiful, she was nearly exceedingly rich, she had been tragically widowed, there was an exotic distinction about her descent from an Orleanist family which had never lost its French character, though it had been settled in St. Louis when that was a fur station in Louisiana. Therefore many people liked meeting her. All sorts of houses were open to her, from the kind where the dirt-rimmed chandeliers seem like snuff-droppings on the bosom of the ancient Faubourg Saint-Germain air, to the kind where the modernist furniture looks like the entrails ripped out of loco-motives. Isabelle went to most of them; and in between her visits she

*[Dedicated to Henry Maxwell Andrews, whom Rebecca West married in 1930:]
"... Vivamus quod viximus, et teneamus
Nomina, quae primo sumpsimus in thalamo."

115

rode horseback, hunted the wild boar down in the Landes, sailed a boat at Cannes, played tennis with the aces, and enjoyed the beating because there was beauty in the inflicting of it. The game was too fast for her body, but her mind could always follow it.

There were times, indeed, when she completely abstained from doing any of these things. She would lie for hours on a chaise-longue, so inert that the folds of chiffon which dripped from her body to the floor hung as steady as if they were stone, her clear face upturned to the ceiling, still bright but not brilliant according to its custom, like a star reflected in tranquil waters. But even then her right hand moved ceaselessly, turning on her wrist as though it were throwing a shuttle. There was indeed a shuttle at work, but it was behind her brows. Her competent, steely mind never rested. She had not troubled with abstract thoughts since she had left the Sorbonne, but she liked to bring everything that happened to her under the clarifying power of the intellect. For she laboured under a fear that was an obsession. By temperament she was cooler than others; if she had not also been far quicker than others in her reactions, she might have been called lymphatic. But just as it sometimes happens that the most temperate people, who have never acquired the habit of drinking alcohol, or even a taste for it, are tormented by the fear that somehow or other they will one day find themselves drunk, so Isabelle perpetually feared that she might be betrayed into an impulsive act that was destructive to such order as reason had imposed on life. Therefore she was for ever running her faculty of analysis over in her mind with the preposterous zeal of an adolescent running a razor over his beardless chin.

So, between sport and pedantry, she was busy enough, and on most nights her eyes closed the minute her head touched the pillow. But last night she had lain awake for quite a long time facing the fact, which seemed to be adhering to the ceiling just above her bed, that so long as she was linked with André de Verviers, she was the ally and the slave of everything she hated: impulse, destruction, unreason, even screaming hysteria. The accusation that posited a state of affairs shameful to herself, that was barbed with horrible circumstantial details for which there was not the smallest foundation in fact, that was suddenly supposed to have been annulled—and this she found most disagreeable of all—by a violent embrace which could have no logical bearing on it, and was loathsome to her because she wanted the accusation discussed on its own terms and withdrawn as untrue—this must be her daily bread, so long as she was with André de Verviers. This would have been abominable to her in any case, even had there not been so near at hand an embodiment and a promise of the kind of life she longed to live; even if Laurence Vernon had not come over from Virginia to see her.

She was miserable, but she was young. All that day she had ridden in the Forest of Compiègne. She rolled over, she murmured, "Ah, if only Uncle Honoré were here to tell me what to do!" and suddenly she slept. But after a few hours she was as suddenly awake again. She remembered how she had stood in André's room, shaking herself as if his arms had left bonds about her, wiping her mouth impatiently, and crying out, "Yes, that's all very well, but why did you say you were sure I was having an affair with Marc Sallafranque?"

André had not answered her but had shuffled barefoot past her to the table, poured out a glass of Evian, and sat back on the duchesse sofa, taking a long drink. "Oh, how beautiful you are!" he breathed over the rim of the glass, nodding his head in connoisseurship.

"But you must tell me why you said it!" she cried. "I have the right to know!"

He shrugged his shoulders, laughed, and went on sipping the water. The trees in the courtyard rustled, and a tram wailed outside in the Avenue Marceau; the quality of the sounds said, "You are alone with him late at night." The candles in the silver sconces were guttering; their reflection on the mother-of-pearl veneer of the Venetian furniture said, "Everything is romantic here." She knew pride and humility in acknowledging that as he sat there, his fine hand lifting the glass to his fine face, he was not less beautiful as a man than she was as a woman; and about his eyes and mouth there was the signature of wit. This should have been perfection. It was not.

She implored him, "Why won't you tell me? There must be something you've heard! You see it spoils everything! I can't understand how, if you think I've been unfaithful to you with Sallafranque, you can want to make love to me! It spoils everything."

He stretched out his hand to her, holding it as one does when one summons an animal, palm down, the thumb fluttering against the curved fingers. She perceived that her demands seemed like the begging of a pet dog at meals, to be soothed rather than granted by the wise master. It appeared to him that she was making an error in timing, probably due to her foreign taint, by arguing with him about his accusations. That had served its purpose in making trouble, delicious, exciting trouble, which had scourged the nerves to a climax.

He thought she had come to be nearer to him, and circled her body with a loving, turning snake of an arm. In a way he loved her. He had the extremest preference imaginable for her society and he evidently believed this to be eternal. Though he did not need her money, he was always asking her to marry him. It was extraordinary how little these considerations alleviated her distaste for the cruel, brawling duality of half his dealings with her.

As his lips touched her ear and found a patch of sensitiveness, her nerves made her break out in complaint, and into the wrong complaint, a lesser one than that which was making her feel clumsy with misery. "And you said it before we left the drawing-room," she mourned. "Madame Vuillaume must have heard."

"She is so stupid she would not have understood if she had," said André comfortably; and, seeing a loophole for his Parisian passion for anecdote, he continued, "Did I ever tell you how her husband made his money? It's rather a good story. When Ferdinand of Bulgaria came to Paris in 1912 . . ."

While he was telling the story, she kept her eyes on the parquet, and in its peat-coloured depths she saw the face of Laurence Vernon, and behind it the avenue of cypresses that led from the old post road to his quiet home, Mount Iris. As André finished, she said, "You do not understand, André. I want to leave you. I want all this to stop."

"Oh, my little one!" he exclaimed. He was really alarmed. She must be quite upset not to laugh at a really funny story like that. "You mustn't say such things to your André. I haven't done anything to make you unhappy, have I?"

She cried out, "Of course you have! Again and again! I tell you I loathe all these scenes and accusations and rages. I want this to come to an end. I don't love you."

"Oh, my little one, how can you say such things? Think what wonderful lovers we are! You are too young," he said, a pedagogic tone coming into his voice, "to realize how exceptionally fortunate we are in that respect."

"But that isn't enough. It doesn't make up for the abuse, the excitement, the hatefulness." To her own surprise she began to weep. "I tell you I can't bear it any longer. I can't go on."

"My poor child," he said remorsefully, taking her in his arms. "Stop trembling like that, you're safe with your André. Ah, I see what the matter is." He assumed an air of solemn authority over physiological mysteries. "I have been too much for you, I am afraid. My little darling, I am wicked, I should have been more careful of you——"

"You haven't been too much for me," she said, with some indignation. "When I tell you that I am sick to death of the cruel, lying things you say to me and the tempers you fly into, why should you assume that it's something else that's the matter with me? Particularly when the things I'm complaining about nobody could help hating, whereas what you're talking about nobody would mind very much"—she broke off, and he released her with a pat of the hand.

"When a woman is very tired," he said with a return of midwifely sententiousness, "she does not know what is the matter with her. It is then that a man who loves her understands her far better than she does herself. Come, darling, put on your things, I am going to send you home now."

"Yes," she said, "I am going home. And I will never come here again."

"Ah, my darling," he said, down on the floor, where he was looking for his shoes, "when you wake up tomorrow after a good long sleep, you will have forgotten that you ever said or thought these words."

She sighed in despair and stood looking down on him full of foreboding at his physical power and distinction. He was so finely made, so well dowered with the dignity of grace, that on all fours he was as little at a disadvantage as a tiger. He was an idiot, but his body did not know it. Resting her chin on her clasped hands, she turned and went slowly to the other end of the room. She took her powder-puff out of the bag she had left on the mantelpiece and passed it over her face, peering into the mirror, for here the sconces were not lit, and her reflection swam white in brown darkness shaken by ruddy firelight. With an exclamation of dismay she pressed still closer to the mirror, unable to believe her own expression. She was young enough not to have outgrown the persuasion adults plant in children, that their emotions are trivial and cannot carry the full freight of human joy or woe, so she was surprised to see on her face the mark of utter weariness, of deep suffering.

André's voice called to her from the distance, "Hurry up, darling. You'll be getting cold." At its charm she shuddered. His good looks, his adroitness, his amiability, had lost all power to affect her. They

119

were admirable of their kind, but they were so inextricably entangled
with elements she detested that for her they might never have existed.
But he had a hold on her for the simple reason that, when he and she
were linked by passion, they formed a pattern which was not only
æsthetically pleasing but was approved, and indeed almost enjoined,
by everything in civilization that was not priggish. When, an hour
or so before, he suddenly paused in the denunciations he was hissing
into her face, swayed for a minute and grew paler, and then drew
his arms softly yet closer and closer round her body and pressed his
mouth gently yet heavily on hers, she would have felt stiff-necked and
ridiculous if she had resisted, like a republican who refuses to stand
up in a London theatre when "God Save the King" is played. She
felt herself the victim of some form of public opinion, which was so
firmly based on primitive physical considerations that the mind could
not argue with it, and it operated powerfully even in the extremest
privacy.

She felt that again in the little hall, when he opened the front
door, looked back at her, and shut it again. Looking down on her
tenderly, he murmured, "You have given me more pleasure than any
other woman." She said sharply, "Ha! King Lear!" and wanted to
explain that at last she understood how Cordelia had been cloyed by
her sisters' excessive protestations of affection, but she could not
prevent her body yielding, not to the spirit but to the shape of his
embrace, as water follows the contour of a river-bed.

When they were out in the courtyard, with the spring sky curdled
by starlight above them, and the wind swinging in the tree-tops,
Isabelle felt relieved. The stars were very high, and the wind was
fresh as if it had come from woods and fields a long way off to visit
these imprisoned branches. A vast universe stretched away in all
directions from this house; and she would be a fool if she could not
find some path of escape through it. In the street outside, her long,
low, speed-shaped car made her exultant. Of space there was plenty,
and she had the means to cover it. She called out to wake her chauffeur, softly but sharply, desperately, as if some danger had overtaken
them while she slept, and they had just time to fly.

But once she was in the car and André was bending over her,
tucking her rug about her, her sense of freedom left her. Behind his
subtle, changing expressions there was a deadly composure, sign of
a settled calm which would always leave him in a position to seek
what he wanted in the most workmanlike style. She remembered that

she had come to his house that night only because at a certain time at
Madame Vuillaume's party, when the Princesse de Cortignac and
Monsieur de Gazière were coming towards the alcove where they sat,
he had gripped her wrist. In another moment that couple of *mau-
vaises langues* would have had something to wag about, so she had
to whisper, "Yes, I will go back with you now." She had meant to
shut the door on him as soon as she had got into her car, but he had
managed to delay her passage across the pavement until some other
people had come out of the house behind them. Turning on him to
say, "I only told you that because you forced me, you can't come with
me," she looked past him at the faintly smiling, inquisitive faces of
men and women older than herself, natives of the country where
she was a stranger, compatriots and therefore partisans of André,
watching to see if her movement changed into some dramatic and
betraying gesture. There is nothing more frightening than the faces
of people whom one does not know but who seem to know one, and
be amused by one. So she had smiled up at André and settled back on
her cushions while he took his seat beside her. That was why she was
still with him, hours later, and entangled still further with the trivial
and the time-devouring. And it would always be so. Any night that
he wanted this pleasure, so much sillier than drunkenness, of screaming,
shaking hate, that dared to change at its ugliest climax into the likeness of love, his tactical genius would force her to procure it for him.

She cried out desperately, "I want to leave you!"

He gazed on her thoughtfully, like a cook who has been brought
an unfamiliar kind of game and wonders if she ought to prepare it
like quail or like plover. "My dear," he said gently, "I thought I had
made you too tired. Now I begin to doubt whether I have made you
tired enough. Come back and stay a little longer with me."

"Oh, don't be such a complacent idiot!" she exclaimed. "Will you
stop regarding me as a technical problem in appeasement? I'm just
a woman who intensely dislikes you. Can't you grasp that?"

He bent his face closer to hers. It was like a young moon in its
pale, calm radiance, its remoteness from any human appeal that might
be raised to it. Isabelle flung herself forward and rapped on the glass,
calling to the chauffeur, "*Allez! Continuez! Vite!*"

Then she sat back and shut her eyes, and thought of Laurence
Vernon and his home. Her husband had taken her to Mount Iris two
or three times in the last few months before he was killed. One morning when they were staying in Washington, Roy had found on the

breakfast table a letter from Laurence, whom he had come to know through some reunion at Princeton, saying he had read in the papers where they were, and asking them to come and stay with him as soon as possible, that very day if they could. Roy had said laconically that Laurence was fine, that they must go and start at once, since they must be back at the Aerodrome in a week's time; and she had been put at the telephone forthwith to call up various people and say that they would not be able to come to the party after all. She remembered well how she had sat at the window while she made these calls, rejoicing in the warmth the sunshine sent through her silk morning-gown, and smiling up at the high blue sky between the roofs, because the answering voices were always so exactly what the outer world would have derisively expected from them. They were at first surprised, not conceiving what alternative could possibly tempt anybody from a good Washington party; then they were clouded by the suspicion that the only conceivable alternative to a good Washington party was another and better Washington party, and that there had happened some monstrous overlapping of dates, in which they had been worsted. But she soothed them, saying that it was because of Roy's next big flight that they had to leave.

They left the hotel an hour later and motored south through the warm fall day. Many miles lay before them, they stopped only once for a stand-up lunch outside a road-house. To the end of her life she would remember again the taste of the fried egg sandwich on her tongue, could bite again into the stored coolness of the apple she picked up from the red heap on a trestle table. Looking back on her marriage, she saw it always as a time when tastes were more pungent, colours brighter, sounds clearer and more intelligible than they had ever been before or since. She would never again see the country round Laurence Vernon's home as she saw it the first time with Roy. They had been travelling long hours when the automobile climbed the height of the pass; through air soft with evening, soft with autumn, they looked down on the inspissated fires of the woods that tumbled up and over a dozen ranges which met here and pooled their rivulets in one deep, sinuous, richly growing valley. This had been a battle-field, Roy told her. Boys had drunk like beasts from those rivulets, and had given back blood for water as they drank. As she sighed, Roy pointed out a line of cypresses that had found a level plane running through the contours of hills and dales and marched on in a straight black column. That, he said, was the avenue that led to

Laurence Vernon's home, which would make her forget that there had ever been war in these parts. Every white pillar of the colonnade was intact, though if one looked closely, it could be seen that each and all were pock-marked with bullets. The Gothic chapel by its side was still as it was when the first Vernon in those parts had built it to relieve his nostalgia. Indoors the china and silver shone on the polished table with a lustre that had not been dimmed by the months they had spent buried in the earth while the looting Yankees searched in vain; and as one sat there one could not believe that both Laurence's grandfathers had been killed in Pickett's Charge in their early twenties, and that even Laurence's father and mother had never seen them, for it seemed impossible that this household was not ordered by someone who had at least been in contact all his youth with someone of the old unshattered South.

Isabelle believed what he had told her when, just as they had turned into the avenue, Laurence Vernon stepped forward out of the cypress shadows and stopped the automobile. He climbed in, was introduced to her, told her in precise words how glad he was to welcome her, and settled down beside her, making civil inquiries. The letters on a book that he laid on his lap spelled Plato. Always, every time they visited him, he strolled down the avenue to meet them, an open book in his hand, and always the letters on the cover spelled an ancient name, Plato, or Lucretius, or Plotinus. Those books had made her wonder if she might not work out some spiritual equivalent of the Einstein theory regarding the re-entrant nature of time, for it was plainly through reading these writers of the remote past that Laurence owed his serene command over the present. Perhaps we are all of us born with one foot on the present, and can grip it with the other only if we swing it far enough back into the past. Her husband, dear Roy, had never made the experiment, and he seemed as if he had to hop about, whirling his arms and legs, to keep his balance on the moment. There was always a fine, fairish glaze on his skin, a dampness about his red-gold curls, as if the sweat of effort had no chance to dry on him. But Laurence, with his fine short pointed brown beard, which he never fingered, his clear brown eyes, which never sparkled, his trim body in his formal and unnoticeable clothes, seemed to rest as comfortably in the hour as if it were a library chair: so comfortably that he could think with a coolness and detachment that she knew to be rare triumphs over the modern world. During that and other visits she learned that he had thought himself right out of the

123

illusions common to the Old South. He preferred the classical to the picturesque any day; he knew that any tradition festered which did not in every generation take fresh vows of service to the timeless gods of justice and reason. But he had not made the error that others who have performed that feat of divestment have fallen into, by adopting the illusions of the New North. He was full of schemes for bringing money down to the South, for developing the resources of his country and making her nobody's old downtrodden mammy; but he was fighting—if one could use that word of an activity in which there was no passion—every attempt to enslave the people by the same conscienceless industrialism as has made the Yankees the drab men-machines they were. When he told her what he was doing, she felt, not only in the interest of the first hearing, but all the many times after, "Laurence is what I would have been if I had been a man. He is living the life I would have liked to live."

They had always known they were the same sort of people, she believed. There had been a moment once, when his recognition of that had struck her mind as clearly as if he had spoken it aloud, in the dining-room, when his neighbour Mrs Bellamy had come in to take port. It had been a recognition without the smallest practical consequences, it had even been without any emotional effects. For across the table had sat Roy, who had a power over her that made mere community of tastes seem a good that was indisputable but no occasion for enthusiasm, like a plate of cereal; and as for Laurence, everybody knew that he would marry Nancy as soon as her invalid husband was dead. But that arrangement obviously might leave some of his mind free for other imaginings. When Southerners said, "Why, Mrs George Fox Bellamy, she was Nancy Rivers Taylor," it sounded glamorous, because of the southern habit of speaking the maiden style of every matron as if it had been the name of a beauty, but this woman's thirties were certifying her as insipid, and the trailing cut of her chiffon dress hinted that she had a silly conception of romance. Still, the Bellamy place was but a bare five miles from Mount Iris, and Laurence was much too busy to go far afield seeking for a woman; and there was just enough there, in a water-colour way, to make a man who needed to fall in love able to find his need in her. There could be no question but that vows had been exchanged. If they had not, Laurence would not have risen suddenly from table and closed the French window, for no one of the party was cold, and his acute perceptions must have known it. She had known from his face that

that had been a symbolic gesture by which he reminded himself where his obligations lay, by which he shut up the wild thing that had threatened to come out of the unfettered darkness and break up the order he had imposed on his emotions. Isabelle had remembered that when she had come to life after the disaster and realized that no amount of grieving can put together a crashed aeroplane or anything that was in it. It had seemed sensible to come to Europe and treat her life as a room that had to be completely refurnished.

It was her fault for not having attributed due importance to the chiffon dress. It should have told her that Nancy was wholly given to the trailing and the asymmetrical, and when it came to the point, would commit any folly to escape being incorporated in the formal design made by Laurence and Mount Iris. There, Isabelle was conscious, she had for a moment stopped thinking. She should have foreseen that, when the invalid husband died, Nancy would be dismayed by a situation no longer irregular; that she would fling herself into a marriage with a stranger that, for no reason that the character of the involved persons could suggest, gave the disorderly impression of an elopement; and that Laurence would come over to Europe. She should have foreseen that one day Laurence would be shown into her drawing-room and that she would know, as she smiled rather blankly into his more ardent eyes, how justly she had read the meaning of that moment in his dining-room. Now he and Mount Iris were hers for the taking. The thought made her breathe slowly for a minute. It was not greed that she was feeling, for she could have acquired as good a home as Mount Iris by purchase, and several better ones by marriage. It was the most naïvely good part of her that was pleased. She wanted Mount Iris for the life that Laurence lived there, because it seemed to exclude all the heated sort of wrong she feared more than anything else in life. She could imagine herself sitting at dusk, in the hall, looking out at the white afterglow that was divided by the dark pillars of the colonnade, while Laurence walked up and down, passing as a black silhouette across the strips of light, as an ordinary clothes-coloured figure across the strips of darkness, his head down, his step regular and slow. He would be thinking over the material the day had brought him; he would be weaving an intellectual protection for him, for her, for their children, from the arrows that the passion-governed world without shot so recklessly. She trembled in an ecstasy of gratitude; and then was still, as she remembered that at the moment Mount Iris was wholly inaccessible to her.

She had treated her life as a room that had to be completely refurnished. A week after she had landed in Europe, she went to a ball in one of those houses which are in the heart of Paris yet have an ivied cryptic woodland looking in at all the windows that do not give on the streets. She had thought as she went through the shabby-gorgeous rooms, among the plain and unperturbed people, "This is utterly unlike America." America then seemed to her a lying continent that by a gloss of comfort and luxury disguised itself from what it was, a desert stretching fifteen hundred miles to the field where Roy lay among the ashes of his plane, and fifteen hundred useless miles beyond. "This was the place where my forebears lived; it is more truly my country than America. Perhaps it will be kinder to me." It was then that for the first time she caught sight of André de Verviers. He would have been easy to see in any case. His square but not broad shoulders, his long waist and narrow hips, gave him the tense, shaped appearance of a figure on a medieval church carving, and his head, though decently and masculinely moderate in its beauty, was so definitely cut that it at once impressed the mind as deeply as if long years had made it familiar. But he was specially easy for her to see because he had already turned on her a look of brilliant and candid interest. It had the same meaning as the first look Roy had ever given her. It said, "You are beautiful. Your beauty is so far over the boundary line of argument that I am sure I do not need any more time for deliberation before I commit myself to that opinion. So here and now I claim that you and I are the same sort of person, and that we could be happy companions." A storm of grief ran through her because for nearly a year now Roy had been unable to prove that claim. She preferred him to everyone else, alive or dead. Then she swung about, feeling dogged about this unknown man, bobbing her head up and down under the tide of an adjacent bore's conversation, saying, "Yes, yes," "Yes, yes," waiting till she should find him at her elbow with an introducing friend.

It had seemed certain that their meeting was fortunate. Isabelle had felt no misgiving that day when they were riding in the forest, under the fine black bones of the winter trees, and there suddenly fell from the dark purple sky raindrops like spinning pennies. She and André both transferred to the rainstorm the excitement they felt about the storm of feeling that was gathering within them, and while she exclaimed in fear, he cried out that they must hurry, they must gallop, to come in time to a hunting-box he knew nearby. The trees

grew thinner before them; they found themselves crossing a tongue
of open country, which now looked livid and fantastic because it was
suffused by a peculiar grey-green light like the colour of water in a
chalk-pit. The dull emerald of the winter grass had become sharp and
acid, the few houses looked like painted paper; and on the white road
a black string of orphans, and the two bunchy nuns at their tail,
seemed stricken with madness as they bent and gesticulated under the
invisible missiles of the rain. "Oh, it all looks so strange," she gasped.
"It looks as if the end of the world was happening. I want to see
this," and she tried to stop her horse. But André was beside her, his
hand on her reins. "Hurry, hurry!" he cried. "We must make haste!"
They were over the road, they were thundering up a hill, they passed
through iron gates and were in a wide avenue in the forest, the smell
of a wood fire came to their nostrils. They were in front of an old grey
house, soft with the stone embroideries of the Renaissance, which
were softer here with moss and fern, flanked on each side by new
stables and cottages. When they jumped down from their horses, they
were both pale and were breathing deeply, as if they had escaped
some real danger.

An old groom came out of one of the cottages, and André hailed
him by his name, but Isabelle turned aside abruptly, because she
could not bear to feel anybody's eyes on hers. In the centre of the
courtyard was the statue of a lion, and though the rain was still falling, she went to stand in front of it. A few dead leaves were rustling
in the trap of its open jaws. Presently she heard André's step on the
gravel and felt his hand on her arm. He told her that he had telephoned for his car and his groom and that, though the lodge was
closed and fireless, they could take shelter in the groom's cottage
while they were waiting. She murmured acquiescently, and then he
said, in a lower tone, and with some stumbling, "There is a woman
watching us from behind the curtains in one of those upper windows.
You cannot think how shy that makes me feel. I am young and
awkward again, as if I were a boy. But I must say what that woman
guesses I am saying, even though the thought of her guessing makes
me want to die of confusion. I love you, I love you, I love you." She
went on smiling at the dry leaves that turned about in the vault of
the beast's jaws. A little rivulet ran down from the brim of her hat to
her shoulder. After a silence he told her. "But you must say you
love me. Say it, say it. You do not understand how naked and un-
armed I shall feel until I hear you say it." She tried to say it, but no

sound came. Then she forced her voice, and only achieved a cracked whisper that she stopped out of shame. He laughed, saying, "My little one, my dear little one, you need not tell me any more, now I know that you are feeling helpless and childish as I am."

Yet their meeting had not been fortunate. Worse than that, it had confused Isabelle's ideas of what might be reckoned as good fortune. She had been stunned at finding that a passionate love-affair was not, as her marriage had led her to believe, a prescription for general happiness. It was an indisputable fact that both André and herself found a great joy in each other's company, that as soon as the one came into the room the other felt an electric invigoration of the whole body, a saturation of every movement of the mind by pleasure. It was an indisputable fact that when André took her in his arms, there began for both of them a period of intense delight which softened and broadened down into contentment. To her the logical consequence of these facts was a pervasive mutual kindness, which would give them an armour against the world, so that they could go about calmly, laying out their lives to the best advantage. Hurry and panic, it seemed to her, should have been eliminated from their experience as soon as they recognized the nature of their feelings. And for about a week after they had been like children dazed by sudden passage to fairyland, he had been simple and kind, they had lunched at little places in the country, they had lunched at big places in town and felt invisible, they had met at night at parties where everybody else was invisible. Then life had unfolded in exquisite order, though following no plan. But suddenly he became no longer at all simple, and often not kind, and their life was full of plans but empty of order.

First Isabelle began to notice that whatever they arranged André wished to alter so soon as she had fallen in with it. If she told him that one day soon she must go and spend a day with Blanche Yates at her château in the valley of the Chevreuse, and it was agreed that Thursday was the day they best could spare, the memory of the agreement went from him before their next meeting. By that time Thursday had come to mean to him the one possible day for taking her to see his cousin Berthe, who had such a charming house near Meaux. To begin with, she dealt with such situations by reminding him of their agreement, and then, when he denied it on one ground or another, by trying to find out what these powerful reasons were which made it imperative they should go to Meaux on that particular day and made him ready to put her to the vexation of writing apologetic letters. There were always none; but at that she only fell silent. If he had this queer streak of eccentricity in him, to suffer it was a small price to pay for the exorcism he had performed over her loneliness and despair. She wrote to Blanche, she went to Meaux. But that did not give them peace. She had said to herself, when she had first made these concessions, "I shall hate it if I see that because I am giving in to him he feels triumphant," but she hated it still worse when she saw that what he was feeling was disappointment. After a time she had to admit that he had made his unreasonable demands only in the hope that she would resist them, and that hope made him screw up his demands to a higher and higher pitch of unreason, with the horrid furtive avidity of a drug addict who manœuvres towards the gratification that he dare not name. She had told herself again, but a little wearily, that this was not too great a price to pay. But she was relieved when, very soon, the amount of change and whim he was imposing on their common affairs became so great that it began to make his own life quite uncomfortable. In shifting backwards and forwards the date of a visit to a village on the Seine, which was said to be very beautiful in the springtime, he forgot an engagement to dine with a Bourbon duke, which greatly upset him. At once he abandoned that form of sport with her.

But still that did not mean peace. For it was then that André began not to feel but to make use of jealousy. One afternoon, when she went to visit him, he greeted her with bitter reproaches about certain men whom she liked and who liked her. Smiling, she offered him her promise never to see any of them alone again. She had every sympathy with the jealous. To lose her lover to another woman would, she knew, cover her with shame. If in a contest where she had wanted to be first she came in second, she knew that her flayed pride would turn round and round trying to argue away the fact of her defeat, and that her mind would flay it again by coldly asserting the flaws in all such arguments. Of course she would not expose André to the fear of such a hurt. Nor was the sacrifice entailed anything but trivial, since none of these men gave her anything like the happiness she received from André. The cry of exultation with which André heard her promise and caught her in his arms shocked her by its excessiveness. She felt an uneasy suspicion that she had been given a part to act in a play which had seemed innocent only because she had seen just her own lines and cues, but which offended all her sense of values once she heard the other actor's words. That suspicion vexed her again when during the next week or so he made some sudden raids on her hotel sitting-room. She saw that when he always found her alone or in the company of women, he was pleased, and even touched, to a degree that struck her as false in taste. An expression of almost maudlin pity used to pass over his face, as if he were a gambler who, in passing through the heated rooms of a gaming-house, had found the strayed child of some officer of the place quietly playing marbles in a corner. She wished he would take it more simply, as her performance of a sensible and not very difficult promise. But she liked even that expression better than the one she saw on his face when he rose to go. He looked wistfully round the room as if to visualize a delight he had hoped it might have offered him, and she knew that he would have liked to find her with a lover, so that he could make a scene. Or, rather, his desire took a form less brutal and perverse, more purely silly. What he really wanted was to find her with a friend whom he could have pretended to believe her lover, so that he could make a scene.

Nevertheless she had kept to her cloistral ways, though she was conscious that there had crept into her attitude more of the ramrod stiffness of a sentinel rather than the shy recession of a votary of love taking the veil. She would not let this brawl enter her gates, and that was all. But she was to lose her resolute calm, and the force that sustained it, during the time he led her to think he was deceiving her with Princess Natalie Avitzkin. He said he had not done this, that it was she who had misread inevitable movements, which meant no more than that he was doing his social duty, and built fantastic dreams on them; but she knew he spoke falsely. It could not be by accident that he had so perfectly forged the appearance of surfeited ardour hankering after change. Perhaps they might speak of Natalie and how she had looked at the Opera, her fairness giving out rays as she sat in front of the blackness of a box, though Isabelle would not say that it had struck her that he had bowed a little too long and too low before that box. A little later he would talk of the paramount beauty of golden hair, and then would break off in embarrassment, and lay a kind hand on her dark hair, as if he were caressing a child about whose future he knew a sad story. At meals he would become absent-minded and stare into the distance, and then come to himself with a start and be uneasily cheerful and affectionate. He became hesitant and distracted about appointments, and at last presented himself with a melancholy air of bearing up nobly under his own penitence. That evening she dismissed him quickly and coldly, contriving that they should be interrupted, and telephoned to the American Express Company to reserve a compartment for herself and her maid Adrienne on the train for Berlin the next night. She had read that her old Professor of Archæology was staying there till he went on an expedition to Siberia, and she knew that he would probably be glad of her as a bottlewasher and a financial aid.

When André rang up the next morning, Isabelle would not speak to him; and she heard a sound as if her coldness had been so pleasing that the air had been forced out of his lungs in a spasm of delight. She turned away from the telephone, foolish with misery. It appeared to her proven that he had divined her plan of departure and was so eager to be rid of her that he rejoiced. To be able to answer any of the other people who rang her up that day, she had to affect an air of mænad joy, as if it were with an impulse to hysterical laughter that she was struggling. "Yes, I am going to Berlin, and then to Russia!" she cried, as if she were going there to be whirled up in the vortex of some orgy so riotous that already it was pulling her off her balance. She never knew who among them told him; but an hour before she had to leave the hotel for the station there was a knock on the door. Her maid opened and then turned round to her, silently asking what she was to do. André leaned against the doorpost, so white that she forgot the trouble that was between them, and asked herself what frightful physical cause, what sudden malady or overdose of drug, could have changed him to this. But in a croaking cry he asked, "You are going to Russia?" and she remembered everything, and stiffened. "Of course," she said. Adrienne went. He flung himself forward on Isabelle; they collapsed together in trembling entanglement on the top of a shoe box. "But—but—" he stammered, and had to begin again in French, for he had forgotten all his English, though normally he spoke it almost as fluently as his own tongue. "You were really going to Russia?" She whispered, "Yes." He took possession of her again in a long kiss, which was honest, which gave himself to her, so that she was not ashamed of her return. From this embrace he broke away to gloat on the look of her and cry out, "You were going to Russia! You were going to leave me, just because I made you jealous!" He was trembling and running with sweat, he looked like a man who has escaped by a hairbreadth from a great danger, who had stepped aside just as the propeller begins to whirl and has felt its breath on his brow, who has arrived so late that the gates of the elevator are clanged in his face and he sees it drop like a stone down the shaft. "You were going to do that to me! But I tell you we belong to each other!"

There had followed a whole month of peace, during which they had progressed with their love and had done much towards changing it into permanent kindness. But even then she had been disquieted, and had sometimes raised her fingers between his lips and hers, and shuddered with a lightning flash of enmity as she lay in his arms. For he had cried out, "You were going to leave me, just because I made you jealous!" although she had never told him that he had made her jealous. She felt it as their common misfortune that a sentence which was wrung from him in what was perhaps the sincerest moment of his life should be damnable and unforgettable evidence of his insincerity. She felt the sham hope, the real despair, of a woman whose husband has just come out of a clinic after the last of a series of cures for morphinism, and is doing very well, just as he always has done during the first few weeks after treatment. Not in the slightest degree was she surprised when he began to wriggle through the one loophole she had left him. She had dismissed all her admirers, except Marc Sallafranque. Marc had to stay. He had to stay, for one thing, because to dismiss him would have conceded that André and she were two insane persons gibbering at one another, since it was perfectly obvious that she could not possibly entertain Marc as a husband or a lover. He was too grossly, too comically successful as an industrialist, his very name had passed from him to the article he manufactured. A Sallafranque was no longer a man, but a cheap car. A woman might as well ally herself with Monsieur Eau-de-Cologne or Monsieur Pâté de Foie Gras. Moreover, though he was not unlovable, he was grotesque. He was tall enough but he looked short, because his body was overweighted with the cylindrical fatness of a robust little boy, and his square jaw went straight down into a bull neck almost the same size round as his head, so that he seemed made all of one thick, rubbery piece. In the midst of this podginess his melting brown eyes, his snub, dilating nostrils, and his wide mouth made a muzzle like a terrier's, expressing a purely sensuous gaiety and melancholy so candidly that one would no more deal with him by cold reason than if he were a terrier, and one felt at no time that one was dealing with a man. It was a terrier that did funny tricks, too. He was comically violent; when he wanted to go upstairs in a hurry, he would put his feet together and hop up several steps at a time, with great springs of his strong legs, and once, when he had grown impatient in a restaurant, he had rushed on a waiter carrying in a pile of plates and had dealt them like cards on the floor around him. It was impossible to think of him without laughing, but the laughter was always kind, for he was so good, so generous, so guileless, so bravely humble in his subservience. It would have been as absurd and insulting and heartless to count him among the admirers who must be dismissed as if he had been a trusty footman. But not doing so had given André his chance. They happened almost every third day now, these revolting scenes, when he pretended to believe her capable of being unfaithful to him with this grotesque, when his voice pattered out accusations against her on one persistent note till she swayed and had to clap her hands over her ears, when his arms would sweep out in menace, not against her, but against the order of the room, so that a vase would be hurled from the mantel-piece and crash on the hearth, until he drew her to him in a recon-ciliation which would have been shameful to both of them if he had believed half of what he had been saying, which was an irrelevant climax to an evening of slapstick idiocy if he had not.

And she could not get rid of him. It had earlier been the intention of both of them to be married in June, and that was still his intention. She was grimly conscious of his power to carry it into effect. He would see to it, by such technical devices as he had employed that very evening at Madame Vuillaume's party, that they should constantly be alone together, and that the generic woman in her who loved the generic man in him should have endless opportunities to betray the individual woman in her who loathed the individual man in him. He might even draw so much public attention to their continuing rela-tionship, that she would find it socially necessary to marry him. What he would make of marriage she would not let her mind run forward to discover fully; if she had been threatened with cancer, she would shrink from precise foreknowledge of her ultimate torture. Marriage with André would not be torture, but it would be tomfoolery. In spite of herself, infuriating visions passed before her. At the very best, he would practise private fidelity to her and public flirtation with innumerable conspicuous women, so that she would be ridiculed by the world as a complaisant wife, and yet would have no reason to complain. Nothing sane could proceed out of their marriage, because it would have to be based on André's assumptions about love, which had the madhouse trick of cutting up the mind into inconsistent parts. He was himself two people in his attitude to passion. When he was her lover, he was grave and reverent, but too often there was afterwards this solemn clowning about sex, this midwife chatter about the bringing to birth of pleasure. Don Juan, it seemed, was a case of split personality; his other half was Mr Gamp. And he did what he could to draw her with him into the madhouse, for he tried to split her personality into two. It was suggested to her that her beauty and her capacity for passion were a separate entity, a kind of queen within her, and that it was to this that his loyalty was given, and that the rest of her was a humbler being, who ought to feel grateful that this superior part had caused her to be associated with such a grand gesture of chivalry. She, Isabelle, was supposed to be possessed by la femme as by a devil. Such an hypothesis made her feel as if she had been plucked back to the dark ages, to find her way among the cobwebby delusions of alchemists.

But in Laurence Vernon's mind she would find unity. He would have but one image of her there and that distinct as the figure on a Greek coin. He would have but one clean-cut image of their marriage, as simple as the year in the mind of a farmer. In the spring he would lay the foundation of his plans for public things and she would have her children, in the summer they would admire to see how their work fared in the heat of the day, in the autumn there would be harvest, and since the days grow shorter and they would have so much to talk over, no doubt winter also would not hang on their hands. Men grow weary of many things, but not of the seasons of the year. The thought of how she was being cheated of a profitable simplicity for a complexity that was sheer loss made her have tears to wipe from her face as her automobile stopped at her hotel. It made her mutter miserably as she fell asleep. It had made dawn look colder than its own greyness when she woke, as it looks to those who have been roused by recollection of their bankruptcy. It made her sit up in bed and stare when there came a knock on the door, as if that must mean sudden danger, and pull on her dressing-gown and rush to turn the key as if the world were so full of such dangers that precaution was worn out, and there was nothing to do but put down the head and charge them.

There stood in the corridor outside nothing more terrible than two women, their arms full of flowers; but at that their arms were full of importunities, of threats to her peace. For even if some of the flowers they carried were from Laurence, the others must come from undesired

134

intruders. Crossly she told them, "You have knocked at the wrong door, you will find my maid in the salon along to the left," but they bowed their heads before her sharp tone so meekly that she repented. She was always susceptible to the pathos of the army of plain women in drab gowns who moved about Paris, carrying to their more fortunate sisters their flowers and dresses and hats, serving the central purpose of the place but not partaking of its full glory, like lay sisters in a sternly governed convent. She ran back to the table by her bed, found a few francs for them, and came back, holding out her arms for their flowers.

"Ah!" she sighed, as she took the first sheaf, and knew it was from André, since it was made of the red and white roses which he always sent her, as symbols of something or other. "These I don't want, not at all. Will you not take them away with you, Madame, to use in your own home?"

The women exchanged glances of embarrassment. It was as if a visitor to the convent should from kindly ignorance propose to a lay sister that she should avail herself of some privilege strictly reserved for the nuns.

"But no, Madame," one of the murmured hesitantly, "that's not really possible. Why, Monsieur de Verviers might get to hear of it, and he's one of our best customers. It would never do to annoy him."

"Life is difficult," said Isabelle, and they agreed, pleased as French people always are when they are offered an established truth to rest on, as it were, in the course of their day's work among unresolved experience; and she said good-bye and shut the door. First she put André's flowers in the waste-paper basket, and then looked at the card to be quite sure they had come from him. "Darling, last night you were more wonderful than ever," he had written, and she groaned aloud. It was evident that, early though it was, he had already been out and about for some time, feeling marvellously well. She saw herself successfully pursued by him through life, as one is by the income-tax authorities.

Shuddering, she turned to the other flowers. She knew at once that Sallafranque had sent the immense and aerie sheaf of cattleyas, so fragile that they seemed not like flowers at all but like assemblies of tiny winged creatures which might decide at any moment to swarm in other shapes, or to disperse into a rising cloud. It was odd that this human barrel should choose always the most delicate and exotic flowers as the ambassadors of his so simple feelings. Since his puberty, gardens the size of a department must have lost their blossoms in the service of his desires. His card was sealed in its envelope, and was scrawled with yet another request that she should marry him at once, so honestly and humbly put that tears came to her eyes, and she put it by to slip into a pocket of her dressing-case, where she kept valuable papers. There remained the pale gold roses, which she hoped Laurence had sent her. He had indeed, and on his card he reminded her that she had promised to lunch with him that day at Laurent's, and begged her not to fail him, since he wanted to discuss what he thought the most important matter in the whole world.

Her heart beat so strongly that, had she not preferred restraint to all things, she would have run about the room, crying aloud, so nearly all was well. Being as she was, she lay down on the bed and kept quite still. She looked at the flowers to quieten herself with their beauty, and her thoughts went to the two plain women in their drab gowns who had so gently borne with her harshness in the corridor. Her conscience smote her that she should have so much and they should have so little. But her feeling of remorse was lessened by the suspicion that the difference in their states was in its practical effects not altogether to their disadvantage. If she had been poor like them, she would have had to eat her heart out in widowhood among her familiar and vigilant surroundings until the proper and valid distraction was offered; she would not have been able to run about the world making experiments in oblivion, and she would not have experimented so rashly. The high degree of security she enjoyed thanks to her money had persuaded her that practically nothing she could do could bring her into serious difficulties.

André, too, she thought, would have been in some ways the better without his wealth. Had he been a poor man, he would not have been free to spend his whole life proving a silly point about his power by leaving women who wanted him to stay with them and staying with women who wanted him to leave them. Really, she reflected, he was not a fool, for he knew that perfectly well. In realizing exactly what he owed to the *status quo* he was cleverer than the more intellectually active Laurence or the more practically effective Marc Sallafranque, who both regarded their lives as purely individual achievements, which they could have made the same in any world. André was well aware that anything that threatened the existing conditions of society threatened him with extinction. He spoke with equally personal dread of the growth of Communism, of the rearming of Germany, of the imprudence of anyone belonging to his own class who, by adoption of an extreme religious or political faith, or by a gratuitous divorce, or by clamant bad manners, became the subject of adverse public comment. The structure must not even be shaken.

At that Isabelle sat up in bed and stared at the opposite wall. That, of course, was the secret of her attraction for André. He had recognized her fundamental temperance, her inaptitude for any kind of violence; he knew that in her company he could play with danger to his heart's content, that no matter how he challenged her to misbehaviour, she would perpetually be moderate. He loved what he feared, as spirits sapped with luxury always do. The thought of screaming and shouting men made his heart stop with terror; it gave him therefore an immense pleasure to raise his voice and hear what a scream and a shout sounded like; and he knew that in the stillness of her atmosphere all such violent noises were at once annulled. Suddenly she realized the true nature of the problem before her. All she had to do was to convince him that his impression of her character was false: that she had within her a mænad, who might some day break loose, answer his raised voice by her own screams and shouts, and invoke the forces of disorder. A single uncontrolled gesture would bring about this change of view, for the first hint of this hidden self of hers would make him so nervous that he would lose his usual critical faculty. But control was obstinately a part of all her nature, even including her imagination. She murmured, "But what can I do, what can I do?" and slid her feet out of bed, feeling for her slippers, as if moving her body would make her mind move too. She rose and pulled on her peignoir, and then became suddenly motionless, staring again at the wall; and indeed she saw what she had to do as if it were written there. Shuddering with distaste, she said, "That would do! Yes, that would do!" and went to the waste-paper basket and took out André's flowers.

II

She liked so little what she had to do, and knew so well what happiness lay on the other side of doing it, that all the morning she was trembling with nervousness. Her hands shook, her mind shook; she was a trifle stupid. When Sallafranque rang her up and asked her at what time he might see her, a rush of tenderness for his affectionate simplicity made her desire that he might know about Laurence and herself sooner than anybody else and count as her first friend to be adopted as their friend; so she told him that she was lunching with a friend at Laurent's and that, if he called for her at half-past two, he might hear great news. He answered with a bubble of joy which she took as proof of his good nature, his readiness to rejoice in the pleasures of a friend as if they were his own, until he had rung off. Then she realized that he had thought she meant she was going to promise to marry him. She would not have exposed him to such humiliation for anything in the world. But she did not see how she could ring him up and make the matter plain without a degree of indelicacy which, in this already sullied day, she felt reluctant to undertake. Besides, the morning was getting on, and she had arranged to have a manicure and a face massage, as an anticipatory rite of purification for the disorderly act she was to commit later in the day.

At half-past twelve she took André's roses in her hand and looked at herself in her long mirror, not that she needed reassurance of her beauty, which had ceased to be relevant to any serious purpose of her life, since by now Laurence must have received some final impression of her appearance. What she needed was to recognize herself as the person she knew, who she had been all her life, who was incapable of being forced to make a scene by the pressure of passion. She waited till it was nearly twenty-five to one, to make quite certain that André would be out, for though he ought to allow a full half-hour to get to Versailles for that lunch, he would perhaps not hurry, since his hosts were not French. Then she went down to her automobile, and told the chauffeur to drive to André's house. As the car travelled up the Champs-Élysées she looked ahead at the Arc de Triomphe, raising against the whitish spring sky a shape appropriate less to architecture than to furniture, as if it were a wardrobe storing the ideal of French miltary grandeur, and she childishly attributed her troubles to her residence in a country where life stamped itself in such spectacular forms. Then she knew the vertiginous pain of a patient who is going to a nursing-home for an operation which is not strictly necessary, which is undergone solely as a precaution against future crises; she wanted to stop the automobile, jump out, to take the chance that some other way of ridding herself of André would present itself. Perhaps her Uncle Honoré would come to France this summer, and would be able to suggest something. It was well known that that old man understood everything. But when the automobile slowed off the

Champs-Élysées into the avenue whose trees marched down to the
Seine, she remembered how often, and with what feelings of humiliation, she had forced herself against her will to make this journey
during the last few weeks. She picked up the roses she had let fall on
her lap, and held them tightly.

"When will Madame want me again?" asked the chauffeur.

"Oh, at once, at once!" she said gaily, and went forward to her
deed.

Decidedly, part of her trouble had been merely that she was in
France, for nowhere else in the whole world would there have been
this courtyard. She had liked coming here, and since it had an air of
liking to be visited by happy lovers, she had humoured it. Yes, that
accounted for at least part of the trouble. She passed through the
archway, and sniffed as always the antique pungency of the concierge's meal, seething in a pot that had no doubt never been emptied
and filled afresh since Paris was Lutetia, that might have begun its
simmering in an even earlier and sterner times, so that the basic
flavour still carried a trace of tender prehistoric child. She was peered
at as always by the concierge's wife, pressing against the dimness of
her window her drooping bosom and features congested by malevo-
lence; how realist are the French to keep at their doorways a perpetual
reminder that the body of man is corruptible and his nature fundamentally evil. Then she entered into the courtyard itself, into the
tender evidence that the French are romantics; that though civilization constrains them to live in great cities, they remain provincials at
heart, and when they have to build high walls, knock them down
again with their minds. This place was like a square in a little town,
not the square where the market is, but the smaller one where the
women sit and gossip over their sewing in the evening. There were
cobblestones underfoot, clean as they are in the country, and trees
tall as they are by village fountains. It was quiet with more than
absence of noise, it seemed to be manufacturing quietness, in which
the toot of a motor-horn in the street outside sounded as feebly as if a
tiny child had set its lips to a toy trumpet. In the very middle of the
square an old dog lay asleep under its flies. To the left was a tall cliff
of dwellings determined wholly by necessity, its windows placed at
ugly intervals, its dark stone scored with pipes. It was entered by a
double door of glass and yellow-painted iron, such as might have
admitted to a lycée. One knew nothing about it except that there
existed behind one of its windows a human being who knew the

139

emotions of fatherhood, for near the entrance was propped up a child's bicycle that some adult had been painting green. One knew also that behind another of its windows was a woman who had once been young, who had learned nothing since, for she was singing an air from *Thaïs* by propulsion of the breath from a bosom choked with syrup, in a manner that one had thought long universally discredited. In fact, there were in that building souls whom metropolitan influences had tried in vain to ravish from their simplicity.

To the right was the house, much lower, only three stories high, where all the shutters were always closed because the banker's widow was still dying at Nice. She had been ill so long that her residence had fallen into some disrepair. The creepers had not been cut back, and tendrils grew about the faded green slats of the shutters. But it was one of those houses which, in emptiness, are fragrant as an empty scent-bottle. One saw the darkness of the rooms peopled with ghosts of women belonging to the eighties, with frizzed light auburn hair set forward on their heads, fawn-dark, faintly Mongolian eyes, long slender waists rising from a fluff of frills like silk-cased spiral springs, and vitally important explanations, long withheld from the noblest reasons, turning to red phthisis between lip and tiny scrap of handkerchief. Beside the lachrymose charm of this home of spectres most other houses would have looked gross and bourgeois, but not this house of André's, which some nobleman had built during the Second Empire as a replica of a Renaissance pavilion in his country park. It was looking its best at this moment, for the grey stone, marked with purplish shadows where the rains had dripped from the rich mouldings, was wreathed with the languid green leaves of wistaria, and its mauve flowers, which, in spite of their fragility, hung with the weightiness of fruit. But it owed little to the benevolence of the seasons; it could depend on its own style, the magnificence that had here curbed itself and been for a moment light, that had with perfect justice scaled down its method of elaboration from pomp and castle-size to the moderate measure of a man living alone except for love. She had cried out when she first saw it, it had seemed so beautiful. It would be beautiful again when André was a ghost like the women in the house next door, and was visible only to such lovers of the past as had a special feeling for this age. Then he would be seen looking out under the broad brows of the mansarded windows purged of his triviality and restlessness by the censorship of man's romanticizing memory, dark and beautiful and grave with consideration of private delights, like a young man painted by Giorgione. It was only in the present that he and his house were intolerable; and that present she was now going to shatter and elude.

She went up the flight of four curved steps that led to his door, rang the bell, and went down the steps again.

In time old Michel hobbled out, his greenish-black trousers concertinaing round his legs. André would not dress his maître d'hôtel properly because his aristocratic relatives were very poor and never renewed their servants' liveries. At this reminder of the complete factitiousness of André's existence she was swept by a wave of irritation, and she began to get the roses into the right position, their flowers in one hand, their stalks in the other.

"Ah, Madame!" Michel called down to her. "Monsieur André did not expect you, he's gone to Versailles for luncheon. But won't you come in and write a note?"

She tried to answer him in the words that she had been rehearsing since the morning; but her lips were dry, her mouth opened and shut but emitted no sound. She could, however, perform her planned action. She broke the flowers in two across the middle of the stalks; she did that easily enough, because she had prepared them with scissors at home. Her pleasure at finding that she could execute at least part of her programme, and that it succeeded so far as to make Michel's eyes pop out of his head and bring him down to the second step, gave her back her breath.

Isabelle cried out, quite loud, "Tell your master that I want neither him nor his flowers!" And she began to tear off the petals from the flowers, the leaves from the stalks, and scatter them on the ground.

"But, Madame!" said Michel. "But, Madame!"

He came down another step, but no further. Horror, even fear, was on his face. She did not wonder. She wished she could stop at once, having made her point. The air from *Thaïs* had stopped, and in the stillness she heard above her a metallic clash, as if someone had very sharply thrown open a window high up in the flats. Perhaps she was being watched. She longed to turn round and run out of the courtyard, but a peculiar motion which Michel had made with his right hand, and a canny narrowing of his eyes, had filled her with alarm. It was as if he were promising himself that when she had gone he would sweep up all this detritus of blossoms, and would spare himself the embarrassment of telling André. She looked down and saw, between the cobblestones and the slab of pavement at the foot of

141

the steps down from the house, a narrow section of earth still wet from the early morning showers. Down on this she cast the most complete red and white roses she had left, and with her heel she ground them into the mud. She knew that Michel, who was clean as a cat, would not dabble in the dirt to retrieve them. André would see them as he came in and would inquire what had happened, and Michel, she knew from the gape of his old jaw, would tell everything; for the savagery she had put into the grinding of her heel on the roses had made him feel concern for the safety of his adored master. Yes, late that afternoon the two men would bend over the muddied petals, and Michel would quaver, "Like a madwoman, I tell you, Monsieur André, like a madwoman!" and André would grow pale with apprehension of hitherto undivined resources of recalcitrant womanhood. He would fling back to the house and spend the evening smoking very quietly in his library; and when her engagement was announced, he would do nothing, absolutely nothing.

She took one last look at the pavilion and its wistaria, and went out of the courtyard, saying to herself, "This is good-bye to all the French thing. It's lovely but it is not really a part of me. Our family's emphasis on its French origin is a piece of snobbery like André's refusal to buy Michel a new livery. By this time our blood has become wholly American. Now I am going back to my own people."

She felt so light-hearted, so freed from the past, that she walked past her own car, and her chauffeur had to call her back. When she got to Laurent's, she wished she had walked, for she was too early. There was no Laurence waiting in the lobby, and she was sorry, for she wanted someone to greet her at once, so that she could release the happy laughter that was welling up in her. She chose a table on the terrace, for she knew he would want to eat out there where the trellis wall shut out all the urban lower part of the landscape, with its babies and nurses and seats and gravel walks, and admitted only the full-foliaged tree-tops and the bright crest of the fountain spray. She ordered some tomato juice, for she would never again need a cocktail to pick her up, since she was never going to be down, and sat at her ease and sipped it, looking at a group of trees, a chestnut and two planes, that were swaying rhythmically together, like gods wrestling together and coming to no falls because their forces, being divine, are equal. But presently she looked at her watch. At first she had been alone because she was too early; now she was alone because Laurence was late. Yet he was never late. Surely he had said Laurent's? She leant back on her chair, and was able to look into the lobby, and there he was, standing quite still with his back to the terrace, his arms crossed on his chest, his head bowed, as if he were pondering something of a desperate nature.

She called to her waiter. "Tell Monsieur Vernon that Madame Tarry is here."

"But I have already told him," he answered.

They both stared at the long, rather stiff, narrow-waisted back. "Perhaps Monsieur is expecting another guest?" suggested the waiter.

"I don't think so," said Isabelle, and smiled to herself. It was touching that even Laurence, the most polished and self-possessed of human beings, should be timid before this moment and should try to stave it off as long as possible. At that instant Laurence chose to swing round, and though he lifted a hand in gay greeting, he showed by a lifting of the shoulders, a compression of the lips, that he found their scrutiny embarrassing. The waiter pivoted on his heel and became part of another group, and Isabelle smiled up into Laurence's face as he bent over her hand. "Had you forgotten you had asked me?"

"No, I certainly hadn't," said Laurence, and sat down opposite her. His body slumped into his seat heavily and clumsily for him. "What's that you're drinking?"

"Tomato juice," she said. She could have wished that he was not taking the approaching moment quite so seriously, for his voice was harsh, his pallor was ghastly.

"I'll not have that," he said. "Waiter, waiter, what have you got that's nearly all gin? A dry Martini, I suppose, is the nearest thing. Well, make it strong." He looked after the waiter with an intensity of gaze that served no purpose, and drummed on the table with his fingertips. He did it so silently that she could make no complaint on the score of her nerves, but she found it odd that he should do it at all. It was incredible that he should be so schoolboyish, so uninitiate. After all, Nancy must at some time or other have received some sort of attacking proposition.

She said lightly, "Well, what have you been doing this morning?"

"Paying a visit," he answered, and added in a tone that was level yet gave the effect of a rebuke, "a visit that would not have interested you. It was far too placid. To Madame Dupont-Gaillard." He fixed her suddenly with eyes full of vehement emotion, that were at once hard and imploring. "You know that name, don't you?"

143

"I've heard it somewhere," she reflected.

"Heard it? Haven't you seen it?" he insisted precisely.

She shook her head.

"Ah, you don't remember," he continued. "She's a teacher of languages, of one language only, really. Her own. She takes in young men who are getting up their French for the diplomatic service; she helps foreign students who are struggling with their University courses. I lodged with her the two years I was at the Sorbonne." He broke his bread and angrily swallowed a crumb or two. "I don't know why, we all got very fond of her. She's a stupid old woman, really, but she's got an absurd bronze wig, and she quotes La Fontaine, and if anyone got sick or homesick she was extraordinarily kind. We all go up and see her quite often when we happen to be in Paris. I went up and called on her this morning. Waiter, waiter, where's that dry Martini?"

"Coming, coming, Monsieur."

"Why, you've just ordered it," Isabelle chided him. He was really very nervous. For the last few minutes he had been talking of Madame Dupont-Gaillard as if he were reproachfully confronting her with an exemplar, though she felt she could hardly be blamed for not wearing a bronze wig, or not quoting La Fontaine, and she knew that he was in no position to judge how she behaved to the sick and the homesick. "Well, what's the matter?"

His gaze, that had been fever-bright, went leaden. "Oh, nothing," he said courteously. "But that's where I was, and I'm sorry I was late and kept you waiting. Nothing's the matter, really . . ." His voice trailed away, he became still paler, he raked the terrace with his leaden gaze, and suddenly galvanized himself into a show of exclaiming interest. "Why, surely that's Michael Baker over there."

"So it is," said Isabelle.

"And that's his new wife, that used to be Claudia Greenway Green, of Nashville, Tennessee." He stood up and looked across the terrace at his friends with an expression oddly fatigued and calculating; and then he looked down at Isabelle's uplifted face. "Shall I ask them to come over and have lunch with us?" he said, very slowly, as if he wanted to show that he understood fully all the implications of what he was saying.

She smiled. At least she could do this sort of thing quite well. Her smile was probably quite convincing. "Why not?"

"Yes," he agreed, "why not?" He held her eyes with his, he would not let them go. "We had nothing we wanted to talk about alone, had we?"

She shook her head. "Nothing. Nothing at all."

He bowed gravely and turned his back on her to go to his friends. The tears rushed into her eyes; his tall stiff back, the white cloths on the tables, the striped black and yellow awning, the gay blue dress of a woman lunching happily with her lover, and the green hedge ran into shining confusion like molten glass. She remembered the infamies she had heard of that men practised on the dignity of women, and with a shout of surprise from her nerves realized for the first time that they might be practised on her. A story came back to her which she had been told by an indignant Frenchwoman, a young widow, whom she had met on board ship during her last voyage. This girl had been a vendeuse with a great French couturier, who had lent her for six months to a Fifth Avenue store; and while she was there she had excited the admiration of a Jewish broker, who whirling her round in night clubs, holding her hand at the Opera, had told her that he was just crazy about her, and could hardly wait to take her down to City Hall. He was repulsively fat and ugly, but he was kind, and she longed for a home and children; so one night she had told him that she was willing to go down with him to City Hall any morning that he chose. At this his jaw had dropped, and he had stammered that he hadn't thought she was a girl to misunderstand a fellow that was just giving her a rush and take it that he was playing the heavy lover. The girl's pride had been broken, and at some loss she had thrown up her post, terrified of staying longer in a country where the code of manners did not preserve the decencies between the sexes. Isabelle had listened to her story sympathetically, but had privately felt that the girl must have been guilty of some indiscretion, even of vulgarity, which had invited this humiliation. Well, she had been wrong. For this same humiliation had befallen herself to the fullest extent. She realized that the tone of every word she had addressed to Laurence since he had arrived in Europe, the quality of every movement she had made in his presence, had been determined by the silent assurances he had given her regarding his intention of asking her to marry him; and that now that he had sharply withdrawn these assurances, there was not one of those words and movements but was ridiculous and shameful.

Now the Bakers were standing over her, offering handshakes, exploding amiably in greetings and professions of surprise. She found herself thinking grimly that Michael's face had grown looser with happiness, that he had been a great deal handsomer when he was married to the first, the notoriously scourgelike Mrs Baker. Then her heart sank. So it was thus that life forced on one unawares the characteristics that earlier had seemed most pernicious and most easily avoidable. Till then she had thought of the hatred felt by the unhappy for the happy as sheer gratuitous vice. The thing that Laurence was doing to her. She would never, she saw, feel free to be honestly friendly with any man again or, as it appeared, with any woman either. She was aware that thousands of women, when asked what they wished to order for a meal, thought fit to announce with a little laugh that they were dieting. It was nothing to their discredit, they might be as useful and agreeable as the many women who wore corsets or sang to their friends after dinner, or did any of those things which, though they were not illegal, she would not do herself. Yet she found herself counting this heavily to Mrs Baker's discredit, and doubting the debit when, after all, she ordered a rich and schoolgirlish repast; and the reason for this injustice was simply that the little bride's face, which was round and wholesome as a cup custard, had plainly never been flushed by any sort of shameful withdrawal of the conventional value attached to her sex. Isabelle understood at last why women are supposed to hate each other. Such an experience as hers was bound to engender a hundred kinds of enmity. Henceforward she would feel abashed before any woman who had not been rejected like herself; she would be cagy in her dealings with any woman who, having suffered such a rejection, would be likely to guess her own disgrace. This was a poisoning of the very springs of sincerity. Even now she was grinning too much, prolonging throughout the meal an affectation of palpitating interest in the honeymooning couple which it would have been natural to have dropped after the first five minutes. But at least Laurence was doing that too. For whatever reason he had decided to hurt her, he was hurting himself too. She was not too sorry about that. So she had grown cruel too.

But suddenly she found herself sincere again. "What, must you really go?" she exclaimed when Michael rose at an incredibly early moment, when some compote had just been put down before her, and said that he and his wife must return to their hotel to be picked up by some friends who were making an early start for the country. Nothing indeed could have been more real than her distress, for it meant that, unless the honeymooners were to suspect how things were, she must stay and finish her meal alone with Laurence. Fortunately he went right out to the pavement with them, and by the time he got back she had only a greengage or two to swallow. But when he was sitting opposite her again, the fineness of his hands, which were all of him her downcast eyes could see, as they lay folded in front of him on the tablecloth, brought a lump to her throat because they were so typical of his general fineness, such evidence that he had been really what she wanted.

"Well, Laurence, this has been very nice," she said, as she put down her spoon and prepared to pick up her bag and gloves. Her dislike of soiled things was so strong that even at this moment, even after there had opened this breach between them, she had to cry out, "Why, what has happened to my gloves! I thought they were clean, and look at all those little brown marks."

"That is blood," said Laurence; "there must have been sharp thorns on those roses."

He raised a half-finished glass of wine to his lips, though a smear of rouge on the rim showed that the little bride had drunk from it.

She looked past him into the distance, at the emerald-green chestnut, the gold-green planes, tossing and writhing together. She felt herself back in the courtyard, her body forcing itself into the unfamiliar and detestable hieroglyphic of rage; she saw Michel's old eyes sagging forward in astonishment; she heard, high up in the sunlit air above her, a metallic clash. She said, "So it was you who threw open the window?"

"Yes," he answered. "That's where Madame Dupont-Gaillard lives, in one of those flats."

She found herself resorting to the pitiful expedient of a little laugh. "Did I look very dreadful?"

"Well, I gathered you were not feeling very pleased with Monsieur de Verviers," he said, resorting to the same expedient. He drank some more of the little bride's wine. "I had no idea," he told her as he set down the glass, "that you were such a mænad."

"I am not," she told him.

He gave a good-humoured smile, as if to tell her she need not keep up pretences with him any longer and could be assured that, now he knew her temperamental peculiarities, he would watch her career with amused and not unkindly interest.

"I have never done such a thing before in my life," she insisted.

147

But he continued to smile, and she became aware that she had raised her voice a tone higher than she had meant. Biting her lips, she began to pull on her gloves, making every movement as calm as she could.

Laurence gesticulated to the waiter for the bill, sat back in his chair, and passed his handkerchief over his lips. Impulsively, as if he were so sorry for having mismanaged their scene together that he must apologize even if this destroyed the pretence that they had had no scene, he said, "I thought you would understand when I told you that I had been calling on Madame Dupont-Gaillard. She has a plate up in the hallway."

"Yes," said Isabelle, "but it is very old, the letters are quite level with the brass, you cannot see what they are."

For now she had remembered how it was that she had heard the name, though she had never seen it. She and André had come in very late, and while he fumbled for his keys under a light, she had stopped by the plate and run her fingers over the hardly perceptible ups and downs of the vanishing letters. "Tell me whose name has time licked off, like a cat cleaning a saucer?" she had whispered, and André had whispered back, "It is an institutrice, Madame Dupont-Gaillard, who like Château Gaillard is in ruins." His whisper had ended on her lips, his arm had clasped her waist more tightly, and they had moved, mouth to mouth, towards his home. With quiet fierceness, with an assumed smile, she turned to Laurence, meaning to tell him of that midnight conversation so that he would guess the parts she would be mum about, meaning to hurt him. Jealousy she knew not to be so strong in his sex as it was in hers; women objected to marrying widowers far more than men objected to marrying widows. But in its lesser quantity it was there, and could be roused and tortured; and if it were tortured enough, her mind sprang on to say, it would go mad and try to prove itself as good as the other male, claiming its own. She had only to speak her story in the right way, with certain hesitancies, and she would end that afternoon in Laurence's arms, and she knew well that, if he were once her lover, she would never lose him.

She shuddered with distaste. She was being swept away into the horrible world of violence that she feared, where one soul delighted in inflicting pain on another, where force and fraud were used to compel victories which were valueless unless they were ceded freely to an honest victor. It would be far better to resign herself to losing all she wanted. She looked across at him as a farewell to what she had wanted, and at the sight of his fine, grave face, on which even this crisis had failed to mark the lines of any expression that was not noble and reasonable, a storm of refusal raged in her. Why should she lose him? And had she tried all ways of keeping him? She had rejected dishonesty, but she had not made full trial of honesty. It was a difficult thing for a woman to be honest; it required from her the full organization of courage. She found that as she coughed to clear her dry throat and leaned forward to make the attempt.

"Laurence," she said, "I want to tell you why I threw down those roses outside André de Verviers' door."

With that detestably distant smile he answered, "I am sure it is a most romantic story."

Lowering her eyelids she spoke it out. "No, not romantic! One would have to be starved of all pleasantness, a tired, homely stenographer or an old hospital nurse, to think it romantic. It is a very silly story, Laurence. When I came over here after Roy's death, I was desperately unhappy and lonely. I wanted a companion with whom I could build up a new life; I have no family to fall back on."

"You are very young," he said reflectively. "One forgets how young you are."

"Oh, not so young," said Isabelle. "No younger than most of the women in the world who have had to make great decisions. That is the special handicap of our sex, the important part of our lives comes before we have acquired any experience. And in my ignorance I thought there was nothing very difficult about the decision that was before me. I merely had to choose a partner, and I looked round and chose André de Verviers."

Laurence made the faintest moan of disapprobation.

"Men do not look the same to women as they do to other men," she reminded him, "and I had no superior tie. I knew of nobody whom I could have loved, who was free to love me. And André is a superb human being, just as Roy was. I thought I could have had some of the same sort of happiness with André I had with Roy. So we were to be married this summer." She pondered for an instant whether she ought to be more precise about her relationship, and decided that she need not. Though men were not very jealous, they thought they were under an obligation to be extremely so, and it would relieve Laurence of this tiresome necessity if she were to leave him the possibility of thinking that André and she had not been lovers. "But, Laurence!" She looked into his eyes. "André isn't any good."

"I can believe it," he nodded.

"It was not so terribly foolish of me to think that he might have been," she defended herself. "What else had Roy got to start with except just that physical faculty, that trick of accomplishment, that André has? Only something hidden, that turned everything he did to gaiety and happiness. Well, it was hidden too, the thing that governed André, and turned everything to fever and violence and disorder."

He murmured sympathetically, "Yes. Yes. I know. One doesn't see it, the thing that governs people . . ."

"And I had, you know, other ideas. I wanted to make something decent of my life. I wanted to marry a man who was devoting himself to some work that mattered, I wanted to help him and have his children, and bring them up well. I wanted to live at the centre of a focus of pleasantness, and harmony, and things coming right. And instead I was tossing about in a whirlpool of useless passion and frenzy and jealousy, that wasn't even real, that was all put on to whip up sensation. I didn't want that, I didn't want it any more than I wanted to marry a drug-taker and be forced by him to take drugs. And I couldn't get rid of him. That was the frightening thing. He wouldn't take any notice when I asked him to go away."

"A man who will not take his dismissal," said Laurence, sounding more southern than was his habit, "is a scoundrel."

"Nothing I could say made any impression. So, at last, I thought of this way." She swallowed the bitterness in her mouth. "This hateful way that you saw."

He raised his eyebrows as if to assure her that she was wrong, that he had not thought it hateful at all.

"You see, André loves violence because his life is utterly peaceful," she explained. "He has a large income, he has an unassailable position, nothing can happen to him, so he likes a little fictitious excitement. But only so long as it doesn't threaten his security. That's why he liked me. He knew I was calm, he knew I could be trusted never to lose my self-control and cause a scandal, however much he stormed. So I set out to pretend that that wasn't true, that I could be dangerous. I took those roses and threw them all over the courtyard so that his servant would tell him, and he would think that he had driven me beyond the limits of self-control, and let me go."

She lived through the moment in the courtyard all over again, and cried out, "Oh, I hated it all so, I hated acting like a madwoman!"

While the blackness was before her eyes, she heard his soothing murmur; but when his face was clear again, it was not wholly kind. She could not quite believe that; she stared. His eyes were kind, but they immediately slid away from hers, and his mouth was pursed, his nostrils dilated. He began to tidy the crumbs by his plate into a little heap, and he seemed wholly absorbed in this task, though his eyes stole back to hers once and he gave her a guilty, insincere smile before he looked back at the tablecloth.

The blood beat in her ears. After all, he was not quite what she wanted. He had understood and accepted all she had told him; he knew that she was the same sort of person as himself, that she had fallen into the hands of the enemy and had suffered outrageously and had taken what means she could to free herself. But he was not going to tell her that he loved her and wished to marry her because he belonged to the vast order of human beings who cannot be loyal to their beloved if a stranger jeers. There had been reason in what she did in front of André's house, but someone who knew nothing of the circumstances, who had merely looked down on her from a window, could not have known that reason, and would have censured her. Perhaps that had happened, perhaps Madame Dupont-Gaillard had leaned against his shoulder as he watched her grind her heel on the roses and had said, cruel as people are when they speak of those they do not know, "Look, she must be mad!" And his fear of what a stranger might say, of what had been said by an old woman who had forgotten how life sometimes drives the poor dog mad, had outweighed all the promise of sweetness there had been between them. Well, it was not the kind of fault that men outgrew.

She fastened the studs at the wrist of her gauntlets, looking at the distance, where the chestnut and the planes rocked together as if they were rooted in a painful place and longed for freedom. She felt a little less humiliated now she knew his disloyalty than she had when she had thought his rejection of her a causeless caprice, but she was far more apprehensive. For she knew that his mind would be ashamed of deserting her, and would try to justify itself by looking on her with a jaundiced eye and imagining in her a thousand defects which would make the desertion seem a necessity. Everything about their intercourse would be vilified. As she thought how her candid unveiling of her plight would then be regarded, she shuddered and looked at her wrist-watch, to find a pretext for an early departure. She saw that it was half-past two, and remembered something that had slipped her mind.

Lifting her eyes to Laurence's, she said gaily, "You understand why I was specially anxious to get rid of André de Verviers at this particular moment, don't you?"

As she had feared, he flushed and looked embarrassed. He might as well have said aloud, "Why, of course I understand. You hoped to marry me. But how can you be so indecent as to talk about it?"

This, she found, she could not endure. To have him thinking of her like that was more disagreeable than any price she would have to pay for putting an end to it.

"How odd it is," she said, taking care not to laugh too extravagantly, "that my excitement over the hateful thing I had to do this morning should have put out of my head what is far more important! Have you noticed nothing about me lately?"

He shook his head, a little stiffly.

"I've sometimes wondered if I haven't seemed a little too frank and free with you, if you might not have thought I had 'gone gay,' considering our friendship was so far from intimate. I would have kept my distance and my party manners properly if there had been only André. But when one is in love, you know, one becomes extraordinarily indiscreet, one treats all other men in a way that must be rather puzzling to them if they haven't got the key."

His eyes had become glassy, he was leaning forward to listen to her.

"Yes, I'm in love!" she told him gaily. "And if I've been successful in ridding myself of André, I shall marry quite soon. And if I've been boring you with an explanation of all the whys and wherefores of this morning's scene with the roses, it's because I've wanted to appear to you with a clean sheet, since I'm a little shy about telling one of Roy's friends about my new choice."

The waiter had laid down a plate of change at Laurence's elbow, and Laurence swept it back to him with a gesture full of hate.

"You see, Roy was perfect." He was, he was, her heart said. He would have sent any stranger to hell rather than think disloyally of me. "And my second husband hasn't, poor dear, anything of Roy's outward perfection."

"Who is it?" asked Laurence. "But who is it?"

"Why, Marc Sallafranque."

"Marc Sallafranque," repeated Laurence. He sat for a second in silence, then exclaimed, "But I thought you didn't like Salla-franque?"

"Ah, you've evidently seen some gestures that were meant for André," she laughed. "But do say you'll approve, and not cast me off. I know he looks the funniest thing in the world, but inside he has a lot of the goodness and sweetness of Roy." She paused, because she had suddenly felt a click in her brain, as if these words which she had spoken for a false purpose had coincided with the truth. "Take that on my word," she said, "and say you'll be my friend." She stood up, but he did not say the word, or do anything but regard her with the queer mask, as of a stricken hyena, that people wear who are making haste laughing at themselves before other people can start laughing at them. Her plan had evidently succeeded perfectly. Its only defect was that it left her in possession of Sallafranque, which was a responsi-bility that she might as well assume fully at once.

"Marc will be waiting in the hall now, I expect," she said. "I told him to come here at half-past two so that you could congratulate us. I'll go and fetch him."

"What, is he here?" said Laurence in tones which betrayed that he had been nourishing even to the end a hope that her story was not really true. "Oh, yes, I'd love to see him."

Isabelle went from the terrace into the hall, leaving him sitting in his chair with far less than his usual elegance, and was in time to see Marc Sallafranque jumping out of his cream-coloured car, which was indeed a Sallafranque, but had a special body put to it, lustrous and inclining to the baroque. He began to hurry towards the door, but turned back to caress the two wire-haired terriers that stood on the seat beside the Negro chauffeur, lifting up muzzles sharp as cut tin and howling because they were not to go with their master. Then he continued towards the restaurant, not seeing her within the darkness of the porch because of the bright sunshine. His lower lip pouted forward, he stared at his feet and from time to time sadly shook his head; he looked like a child going to an interview which might mean a beating.

When he found her waiting for him, he came to a standstill. He took his hat in both hands and held it in front of him and said, "Oh, Isabelle, my little one, my little cabbage, my little angel, I am very stupid, nearly everybody is cleverer than I am, I often do not understand things properly. But say I was not wrong about what I thought you meant on the telephone this morning?"

She nodded and smiled. "You were right."

He continued to stand quite still, and twirled his hat round and round and round, his face growing very red. "Isabelle," he said, "my Isabelle."

She remembered the click her brain had given when she had spoken of his goodness, telling her that the statement she had meant to be false was in fact true; and it shamed her that she was making him so solemnly happy by what she had coldly conceived as a ruse to protect her pride. Penitently she murmured, "I will try to be good to you, Marc."

Tears stood in his rich animal eyes, he ceased to twirl his hat, he crumpled it in his fist. "It is I who must try to be good," he growled. He took her hand and crushed it against his warm, throbbing, rubbery side.

The tears stood in her eyes also, in another moment they would roll down her cheeks. She said, "My dear, I have been lunching here with Laurence Vernon. He is out there on the terrace. You cannot think how much I like him, you must be friends. Come out and meet him."

"Ah yes," said Marc. "I must be very polite to your friends. It will be my only way of winning them, they will be all so much cleverer than I am." But as they went he slipped his arm through hers and tugged her back. "And our marriage," he begged like a dog. "When can it be?"

"As soon as you like."

"Ha, ha! Next week?"

"Next week, if you will."

"But it can't be," he cried, "that I am going to be married to you next week? My God, I am going to be married to you next week?"

A waiter passed them, carrying two glasses of brandy on a tray. Marc's left foot clothed in a yellow shoe shot out and caught him on the behind. The tray clattered on the floor underneath the caisse, a wall was streaked by two brown stains and shivers of glass, the waiter howled, the caissière bent forward a Roman eyebrow and a fortress bosom, the vestiaire ran out holding one grey and two brown hats, chasseurs swarmed, glad that this time nobody could say it was their fault, the maîtres d'hôtel of the inside and outside restaurants ran in and stood like stars in conjunction.

"Ah, mesdames, messieurs," said Marc, "it's only me."

154

"Ah, good day, Monsieur Sallafranque," said the maîtres d'hôtel, laughing.

"Forgive me, Gustave," said Marc, bringing out his wallet. "I had need of a behind just then, for purposes of celebration, and yours was the only one that was handy. But here's something!" He flipped a thousand-franc note on to the man's palm. "And here's another, Madame, for the damage and the nerves of the personnel." It drifted on to the mahogany of the caisse.

The waiter grinned, the Roman eyebrow abated and the fortress became more like a pleasure palace, the vestiaire, the chasseurs, the maîtres d'hôtel flowed backwards like an ebbing tide, in a rhythmic series of obeisances.

"But, Marc," breathed Isabelle, "but, Marc!"

"Ah, little one, don't bother about that!" said Marc. "I am very impulsive, and sometimes I like to do silly things *pour rigolo*, but it doesn't matter. They all know me here; Maman used to bring me here for treats when I was a tiny boy. They all adore me really. Come, darling, where is your friend?"

She had contrived that violence should not make her life a tragedy. It might yet make her life a farce, which she would find hardly more tolerable. They went out on the terrace, Marc's fingers opening and closing on her wrist, to the man who had brought this on her.

II. BIOGRAPHY

St Augustine (1933)

PREFACE

Nobody could be more conscious than myself of the omissions in this volume. I am especially conscious that I have said very little of Augustine's philosophy, of the implications and influence of *The City of God*, and of his doctrine of the Church as a rule of faith. But a full discussion of these matters would make a very large instead of a very small book; and they have been discussed elsewhere, often with talent and sometimes with genius, while there is still room for a simple account of Augustine's personal life and background.

R.W.

TO THE MEMORY OF

FLORA DUNCAN

WHO SINCE OUR CHILDHOOD IN EDINBURGH

WAS MY BELOVED FRIEND

Bene quidam dixit de amico suo:
dimidium animae suae.
(*St Augustine's Confessions*, iv. 6.)

St. Augustine

Seventeen hundred years ago Cyprian, Bishop of Carthage, took up his pen to explain to the Pro-Consul of Africa why he was wrong in supposing that the Christians' refusal to worship the gods was the reason for the wars and famines and pestilences then vexing the world. First he chastised his correspondent as the Fathers of the Church were wont to chastise the pagan. "I have often, Demetrianus," he wrote, "treated with contempt your railing and noisy clamour with sacrilegious mouth and impious words against the one and true God, thinking it more modest and better silently to scorn the ignorance of a mistaken man than by speaking to provoke the fury of a senseless man. We are, moreover, bidden to keep what is holy within our own knowledge and not expose it to be trodden down by swine and dogs." After much hearty thwacking of this sort he went on to propound a theory very strange to find in a man of naturally cheerful temperament and not ungratified ambitions.

"You have said," he wrote, "that to us should be attributed the calamities by which the world is now shaken and distressed, because your gods are not now worshipped by us. Now, since you are ignorant of divine knowledge and a stranger to truth, you must in the first place realize this, that the world has now grown old, and does not abide in that strength in which it formerly stood. This we would know, even if the sacred Scriptures had not told us of it, because the world itself announces its approaching end by its failing powers. In the winter there is not so much rain for nourishing the seeds, and in the summer the sun gives not so much heat for ripening the harvest. In springtime the young corn is not so joyful, and the autumn fruit is sparser. Less and less marble is quarried out of the mountains, which are exhausted by their disembowelments, and the veins of gold and silver are dwindling day by day. The husbandman is failing in the fields, the sailor at sea, the soldier in the camp. Honesty is no longer to be found in the market-place, nor justice in the law-courts, nor good craftsmanship in art, nor discipline in morals. Think you that anything which is old can preserve the same powers that it

159

possessed in the prime vigour of its youth? Whatever is tending towards its decay and going to meet its end must needs weaken. Hence the setting sun sends out rays that hardly warm or cheer, the waning moon is a pale crescent, the old tree that once was green and hung with fruit grows gnarled and barren, and every spring in time runs dry. This is the sentence that has been passed on the earth, this is God's decree: that everything which has had a beginning shall have an end, that everything which has flourished shall fall, that strong things shall become weak, and great things shall become small, and that when they have weakened and dwindled they shall be no more. So no one should wonder nowadays that everything begins to fail, since the whole world is failing, and is about to die."

So it seemed, seventeen hundred years ago, to many citizens of the Roman Empire. The individual might be full of life—it must indeed have taken a considerable degree of vitality for Cyprian to address in such terms an important representative of the government which not only possessed the power to put him to death but was ready to exercise it, as it actually did some years later—but he felt as if he were suspended in a medium of death. All was going very ill in the Empire. Rome, whose greatness had developed out of a peasant state, had passed on to feudal capitalism, until the domination of the landowners and business men was smashed by the joint revolt of the bourgeoisie and the proletariat. In the new state that followed, the bourgeoisie waxed fat and fell into the sin of pride, and ground the faces of the poor; so presently the Empire consisted of rich townsmen and their dependants on one hand, and hungry peasants on the other. But even hungry peasants make better soldiers than townsmen, and the Emperors took them into their armies. At length there came to be an army which knew itself solidly peasant, and more peasant than army. So in the third century there was civil war between army and bourgeoisie; and since the proletariat had had no chance of assimilating the culture of the upper classes, they were unable to frame a policy of deliverance, and anarchy was the result.

Order was restored; but it was rather, a stabilized disorder. During the century after Cyprian's death there accumulated more and more of what he would have taken as evidence of the world's impending doom. Civilization slowed down, it seemed about to stop. There was still the material substance of the Empire, the ground to tread, the seas to sail, the fields where corn and olives could be grown, the hills where ores could be quarried. But the roads were falling into ruin, and the seas were vexed by pirates. Agriculture, through heavy taxation both in money and kind and forced labour, was falling into a rapid decay, for which later puzzled historians tried to account by a mythical exhaustion of the soil. Raw materials went unused because the purchasing power of the community was shrinking. Prices soared, and at the same time currency fell; and a mob of tax-collectors who were licensed brigands skinned the remnants of the moneyed classes. There could be no social unity. This disorder gave every class reason to hate all other classes as if they were enemies from another land. Now the army had lost its identity with the peasants, and it hated and was hated by all.

But the age held worse than this. Poverty is a condition which nations can endure; and the Roman Empire was merely returning to the simple agricultural economy from which it had risen. Moreover, it is probably true that innumerable Roman citizens knew little of what was happening to them, for it was still the policy of the Emperors to bribe the urban populations by beautifying the cities, organizing public amusements, and distributing doles of corn and oil and wine and bacon. It is hardly credible to us that the vast Baths of Diocletian, a minor chamber of which now makes the Carthusians a spacious church, could have been built when the social and economic structure of the Empire had already collapsed; and it must have been much less credible to those who enjoyed its unruined splendours and had every reason for persuading themselves that such good glutting prosperity must inevitably be permanent. But however much the material disasters of the situation might be concealed from the common man, he had suffered a spiritual mischance which, even if he could not recognize it for what it was, must needs have caused him pain and despair. He had been castrated of his will.

In the old days the Roman Empire had given its children considerable freedom in exchange for their submission to the essential discipline necessary for the maintenance of the State. A peasant of sufficient intelligence and enterprise could become a landowner and rise right through the ranks of society to the senatorial aristocracy; and any meritorious family would have no difficulty in achieving the same feat in a few generations. Even common soldiers had considerable opportunities for advancement, and if a slave could win his freedom—and this was often achieved—there was nothing to prevent him or his children from entering the municipal aristocracy. But, paradoxically enough, the civil wars provoked by the clash between the city bourgeoisie and the peasant army put an end to this social elasticity. The reforms of Diocletian and Constantine were the legislative experiments of men who had been imperfectly educated in the bases of the old Roman civilization and whose personal experiences had been too constantly preoccupied with violence and compulsion. Hence they treated the organic as if it were the inorganic, and made every man a peg stuck in a hole. Whether he was born in town or country, he found himself committed to an occupation and a domicile which he could not change. It might be that he was lucky enough to be born into the caste, now in practice hereditary, of public officials; but his luck consisted chiefly of the power to grow rich by corruption and extortion. Numerically it was more probable that he would be born into the ranks of the despoiled, where he would not dare show unusual capacity lest he should be compulsorily raised to the *curia*, a dreadful honour, since the *curiales* were corporately responsible with their goods and persons for the taxes of a whole area. It was true that the proletariat in the streets had their bread and their circuses, but they had no political rights and they had less and less work and money. They had the strictly limited and not satisfying freedom of stray cats to ravage dustbins and fight in alleys. Nowhere was there any release for creative energy. Man could not use time in the only way it can serve him; he had no chance to devise a drama in which he could play his part and reveal the character of his self. Since he needed that revelation for his own enlightenment, since without it he goes out of the world knowing no more than the beasts of the field of anything beyond his sensations, it was as if his life had been cancelled, as if he had been unfairly given over to death while his flesh still promised him preservation from it. So the children of that age sat in an anguished lethargy.

There was but one force which could help them, and that was Christianity. Before the civil wars this faith had gathered many adherents from the oppressed proletariat, who were happy to think that though they were despised by the possessor classes they were the close and kindly treated friends of the Son of God; from the people whose ethical fastidiousness led them to desire some of that peculiar and delicate wisdom which is only learned in defeat, and which was too largely lacking in the counsels of Rome; and from the people who, being of that temperament which finds pleasure in joining movements, were swept into the Church by the proselytizing force of St Paul and his successors. But as conditions grew worse, Christianity exercised a far wider appeal. At its altar the common man found what was wholly wanting in the secular world: a sense of the uniqueness and preciousness of his individuality. Out of his relationship with his God and his Church he could devise the needed drama in which he could play his part and reveal the character of his self. He was given back the will which society had cut from him, he was alive after all. Like an ill dream at the moment of waking, his anguished lethargy fell from him, and he leaped up into the day.

This service done by Christianity to the age produced two conspicuous results. One was the abandonment of the masses to the pleasures of religious controversy to an unprecedented degree. It is possible that this degree has been exaggerated in our minds because we derive our knowledge of it from the reports of those who were themselves fanatically interested in such controversy, and it is the habit of fanatics to believe that the whole world shares their obsessions. But the disorders that occurred at certain crises of doctrinal dispute show that, without doubt, enough of the population could become sufficiently excited about such subtle questions as whether the Father and the Son were of the same or like but distinct substance, for the peace of great cities to be endangered. It seems certain that a large section of the community were as familiar with theological matters as, say, English public school boys are today with the main facts relating to automobiles. This led inevitably to comic fatuities of the sort that Gibbon loved to mock, and to the depreciation of thought by the hasty and facile processes inevitable in group-thinking. But since Christian theology had grown out of Greek philosophy and Hebrew ethics and poetry, and since it dealt with the most important movements of the mind, this preoccupation of the community gave every individual a stimulating education and first-rate material on which to use his wits.

The other important result of Christianity's hold over the age was due to the tendency of men to call on the Church to free them from their material pains as it had freed them from their spiritual impotence. This naturally became more marked after Constantine had made it the official religion of the Roman Empire; he was possibly inspired in his action by the hope that the Christians' unique power of organization would enable them to do this very thing. Hence the thinkers of that age found themselves forced into a position unlike that occupied by the thinkers of any other age. They were inevitably attracted by the Church. There was hardly scope for an original mind outside the Church; that is proven in the pages of history by the transference, so swift and complete as to be dramatic, of all the enduring names from the pagan records to the tables of the Fathers of the Church. But once they were inside the Church, and busy formulating their conceptions of the universe, they were thrust into the thick of practical affairs. The bishop who was investigating the mystery of the Trinity was forced to assume most of the functions of a Roman magistrate, and stand between the masses and the bureaucracy in the position of a popular tribune. But he was not able to abandon his speculative thought. He was obliged to go on formulating his conceptions, because he believed that his ultimate salvation, the inspiration for his practical performances, and his prestige among men were all derived from that source. The pursuit of the fixed truth remained his first duty, yet he had continually to practise the most agile opportunism. This division and conflict of function must occur whenever a Church exercises temporal power, or even whenever it attains great importance as a spiritual institution. But it is doubtful whether it has ever occurred more picturesquely than it did in the third and fourth centuries, or raised more tremendous issues in the lives of single individuals.

Into this world, on Sunday the thirteenth of November, in the year 354 A.D., at a town named Thagaste in the Roman province of Numidia, which is now Souk Ahras in Algeria, there was born the great genius Augustine. To meet the unequalled strains and excitements of the age he brought an unequalled power. That power he derived from Africa, that stony yet not infertile land, which engendered tremendous crops, tremendous men, violent events. Though it was but two days' sail from Tiber mouth, the Romans looked on it as a land of mystery. Even after they had foully murdered their Punic enemies there, it seemed as if an enemy remained. Even when they covered the countryside with camps and factories, cornfields and olive groves, they felt an undispelled wonder in the place, which they conveyed by telling travellers' tales and peopling it with lions that understood language and snakes that banded together to turn back the legions. Perhaps this was because North Africa was edged by the blackness of the unexplored. But perhaps it was also because they knew that this land bred people who, though they were far from being cultureless barbarians, obstinately adhered to their barbarism and had not lost touch with the primitive sources of being which they themselves had covered over with the mild rationalism of paganism.

Pain, which sensible pagans had trained themselves to treat with indifference both in themselves and other people, save when it could be used to add excitement to the public games, was here put to magic uses. Up till the conquest the Africans had worshipped Baal and Tanit, father and mother of fertility, who dispensed great gifts in return for human sacrifices; and this worship was afterwards continued under cover of the cult of Saturn, it is thought without complete mitigation of its harshness. In time the worshippers of Saturn moved almost in a body to the altars of Christianity; but this only brought back in another form this eerie talk of buying favours from the gods by suffering. Above this mob there appeared an army of magicians—prodigious in number, for it must not be forgotten that by far the larger part of Latin Christian literature was of African authorship—who spoke with terrible eloquence of various benefits, including immortality, procured by various sorts of deaths, including that of a god who had been crucified in an undignified sort of way, and those of quite base people who had been very properly executed by the State for refusal to obey the Imperial laws on such trifling matters as idolatry. Rome must have become familiar within her own doors with Christianity as a troubling secret society that gradually changed into something like a branch of the Civil Service; but from Africa and the East—and especially from Africa—must have come the knowledge of Christianity as a powerful threat to reason. Perhaps this accounts in part for Rome's disquieted awe of Africa; but, indeed, with the advent of Augustine came witness that their wildest stories of the land were true, for here was a lion that could understand language, a python whose coils could crush the upright Roman standard.

II

Augustine has himself told us the story of his first thirty-two years in his *Confessions*, with an unsurpassed truthfulness. He is one of the greatest of all writers, and he works in the same introspective field as the moderns. In his short, violent sentences, which constantly break out in the rudest tricks of the rhetoricians, rhymes, puns, and assonances, he tries to do exactly what Proust tries to do in his long, reflective sentences, which are so unconditioned by their words, which are so entirely determined by their meaning. He tries to take a cast of his mental state at a given moment. He will describe how it sometimes happened that when he went riding through the countryside he would see a dog coursing a hare in a field, and could not help being distracted from godly thought by the spectacle, not so much, he says, as "to turn out of the road with the body of my horse, yet with the inclination of my heart," although he knows well that this is a sport of the kind he has renounced the sight of in the public games. Not only is the experience itself depicted with the clear colour and right form of master-painting, but a vast area of his temperament round the point of impact with this experience is illuminated also. One perceives the barbaric vitality which needed to be disciplined and acquainted with mildness, but which itself framed the discipline, so that in the end, though violence bent its neck to mildness, the proceedings were violent.

That no later novelist has surpassed him is proved by the frequency with which he reminds us of the immortal part of Tolstoy and transcends it. This is particularly true of two incidents in the *Confessions*. The first relates how a friend of his, an unbeliever as he himself was in those days, fell ill and was baptized by his family during a spell of unconsciousness. When Augustine visited him during his convalescence he jested with him concerning the baptism, and to his embarrassment and hidden anger was hotly rebuked for making a mock of sacred things. There has never been a better description of the change of temperature brought about in a friendship by a difference on an impersonal matter. The second relates how Alypius, his very mild and chaste friend, was haled by some companions to see the sword-players, sat with his eyes covered, uncovered them at the sound of a great cry from the people, saw blood, and from that moment was inflamed by a mad infatuation for the murderous sport. The passage is so Tolstoyan that one thinks of Alypius as a young Russian landowner. It does not flinch from recording that which is subtle and inexplicable on any rational basis; but there is no pretentious and perfunctory moral judgement attached to it. It is self-sufficent in its veracity as very little of Tolstoy is.

Nevertheless, we must not take the *Confessions* as altogether faithful to reality. It is too subjectively true to be objectively true. There are things in Augustine's life which he could not bear to think of at all, or very much, or without falsification, so the *Confessions* are not without gaps, understatements, and mis-statements. And among these last may be counted the suggestions he makes against his father, Patricius. He speaks of him always in a tone of hatred and moral reprobation, which was probably quite unjustified.

The worst he can say of the poor man is that he failed to exhort his son to chastity or the love of God, that he was ambitious for the worldly success of his son and looked forward eagerly to the time when he should marry and have children, and that he was hot-tempered. But male chastity, a virtue rarely found in vulgar profusion, was notoriously rare among Africans, and to expect such exhortations from any but a professed Christian was unreasonable; and Patricius did not abandon his paganism and submit to baptism till the end of his life. His ambitions for his son cannot be said to be disgraceful, in view of the fact that the Church bases its defence of the family partly on the supposition that the majority of fathers will lay just such hopeful plans for the perpetuity of their blood. And the accusation of hot temper shows a curious lack of generosity in Augustine, particularly when he has to make the grudging admission that this was counter-balanced by an unusual expansiveness of good will; for Patricius must have led a very troubled life.

He was a country gentleman of very narrow acres, and he belonged to the select but unlucky class of *curiales,* who were responsible for the taxes of their district. He must have known all the troubles which are suffered today by owners of agricultural land, and a great many more on top of those, due to the harsher provisions of the Roman tax system and the corruption of the administrative classes. If he was seized with frenzy a thousand times, there were probably nine hundred just occasions for it in the caprice of the weather working on his barren fields, the idleness of slaves, and the exactions of tax-gatherers; and the remaining hundred instances could be accounted for by his marriage to a woman whose good temper was of the sort that causes bad temper in others. Augustine has left for us a vivid description of how it was Monnica's habit to tell women who bore marks of their husbands' blows on their disfigured faces that marriage had made them their husbands' slaves, and blame them for having rebelled against their lawful masters. It is not probable that this invariably represented a fair judgement on all the matrimonial disputes of Thagaste, and in any case it is not the kind of wisdom which one would care to dispense to people who had been recently subjected to physical pain. As if in anticipation of the worst pedagogic affectations, this advice was given "gravely, but with a humorous air," and was followed by a complacent boast that she herself was never beaten, because she made it a rule never to contradict her husband when he was angry, but would wait her opportunity when he was calmer, and would point out how unreasonable his conduct had been. In fact, she was a smooth cliff of a woman on whom the breakers of a man's virility would dash in vain; and such order often causes its counterweight in disorder. Perhaps it would be unfair to expect Augustine to have seen this excuse for his father's choleric behaviour, since children rarely arrive at a just estimate of their parents' relationship. But it is strange that he should not have made some sympathetic allusion to his father's economic troubles, for they must have been brought home to him when he was fifteen, since he had then to be withdrawn from school, and would have had no further education had his father not made the most frantic efforts to collect some funds. It can only be explained by his love for his mother Monnica, which was so strong that he was bound to hate anyone who had a competing claim on her.

If a child looks at the superior force of its father and regards it not as so much protection but as the strength of the enemy against which it has to pit itself, the result is desperation, which may either paralyse it or move it to efforts so great as to be greatness. Plainly the process worked the latter way in Augustine's case; and there were other disharmonies in his surroundings which he took up as challenges to his will. It is probable that he had that feeling of uneasiness about his status which comes to children who are born to parents of unequal rank. For Patricius belonged to the landed classes, and his reluctance to abandon paganism showed that he had affiliations with the aristocracy; but Monnica's family had been firm-rooted in Christianity for generations, which suggests that they belonged to a lower social level. It is quite certain that from both sides alike he derived the embarrassment of belonging to a conquered people racially different from their conquerors. Though Patricius was a landowner, he did not belong to one of those Roman colonist families which were as much the ascendant class as the Anglo-Irish families used to be in Ireland; he was an African like his wife. So Augustine was a Numidian, a brother to the Berber and the Tuareg, one of a people that are non-Semitic, long of limb and sometimes fair-haired and blue-eyed, but of bronze complexion and different mould from Europeans.

Augustine was, moreover, a poor provincial. Thagaste lay in green and pleasant country, among hills well wooded with pines and ilex and watered by many streams. It gave him the beautiful landscape of his mind's eye, on which the artist in him constantly throws open a window, even in those parts of his writings which he most desired to be a blank cell of abstract thought. But though it offered some share of urban delights in a theatre, a forum, and baths, the remains of these show that they were insignificant buildings. Thagaste was, in fact, only a free town of the second or third order, which owed its importance almost entirely to its site at the junction of several roads. He might, when he was older, go to Carthage; the prodigious rumour of that city must have been brought to him from earliest youth by the spectacle of the equipage and outriders of the Imperial Mail halted outside the inns of Thagaste. But he knew that even if he went to Carthage, even if he there became completely metropolitan, he would still be a provincial, because Africa was but a Roman colony. Only those could claim to be truly metropolitan who were citizens of Rome itself. Carthage was a marvellous city. Centuries ago it had been marvellous enough to excite the diabolical envy of Rome; it was the first of all cities to be built by plan, and the plan was stupendous. That pile of buildings which rose to the vast temple of the heathen god Eschmoun had long been effaced by war. For seventeen days the Romans kindled fires there till the home of seven hundred thousand people was a field of ashes, and they dragged the ploughshare about the vitrified ruins. But so potent were the forces which had worked to engender a city at this spot, that after destruction it rose again, second in area and population only to Rome, and the equal of Alexandria. The temple of Eschmoun was now dedicated to Aesculapius, but the same beauty and luxury and African might informed the town. One may know how gorgeous a city Carthage was in Augustine's time from the circumstance that, centuries later, after successive invaders had looted her again and again, the best of Tunis and Pisa was built from her marble residue. But for all that, Carthage was not Rome. It was an African city.

In that lay the secret of its power to be reborn after ruin; and Augustine, who must have felt his own genius as characteristically African, must have known this well. But the Romans, being conquerors, had imposed a standard of values which set their values above African values. When the Africans bent Latin to their own purposes, it was taken for granted that they were spoiling it, though they had done nothing more than develop the archaic forms which had been brought over to them centuries before by their conquerors, and the Romans had done exactly the same thing to make their contemporary Latin. Whenever African and Roman practice differed, it was taken for granted that the Africans were wrong; and, unhappily, in a sense this assumption was warranted. To Rome, the centre of the world, hastened all the most skilled artists and artificers, philosophers and rhetoricians. These, by mingling with each other, and by listening to the criticism of their patrons, who had been educated to expertness by their opportunities for appreciation, could raise their manners and their work to a pitch of accomplishment which could hardly be conceived elsewhere. At the thought of that polished and clannish society any provincial would feel himself clumsy and isolated, even if he knew that he had power within him such as none of these metropolitans could possibly claim. Such was the case of Augustine, and in this matter he reminds us again of Tolstoy. Each alike lived with barbarism at his back, on the fringe of a civilization which stood to him for a refinement and self-possession which he at once hated and envied; and each was ashamed of his envy, because of his consciousness that the crude strength he drew from his barbaric soil was worth infinitely more than any refinement and self-possession.

So life laid down a certain number of challenges to Augustine. He was the son of an overpowering and resented father, he was born of an unequal marriage, he was one of a subject people, he was a provincial, and no migration to Carthage could save him from a still superior metropolitan scorn. Of all these challenges he must have been acutely aware; he had such an inflamed pride that when he was forty-six years old he could write with a blistering pen of how his elders had teased him about the punishments he underwent at school. And all these challenges he could have accepted, as ultimately he did, but the issues were not then clear. They were all associated with his father, or at least the male side of life. But there was also his mother. We know nothing of Monnica save what her son tells us, and that is plainly often a distortion of reality. The fact of her Christianity throws very little light on her character, any more than the fact of Protestantism would tell us much about a woman born in England during the century after the Reformation. It was a natural form of religion for one in her position. What we learn beyond all reasonable doubt is that she was an energetic woman full of good sense and worldly wisdom, whose outstanding virtue was a certain steady self-control which her son, because he himself and his father so conspicuously lacked it, very greatly admired. She was a haven of calm to him, and she was willing to be that for ever. She did not want her son to grow up. Once, over his wine, Patricius told her that he had been watching the boy at the baths and had seen such signs of manhood that they might hope to have grandchildren about them before long. This happened after Patricius had become a Christian catechumen, so it is highly unlikely that he meant anything indecorous, anything other than that desire for heirs which the landowner, bless his optimistic soul, does not lose in the worst of times. But Monnica fell into a shuddering alarm.

It was fortunate that in her religion she had a perfect and, indeed, noble instrument for obtaining her desire that her son should not become a man. Very evidently Christianity need not mean emasculation, but the long struggles of Augustine and Monnica imply that in his case it did. Monnica could have put him into the Church as into a cradle. He would then take vows of continence and annul the puberty she detested. He would worship the eternal power of the Trinity and never use his will in the polity that man has set up for the exercise of temporal power. To him the sword would not be a weapon to which he stretched out his hand, but one to which he bowed his neck, and a son dead is as much a mother's undisputed property as a son not yet born; and she could bear to contemplate this death since it would only happen in fantasy, would only be enacted in the emotional attitude of the Church now that the assaults of Julian the Apostate had failed and Christianity was firmly established. With her smooth competence she must have been able to make the Church a most alluring prospect for one who, with his dislike of his father, and his addiction to unsparing self-criticism, must have hated violence almost as urgently as his pride recommended it to him.

Thus two alternatives faced Augustine. Would he keep to the world of men, and in the field of action or pagan letters become such a great man that his father looked little beside him, that it would become apparent there was no base alloy in him and a subject race could produce masters, that Carthage would forget he was a squireen's son and Rome forget he was an African? Or would he turn his back on the world of men and pass into another world which denied the standard of values held by Patricius, Carthage, Rome, and presented him with another standard that, if he accepted it, would raise him at one step above the greatest man in Rome, would utterly condemn the accomplishments of civilization, and indeed reward him for lacking them, and what was more, would ensure him pre-eminence in the future life as well as in this? The decision was not easy to make, for it was a choice between violence and control, between discord and harmony, between heat and light, and he was torn between love and hate of all these things. History, moreover, was disturbing the simplicity of the alternatives. The Roman Empire had been so mighty that the mere fact of its failure could not displace the legend of its supreme power; the gospel story and the blood of the martyrs had fixed the character of the Christian Church as meek. Yet if one had a disposition to seek the quiet of death, not by immediate flight out of life but by association with dying things, one might find gratification in the service of the Empire; and when the Church was made official and began to exert power in secular affairs it exchanged the coolness of resignation to the tomb for the liveliness and sweat of action. In the conflict that was waged on the battlefield of Augustine's soul there was a great confusion of enemies and allies. Even Monnica could not give him a whole-hearted summons to her side. She could not bear him to assume adult status even in the Church. Hence, though at his birth he was signed with the cross and touched on his tongue with the symbolic salt, she did not insist on his baptism, for reasons which one so conversant with Church custom must have known to be specious. It was the custom among the lax to delay baptism as long as possible, so that as many sins as possible should be annulled by the holy waters and anointment; but Monnica, who prided herself on her orthodoxy, must have been aware that the strictest opinion in the Church favoured infant baptism.

III

The boy hated school. The chief cause of his resentment against it was certainly the humiliation it inflicted on his infant dignity; and he had that precocious insight into character which is as sand in the engine of any educational machine. In a curiously petulant and extremely Tolstoyan complaint against the discipline applied to children to make them acquire learning which will probably only lead them into intellectual folly when they are older, he points out that "my master, if in any trifling question he were foiled by another schoolmaster, was presently more racked with choler and envy at him, than I was, when at a match at tennis-ball, I lost my game to my play-fellow." Human nature being what it is, it usually goes ill with children who notice things like these. It is also possible that he annoyed his masters still further by apparent stupidity, for a literary mind like Augustine's is apt in childhood to flee from drudgery into reverie, and his loathing recapitulation of the chant, "One and one make two, two and two make four," shows what sort of subject he found most difficult. In any case, his natural incapacities were bound to be increased by the alien character of the school work, which was designed for the Romanization of African children. The native culture had been suppressed, and all that education could do was to aim at the exploitation of such talents as the pupils possessed for the benefit of the Roman system; so it offered just the same combination of material inducements and exasperations to the racial genius as the educational system devised by the British for India.

At first Augustine was in school at Thagaste; but later, when he was fourteen, he was sent to study at a much more important town between twenty and thirty miles away, called Madaura, which is now Mdaourouch in Algeria. It was a stimulating place for a boy with literary talents, as it was the Stratford-on-Avon of Africa. Apuleius had been born there two centuries before. Of all African writers he is the best known to us today, because Walter Pater inserted in *Marius the Epicurean* a translation of the delicious story of Cupid and Psyche from *The Golden Ass*, and made Apuleius himself one of his characters; and he symbolized literature in the popular mind of his land just as Shakespeare symbolized it for ours. He was the centre of a national cult. This was not only because of his rich imagination, which enabled him to write the first and probably the finest picaresque novel ever written, and to inseminate the later geniuses of Boccaccio and Cervantes and Le Sage, nor because of his romantic style, which firmly resisted the standardizing and rationalizing influence of Roman literature and asserted the varied forms and colours of life. It was chiefly because he dealt so often with magic, an approach to the secrets of the universe very dear to the African mind, which, having kept its primitive vigour, constantly created symbols which are next door to spells. Everything Numidian in Augustine must have answered to Apuleius' appeal, and his ambition must have longed for like fame. But all the Christian in him must have recoiled, not because the Church disbelieved in magic, but because it believed in it and feared it. The special reason it forbade Christians to take part in the worship of the gods was that it believed the gods to be demons, and the ceremonies of their service to be magical practice. Apuleius, to devout Christians such as Monnica, must have been a doorkeeper of Hell.

But during boyhood the Christian influence had not much power over Augustine. He himself says that this period was full of abnormal depravity, particularly during his sixteenth year, which he had to spend at home, as his family could no longer afford his school fees. But it is quite possible that this is a distortion of fact due to the excessive development in him of the sense of guilt, which we all have, and which seems to be due rather to an inherent shame of the human being at its common experiences than to acquired shame at individual experiences. Certainly he confesses to homosexual relationships in a sentence which, with characteristic insight, puts its finger on the real offence of homosexuality, by pointing out that it brings the confusion of passion into the domain where one ought to be able to practise calmly the art of friendship. No doubt there was a time when he was a horrid little boy, but there have been a lot of horrid little boys since the world began. The only other sample of his iniquity he gives us is a raid which he and some friends made on a neighbour's pear tree, which he describes in a passage that takes one's breath away by its penetrating analysis of the gratuitous character of adolescent delinquency. He and his friends did not want the pears. They picked far more than they could eat, and threw them to the hogs. It was simply a demonstration against order, the cherished work of the adult; in fact, it was an *acte gratuit* of the sort that fills M. André Gide with such ecstasy. But it is very unlikely that Augustine, if he had really had a past of unexampled viciousness, would have cited such a commonplace piece of schoolboy mischief.

Whatever that side of his life may have been, it did not interfere with his intellectual growth. His literary interests continued, before and after his father had scraped together enough money to send him to the schools at Carthage. He must have been debarred from much pleasure that would normally have come his way during training as a rhetorician by his dislike of Greek. Though he forced himself to acquire some knowledge of it, his natural hatred of suavity inclined his heart against it. But from boyhood he greatly enjoyed the poetry of Virgil, and loved to bewail with proper feeling the exile of Aeneas and the death of Dido, and to put forth new versions of the lament of Juno on the departure into Italy of the Trojan king. By such studies he acquired a mastery of language that won him a high place in the Rhetoric Schools of Carthage; and we hear of him being crowned in a poetical competition. The intellectual and artistic activity that seethed round him there, particularly in the theatres, excited him greatly.

All went very well with him. Presently his father died; it shows how much Augustine had disliked him that, though he was particularly sensitive to the tragedy of death, he chronicles the event with complete indifference, and only mentions it to explain why his allowance was coming to him from his mother. He had set his sexual life in order. At first he had been promiscuous, though not from entirely sensual motives; he says that he delighted—and from the form taken by his religious devotions we know this to be true—in the emotions of loving and being loved. There was an obvious way out of this situation. He himself expresses wonder and resentment that his parents had not arranged for his marriage at the early age which was customary in Africa. But although Patricius had been willing to do this, Monnica had not. She had pleaded that an unsuitable marriage might give him a "she-clog" on his ambitions. But Augustine settled the matter in his own way by falling in love with a woman to whom he joined himself in a bond of fidelity that was virtually marriage. There was probably some valid reason why he did not marry her; she may have been a manumitted slave, in which case her marriage to a man of superior class was forbidden by Roman law, but she would not be despised by society if she entered into concubinage with him.

However that may have been, the union was so happy that it became permanent, and Augustine avows that he was strictly faithful. He records this relationship in a passage which is puzzling enough read by itself. "In those days I kept a mistress not joined to me in lawful marriage; but one found out by wandering lust empty of understanding; yet had I but that one, towards whom I truly kept the promise of the bed; in whom I might by mine own example learn experience, what difference there would be betwixt the knot of the marriage covenant, mutually consented unto for the desire of children, and the bargain of a lustful love, where though children be against our wills begotten, yet being born they even compel us to love them." This means nothing at all save that their bodily relations had been happy, for when he wrote this passage in his *Confessions* he had come to believe that sexual pleasure was a deadly shame. Later still, in *The City of God*, he was to indulge in wistful speculations, so naïve and so detailed that a fairly robust translator leaves them in what Gibbon called "the decent obscurity of a learned language," as to the

manner in which the business of propagation might have been conducted had not man fallen and been under the disgraceful necessity of
soiling himself with enjoyment. For there was to grow in him to
morbid proportions as he grew older that unhappy attitude to sex,
consisting of an exaggerated sense of its importance combined with
an unreasoning horror of it, which is not uncommon among men but
rare among women other than those affected with hysteria. The cause
of this attitude may lie to some extent in the less dignified anatomy
of man, a point on which Augustine copiously complained; but it
may lie to some extent in the disadvantageous situation of man in the
sexual act, who finds that for him it ends with physical collapse and
the surrender of power, whereas for his partner it ends with motherhood and an increase of power. In any case, this tendency had not
yet developed in Augustine, and he was happy enough to call the
child that compelled his love Adeodatus, "given by God." It is true
that it is not safe to draw too definite conclusions from this name,
because it was the custom in Christian Africa, as in Puritan England
and America, to attach to children such pious labels as Born-in-grace,
As-God-wills-it, Praise-God, and God-be-with-him. Yet even though
that custom existed, Augustine, to whom words meant much, to
whom talk of God meant more, would hardly have called his child
by that name if his mind had not been at rest in his family. The name
of the child's mother we do not know. Both she and the young man
whose death Augustine lamented in chapters which are the supreme
analysis of grieving friendship in all literature, slink nameless through
his pages. It is as if he felt that they had no right to be there, that
there should have been no one in his heart except Monnica.

But in spite of Augustine's immense gifts and early promise, and
in spite of the order he had imposed on his personal life, he did not
succeed as a rhetorician. Slowly the shadow of failure passes over the
pages of the *Confessions*. He can hardly bear to write of it; but he
preserves the mournful dignity of a sick lion, and is nobly unem-
bittered, speaking no jealous word against his successful rivals. It is
true that he had always a following of admiring friends, but these
were not eminent nor even always very discerning young men.
Certainly he produced no work except a treatise on the Beautiful and
the Good, which attracted no attention whatsoever, and seemed the
most unlikely candidate for fame. This impotence of his genius can
only be explained by the fatality that his vocation was obviously
for imaginative writing and that he had renounced the use of the

imagination. His hostile attitude to art, which is dogmatically expressed in several places in his work, has very deep roots. It is, of
course, not uncommon. Art is bound to come under the censorship of
our sense of guilt, which suspects all our activities if they are not
part of processes that we hope will redeem us from our stains, not by
giving pleasure but by withholding it; and it is bound to incur the
disapproval of the death-wish we all have in varying degrees, since by
analysing experience it makes us able to handle experience and increase our hold on life. But Augustine's hostility to art was given a
special vigour, because it proceeded not only from these causes but
from the political situation which had such a dynamic effect on him.

Augustine's case falls under a few headings. He examines the
poetry of Virgil, and declares it absurd that he should have been
taught to lament the death of Dido when he was still indifferent to
his own spiritual death, "caused by not loving Thee, O God, light of
my heart and bread of the inner mouth of my soul." He objects to
the stories of the gods, because they frequently represent them as
engaged in lecheries and crimes which the people are tempted to
imitate because they hear them recounted with praise and admiration.
And he objects to stage plays, because they arouse in the audience
factitious emotion of a hysterical and unprofitable sort. Now, this
must remind us at once of Tolstoy's *What Is Art?* which makes
exactly the same points. It is true that Augustine's case against art is
more logically put than Tolstoy's, shows greater cultivation, and is
devoid of many of his absurdities. It would never have occurred to
Augustine to lay it down that society, having organized herself so
badly that a section of her population is illiterate and inexperienced,
should limit the understanding of that section, disregarding the fact
that only by the unfettered exercise of those functions can she discover the faults in herself which lead her into bad organization; and
his denigration of pagan activities never took such an idiotic form as
Tolstoy's proud citation of the comminatory remarks passed by his
daughter, "a gifted art student," on the works of Renoir, Manet,
Redon, and Pissarro. But Tolstoy comes very close to Augustine when
he complains that all works of art which arouse other feelings than
love of God and brotherliness towards men are deflecting our forces
from another end; that when people are rewarded by fame and wealth
for the power to create beauty through music or painting or literature,
this is discouraging to children and peasants, who only admire people
for being very strong or very good; and to create an artistic illusion,

as in Wagner's operas, is to switch the audience into a world of nonsense.

Each of them is a man living on the fringe of a great civilization which, by conquering or ignoring the culture of his native land, has imposed its culture on him. Consequently it forces him and his people to apply its standards to their art; but as no people can create according to any standards other than those they find in their own breast, this means that they are prevented from full artistic achievement. But the affected people will not complain of this grievance, since that would amount to confessing that they have been conquered, and that the conquerors have really succeeded in doing them harm. So they try to annul the whole question by wiping out art. They declare that art is reprehensible unless it has an explicit religious and moral content; and as this is just what authentic art never has—since its business is to press ahead and discover the yet unformulated truths which can afterwards be formulated in terms of religion and morals—they therefore wipe out all the superior artistic achievement of the conquerors. It may be beautiful, but it is not good. So the conquered lift themselves to a level with their conquerors, or are possibly even above them; and even individuals whose gifts could triumph over any limitations are forced to adopt this attitude because of their smarting national consciousness.

This was the process that robbed Africa of a name which should have ranked higher than Apuleius, and Latin literature of a name that might have ranked with Virgil, and that made Augustine the instrument of the Catholic Church, and the Catholic Church the instrument of Augustine. He never essayed the imaginative work for which he had such an unsurpassed endowment; and he found sanction for the surrender in a pagan book, Cicero's *Hortensius*. This is now lost, but we can judge its quality from certain quoted passages. It seems to have been bland rather than stimulating, and perhaps its appeal to Augustine lay in its confirmation of the wisdom of his flight from the more artistic opportunities of a rhetorician's life. "In the next world," it asked, "what need will there be of eloquence? *There* no legal processes will be needed. There our blessedness will consist in the study of virtue and the advance of knowledge. Other objects of endeavour are matters of necessity; this only is a matter of delight." The book filled him with a desire to be a philosopher, so ardent that one wonders why, in a being whose ardour must have had such a compelling quality, it did not procure him success. But he had not, perhaps, the perfect equipment for a philosopher. He was under the practical disadvantage of being unable to keep discipline among his pupils; and he lacked many of the intellectual qualifications for philosophic discussion. Only once—when he had a story to tell, in his *Confessions*—did he show any sense of form; and that can only be said if one lops off the philosophical chapters at the end. Nearly all his religious treatises are integrated by religious fervour rather than by any recognition that a work should have a beginning, a middle, and an end. He was, moreover, apt to grow passionate, personal, and careless of logic in argument. But not only was he unrewarded by success in philosophy, it brought him no more inner peace. The book *Hortensius* could not satisfy him, since nowhere was there written in it the name of Christ, for which he listened always, like a child waiting for its mother's voice to call it in from its play to feed and rest. Feeling that lack, he laid the book aside and turned to the Holy Scriptures; but he was repelled by the contrast between the ruggedness of the old Latin version and the Ciceronian pomp, the pagan polish which he envied and loathed and admired more than anything else in the world. It was then that he was seized upon by a force which introduced a new element into his life, which had nothing to do with Patricius or Monnica, which was of neither Rome nor Africa, which came out of Asia. He became a Manichæan.

We know little enough of Manichæanism, for it rose as a rival to the Church just at the time when Constantine made Christianity the State religion and the bishops and magistrates joined to destroy the heretical writings. Hence we are forced to derive our knowledge of its doctrines and origins chiefly from accounts of its opponents, but what we know is enough to show us that it was not so much a religion as a work of art. The founder was a Persian called Mani, who was born about a hundred and forty years before Augustine, in 215 A.D. Tradition describes him as wearing the dress of a Persian sage, and we can well imagine him with a mantle of changeable blue taffeta, one green shoe and one red, an ebony staff in the right hand, and a book of mysteries under the left arm; for through the ages we suspect something fantastic and bedizened about his genius. But tradition also tells us that he was a great painter, and won fame both by decorating temples and illuminating manuscripts; and that too we can believe, for every shred of knowledge we have about his work tells us that here was a man so immersed in the artistic process that he knew no other. The myth he created has grandeur and profundity.

Light and darkness, good and evil, are the same pair under different names. Some might say that the pair is also known under the name of matter and spirit, but it is doubtful if Mani ever advanced so far in the way of abstract thought as the conception of matter. Being an artist, he worked with the concrete, and gave the kingdom of light a personal ruler who was God, and put the kingdom of darkness under the lordship of Satan and his angels.

For long the two kingdoms were unaware of each other. Then Satan made war on the kingdom of light, and God begat Primal Man on His consort to be His champion and defender. But Primal Man was vanquished and thrown into captivity. God Himself then took the field, routed evil, and released the captive. But meanwhile there had been wrought a malicious and not easily reparable confusion of the two kingdoms. Seeds of darkness had been scattered widely in the soil of light, innumerable seeds of light found themselves sown deeply in the darkness. These elements must be sorted and returned to their own. For this purpose the universe was created. It is planned as a means of deliverance for the stolen particles of light. In the sun dwells Primal Man, and in the moon dwells Primal Woman, and the signs of the Zodiac, like dredging buckets on a revolving wheel, raise the rescued particles to be cared for by these two and returned after purification to their proper kingdom. On earth man plays out a peculiar drama of division. He is the work of Satan, who placed in his dark substance all the particles of light he could steal, so that he could control them. Man is, therefore, a house divided against itself. Demons seek to aid the darkness in him by preaching him false religions, of which Judaism is the worst; and certain activities, notably the eating of flesh, the taking of life, and sexual darkness, cause dark victories. The light in him is enfranchised by the teaching of the true prophets, Adam, Noah, Abraham, Zoroaster, Buddha, the phantom Christ who made use of the Messiah of the Jews, who was really a demon, Paul, and Mani himself. When all the particles of light are liberated the kingdom of light will be perfected, the good angels who maintain the present universe will withdraw the prop of their power from it, and it will collapse into fiery nothingness. The kingdom of darkness will not be annulled. It is a part of reality. But the kingdoms will be distinct and separate.

It is a beautiful myth, and how nearly it corresponds to a basic fantasy of the human mind is shown by its tendency to reappear spontaneously in age after age. Moreover, it has the practical advantage of presenting the ordinary human being with a hypothesis which explains the extraordinary and unpleasant things which are constantly happening to him externally and internally and suggest that all is going as well as can be expected. It is not surprising that Augustine remained under its spell for nine years, particularly as it gave him the opportunity to take back art into his life under the title of religion. But it must be admitted that there is a profound mystery about his adherence to Manichæanism, for his later attacks on it show very imperfect knowledge of its doctrine, and are even tainted with that vulgarity and crudity which one finds in attacks on creeds made by people whose knowledge of those creeds has been acquired only for the purpose of attack. These inconsistencies can only be explained by supposing that, as so often happens to very gifted people in their youth, he passed through a period of moonish reverie, during which he thought a great deal of Manichæanism but not very alertly, and attended at their services regularly but did not listen very vigilantly. Certainly the fundamental elements of Manichæanism sank into him; to them he owed the recognition of dualism as a source of distress which he imported into Christianity. Certainly also he converted several friends to it, and professed it with sufficient vehemence to defy the disapproval of Monnica, who forbade him her house when he returned to Thagaste.

This appears a curiously harsh action, for the incident occurred at the very beginning of his adherence to Manichæanism, when he was an exceedingly young man; and, as she herself reveals in an anecdote, it was contrary to the advice given by the Church to the relatives of infidels. But there was probably a sufficiently poignant cause for Monnica's distress. She had been left by her husband in straitened circumstances, and she must have found the necessity to maintain her son and his concubine and child a heavy burden; and meanwhile her position in the Church must have improved. Widows who had taken vows of celibacy were granted special privileges by the Church, as if they were being rewarded for a triumph over the turbulent quality of maleness. There is something very sinister about the emphasis with which they are exhorted to dignity and sobriety; so might mutes be bidden to behave when returning from the successful accomplishment of an interment. In its mixture of material and spiritual exasperations her situation might possibly be compared to that of a necessitous lady, well-known for her piety and good works in Anglican circles, with a son for whom she could easily get an excellent living if he would only be ordained, but who insists on being an unsuccessful journalist and an enthusiastic Theosophist. In any case, we cannot accuse her of harshness, only of a harsh intention, which broke down under the comfort she administered herself as human beings were able to do in those days when dreams were believed to be divine communications. It seemed to her in her sleep that she was standing weeping on a wooden rule and was approached by a radiant young man who enquired the cause of her sadness. She explained that she was weeping because of her son's Manichæanism, and he bade her look about her and see that where she was there was Augustine also; and when she turned about, there he was, standing beside her on the rule. So she took this as proof that he would return to grace, and she admitted him again to her table and her fireside. When she told him her reason for relenting, he pointed out that the dream might have another interpretation: it might mean that she would become a Manichæan. But she answered, "No, it was not told me, thou art where he is, but where thou art, there he is." With Augustine's genius for recording subtleties, he notes that what struck him most was not his mother's dream, even with its suggestion of supernatural intervention in his affairs, but the the characteristic cool shrewdness of this answer. It rings through the Latin today, his adoring recognition of Monnica's essential quality: what she wanted fitted in with what was, as neatly as if she were playing cup-and-ball. Such a woman could afford to wait. The son of such a woman could afford to wander, knowing he would be brought home at last.

IV

So for nine years Augustine wandered in his only half-attentive pre-occupation with Manichæanism. Then he began to weary. This faith was a work of art; so he renounced it, partly because of his hostility to art, partly because in fact no work of art can take the place of a religion. A work of art is the analysis of an experience, an expression of the consciousness of the universe at a particular moment. Religion aims at the analysis of all experience, at an expression of the con-sciousness of the universe through all time. It claims through revela-tion and prayer to arrive at the final knowledge which art can con-ceive of existing only at the inconceivable moment when all works of art have been created. Augustine became aware that Mani could not make this claim. He was an artist, and a romantic artist at that. Digging in his mind with the purpose of formulating yet unformulated truths, he brought up the false with the true, the trivial with the weighty, the superficial fancy that masks the deep fantasy. For a time Augustine tried to allay his doubts by working under a certain Manichæan bishop named Faustus, but he was left unsatisfied. He is careful to state that this was not because Faustus had a beautiful faculty of eloquence; one realizes how long the "plain blunt man" has been about his horrid work when one finds Augustine protesting that "nothing is true because roughly delivered, nor false because graced in the speaking." He was dissatisfied because he found Faustus a poor scholar, unable to explain the discrepancies between the philosophers' and the Manichæans' views on natural science, and not very interested in them. He seemed to have no appetite for finality, he was content to work on half-apprehended hints, the symbols used by others set working in him his own imaginative set of symbols and not an imperative desire for understanding. In fact, he was an artist as Augustine was, and as Augustine longed not to be. So Augustine detached his heart from Manichæanism, and in a burning sentence compressed his case against its teasing artistic quality, its substitution of Jesus who was a phantom for the Very Son of God: "These were the dishes wherein to me, hunger-starven for Thee, they served up the sun and moon."

But Augustine did not make his way straight to the Church. He knew he could afford to wander a little longer. He decided to go to Rome. Friends had promised him there a position of better pay and greater dignity, among more disciplined students. So, with his concubine and his son, he set sail for Ostia in his thirtieth year. This step was passionately opposed by Monnica, who travelled from Thagaste to beg him not to go. He was able to get on board the ship only by telling her that he had a friend whom he had to see off on a voyage, and by bidding her wait for him in an oratory erected to St Cyprian, close by the harbour; and on discovering his deception she fell into an agony of sorrow. Perhaps because of this, he did not feel happy on his travels. For Rome in her pride, the ruins of which strike us with amazement, he has not one word of praise. He knew there the misery of a proud provincial who cannot compel the metropolis to recognize his powers, and a sickness, probably malaria, overcame him. His friends, who included the mild Alypius, now an assessor in the Italian Bounty office, helped him to find pupils; but

Roman students, though orderly, had a mean habit of not paying. Worst of all, in his search for belief he had come on a blank wall. He fell for a little time under the influence of the Sceptical philosophers, who held that we can know nothing about the nature of things, and therefore should withhold judgement on all fundamental problems and cultivate imperturbability. But this was not a philosophy that could satisfy a man with a mind like a fountain of enquiry; as well might a lion resolve on vegetarianism. He abandoned this line of thought as soon as he received his first summons to greatness, which, oddly enough, resulted from a visit paid by Symmachus, the pagan Prefect of Rome, to the young Emperor Valentinian and his mother Justina at the Imperial Court at Milan, for the purpose of explaining why the Senate had rebuilt an altar to Victory which had been dismantled out of respect for the Christian religion. For the Milanese had asked Symmachus, who was a well-known amateur of letters, to send them from Rome a good professor of rhetoric; and Augustine was recommended to him by some Manichæan friends.

This was Augustine's first success since his student days, and it was considerable, for though Milan was smaller than Rome, it had the prestige attaching to the Imperial residence. It had an enormous effect on him, because it brought him under the spell of Bishop Ambrose. Augustine was bound to become infatuated with this man, because he was everything that Augustine was not, and pretended to hate, and longed to be. Ambrose was an aristocrat, the son of a prefect, who had himself been a lawyer, a magistrate, and the Governor of Liguria before he was chosen, much against his wishes and in spite of the fact that he was not yet baptized, bishop of the most important see in North Italy. He was a superb human being, a princely leader, a successful negotiator, a fluent preacher, a notably fine Greek scholar. Augustine could not take his eyes off him. He listened to all his sermons in the basilica, he called on him constantly at his home. But it is obvious that Ambrose felt no reciprocal emotion towards the new professor of rhetoric, this awkward Numidian, who had come on the recommendation of his enemy Symmachus (whom he had neatly worsted in this matter of the restored altar) and was understood to have Manichæan associations. One might as well expect an Archbishop of York to receive with open arms a young Maori who had been appointed to an educational post in York on the recommendation of some well-known Secularist such as Mr J. M. Robertson, and who showed sympathies with Theosophy.

184

The resultant relationship is the subject of a passage in the *Confessions* which is a masterpiece of honest and subtle observation, and a most amusing example of the triumph of repressed feeling. "As for Ambrose himself, I esteemed him a very happy man according to the world, whom personages of such authority so much honoured; only his remaining a bachelor seemed a painful course unto me." In that phrase rings an implied criticism, a covert pride. The other man gets worldly success, but if he had real power, of which virility is the symbol, could he bear to be celibate, as I cannot bear to be? But Augustine goes on to explain that he knows nothing of "what hopes he carried about him, what strugglings he felt against the temptations his very eminence was subject to," for when Augustine went to see him he was either engaged with many people, or was refreshing "his body with necessary sustenance, or his mind with reading." There was no trouble about seeing him. Anybody could go into his room; but nobody was announced, and he ignored everybody. Simply he went on reading. He did not even read aloud, perhaps because he feared lest his audience should break in with demands for an exposition, or perhaps because he was husbanding his voice; "with what intent soever he did it," says Augustine loyally, "that man certainly had a good meaning in it." There was nothing for his visitors to do save go away. One perceives clearly under the surface of Augustine's prose what he was thinking as he sat in the quiet room and looked at the prince of the Church, so reasonably and yet so insolently turning over the pages of his books and withdrawing into his superb self. He was rightly supposing that posterity would see Ambrose not as the prince of the Church who in self-protection had turned a blank face on the tiresome provincial, but as a prince of the Church who lost his opportunity to speak like an equal with a king of the Church. But the lion knows only a blunt and honourable form of malice. His honesty, his delicate discrimination, made him continue to realize that this man was a marvel of precious distinction.

So the influence of Ambrose continued to work on him, powerfully as if he were his father, but without arousing resistance, as if he were a father so gentle that no son could feel him as a challenge. Ambrose's sermons must have pleased the demand of the artist in Augustine for suavity by their fine Italian Latin and gracious style; and presently the ordered thought behind them began to resolve his deep and troublesome perplexities. It happened that Ambrose was greatly given to subjecting the Scriptures to allegorical interpretation, a method of exegesis which the Greek theologians had borrowed from the cultured pagans, who had long used it to excuse the cantrips of the immortals, and thus he was able to smooth away Augustine's disgust at the barbarism of the Old Testament. He also smoothed away Augustine's objection to authority, and made him agree comfortably that, just as he was able to accept the fact that he was the son of Patricius and Monnica though he had no first-hand knowledge of it, even so might he be able to take other truths at second hand. Moreover, Ambrose was able to insinuate into Augustine's mind, past his marked preference for the concrete, the conception of a spiritual substance; hitherto one of his chief difficulties in accepting the Christian God had been that he could not see how He could exist without being corporal. So complete was the victory of Ambrose's suavity that when Monnica came to her son from Africa, as she did about a year after his establishment in Milan, he was able to tell her that he had become a Christian catechumen, and was only waiting for some direct mark of the divine will be to be baptized. One can see how keen and new his enjoyment of gentleness was, and how alien from his violent and senseless temper, by his wonder at Monnica's cheerful obedience when she was forbidden by the sexton at a Milanese shrine to practice her country custom of offering her fellow-worshippers bites and sups from a little basket containing wine and cheese-cakes, so as to make a little feast of remembrance. The custom had been forbidden by the Bishop because it had led to disorderly picnicking. Augustine apparently would have thought it natural if she had made some rebellious scene, and, linking the two who had opened to him the springs of mildness, he happily wondered whether she would have resigned herself so easily to the breaking of her country custom had it not been enjoined by marvellous Ambrose.

But he would not go at once into the fold. He would take his own time. He was a lion, not a lamb. He and his friend Alypius, who had followed him from Rome, and Nebridius, a young man whose infatuation for Augustine had made him leave his home in Africa simply to be with him, gathered together in a gentle and rather amateurish little company of truth-seekers. They read—or rather Augustine read and expounded to the others—the works of the Neoplatonic philosophers. It throws a curious light on Augustine's equipment for his career that he had not yet read them, and that he had to read the *Enneads* of Plotinus in the Latin translation of Victorinus. Naturally they were enchanted by that delectable philosopher, who has sustained so many of the finest human beings even to our own day. He offered them a philosophy which was very near to a religion, which was, indeed, very near to being Christianity, since from its foundations it had constantly borrowed from Christian thought and repaid its loans by influencing Christian thinkers. Many Christians, such as Origen and Eusebius and Athanasius and Hilary of Poictiers and Ambrose himself, had been deeply influenced by Neoplatonism, which put before them ideas hardly at all alien from the Christian faith. It held that the first duty of human beings is to seek the knowledge of God; that God is a Trinity; that evil is nothing but nihilism, a patch in the matter which is the dark substratum of the universe accidentally uninvaded by God; that we can only come to the knowledge of God by chastity and temperance of body and mind, and by the practice of contemplation in degrees of increasing intensity, rising to mystical ecstasy. It was a system of thought as elevated as Christianity, but lacking in the one element that would bind Augustine's soul.

What that was one may see if one contrasts the Neoplatonic and the Christian Trinity. The first person of the Neoplatonic Trinity was pure Existence, Goodness, or Unity, present everywhere in the finite world, yet infinite, the supreme reality on which all other things depend. From this proceeds Universal Mind, which only knows the world of ideas, of abstract thought; it knows nothing of the material world and plays no providential part in the affairs of man. From this proceeds the World-Soul, which is immaterial like Mind, but stands between Mind and the material world, and has elected to confuse itself with the world of phenomena; it creates souls of various kinds, including those of men, which are capable of rising to union with it or sinking into matter. In this Trinity the First Person has no knowledge of the Second or Third persons, being superior to thought; and the Second Person has no knowledge of the Third. No love is felt by a superior for an inferior, only by inferiors for their superiors. This is entirely different from the gracious conception of the Christian Trinity, which lives in loving, reciprocal relations and cultivates a common aim in the redemption of mankind. Above all, it lacks the figure of Christ. "No man in these books," writes Augustine at the end of a burning chapter, "hears him calling, Come unto me, all ye that labour."

This delicate Neoplatonism had no real chance of holding Augustine, whose most severely abstract thought is damp with his sweat.

But it enchanted the three Carthaginians with its grace, its polish, its manifest "superiority," and they wished that they too could be philosophers and spend their days in the pursuit of wisdom. But how was it to be done? Augustine was still not meeting with the worldly success for which he hoped. There is a pathetic chapter, which leaves the very taste of failure in the mouth, describing how he paced the streets of Milan, trying to grind out a sycophantic oration in praise of the Emperor, and saw a drunken beggar, and wished he could change places with him. One feels sure that that oration was not a success. Augustine must have been one of those innately, indeed involuntarily, sincere people whose sincerity is never more glaringly apparent than when they try to be insincere. For this reason, and others, he could only make a living by toil so continuous that it left him no leisure for thought. The mornings were taken up by teaching, and the rest of the day had to be spent keeping up influential connections and writing discourses for sale to his scholars. Alypius and Nebridius could not offer any relief, for since they had been pulled out of their natural orbits by his attraction, they were under a like necessity. Though they were all sure that if they could but study the Catholic faith they would find therein redemption, they had not the time to read or even to find out what books they ought to read and how to get hold of them. Wistfully they debated among themselves how they ought to proceed. It was mentioned, perhaps with deliberate restraint, that Ambrose was too busy to advise them. The only hopeful prospect they could see before them, which indeed offered a very pleasant contrast to their plight, lay in the possibility of inducing one of their more powerful friends to procure them some post, and of then making a sensible marriage with a wealthy wife.

To this Alypius at first demurred. He was a gentle soul to whom one's heart goes out through the ages because of his confession that, though he had sternly refused all bribes when he sat on the Assessor's bench in Rome, he had been sorely tempted to take advantage of the custom by which praetors got their books at cut prices. He had also, much earlier, been the hero of an endearing adventure in Carthage, when he was arrested because, coming on the scene of an interrupted burglary, he had wondered why the burglar was running away so fast and why he had left all those tools lying about, and was thoughtfully examining them when the police came and fell into a natural misapprehension. On him had been bestowed the gift of chastity, for he had, Augustine says, "made a trial of that act in the beginning of his youth, but having not engaged himself by it, he was sorry for it rather, and despised it." He saw, therefore, no excuse for introducing the complication of marriage into such a colony of philosophers as they had planned, ten strong, with a rich friend from Thagaste as patron, governed by two officers annually elected, "whilst the rest were quiet." But Augustine would not have it so. He urged that many great and good men had pursued wisdom in the married state, and that he himself could not live without sexual intercourse. It was his habit to write of himself as if specially ferocious lust had been his governing characteristic, though a man who was faithful to one woman for fourteen years in a community where temptations abounded and moral judgements were lax cannot really have been the prey of uncontrollable sensuality. But such were his representations that Alypius, always very amenable to argument, admitted that perhaps he had formed his adverse opinion of sexual intercourse too hastily, and that he was prepared to try it again. So all three looked for deliverance to a moneyed marriage.

All this reads like harmless chatter in a garden, the construction of castles in Spain; but suddenly it precipitates into real and very ugly fact. Abruptly Augustine tells us that negotiations were begun for his marriage with a suitable bride, and, thanks to Monnica, were soon concluded. This involved his separation from the woman with whom he had lived for fourteen years. She was packed off home again to Africa. That she was not a loose woman, that their relationship had been serious, she proved by taking a vow of celibacy. It is, of course, possible that the loss of Augustine may have inflicted no great hardship on her. After fourteen years of companionship with a violent and blundering man, the pain of separation might well have been assuaged, and even rendered unnoticeable, by the new-found pleasure of tranquillity, and the peace of the religious life may have seemed to her an exquisite self-indulgence. What is indefensible in the incident, what makes it seem a sickening outbreak of barbaric cruelty amidst all this talk of religion and philosophy and this gluttonous enjoyment of culture, is the separation of the woman and her child. The boy Adeodatus stayed with Augustine and Monnica.

Nothing can make this incident other than horrible; but examination reveals possible causes for it which make it not so wanton and gratuitous as it might appear in its beginnings. It is plain that the moving spirit in the incident was Monnica. Augustine tells us so, and he proves it when he speaks of the departure of his concubine as something that was done not by him but to him. "When that mistress of mine which was wont to be my bedfellow, the hinderer as it were of my marriage, was plucked away from my side," he says in a sentence which would arouse our sympathies by its conclusion—"my heart cleaving unto her was broken by this means, and wounded, yea, and blood drawn from it"—were it not that neither then nor at any other time does he utter one word of sympathy with the sufferings of the woman. It can hardly be doubted that he was a passive agent, it is unlikely that he would not have had fortitude to persist in it in despite of these feelings. But while one may accept his story of Monnica's responsibility, one cannot accept his explanation of it. He says that she wanted him to be married so that his sexual life could be regularized and he could be baptized; but that really will not do. If that had been her motive, she would not have chosen him a bride who was so young that there could be no question of marriage for two years, which means that she was probably about twelve or thirteen. For she must have known that with Augustine's strong views on his sexual insatiability he would be bound to take a concubine to fill in the intervening two years, and that the baptism would therefore have to be postponed for that period. A whole-hearted interest in his baptism would have led Monnica to search for a bride who was immediately available.

There must be some other explanation, and it is probably of a financial kind. In writings dated a short time after this period. Augustine describes himself and his family as having been in dire need, and one of his letters written in later life speaks explicitly of the smallness of his patrimony, and declares that in entering the Church he passed from poverty to wealth. Out of a meagre estate Monnica was obliged to provide not only for herself and to help Augustine, Adeodatus, and his mother, but to support entirely another son and daughter. For Augustine was not, as the parts of the *Confessions* dealing with his childhood and youth would lead the reader to suppose, an only child. The flat omission of any reference to his sister, and of any but a late casual reference to his brother, gives point to his uneasy description of jealousy in children of tender years. He must have enjoyed cutting these other claimants on Monnica's attention out of the literary perpetuation of his life, cancelling their existence with his pen. Such love would make him long to be dependent on his mother in every possible way, and he would ignore as long as he could her complaints that she found it beyond her power to provide for him. But no doubt the disturbed economic condition of the country caused a failure of supplies that at last convinced him. Moreover, Monnica was probably in a nervously exhausted state which forbade her carrying her accustomed burdens, for the Empress Justina had become an Arian heretic and had harried the orthodox Christians of Milan, until Ambrose, fortunate indeed if he were a seer, and not blameworthy if for once the artist became a charlatan, discovered in a vision the remains of two martyrs beneath his church, and thus proved himself the object of divine favour. Since the cupboard was bare, and since her son would not enter the Church and become a priest, the tired and desperate woman can have seen no hope for the family except in a rich marriage for him; and the dismissal of the concubine would inevitably follow, since the parents of the bride would obviously insist on the rupture of any long-standing tie. The situation has occurred again and again in every society where men marry for money; innumerable plays and novels have shown us the worried dowager forcing her son to send away his beloved mistress and take a rich wife. What is a little startling is to see the drama enacted by persons who were subsequently raised to the status of saintship.

Augustine was in a peculiarly bad state to suggest any alternative to the scheme. Since he had arrived in Milan he had developed enormously in some respects, but in others had regressed. He had become more and more unwilling to cope with his environment, he had become more and more desirous of withdrawing from adult life and settling down in dependence on someone. This was indeed a very profound tendency in him, which went much further than merely wanting to live in a little closed colony on the bounty of a patron. In the *Confessions* he addresses God in very curious terms: "And thou art my Lord, since thou dost not stand in need of my goods." Much later he recommends Heaven to a catechumen by the odd promise that not only will he never feel ill or tired or needy there, but no one else will either, so that he will never be under any obligation to do anything for anybody. This fundamental determination to take and not to give explains why he never performed any action during his seventy-six years which could possibly be held up as a pattern for ethical imitation; and at this point it certainly determined his sexual life. A very short time afterwards he writes of the desirability of a wife as consisting entirely on the condition that "by means of her ample patrimony, it were possible that all those whom you wish to have living with you in one place could be comfortably supported, and that by this reason of her noble birth she could bring within your easy reach the honours necessary for a man to lead a cultured existence"; and in his accounts of his conversations with Alypius he expressly states that though they wanted to be married, they felt no desire to have children or fulfil any of the duties of family life. In other words, what he wanted to do in marriage was not to accept responsibility but to find someone to be responsible for him; not to be a father, but to be dependent on a woman as a child on its mother. This desire was so strong that he would fall in with any plan that would punish the woman who had proved to him that he was not a child by making him a father; and it would give him great pleasure to take that child from her and hand it over to his own mother, with whom they could then live as if they were brothers instead of father and son. And though Monnica may have initiated the plan for other reasons, her feeling of superiority to other women shows that she had an intense desire to be the only woman, which must have been gratified by its consequences.

Once the deed was accomplished all should have gone well. Yet Augustine was miserable. The thing in him that wanted to go back and be a child was not all of him; there was a thing in him that wanted to be adult, and this raved. He took another concubine, but still ached for the companion of fourteen years. A dark sentence hints that he found he had unleashed again the homosexual tendencies which had troubled his boyhood. But, worst of all, what he had done seemed senseless. Now that ease and honour were within his reach he began to doubt their value. Even the need to search for wisdom seemed not so imperative. "Nor did I desire as now to be made more certain of thee, but to stand firmer in thee," he writes of this time. In his depression he went to visit Simplician, a priest of great reputation, who had received Ambrose into the Church; if Augustine could not get attention from Ambrose, he would get it from one who was as a father to Ambrose. He told Simplician in what spiritual difficulties he found himself, and mentioned that he had been reading Victorinus' translations of Plotinus and Porphyry, and at that Simplician rejoiced, for he regarded the Neoplatonists as powerful auxiliaries to the Christian faith, and had himself baptized Victorinus. Proudly he told the story of that distinguished conversion. Victorinus had been the fine flower of pagan scholarship, and such a mighty mocker of Christianity and champion of the gods that his statue had been placed in the forum, an honour usually conferred only on men of action. He had been converted to the new faith by studying the Scriptures in order to prepare a philosophical campaign against it, but at first could not bear to kick away the foundations of his life by a public avowal. Not for long did his fine mind permit him the weakness of suppressing the truth, and he chose to make his profession as publicly as possible. "So soon therefore as he was mounted up aloft, every one that knew him whispered his name to one another with the voice of congratulation. And who was there that did not know him? And there ran a soft whisper through all the mouths of the rejoicing multitude, Victorinus, Victorinus." Augustine's record of it shows how he was thrilled by the story of this philosopher who set aside all the highest pagan honours for this subtler form of acclamation, which he had evidently found more intense, with that special and alluring intensity of which Christians, apparently, alone possess the secret.

But Simplician could not help Augustine. No outward help, indeed, could solve his problem, which lay now not in uncertainty as to what he should do, but in a paralysis of the will that prevented him doing what he wanted. He knew now that he wanted neither a wife nor a position, that his happiness must lie in celibate membership of the Church. But he drifted on, unable to break any of the links that bound him to the distasteful pursuit of worldly well-being, performing his work mechanically and resentfully, and spending every moment he could in church. Perhaps it was because he was in an alien country that nothing in his surroundings had the power to say the word which would awaken his will from its unnatural sleep. When at last the awakening came, it was an African, one Pontician, who contrived it. He was a court official who called one day on Augustine to ask him some service, and found him sitting with Alypius. While they were talking he picked up a book which was lying on a games table, and was pleased to find, since he was a devout Christian, that it was no treatise on rhetoric, but St Paul's Epistles. When Augustine told him he read many such works, he began to talk to them about St Anthony of Egypt, of whom, oddly enough, neither of them had ever heard, though he was an inspiration to the contemporary monastic movement; but from another sentence it appears also that they were unacquainted with the idea of monasticism, which broke on them as a revelation of delight. But it was not the life of St Anthony which impressed them so much as a story

Pontician told about its effects on two of his friends, young men of noble birth.

He had been, he said, at Treves, when the Emperor had gone to see the chariot races; and he had gone with three other court officials to walk in some gardens by the city wall. He had stayed behind with one of the party, and the other two had wandered off and had come by chance on a little cottage where some Christians lived, where they had rested for a while. As they were sitting there they picked up a little book, which was a Life of St Anthony. They were so impressed by his retreat into the desert to find God that presently one of them cried out: "Tell me, I entreat thee, what preferment is that unto which all these labours of ours aspire? What are we at? What is it we serve the State for? Can our hopes at Court rise higher than to be the Emperor's friends? And in this Court what is there not brittle and full of perils? And by how many dangers arrive we at last at one danger greater than all the rest? And how long shall we be getting thus high? Whereas if I be desirous to become the friend of God, lo, I am even now made it." And both he and his friend, being found later by the other two, refused to return to Court and stayed there in the cottage, living the religious life; and the women to whom they were betrothed, on hearing what their lovers had resolved, dedicated their virginities to God.

This story filled Augustine with shame. In its picture of men pre-ferring the honour of Christian baptism to worldly honours it con-firmed the moral of the story of Victorinus which had moved him so strongly. It pricked his pride and gave him a feeling of sordid inferi-ority to realize that the kind of people he most respected despised the secular distinctions which he had pursued all his life long. He felt ashamed and squalid and foolish, and as soon as Pontician had gone a kind of frenzy came on him and he cried out to Alypius, asking what sickness it was in them which prevented them from taking part in this movement to the highest. The Epistles in his hand, he rushed out into the garden, Alypius following him, for he was afraid to leave him in such a state. They sat down as far from the house as possible, and Augustine fell into a passion of rage against his own inertia. Of doubt there is not a shadow; God is so entirely taken for granted that He is almost ignored. The source of his distress lay purely in the inability of his will to make the decision to renounce the world. There was a debate in him between his sexual impulses and his desire for continency, which ended in a flood of tears. He rose and left Alypius, and flung himself down on the ground under a fig tree, vehemently asking the Lord why He would not put an end to this period of helplessness.

He was lying thus, shaken with prayers and weeping, when he heard a voice from some neighbour's house, a child's voice; it might have belonged to a boy or a girl. It was chanting in a sing-song, "*Take . . . up . . . and . . . read! . . . Take . . . up . . . and . . . read!*" It chanted it over and over again, and Augustine began to suspect the sound. He tried to think if such words were part of any children's game he knew, and he could remember none. He stood up; and he was sure that the words were a message from God telling him to take up the Epistles of St Paul and take the first text he should read as a sign. Hastily he rushed back to the place where he had dropped the book at Alypius' feet, and snatched it up. The text his eyes fell on read, "Not in rioting and drunkenness, not in chambering and wantonness, not in strife and envying, but put ye on the Lord Jesus Christ, and make no provision for the flesh, to fulfil the lusts thereof." Light flooded his heart; again his will moved like a living thing.

Intricate was the workmanship of this omen. It is well to note that Ambrose had been called to baptism and the episcopate when he was attending a basilica, in his capacity as Governor, to quell a riot that had broken out over the election of a bishop; and a child's voice had chanted again and again, "Bishop Ambrose! Bishop Ambrose!" It is well to note, too, that the Epistles of St Paul were the foundations of Ambrose's preachings. One might think that the omen might have been more fortunate, for indeed it would be difficult to open the Epistles of St Paul and not find some encouragement to adhere to the Church, and it would have been better for the world if Augustine's eyes had fallen on a text that added graciousness to purely negative moral admonition and gaunt invitation to enrol under the right banner. Nevertheless it was the sign for which he had waited, and he was free and happy. He cried out his joy to Alypius, who, always willing to follow his friend's lead, took up this new project of sudden conversion as cheerfully and obediently as he had taken up the idea of marriage. The text he drew was, "Let him that is weak in faith receive." So together they went back to the house, and found Monnica, and told her they were at last ready to receive baptism. *Exultat et triumphat.* She was at last happy; for, as Augustine says, she knew a much greater joy than she could have had from grandchildren—and indeed she had one of these—since her son was delivered over to her and her way of thinking, wholly and for ever.

V

Augustine and his friend did not immediately announce their conversion. They could not be baptized at once, for it was then summer, and at that time baptism was administered chiefly during the night between Holy Saturday and Easter Monday; and they shrank from passing the intervening period in the atmosphere of controversy which any avowal of their intention would create about them. But Augustine's tempestuous spirit could not bear this time of prudent waiting, and cut all ties with this hateful life at once. It called to its aid an illness which, by affecting his chest and throat, made it impossible for him to continue teaching. Meanwhile his affairs had been settled so that he could leave Milan. History rarely tells us who picks up the pieces after the great man has gone by, so we do not know who placated the parents of the affianced bride and who dismissed the new concubine, but it was probably Monnica. At any rate, Augustine records no part of his own in these proceedings. In October the whole household were able to go with his mother and his brother and some pupils, all of African origin, to a friend's simple villa at Cassiciacum, which is now Cassago, on the slopes that rise from the Lago de Varese to the uplands known as the Field of Flowers. There he taught and wrote some treatises, which distress one by the intimations of the suppressed artist in him, both in his descriptions of the fruitful Italian autumn and in his amazing character-sketches of his pupils. But they also exhilarate by the spectacle of genius finding its feet on the ground it prefers. They glow with fulfilled happiness.

In April of the year 387, when he was thirty-three years old, he was baptized by Ambrose at Milan, in the company of his friend Alypius and his son Adeodatus. It was a long ceremony. He had attended the basilica daily throughout March and April to receive instruction in the fundamental truths of the faith, which was often imparted by an exorcist, who had power to expel demons. On Easter Eve he kept vigil, and after midnight knelt before the altar and was touched by Ambrose on the ears and nose in what was known as the mystery of opening. Then they went to the baptistry, where they stripped naked and were anointed by the priests and deacons, who afterwards asked them if they renounced the devil with all his works, and the world with all its luxury and lusts, and bade them spit on Satan. Meanwhile the Bishop exorcized the cistern which was then the font, driving out of it the creature of water, and prayed that the presence of the eternal Trinity might descend upon it. Then the clergy went down into the font with the candidates, and the Bishop stood beside it. He asked each candidate, "Do you believe in God the Father?" and was answered, "I believe." Then the candidate was immersed; that is, he was buried. Then he was asked, "Do you believe in our Lord Jesus Christ in His cross?" and answered, "I believe." and was immersed again; that is, he was buried with Christ, for he who is buried with Christ rises with Him. Then he was asked, "Do you believe also in the Holy Spirit?" and he said, "I believe," and was immersed again; that is, by manifold lustrations they wiped out their manifold lapses. Then the Bishop sprinkled drops of an unction made of oil and balsam on the heads of the candidates, and announced that thereby God had remitted their sins and called them to life eternal; and afterwards he and the presbyters washed their feet. Ambrose approved of this rite, which was not universal, because he thought that though the sprinkling of the head might remove the sins of the individual, this washing of the feet was necessary to remove his hereditary sins. Then the newly baptized were dressed in clean white robes and given candles to carry. They must have been dazed with excitement and fatigue following on a fast of three days; and a frenzied routine must have streamed past them, for hordes were pressing in to take advantage of the Church's salvation at this time. To complete the rite, the Bishop laid hands on them and called down on them the sevenfold gifts of the Spirit. Then they went out from the baptistery in procession to the basilica, and at the Easter Sunday mass received for the first time the bread and wine of the Eucharist.

But when Easter week was over and Augustine was no longer under the necessity of attending the basilica in his white baptismal robes for mass and vespers each day, he and his mother and brother turned their backs on Milan and set out for their own country. Alypius and a new-found friend, Evodius, went as well, and were with him in the intention of founding a religious house somewhere near his home in Africa. Behind them Italy was crackling like dead wood set alight. The usurper Maximus was gathering his hordes; only a few weeks later he was to cross the Alps and sweep down on Milan, while the Roman Emperor fled first to Aquileia, then across to Thessalonica, on a long journey that ended only in captivity and death. By June, Augustine and his companions had reached Ostia, the port of Rome, and were living together in a house remote from the bustle of the harbour, resting quietly until their ship should set sail. They were all, one feels as one reads Augustine's record, exhausted and happy. One day Augustine and Monnica were sitting by a window that looked over a garden, and as they talked their happiness soared to a climax. They forgot the distressful past, the struggles he had had, and the struggles she had had with his struggles. They talked of the purity of life with God, unstained by sensuous experience, and they were lifted up towards it.

"And when our discourse was once come unto the point, that in respect of the sweetness of that life, not the highest pleasures of the carnal senses, bathed in the brightest beam of material light, was worthy neither of comparison nor even of mention, we, cheering up ourselves with a more burning affection towards the Self-same, did by degrees course over all these corporeals, even the heaven itself whence both sun and moon and stars do shine upon this earth. Yea, we soared higher yet, by inward musing and discoursing upon Thee, and by admiring of Thy works; and last of all, we came to our own souls, which we presently went beyond, so that we advanced as high as that region of never-wasting plenty, whence Thou feedest Israel for ever with the food of truth, and where life is that wisdom by which all these things are made, both which have been, and which are to come. And this wisdom is not made; but it is at this present, as it hath ever been, and so shall it ever be: nay, rather the terms to have been, and to be hereafter, are not at all in it, but to be now, for that it is eternal; for to have been, and to be about to be, is not eternal. And while we were thus panting and discoursing upon this wisdom, we arrived at a little touch of it with the whole effort of our heart, and we sighed, and even there we left behind us the first fruits of our own spirits enchained unto it, and we came back to the sound of our own voices, where words uttered have both a beginning and end. For what is like Thy Word, our Lord, which knows no change, which is without age, and makes all things new?"

The ecstasy does not fall, it rests in the air, circling in its strength. "We said, therefore: If to any man the tumults of the flesh be silenced, if fancies of the earth and waters and air be silenced also; if the poles of heaven be silent also; if the very soul keep silence within herself and by going beyond the self surmounts the self; if all dreams

198

and imaginary revelations be silenced, every tongue, every sign; if everything subject to mortality be silenced—yea——" Augustine is writing ten years later, but at the recollection of this ecstasy his flesh is swept with a tremor, his words fall into confusion, it is hard to untangle the Latin—"if all these be silenced and He speak alone, not by them but by Himself, so that we may hear His own word; not pronounced by any tongue of flesh, nor by the voice of the angels, nor by the sound of thunder, nor in the riddle of a resemblance, but by Himself alone (and lo! we two now strained ourselves and with rapid thought touched on that Eternal Wisdom which is for ever over all)—could this exaltation of spirit have continued without end, and all the other lesser visions been quite taken away, and that this exaltation should ravish us and swallow us up, and so wrap the beholder in these more inward joys, so that his life might be for ever like to this very moment of understanding which we now sighed after: were not this as much as Enter into thy Master's joy? But when shall that be? Shall it be when we shall all rise again though nothing of us will not be changed?"

It was the peak of Augustine's experience. It is perhaps the most intense experience over commemorated by a human being. Some, however, have doubted if it were distinctively Christian, and have considered its lack of any reference to the personages or doctrines of his new faith as proof that he was still a Neoplatonist at heart, and that this was but an ecstasy such as Plotinus had achieved in full paganism. But their doubts are groundless, since even the most devout Christian mystics have found that only lesser visions and revelations bear traces of the detail of their faith. The highest state of mysticism is bare of everything but the knowledge of God. Yet Augustine himself lets us doubt whether religion had been the sole cause of the excitement he and Monnica had felt. He himself makes us wonder whether what happened to them at the window was not, in part at least, an extraordinary manifestation of ordinary human love: whether the souls of Augustine and Monnica had not known then such a peaceful mutual adaptation of the will, such a severe identity of purpose and process, such a triumphant duplication of the might of the self by absorption of another self as all men seek from birth to death. For he says: "Such discourse we then had, though not precisely after this manner, and in these self-same words, yet, Lord, thou knowest, that in that day when we thus talked of these things, that this world with all its delights grew contemptible to us, even as we were speaking of it." This is a curiously apologetic sentence. It suggests that when he came to write the *Confessions* he had fallen into the habit of expressing everything in religious terms, but that his violent honesty had tugged at him as he described this particular intense experience, and reminded him that really it was not so; and the particular point in which he assures us his account is truthful is a very small part of the whole. Our suspicions are confirmed when he continues: "Then said my mother: 'Son, for mine own part I have delight in nothing in this life. What I should do here any longer, and to what end I am here I know not, now that my hopes in this world are spent. There was one thing for which I sometimes desired to be a little while reprieved in this life; namely, that I might see thee become a Christian Catholic before I died. This hath the Lord done for me, and more also, for that I now see thee having contemned all earthly happiness, to be made His servant; what then do I here any longer?'" This reads very much as if it were the first time religion had come into the conversation by the window, as if they had been speaking till then only of their life on earth. But to suspect a human basis for the experience is not to belittle it or to deny that its ultimate significance for Augustine was religious.

Perhaps it was because the marsh-fever was already on Monnica that she felt the weariness of life; perhaps it was that which had fanned her being to the flame that had ignited them both. Five days later she was gravely ill. She was a bad subject for such a malady, or rather, it was in a position to do her a great service. She was fifty-five, and her middle years had been spent in a tedious struggle for money and an effort to get her brilliant and helpless son on his feet. On the ninth day she lost consciousness; and when she came to herself she looked up at Augustine and his brother and said, "Here you must bury your mother." Augustine was silent, but his brother bade her take heart, since she had better not lay her bones in a strange land, and think of going home. She looked sadly at him, and then turned to Augustine, saying, "Hark at him!" Then she exhorted them to bury her anywhere, but always to remember her at the altar of the Lord. After that the progress of her malady silenced her; but she had said enough to put Augustine into a blaze of joy. Always before, Monnica had been at pains to make sure that she should be buried beside her husband. She had had a grave made ready beside his, so that she might enjoy his company in death as in life, and that her neighbours might hand down the tale of how God had granted her to travel far beyond the seas and to lie at last under the same earth as her man. Augustine thanked God that out of the fullness of His goodness He had thrust this empty conceit out of his mother's heart. She was not changing her plans because of the fatigue and delirium of her sickness. When she had talked about dying, at the window before she had begun to ail, she had said nothing about being buried in her own country; and later he heard that she had told some of his friends in his absence how little it mattered to her where her bones rested, since no place was far from God. It was in full sanity that she was giving him her body to bury alone, in a country where she had never been with her husband, where she had travelled only for her son's sake. Fervently he thanked God for having worked this miracle, which removed an ancient offence, which at last made all things seemly.

But he had to pay a price for this violent and final delight. His mother lay dead, and he had to close her eyes. As he stood with the tears of agony running down his face, the boy Adeodatus broke out into loud cries. His mother had been sent away from him the year before, and now the only other woman in his life had gone; he himself was to die a year later. They turned and silenced him. Had they not the promise of Monnica's immortality? They were feeling sad only because "the most sweet and dear custom of living with her" had been too suddenly broken. Augustine tried to comfort himself by remembering that in her last hours she had called him a dutiful child, and had boasted that he had never uttered a harsh word to her. But a dead body presents its case against the world with tremendous forensic power. He saw that whatever honour he had paid her was as nothing compared with her slavery to him. Though Evodius took up the Psalter and began to sing, and the Christian brethren came to put all things in order for the burial, he could not loosen the constriction of this pain at such thought. But his pride made him tearless, then and at the graveside, though his agony would not be abated even when he reminded himself that Christianity had wiped out death and substituted for it immortality. He went out from the burial-place to have a bath, telling himself with pathetic pedantry that the Greek word for bath meant that which drives sadness out of the mind. But he learned that sorrow cannot be sweated out. In bed, however, he slept, and woke a little comforted, with some lines from a hymn written by Ambrose ringing through his head. The words came out of the darkness like a kind, fatherly message, and he began to know the relief of prolonged weeping.

It is odd that the two stories he tells of his mother when he writes of her death, to prove what a miracle of holiness then passed, both end in violence. The first refers to Monnica's early married life. Her mother-in-law, it seems, was prejudiced against her by the tale-bearing of some servants, but she had kept her head so well and behaved with such patient good temper that in the end the mother-in-law had reported the servants to her son, who had them well beaten. The second is a grim and ugly anecdote of Monnica's childhood. There had been in her father's house a privileged servant, one of those horrid old women that by length of service and toadying to the elder members of the family win the right to bully and torment the others. It was her malicious pleasure to forbid the children to drink water between meals, at which they got a severely rationed supply. Her reason for this restriction, which was sheer cruelty in thirsty Africa, was that if the children got into the habit of drinking water freely when they were young, they might drink as much wine when they were older. So when little Monnica was sent down to the cellar to draw wine for her parents, she used to take a sip for herself; and this habit grew on her till she found herself taking whole cupfuls. She was not detected by her parents nor by the old woman; and the habit might have grown into a disposition towards drunkenness, had not one day a maid with whom she used to go down to the cellar lost her temper with her and hit her savagely on the teeth, calling her a little sot. This unpleasing sequence of events seems to Augustine a beautiful proof of the Lord's wisdom that can "by the fury of one soul thus cure the ill custom of another."

These stories make a strange tribute for a loving son to lay on the grave of his mother; but perhaps that tribute records a perception that even as Monnica was calm, so too is the heart of the whirlwind. She was modest and sober and restrained as a Christian woman should be; but she survived like a conqueror, and all about her that was not of her way of thinking fell like the conquered. Patricius had long been in the grave. In Augustine's mind she had annihilated great men and vast cities: Virgil and Mani had passed like blown wraiths, the walls of Carthage had fallen, it was as if Rome had never been built. Even the world of flesh about him she seemed able to alter and destroy. Milan was no longer the pompous seat of the Imperial Court; it was an inn at which he had stayed on his roundabout journey home to her, and it had closed its doors after he had gone. All the land through which he had passed was wiped out now as if it had served its purpose and was needed no more. All Italy, all paganism, all profane existence was going up in flames. Monnica alone was left victorious, and her death did not put an end to her victory. It only meant that as she swept the board of this world, so she was to sweep the board of infinity and eternity. Years later, when Augustine was considering the transmigration of souls, he writes: "Plato has declared, to be sure, that human souls return to earth after death to the bodies of animals. Plotinus also, Porphyry's teacher, was of like opinion, but Porphyry rejected it; and that very rightly. He believed with Plato that souls pass into new bodies, but into human bodies. Doubtless he shrank from the other opinion because he saw that if it were true, a woman changed into a mule might carry her son astride her. He forgets that his own system means that a mother changed into a young girl might make her son incestuous." Others, thinking of transmigration, might see a myriad of souls in flux about the generative gates to earth, but not so Augustine. For him these souls did not exist. For him there was then and thereafter to be nothing in the universe save his mother and her son.

VI

The time of Augustine's genius had come. There was nothing but his mother and her son in the universe, but she was not in the visible universe. Therefore she must be in the invisible universe. This laid him under the urgent necessity to prove beyond all shadow of doubt that the invisible universe existed, to study the plan of its structure and the nature of its substance. He had received the stimulus which was to make him one of the first four Doctors of the Church. But he could not settle to his work at once. For he missed the summer sailings of that year, went to Rome, where he wrote several treatises against the Manichæans, and did not complete his journey to Africa till the following August. This delay must have gone against the grain, and he nowhere explains how he came to submit to it; but some have suggested that he was recalled for the purpose of writing these treatises by Siricius, the new Pope, who was a great harrier of the Manichæans. Once in Africa, Augustine went to Thagaste and wound up his father's estate, and used his share as a foundation for a small religious house, the first Augustinian monastery. There he lived very happily for three years, writing busily, confirming himself in the possession of the Christian tradition, and preparing himself to hand it on and extend it by his own work; and there he might have spent all his days had it not been for the tendency of his age to call on its men of thought to be men of action.

It happened that in the seaport town of Hippo Regius, which is now Bône in Algeria, a high official told someone that he thought he might have strength to renounce the world if he could but talk with the monk Augustine; and this came to Augustine's ears. He set out to help this convert with an easy mind, for Hippo was among the towns he could visit in safety. Involuntary episcopacy is one of the few perils which man has been able to eradicate since the time of Augustine, and it is hard for us to realize that it was then a hovering terror, almost as the press-gang once was in England. Not only was the Government official of high character liable to be called on to perform duties and take vows towards which he felt no inclination, but also the religious man who had found his proper vocation in the monastic life was apt to be forcibly transferred to the way of service he had already rejected. Augustine, therefore, took pains to avoid, in any travels he had to undertake, all towns which were without a bishop. But he went to Hippo in perfect confidence, and even lingered there when his convert showed signs of vacillation, because it possessed a worthy bishop, one Valerius, and no town was allowed two bishops. It was unfortunate that Valerius was a Greek, who was far from fluent in Latin and knew no Punic at all, and was therefore of little use to a population that spoke Latin and Punic; and that advancing age was depriving him of the power to show any compensating ecclesiastical merits. The congregation badly needed an energetic and learned pastor who could preach against the heretics and schismatics that were seriously threatening the existence of the Catholic Church locally, and who could bring money to the treasury to enable alms to be distributed. Augustine's fame had spread over the countryside very quickly. When he came to the basilica they knew they saw the man they needed, and they determined to get him by ordaining him as a presbyter, though that did not quite give them what they wanted, since in the Western Church presbyters did not preach. They seized him and dragged him by force to the altar, crying, "Augustine the presbyter! Augustine the presbyter!" After that there was no help for him, though Augustine wept aloud.

It shows what an air of pride the man must have had, that those around him assumed he was weeping because he had been made a presbyter instead of a bishop. But his tears came from a deeper cause. Thereafter his work of establishing the existence of the invisible world was to be interrupted by appeals that he should establish the continuity of the visible world; and he was to run backwards and forwards between the two tasks, making adjustments in the visible world according to his conception of the invisible world, and altering his conception of the invisible world according to his experience of the visible world. This cannot be regarded as a misfortune. The capability he showed in his new duties proved that he had an immense amount of energy to spend in action, and if this had been given no outlet the atmosphere of the religious house at Thagaste might well have become so tense that it would have remained the last as well as the first Augustinian monastery. The abduction of Augustine by the congregation of Hippo was probably most helpful for his genius.

These new duties were more onerous than Augustine can have feared even when he wept, for Valerius set aside Church custom and made him use his mastery of the Latin tongue in the pulpit. He had to preach constantly, at least once a day, and his dramatic temperament obliged him to make each sermon an important performance. One of his most vivid letters describes with what thunderbolts he preached down the custom of merrymaking in the graveyards and churches on saints' days; thus he introduced into Africa the prohibition which Ambrose had forced on Milan, which Monnica had cheerfully obeyed. In the same letter one learns of animated correspondence with the Primate of Africa. He was becoming an expert player of the administrative game. Besides these duties he had to give much time to the instruction of catechumens, a task which he came to perform with the joy of the virtuoso, as one may see in his treatise On Catechizing the Uninstructed, which is still the best handbook ever written for people who have to speak over and over again on the same subject and so run the risk of boring themselves and other people. Soon he had to bear the whole burden of the see on his shoulders, supervising the Church property, organizing charitable relief, and acting as Cadi to disputants, for Valerius was afraid that his able presbyter might be stolen from him by some bishopless town, and he persuaded the Primate of Africa to override precedent and allow Hippo to have two bishops. The Primate of Numidia for a time opposed the consecration of Augustine on the grounds that he had used magic to secure to himself the possession of a female penitent, but this accusation seems not to have cast the shadow over the proceedings that it would have done at a later date. After the story had been disproved, the Primate showed eagerness to make amends by himself consecrating Augustine.

The grip of the visible world on Augustine was strong, but he, being one of the strongest among the sons of man, could throw it off. He had founded in Hippo the second Augustinian monastery, and there he lived. Every moment that he could, he went to his cell and shut out all thought of his priestly duties, and the scene where he fulfilled them. This last exclusion must have been a great effort, for the scene was very beautiful. Hippo was a little Naples, set in a blue bay, and behind it was a plain, rich with vineyards and olive groves and farm-lands, and watered by a river that wound down through piney heaths from an amphitheatre of wooded mountains on the south. From innumerable vivid phrases in Augustine's writings, which escape him before the censor at the back of his brain can act, we know how that landscape and the life it nourished delighted his strong senses. But he cancelled them with his will, and on the nothingness which was left in their place he drew another landscape, another life, which were not an atom less real because they could not be seen. Why, the seen world depended for its reality on the unseen. He points out that parents and children could not believe in each other's love if it were impossible to believe in the unseen, and then society would fall apart, and man pass away. Nor need the unseen remain the uncomprehended. He smote his own breast, and knew he knew who smote and who was smitten; he anticipated Descartes' *Cogito, ergo sum*, and matched the self of which man is certain against the most extreme uncertainties man recognizes in the universe, as if he were cheering two cocks fighting in a pit. It was a spirit very necessary in that period when—as happens in all periods of extreme political and economic disorder—the proper philosophical scepticism as to the infallibility of man's mental instrument had suffered a morbid degeneration into hysterical coma. He stoutly maintained that consciousness could investigate its own laws, and that that was worth doing, which the Sceptics had come very near to denying. He glorified reason, and bade us put "far from us the thought that God detests that whereby He has made us superior to other animals, far from us an assent of pure faith which should dispense us from

206

accepting or demanding proof." But he insists that faith should precede reason. At first this seems contradictory and lacking in faith, which surely should hold that since the truths of religion really are truths, reason is bound to lead to them. But, in fact, this proposition reveals Augustine's astonishing power as an introspective psychologist. He perceived that reason, the working of the conscious mind, was not a mechanical process which inevitably turned out truth as its finished product. There was something else in a human being which decided what reason should work on, and how it should work, and unless this something decided that the finished product should be truth it might well turn out to be a mere rationalization of error. He was able to realize this because, as his attempts to define memory show, he was well aware of the existence of an unconscious mind; and that realization must have been given point by his knowledge that, if he had tried and failed to find truth during his twenties, it was because this hidden part of his nature had preferred to remain in error. Hence he had cause for maintaining that unless the whole of a man gave allegiance to a theory of values which recognizes knowledge of the truth as an essential good, he could not be trusted to use his reason with integrity; and as for him Christianity was the means by which such a theory could be propounded to the whole of man, his argument that faith should precede reason has a sound psychological basis which it is not easy to dispute.

It was difficult to draw the map of the invisible world on the blackness of nothingness; and he bore heavily on the outlines that one whom he had loved and trusted had traced before him. There can be recognized in the Augustinian system the distinctive draughtsmanship of Ambrose. The sermons of Ambrose dealt much with sin, which, since he was greatly influenced by Greek thought, he regarded as not-being, and rejected with a Stoic passion for the good life. The root of sin was regarded by him not as sensuous, not as a mere matter of fleshly appetites, but as situated more deeply, in man's perverse use of his free will. Only could its root be torn up if man won through his faith in Christ the right to lay hold on the strength of God. Again and again he cries out humbly and proudly that the soul must not boast because it is upright, but because it has been lifted up by the Lord; and if these passages are translated—left untranslated their distinctively Italian Latin is a guide—it is hard to believe that they were written by Ambrose and not by Augustine. For that position was the foundation of Augustine's system, though he added to it the quality which one would expect from the drama which had led him to the creation of that system, the quality which Ambrose could not have contributed, and probably would not if he could. He added to it his characteristic ardour. He suffused the existing Christian system with a greater passion of love than it had known since the immediate influence of its founder had passed away. In the intervening centuries the sense of God as a judge who tried man on moral grounds had degenerated into a too narrowly legalist attitude towards religion; it was felt that salvation was a matter of the performance of a contract between God and man, whereby retribution was demanded and merit was supplied. But now Augustine depicted the relationship between God and man as being passionate and eventful and subject to woeful alienation followed by happy reconciliation, like the relationships of the flesh.

But though the saints have decided that sin has not its roots in the flesh, it can hardly be denied that thought springs from that soil. Augustine was never more bitter than when he was denouncing those who represented God as having human form and human passions, yet all his conceptions of God are determined by the passions which are imposed on humanity by its form. We know, not by deduction but from Augustine's own statement, that his most intense experiences were those arising out of the relationship between himself and his parents. It is not surprising that he depicted the relationship between man and God, which must inevitably engender the intensest of all experiences, as a magnified form of the relationship between a child and its parents. Always it had been understood that by the operation of God's grace Christ had the power to abrogate man's sins; but Augustine made it appear that God continuously rained grace on mankind, continuously transforming him from the filthy subject of original sin to one bearing resemblance to God, even as parents love their children and train them up from angry helpless babes to civilized adults. Man attains resembance to God, but is never the same as God, just as a child grows up to be an adult like its parents, but never becomes its parents. While it grows it shall bask in love, but that love can be withheld if the child is not good, and even if it is. With a curious wild gesture, that passed on to the invisible world the guilt of not declaring its ultimate motives which lies so heavily on the visible world, Augustine laid down that God's love can be withheld for reasons beyond man's comprehension.

He invented the doctrine of predestination: which is the doctrine that God chooses some to be saved, and some to be damned. This is, of course, not a question of judgement by faith or by works. For since man can hold forth or achieve works only by God's grace, it follows that he can lack them only by God's determination to withhold His grace. There must be justice in this, but the cause is not communicated to the victim, it remains God's secret. "When of two infants, whose cases seem in all respects alike, one is by the mercy of God chosen to Himself, and the other is by His justice abandoned: why, of these two, the one should have been chosen rather than the other, is to us an insoluble problem." He found his sanction for this idea in the preaching of St Paul, but to explain his warm liking for it one need only look to the nursery and see if a beloved child does not sometimes feel an intensification of its rapture at thinking of other children not so loved, and that for no other reason than that they are they. Yet, since a child must believe its parents morally right, it must believe their action in withholding their love to have some moral justification. It must believe them right in all things, if it is fully to participate in the most grievous and joyous of all experiences, the cycle which Augustine has made the pattern of Christian piety. The child must be naughty and run away, get dirty and hungry and tired, and know the terror of loneliness and a pricking conscience; and then suddenly be picked up and carried safe home again, to be washed and fed and rocked to rest, to be loved and forgiven. So the mystic sees himself as the child of God, playing truant in time and the finite, being brought home to the eternal and the infinite.

But how can this condition of things have come about, if God is omnipotent? For then He must have permitted, nay, even caused, the preliminary aberration, the sins that occasioned the repentance. This was a terrible charge. For though Augustine had the lightest possible sense of ethical responsibility, he had the heaviest sense of sin. Regarding the consequences of his actions he was as indifferent as almost any man who has been self-conscious enough to record his own emotions, but he had an excessive share of that feeling of guilt which exists quite unrelated to any individual experience in the mind of almost every human being. It seemed to him as if humanity was saturated with the obscene, not by reason of what it did but of what it was; and his years in the Manichæan camp had confirmed him in this attitude. He could not bear to think that God could be the author of this filth by which he was haunted, and he set himself to shift the responsibility on to man's will and the fall of Adam. To do this he had to create a complete philosophical system that must explain every phenomenon of the invisible and visible worlds. Though that system is not entirely satisfactory, though it abounds in false assumptions and contradictions, it still remains one of the most stupendous works of man. Augustine's errors were the result of his position in time, and so are not disgraceful. It was for him to be the great romantic artist, leaning far out to the apprehension of yet unformulated truths, and bringing in the false mingled with the true in an immense mass of material which was reduced to order eight hundred years later by the great classical artist, St Thomas Aquinas. We have here one of the first and most impressive demonstrations that all classicism depends on a previous romanticism.

But from this task Augustine was perpetually called away to the routine of his episcopal office. As the state of disorder in Africa grew wilder his sermons had to be more and more authoritative and dynamic, more and more catechumens pressed forward for instruction, the administration of the Church funds became more complicated: when a man left his money to the Church instead of his kin, Augustine was constrained to return it for fear that heretics and schismatics should gossip, but had to face the anger of those in his flock who needed bread. There was Church discipline to be maintained. He had, for example, to deal with two deacons who had accused each other of attempted seduction. He sent them together on what must have been a very embarrassing journey to the tomb of St Felix of Nola in Italy, hoping that the relics of the saint would make some discriminating gesture. There were also fussy parishioners who had rather more conscience than ought to be in private hands. "May a Christian use wood taken from one of the idols' groves which have been chopped down as part of the State campaign?" asked one Publicola. "May a Christian put a wall round his property for defence against an enemy? And if some others use that wall as a place to fight and kill, is he then guilty of homicide?" "If a Christian buy in the market-place meat which has not been offered to idols, but rather suspects it may have been, and in the end decides that it has not, does he sin if he eats it?" Augustine answers, "Better not! Yes! No! No!" and wearily gives reasons, but obviously refrains only with difficulty from adding, "and try not to be so silly."

The correspondence for which he had a greater taste was of the kind which he initiated with St Jerome six years after he had gone to Hippo; though that took a turn which he hardly enjoyed. Jerome was a saint in the highly technical sense of the word, being a literary genius of repellent disposition and venomous tongue. But he was like the juggler who was found performing his tricks before the Virgin's altar because he had nothing but his professional skill to offer up to her. Such as his qualities were, he laid them without reservation at the service of his religion. He was fifteen years older than Augustine, and was a famous scholar who still kept the world busily admiring him and hating him even though he had retired to a monastery at Bethlehem when the correspondence between them started. A rumour had spread abroad that Jerome was translating the Scriptures from the original Hebrew into Latin, and this came to Augustine's ears. He wrote to Jerome, begging him to abandon this enterprise and to confine his attention to the Greek Septuagint translation of the Scriptures, and calling him to account for having ascribed a pious fraud to St Paul in his interpretation of a perplexing passage in Galatians. His letter arouses tenderness and apprehension in the reader. It is as if one watched a St Bernard puppy, as yet unaware that cats do not like dogs, gambolling up to make friends with a Persian. But it is also an abominable letter. Augustine was no scholar at all compared with Jerome; he was the newly appointed presbyter of a fourth-rate diocese, while Jerome was a world-renowned religious leader; they were strangers. Yet Augustine's approach to him would be considered pert and familiar even in a close friend and equal. He expresses doubt whether the Greek translators can have left so many points unsettled that Jerome thinks it worth while translating them all over again. "Now, these things were either obscure or plain. If they were obscure, it is believed that you are as likely to be mistaken about them as the other translators. If they were plain, it is not likely that the others should have been mistaken about them. Having stated the ground of my perplexity, I appeal to your kindness to give me an answer regarding this matter." He went on writing letters in this strain for years, careless of the fact that Jerome did not answer them. "Wherefore I beg you," he says, "apply to the correction and emendation of your book a frank and truly Christian severity, and chant what the Greeks call a palinode. For incomparably more lovely than the Grecian Helen is Christian truth. I do not say this in order that you may recover the faculty of spiritual sight— far be it from me to say you have lost it!—but that, having eyes both quick and clear in discernment, you may turn them towards that from which, in unaccountable dissimulation——" and so on.

There is more here than simply a failure in manners. There is a failure to be civilized. Augustine shows no signs of realizing that Jerome, like himself, was working under the direction of conscience, that he had his own approach to truth which might even afford as good results as Augustine's, and that he might be hurt by an attack on his life-work. Worst of all, he exhibits towards Jerome that kind of sadistic indelicacy which lays impudent fingers on hidden wounds. It happened that, some time before, Jerome had parted from his life-long friend Rufinus after one of those bitter quarrels that spring up between specialists. Jerome believed that Rufinus had betrayed that obligation of honesty which binds scholars, and, what was more, had involved him in this betrayal, so he turned and rent him. This was, as Jerome's writings show, a source of agony to him; the quality of his venom always suggests that his cruelty was a defence put up by an extreme sensitiveness and need for love. It seemed to Augustine good that he should intervene in this private matter. "If I could anywhere meet you both," he exclaims unctuously, "I would throw myself at your feet, and there, weeping till I could weep no more, I would appeal with all the eloquence of love——" and so on. These indiscretions were punished by Jerome in a series of masterpieces of murderous irony which make Wilde and Whistler seem clodhoppers and Voltaire and Gibbon mealy-mouths. He had even greater justification than the content of the letters, for Augustine had allowed copies of them to be widely circulated through the Church before he had waited to make sure that Jerome had received them and had an opportunity to answer them. It was therefore very handsome of Jerome to write a year later holding out his hand in a good-natured gesture of reconciliation. But Augustine used a clumsy and ungracious misinterpretation of a charming phrase of Jerome's—"Let us play in the fields of scripture without wounding each other"— as an excuse for a priggish rejection of his advances.

Looking back, one sees that Ambrose may have had his reasons for not reciprocating Augustine's affection; and in a letter to Jerome Augustine tells a vivid story which reveals what weariness and irritation must have afflicted the more urbane type of churchman at this time. In Oea, which is now Tripoli, a certain bishop was reading the Scriptures to the congregation, using Jerome's version, and came on the passage in the book of Jonah in which it is described how the Lord God caused a plant to grow into a lofty shelter for the disaffected prophet. The plant named in the original text is a kind peculiar to Asia, and the earlier translators, in a desire to make the passage intelligible to Europeans and Africans, had called it either a gourd or ivy; and while the Septuagint translators had chosen the gourd, Jerome chose the ivy. The congregation had been previously accustomed to use the Septuagint version, and when the point came in that admirable short story where they had always heard the word "gourd" and they heard "ivy" instead, they were angered, like children who are listening to a familiar fairy-story and are told that instead of three bears three gazelles came in to the little house in the wood. But these were dangerous children. They raised a riot in the basilica, and the terrified bishop had to let them send out for the opinion of the Jewish residents in the town as to the meaning of the original Hebrew word; but this opinion was given less in care for philological accuracy than in the hope of prolonging Christian dissensions, and in this it was entirely successful. It must have been infuriating for a learned man like Jerome to have it suggested that he should gag his scholarship lest it should offend such foolish assemblies of the childish and the unlettered; and the incident reveals how unjust it is to regard Christianity as a mob-religion that wiped out the individualized culture of paganism. The cleavage between the mob which wanted to reduce everything to the level of their own rudimentary understandings, and the individuals who wanted those who could extend human knowledge to be given full licence to do so, was as marked within the Church as without it. The State had bred a vast part of its population simply to do the dirty work of the world, and now that it had lost the power to regiment this artificially created army of inferiors they wandered loose and looting over the whole social system. One of the most interesting of Augustine's writings, from a historical point of view, is his treatise, *Concerning the Labour of Monks*, which deals with the problems created by the monks who refused to obey the apostolic injunction that they should support themselves by their own hands, and who claimed the right to live like the lilies of the field and rely on alms from the faithful. These monks, it appears, were either workmen who could no longer face the impossible struggle for subsistence, or the freed slaves of landowners who had been obliged to free them on becoming Christians, and who may have become Christians for the express purpose of being able to hand their properties over to the Church and disembarrass themselves of the intolerable burden of taxation. The Church, which was yet inexperienced in handling the problems arising out of monasticism, gave itself no liberty to turn away these workmen and freed slaves if they declared their desire to be monks; but it was perfectly aware that when they refused to work they were actuated by other than religious considerations.

Africa, indeed, was groaning like a rotten branch that high winds are tearing from a dying tree. Gildo, a Moorish prince of savage genius and immense wealth, who had been made military governor of Africa in reward for his apparent fidelity to Rome, had covered the land with the horrors of revolt from 394 to 398; and from the Imperial edicts which for ten years after deal with the rebels and informers against them one may learn of the horrors involved in the suppression of that revolt. The subdued provinces had suffered the worst punishment that can be inflicted on rebels. They had no confidence that their conquerors would continue to rule them. For the Goths were coming down on Italy slowly and irresistibly as age, and the Vandals were following them as death follows age. But all this was as nothing to Augustine. Though he was young in the Church, and though Hippo was a diocese of little importance, he had become the mind of the African Church, and when heretics and schismatics put forth false doctrine it was from him that a lead was expected. He had to deal again with Manichæanism, and he shows again a curious lack of sympathy for all its doctrines save its belief in the evil of the flesh. He attacks Mani's poem about the universe as if it were a literal statement of fact, and it is as if a clever counsel were bullying Dante. "But can you point us out on the map these places you say you visited, Heaven, Purgatory, and Hell? Are you aware that the measurements you give of this place are not mathematically credible?" But the treatises are interesting to a modern reader, because they will very often make him feel as if he were watching a Tolstoy who developed much further than he actually did, rebuking a Tolstoy at the stage at which he stopped. When Augustine points out that there is really much more to the religious life than giving oneself gooseflesh over the fact that some things strike one as dirty and others do not, it appears as a grave indictment against the nineteenth century that it allowed itself to be impressed by a teacher whose experience was limited to only a small part of Augustine's spiritual progress.

The Pelagian controversy came later and occupied him longer. Pelagius, a monk, and Celestius, a pious layman, came forward with propositions that struck at the bases of the Augustinian conception of religion, which were again and again to be revived and to contend with it throughout the next fifteen hundred years. They held that man's will is free, and that he can use it to become virtuous and be rewarded by God. This is a superficially attractive proposition, and its prophets laid it down because the moral stagnation of Rome made them feel that virtue must be preached anew. But it has the disadvantage of lacking, even from the least orthodox point of view, full correspondence with reality. If we examine ourselves carefully we cannot claim to have free will. We exercise what looks like a free faculty of choice, but the way we exercise that faculty depends on our innate qualities and our environment, and these always bind us in some way or another to the neuroses which compel us to choose death rather than life. We cannot break this compulsion by the independent efforts of our minds, for they cannot function effectively unless they learn to depend on tradition. Augustine's view that we are full of original sin, that we do not enjoy the free use of our wills, and must link ourselves to the eternal if we are to be saved, is at least a symbolic interpretation of something that the most secular-minded must allow to be true. Since the triumph of Pelagianism would have meant not only the establishment of an inexact psychological statement but the limitation of Christianity to a narrow Puritanism, it is as well that Augustine was at hand to fight it. His lack of ethical interests made him, perhaps, not such a deadly opponent as he might have been if he could have fought Pelagius and Celestius nearer their own ground. But the intellectual problems involved were delightful to him, though sometimes they baffled him.

For instance, what was the origin of the soul? It was necessary to know for certain. For if the soul of each infant is generated by the souls of its parents as its body is generated by their bodies, then it inherits its spiritual as well as its physical attributes from Adam, and it is natural enough that it should inherit the sinfulness brought about in him by the Fall. But if the soul of each infant is newly created by God, then where does its sinfulness come from, since God could not possibly create evil? Augustine was obliged to confess that he did not know. But he told two bishops who asked him that perhaps Jerome knew, and that they had better write to him and find out. It says much for the older man that he and Augustine were again on friendly terms. Later on, Augustine himself wrote Jerome a long letter asking him to confirm his belief in "that most firm and well-grounded article in the faith of the Church of Christ," that new-born children can be delivered from perdition only by baptism. But Jerome sent no very satisfactory answer. He replied courteously to the bishops. With the exquisite capacity of compression which comes of long and disciplined use of the pen he set down the various theories regarding the origin of the soul, but could go no further. He manages just one flick of the pitchfork and flourish of the forked tail to show that the old imp in him is not dead yet. The bishops, he says, had better apply to "that holy man and learned Bishop Augustine, who will be able to expound you his opinion, or rather, I should say, my own opinion stated in his words." More than that he could not do. There had been a time of late when he had been so miserable that he had forgotten his own name, and had kept silent, knowing it a time for tears. He had been forced to lay his studies on one side till his eyes were less constantly dimmed with weeping. For he was an old man, over seventy, and he could not bear such ill news as the Sack of Rome by the Goths.

No man had cursed Rome more roundly than Jerome, but no man had been more aware of it. The hard brightness of its street-scenes, and the tumult of its human babble and its traffic noises, assault the senses from his page. Such intense consciousness is usually the effect of love: and though it is sometimes the effect of hate, such hate is not very far from love. Whether he loved or hated the place, it had been his home for many years, and now it was gone. To tell him how completely it had gone, men and women whom he had known as rich and powerful passed hungry and footsore by the gates of his monastery at Bethlehem, content to beg if they might find safety in the sacred places of the Holy Land. But he did not believe safety was to be found any more upon earth. It had died at the heart. After Rome had fallen, had not the Arab tribes seethed in rebellion across the desert so that he and his brothers and sisters in God had trembled for their lives? He knew much more than an old man's terror at these mishaps. For he too had believed in the creation of an invisible world, though almost certainly he had not believed that it could be achieved all at once by one excited man. He had seen it being created touch by touch, not by successive generations of men, who would correct each other savagely if need be and error crept in, but who would persevere in the great task with perfect loyalty, age in, age out. But they could not do that if they were fighting for their lives with Goths and Arabs. And if they could not, what would be the good of their lives? They would die like beasts, not knowing their own nature or purpose. So he did not answer Augustine's letter to him about the origin of the soul, nor yet his later one on the saying in the Epistle of St James, that "whosoever shall keep the whole law and yet offend in one point, he is guilty of all." For the years did not take from him his horror at the Sack of Rome.

But the news affected Augustine very differently. He was not appalled by it. In his sermons he made a shrewd guess that it was not such an immediate catastrophe as might be supposed, and that the congregation he addressed need fear no immediate alteration in their state; and this was indeed the case. But had Africa lain under an immediate menace he would have been reluctant to admit it, for the news had filled him with a passionate exaltation. He was as happy when he heard of the Sack of Rome as he was when his mother no longer wanted to be buried by the side of his father. To commemorate his emotion he turned aside and wrote, ostensibly to answer the charge that Rome had fallen because the gods were angered at the apostasy of their people towards Christianity, a book called *The City of God*, and though he took many years—probably thirteen—to write it, there is the same intense glee inscribed on the last pages as on the first. That glee is not to be dismissed as malignant, though that it certainly is in part. It is also one sign of the vigour of a conflict which engendered enough dynamic power to make *The City of God* a work of genius. For that it certainly is, though it is also a shocking and barbarous book. A student is reported as having said of it that "this is not a book, it is journalism; whenever St Augustine had nothing else to do, he sat down and wrote a bit of it"; and if he erred in too roseate a conception of the journalist's life, he conveyed correctly enough the sense of extreme incoherence which baffles and even disgusts the ordinary reader of this book. The disgust arises, perhaps, because there is here more than the formlessness which was imposed on Augustine by overwork and liability to interruption. There is also the disorder which comes from abandonment to a base passion. Though Augustine was a saint and a genius and a most lovable child of earth, he was often not a gentleman, and he is never less gentlemanly than in his jeers at the plight of the Romans and his ill-natured allegations that all their virtues were really vices. Elsewhere in one of his letters Augustine lets fly an accusation at the pagan world which touches the spot of its rottenness. "These learned men," he called the philosophers, "whose ideal of a republic or a commonwealth in this world was rather investigated or described by them in private discussions, than established and realized by them in public measures." But in *The City of God* little enough of the criticism of the pagan world is on such high ground. There is a wholesale rejection of all the treasures of art and science, of law and organization, that Greece and Rome had laid up for humanity; it is like seeing a giant child wrecking a museum. There are innumerable cheap jokes against polytheism, flushed and interested researches into obscene rites, and ungracious attacks on the Platonists.

Yet tangled up with these is wisdom, and more than wisdom. There is a sudden magnificent attack on Imperialism. He sees and presents in perfectly ordered paragraphs—though these are scattered far apart in irrelevancies—the psychological advantages that small States enjoy compared with great Empires. The conquering spirit that had made Rome cross the seas to Africa is destroyed in a blaze of fiery criticism. It was loutish stupidity. It had not the dignity of evil pride, it was more mockable than that, it had defeated its own ends, and had led straight to ruin and this sweet Sack of Rome. Such States as do these things, being without justice, are loathly things, mere robber bands; and in a State without God there can be no justice, for justice and all such things come of God. Yet the State cannot be wholly of God, because it is caught in the coarse foul mesh of material reality. Yet it must be. For without States there could be no kings and emperors, and kings and emperors can do what no common man can do to punish the heretics and schismatics that lay villainous hands on the faith of the Church of Christ. He flags, he rambles, he reverts to his unfortunate wistful obsession about the means of generation that would have been possible had man's constitution been ever so little different. But his genius restores him. He sees again a vision such as he and his mother saw when they leaned from the window, a little time before she died, having accomplished all that she could do for him. It was a vision that showed history as the mass movement of predestination, as the organization in grace of those whom God has chosen not for their merits but out of His goodness, to enjoy not war but peace, not sin but beatitude.

"Accordingly, two cities have been formed by two loves: the earthly by the love of self, even to the contempt of God; the heavenly by the love of God, even to the contempt of self. The first glories in itself, the second in the Lord. The first seeks glory from men, but the greatest glory of the second is God, the witness of conscience. The one lifts up its head in its own glory; the other says to its God,

'Thou art my glory and the lifter up of mine head.' In the one, the princes and the nations it subdues are ruled by the love of ruling; in the other the princes and the subjects serve one another in love, the latter obeying, while the former take thought for all. The one delights in its own strength in the persons of its rulers; the other says to its God, I will love Thee, O Lord, my strength. Therefore the wise men of the first city follow either the goods of the body or mind or both, and those who have known God glorified Him not as God, neither were they thankful but became vain in their imagination, and their foolish heart was darkened, professing themselves to be wise. But in the other city there is no human wisdom, but only godliness, which offers due worship to the true God and looks for its rewards in the society of saints, of holy angels, as well as holy men, that God may be all in all."

VII

It might seem that the victory was wholly with Monnica and the Church. Yet it was not so. In the forty-four years of life that followed Augustine's conversion he never for one minute ceased to be the loyal servant of Christianity and the active enemy of paganism; but the nature of man is so constituted that it can contrive the extremest treacheries without itself knowing what it has done. We must suspect a profound and subtle form of such treachery when we notice the change that passed over Augustine's character after middle life. He retained the curious quality which made him lovable in spite of his complete egotism. That one can see from his friends' letters. But in other respects he knew a complete reversal of his previous tendencies. When he tells the fussy enquirer, Publicola, that "as to killing others in order to defend one's own life, I do not approve of this, unless one happen to be a soldier or public functionary, acting not for oneself, but in defence of others or of the city in which one resides, if one act according to a lawfully given commission and in a manner becoming that office," we may smile at the brisk official tone, and may mark what seven years of the priesthood have done to the scholar who in youth was sealed and dumb with individualism. We must laugh aloud when, fourteen years later, he writes in a letter discussing the evils of demon-worship: "Apuleius, though born in a place of some note, and a man of superior education and great eloquence, never succeeded, with all his magical arts, in reaching, I do not say the supreme power, but even any subordinate office as a magistrate in the Empire." It is true that this sentence has some justification, considering Apuleius' worldly ambitions, but the old Augustine would surely have reflected that if the demons had given Apuleius his genius, that might be reckoned as supreme power. The mind of the new Augustine seems to have taken an official turn; and letter after letter, treatise after treatise, shows that it had. He had become a conservative. He stood by the organization, he felt under an obligation to make it work. The importance of making it work outweighed the importance of making his own psychical organization work. So he became hurried, impatient, high-handed. He became, in fact, Patricius.

Year by year he gradually transferred his allegiance to the ideals of his father, which had been associated with the State, adherence to Rome, and the cultivation of a robust antithesis to the Christian ideal of meekness and passivity, while he apparently continued to serve the ideals of his mother, which had centred round the Catholic Church; and how he did it can best be illustrated by his relations to the Donatists. These were schismatics who already had a long history behind them. When Diocletian was persecuting the Christians in 305, the magistrates were obliged to demand that the Christian clergy should surrender their sacred scriptures for destruction. The clergy that refused were slain. But Mensurius the Bishop of Carthage thought of a neat evasion, and he and his archdeacon Cecilian presented the magistrate with a selection of heretical writings. Thus they gained safety for themselves and their congregations; but several years afterwards, when Mensurius died and Cecilian was made bishop in his place, a number of Numidian bishops objected on the ground that the two had really handed over the sacred scriptures, and that Cecilian was therefore a "traditor"; and that this made it impossible that he should be consecrated a bishop, since only sacraments administered by a righteous priest were valid. This contention, after being debated in many courts, was quashed. It had the sole merit that it might have done something towards raising the character of the priesthood; otherwise there was little to be said for it. The evidence in the particular case debated was weak; and the underlying principle was illogical, since the real dispenser of the sacraments must be Christ, and it is inconceivable that a relationship decreed by Him can break down through the personality of the mediator. Moreover, it destroyed the continuity of the Church as an imaginative conception, to be replaced by a wild and uncomforting fantasy. One might as well say that people would lose their capacity to appreciate art if the artists of one generation failed to attain a certain standard of proficiency. But worst of all were the practical effects of the schism. Christian communicants obviously could not suffer themselves to be deprived of the means of grace, and if they were liable to suspect that this was happening on account of the behaviour of their priests, the Church would have become a bear-garden.

It indicates the misery of Africa that such a poor and unattractive schism should have gained a whole army of adherents. Its original power is said to have lain in the circumstance that though Mensurius and Cecilian had not handed over the sacred scriptures, a great many other ecclesiastics had, and were eager to avert suspicion by accusing other people of their fault. But its later strength was drawn from the poverty of the land. There were a vast number of Africans who were submerged in suffering by their economic conditions, and who consequently needed a religion that glorified suffering. This they had found in the Catholic Church when it was a persecuted religion; but they found it there no longer now that the Catholic Church was the triumphant ally of the Roman Empire. Many such people joined the Donatists for no other reason than to find themselves again in a harassed minority, and Augustine's writings suggest that the Church itself had been partly to blame for this by its emphasis on the cult of the martyrs. These schismatics were joined by a number of desperate people, who formed bands called *Circumcelliones*. Scholarship handsomely offers us the choice of translating this word as either "the chaste ones" or "those who hang round the huts." They were, in any case, hungry African nationalists who hated the Roman power which had let them be born into this ruin, and considered themselves justified in robbing and murdering the oppressing classes. The Donatists had no relish for these allies, and tried to cast them off. In 340 the Numidian Donatist bishops had appealed to the Roman military governor to send troops against the local Circumcelliones, and after the pitched battle outside Octava that followed they would not permit the bodies of the rebels to be buried in the basilicas. But the forces drawing them together were strong. Two commissioners, Paul and Macarius, were sent from Rome to bring the schismatics back to the parent church, and they made themselves as well loved in Africa as Cromwell in Ireland. A silence fell; but it was the sign of sullen fear, not death. The country was still hungry and governed by aliens. Then Julian the Apostate came, and ordered the restitution of the churches to the Donatists. They came back like a pack of wolves for their revenge. But after three years he was gone, and the Catholics were taking revenge for that revenge. Imperial edict beat down the Donatists, while the misery of the country brought them more and more recruits. When Augustine came back from his sojourn in Italy there were Donatists in almost every African town, and in many places, including Hippo, they outnumbered the Catholics.

There could be no satisfactory method of dealing with Donatism. It raised problems of which no solution has ever been found; for there can be little doubt that the prime causes of the movement were economic. There is room for debating how far and how drastically it was necessary to deal with it. The opinion that sacraments were valid only if administered by righteous priests was unsound, but so little offensive that St Cyprian had held it till the day he died; and in all other respects the Donatists were rigidly orthodox. They were, therefore, disseminating no very dangerous poison in the public mind, and one would have thought that Augustine and his friends could easily have preached down their single and obvious error. But once a Church acquires property, and takes over administrative duties from the State to the extent to which Christianity had done during the fourth century, schism becomes not only a difference of opinion about ecclesiastical organization but an attempt at malversation. It is as little a matter for tolerance as an attempt of certain shareholders in a company to take out their capital and seize part of the company's plant. Nor could tolerance have been stretched far enough to excuse all the doings of the Donatists. One cannot believe all the accusations brought against them by their opponents. Augustine's tales of their immorality are the same sort of thing he told about the Manichæans, and the evidence of his contemporaries goes to show that in this he was unjust. In reading patristic literature one's incredulity is constantly aroused by the frequency with which persons holding unsound doctrines are also guilty of the grossest misdemeanours, often of kinds that one would think most incompatible with strong religious interests. Other accusations against the Donatists are frivolous. Augustine's famous story of the Donatist baker at Hippo, who would not bake bread for Catholics, proves on examination to have taken place forty years before he wrote, during the terrorist period under Julian the Apostate. The Donatists' desire to avoid social intercourse with their enemies was such as the world has since seen mutually displayed by Jews and Gentiles, Catholics and Protestants, Anglicans and Nonconformists; so it cannot be taken as proof of exceptional naughtiness. But there can be no denying that many of them thieved, burned churches, beat people with clubs, threw vitriol over bishops, and murdered their opponents; and the standard of civil order was so low that they could do these things with impunity.

Augustine's treatment of Donatism was therefore determined, and not very pleasantly determined, by two essential facts: that the Church could not exercise tolerance towards it, and had to perform the duty of suppressing its offences against order. What is significant is the spirit in which he carried out this treatment. It was in no way different from the spirit in which his father, or any other good Roman citizen, would have waged war against rebels who had risen against the Empire. The extent to which Augustine had changed since his youth can be measured by the contempt he pours on Donatism because it was purely African. In the early days of his return to Thagaste he had formidably rebuked a pagan scholar of Madaura who had reproached the Christian Church with provinciality and had jeered at the Punic names of some of the martyrs. Later he himself jeered at the Donatists, because their church, which had for head-quarters in Rome only an insalubrious cave presided over by an obscure bishop, had neither the majesty nor the magnitude of his own church, which was coincident with the Empire. He begged the question at issue as Imperialists do when they deal with rebels: he treated it as a crime in his opponents that they resisted his authority, and ignored the arguments by which they tried to prove that authority lay not in him but in themselves. He was growing to find the arguments of others as negligible as people do when they can back up their own by force, for he had the ear of the Court, which was now at Ravenna, and could inspire the promulgation and enforcement of edicts providing for the imprisonment, expropriation, physical chastisement, and exile of all heretics and schismatics. Like a bluff old soldier, inured to the rough justice of campaigns, he recommends the application of this medicine to the lawless and the law-abiding alike. "As to those who had not, indeed, a boldness leading to acts of violence, but were pressed down by a kind of inveterate sluggish-ness of mind, and would say to us, 'What you affirm is true, nothing can be said against it, but it is hard for us to cast away what the tradi-tion of our fathers has handed down to us,' why should not such

223

persons be shaken up in a beneficial way by a law bringing upon them inconvenience in worldly things, in order that they might rise from their lethargic sleep and awake to the salvation which is to be found in the unity of the Church?" He was indifferent to the effects of the persecutions he was thus initiating, not because he was cruel, but because his imagination had completely disappeared, as it sometimes does in men of action. The extremists among the schismatics were passing through an epidemic of suicidal mania which bears heartrending witness to their misery. They did not care how they died so long as they died. They insulted judges so that they should inflict the death penalty, and waylaid travellers whom they forced to kill them, threatening them with death if they did not. Those who died thus at the hands of others hoped for a martyr's crown; but others were amply content merely with death, and drowned themselves, threw themselves over cliffs, or set themselves alight. To these unhappy creatures Augustine addressed priggish rebukes, or was mildly facetious at their expense. To a Donatist priest, who, to avoid arrest and forced conformity, first threw himself down a well, and then, when he was arrested and put on a horse to be taken before the authorities, flung himself down on the ground and inflicted grave injuries on himself, Augustine wrote a brisk and cheerful letter beginning, "If you could see the sorrow of my heart and my concern for your salvation, you would perhaps take pity on your own soul . . ."

With the Conference of Carthage in 411, which was the reward of Augustine's efforts, and brought together the beaten Donatist bishops to go through a travesty of reconciliation with the Church, he rejoiced as one cannot imagine a trained philosopher rejoicing at an intellectual assent extorted by force. Nor did he show doubt later, when his firm way with schismatics brought blackness into a situation dark enough already. Heraclian, the Governor of Africa, who had rebuffed a part Gothic, part Roman, rebel expedition which had sailed from Italy in 410, himself became a rebel, and in 413 took a fleet to the Tiber. He was routed, and was beheaded at Carthage; and again unhappy Africa was subjected to the miseries that attend the suppression of a revolt. Count Marinus was sent to discover and pass judgement on all Heraclian's supporters, and his commission gave endless opportunities to the informer who wanted to satisfy a judge. So the Donatists denounced two brothers who were both State officials and had been active in the enforcement of the Imperial decrees against schismatics. One had been President of the Conference at Carthage. Though they were innocent of any share in the revolt, they were suddenly executed. There is a letter from Augustine to the official whom he believed to be responsible which is an outburst of rage like a thunderstorm: like one of those outbursts for which his father was famous in Thagaste. But he shows no sign of recognizing that perhaps a Capitoline type of tragedy follows from a Capitoline policy of oppression. It might be said that in that lack of recognition he was of his time, and therefore no blame attaches to him. But that is not true. He had come from Italy with other views, which permitted his first letters on the Donatists to be kindly and tolerant; and they were still held by others. "Reflect," Nectarius writes to him, "reflect on the appearance presented by a town from which men doomed to torture are dragged forth; think of the lamentations of mothers and wives, of sons and fathers; think of the shame felt by those who may return, set at liberty, indeed, but having undergone the torture; think what sorrow and groaning the sight of their wounds and scars must renew. And when you have pondered all these things, first think of God, and then think of your good name among men."

There was nothing but violence in his life in the visible world, even when he turned from baiting heretics and schismatics. The church at Hippo was very different from the quiet church to which Monnica and Ambrose had led him. What it was may be judged from the curious letters that passed after Melania and Pinian had visited him. Melania was the heiress of one of the wealthiest families in Rome, and when the Vandals had drawn near she and her husband Pinian and her mother Albina had started on travels which eventually led them to their African estate, which was near Thagaste. They were enormously rich. It is said that they owned estates not only in Rome, Africa, and in several parts of Italy, but also in Sicily, France, Spain, and Great Britain. They were also very pious, and made such gifts to the Church that they ultimately beggared themselves. They became very friendly with the Bishop of Thagaste, who was Augustine's old friend Alypius; and when Augustine wrote to them excusing himself from visiting them on the grounds of his bad health, the severity of the winter, and the fretful exigency of his congregation, they persuaded Alypius to take them to Hippo. But when a visit to the basilica was proposed, Pinian, as a precaution against the peril of involuntary priesthood, made Augustine promise not to ordain him

225

even if the congregation demanded it. It is relevant to note that Augustine, though himself a victim of compulsory ordination, had come in a very few years to apply it himself; there exists a very sinister letter in which he bids one Castorius try to like being a bishop, since that is certainly what he is going to be.

Pinian's precaution was, however, of no avail. The congregation immediately recognized the wealthy and pious visitors, and shouted to Augustine that he must forcibly ordain Pinian as presbyter; and when Augustine told them of his promise they were damped only for a minute, and suggested that he should either break it, or evade it by arranging for another bishop to perform the ordination. Meanwhile Melania and Pinian fled in terror into a recess in the choir. Augustine flatly refused to do the mob's bidding, saying that if they insisted he himself would cease to be the bishop, and then a riot broke out. It was so severe that, as Augustine admits, he was alarmed for the safety of the buildings, and dared not take Alypius through the crowd, because they were shouting insults at him for having forestalled them and secured the rich man for his own congregation, and seemed likely to attack him. While Augustine stood facing this disorder and wondering what to do, Pinian sent a monk to tell him that he wanted to swear to the people that if he were ordained he would at once leave Africa. But Augustine saw that this would only make the crowd more dangerous, and while he was pondering what to do he received another message from Pinian, who, alarmed by the increasing tumult, offered to withdraw this defiant oath and make the more conciliatory promise that he would consent to settle down in Hippo, provided he were not forcibly ordained. Augustine went to discuss this offer with Alypius, but he, doubtless remembering the occasion in his youth when he was found minding the burglar's tools, and reflecting that he would have to face not only Pinian and his wife but his notoriously forceful mother-in-law Albina, tersely replied, "Please don't ask me."

Augustine then saw nothing for it but to announce this second promise to the crowd, who, however, accepted it only with the shrewd proviso that Pinian must also promise that if he were ordained it should be in their church. Augustine went back and put this to Pinian, and they set about framing the terms of the oath. Pinian insisted on certain conditions being stated to cover such necessities as might compel him to leave Hippo, and of these he named first of all an invasion of barbarians. It must be remembered that these unhappy

226

people had fled Rome before the Goths, and that rebellious Africa was known to be half-hearted in her own defence. But Augustine objected to this condition, on the curious ground that the people would regard it as a prophecy of evil; and Melania was not allowed to mention the possible effects on their healths of the climate, though a Roman lady might well have shrunk from permanent residence in North Africa. Finally Pinian insisted on including a general clause to cover all necessities, but Augustine was right when he warned him that the mob would not tolerate it. When the clause was read, such a riot broke out that the terrified Pinian eagerly took an oath without reservation to become a permanent resident of Hippo and be ordained there or nowhere. At this "the people recovered their cheerfulness once more," and after giving thanks to God, demanded that the oath should be properly signed and witnessed. Pinian gave his signature, and when Alypius and Augustine were urged to witness it, "not by the voices of the crowd, but by faithful men of good report as their representatives," Augustine was willing to do so. But Melania sternly forbade him to put his episcopal signature to such a discreditable document. From her gesture we can see how profoundly shocked the Roman visitors were by those African disorders; and it is characteristic of Augustine that he records the rebuke without realizing its significance. Once the oath was recorded, the people let the party leave the church, and by the next day all three visitors had fled back to Thagaste. Once there, Pinian and Melania did not hesitate to declare that there could be no question of keeping an oath extorted in such circumstances, and to make the most definite allegations that not only had the congregation of Hippo shown unpardonable cupidity in attempting to kidnap a wealthy stranger, but that Augustine had acted as their accomplice.

Of the full force of this accusation Augustine must be acquitted. He had not wanted the Romans to come to Hippo; his invitation to them had been so lukewarm that it might have been taken as a hint that they should stay away. But he was guilty of a great deal. Even Alypius, lifelong slave as he had been to his admiration for Augustine, felt that this time his idol had gone too far, and when he got home he sat down and wrote a stinging complaint against the threats and insults to which he had been subjected at Hippo, and the blackmailing of Pinian. How much justice was on his side can be judged from Augustine's bland and unscrupulous replies to Alypius' and Albina's remonstrances. He makes no apology for the shocking manners and morals of his flock, nor for his own failure to have them under control, and mentions with an air of satisfaction that only one of the monks from his own monastery took part in the riot. He minimizes their offences. "Even if there were mixed in the crowd some who are paupers or beggars, and even if they did help to increase the clamour, and were actuated by the hope of some relief to their wants out of your honourable affluence, even this is not, in my opinion, base covetousness." And as for the oath: "Tell me, I beseech you, what hardship deserving the name of exile, or transportation, or banishment, is involved in his promise to live in Hippo?" So might a general defend his beloved legionaries. They may sometimes raise Cain round the camp-fire and try their hand at a bit of looting and bonneting civilians, but that only shows their high spirits. With an altogether pagan verbalism he insists that Pinian must keep his oath, since an oath is an oath however it was extorted. To give his views a Christian appearance he makes perfunctory allusions to the Scriptures, but he speaks much more of the etiquette of the battlefield, of Regulus and his oath to the Carthaginians, and of the Roman censors who refused to inscribe on the roll the names of the senators who had committed perjury even though they were compelled to it by the fear of death. Had not this bluff and jolly buccaneer been a priest, one would never have guessed from those letters that he had even been baptized.

Augustine wrote as one who can think only in terms of Roman order; but as the proceedings at Hippo show, he lacked its substance. His congregation had the licence but not the discipline of soldiery. What dangers were latent in the situation can be guessed from the letter which he wrote to Count Boniface in 417. This is a very long and full recital of the benefits derived from that "function of Christian charity" known as persecution, which is "unwilling to spare the brief fires of the furnace for the few, lest all should be abandoned to the everlasting fires of hell"; and interesting as it is in its revelation of how imagination can be killed in a man by cruel duties, it derives still greater interest from the person to whom it is written and the reasons for which he had invited such a letter. Boniface was a Greek who had defended Marseilles against Ataulf and as a reward had been appointed to Africa first as a commissioner to the Imperial Government, then as the military governor. He was an able man, and was both a sincere believer and the husband of a very pious wife. At that time Imperial servants had much reason to profess Christianity, for both the Emperor Honorius and his dominating sister Placidia were devout. Boniface would therefore be moved by temperament, affection, and ambition to accept the orthodox Catholic policy. But it is evident that Augustine's letter was an attempt to allay doubts which were vexing Boniface as an official. It was not quite as certain as might have been wished that the persecution of the Donatists was producing unity rather than disunity: that Augustine's use of the Roman formula was not, considering the special African circumstances, an ultimate injury to Rome. There was to be nothing so simple, in this most complicated man, as a final victory for Patricius.

VIII

Rome needed no further enemies. She had enough. In 416 Wallia the Goth sent a fleet to attack Africa. It was shattered by storms near Gibraltar, and though he had to make peace thereafter to get food for his starving army, and become an ally of Rome in her war with Spain against the Vandals, this was no true victory for the Empire. It registered no recovery of health. About the edges of tortured Africa tribesmen eroded civilization by their incessant raids. During the next few years the Empire failed at the heart as well. The weak Honorius suddenly turned in hatred against his sister Placidia, and Old Rome stood by him, while all the new barbarian allies on whom the dying Empire had come to depend stood by her. There followed after this a quarrel between Boniface and a general called Castinus. It has been conjectured that the reason for this was that Boniface had been put forward as commander-in-chief by Placidia, and that Castinus was the candidate preferred by Honorius. In any case, Boniface was an unhappy and disillusioned man. His beloved wife had died in 418, and he had been so stricken by grief that he would have resigned his military career and become a monk, had not this intention so shocked and alarmed Augustine that he travelled all the way from Hippo to Boniface's camp in southern Numidia in order to dissuade him. We see the official trend of Augustine's mind in his own description of this interview; it appeared to him Boniface's plain duty to abandon his desire to go into seclusion and cultivate the spirit when he had the opportunity of maintaining the peace and unity of Roman Africa in the Imperial service. But now Boniface found difficulty in going on with his work, since he lost his bid for the command of the forces, though he had made an attempt to consolidate his position among the allies by marrying a barbarian princess, who had to be hastily converted from Arianism to Catholicism before the ceremony could take place. He had to retire to Africa, whence he watched with some satisfaction the defeat of Castinus in Spain, and set up as a pro-Placidian governor. He sent all his revenues not to Honorius but to Placidia, who was an exile at Constantinople, and waited his time.

In 423 Honorius died, but his time did not come. To keep Placidia and her children out of power, Castinus, who had still command of the forces, put on the vacant throne a State official named John; and then he revived his feud with Boniface. All available forces were sent against him to Africa. But Placidia's son, Valentinian, dethroned John and replaced Castinus by a general called Felix. But still the time had not come for Boniface. There was some silly court intrigue, and Boniface was shabbily rewarded for his loyalty to Placidia, and, still worse, knew that Felix had conceived a grudge against him. There can be no exaggerating the plight of Boniface, who had waited so long for order to be restored in Italy, and then found that it was no order; who had hoped to be a firm administrator supported by a strong central government, and who found himself in a noose at the end of an immensely long coil of rope. When Felix recalled him to Italy in 427 he refused to go, and stood forward frankly as a rebel. Gildo and Heraclian had already shown how inevitable it was for any able-spirited man to feel that Africa must cut the now unnatural tie with decaying Rome.

The first expeditionary force sent over by Felix, Boniface defeated easily. But the second, which was composed largely of Gothic mercenaries, and led by a German general, was more formidable. It was for fear of it, some historians tell us, that Boniface treacherously appealed to the Vandals and let them into Africa: but such historians wrote a century later. The evidence of the one contemporary historian who writes in any detail makes it seem more probable that the Vandals, who had for long been casting covetous glances at Africa and had since 419 moved their headquarters to the south of Spain, had planned an invasion quite independently, and that the contending parties in the State had both tried as a last resort to enlist the support of the invaders. By 425 the Vandals had made a landing near Tangier. Though this was then treated as a part of Spain, and not of Africa, it was near enough to fill any governor with the most piteous and desperate forebodings of a breaking world.

To Boniface, at the time of this rupture with Felix, Augustine wrote a letter which is amazing in its vigour for a man of seventy-six. It is, however, not at all a wise letter, and it illustrates painfully two of Augustine's chief failings in its ill-timed garrulity about sexual matters, and in its inability to realize that other people also had tragedies and consciences. Augustine begins by expressing regret that Boniface should have married a second time, and claims, in the blandly unscrupulous tone noticeable in the letters about Melania and Pinian, that he had no moral right to remarry, because he had expressed the intention of not doing so in the interview in the south Numidian camp. "When I learned of your second marriage," Augustine writes, in the manner of the worst kind of headmistress, "I was, I must confess it, struck dumb with amazement"; yet no oath or promise had been given. There follows gossip about concubines, and an allegation, which no commander of forces would find helpful, that many persons were following Boniface because they were "desirous of obtaining through this certain advantages which they covet, not with a godly desire, but from worldly motives." It goes on to complain that Boniface was not dealing as he should with the invasion of Africa by savage tribesmen from the interior—("I need say nothing more on this subject because your own reflection must suggest more than I can put into words")—and accounts for this by a thinly veiled accusation of treachery. These denunciations were for long regarded as weighty evidence against Boniface, but they cannot be taken seriously by a generation which can remember the speeches made during the war in which the lesser sort of public man used to account for the Cabinet's failure to do anything about winning the war by the hypothesis that it had been bribed by German gold. We know little of Boniface beyond his early piety and his grief for his dead wife, but we can guess how he or any other able man would have felt as he sat trapped between the Imperial Government, the Vandals, and the tribesmen, and what a vexation this letter must have been to him; particularly as he had already begged Augustine with some impatience not to write of matters about which he knew nothing.

But there are certain points in that letter which are significant. One is its discourtesy. It is amazing that a bishop could with impunity write a letter to the representative of government in Africa covering him with insults and even making slighting references to his wife. This was partly due to Augustine's charm. It is not at all irrelevant to his theological system, with its emphasis on salvation by grace and predestination, that he was one of those people who never deserve forgiveness but always receive it. Monnica he had often offended, but she counted nothing against him. We read of him raising the just anger of Jerome, Alypius, Melania, and Pinian, and then we read later that they are friends again, though there was no reconciling tie of blood. But it was partly due to the position of the Church, which alone spoke with authority in that world of collapsing institutions. That Augustine took advantage of this position to show indifference to his correspondents' feelings is not altogether the fault of his egotistical temperament. He was following a fashion. The early Christians cultivated aggressiveness as a noble defiance of the pagan State, an advertisement that they enjoyed heartening knowledge of the next world and need fear nothing in this. When Cyprian wrote the letter quoted at the beginning of this book, there was great courage in his insolence, for he was addressing the representative of the power which a few years later cut off his head. But the tide turned, and the Church became the ally and even the dictator of the State, far too quickly for Christians to drop the habit of insolence when the occasion for it passed. Hence the curious rudeness that broke out between Christian correspondents when they happened to differ. "Thou biddest me take back this lie; cease thou to be a liar thyself," writes Jerome to Rufinus, and the passage has many parallels in patristic literature. Hence, too, the harshness of language which the orthodox used of heretics and schismatics, and hence, since it is difficult to use harsh language about a man and retain the capacity to treat him justly, the violence of even those persecutions which were initiated with the intention of suppressing violence. What damage this provocative habit had caused can be guessed from one of the accusations which Augustine made against Boniface. He had, it seems, let some of his household lapse from Catholicism into Arianism, and his infant child had been baptized into that heresy. Since he must have longed for national unity more than anything else, it looks very much as if he had come to doubt whether Catholicism was an unmixed blessing for Africa, and was inclining towards treating the heresies with tolerance. Augustine's lack of such doubts, his comfortable persistence in the habit of rebuke, and his assumption that the situation could be satisfactorily dealt with by determined offence and puritan manners, make him seem by comparison insanely rash, but there must be remembered the strain which that time laid upon the imaginative man. There was innate in Augustine the desire that the world should go up in flames which marks the romantic artist; and this had been stimulated by the apprehension of the age, which Cyprian describes, that the world itself was on the eve of death. This apprehension had itself been inflamed to fever by the chiliastic fantasies of Christianity, its sumptuous visions of the last things and their replacement by the divine.

If Augustine had had full prescience he might, indeed, have awaited the future with composure, since, though the old order was ended, it was to be succeeded by a new one which was, century in, century out, to be dominated by his spirit. It was not only that all the important subsequent manifestations of the religious spirit were to show signs of his influence, that his insistence on the unity of the Church was to confirm Catholicism as his doctrine of predestination was to beget Calvinism. It was also that humanity, and in particular the artist, was to think and feel as much as he thought and felt; that a great many people have recognized a peculiar fitness in the designation "the first modern man," which was bestowed on him by two German writers. Augustine took as his subject-matter, with a far greater simplicity and definiteness and vigour than any earlier Christian writer, a certain complex of ideas which are at the root of every primitive religion: the idea that matter, and especially matter related to sex, is evil; that man has acquired guilt through his enmeshment in matter; that he must atone for this guilt to an angry God; and that this atonement must take the form of suffering, and the renunciation of easy pleasure. Instead of attempting to expose these ideas as unreasonable, or to replace them by others, as nearly all the ancient philosophers had done, Augustine accepted them and intellectualized them with all the force of his genius. It would be easy to prove how closely the modern world has followed in his steps by examining the works of its great artists; the Augustinian content of Shakespeare alone is impressive. But the point can be more briefly proven if it be considered that the unique position of Goethe is due very largely to his freedom from Augustinian conceptions; and that today, fifteen hundred years after Augustine's death, after a raking attack on the supernatural and a constant search for a rational philosophy lasting several centuries, the greatest artists still restrict themselves to his subject-matter. Lawrence tried to investigate the complex of ideas and test its validity by exposing himself to its emotional effects, which had long been disregarded in the one-sided discussion of its intellectual bases. Proust made a colossal effort to justify his sense of dualism by marshalling all the evidence for the horrid oddity of matter collected by his senses, and to soothe the sting by propounding that experience could be converted into beauty by being removed into the immaterial and therefore clean world of memory. James Joyce in *Ulysses*, representing the spirit by the unstained boy Stephen Dedalus and matter by the squatting buffoon Leopold Bloom, finds a myth that perfectly expresses the totality of facts and emotional effects of the Augustinian complex. It is the ring-fence in which the modern mind is prisoner.

But the content of the artist's mind is not peculiar to itself. Its sole peculiarity lies in its exceptional consciousness of a content which we know it shares with the rest of men, since if it did not, works of art would not be generally comprehensible communications. Since that content is common to all, men of action as well as artists must be dominated by this same deep fantasy of dualism and the need to wipe out guilt by suffering; and perhaps it is this which causes the pain of history, the wars, the persecutions, the economic systems which put many to the torture of poverty and raise up rich men only to throw them down, the civilizations that search for death as soon as opportunities for fuller life open before them. There is confirmation for this suspicion in the life of Augustine, who as an artist and philosopher was so explicitly dualist and tragic, who as a man of action had some hand in a policy that dealt the final blow to a system which had once promised ease to man, and submerged his land in disaster.

In 429 Gaiseric and the whole of the Vandal forces left Spain behind them and launched an attack on Africa. The Romans and Boniface dropped their feud. They tried to make a treaty with the Vandals, but they were no longer in a position to exact consideration. Boniface then went out against the invaders at the head of a force of Romans and Visigothic mercenaries, but he was beaten. The Vandals broke over the country like a wave. There was ground for terror, but the old man did not feel it. We have four important letters belonging to these last months. One is an exultant account of the conversion of a physician named Dioscorus, who had promised to be baptized in panic at his daughter's sickness, but after her recovery had forgotten his vow until the Lord smote him with blindness. During the baptismal rite he omitted for some reason to repeat the Creed, so although the Lord gave him back his sight He afflicted him with partial paralysis and total loss of speech. After he had confessed his omission and written out the Creed, the Lord removed the paralysis, but left him dumb. "So," writes Augustine, "that frivolous loquacity which, as you know, blemished his natural kindliness, and made him, when he mocked Christians, exceedingly profane, was altogether destroyed in him. What shall I say, but 'Let us sing a hymn unto the Lord, and highly exalt Him for ever! Amen.'" The second is a letter to an Imperial Commissioner, bidding him remember what he himself seemed sometimes to have forgotten, that "it is a higher glory to slay war with a word, than to slay men with a sword"; and the third is a touching expression of gratitude, pitiful in its suggestion of old age, for praise that this Commissioner had bestowed on his books. The fourth is a letter to a priest who had enquired of him whether he might forsake his church and flee before the invaders, since he could not see what good he did by waiting to see men slain, women outraged, churches burned, and himself put to the torture. The old man reminds him of the unhappy mob that took refuge in the churches when the enemy were near, crying out in fear, begging for the Sacraments. "If the ministers of God be not at their posts at such a time . . . !" He himself stood firm at Hippo, though Boniface was soon to retreat to it, though it was soon to be besieged. One remembers the story that the Roman legionaries had told long before, of lions met in the Numidian sands that knew the human tongue. This one could still wake echoes with a good round-mouthed roar, though it was in its seventy-sixth year.

Perhaps there was some truth in the other story that the Roman soldiers used to tell of Africa, the story of pythons that put legions to flight. For as the Vandals swept across the country, out ran the Donatists to meet them, eager to change masters, frantic to avenge themselves on the State and Church which Augustine had made them hate. No defending force could stand its ground against such ubiquitous treachery. The legions had to break and run, vanquished years before by the correspondence which had passed backwards and forwards between Ravenna and Hippo, weaving of complaint and edict and enforcement a shroud for Roman Africa. Augustine had seemed in later life a copy of Patricius, but he used the high-handed, choleric method of Patricius to destroy the system with which Patricius had been identified in his mind. It was as if a python had wound itself round the Roman standard and very slowly crushed it with its coils.

Throughout the siege, the text was on Augustine's lips, "Righteous art Thou, O Lord! and upright are Thy judgements." Sitting at table among his monks and the fugitive priests who had come for shelter to his monastery, he uttered the stoic and not specifically Christian prayer: "I ask God to deliver this city from its enemies, or if that may not be, that He give us strength to bear His will, or at least that He take me from this world and receive me in His bosom." Presently it became apparent that the last part of his prayer was to be answered, and he took to his bed. He would have driven the world out of his cell, but a man brought him his sick son to cure by the laying on of hands. Augustine answered bluffly that if he had any power to cure the sick the first person he would use it on would be himself. The man persisted, however, that an angelic voice had told him to make the demand. So Augustine laid hands on the boy, and he was cured; but the old man was not yet to be allowed his rest, for there came to him petitioners who wanted his prayers for some who were possessed by devils. At that Augustine burst into tears. He prayed very vehemently for the afflicted, and the devils went out of them. Then he became so ill it grew plain he must be left in peace. Except for the physicians and the monks who took him food no one disturbed him, and he lay contemplating the Penitential Psalms, which he had had copied out in very large writing on the walls of his cell, and abandoning himself to weeping. At the end of ten days the parts of Monnica and Patricius which had joined to make his body and soul had weakened and dissolved; and outside the convent the civilization which was as a body to the soul of Rome and Africa also suffered death. Nothing remained except the Church to which his mother had given him, the Mother Church, where as much of the human tradition was stored as would permit man to repeat in another place the cycle of building up and tearing down to which, as yet, he has been limited.

III. POLITICAL AND CRIME
REPORTAGE

FROM Greenhouse with Cyclamens I [1946]
From A Train of Powder (1955)

Mr. Setty and Mr. Hume
From A Train of Powder (1955)

FROM The New Meaning of Treason (1964)*
Revised and expanded from *The Meaning of Treason* (1949)

*British title: *The Meaning of Treason*, Revised Edition [1964]

FROM Greenhouse with Cyclamens I [1946]

From A Train of Powder

1

There rushed up towards the plane the astonishing face of the world's enemy: pine woods on little hills, grey-green glossy lakes, too small ever to be anything but smooth, gardens tall with red-tongued beans, fields striped with copper wheat, russet-roofed villages with headlong gables and pumpkin-steeple churches that no architect over seven could have designed. Another minute and the plane dropped to the heart of the world's enemy: Nuremberg. It took not many more minutes to get to the courtroom where the world's enemy was being tried for his sins; but immediately those sins were forgotten in wonder at a conflict which was going on in that court, though it had nothing to do with the indictments considered by it. The trial was then in its eleventh month, and the courtroom was a citadel of boredom. Every person within its walk was in the grip of extreme tedium. This is not to say that the work in hand was being performed languidly. An iron discipline met that tedium head on and did not yield an inch to it. But all the same the most spectacular process in the court was by then a certain tug-of-war concerning time. Some of those present were fiercely desiring that that tedium should come to an end at the first possible moment, and the others were as fiercely desiring that it should last for ever and ever.

The people in court who wanted the tedium to endure eternally were the twenty-one defendants in the dock, who disconcerted the spectator by presenting the blatant appearance that historical characters, particularly in distress, assume in bad pictures. They looked what they were as crudely as Mary Queen of Scots at Fotheringay or Napoleon on St Helena in a mid-Victorian Academy success. But it was, of course, an unusually ghastly picture. They were wreathed in suggestions of death. Not only were they in peril of the death sentence, there was constant talk about millions of dead and arguments whether these had died because of these men or not; knowing so well

239

what death is, and experiencing it by anticipation, these men preferred the monotony of the trial to its cessation. So they clung to the procedure through their lawyers and stretched it to the limits of its texture; and thus they aroused in the rest of the court, the people who had a prospect of leaving Nuremberg and going back to life, a savage impatience. This the iron discipline of the court prevented from finding an expression for itself. But it made the air more tense.

It seemed ridiculous for the defendants to make any effort to stave off the end, for they admitted by their appearance that nothing was to go well with them again on this earth. These Nazi leaders, self-dedicated to the breaking of all rules, broke last of all the rule that the verdict of a court must not be foretold. Their appearance announced what they believed. The Russians had asked for the death penalty for all of them, and it was plain that the defendants thought that wish would be granted. Believing that they were to lose everything, they forgot what possession had been. Not the slightest trace of their power and their glory remained; none of them looked as if he could ever have exercised any valid authority. Göring still used imperial gestures, but they were so vulgar that they did not suggest that he had really filled any great position; it merely seemed probable that in certain bars the frequenters had called him by some such nickname as "The Emperor." These people were also surrendering physical characteristics which might have been thought inalienable during life, such as the colour and texture of their skins and the moulding of their features. Most of them, except Schacht, who was white-haired, and Speer, who was black like a monkey, were neither dark nor fair any more; and there was amongst them no leanness that did not sag and no plumpness that seemed more than inflation by some thin gas. So diminished were their personalities that it was hard to keep in mind which was which, even after one had sat and looked at them for days; and those who stood out defined themselves by oddity rather than character.

Hess was noticeable because he was so plainly mad: so plainly mad that it seemed shameful that he should be tried. His skin was ashen, and he had that odd faculty, peculiar to lunatics, of falling into strained positions which no normal person could maintain for more than a few minutes, and staying fixed in contortion for hours. He had the classless air characteristic of asylum inmates; evidently his distracted personality had torn up all clue to his past. He looked as if his mind had no surface, as if every part of it had been blasted away except the depth where the nightmares live. Schacht was as noticeable because he was so far from mad, so completely his ordinary self in these extraordinary circumstances. He sat twisted in his seat so that his tall body, stiff as a plank, was propped against the end of the dock, which ought to have been at his side. Thus he sat at right angles to his fellow defendants and looked past them and over their heads: it was always his argument that he was far superior to Hitler's gang. Thus, too, he sat at right angles to the judges on the bench confronting him: it was his argument that he was a leading international banker, a most respectable man, and no court on earth could have the right to try him. He was petrified by rage because this court was pretending to have this right. He might have been a corpse frozen by rigor mortis, a disagreeable corpse who had contrived to aggravate the process so that he should be specially difficult to fit into his coffin.

A few others were still individuals. Streicher was pitiable, because it was plainly the community and not he who was guilty of his sins. He was a dirty old man of the sort that gives trouble in parks, and a sane Germany would have sent him to an asylum long before. Baldur von Schirach, the Youth Leader, startled because he was like a woman in a way not common among men who looked like women. It was as if a neat and mousy governess sat there, not pretty, but with never a hair out of place, and always to be trusted never to intrude when there were visitors: as it might be Jane Eyre. And though one had read surprising news of Göring for years, he still surprised. He was so very soft. Sometimes he wore a German Air Force uniform, and sometimes a light beach suit in the worst of playful taste, and both hung loosely on him, giving him an air of pregnancy. He had thick brown young hair, the coarse bright skin of an actor who has used grease paint for decades, and the preternaturally deep wrinkles of the drug addict. It added up to something like the head of a ventriloquist's dummy. He looked infinitely corrupt, and acted naïvely. When the other defendants' lawyers came to the door to receive instructions, he often intervened and insisted on instructing them himself, in spite of the evident fury of the defendants, which, indeed, must have been poignant, since most of them might well have felt that, had it not been for him, they never would have had to employ these lawyers at all. One of these lawyers was a tiny little man of very Jewish appearance, and when he stood in front of the dock, his head hardly reaching to the top of it, and flapped his gown in annoyance because Göring's smiling wooden mask was bearing down between him and his client, it was as if a ventriloquist had staged a quarrel between two dummies.

Göring's appearance made a strong but obscure allusion to sex. It is a matter of history that his love affairs with women played a decisive part in the development of the Nazi party at various stages, but he looked as one who would never lift a hand against a woman save in something much more peculiar than kindness. He did not look like any recognized type of homosexual, yet he was feminine. Sometimes, particularly when his humour was good, he recalled the madam of a brothel. His like are to be seen in the late morning in doorways along the steep streets of Marseilles, the professional mask of geniality still hard on their faces though they stand relaxed in leisure, their fat cats rubbing against their spread skirts. Certainly there had been a concentration on appetite, and on elaborate schemes for gratifying it; and yet there was a sense of desert thirst. No matter what aqueducts he had built to bring water to his encampment, some perversity in the architecture had let it run out and spill on the sands long before it reached him. Sometimes even now his wide lips smacked together as if he were a well-fed man who had heard no news as yet that his meals were to stop. He was the only one of all these defendants who, if he had the chance, would have walked out of the Palace of Justice and taken over Germany again, and turned it into the stage for the enactment of the private fantasy which had brought him to the dock.

As these men gave up the effort to be themselves, they joined to make a common pattern which simply reiterated the plea of not guilty. All the time they made quite unidiosyncratic gestures expressive of innocence and outraged common sense, and in the intervals they stood up and chatted among themselves, forming little protesting groups, each one of which, painted as a mural, would be instantly recognized as a holy band that had tried to save the world but had been frustrated by mistaken men. But this performance they rendered more weakly every day. They were visibly receding from the field of existence and were, perhaps, no longer conscious of the recession. It is possible that they never thought directly of death or even of imprisonment, and there was nothing positive in them at all except their desire to hold time still. They were all praying with their sharp-set nerves: "Let this trial never finish, let it go on for ever and ever, without end."

The nerves of all others present in the Palace of Justice were sending out a counter-prayer: the eight judges on the bench, who were plainly dragging the proceedings over the threshold of their consciousness by sheer force of will; the lawyers and the secretaries who sat sagged in their seats at the tables in the well of the court; the interpreters twittering unhappily in their glass box like cage-birds kept awake by a bright light, feeding the microphones with French and Russian and English versions of the proceedings for the spectators' earphones; the guards who stood with their arms gripping their white truncheons behind their backs, all still and hard as metal save their childish faces, which were puffy wih boredom. All these people wanted to leave Nuremberg as urgently as a dental patient enduring the drill wants to up and leave the chair; and they would have had as much difficulty as the dental patient in explaining the cause of that urgency. Modern drills do not inflict real pain, only discomfort. But all the same the patients on whom they are used feel that they will go mad if that grinding does not stop. The people at Nuremberg were all well fed, well clothed, well housed, and well cared for by their organizations, on a standard well above their recent experience. This was obviously true of the soldiers who had campaigned in the war, and of the British and French civilians at work in the court; and it was, to an extent that would have surprised most Europeans, true of the American civilians. It never crossed the Atlantic, the news of just how uncomfortable life became in the United States during the war: what the gasoline shortage did to make life untenable in the pretty townships planned on the supposition that every householder had an automobile; how the titanic munitions programme had often to plant factories in little towns that could not offer a room apiece to the incoming workers; what it was like to live in an all-electric house when electric equipment was impossible to replace or repair. By contrast, what Nuremberg gave was the life of Riley, but it was also the water-torture, boredom falling drop by drop on the same spot on the soul.

What irked was the isolation in a small area, cut off from normal life by the barbed wire of army regulations; the perpetual confrontation with the dreary details of an ugly chapter in history which the surrounding rubble seemed to prove to have been torn out of the book and to require no further discussion; the continued enslavement by the war machine. To live in Nuremberg was, even for the victors, in itself physical captivity. The old town had been destroyed. There was left the uninteresting new town, in which certain grubby hotels improvised accommodation for Allied personnel, and were the sole places in which they might sleep and eat and amuse themselves. On five days a week, from ten to five, and often on Saturday mornings, their duties compelled them to the Palace of Justice of Nuremberg, an extreme example of the German tendency to overbuild, which has done much to get them into the recurring financial troubles that make them look to war for release. Every German who wanted to prove himself a man of substance built himself a house with more rooms than he needed and put more bricks into it than it needed; and every Germany city put up municipal buildings that were as much demonstrations of solidity as for use. Even though the Nuremberg Palace of Justice housed various agencies we would not find in a British or American or French law court, such as a Labour Exchange, its mass could not be excused, for much of it was a mere waste of masonry and an expense of shame, in obese walls and distended corridors. It recalled Civil War architecture but lacked the homeliness; and it made the young American heart sicken with nostalgia for the clean-run concrete and glass and plastic of modern office buildings. From its clumsy tripes the personnel could escape at the end of the working day to the tennis courts and the swimming pools, provided that they were doing only routine work. Those who were more deeply involved had to go home and work on their papers, with little time for any recreation but dinner parties, which themselves, owing to the unique character of the Nuremberg event, were quite unrefreshing. For the guests at these parties had either to be co-workers grown deadly familiar with the passing months or VIPs come to see the show, who, as most were allowed to stay only two days, had nothing to bring to the occasion except the first superficial impressions, so apt to be the same in every case. The symbol of Nuremberg was a yawn.

The Allies reacted according to their histories. The French, many of whom had been in concentration camps, rested and read; no nation has endured more wars, or been more persistent in its creation of a culture, and it has been done this way. The British reconstituted an Indian hill station; anybody who wants to know what they were like in Nuremberg need only read the early works of Rudyard Kipling. In villas set among the Bavarian pines, amid German modernist furniture, each piece of which seemed to have an enormous behind, a triple feat of reconstitution was performed: people who were in Germany pretended they were people in the jungle who were pretending they were in England. The Americans gave those huge parties of which the type was fixed in pioneering days, when the folks in the scattered homesteads could meet so rarely that it would have been tiring out the horses for nothing not to let geniality go all up the scale; and for the rest they contended with disappointment. Do what you will with America, it remains vast, and it follows that most towns are small in a land where the people are enthralled by the conception of the big town. Here were children of that people, who had crossed a great ocean in the belief that they were going to see the prodigious, and were back in a small town smaller than any of the small towns they had fled. ◇ ◇ ◇

◇ ◇ ◇ It might seem that this is only to say that in Nuremberg people were bored. But this was boredom on a huge historic scale. A machine was running down, a great machine, the greatest machine that has ever been created: the war machine, by which mankind, in spite of its infirmity of purpose and its frequent desire for death, has defended its life. It was a hard machine to operate; it was the natural desire of all who served it, save those rare creatures, the born soldiers, that it should become scrap. There was another machine which was warming up: the peace machine, by which mankind lives its life. Since enjoyment is less urgent than defence it is more easily served. All over the world people were sick with impatience because they were bound to the machine that was running down, and they wanted to be among the operators of the machine that was warming up. They did not want to kill and be grimly immanent over conquered territory; they wanted to eat and drink and be merry and wise among their own kind. It maddened them further that some had succeeded in getting their desire and had made their transfer to peace. By what trickery did these lucky bastards get their priority of freedom? Those who asked themselves that bitter question grew frenzied in the asking, because their conditions became more and more exasperating. The prisoners who guarded the prisoners of Nuremberg were always finding themselves flaring up into rage because they were using equipment that had been worn out and could not be replaced because of the strain on the supply lines. It could not be credited how often, by 1946, the Allies' automobiles broke down on German roads. What was too old was enraging; and who was too new was exasperating too. The commonest sight in a Nuremberg office was a man lifting a telephone, giving a number, speaking a phrase with the slurred and confident ease that showed he had used it a thousand times before to set some routine in motion, and breaking off in a convulsion of impatience. "Smith isn't there? He's *gawn*? And you don't know anything about it? Too bad. . . ." All very inconvenient, and inconvenient too that it is impossible to imagine how, after any future war, just this will not happen—unless that war is so bad that after it nothing will happen any more.

The situation would have been more tolerable if these conquerors had taken the slightest interest in their conquest; but they did not. They were even embarrassed by it. "Pardon my mailed glove," they seemed to murmur as they drove in the American automobiles, which were all the Nuremberg roads then carried save for the few run by the British and French, past the crowds of Germans who waited for the streetcars beside the round black Nuremberg towers, which were hollow ruins; or on Sundays, as they timidly strolled about the villages, bearing themselves like polite people who find themselves intruding on a bereaved family; or as they informed their officers, if they were GIs, that such and such a garage proprietor or doorman was a decent fellow, really he was, though he was a kraut. Here were men who were wearing the laurels of the vastest and most improbable military victory in history, and all they wanted was to be back doing well where they came from, whether this was New York or the hick towns which comedians name to raise a laugh at the extreme of American provincialism. Lines on a young soldier's brow proclaimed that he did not care what decoration he won in the Ardennes; he wanted to go home and pretend Pearl Harbor had never been troubled and get in line for the partnership which should be open for the right man in a couple of years' time. A complexion beyond the resources of the normal bloodstream, an ambience of perfume amounting almost to a general anaesthetic for the passer-by, showed that for the female the breaking of traditional shackles and participation in the male glory of military triumph cannot give the pleasure to be derived from standing under a bell of white flowers while the family friends file past.

Considering this huge and urgent epidemic of nostalgia, the behaviour of these exiles was strangely sweet. They raged against things rather than against one another. At breakfast in the Grand Hotel they uttered such cries as, "Christ, am I allergic to powdered eggs with a hair in 'em!" with a passion that seemed excessive even for such ugly provocation; but there was very little spite. The nicknames were all good-humoured, and were imparted to the stranger only on that understanding. When it was divulged that one of the most gifted of the interpreters, a handsome young person from Wisconsin, was known as the Passionate Haystack, care was taken to point out that no reflection on her was implied, but only a tribute to a remarkable hair-do. This kindliness could show itself as imaginative and quick-witted. The Russians in Nuremberg never mixed with their Allies except at large parties, which they attended in a state of smiling taciturnity. Once a young Russian officer, joyously drunk, walked into the ballroom of the Grand Hotel, which was crowded with American personnel, and walked up to a pretty stenographer and asked her to dance. The band was not playing, and there was a sudden hush. Someone told the band to strike up again, the floor was crowded with dancing couples, a group gathered round the Russian boy and rushed him away to safety, out of the hotel and into an automobile; and he was dumped on the sidewalk as soon as his captors found an empty street. It is encouraging that those men would take so much trouble to save from punishment a man of whom they knew nothing save that he belonged to a group which refused all intercourse with them. ◇ ◇ ◇

◇ ◇ ◇ But that there had to be a trial cannot be doubted. It was not only that common sense could predict that if the Nazis were allowed to go free the Germans would not have believed in the genuineness of the Allies' expressed disapproval of them, and that the good Germans would have been cast down in spirit, while the bad Germans would have wondered how long they need wait for the fun and jobbery to start again. It was that, there in Germany, there was a call for punishment. This is something that no one who was not there in 1946 will ever know, and perhaps one had to be at Nuremberg to learn it fully. It was written on the tired, temporizing faces and the bodies, nearly dead with the desire for life, of the defendants in the dock. It was written also on the crowds that waited for the streetcars and never looked at the Allied personnel as they drove past, and it was written on Nuremberg itself, in many places: on the spot just within the walls of the old town, outside the shattered Museum of Gothic Art, where a vast stone head of Jehovah lay on the pavement. Instead of scrutinizing the faces of men, He stared up at the clouds, as if to ask what He Himself could be about; and the voices of the German children, bathing in the chlorinated river that wound through the

247

faintly stinking rubble, seemed to reproach Him, because they sounded the same as if they had been bathing in a clear river running between meadows. There was a strange pattern printed on this terrain; and somehow its meaning was that the people responsible for the concentration camps and the deportations and the attendant evocation of evil must be tried for their offences. . . .

It might seem possible that Britain and America might have limited their trials to the criminals they had found in the parts of Germany and Austria which they had conquered, and thus avoided the embarrassment of Soviet judges on the bench. But had they done so the Soviet Union would have represented them to its own people as dealing with the Nazi leaders too gently, to the Germans in the Eastern Zone as dealing with them too harshly. So there had to be an international tribunal at Nuremburg, and the Americans and the British and the French had to rub along with it as best they could. The Nuremberg judges realized the difficulty of the situation and believed that the imperfection could be remedied by strict adherence to a code of law, which they must force themselves to apply as if they were not victors but representatives of a neutral power. It was an idealistic effort, but the cost was immense. However much a man loved the law he could not love so much of it as wound its sluggish way through the Palace of Justice at Nuremberg. For all who were there, without exception, this was a place of sacrifice, of boredom, of headache, of homesickness. ◇ ◇ ◇

◇ ◇ ◇ So the Germans listened to the closing speeches made by Mr Justice Jackson and Sir Hartley Shawcross, and were openly shamed by their new-minted indignation. When Mr Justice Jackson brought his speech to an end by pointing a forefinger at each of the defendants in turn and denouncing his specific share in the Nazi crime, all of them winced, except old Streicher, who munched and mumbled away in some private and probably extremely objectionable dream, and Schacht, who became stiffer than ever, stiff as an iron stag in the garden of an old house. It was not surprising that all the rest were abashed, for the speech showed the civilized good sense against which they had conspired, and it was patently admirable, patently a pattern of the material necessary to the salvation of peoples. It is to be regretted that one phrase in it may be read by posterity as falling beneath the level of its context; for it has a particular significance to all those who attended the Nuremberg trial. "Göring," said Mr Justice Jackson, "stuck a pudgy finger in every pie." The courtroom was not small, but it was full of Göring's fingers. His soft and white and spongy hands were for ever smoothing his curiously abundant brown hair, or covering his wide mouth while his plotting eyes looked facetiously around, or weaving impudent gestures of innocence in the air. The other men in the dock broke into sudden and relieved laughter at the phrase; Göring was plainly angered, though less by the phrase than by their laughter.

The next day, when Sir Hartley Shawcross closed the British case, there was no laughter at all. His speech was not so shapely and so decorative as Mr Justice Jackson's, for English rhetoric has crossed the Atlantic in this century and is now more at home in the United States than on its native ground, and he spoke at greater length and stopped more legal holes. But his words were full of a living pity, which gave the men in the box their worst hour. The feminine Shirach achieved a gesture that was touching. He listened attentively to what Sir Hartley had to say of his activities as a Youth Leader; and when he heard him go on to speak of his responsibility for the deportation of forty thousand Soviet children he put up his delicate hand and lifted off the circlet of his headphones, laying it down very quietly on the ledge before him. It seemed possible that he had indeed the soul of a governess, that he was indeed Jane Eyre and had been perverted by a Mr Rochester, who, disappearing into self-kindled flames, had left him disenchanted and the prey of a prim but inextinguishable remorse. And when Sir Hartley quoted the deposition of a witness who had described a Jewish father who, standing with his little son in front of a firing squad, "pointed to the sky, stroked his head, and seemed to explain something to the boy," all the defendants wriggled on their seats, like children rated by a schoolmaster, while their faces grew old.

There was a mystery there: that Mr Prunes and Prisms should have committed such a huge, cold crime. But it was a mystery that girt all Nuremberg. It was most clearly defined in a sentence spoken by the custodian of the room in the Palace of Justice that housed all the exhibits relating to atrocities. Certain of these were unconvincing; some, though not all, of the photographs purporting to show people being shot and tortured had a posed and theatrical air. This need not have indicated conscious fraud. It might well have been that these photographs represented attempts to reconstruct incidents which had really occurred, made at the instigation of officials as explanatory glosses to evidence provided by eye-witnesses, and that they had found their way into the record by error. But there was much stuff that was authentic. Somebody had been collecting tattooed human skin, and it is hard to think where such a connoisseur could find his pieces unless he had power over a concentration camp. Some of these pelts were infinitely pathetic, because of their obscenity. Through the years came the memory of the inconveniently high-pitched voice of an English child among a crowd of tourists watching a tournament of water-jousting in a French port: "Mummy, come and look, there's a sailor who's got no shirt on, and he has the funniest picture on his back—there's a lady with no clothes on upside down on a St Andrew's Cross, and there's a snake crawling all over her and somebody with a whip." There had been men who had thought they could make a pet of cruelty, and the grown beast had flayed them.

But it was astonishing that there had been so much sadism. The French doctor in charge of these exhibits pondered, turning in his hand a lampshade made of tattooed human skin. "These people where I live send me in my breakfast tray strewn with pansies, beautiful pansies. I have never seen more beautiful pansies, arranged with exquisite taste. I have to remind myself that they belong to the same race that supplied me with my exhibits, the same race that tortured me month after month, year after year, at Mauthausen." And, indeed, flowers were the visible sign of that mystery, flowers that were not only lovely but beloved. In the windowboxes of the high-gabled houses the pink and purple petunias were bright like lamps. In the gardens of the cottages bordering a road which was no longer there, which was a torn trench, the phloxes shone white and clear pink and mauve, as under harsh heat they will not do, unless they are well watered. It is tedious work, training clematis over low posts, so that its beauty does not stravaig up the walls but lies open under the eye; but on the edge of the town many gardeners grew it thus. The countryside beyond continued this protestation of innocence. A path might mount the hillside, through the lacework of light and shadow the pine trees cast over the soft reddish bed of the pine needles, to the upland farm where the wedding party poured out of the door, riotous with honest laughter, but freezing before a camera into honest solemnity; it might fall to the valley and follow the trout stream, where the dragonflies drew iridescent patterns just above the cloudy green water, to the edge of the millpond, where the miller's flax-haired little son played with the grey kittens among the meadowsweet; it would not lead to any place where it seemed other than plain that Germany was a beautiful country, inhabited by a people who loved all pleasant things and meant no harm.

Yet the accusations that were made against the leaders in the Palace of Justice at Nuremberg were true. They were proved true because the accusers did not want to make them. They would much rather have gone home. That could be seen by those who shamefully evaded the rules of the court and found a way into one of the offices in the Palace of Justice which overlooked the orchard which served as exercise ground of the jail behind it. There, at certain hours, the minor Nazi prisoners not yet brought to trial padded up and down, sullen and puffy, with a look of fierceness, as if they were missing the opportunity for cruelty as much as the company of women or whatever their fancy might be. They were watched by American military guards, who stood with their young chins dropped and their hands clasped behind them, slowly switching their white truncheons backwards and forwards, in the very rhythm of boredom itself. If an apple fell from the tree beside them they did not bend to pick it up. Nothing that happened there could interest them. It was not easy to tell that these guards were not the prisoners, so much did they want to go home. Never before can conquerors in charge of their captives have been less furious, more innocent of vengeance. A history book opened in the mind; there stirred a memory that Alexander the Great had had to turn back on the Hydaspes because his soldiers were homesick.

5

Monday, September 30, 1946, was one of those glorious days that autumn brings to Germany, heavy and golden, yet iced, like an iced drink. By eight o'clock a fleet of Allied automobiles, collected from all over Western Germany, was out in the countryside picking up the legal personnel and the visitors from their billets and bringing them back to the Palace of Justice. The Germans working in the fields among the early mists did not raise their heads to look at the unaccustomed traffic, though the legal personnel, which had throughout the trial gone about their business unattended, now had armed military police with screaming sirens in jeeps as outriders.

This solemn calm ended on the doorstep of the Palace of Justice.

Within there was turbulence. The administration of the court had always aroused doubts by a certain tendency toward the bizarre, which manifested itself especially in the directions given to the military police in charge of the gallery where the VIPs sat. The ventilation of the court was bad, and the warm air rose to the gallery, so in the afternoon the VIPs were apt to doze. This struck the commandant, Colonel Andrus, as disrespectful to the court, though the gallery was so high that what went on there was unlikely to be noticed. Elderly persons of distinction, therefore, enjoyed the new experience of being shaken awake by young military policemen under a circle of amused stares. If they were sitting in the front row of the gallery an even odder experience might overtake them. The commandant had once looked up at the gallery and noted a woman who had crossed her ankles and was showing her shins and a line of petticoat, and he conceived that this might upset the sex-starved defendants, thus underestimating both the length of time it takes for a woman to become a VIP and the degree of the defendants' preoccupations. But, out of a further complication of delicacy, he forbade both men and women to cross their ankles. Thus it happened that one of the most venerable of English judges found himself, one hot summer afternoon, being tapped on the shoulder with a white club by a young military policeman and told to wake up, and uncross his legs.

These rules were the subject of general mirth in Nuremberg, but the higher American authorities neither put an end to them nor took their existence as a warning that perhaps the court should be controlled on more sensible lines. <> <> <>

6

The next day, the last day of the trial, there was something like hatred to be seen on the faces of many Germans in the street. The Palace of Justice was even fuller than before, the confusion engendered in the corridors by the inefficient scrutiny system was still more turbulent. There were some bad officials at Nuremberg, and that day they got completely out of hand. One of them, an American, male and a colonel, had always been remarkable for having the drooping bosom and resentful expression of a nursing mother who has had a difficult parturition, and for having throughout the trial nagged at the correspondents as if they were the staff of the maternity ward that had failed him. Hitherto he had not been arresting; the mind had simply noted him as infringing a feminine patent. But standing this day at the entrance of the gallery, staring at obviously valid passes, minute after minute, with the moonish look of a stupid woman trying to memorize the pattern of a baby's bootee, he was strangely revolting in his epicene distress.

The defendants were, however, quiet and cool. They were feeling the relief that many of us had known in little, when we had waited all through an evening for an air raid and at last heard the sirens, and, ironically, they even looked better in health. In the morning session they learned which of them the court considered guilty and which innocent, and why; and they listened to the verdicts with features decently blank except when they laughed. And, miraculously enough, they found the standing joke of the judges' pronunciation of German names just as funny today as before; and the acquittals amused them no end. Three of the defendants were found not guilty. One of these was a negative matter which caused no reaction except comradely satisfaction: that Hans Fritzsche, the radio chief of Goebbels' Propaganda Ministry, should have been found innocent recalled the case of poor Elmer in the classic American comedy, *Three Men on a Horse*. Elmer, it may be remembered, was a gentle creature, who neither smoked nor drank nor used rough words, and when he was found in a compromising attitude with a gangster's moll, and the gangster was wroth, one of the gang inquired, "But even if the worst was true, what would that amount to, in the case of Elmer?"

But the acquittals of von Papen and Schacht were richly positive. The two old foxes had got away again. They had tricked and turned and doubled on their tracks and lain doggo at the right time all their lives, which their white hairs showed had not been brief; and they had done it this time too. And it was absolutely right that they should have been acquitted. It would only have been possible to get them by stretching the law, and it is better to let foxes go and leave the law unstretched. Von Papen had never performed an official act, not even to the initiating of a faintly dubious memorandum, which could be connected with the commission of a war crime or a crime against humanity. He had intrigued and bullied his way through artificially provoked diplomatic crises with the weaker powers, he had turned the German Embassy in Vienna into a thieves' kitchen where the downfall of Schuschnigg was planned and executed; but this skulduggery could not be related to the planning of aggressive warfare, and if he had been found guilty there would have been grounds for a comparison, which would have been quite unfair but very difficult to attack on logical grounds, with Sir Neville Henderson. As for Schacht, he had indeed found the money for the Nazis' rearmament programme, but rearmament itself had never been pronounced a crime; and it is impossible to conceive an article of international law which would have made him a criminal for his doings and not given grounds for a comparison with Lord Keynes. Indeed, the particular jiggery-pokery he had invented to make Germany's foreign trade a profitable racket, particularly in the Balkans, was so gloriously successful, and would have produced such staggering returns if it had been uninterrupted, that he cannot have wished for war.

But, all the same, these were not children of light, and the association of innocence with their names was entertaining. When the verdict on von Papen was pronounced the other defendants gave him good-natured, rallying glances of congratulation; and he looked just as any Foreign Office man would look on acquittal, modest and humorous and restrained. But when the defendants heard that Schacht was to go free, Göring laughed, but all the rest looked grim. A glance at Schacht showed that in this they were showing no unpardonable malice. He was sitting in his customary twisted attitude, to show that he had nothing to do with the defendants sitting beside him and was paying no attention to the proceedings of the court, his long neck stretched up as if to give him the chance to breathe the purer upper air, his face red with indignation. As he heard the verdict of not guilty he looked more indignant than ever, and he tossed his white hairs. Had anyone gone to him and congratulated him on his acquittal he would certainly have replied that he considered it insulting to suppose that any other verdict could have been passed on him, and that he was meditating an action for wrongful imprisonment. There was, to be sure, nothing unnatural or illogical in his attitude. The court had cleared him with no compliments but with no qualifications, and the charges which had been brought against him were definitely part of the more experimental side of Nuremberg. Why should he feel grateful for the acquittal that was his right? There was no reason at all. But it must have been trying to be incarcerated over months in the company of one whose reason was quite so net and dry, who was capable of such strictly logical behaviour as Schacht was to show over the affair of the orange.

This was quite a famous affair, for it amused the other defendants, who laughed at it as they had not been able to laugh at his acquittal, and told their wives. That was how it got known, long before one of the court psychiatrists told it in his book. Each defendant was given an orange with his lunch; and of the three acquitted men two had the same inspiration to perform a symbolic act of sympathy with their doomed comrades by giving their oranges away. Von Papen sent his to von Neurath, and Fritzsche sent his to von Schirach. But Schacht ate his own orange. And why not? Why should a man give up an orange which he had a perfect right to eat and send it to somebody else, just because he had been acquitted of crimes that he had not committed and the other man had been found guilty of crimes that he had committed? The laughter of his fellow prisoners was manifestly unjust. But surely they earned the right to be a little unjust, to laugh illogically, by what happened to them later at the afternoon session.

Something had happened to the architecture of the court which might happen in a dream. It had always appeared that the panelled wall behind the dock was solid. But one of the panels was really a door. It opened, and the convicted men came out one by one to stand between two guards and hear what they had earned. Göring, in his loose suit, which through the months had grown looser and looser, came through that door and looked surprised, like a man in pajamas who opens a door out of his hotel room in the belief that it leads to his bathroom and finds that he has walked out into a public room. Earphones were handed to him by the guard and he put them on, but at once made a gesture to show that they were not carrying the sound. They had had to put on a longer flex to reach from the ground to the ear of a standing man, and the adjustment had been faulty. His guards knelt down and worked on them. On the faces of all the judges there was written the thought, "Yes, this is a nightmare. This failure of the earphones proves it," and it was written on his face too. But he bent down and spoke to them and took a hand in the repair. This man of fifty-three could see the fine wires without spectacles. When the earphones were repaired he put them on with a steady hand and learned that this was not a nightmare, he was not dreaming. He took them off with something like a kingly gesture and went out, renouncing the multitudinous words and gestures that must have occurred to him at this moment. He was an inventive man and could not have had to look far for a comment which, poetic,

255

patriotic, sardonic, or obscene, would certainly have held the ear of the court and sounded in history; and he was a man without taste. Yet at this moment he had taste enough to know that the idea of his death was more impressive than any of his own ideas.

A great mercy was conferred upon him. At this last moment that he would be seen by his fellow men it was not evident that he was among the most evil of human beings that have ever been born. He simply appeared as a man bravely sustaining the burden of fear. This mercy was extended to all the prisoners. It must be recorded that there was not a coward among them. Even Ribbentrop, who was white as stone because of his terror, showed a hard dignity, and Kaltenbrunner, who looked like a vicious horse and gave no promise of restraint, bowed quietly to the bench. Frank, the governor of Poland, he who had repented and become a good Catholic and wore black glasses more constantly than any of the others, gave an odd proof of his complete perturbation. He lost his sense of direction and stood with his back to the bench until he was spun round by the guards. But then he listened courageously enough to his sentence of death.

There was a deep unity in their behaviour as there was a unity in their appearance. The only diversion was the mad little slap Hess gave the guards when they tried to hand him his earphones. He would not wear them, so he did not hear his sentence. The Service defendants, too, were distinct in their bearing, for they had experience of courts-martial and knew the protocol, and bowed and went out when their sentences were delivered. The others seemed to believe that the judge would add to their sentences some phrase of commination, and waited for it, looking straight in front of them; and, curiously enough, they seemed to be disappointed when the commination did not come. Perhaps they hoped that it would also be an explanation. That was what all in the court required: an explanation. We were going to hang eleven of these eighteen men, and imprison the other seven for ten, fifteen, twenty years, or for life; but we had no idea why they had done what they did. All but Streicher had Intelligence Quotients far above the average, and most of them had not been unfavoured in their circumstances. We had learned what they did, beyond all doubt, and that is the great achievement of the Nuremberg trial. No literate person can now pretend that these men were anything but abscesses of cruelty. But we learned nothing about them that we did not know before, except that they were capable of heroism to which they had no moral right, and that there is nothing in the legend that a bully is always a coward.

Then the court rose. It did so in the strict physical sense of the word. Usually when a court rises it never enjoys a foot of real elevation; the judge stalks from the bench, the lawyers and spectators debouch through the corridors, their steps heavy by reason of what they have just heard. But this court rose as a plane takes off, as gulls wheel off the sea when a siren sounds, as if it were going to fly out out of the window, to soar off the roof. The courtroom was empty in a minute or two, and the staff hurried along the corridors into one another's offices, saying good-bye, good-bye to each other, good-bye to the trial, good-bye to the feeling of autumn that had grown so melancholy in these latter days, because of the reddening creepers and the ice in the sunshine, and these foreseen sentences of death. ◇ ◇ ◇

◇ ◇ ◇ The trial had begun its retreat into the past. Soon none of us, we thought, would ever think of it, save when we dreamed of it or read about it in books.

7

Yet we were soon to think often and gravely of Nuremberg and its prisoners. ◇ ◇ ◇

◇ ◇ ◇ The executions were to take place on October 16. Some time during the preceding night Göring killed himself. The enormous clown, the sexual quiddity with the smile which was perhaps too wooden for mockery and perhaps not, had kicked the tray out of the hands of the servants who were bringing him the wine of humiliation, the glasses had flown into the air and splintered with a sound too much like laughter. This should not have happened. We are all hunters, but we know ourselves hunted by a mightier hunter, and our hearts are with the hunted, and we rejoice when the snared get free of the snare. In this moment visceral mournfulness changed to visceral cheerfulness; we had to applaud for the flesh that would not accept the doom that had been dealt to it but changed it to an expression of defiance. All those people who had fled from Nuremberg, British and American and French, who were scattered over the world, trying to forget the place of their immurement, would straighten up from whatever they had been bent over and burst out laughing before they could help themselves, saying, "That one! We always knew he would get the better of us yet." Surely all those Germans who walked through the rubble of their cities while their conquerors drove, they too would halt, and throw back their heads, and laugh, and say, "That one! We always knew he would get the better of them yet."

Göring should not have been permitted even this small amelioration of his doom. True, we now know some reasons for feeling that he might have been allowed to get a little of his own back. Like all the Nazis, he had been plagued by the attentions of the psychiatrists who haunted Nuremberg Jail, exercising a triple function of priest and doctor and warder hard to approve. They visited the men in the cells and offered themselves as confidants, but performed duties at the behest of the court authorities. When some of the defendants seemed to be taking an unrepentant pro-Nazi stand in their line of defence, one of the psychiatrists worked out, at the commandant's request, a plan for a new seating arrangement at the lunch table in order to break up this group and expose them to other influences. It is not easy to think of an accused person on trial before a national tribunal being subjected to such manipulation by prison officials. There was no silver lining to this cloud. One of these psychiatrists has related, without humorous intention, that when Göring asked him what a certain psychological test had revealed about his character, he replied that it had shown that he lacked the guts to face responsibility. Göring had also the benefit of spiritual care of a remarkably robust kind. He asked the Lutheran chaplain to give him Holy Communion on the night before the executions, but the chaplain refused, on the ground that he was probably shamming.

Nevertheless Göring should not have been given the chance to use his courage to weaken public horror at his crimes, to which his courage was not relevant. The Nazis were maniacs who plastered history with the cruelty which is a waste product of man's moral nature, as maniacs on a smaller scale plaster their bodies and their clothes with their excreta. Since sanity is to some extent a matter of choice, a surrender to certain stimuli and a rejection of others, the nature of mania should never be forgotten. It is unfair, not only to Germans, but to all the world, if the vileness of the Nazis be extenuated; and it was unfair that this Nazi of all Nazis should have been allowed to disguise his gross dementia. This suicide meant a long-term danger too, had it not been for the severity of the following winter. Germany was to be ice-bound and waterlogged and had no time to think of reviving the Nazi party; and if that stretch of bad weather broke Europe's heart, it also broke the continuity of popular political thinking and forced it on to a fresh phase not shadowed by resentment at conquest. But the Allies had failed idiotically in a prime matter. All to no purpose had the military policeman in the VIP gallery shaken the venerable Lord of Appeal and bidden him wake up and uncross his legs. All to no purpose had his colleague waved his club round the ears of the judge and asked him how the hell he had got in. All to no purpose had the maternal colonel shadowed our passes with his pendulous bosom. The cyanide had freely flowed. ◇ ◇ ◇

◇ ◇ ◇ The ten men slowly choked to death. Ribbentrop struggled in the air for twenty minutes. Yet it would be treachery against truth not to concede that justice had been done. Each one of these men who had been hanged had committed crimes for which he would have had to give his life under German law; and it would have then been an axe that killed him. But there are stenches which not the name of justice or reason or the public good, or any other fair word, can turn to sweetness.

Mr Setty and Mr Hume

From A Train of Powder

The murder of Mr Setty was important, because he was so unlike the man who found his headless and legless body. It was news, after the pattern which was established when the Wise Men came out of the East and questioned their way to the stable where the King of the Jews had been born; for they were of course neither kings nor philosophers, as has often been pretended, but newspapermen, and they had seen no star, but had received the call not heard by the ear but felt by the nerves, which announces that somewhere there is news. For news is always an incarnation. Interest comes when people start to act out an idea, to show what a thought is worth when it is worked out in flesh and blood; and both Mr Stanley Setty and his discoverer, Mr Tiffen, were engaged in such dramatization.

Mr Setty had no apparent connection with ideas. He was one of those cases of abnormally unlucky precocity followed by abnormally lucky maturity, which, though the good luck adds up to nothing impressive, nevertheless present modern England with a disquieting problem. He was born Sulman Seti in Baghdad in 1903. He was brought to England by his parents when he was four, and at fourteen was working in a Manchester cotton mill, as the law then permitted. Two years later he and his brother set up in business as shipping merchants with a registered capital of something like three thousand pounds. After two years a receiving order was granted against the little lads, who owed about twenty-five thousand pounds and had only five pounds' assets. As Mr Setty was still only eighteen he could not be made a bankrupt, a status reserved for adults. Four years later, in 1926, he had saved five hundred pounds and started up in business again, calling himself a shipping merchant, but dealing in every kind of merchandise on which he could lay his hands. A year later he had run up twelve hundred pounds' debts, and he ran away with two hundred pounds he had abstracted from the till to

Italy, where his father lived, in hope of getting help from him. But blood ran thinner than water, and he was back in Manchester in the following spring without a penny. He rapidly tried to mend his fortunes by gambling on horses and dogs, but soon acquired another three thousand pounds of debts.

Meanwhile a receiving order had been made against him, and in August 1928, at the age of twenty-four, he was sentenced by a Manchester court to eighteen months' imprisonment, having pleaded guilty to twenty-three offences against the Debtors' and Bankruptcy Acts, such as having kept no proper accounts, left his place of business with the intention of defeating or delaying his creditors, and having used the two hundred pounds with which he went to Italy for his own purposes instead of handing them over to his creditors. His counsel made a moving plea for Mr Setty, putting the blame for his misadventures on the community, which should never have allowed him to be a master or employer—he had "evidently not the mentality to deal with sums of money or large quantities of goods."

Ten years later, in 1938, just before the war, he appeared before another court, still, according to his own account, a shabby and woeful figure. He applied for his discharge from bankruptcy, explaining that he was working as a dealer on commission and that his earnings were pitiful, amounting to two or three pounds a week, and that he wanted to raise some capital and start up in business again. This ambition he could, of course, not gratify until he got his discharge, since as an undischarged bankrupt he could not have a banking account and could not obtain goods on credit without disclosing that he was an undischarged bankrupt. Now it is not difficult for an English bankrupt to get his discharge. He has to submit to an inquisition concerning his means and his character, which he is likely to remember with a smart of shame for the rest of his life, but the findings of the inquisitors are not unmerciful. If a man seems to have failed through ill luck or a local or historical crisis, or if he has worked really hard to pay off his creditors, he can usually get his discharge long before he has paid his debts in full. A percentage of thirty to sixty is often accepted. But the judge to whom Mr Setty made his application evidently found reason to harden his heart beyond the habit of his kind. He gave him a blank refusal, remarking grimly that Mr Setty appeared to be planning to set up business "in a way which might or might not be for the benefit of the business community."

It would be interesting to learn the present income of the counsel who pleaded that Mr Setty had "evidently not the mentality to deal with sums of money or large quantities of goods," or of the judge who refused him his discharge. There is not a chance in the world that the judge, anyway, could enjoy anything but a fraction of the lordly income which, when the clouds of war cleared away, Mr Setty was seen to be enjoying. His address was now impressive. He was not as grand in this respect as his brother, Mr Max Setty, owner of the most fashionable night club in London, The Orchid Room, who lived in an apartment close to the American Embassy in Grosvenor Square, which, fifty years ago, was inhabited exclusively by peers of the realm and bankers. There was perhaps more restraint in his choice of the apartment, which Mr Setty shared with his sister and her husband, Mr Ali Ouri, who is one of the wealthiest Arab landowners in Israel. It is soberly distant from the West End, in the grey stucco district north of Hyde Park. He did nothing to disturb the sedate atmosphere. He did not drink, he gave few parties, he dressed quietly but expensively. He could afford it. He never carried less than one thousand pounds on him, and it was known that, if he was given an hour or two of notice, he could produce five times that sum.

But he still had no banking account. He was still an undischarged bankrupt. He still had no office. Because his ostensible business was dealing in second-hand automobiles, he had a garage in Cambridge Terrace mews, a dead end of old coach houses converted into garages, hidden away behind the stately houses that look on Regents Park. But chiefly he carried on his trade on the pavements and in the public houses and snack bars of Warren Street, that warm, active, robust, morally unfastidious area which has a smack of Dickens' London. This meant, of course, that he was hard to tax. The Inland Revenue must have found it very hard to find out what his profits were and assess him; which meant that the assessment of all other British subjects had to go up. But it meant more than that. This is the centre of the second-hand automobile market, and there, at that time, flourished a curious medley of the legitimate and the illegitimate. Countless automobiles were bought and sold here without blame in the sight of God and man; but there was also a trade in English automobiles designed for export and banned in the home market, in foreign automobiles which had been illegally imported, in new automobiles which were not allowed to be resold under the twelve months' covenant, in stolen automobiles, and in petrol which was drastically rationed.

Mr Setty was active in the purely legitimate trade, but even there something strange was suggested. He was said, by those who knew him only as an automobile dealer, to do business on a scale suggesting that he had capital to the amount of about fifty thousand pounds. He bought many cars, and he often paid large prices for automobiles which used a high amount of petrol at times when the ration of petrol was still small, and would have to keep them for a considerable time before he could resell them. Yet, in 1938, when he had asked for his discharge from bankruptcy, he had represented that he was earn-ing from two to three pounds a week, and a court which was scrutin-izing his affairs with a hostile eye made no suggestion that it disbelieved this story and that he could afford to pay out a dividend to his creditors. It is hard to imagine how in the intervening eleven years he could have accumulated fifty thousand pounds' capital. Taxation alone would have made that impossible, no matter what gifts he might have developed in the meantime. But there was no registered company behind him, and he seemed to have no associates.

He was also a curbside banker. Anybody who wanted to cash a cheque without passing it through a bank came to him and he gave them money for it with a discount, which he never made unreason-able, and passed it on to an associate who had a banking account. Here again is a field where the legitimate and the illegitimate are mingled. The most honest of undischarged bankrupts may like to have some means of cashing the cheques he receives in the way of business other than by explaining his state over the counter of his customer's bank; and we also have a legacy handed down from Tsar-dom. Up till the first five years of this century Great Britain took in countless immigrants from Russia and Poland, and many of these, partly from the inferiority complex the alien feels before the native, and partly from a peasant fear of being swindled by lettered men, never learned to use a bank. Survivors of that generation, and even some of their children, go on cashing their cheques with the man who has never let them down yet and is always to be found outside the Three Feathers between five and seven, even when those cheques run into thousands of pounds. But after the Second World War the curbside banker was used more and more by people who wanted to evade taxes or cover up illegal transactions, such as currency frauds or payments for illegal imports slipped in on false invoices. Nobody

263

can tell now what branches of the profession were cultivated by Mr Setty, since he had no papers. The figures were all in his head, which is perhaps why in the end it was cut off. But certainly every day he handled thousands of pounds.

It could be taken for granted till now that the English racketeer has been less well acquainted with violence than his American counterpart. He and his friends exchange endless cruelties, they cheat one another and squeeze one another in blackmail and railroad one another into prison, but they rarely draw a gun. A beating-up is the furthest most of them ever go, and that is not common nor drastic. But Mr Setty had all that summer been showing signs of acute apprehension. Nothing would induce him to get into any automobile but his own, which is an unusual form of shyness in an automobile dealer, and he went less and less to his own garage; and, indeed, Cambridge Terrace mews at certain hours might feel uncommonly like a mousetrap to a nervous man. His garage lay across the dead end of the mews, and, going in or out of it, he could be covered by a single enemy. He would not go into a strange garage, or go upstairs into an office or warehouse. His clients had to seek him where he stood in the open street or in a public house. All the same, on October 4, he disappeared. He told his family that he was going to look at an automobile in Watford and drove off in his Citroën, which later was found abandoned near his garage.

His family were quick to take alarm. Very soon they offered a thousand pounds reward to anybody who could find him for them. Remoter relatives, including a sister named Mrs Sadie Spectreman, converged on the apartment house, the other tenants of which were startled by their new knowledge of their neighbour. A Miss Constance Palfreyman told the reporters that no, a day had never been actually fixed for the wedding, but they had hoped it would be soon. While this group mourned and wondered, the police remained quite calm. Three days after Mr Setty's disappearance his sister and her husband reported a bizarre circumstance: they went out for the afternoon, after turning the key in two mortice locks in the front door, and came back to find it swinging wide open. Coldly the police issued a notice to the effect that they had found no indication that the apartment had been entered. There was as cold a tone about all their announcements. Indeed, they inspired an announcement which was bound to leave any reader suspecting that they thought that Mr Setty had come to no harm and had left home for his own purposes.

Then, suddenly, part of Mr Setty appeared. Off the Essex coast, some distance north of the Thames estuary, there is a marsh, a curious spring cushion of mud and grasses, patterned with a net of rivulets, and frequented by a great many duck and widgeon. On October 22, Mr Sidney Tiffen, a farm worker who was taking a week's holiday but not leaving home for it, went out in his punt to get some game. He saw something grey being lifted off the hummocks by the tide and thought it was a drogue, the target, not unlike the windsock of an airfield, which a training plane trails behind it in fighting exercises. As he had earned five shillings often enough by picking up these drogues and taking them back to the R A F station not far away, he paddled over to it. When he got there he found that it was not a target but a grey bundle tied up in a thick piece of felt, like the carpet of an automobile. It was so carefully secured with such stout rope that he deduced the packers must have thought it valuable, and wondered if this was flotsam from a wreck. As it was too heavy and unwieldy to take in his punt, he cut it open and found himself looking on a body, swaddled in a cream silk shirt and pale blue silk shorts, from which the head and legs had been hacked away. He drove a stake into the mud and tied the torso to it, then paddled ashore and went two miles over the marshes to fetch the local policeman. Eventually the body was carried ashore and its fingerprints were taken. The murderer who hopes to commit the perfect crime should exchange references with his victim. Mr Setty's enemy had not known that he had ever been convicted, so he had not cut off his hands. Thus Scotland Yard was able to identify his body in a few hours. Seven days later a man of twenty-nine named Brian Donald Hume, owner of a radio shop in a London suburb and managing director of a small factory producing gadgets for domestic and workshop use, was arrested and charged with the murder of Mr Setty. In court he was accused of having dropped the body on the marshes from an airplane.

Very soon the experienced newspaper reader began to suspect that Mr Tiffen was, in some way, an exceptional person. The legal restrictions on crime-reporting in Great Britain are far beyond American conception. They are admirable, and it should be our pride to obey them, for they go far towards preventing trial by prejudiced juries. If a gentleman were arrested carrying a lady's severed head in his arms and wearing her large intestine as a garland round his neck and crying aloud that he and he alone had been responsible for her reduction from a whole to parts, it would still be an offence for any newspaper to suggest that he might have had any connection with her demise until he had been convicted of this offence by a jury and sentenced by a judge. Therefore the veins swell up and pulse on the foreheads of reporters and sub-editors, and somehow their passion seeps into the newsprint and devises occult means by which the truth becomes known. The experienced newspaper reader can run his eye over the columns of newspapers which are paralysed by fear of committing contempt of court (and this fear has justification—only the other day the editor of an English tabloid was sentenced to three months in jail for stating, quite truly, that a man had confessed to a murder for which he was afterwards hanged, and served every day of it), and can learn with absolute certainty, from something too subtle even to be termed a turn of phrase, which person involved in a case is suspected by the police of complicity and which is thought innocent. It was at once apparent that Mr Tiffen was regarded by the police as guiltless of any part in Mr Setty's murder, although his story was precisely that which would have been told by an accessory after the fact who had been paid to take Mr Setty's body out to sink on the flooded marshes, had found it more difficult to do than he had anticipated, and had in panic resolved to try to clear himself of suspicion. There was also discernible to the eye of any newspaper writer the sort of block round Mr Tiffen's name which comes when a reporter would like to write more fully about a person or an event but is stopped by some consideration, most probably lack of space, but sometimes a matter of emotion.

A friend had a legitimate reason for visiting Mr Tiffen, so one evening, after a fifty-mile drive from London, we came to a little town on the east coast just north of the Thames estuary and got out in the high street. In a tower a big clock, pale orange like a harvest moon, bright above the low mist, told us that it was too late to look for Mr Tiffen at his home some miles away. We found a hotel and dinner, and then went out to find a public house where Mr Tiffen might go, for it was Saturday night and not impossible that he might have come in from his village for a glass of beer and a game of darts.

We found the public house which was Mr Tiffen's favourite port of call, but he was not there. A man can be judged by his public house, and we left thinking well of Mr Tiffen. We had settled down to watch a game of darts, and only gradually realized that we had strayed into a private room, reserved by custom for the use of some

266

friends who met there every Saturday night. But the people saw that we did not know and made us welcome; and they were pleasant too to a girl who belonged to that wistful company who love playing games and are duffers at them all. Each time she lifted her hand to throw a dart her eyes shone like a begging dog's; and each time it fell somewhere out of the scoring areas, often right off the board into the wall behind. They were just right for her, not so sorry for her that they rubbed in how bad she was, but sorry enough to dispel any suspicion that they were knocked speechless by her ineptitude. By such signs a gentlemanly society reveals itself, and it looked as if Mr Tiffen might be a gentleman. We went back to our beds, and the next morning showed us the river like grey glass, with a hundred or so little boats lying in the harbour basin. On the opposite bank the sea walls which kept the estuary from doing harm were darker grey, the trees rising above them were black and flat like so many aces of clubs, and some barns were red. Yachtsmen and yachtswomen came down and breakfasted, glossy with content because they were presently to get into their boats and sail off into the shining water, as if taking refuge in a mirror. We drove away through the little town, at the very moment when the lie-abed leisure of Sunday morning changes to the churchgoing bustle, into a countryside that was the simplest arrangement of soil conceivable. It was featureless as the flats of Holland and Belgium it was facing across the North Sea. Some force had patted this piece of it into rising ground, but not very hard; the plateau was quite low. It was cut up by hedges into green pastures and fields of fat black earth. There were a few trees, some farms and cottages, no great houses. It could be seen that a ragged and muddy coastline had kept the railways out of this corner of England, and the sea winds and heavy soil had limited the size of the settlements. Here society had been kept simple; and what simplicity can do if left to itself was shown to us when we halted at a cottage to ask the way, and a woman, young but quite toothless, with several tubby children at her tubby skirts, stared at us without answering, without ill will, without good will, neutral as dough. I wondered whether the reporters' pencils had halted on Mr Tiffen's name because he belonged to this recessive phase of the bucolic, and it had struck them as painful that the worst of town life, in this murdered body, should in its finding have come in contact with the worst of country life.

Before long we found his village. We passed a prim edifice with

"The Peculiar People" painted across its stucco forehead, towards which some lean and straight-backed men and women were walking with an air of conscious and narrow and splendid pride. That strange faith which has no creed and no church organization but believes simply in miracle, in the perpetual re-creation of the universe by prayer, is about a hundred and ten years old. Each death which has occurred during that period is a defeat for it, since all sickness should be prayed into health by the faithful, but these people walked away from us with the bearing of victors. People were streaming towards the church too. We stopped a boy of twelve or so, who must have been a choirboy, for he was carrying a surplice, and asked him the way to Mr Tiffen's house. He smiled at us; the little frown between his eyebrows registered not ill nature but his sense of a conflict between duties. He had to hurry if he was to be in time for church; but one had to be polite to strangers. So he paused to give us full directions, detailed enough to bring us to the housing estate where Mr Tiffen lived. A few houses built of yellow wood stood among others built of alternate slabs of concrete and breese on land which had obviously been a field till about five minutes before.

The door was opened by a young woman. She was at the opposite end of the scale of rural society from the family made of dough. Completely articulate, she explained that she was Mr Tiffen's married daughter, and kept house for him, and was sorry, Dad had gone to see Gran, he always did on Sundays. We asked where Gran lived, suggesting that we might follow him, and, though she was careful not to discourage this, lest she should be implying that Dad would not find our company agreeable, her gaze softened with pity. She did not think we could follow him. Gran lived four miles away in the old coast-guard's cottage. Well, that was all right, we had an automobile and four miles was nothing. Yes, but the cottage was on the sea wall. Two miles was as far as we could go by road, after that the way across the drained marshes, muddy and hard to find. Oh but we went anywhere. And how long ago had Mr Tiffen started? Half an hour? Was he driving as far as the road went, or did he ride a bicycle? Oh no, he walked. We reflected on the remarkable filial piety of Mr Tiffen, who walked eight miles every Sunday to see Gran, and hurried off, saying that we would catch him up.

But we never did. He was not on the road, and he was not in sight when we left the car among the hayricks in a farmyard on the edge of the marshes. We could see Gran's house in the distance, a small

268

coal-black square under the sharp pie-crust edge of the sea wall which
bounded the landscape, and there seemed to be no living thing between us and it. This was, of course, an illusion. The air was alive
with the cries of countless marsh birds. All here was lively. To town
dwellers winter is a season of death, but here it was a brisk cleansing
process. The earth was being tilted so that the heat which had collected during the summer drained away, freshness was flowing in.
Growth had not stopped. Through the black fatness of some fields the
winter wheat and oats were sending up green blades bright as paint,
the ploughed fields lay cut up into dark shining bricks as obviously
nourishing as butter. On that nutrient material we slid and skipped
and fell as we worked our way across the flatlands to the sea wall by
the sides of the deep irrigation ditches. We kept at it hard, pausing
only once when we came on a dead fox, which looked less pathetic
than would seem possible for a dead animal, because it was still a
trim and barbered wise guy. We crossed an irrigation ditch, jumping
from one slope of dark butter to another, and got to the sea wall, and
clambered up through the long wet grasses that clothed it.

The tide was out. So far as the eye could see there stretched the
matted bents of the mudflats: a soft monotony blended of grey and
green and blue and purple. It had a quilted look, for the thousands
of rivulets which cast a network over it followed the same course day
in, day out, and had worn down the mud into channels between the
hummocks some feet deep. To the small creatures which lived here
this must have been a most fantastic landscape. At the bottom of
these deep channels the tiny streams, only a few inches wide, had
their established, deeply graven waterfalls, their rapids which tested
to the utmost the gallantry of straws, the lakes with bays and beaches;
and on the islands grass roots found purchase on the mud by gripping it and one another so that they grew into cushions of jungle, one
plant rising on another like minute vegetable pagodas. The scene was
incised and overstuffed with profligate ingenuity; and it was odd to
think of all this elaboration being wiped out twice in every twenty-
four hours, the rivulets losing their identities in the rough inundation
of the tide, the springing grasses, so obstinate in their intention of
making dry land out of mud, becoming the bottom of the sea. There
was the same spendthrift and impermanent fabrication going on at
ground level as there was over our heads, where great clouds, momen-
tarily like castles, temples, mountains, and giant birds, were blown
by the cleansing winter wind to the edges of the sky, here not clipped

away by hills or streets and astonishingly far apart. There could not have been a more generous scene, nor one which was less suited to receive the remains of Mr Setty, who from infancy had been so deeply involved in calculation, and so unhappily, who had tried keeping figures outside his head and got sent to prison for it, and had kept them inside his head and got killed for it.

Gran's cottage lay about a quarter of a mile away on the landward side of the sea wall, not small, containing at least eight rooms, but nonetheless a deplorable habitation. It was built of brick covered with tarred weatherboard which was falling away in splinters, and the windows of one half of it were broken. The only approach to it was by a couple of planks laid across an irrigation ditch. It seemed unlikely that Mr Tiffen would allow Gran to live there, or that she would consent to do so, unless they were sunk so deeply in poverty that they had forgotten how to make demands. The young woman who had received us at Mr Tiffen's home was perhaps a sport from a rough stock; or, just as probably, we had mistaken for gentleness what was really the inanition of anæmia. We fumbled at a door, but of course it led only into a woodshed, for it was on the seaward side, and here the front door would have to face landwards, or on many days it would be impossible to open and shut it against the gales. As it was, so strong a gust blew on us as we knocked at the right door that we were pulled inside, and thus were suddenly confronted with the character of the Tiffen family, and gaped. It did not matter. They were expert in all forms of courtesy, and knew how to receive guests, and how to give them time to recover themselves if they had lost their self-possession.

They were sitting in a room which was surprisingly warm. The house was much better than we had thought; it kept out the weather, this room had a pleasing and individual shape, the fire was drawing well in the grate. There were four of them, sitting round a table, drinking cups of tea and eating mince pies, and they were obviously an elect race. If they were not eminent it was because generation after generation had chosen not to be, having the sense to know that they would have more fun and do as good a job by remaining obscure. Gran, who was eighty-four, had been a beauty. She was still pleasing to the eye, with abundant white hair and a very white skin, and a plumpness which seemed an accumulation of satisfaction. Her daughter sat beside her, red-cheeked and blunt-featured like a Brueghel peasant, but aristocratic and artistic by reason of her unusual powers of perception. Beside the fire, next to me, sat her husband, and it could be seen that she had taken to herself a man who might have been outside the tribe but was one of the same kind. He had a good head and body, he bore himself with dignity, he made sensible remarks in beautiful English. It was to be noted that on the walls there hung two religious prints, one of them a copy of Leonardo da Vinci's "Last Supper," and numerous photographs of weddings, in which both brides and bridegrooms looked thoroughly pleasant human beings. Obviously the Tiffens, whom I realized had been look-ing after my interests in many ways which I had never suspected, had been carrying on successful experiments in eugenics on quite a large scale. There remained Mr Tiffen, who was sitting over in the window, instantly affording a complete answer to the problem of why the reporters' pencils had checked for a moment when they came to write of him. He was a small man, with dark hair which was tousled because he constantly ran his hands through it in wonder. It could be seen that he was not a rich man, because his spectacles were the cheapest kind that are made; but he needed nothing, he could get everything he wanted out of what he had, save certain things which the nature of things denied him. But he was thinking of that denial in a way which made it something other than a frustration.

Our friend settled with Mr Tiffen the matter which was the cause of our visit, and Mr Tiffen thanked him, and told us all was going well, and set about making our visit a pleasant social occasion. We spoke of the agreeable warmth of the house, and it turned out that Gran's tenancy of it was quite a story. She had gone there as a young woman because her husband had been a coast guard, a member of a marine police force recruited from time-expired naval men, which used to be quartered at regular intervals along the British coastline, but has been superseded since the advent of the combustion engine by smaller mobile forces operating from the harbour. In the old days there had been a row of these houses, and she had had plenty of company; there may have been a dozen adults set down here on the marshes. When the coast guards were disbanded the pensioned men and the widows were allowed to stay on, and as they died off the houses were pulled down. "And quite right too," the women agreed, their voices rising. They were not archaic. They were part of the modern England which was building itself anew. "No woman," they said, "ought to be asked to live like this. There's no water here ex-cept the rainwater in the cisterns on the roof."

Now the family who had lived in the other half of this house had gone; that was why the windows had not been mended after having been broken by the winter gales. So Gran was the last one to linger here, and a mercy it was she had held her ground and not gone up to the village when she could have, before the war, for now her son-in-law and daughter were living with her, and glad they were to have a roof over their heads, for they had lost their home while he was serving in the Navy during the war. Of course it was very hard on the son-in-law to be down here on the sea wall, for he was a builder and never worked nearer than the village and sometimes farther away, so in the winter he had to do the two-mile walk across the marshes in the darkness of early morning and late afternoon. But goodness knows what they would have done if Gran had not been able to take them in; and she could do that only because of the trouble that had fallen on Mr Tiffen.

Sorrow ran through the group like wind through the branches of a tree. It was because of that trouble that Mr Tiffen had been so upset when he found Mr Setty's body. He could not get over it, although it had happened some years ago. He had had a wife, the mother of the girl we had seen in the village and of some sons. She was forty-two years old and had hardly had a day's illness in her life except for childish troubles. She and Mr Tiffen and the children had all lived along of Gran, and all had gone well, none of them had a care in the world. One day she had gone shopping in the village and seemed full of unusual happiness. "I've never seen you looking so well," the grocer had said, and she had answered, "I don't know what's the matter with me, I feel on top of the world." He was not the only one; everybody she met that morning remembered how she had laughed and joked. Then she turned homewards across the marshes. Gran and the children were at the windows, waiting for her; and they saw her pause as she stepped off the plank over the ditch and fall to the ground. They found her lying among the parcels spilled from her shopping bag, dead of heart failure. The faces of these four people asked why there should be all this fuss about murder when death is the real wonder. Think of it, a body is in the state in which all living bodies are, and shows no signs of alteration; it is loved; many people wish it to go on just as it is. Suddenly it is dead; it becomes necessary for those who love it to let the undertakers take it away and bury it. This is much more difficult to understand than somebody dying because they have been stabbed or shot or poisoned by somebody that hates them. Natural death seems far less natural than unnatural death.

After Mr Tiffen's wife died he could not bear to stay in this house. He saw her everywhere in it. So he moved into the council house in the village which we had visited that morning. He had had to pay a great price for it, for council houses are given only to farm labourers; they have priority. He was a fisherman and a fowler, and had been so all his days and loved that life, and he hated agricultural work. But to get one of these council houses he left the water and took a job with a nearby farmer. It irked the family that had he got over his feeling about the haunting of Gran's house and had wanted to come back there, he still could not have exchanged quarters with his brother-in-law and handed his council house over to him, who would have found it most convenient for his building work. The regulation which gave these houses to farm labourers could not have been set aside, and this is reasonable enough, for there is a much greater dearth of farm labourers than of builders; but it is hard for people of independent character, as fishermen tend to be, to accept gladly something that so overrides their wills. That, however, did not vex Mr Tiffen himself; he still missed his wife so much that he could not have borne to go on living in this house.

It was because of his thoughts about death that he had turned so squeamish over this body, and had not been the same man since he had had to touch it. He had been in two minds about taking any notice of it, but it was such a great parcel that someone might have set store by it; it wasn't just a thing you could let go, and once he had seen what it was he had to do his duty by it, though nobody likes handling that sort of thing, really. It was not easy to handle either. He had got the stake into the mud easy enough to tie it to, but he had tried to get the rope between the arm and the body, it made a neater job that way, but then the arm had dropped off and to keep it he had had to put the rope round both arm and body, and that was a business. Then he paddled the punt back to the sea wall, about a hundred yards it was, and he went the two miles over the marshes to the police station, and he found a constable there, about midday it was, and he brought him down to look at it. They sat in the punt together and looked at the great thing held up above the grey waters by the stake, and the constable said to Mr Tiffen, "There's something wrong here," and Mr Tiffen answered, "Yes, I think there's something wrong here." Then the constable said, "It's

273

my opinion this is a murdered body," and Mr Tiffen said, "Yes, I do think it is a murdered body."

These comments on a torso which had been found wrapped in felt and tied up with rope might seem comically obvious; but they were said for a purpose. The constable and Mr Tiffen saw the remains of a human being who had been dispatched without mercy, and they had neither of them ever seen such a thing before, and they knew that if too many of such things happened it would be the doom of their kind. They were deeply moved and had a sound instinct to find words to express their feelings, so that they would commemorate their emotion and make it more powerful. Doubtless they fumbled in their minds among the texts from the Bible and verses from the Church Hymnal and tags from Shakespeare they carried in their minds. But murder is so rare an event that there is no widely known formula for expressing the feeling it arouses, and so they had to do what they could for themselves. They did it well enough, for as Mr Tiffen solemnly repeated what they said, their holy loathing of murder was manifest, and as we listened we were moved back several stages nearer the first and appropriate shock caused by Cain. His talk told then of the fatigue and tedium which follows catastrophe. The constable had said it was not for him to handle the body and that he must telephone headquarters, and then there was much running backwards and forwards that went through that day into the next. For darkness had fallen by the time the great ones were all assembled and ready to take Mr Setty ashore, and they could not find him, and had to wait till he showed up across the flats on his stake through the morning light.

Mr Tiffen acted as guide, made a statement to a Scotland Yard Inspector, learned who the dead man was and that he had reason to expect a thousand pounds' reward, and went home feeling deadly tired and nauseated by the thought of the parcel, though believing that a sleep would get him over that. But it did not; and the next night a chill came on him. He shivered and piled on the bedclothes, and his son-in-law brought him his army greatcoat to lay on top of him, and there is real warmth in those army greatcoats, but still Mr Tiffen shivered so that the bed rattled. In the morning his son-in-law brought him a cup of tea, and he said he did not want it. His son-in-law said, "Go on, try it, Dad, you must have something," but he only brought it up. He was like that for a week, and all that time he was away from work; it was as if he had a real chill, but it was not that, it was the shock of handling the body. Of course he had brought in bodies before. In the war he had found several R A F men and a couple of German sailors out on the marshes, but that was helping them to Christian burial, you didn't think anything of it. But this was different. Mr Tiffen's brother-in-law agreed that it was different, something apart. He had brought in a suicide, a woman that had drownded herself (they all four used the old form of the past participle), and had thought nothing of it, but he would not have done what Mr Tiffen did, not for anything. "Come to think of it," said Mr Tiffen's sister, "have you seen anything in the papers about them burying the body? I haven't." "They ought to lay it at rest," said Gran. "Well, I suppose it's awkward for them having only the one part of it," said the sister. "It'd be better if they got the whole of it. I go up all the time to Mum's room with the binoculars, to look if I can see another parcel coming in, but I never see anything." "You never will," said Mr Tiffen, "all the rest is at the bottom of the sea. And it is awkward for the family. Nice people, they seemed too. They were at Bow Street when I went up to give evidence. Mr Setty's sister's husband came right across the room to shake hands and thank me for the trouble I'd taken, very civil."

Death was a sacred mystery to these people and a loathsome obscenity; but also it had sometimes to be inflicted, and the risk of it suffered, in the way of duty. Gran had brought in cups of fresh hot tea, and for a minute or two we all drank and were silent. My eyes went to two photographs of destroyers on the walls, and Mr Tiffen's brother-in-law said, "My ships in the war. We're all in the Navy here." "All in the Navy," nodded Gran, and sure enough all the bridegrooms in the wedding groups wore naval uniform. So death was not altogether terrible here, for it was part of a familiar and accepted and enjoyed discipline. Indeed, they had subjugated death still further, for though it was solemnly realized, it was also domesticated, a part of household economy, not taken too seriously, carelessly dispensed to the birds and beasts and fishes, along with love.

"It came of being my holiday then that I came on this thing," grieved Mr Tiffen, "for, it being my holiday, of course I went down on the marshes and got out in my punt; that's what I like to do, have a bit of shooting in my punt." "He is a proper wonder in his punt," said his brother-in-law; "nobody can do more with a punt gun than he can." "Only time," said Mr Tiffen sadly, "that I ever had anything to do with the police before all this fuss and bother was to go to the police station and get a licence for my gun. Duck we can get," he said more happily, "and widgeon. There's many like widgeon better than duck, it's richer. It's a nice kind of sport too. It's not like other shooting, you know. You don't wait for the birds to rise. You paddle along, quiet as you can, lying down in the boat, facing forward, till you see a nice lot of birds settled on the water, and you get to the right distance, so that the shot splays out amongst them, and you get the lot." "Twenty or thirty he gets at a time," rejoiced his brother-in-law. "We take what we want," said Mr Tiffen, "and we get rid of the rest easy enough. I don't even have to send them to market; I just take them home to the village and sell them up and down the street. People are glad to have them to make up the meat ration." "He has his fun and makes good money out of it," said the brother-in-law. Mr Tiffen's glasses shone with satisfaction. The times had got him with his back to the wall; they had made him a farm worker when he was a fisherman and a fowler, but he had found the only loophole, he had an exceptional gift, and, in his several ways, he was enjoying exceptional rewards.

We asked him questions about this gun which brought down twenty and thirty birds at a time, and they were foolish questions, since neither of us had ever shot from a punt. We were worried about the kick of such a wonder-working gun, because we thought it must be fired from the shoulder, like other guns. "No, no," said Mr Tiffen patiently, "you haven't got this right. The boat takes the kick, not my shoulder. It isn't near my shoulder, it's lying on the floor of the punt. There's a couple of ropes like a cradle at the back of it like, to take the kick. It's got no sights, I just look along the barrel, and when I get it lined up on the birds I ship a paddle and pull the hammer-trigger with my hand. But you come out and see for yourselves the way it is." "Yes, you ought to have a look at that punt and that gun," said the brother-in-law, "you won't see better." "I never saw better," said Mr Tiffen. "I don't know who made them. They belonged to an old man used to live round here. I bought them when he died. I was young myself then. Come and have a look at them. It's just a step along the sea wall."

Outside the warm house the air came through our clothes to our skins; it was as if we had dropped into a swimming pool, we shivered and said "Brrr," but liked it. We walked in single file along the top of the sea wall, Mr Tiffen going first. His feet were very small, and he put them down lightly and firmly as if he were a ballet dancer.

Like us, he had come over two miles of drained marsh, and he had explained that we had not overtaken him on the road because he had come by a short cut of his own across the fields. But though we were muddied to the knees there was hardly a speck of dirt on his neat brown boots. We stopped to look over the blue-green mudflats and listen to the cry of the seabirds. It was as if the still air were striped vertically with the pure, thin, ascendant notes. "The teuks those are," said Mr Tiffen. "Some call them red shanks."

Staring out to the sea, which was now just visible as a dark shining line on the horizon, he ran his hand through his hair and said, "An unnoticing man he must have been, a most unnoticing man. This Hume, the man they said had done the murder. You see how it happened that the body was laying about so that I found it? He dropped it from the plane where he saw deep water. That is why I say he must be a most unnoticing man, for they tell me he was round here during the war with the RAF. He should have noticed that all round the coast here there's places where it's deep water just twice in the month, when there's a full moon and a new moon, and all the rest of the time there's shallow water. When he dropped this parcel here the sea was flooding over the flats; it was near to the top of the sea wall, I grant you that. But the water runs away, after that there's only a foot or two of water even at high tide; that parcel was bound to lie about on the mud when it was low tide, same as it was doing when I found it. You'd think a man would know more about tides when he's been in the neighbourhood, like?" The face he turned on us was deeply lined by the strain of acute observation carried on all his life long, of a constant conversion of the knowledge he thus gained into wisdom. But for once he was inquiring into something which would remain for ever unknown to him. It was not for him to understand the peculiar bargain this age had driven with some of his fellow men: teaching them to perform one enormously complicated operation, such as flying a plane, but in exchange taking away their knowledge of certain very simple things, such as the pull of the moon on the sea, and the unlikelihood that a man can kill another man without being found out, or even the nature of murder.

The punt was lying in one of the channels, and we went out to it over the mud, again appreciating how neat Mr Tiffen was on his feet. If we followed his trail exactly, treading on the tufts of grass where he had trod, we remained dry-shod; if we strayed, we slid on stuff like toothpaste. For a little we hung over the punt and made clucking noises as if it were a baby. It had that mysterious secondary colour, apart from its paint, which very old boats have, and it looked too fragile to carry its gun, which looked like a drainpipe. "Do you ever capsize?" we asked. "Well, I did when I was very young," said Mr Tiffen, and laughed as if he remembered a story against himself.

Just then the clouds broke. Circles of amber brightness travelled towards us over the mudflats and broadened out, and we were suddenly in full sunshine, and quite warm. We were surprised, but Mr Tiffen told us, "It often gets hot like this down here, even in the wintertime; the coastline runs all twisted here, and the way this bay lies the sea wall shelters you from the east wind. Why, it wasn't long ago, we were right into November, that I came down here and found a great seal sunning himself in that channel over there. The punt was here, and he was over there, sitting up against the bank as if it was his own armchair. I said to myself, 'Well, I've never shot a seal and now I'm going to get one,' and I had my shotgun lying down here at the foot of the wall, and I came back and fetched it, and I was creeping up on him when he looked round at me and started shaking his head. You know, moved it from side to side, the way old people do when they're just sitting and are comfortable. Like this." Mr Tiffen made a movement which brought before the mind's eye all the seals in zoos and circuses that look like old gentlemen, all the old gentlemen that look like seals. "After that I couldn't shoot him. I hadn't the heart to take his life. Not after he'd looked round at me and shook his head that way. I lowered my gun and let him be." His face deeply creased with smiling tenderness, Mr Tiffen looked round at his marshes, his sky. "It was a nice day, just like this," he said.

2

The person accused of the murder of Mr Setty, Brian Donald Hume, was twenty-nine years old. It was alleged that he had invited Mr Setty to his flat in Golders Green and stabbed him to death, on the night of October 4, and cut him up into several pieces and packaged them on the afternoon of October 5; and that later that day he had taken some of these packages up in a plane and dropped them in the North Sea off the east coast, and that the next day he had dropped some more. He was a middle-sized young man, with an abundance of black hair, a face much fatter than his body, a mouth like a woman's and deep-set dark eyes burning with eagerness. Whatever it might be that was going to happen next, he would greet it eagerly just because it was an event. He had a much greater lust for life than most people who get into the dock. He looked foreign; he might have been a Turk or an Arab.

The first sight of him suggested that he was a spiv. He wore the checked sports jacket, the pullover, the flannel trousers, all chosen to look raffish, which was then the uniform of the spiv, and he had the air of self-conscious impudence which is the spiv's hallmark. That in itself made it surprising that he was charged with murder. Spivs were then busy dealing on the black market in automobiles and petrol, meat and poultry and sugar, foreign currency and building materials. Though they broke the law in handling these goods, and some of them got involved in warehouse robberies and automobile thefts, most of them would keep their hands clean of murder. We still get most of our murderers and hang most of those we catch. It would have been surprising if Hume had been one of the spivs who disregarded this reason for caution, for though it was apparent that he wanted to live, it was apparent that he had suffered some head-on collisions with life in which he had come off badly. He was brassy but wistful.

The court was filled by the relatives and friends of Mr Setty, who were not wistful. Rumour said that they were kin to the two great Shashoua brothers, who had built a flamboyant opulence for themselves in England during the first forty years of this century. They were no fools. Ben was an automobile dealer in the early days when it took real intelligence to find out what makers were worth following. Abraham was in the textile trade and kept going in that legitimate business until the great textile slump of the early twenties. Ben, who was the more picturesque, was in the end deported. This was not because any criminal proceedings were ever brought against him. It was simply felt that England and he were working at cross-purposes. He revelled in litigation; in the last twenty years of his residence in England he brought twenty-four actions in the court, and must have been an ill-used man, for he won fifteen. The other brother, Abraham, went bankrupt for a hundred and fifty thousand pounds and paid his creditors a half-penny in the pound. He greatly enjoyed all the technicalities of the proceedings and ranks as a very great concert bankrupt. At one point he raised his creditors' spirits by returning to his birthplace in Mesopotamia to realize some property he owned there, spending three years on the task, surely in courts and gardens where fountains splashed, and returned with the proceeds of the sale, which amounted to thirty-five thousand rupees, but presented an expense account for forty thousand rupees. When he had lived fifty fantastic years an automobile ran over him in a country lane; and a year afterwards his widow, Iris Shashoua, gently and ceremoniously killed herself because she could no longer bear to live without her beloved husband.

The relatives of the Shashouas who were in court belonged to a later and less adventurous generation, which never got its names in the papers; but they had kept the Baghdad quality. Mr Setty's sister, Mrs Ouri, was no longer a young woman, and she had wept the flesh loose from the bones on her face; but she had the arched eyebrows and oval face and bland symmetry which Arabian romancers would have ascribed to a girl lying on a mother-of-pearl bed, fanned by a Negro eunuch, behind the latticed windows of a palace. Like most other women in London, New York, and Paris at that date, she wore a black Persian lamb coat and a hat like a coronet; but it might have been the mourning wear prescribed by ancient custom for women of rank in some walled town on the bare rocks above an Asiatic plain. What the men of her rank in that same city wore at such a time seemed to be shown by her cousin, though he was actually wearing a camel's hair coat; but his skin was amber, his black hair was crimped like the long tresses and beards of the men sculptured on the monuments of dead civilizations, his features were heavy, not coarse or stupid, but weighty, as if his maker had determined to keep him in scale with retinues of elephants, and masonry built massively, as can be done where there is a multitude of slaves.

These two told how last they had seen Mr Setty. As his sister had walked in a street in the quarter where the automobile market is carried on, she had seen him drive by in his resplendent automobile, a yellow Citroën limousine with scarlet upholstery, some time between five and half-past on October 4. His cousin had seen him driving by, a little later, as he stood waiting for a bus. This seemed an improbable statement when he made it, for he would obviously have travelled either by elephant or by a limousine as spectacular as his cousin's; but indeed he could be seen every afternoon going home from the Old Bailey on the bus, which he made, by the mere act of boarding it, the rickety and ill-proportioned contrivance of an immature civilization. These two family witnesses were followed by two young automobile dealers, who told how Mr Setty had visited their office later that evening, and how they had introduced Hume to Mr Setty some time before. These young men were in the same line of picturesqueness as the Shashoua kin. Their clothes also reversed the drabness of the West and sent the mind back to the valleys of the Euphrates and the Tigris. One of them was solid and sleek, and was dressed in such richly coloured and finely woven stuffs that it seemed hard to believe that he did not keep his automobiles in a cave guarded by a jinni; the slenderness of his partner was so treated by his tailor that it came back to the mind that slim young men were often likened to the crescent moon in the Arabian Nights. Yet for all this gorgeousness of apparel they were not Shashouas.

The Setty relatives looked as if their interior lives matched their exteriors to some degree in picturesqueness, as if they intensely experienced love and hate and joy and grief, and could find words to express how these fires burned. These younger people's tongues were dead in their mouths. They gave their evidence in tired jargon. They could not say "no," they had to say "definitely no"; they could not use the word "about," they had to put in its place "approximately." They painted no pictures for their listeners, and their faces were never lit up by their minds.

These young men had had legal troubles of a complex kind which the Shashouas would have rolled over their tongues with the ecstasy of connoisseurs, and were quite unworthy of them. Shortly after the war, when it became obvious that the bulk of British automobiles must go abroad and only a few could be kept for the home market, the British Motor Traders' Association made a rule that none of its members should sell a new automobile without making the purchaser sign a covenant binding himself not to resell it for twelve months. This was a sensible enough provision, for it might well have happened that the auto trade passed out of the hands of the legitimate traders and became a matter of private sales at huge profiteering prices, which would encourage auto-stealing and the passing off of stolen autos as new ones.

Some dealers, however, had contended that the covenant was an illegal restraint of trade and refused to observe it; and these two young men were among their number. They therefore had been defendants in an action brought in the civil courts by the British Motor Traders' Association, a case which lasted a month and was remarkable for the number and brilliance of the attorneys involved. It would have been as good as a vintage claret to the brothers

Shashoua. These young men showed in the witness box that they had never understood what had happened in court and blundered over the simplest legal terms.

Their ingenuousness went deep. When Mr Setty's cousin and sister were in the box they looked at Hume with sombre courtesy. They and he were walking along the same road, and it had led them into the Valley of Skulls, which was no place for brawling. But when these two young men spoke of Hume it was as if the three of them were hobbledehoys quarrelling in a school playground. They knew him quite well, and it was through them that Hume had met Mr Setty. Hume had put his name down on the waiting list of an auto-mobile manufacturer, and when he got his new automobile sold it to these dealers, who afterwards introduced him to Mr Setty as a possible scout for used automobiles. As a result of this contact these dealers had formed a poor opinion of Hume, and from the deals of his which were traced they seem to have been right: he once bought a new car and sold it shortly afterwards at a loss of thirty per cent, which was something of an achievement in those days. But they expressed their opinion with a curious infantilism. They were the big strong popular boys who were good at games, and Hume was the little odd-come-short who sometimes tried to suck up to the gods of the school but only got jeers and cuffs as a reminder that he must keep his place. When the sleeker of the two told how Hume had tried to borrow a couple of shillings from him so that he could make up a pound to buy a postal order to send off with his weekly football-pool coupon, he might have been saying that everything about the wretched little beast was paltry, he never even had enough pocket money. But if they showed no respect for Hume's danger, they also showed none of the resentment towards him which might have been expected, con-sidering that in his statement he had suggested that Mr Setty had been murdered by associates of this pair. Thus he must have brought on them hours of questioning in a most disagreeable connection; but, like many people who come into the law courts, they had the virtues as well as the defects of childhood.

It was Hume's story, unsupported by any other evidence, that he had come into possession of Mr Setty's body through his meeting with three men, who, he said, were well known to these two young dealers: a tall fair man in his thirties named Mac or Max, who wore a single-stone ring which he was always polishing, a younger man wearing steel-rimmed spectacles who was called The Boy, and a Greek or Cypriot in a green suit who was called Green or Greenie or G. They had asked him to take up in a plane some hot presses, with which they had been printing forged petrol coupons, and drop them in the sea. Hume declared it was natural that they should make such an inquiry of him, since he was known for making illicit air trips to the Continent, some in connection with the purchase of planes and munitions for the Middle East. He consented to do the job for about four hundred dollars, and the three called at his flat with two parcels on the afternoon of October 5, the day after Mr Setty disappeared. These parcels were supposed to have contained the head and legs of Mr Setty, but, according to Hume, he never doubted that they were presses, and he went to his flying club and got rid of them in the sea just beyond the Thames estuary. He then went home, and found the three men waiting in the street below his apartment with a third parcel, which he took up the next day and dropped in the same area. He admitted that he had suspected that this third parcel contained part of a corpse, but he pleaded that he had been too frightened to go to the police, either then or when it was announced in the newspapers that the parcel had been found and what it was.

Certainly something extraordinary had happened in Hume's flat on those days, though it was not a place which most criminals would have chosen for a dangerous operation. It was a duplex flat in a line of houses, with shops underneath, that hugs one angle of a busy crossroads. The spot is well known to all connoisseurs of Victorian thrillers; for it was here that, in the first chapter of Wilkie Collins' *The Woman in White*, the drawing master, Walter Hartwright, met the escaped lunatic walking through the night in her dressing gown. Then hedges divided it from fields. Now it is the heart of a suburban shopping centre. The intersection is dominated by Golders Green Station, and Golders Green Theatre stands beside it. At the end of the line of houses where Hume lived there is a cinema. A line of streetcars links this spot with the farther suburbs, many bus routes run through it; it sees more than suburban traffic in the way of automobiles, for this is a short cut between West London and the Great North Road. There was a bus stop right opposite Hume's front door, and an electric standard that pours brightness on it when daylight has gone. The shops round about serve a wide district, in which German is heard as often as English, for many refugees from Hitler's Germany have settled there, and perhaps for this reason it keeps later hours than most London suburbs. At all times a policeman on point duty stands fifty yards or so away. The back entrance of the premises can be reached only by a narrow road behind the line of houses which runs past a garage and is overlooked by a number of flats. The neighbours would take note if any automobiles used it late at night.

Even inside his home Hume had less privacy than many. He lived in the upper of two duplex apartments over a greengrocer's shop, and the structure was as insubstantial as cheap suburban architecture usually was fifty years ago. A dark, steep, and narrow wooden staircase with a murderous turn to it led past the front door of the lower duplex flat, which was inhabited by a schoolmaster and his wife, up to Hume's own front door, which opened on a slit of lobby. To the left was a living room, looking over the street; to the right was a smaller dining room, long and narrow, with a pantry beyond it, and beyond that again, an attic kitchenette, with the slant of the roof coming fairly low. None of these rooms was large. The living room was perhaps fifteen feet by eleven, and the dining room fifteen feet by eight.

Another steep and narrow and perilous stairway led up to a bedroom, a nursery, and a bathroom. The rooms were sparsely furnished, which meant nothing, for furniture was the last painful shortage in Britain, and only a very well-to-do young couple could then set up a brand-new comfortable home. But the place had been furnished according to the memory of a pattern established by the educated and fairly prosperous middle class. Somebody living here had been brought up in the kind of home where they took in *Punch*. The convention of interior decoration on that level of culture is simple and airy, so there were no nailed-down carpets and linoleum, no heavy curtains. The cheap wood floors, which were insufficiently caulked between the widely spaced boards, might as well have been gratings. If anybody shouted or screamed in any room in this apartment, or if anything heavy fell on the floor, it would have been audible in all the other rooms, and almost certainly in the apartment below, and probably in the houses to the right or the left.

There were three people living in this apartment: this nearly handsome, faintly raffish young ex-pilot, as his intimates considered him, Brian Donald Hume; his wife Cynthia; and their baby daughter, who was just over two months old. Cynthia Hume had an unusual and very strong personality. She was twenty-nine and looked six or seven years younger. She had soft dark hair, gentle eyes, a finely cut and very childish mouth, and an exceptionally beautiful creamy complexion. Her fault was that she appeared colourless. If she had been more definite in appearance she might have had the chiselled dignity of a Du Maurier drawing, of Mimsey in *Peter Ibbetson*, but she was too shadowy for that. In compensation she had a low-pitched and very lovely voice, and a charm that, had she been a mermaid, would have drawn all navies down into the deep water, man by man. Nobody could talk with her for more than ten minutes without feeling that she was infinitely kind and tender and simple and helpless, and that to succour her would be bliss. The only unfavourable suspicion she ever aroused was a doubt as to whether her look of childishness might not spring from a lack of adult intelligence. The doubt was unfounded. She was not intellectual but she was shrewd. Perhaps she was too languid to use her shrewdness to avert catastrophe; but she could survive catastrophe.

Her father was the chief examiner in a Midland Savings Bank which had four hundred branches, her mother was a woman of strong character and abounding affections. After she had been at a provincial university for a term or two she went into the Women's Auxiliary Air Force, at the age of nineteen; and life in the women's services did its curious trick of making a girl into a woman before her time and at the same time keeping her for ever a little school-girlish. She made an unsuccessful marriage, which took her into the night clubs and restaurants of the West End of London. She got a divorce, which neither she nor her family took lightly. She was secretary in a fashionable restaurant when, late in 1948, she married Brian Donald Hume. Ten months afterwards she had a baby, suffering a difficult and dangerous confinement. Now she was breast-feeding the baby, as well as looking after it herself, and doing all its laundry. She also did all the housework with no help except a weekly visit from a domestic worker. If she had a pretty air of sleepy remoteness it was not because she had assumed it in order to seem voluptuous and exciting. It was because she was tired, and by nature turned all things to favour and prettiness, even fatigue.

Nothing is known of what happened in this apartment on the night of October 4. Hume said he was at home, though at first he put up a false alibi; and Mrs Hume said that that night was to her like any other evening. She could bring back to her mind nothing about it, until she looked at an old copy of the *Radio Times* and recognized one of the programmes as one she had listened to when she sat in the living room after supper, waiting to go upstairs to give her baby its ten o'clock feed. It was, in obedience to the sinister pattern of this murder case, an account of the trial of Landru. For the rest it was, as she kept on repeating, just like any other evening. She and Hume slept in a double bed, and he had come to bed as usual. At no time did she wake up and find him gone. And when she rose at six in the morning to give the baby its first feed, he was still there.

But if we know nothing about the night of October 4, we know a great deal about October 5. That day was built up all over again, as solid as when it was first lived, when it had seemed buried for months deep in the past. A procession of people passed through the witness box and showed what it is that the virtuous apprentice receives as his reward. They toiled and they spun and they were in no way like the lilies of the field; a bank manager, the manageress of a dyeing and cleaning establishment, a charwoman, a house painter, a taxi-driver, and so on. Not for them tailoring that recalled the dyes of Tyre, the weavers of Arabia. Drab they dressed and drab they lived, but somehow their tongues were alive in their mouths. They said "no" and "about" instead of "definitely no" and "approximately." Because of their simple and economical use of language they achieved magic. It was as if all sorts of objects came floating over the house-tops from Golders Green to the Old Bailey to build up that day anew; a trail of five-pound notes, a carpet, a prescription, a carving-knife, a cup of tea, a piece of rope. But the magic was mischievous. Reconstructed, the day suited no one's convenience.

Hume had started the morning, it appeared, between ten and eleven by going to the local branch of the Midland Bank and paying seventy pounds in five-pound notes into his account, which was about two hundred and fifteen pounds overdrawn. Then he went home, and sometime that morning the family doctor called and looked at the baby, whose stomach was out of order, and prescribed some medicine for it and advised Mrs Hume to take it to the Children's Hospital in Great Ormond Street. Hume listened to his instructions as to how he was to get his wife and child there, and asked for a prescription for sleeping tablets. Then he went out and had these two prescriptions made up at a drugstore. Later, not long before one o'clock, he went to the dyeing and cleaning establishment, which was a few doors away from his apartment, presided over by Mrs Linda Hearnden. This was a middle-aged woman with a delightful smile, unfussed over good looks, and perfect manners. She had a peculiar horror of the crime which had been committed, and had never become used to the thought of it, as most witnesses do during the preliminary proceedings in the lower court. She was still taut with disgust, but she took time to be fair to Hume. She told how he had come in and asked if she could accept a carpet for cleaning and dyeing, and how, when she said she could, he had brought down the light carpet from his sitting room, rolled up and tied with rope, and asked her to get it dyed a darker green, and how she gave an estimate without having it unrolled; and she would not accept the prosecution's suggestion that she had judged this by guesswork because he had not wanted to unroll it. The prosecution was hoping to prove that he had tried to prevent her from seeing a stain on the carpet which had, since the carpet was cleaned, been identified as the result of a flow of some human secretion, probably blood. But she would not have it so. If the carpet was not unrolled, it was a matter of her unwillingness to have it spread out over the shop, not of Hume's reluctance.

After he had handed over the carpet he went upstairs again and soon came down with a carving knife, which he took to a garage round the corner and handed to one of the mechanics, asking him to sharpen it. The mechanic had the impression that he said to him, "The joint is on the table, and I want to get back quickly." But he did not give the mechanic time to sharpen it properly. He took it away as soon as the mechanic had given it a rough edge and would not let him finish it on the oilstone. This irritated the mechanic, and when Hume offered him half a crown he would not take it, saying he had not been allowed to make a thorough job of it. He was a proud and tetchy man, and was extremely annoyed by the process of cross-examination, refusing to play, and regarding it as he might have regarded an attack by any stranger on his truthfulness. He stood crossly answering questions about times and Hume's words and manner, knitting his brows in peevish concentration, while without his knowledge his hands calmly played with the carving knife, noting its properties, bending back the blade, testing the edge, feeling how it lay in the handle, balancing it to see if the proportion of blade to handle was right. Matter was having a highly intelligent conversation with matter, while his and the lawyers' minds were having a much less brilliant exchange. But he got it plain that he felt sure that Hume had spoken of a joint on the table; and for all he knew this might not have been an exceptional occurrence, for though Hume had never asked him to sharpen a carving knife he might have asked other mechanics at the garage to do it; and that if there was an urgency in Hume's manner it was nothing more than his habit. "It's his nature," he said, in a phrase which sounded sinister when used of a man on trial for his life, "that he's here today and gone tomorrow."

Hume went back to his apartment, and he and his wife ate lunch and washed up the dishes. Then, a few minutes before two o'clock, there arrived Mrs Ethel Stride, the charwoman. Under a little round hat she had the prim small face of a kindly cat, and she looked ahead of her with the still integrity, the dedication to exact vision, that shines in the eyes of a cat. She knew the truth, and she told it. Why? Because she had sworn to tell the truth, the whole truth, and nothing but the truth, and she believed in keeping oaths; but even if she had taken no oath she would still have told the truth, because she believed that to lie was wrong. Simply she told the truth.

When she entered the apartment, a few minutes before her regular time, Hume met her and asked her to go out and buy a floor cloth because he had ruined one by trying to wash a stained carpet. Casting an eye round the apartment, she saw that the carpet was missing, and also a floral rug in the lobby. He also talked to her about the floor round the carpet, saying that he was going to have it stained again. He then gave her the money for the floor cloth, and she went down the street to buy it, and then remembered that the shop which kept the best kitchen articles was still shut for the lunch hour. So she turned about and went back to the apartment. Again Hume met her, for Mrs Hume was upstairs feeding the baby before she took it out for the afternoon, and he told Mrs Stride that she was to go up and work there, because he wanted to tidy up a cupboard in the kitchen to make room for coal to be stored in the winter, and he said that he did not want to be disturbed while he was doing it, "on no account and in no circumstances." If the telephone rang she was to answer it and say that he was not at home.

So Mrs Stride went upstairs and cleaned the Humes' bedroom and the nursery and the bathroom. Presently Mrs Hume went out with the baby, and Mrs Stride went on with her work, using the vacuum cleaner from time to time but listening for the telephone bell. She never heard it. After Hume had been in the kitchen for about an hour he came out and asked her to make some tea for him. She brewed it in the scullery, and at the same time went into the kitchen, which she found quite orderly. Then Hume went out of the flat, carrying two parcels, one under each arm. One was square, a cube with sides of about eighteen inches, and this is presumed to have been Mr Setty's head; the other, which was a long, bent shape and considerably larger, is presumed to have contained his legs. Mrs Stride had seen no joint of meat in the apartment that needed carving, not in the refrigerator nor in any cupboard. Nor had she seen anything unusual in the flat, no sign of a man's body with the head and legs cut off, no blood. Nor had she heard any sounds like the sawing of bones. Nor had she smelled anything that might have been blood or a corpse.

Mrs Stride told the truth; and she was very intelligent, she had keen perceptions, she had sound powers of deduction, and she handled her memory well. When she was asked whether she would have heard Hume if he had been sawing bones, she said that she thought she could, but it was so quiet that she almost thought Mr Hume had gone out. When she was asked if she thought that she could have heard the doorbell ring when she was working upstairs, although she was using the vacuum cleaner, she deliberated and said that she believed she could, because the vacuum cleaner was a Hoover. Had it been an Electrolux, which made a different kind of noise, she might not have been able to hear a bell while it was working, but she could hear most things through the noise made by a Hoover.

When Mrs Stride had left the witness box she had, by her measured and conscientious evidence, performed one of the most spectacular acts which have ever amazed a law court. She had, on the first day of the trial, wholly destroyed both the case for the prosecution (whose witness she was) and the case for the defence. For the prosecution claimed that Hume had enticed Setty into his apartment and had there stabbed him and cut up his body, and the prosecuting counsel laid stress on the fact that Hume went to the garage at lunchtime on that day and asked a mechanic to sharpen a carving knife, saying, "It may be that he had already blunted it by cutting up a body and maybe he wanted it to be sharpened for more cutting." But it was abundantly clear from Mrs Stride's evidence that he had done nothing, in that eggshell of an apartment, of the hauling and pitching and dragging which would have been necessary if he were cutting up the body of a man weighing over a hundred and eighty pounds, and that he had certainly not been sawing through a spine and through thigh bones. If he had cut up anybody there the night before, there would have been some blood somewhere, which Mrs

Stride, who performed her duties with fervour, would certainly have noticed.

Another significant matter which was fatal to the prosecution was established when she was in the witness box. Hume was no fool, and he knew just what Mrs Stride was. His face showed that he was following her evidence with the utmost appreciation of her character; and it was confirmed by his friends that he was in fact extremely fond of her and had often had long conversations with her about serious problems of conduct. He knew that she was intelligent and observant and honest, and he would certainly not have allowed her to come into the apartment had there been a body lying there still to be dismembered or only just dismembered. He would have met her at the door and made some excuse why she should not enter. One is glad to welcome a domestic worker arriving, but not so glad as all that.

But when the mind turned back towards Hume's account of the three men who had come to his apartment and left parcels on him which they said and he believed were presses, it was evident that Mrs Stride had killed that story too. She had heard nobody come to the flat. It was a Hoover, not an Electrolux; the apartment had been so quiet that she thought Mr Hume had gone out; and Hume had declared in his statement that the men had come at the time when she was in his apartment.

They drank their cups of tea together, these two, and Hume went down the stairs with Mr Setty's head under one arm and Mr Setty's legs under the other, and his pet dog, Tony, a mongrel Alsatian, at his heels. He packed the parcels into the back seat of an automobile hired from the nearby garage where he had had the knife sharpened at lunchtime, and with the dog beside him he drove off to Elstree Airfield, the headquarters of his flying club, about eight miles away. That morning he had telephoned to ask for an Auster plane to be kept ready for him, and he and a groundsman took the parcels out of the automobile and put them in the plane, the head in the co-pilot's seat, the legs in the passenger seat behind. Before he went up he paid the cashier of the flying club twenty pounds in payment of an outstanding account, in five-pound notes.

He took off from the airfield about half-past four and flew east, leaving London on his right and heading for the Thames estuary and the North Sea. He says that at a thousand feet up and four or five miles out to sea he opened the door, holding the controls with his knees, and threw both the parcels out of the plane into the water below. Then he came down at Southend Airfield, a mile or two inland from the Thames estuary, at half-past six. He could not take the plane back to Elstree because it was getting dark and he had no night-flying certificate, and he tried to get a member of his flying club whom he met on the airfield to fly him back, without success, since this man was staying down there with his family. As a result of this meeting the man had a good look at the plane and was able to give evidence that it was empty, that the parcels were not there.

As Hume could get nobody to fly him back to Elstree, he took a taxi back to London and paid the driver with a five-pound note. This turned out to be one of those which had been handed over to Setty by a friend named Isidore Rosenthal, an automobile dealer, who had got a cheque for a thousand pounds cashed for him on the morning of October 4. It was Hume's story that when he got back the three men were waiting for him, and that they handed over a third parcel to him, promising to pay him more money if he would drop it into the sea from the plane as he had done the first, and after haggling and coaxing he agreed. Nothing is known as to what happened that night in Hume's apartment. To Mrs Hume it was, again, like any other night. But though October 5 must have been a very long day for Hume, he was out quite early on October 6. By nine o'clock he was being driven in another hired automobile to fetch the one he had left the previous day at Elstree, with the dog in it. The driver who took him there said that he had other parcels with him, which he moved into the automobile already at Elstree. This he denied, but the theory of the prosecution was that these contained the dagger with which Mr Setty had been killed, the saw with which his bones had been cut up, the suit which Hume had worn during the murder and the butcher's work, and such oddments. Hume drove back to his apartment and was in good time to send his wife and his baby off to their appointment at the Children's Hospital.

Later he concerned himself again with interior decoration. He went to a painter who worked in the neighbouring garage and asked him to stain some boards in the living room and in the lobby, and this the man did in the lunch hour. When he had finished the job Hume asked him to lend him a hand with a parcel he had to carry down to his automobile, and produced what was in fact Mr Setty's torso, tied up in felt with rope. It was very heavy, and the painter could not lift it by himself. He was trying to make it an easier job by putting his hands underneath it, but Hume stopped him and told him to carry it by the rope, because it was valuable property. This was plainly nonsense, since it is safer to hug a parcel to one's body than carry it by the rope which binds it. Holding the parcel up between them, the two men staggered down the staircase. At the awkward turn Hume lost his footing, and the two men slithered down the last few steps, with the parcel bumping about on top of them. It was at this point that Hume, according to his statement, heard a gurgling noise from the parcel and began to suspect that it might be part of a corpse, and even of Mr Setty's corpse. By this admission he convicted himself out of his own mouth of being an accessory after the fact of murder, a crime which can be punished by life imprisonment; for as soon as he formed this suspicion it became his duty to report it to the police. But he drove the parcel off to the airfield at Southend, where, with the aid of a groundsman, he manœuvred the gross package into the plane he had abandoned there on the previous evening. Again he took it over the coast, and over a patch of water, which he believed to be deep sea but which was actually a mudflat flooded by the strong tide of the new moon, he prepared to tip out the torso. This time things went wrong when he opened the door, and the plane went into a vertical dive, during which the parcel fell out into the sea. He made a disorderly landing in a playing-field south of the river, in Kent, and though he went up again he did not succeed in getting back to his home airfield at Elstree but had to come down, still on the wrong side of the river, at Gravesend, at about a quarter to six. It was noted that he had brought nothing in his plane. He then crossed the Thames and got somehow to Southend Airfield, where he reclaimed the hired automobile, and got back to Golders Green the next morning. He must have been very tired. During the previous forty-eight hours he had made two flights, amounting to at least three hours, in bad weather and failing light, driven a hundred and fifty miles, attended to a large number of small commissions, and done more than many a father would in the way of aiding his little daughter to overcome her stomach ache.

There was no doubt that Hume was in grave danger. Though Mrs Stride had made it almost impossible to believe that the prosecution could prove that Hume, singlehanded, had stabbed and dismembered Setty in his apartment, the jury might well be persuaded to believe that it had an alternative proof in the assumption that Hume would hardly have taken so much trouble to dispose of a corpse unless he had had something to do with the murder. This was the more likely because Hume's story of the financial inducements which had led him to take on the responsibility for the parcels was quite incredible. He said that the three men had promised him a hundred pounds on their first visit, which they had raised by fifty pounds when they left the third parcel; that is, about four hundred and twenty dollars in all. Of that he must have spent more than a third on the hire of automobiles and the plane, to say nothing of tips to attendants and the cost of dyeing the carpet and staining the floor. But Setty had had a thousand and five pounds on him, mostly in five-pound notes, of which two were traced back to Hume. One he had given to the taxidriver who brought him back from Southend, the other he had paid across the counter of the Stationery Department in Fortnum and Mason's for an address book. None of the other notes were traced, but those two were enough.

So they were saying gravely, the policemen and the reporters and the people in the streets, "He'll be topped, he'll be topped right enough"; and during that day the thought of death began to fill the court. It is strange how a man looks when that threat overhangs him. His life withdraws from the skin, leaving it blue, and seeks the concentrated shelter of the heart, so that the strong fluttering of the pulses disturbs the calmness of his hands and makes his head shift from side to side on the uncomfortable pillar of the throat. His eyes were fixed on the court in something more than attention, as if he were thinking that what he saw had a new and ultimate value, because it might be the last thing he would ever see. But his grasp of experience failed as the hours went by. Presently it was plain that he wanted the day to end with an exhaustion that had the intensity of appetite, that was as painful as hunger and thirst. It was a relief to all of us when four o'clock came, and he rose from his carved chair and gathered his red robe about him and, clutching the black cap which the judge must carry when he tries a murder case, walked out past the bowing aldermen. For the man we had been watching as death threatened him was Mr Justice Lewis, not the man whom he was trying on a capital charge. A serious operation was performed on him a few hours after he left the court, and another was performed a week or two later. He died about the time that Hume would have been hanged had he been convicted and his appeal disallowed. This murder trial, which was doing nothing in order, which had the air of a morality play in its presentation of contrasting types of good and evil, was directing attention to the cruelty, not of capital punishment, but of natural death.

3

Because Mr Justice Lewis had been taken with a fatal illness during the first day of the Hume trial a new judge had to take the case. Instead of Sir Wilfrid Lewis, sixty-eight years old, a Fellow of Eton College and the University College, Oxford, a passionate Churchman, slender and refined, like the statue of a bishop in a French cathedral, we now had Sir Frederick Sellers, fifty-seven years of age, a North-countryman, educated at a grammar school and Liverpool University, a fine soldier in the First World War, with the unusual distinction of two bars to his Military Cross, a Liberal politician, handsome and hearty. That, of course, made a difference to Hume's fate. In the English system the tone of a trial is set by the judge, no matter how brilliant the advocates be. To let Mr Justice Sellers get the reins in his hand, most of the witnesses who had given evidence on the first day were required to repeat their evidence. This was a great hardship to them. Mr Setty's sister was still perfectly dressed, but the smoothness of her face was dishevelled. The manageress of the dyeing and cleaning establishment was still smiling and moving at a leisurely pace that was a kind of courtesy towards time; she would let every moment have its chance, would do nothing to push it out of the present into the past sooner than need be. But it would not have been surprising if she had wept. The person most likely to resent this lengthy recapitulation, Hume himself, showed no displeasure. He sat in the dock showing the heartiest appetite for events, this repetitive event, any event at all.

But soon an incident occurred which would have diverted anybody. There was suddenly a fluttering conference between Hume's solicitor and his counsel, into which the prosecuting counsel was drawn. Then Hume's counsel, Mr Levy, rose and complained to the judge that Hume's solicitor had intercepted a telegram addressed to Mrs Hume by the representative of a national newspaper which showed that he was trying to prevent her from giving evidence for her husband. At this a shudder ran through the court. The lawyers were genuinely shocked, and the newspapermen and women thought that one of their craft must have temporarily gone out of his senses. To interfere

294

with a witness is a misdemeanour in English Common Law and carries such heavy penalties that, in fact, it is rarer in England than in other countries for witnesses, even in the gangster world, to be spirited away and intimidated. It is contempt of court of the worst kind, and the judge in the case can, if he be so minded, stretch forth his hand and say to the offender, "Here you go to jail, now," and he goes to jail there and then, and stays there until the judge decides he has purged his contempt or he makes a successful application against the judge's decision under the Habeas Corpus Act. Mr Justice Sellers read the telegram, looked astonished, and told the officers of the court to go and find the writer and bring him to court forthwith. In imagination one saw a surprised man taking off his eyeshade in a room of clattering typewriters, and one's heart bled for him.

The tide of recapitulated evidence flowed on, and then Mr Levy rose again and said that a further communication from the same representative of a national newspaper had arrived in the form of a letter addressed to Mrs Hume, care of Mrs Hume's solicitors, and that they had got her permission to open it and had found that it was a letter on the same lines as the telegram. The judge read it, and looked more astonished, and directed that the sender of the letter and the telegram, who had meanwhile been brought from his office to the Old Bailey and was standing under guard outside in the corridor, should be brought into court. There then appeared, to the wonder of all the press, the crime reporter of a sensational but serious-minded Sunday newspaper, which likes torsos but supports labour.

This crime reporter was a man in his thirties who was supremely good at his job. He had been in the Navy during the war and found himself in command of a small boat that was continually attacked from the surface of the water and the depths of the water and the sky above, and had to attack as continually other craft and bring trouble on itself. He has a feeling that some criminals, and the relatives of accused persons, are much in the same position. Consequently he appears among the cast of every criminal drama not wholly damnable, proffering sympathy and doing odd chores. He gets news for his paper out of his process, but that is only because he is a loquacious man and has to express himself by speaking or writing; and if he were a millionaire and never wrote another line he would still be found getting the best out of the National Health Service for the murderer's baby, running errands for the corpse's grandmother. But he had a respect for the law. It seemed impossible that he could have interfered with a witness in a case under trial.

The judge remarked tremendously that there was such a thing as the Common Law of England, and Mr Webb explained politely that he knew Mrs Hume apart from this case, having met her a year before. He had often seen her since the arrest of Hume and had promised her mother to be her escort if she came down to the Old Bailey to give evidence, but he had understood that she was not going to do so. The letter and the telegram, however, had nothing to do with that. They had been sent in order to dissuade her from writing an article a certain newspaper had wanted from her, which was to be called "I Was a Murderer's Wife."

At this point the judge said, "Perhaps you had better not say too much about that." Everybody in court knew that a Sunday newspaper was paying the expenses of Hume's defence. It might or might not be the newspaper which had tried to commission this article from Mrs Hume. The situation obviously had its delicacies. The judge then read the letter and the telegram again and said, "On that explanation I will say nothing more about this; but you should be reminded that to interfere with a witness is a Common Law misdemeanour." This was manifestly not quite logical. If Mr Webb's explanation was accepted, then it was unnecessary to warn him of the danger of committing a misdemeanour which, according to that explanation, he had never had the slightest intention of committing. But the step the judge had taken was better than logical; it was eminently sensible. It would be disagreeable to have a discussion before a man on trial for his life concerning an invitation to his wife to write an article which would plainly be useless unless he were hanged, particularly if it might distress him to know who had made the offer. Moreover, the whole business of having a murderer's defence paid for by a newspaper which wants the inside story of the murder in order to increase its circulation, matter of established custom though it be, cannot well be presented in a way which adds to the dignity of the legal profession. Best to pass over the incident as smoothly as possible, while giving the defence lawyers no chance to feel aggrieved and raise these delicate points again. Nobody can say that these thoughts passed through the judge's mind. But they passed through a number of other people's minds, and the situation suddenly and beautifully disappeared. We found ourselves out in the street, looking for lunch.

In the afternoon the stream of witnesses went on. The twenty-fifth was Mr Tiffen, the fowler and fisherman from the Essex marshes who had found Mr Setty's torso. He had difficulty over taking the oath. The clerk gave him the printed card which he handed to all witnesses to read from, but he returned it to him; after some whispering the clerk spoke the oath and he repeated it after him. This man whose good manners and good sense and store of information were the wonder of everyone connected with this case could not read. Forty years ago, when he was a child living eight miles out of a village on the marshes, no education authority worried its head about him. It made one proud that in modern England such a child would be under no handicap at all. They would get it to school all right. If we can teach his kind, without spoiling its simplicity, we are safe. He gave evidence in language as strong and bare as the Bible. Met afterwards in the corridors, he was behaving much as if he were in church, but happiness was sparkling on his glasses, for he had just before Christmas been paid the thousand-pound reward which Mr Setty's relatives had offered for news of him. He had given, he said, a hundred pounds to his two grandsons, Peter Perrin, who was getting on for eighteen months, and Robert John Warner, who was six months. Then, with the tenderness of a lover speaking of the planned honeymoon, he spoke of a fishing boat. It wasn't any use getting it now. To get one of the houses built by the rural district council he had had to become a farm labourer, but when he was fifty they wouldn't bother him no more; at that age this controlled labour business had to let you go. Then he would go back to fishing. He had been out with the boats since he was eight. It would be two and a half years till he was fifty, but that was none too long to think about buying a boat. You had to turn it over well in your mind. As for the rest of the money, he would keep it to help anybody in the family that was in trouble and to look after himself when he got old. He spoke of age with prudence but without terror; nothing, it appeared, could really touch a man who was about to buy himself the perfect boat. Now he was going to visit his sister who lived down by the docks. A bus went from the corner and he would go straight there, and tomorrow he would be back in Essex.

There followed the expert witnesses for the prosecution, the chief of the Scotland Yard laboratory and a pathologist, who proved conclusively that a murder had been committed in a way which was completely impossible. On the living-room carpet there was a large stain caused by some human secretion, most probably blood, which

they had talked about earlier; there were traces of blood on the linoleum in the lobby; and in the dining room there was human blood
on the floorboards and on the lath and plaster ceiling below; and
there were traces of blood, though it was not proved to be human,
on the stairs leading to the upper floor. These stains evoked a perfect
picture of Mr Setty being stabbed in the chest with a dagger five
times, as we knew he had been, while he sat or stood in the living
room, and then staggering out of the room into the lobby, where he
went through a door which he might have thought led out to the
stairs and safety, but which in fact led into the dining room, where
he slumped and died face downward on the boards. These bloodstains
showed that a considerable amount had been spilled, perhaps a fifth
of all the blood a man of Mr Setty's size might have in his body.
Where it was proved to be human, it belonged to O group; and that
was Mr Setty's group. This was not conclusive, for O is the largest
blood group and includes about forty-two percent of the population;
but it would have been nicer for Hume if there had not been this
coincidence.

The case was all sewed up, except that the murder could not have
possibly been committed in this way. It is not to be believed that
Mr Setty, when someone began to stab him, refrained from uttering
a loud cry; and that, when he had been stabbed five times in the
chest, he would have refrained from putting his hand to the wound,
or that, as he walked across the room with the faltering step of a
dying man and crossed the lobby and went into another room, he
would also have refrained from supporting himself by leaning on the
furniture or against the walls. But there was not a single fingerprint
of Mr Setty's to be found in the whole flat, nor any sign of blood on
the furniture or on the walls, though these were of a substance which
would have soaked up the stain and retained it indefinitely. But even
if Mr Setty had remained taciturn and erect while being murdered,
Hume could not have counted beforehand on this unusual behaviour;
and a single cry, a single lurch, might have been enough noise to be
remembered and to hang him. If the noise had been loud enough it
might have brought an inquiring policeman in at that very minute.
But once Hume had taken these risks, why did he let a dying man,
who could have been easily restrained, stagger from room to room,
leaving a trail of blood behind him?

It might have been, of course, that Mr Setty did not grasp the
knife (and his unscarred fingers showed that he had made no attempt

to do so) and had left no fingerprints on the wall and the furniture because he was unconscious when he was killed. He might first have been hit on the head with a cosh; but that is most unlikely, for murderers rarely change instruments in the middle of a murder. Or he might have been drunk; there was a good deal of alcohol found in his stomach. But in that case his assailant would hardly have stabbed him five times when once would have done; and as his stab wounds were all in the front of his body, if he had been unconscious and therefore presumably lying flat or leaning back, the blood would have run back into his chest cavity, and no doctor spoke of this having happened. Nor would a murderer, having an unconscious man at his mercy, have stabbed him where his blood was likely to fall on a carpet or have carried him into another room without wrapping him in a blanket or some absorbent material. It was impossible to believe that Hume had murdered Mr Setty in this apartment singlehanded, and it was even more impossible to believe that he had murdered him with the aid of accomplices, for in that case it was even less likely that the dying man would have been allowed to stagger from one room to another, or that his corpse should have been borne unwrapped to drop a trail of blood. It was also impossible to believe that Hume had, alone or with help, dismembered the body in the apartment. The bones had been severed with a saw, and one of the pathologists assured the court that that must have been a very noisy proceeding, adding, "It is quite impossible to go on dictating to one's secretary if human bones are being sawed through in the vicinity." There was no table in the whole apartment long enough to lay Mr Setty's body on during the dissection, and if such dissecting had been done on the floor it would surely have left bloodstains of a more diffuse, sprayed sort than any which were actually found.

It is certain that in essence Hume's own story was true, and that Mr Setty's corpse had been left at his apartment already dismembered and packaged; and that he was not the murderer but only an accessory after the fact. This would do away with all the difficulties inherent in the theory of the prosecution; it did not ask us to believe that Mr Setty, who had been noted for a timidity so extreme that he never would travel in any automobile but his own, would visit the apartment of a man in whom he had no reason to feel confidence. It suggested an explanation of the patches of bloodstain all over the apartment. Supposing that Hume had opened the door to some visitors and invited them to come into the living room, they may have brought all or any of the packages and dumped them on the floor. Hume may not have known at first or indeed for some time what the packages contained, but may simply have noticed that they were exuding a sticky fluid and suggested that they might be moved to the kitchen and put in the sink or the coal cupboard, if it had been proposed that he was to keep them and dispose of them. But unfortunately for Hume the details of his story annulled all benefit the outline of it might bring him. For he said that the three men who had come and left the first two packages had come between two and three on the afternoon of October 5; but he had sent the bloodstained carpet to the dyer that morning before lunch, the floral rug in the bloodstained hall had disappeared by the time Mrs Stride had arrived a few minutes before two, and he had spoken of his intention to have the floorboards revarnished soon after her arrival. These circumstances, and Mrs Stride's firm assertion that there were no callers at the apartment during the whole afternoon, knocked Hume's defence to pieces. For that reason this murder seems likely to rank as one of the great unsolved mysteries. The possibility that Hume murdered Mr Setty can definitely be excluded. But who murdered Mr Setty, and how, and where, is known to nobody except the murderer. Not for lack of evidence. That is piled sky-high. There is so much that whatever theory the mind may base on that evidence, there exists some fact which disproves it.

The case was the stranger because the prosecution was so curiously conducted by Mr Christmas Humphreys, who had just become the senior prosecuting counsel for the government. He is the son of a very famous old judge, who presides over trials with a merciless, humorous, savage, solemn kind of common sense, often shocking to everybody in court except the prisoner, who, out on a limb where at last he knows what's what, can see what the old man is driving at. His son, who is getting on for sixty, looks as if he would be the conventionalist of all time, and would enjoy few activities outside the law except going back to his old college and having dinner with the dons at the High Table in Hall. He is in fact a passionate joiner of the wilder type. He starts near the centre by being chairman of the Ballet Guild and of a group that reads poetry aloud, then gets off to the left with osteopathy and psychoanalysis, then the Bates system of curing eye defects without spectacles lures him, and he runs along into herbalism and the movement against the use of artificial fertilizers. His top note is Buddhism. He is probably the only English-born Buddhist at the Bar. Conversions of any kind are uncommon among lawyers, who rarely want to become anything except judges.

This was the first case he had conducted as senior prosecuting counsel for the government, and it was therefore watched with interest. This turned to dismay. On rising to cross-examine this man who had been accused of the appalling crime of stabbing and cutting up Mr Setty, Mr Christmas Humphreys asked him, in accents cold, with a loathing which suggested that he had detected him doing something far, far worse, whether he had not taken a blond girl called Teresa out to a night club and paid the bill with a rubber check. It was of course pleasant to think of him doing anything so relatively innocent, but Mr Humphreys suggested that this was the kind of thing that stabbing and cutting up people led to if done too often. He also alluded with horror to the fact that Hume had an overdraft at his bank, though British banks indulge, to an extent which Americans find astonishing, in the amiable habit of letting their clients run into debt with them, if they either deposit security, or get a solvent friend to give a personal guarantee, or exhibit symptoms of future solvency. Such is the economic disorder of England today that probably at least half the people in this court were living on overdrafts. There were many faces which failed to light up as Mr Humphreys suggested that Hume had been so distressed at having an overdraft that Mr Setty's notes had offered him an irresistible temptation. Other suggestions of his brought forward as a reason for the butchery included even more common signs of indigence. He made much of the fact that Hume had pawned a suit. Yet it is part of the curious economics of pawnbroking that there are many objects for which pawnbrokers give much more than their second-hand value; and a large section of the population pawns things all its life, and a still larger section pawns things quite a lot when it is young, and yet neither habitually engages in murder. He cut an even wider swathe when he mentioned portentously that Hume had often been some days late in paying the rent. By this time the court was looking on Mr Humphreys with awe as a financial virgin, who felt as strongly about his state as the Lady in Comus felt about hers and would have claimed at any moment that So dear to Heav'n is Saintly solvency That when a soul is found sincerely so, a thousand liveried Angels lackey her.

Rage rang in his voice, and it was very odd to remember his last book. He is quite an accomplished writer. His book on *The Great*

Pearl Robbery of 1913 is one of the classics of criminal literature; it conveys the peculiarly cosy character of British crime as it was before the First World War far better than any detective novel. He has also published several works on Buddhism, the chief of which is *Concentration and Meditation*. The last, *Via Tokyo*, is the record of his trip to Japan as a junior counsel for the British government in the International War Trial. It contains little about his legal mission, for he is preoccupied by his awed delight in the stillness and formality of the East, as they were exhibited in the Buddhist shrines and schools of dancing which he visited in Japan and the countries through which he travelled.

The emotional climax of his journey was his surrender to the Zen sect of Buddhism. This is a rarefied form of the faith, in which stupidity is regarded as the first enemy, to be overcome by the intellect, which when it has been trained to its highest capacity, becomes the second enemy, to be overcome by the development of a higher faculty of wisdom. The means by which the intellect is transcended includes the asking of *koan*, refined conundrums for which there is no logical answer, and the practice of *mondo*, dialogues between master and pupil which sound like nonsense because they are carried on above the plane where sense holds good. As the pupil progresses he is rewarded with flashes of *satori*, immediate understanding, and his ultimate aim is to stop thinking and have no need for thought, because as soon as he becomes aware of a problem he himself becomes its solution. He enters into it by intuition, as he can enter into all things in the universe, without effort, by tranquil acceptance. *Via Tokyo* shows that its author is in love with tranquillity. In one of the poems which are scattered through the volume he writes of his regret that he must leave "the golden cool serene" of his room in a Japanese house; and his pages are covered with his desire to discard all hot emotions and intellectual superfluities and make himself an empty chalice to receive the wine of mysticism.

Yet the Old Bailey has not for many years witnessed anything like Mr Christmas Humphreys' cross-examination of Hume. It was Hume's intention to be gaily impudent, and he soon found a way of mentioning that an escaped criminal lunatic called the Mad Parson, for whom all the police forces of England were searching, had lived for months unmolested in lodgings directly opposite the London police station where he himself had been detained and examined. But nobody can be funny for long when he is being tried for such a crime; there is something in everybody which forbids it. Soon Hume began to bicker and yelp and snarl, and nothing was said to him which might have exorcised him. Mr Humphreys had several times described Hume as an inveterate romancer, so it happened that when he said to Hume, "I suggest that you stabbed Setty in the sitting room and that he died in the dining room," Hume snapped back, "Now you're romancing," and when Mr Humphreys went on, "And that you cut him up that night," Hume pouted out his lips in insolence and sneered, "Absolute baloney." The horrid subject matter was being discussed in too appropriate a style. From Mr Humphreys' book it had appeared that one of the most intense pleasures he had experienced on his journey to the East, indeed, perhaps in all his life, was his stay in a Zen monastery, the Temple of Full Enlightenment, founded seven hundred years ago, a place of mellowed wood and grey-green tiles, set among flowering trees below a sandstone cliff. There was a Great Bell there, older than the Temple, at the top of a rising venue of worn grey steps. In this home of pure mysticism, purged of formality, nobody minded the bell being sounded at any time by anybody who was moved to sound it. So he used to go up the long steep stairs to the bell whenever he had time to take refuge in this Temple, and strike it to announce his coming, fusing himself with its ancient, harmonious voice.

There was a war of philosophical principles here. Mr Humphreys is a fastidious person who is displeased with what man has made of the earth, and has therefore always distrusted the common practices of mankind and has put his faith in any alternative which has been less generally adopted. Ballet is not ordinary motion, therefore he adored it; prose is more habitually used than poetry, therefore he wrote poetry and read it aloud; he would not be satisfied by any rationalist view of the mind, he enjoyed the psychoanalytic reinstatement of the primitive; he rejected the findings of orthodox medicine for osteopathy and herbalism; he waved away modern agriculture; he would have nothing to do with the Christianity which lay at his hand shaped for the use of his Western personality, he insisted on going out of Europe into Asia to find a religion hardly modified by the spirit of recent centuries, which treated as insignificant that pampered darling of the West, the self.

But Hume had nothing against the self. He showed this when the cross-examination became such a bitter wrangle that the judge had to check it, and reminded him that he must not answer counsel violently, telling him that the purpose of the trial was to make a necessary investigation and that there was nothing personal behind the questions put to him by his cross-examiner and therefore no occasion for heat. To this Hume replied, "But my life is a personal matter to me." This was not only a very sensible remark, which the judge did not reject, it was a proclamation made with immense Byronic pride. Yet he made no claim that the life he wished to preserve showed any merit. No man ever went into a witness box to defend himself against a capital charge and took such trouble to convince the jury that he was of bad character. When he was asked whether he would call himself an honest man, he answered that perhaps it would be better to call him a semi-honest man; and his grin gave a deep nastiness to the phrase. He was announcing that he would not be good but he would not be bad either; he was presenting them with a problem of confusion and defied them to solve it. He had a deep love of chaos, and he was for the self because it can carry such a load of the stuff. It was his intention to revolt all who have tried to establish order and to torment them by declaring that let the ballet be what it may, there would still be cripples who cannot dance and louts that will not, there will be blindness which cannot be cured by exercises, sickness which will not yield to herbal iodine and sickness which resists psychoanalysis, fields which will be barren for all the dung that is spread on them, and souls which refuse the gift of peace from Christianity or any other faith. Hume spoke with the voice of the spirit that denies.

It seemed odd that a person so strong in dissent should have lived the ordinary existence of which we had been told. He had been an RAF officer who had done well in the war, having won a decoration in the Battle of Britain, and had been invalided out of the service. Since then he had made a living in various ways, some of which were quite ordinary jobs of electrical engineering, and others of which, such as dealing in planes for the Near East, were more unusual and probably dovetailed with more dubious ones. He had had bad luck; he had started a factory in Wales to make plastic switches and it had been destroyed by two fires. He had his gay side and was seen about in night clubs, often with notably good-looking girls. But he was making a good living by acting as a commercial pilot. It was a very ordinary story. What made it extraordinary was that, though everybody who knew him, including his wife, to whom he was a devoted husband, believed it, not one word of it was true.

There had been some strange circumstances connected with his birth. His mother was a schoolmistress and called herself his aunt and when he was three he was sent to some sort of institution which he always described as an orphanage, at which he stayed until he was ten. He interpreted this to mean that he was illegitimate and that he had been sent to this institution because his mother hated him and wished to cast him off. But there are reasons for disbelieving that the story was as simple or as sinister. His mother, an intelligent woman, sister of a well-known scientist, was married at the time of his birth, and it is possible that she may have concealed her relationship to him in order that both of them should escape the shadow of some curious calamity; and certainly many women have sent their young children away to boarding school not because they wanted to but because their circumstances prevented them from looking after them at home. In the village where she lived at the time of the trial she was liked and respected, and as in his childhood she took Hume back from his boarding school to make his home with her, and as she makes a later appearance in his story as conferring with somebody who wanted to be his benefactor, it seems unlikely that she behaved badly to him. Apparently the psychoanalysts are right, and the mind of a child cannot stand any prolonged separation from its mother during the first five years. In any case he continually spoke with rage of his mother, and went on and on through the years about her cruelty in leaving him in the orphanage. He once had a long conversation on the subject with Mrs Stride, the daily help who gave evidence at his trial, and she gravely told him not to wear himself out by making a fuss over it, and said that she had a right to tell him that, because her father had died young and her mother had had to let her go away for a time, and she knew what it was to have that happen to you when you were a child. But you just had to forget it and get on with life.

He was a clever boy. He won a scholarship that might have taken him through a secondary school and given him a good chance of going to the university; but in a frenzy he rushed out into the world and earned his living as a kitchen boy in various hotels. It is strange that wherever this boy went, who was bitter because he believed his mother had failed to love him, the earth opened and there appeared people who were willing to give him deep and disinterested affection. One winter's day in 1934, when he was fourteen, he was seen by a motorist walking across a common in the suburbs of London, dragging a heavy suitcase and weeping. The motorist stopped and gave him a lift and asked him what his trouble was. Hume told him that he was running away from a job as a houseboy in a hotel where they had ill-treated him, and was going to the docks to find a ship that would take him. The motorist, who was a builder, offered him a job in his own business, bought him a suit of clothes, and got one of his own foremen to take the boy in as a lodger. This was amazing good luck, for the foreman's wife, an elderly woman named Mary Clare, immediately became his loving and beloved mother.

There began what should have been a happy life for him. By day he learned with some aptitude the craft of electrician; and in the evening he sat with his new mother in the kitchen and enchanted her and was enchanted by her. For a time he became a Communist and had a contented time planning revolution, but politics had hardly any chance with him because of his obsession with planes. When he was working on the wiring of a new house they could always tell where he had been, because he had scribbled drawings of planes on the plastered walls. It was this passion for planes which made him leave that business and take a job in an aircraft factory, and later another one in a Metal Engraving Company which had some connection with aeronautics. At the same time he joined the RAF Volunteer Reserve, and when war came he enlisted in the Royal Air Force.

Very soon he had a serious accident when flying. Probably he cared too much about it. Shortly afterwards he had an attack of cerebro-spinal meningitis, and he was declared unfit for flying duty and put on the ground staff. Eighteen months after he had volunteered he was declared unfit for any sort of duty in the RAF and was invalided out. Then he took a job as one of the spotters who sat on the roofs of factories and offices and gave warning when a German plane was actually in the neighbourhood, so that the workers need not break off and go down to the shelter when the sirens sounded, which might announce the arrival of a plane anywhere within a hundred miles. At the same time he was trying to get back into the RAF through other avenues, and once got a call to an Aviation Selection Board, but was turned down. It happened about this time that Mary Clare, who had again given him a home, took in her own daughter and her husband, who were homeless owing to the war, and the girl had a baby. Hume became bitterly jealous and complained that Mrs Clare gave the baby too much of her attention and that it cried so much that he got pains in his head. He became such a plague that she was forced to ask him to leave the house.

Shortly afterwards he revisited his benefactor, who had picked him up on the common six years before. He was in sergeant-pilot's uniform and told a story of having played a gallant part in the Battle of Britain. He gave his benefactor and some of the workmen souvenirs, parts of planes he had shot down and a German machine gun. Later he turned up again in officer's uniform, wearing the ribbon of the Distinguished Flying Medal; and in this rig-out he went to the Metal Engraving Company works, where the firm gave him a substantial cheque in appreciation of what he had done for the country. Then his benefactor received a visit from the police, who told him that Hume had been using his name in the town to recommend himself to people on whom he played the confidence trick; and shortly afterwards he was arrested for masquerading as an RAF officer. He had for some time been carrying on a peculiar fraud, which required great talent and resourcefulness. After Mrs Clare had asked him to go he had lodged with an ex-officer of the RAF, and had bought his uniform from him and had borrowed an RAF identity card. Thereafter he had travelled from one airfield to another all over the country, living in the messes, getting pilots to take him up for flights, and finally cashing worthless cheques and going on his way to another airfield. He even consulted an RAF medical officer and got him to certify him as unfit for duty, so that he had a certificate to convince any military policeman or anybody else who questioned him that he was on sick leave.

So ingenious was this plan of campaign that the police at first thought that Hume must be a spy. But they found out that the story was a simple one of imposture, and he was bound over to come up for judgement after being kept in prison for some time under medical treatment. While he was jailed he wrote to Mrs Clare, who sent him sweets and food. But when he came out he did not go to see her. He cut himself off from his second chance of a contented home life because it was more important to him that he should be able to go on pretending to be a pilot. His marriage was a supreme episode in that impersonation; and there are glimpses of other delights. One summer he appeared at Torquay, the best of the south coast seaside resorts, with an American accent and a large American automobile, saying that he was a Pan-American Airways pilot. He became very popular, and when there was a town carnival he was asked to drive the carnival queen in the procession, which he did, bringing out a scarlet and gold uniform for the occasion. He gave the right impression of being very good-humoured about doing something which he could not, of course, really like doing.

It is an obvious enough story. He suffered from the neurotic's incapacity for love and could not compensate for that lack by exercising power, so pretended to be powerful. But it was much more than that. The idea of flight had had some treatment in his mind which made it tremendous. When Mr Humphreys, listing his lies, asked him whether it was not true that he had pretended to be a pilot though he had failed his tests, he was convulsed with grief and fury as he shouted back that he had not failed his tests, he had never taken them, he was not allowed to take them, because he had concussion. "You have no right to say I failed," he cried, as if Mr Humphreys were in some magic way killing him by using those words. He too had his religion, he could not bear to have it violated, he was a fervent worshipper. That was to be seen in his apartment, which was a temple of flight. The upper parts of all the walls were obsessionally covered with photographs of planes, of aviators, of air battles, with parts of planes, with cartoons about flyers. Many boys and girls are infatuated with flying, but their rooms are not quite like these, though the fetishes are the same. In his apartment there was a wall on the staircase to the upper floor which took the light. On this wall there were arranged such pictures and such plane parts, and a medal. They were arranged in a pattern like the outline of a great bird with wings. This was not planned; it was an achievement of the daemon within Hume, who had ideas about flight beyond the sphere of aeronautics, who allowed, indeed, some pictures on his walls which were neither of planes nor aviators, which were of birds with strong wings, wild swans, wild geese, creatures of dazzling plumage, cleaving air so high and pure that it is not air at all. Hume had mistaken the nature of his spirit. This was not denial, it was affirmation.

Purity is the justification of flight here. You rise and leave your abhorred mother and the orphanage far below. Above the pictures and the plane parts on the walls was a cartoon representing a pilot as a knight in armour, saving the world from evil. There was no indication anywhere in the apartment that Hume was attracted by the idea of murder. There were on his shelves no detective stories, only books, mostly of a high standard, about flying and adventure. But there were in these pictures hints that added up to a broad statement that a man had lived here who would find it ecstasy, the perfect realization of a fantasy which had absorbed him from childhood, to take a corpse, reeking emblem of our human corruption, defy its nastiness by expos- ing it to the purification of flight, and cast it down through the clean air into the clean sea, which would keep it and cover it and annul it forever. It was extraordinary that somewhere an unknown man had found it pleasing to his soul to kill and cut up an enemy, thus giving Hume an opportunity to do the equally strange thing that pleased his soul; but none more extraordinary than that the corpse should ultimately have been picked up by Mr Tiffen, who was as strange as these others in his great goodness, and therefore was able to pity Mr Setty in a way that performed the miracle Hume had thought the air and sea would do, and took the horror from the crime.

It must not be thought that Hume got his ecstasy for nothing. He had had to win it by great courage. He had either been connected with the RAF or posing as a flyer for about twelve years, but not till the last year had he taken flying instruction sufficient to get a licence. Then he only got a civilian "C" licence, which enabled him to fly solo but included only one hour's instruction in navigation and none at all in night flying. It was the opinion of the airfield staff that he had no gift for flying, and in any case he must have lacked practice. In his work as an electrician he showed a curious mixture of flashes of unusual aptitude combined with an unusual unhandiness and failure to grasp essentials. It is to be noted that the times of his two flights with Setty's body over the sea, running into the evening, are fantastically long; he should have been able to do the job well before dusk fell. He landed in the most odd places, twice coming down south of the river when he wanted to be north. He owned to the police that he blundered about, losing his bearings, misjudging his height so that once he nearly flew into the water. It was bad weather. It was sheer accident that he did not die for his ideal.

Surviving that phase of danger, he tried again for martyrdom. When he was telling the story of how the three men had given him the parcels his life depended on whether he was believed; but his desire to alienate his hearers grew here to a perverse climax, and he told the story so that nobody would wish to believe it. When he was describing how he had handled the third parcel, how, as he lifted it, it made a gurgling noise and he saw a pool of blood under it, he said, "It put the fear of Christ up me," and leered. There was nothing spontaneous in the brutality of his speech. He was using the name of Christ in the hope that some believers would consider it blasphemy, he was speaking of the dead flesh with planned callousness so that he should affront the pitiful, and he was feeling a sensual pleasure at the thought that he was disgusting people so much that presently they would turn round and hurt him, perhaps to the ultimate degree. He worked still further to that end by altering the time when this incident had occurred to an hour different from the one he had given in his original statement, thus making it less easy to believe. At such moments his plump face lost masculinity and youth; he might have been a smiling middle-aged woman dressed as a man. He was invoking chaos, and it came. But he did not appear a murderer. It was impossible to imagine him leaving the world of fantasy long enough really to kill a man. But the three men he described as leaving the corpse with him, they too seemed to belong to the world of fantasy.

It is true that there were two witnesses who confirmed the existence of the three men. One was a retired army officer who seemed odd to English eyes, because he was exactly like the American idea of an Englishman. Tall and rigid, with a long and fastidious face, and a voice strangled with punctiliousness, he gave evidence that he had once lived in the mews where Mr Setty had his garage, and that it had rapidly degenerated from a citadel of respectability to a haunt of spivs. His head went back, his nostrils dilated. One saw the gipsies come in, some in black and some in yellow. He was of opinion that among the spivs there had been two called Maxie and The Boy, and one who had answered to the description of Greenie. This took us not very far; but the second witness was to take us much further. This was a man in his early thirties who described himself as a writer. He was an attractive young man, with thick golden hair, a sensitive face, and a well-bred voice. Before he gave evidence he looked round the court with a diffident smile which told that he liked being liked. He gave evidence which, if it were accepted, went far to making Hume's story credible. He said that he had been in Paris the year before, and had got into touch with a gang engaged in the smuggling of arms into Palestine and automobiles into Britain. Two strong-arm men attached to this gang were known as Maxie and The Boy and answered to the description given by Hume. He had got into this company, he explained, because he had met a man in a night club who had offered to cash some travellers' cheques for him, and so he had gone back with him to his hotel, at which place the obliging gentleman was arrested by the police; and the mere fact that he had been present at the arrest had made the other members of the gang accept him as one of themselves. He had collected a great deal of information about them and had sent a report about them to both the French Sûreté and the British Embassy. This last statement could be so easily verified that it compelled belief in his evidence. But alas, this was—let him be known as Philip—a poor soul born to vex a respectable family, well known to every contemporary amateur of crime by reason of his frequent convictions. Yet he is no criminal, merely one of the wild asses of the world, and nobody, not even the police, is ever very angry with him, though, to be sure, larceny and forgery and bigamy cause some inconvenience. It was most strange that he should have come out of safe obscurity and visited Scotland Yard, which for him was putting his head in the lion's mouth, for the purpose of giving testimony in support of Hume's story of the three men. He had never seen Hume in his life before, but there was a bond between the two of them. For Philip's first conviction and Hume's only conviction had been for the same offence: for unlawfully wearing military emblems and representing himself to be a member of His Majesty's Forces. It is most probable that Philip did not know this when he volunteered to give testimony for Hume. These two naturally flew in the same flight, in bad weather and poor visibility, losing their bearings and diving so deep that the waters rushed up at them.

It would have been better for Hume if his wife had mentioned the three men when she murmured her evidence. But she, like the char-woman Mrs Stride, gave testimony that wrecked both the case for the prosecution and the case for the defence. She declared that she had been in the apartment throughout the night when, according to the prosecution, her husband had stabbed and cut up Mr Setty, and had seen and heard nothing unusual; but with equal, gentle firmness she declared that she had seen no three men in the apartment at the time when Hume said they had visited him. And her evidence was certainly true, for she had not sought to prove that she was away from the apartment on the night of the murder, which a perjurer in her position would certainly have done. Yet many people regarded her with suspicion. Even if Hume had merely received the parcels and put them in the coal cupboard, wouldn't she, the housewife, have been bound to know something about that? And why hadn't she asked her husband why he suddenly wanted the dining-room carpet cleaned, and where the rug in the hall had gone? These questions showed the prevailing ignorance of nearly all men and the more articulate kind of woman regarding the common lot of the inarticulate woman. A mother only three months past a dangerous confinement, who was feeding her baby and was worried about its illness, would be just getting round to the things she had to do, and would not be worrying about the coal cupboard, which was below eye level, and could only be inspected if she went on her knees. As for the carpet, it was light green, they had tried to buy a dark green one when they were furnishing and had been unable to get one, so they had taken the lighter one and had promised themselves to have it dyed as soon as it got dirty, and it was dirty by this time, it had been down for over ten months. She had not asked why Hume wanted it dyed at that particular moment for the same reason that she had failed to ask where the rug had gone, because she was the kind of woman who accepts everything that men do. The creatures are irrational, but they are useful, and it might impair their usefulness to vex them with reasonable propositions. The disappearance of the rug, moreover, had appeared to her, when she hazily thought about it, as possibly to be explained by her husband's habit of pawning things, which often sent her possessions away on temporary holidays.

But the suspicion that many men and some women felt about Mrs Hume was derived not from dissatisfaction at her explanations of her conduct, but from her own reactions to her intense femininity. Her face, her body, her bearing, and above all, her soft, preoccupied voice, made an allusion to something outside the context; and they believed this something to be the truth about the murder. One might as well suspect a tree that has blossomed because it is spring of making signals to another tree. What her whole being was alluding to, definitely though with dignity, was sex; the whole process, not short-circuited. When her eyes darkened, and she knitted her delicate eyebrows and then smoothed them out again, and smiled, the suspicious imagined that she was thinking. "How terrible it was that night I helped him to wash out the bloodstains in the apartment, but thanks to the lawyers I have got out of all that trouble scot free." But those who knew her, and these included some not unskilful in extracting secrets, were aware that at such times she was pondering such thoughts as these:

"This apartment is not very convenient now we have a baby. I wish we had a proper house, with a garden. Then I could put baby out in her pram to sleep in the mornings. And I could hang the diapers out to dry, instead of putting them on that horrible pulley outside the window, which is so stiff and heavy. Also, it would be more convenient for keeping the pram; I have to leave it on the stairs now, and people have to push past it. But I must not grumble. After all, Golders Hill Park is just up the road, and it is a very pretty park. It is a big house with beautiful gardens, and the London County Council has taken it over and keeps it just as it used to be before; you might think you were visiting a friend's home. It will be nice, taking baby up there in the summer, when the band plays. And they have a little zoo there, with kangaroos. It will be amusing when baby is old enough to notice them."

Her thoughts were not of this simplicity because she was stupid but because she was a pragmatist and these were the thoughts which were most useful for her to think in her present situation, while she was the mother of a young child. It was very difficult to make people believe that what seemed interesting and exciting to her about her life at present was not that her husband had been caught disposing of a corpse, but that she had just had a baby. Yet, when the bloodstained facts of history are considered, it is apparent that this must have been the standard feminine attitude throughout the ages.

She was a troubling figure to anybody who had begun to doubt the value of life as a thing in itself, who had decided that life ought to be rejected if it were this and not that. Passive and yielding and drowsy with the fatigue of doing all that has to be done for a young baby, she had the massive resolution of a battleship or a bomber. She meant life to go on, whatever it was like. That was how she came back into the case, at the very end. Her husband's counsel, Richard Levy, had made a closing speech that put him in the first rank of criminal lawyers. He was already well known at the commercial bar, where the great fees are made, and much esteemed by his fellows; but this speech took him a stage further. What he did for Hume was not to expatiate on his story of the three men but to prove that the prosecution's story was at least as vague, and cite the evidence of Mrs Stride and Mrs Hume as proof. It was a superb speech, as free from humbug and tricks as Euclid, and it lived in the memory by its logic and lucidity. It showed the strength of the best sort of Jewish mind, which becomes majestic as it pursues an argument, because justice is the product of sound argument, and Jehovah is a just God.

Nevertheless its majesty moved Mr Christmas Humphreys to one last transport of what looked like indecorum but was acute spiritual distress. He could not abide the use that Mr Levy made of Mrs Hume's testimony that she had seen no murder done in the apartment; he had used it as conclusive proof that no murder had been done. Mr Humphreys said, "I am not prosecuting Mrs Hume. I am not defending her. She is first and foremost the wife of the man she loves. There is a law older than the law of England or any man-made law; a man and a wife who love one another stick together. I do not say that Mrs Hume had no part in this murder. I say I have no evidence whatsoever that she had any part in it. I certainly do not agree necessarily that she had no part in the cutting up of the body and the tidying up of the apartment. That is entirely a matter for you to consider if you wish." These were strange words. They suggested to the jury that they should consider whether Mrs Hume was guilty of murder or of acting as an accessory after the fact, though she had not been charged with either offence nor given an opportunity of being legally defended against such charges, and the jury had no means of expressing its conviction of her guilt, or, what was more important, her innocence. This left Mrs Hume at the end of the trial in a position in which the process of justice should never leave anybody. This was peculiarly unfortunate, as there was not a shadow of evidence that she had committed any offence whatsoever. But there are philosophical divergencies which go deep. "Now let the unravished heart arise, and find Communicable light," Mr Christmas Humphreys remarks in one of his poems. But Mrs Hume was the female whose heart, not to be ravished by any calamity, found communicable light and communicable shadow too, and went on producing life in its unreformed state.

When the jury disagreed and had to be discharged there ran through the court the relief which is always felt when a man escapes conviction on a capital charge, a relief which is not so much of the mind as of the bones and blood and nerves, feeling for their kind. But it was succeeded by distress. For one thing, it is in England something of a scandal, reflecting credit on no person connected with the trial, when a jury disagrees on a murder charge. It happens very rarely; nobody at the Old Bailey that day could call to mind more than two such cases in the last fifty years. Theoretically the Director of Public Prosecutions should not charge a man with a capital crime unless it has got enough facts to shape a story which a jury can either believe or disbelieve. But this odd crime had made it impossible for the prosecution to stick to this theory, for there were so many facts

314

which made it look as if Hume had murdered Mr Setty that it would have been giving a licence to murderers not to bring him to court.

There were, however, deeper reasons for discomfort. The position of man is obviously extremely insecure unless he can find out what is happening around him. That is why historians publicly pretend that they can give an exact account of events in the past, though they privately know that all the past will let us know about events above a certain degree of importance is a bunch of alternative hypotheses. But they find such hypotheses. Here, however, was a crime that was not in the past but in the present, and was much simpler than any important historical event. But it remained a secret: a secret which was in the hands of a talkative spiv, yet was unbreakable. If we could not find out the nature of a monstrous act which we knew to have been committed in the insubstantial shelter of Hume's flat, we were more helpless than we had thought, and anything could creep up on us. It also made for misery to contemplate Hume. It seemed a symbol that two judges had sat on the bench, coming out of different centuries to try him, the one so like a medieval churchman, the other so visibly a man of our times, liberal and reasonable, and that there was no verdict. Hume could not be thought of as a coherent person, and made limbo a real place.

The legal situation created by the disagreement of the jury was tidied up within a few minutes. Another jury was sworn in, and Hume was again charged with the murder of Mr Setty, and asked to plead, and he pleaded not guilty; then the prosecution announced that it intended to offer no evidence, and the judge directed the jury to return a verdict of not guilty. This procedure was not automatic. Two days later another jury, in the North of England, failed to reach a verdict after the trial of two men on a murder charge which lasted thirteen days, the longest murder trial that has ever taken place in Great Britain. The men were on trial again within a week, and one of them, a man named Kelly, was condemned to death and the other was acquitted, within a fortnight. But there was plainly no use retrying Hume's case. Not that he went free. There was another indictment against him which charged him with being an accessory after the fact of murder; and he pleaded guilty to this offence, having confessed to it in his statement, and was sentenced to twelve years' imprisonment. Then came the last strange feature of the case. It did not come to an end.

We all waited for more to happen. Hume was a man who would

have to talk, who would have to go on making drama. In prison it would be safe for him to talk. He had said that he had wanted to go to the police and tell them about the part he had played in getting rid of the body when the news of Mr Tiffen's find on the marshes had been published in the papers, but had been frightened into silence by a telephone call from the three men who had left the parcels with him. It might be perfectly true that from some quarter he had been threatened; he would be protected from such intimidation now. That he should have a new story to tell became more certain as certain facts about the old one sunk into our minds. In fact there had been three men, Mac or Maxie, The Boy, and Greenie. It was slowly realized that the description of Mac or Maxie quite closely fitted one of the policemen who were in the police station where Hume was examined; and as for The Boy and Greenie, there is a novel, by Graham Greene, called *Brighton Rock*, which had been turned into a film. The chief character is a nasty little gangster, who, like Hume, had been brought up in an orphanage, and he was known as The Boy and as Pinkie.

But, though there were rumours that Hume had made a statement in prison, nobody has been charged with the murder of Mr Setty; and Scotland Yard has indicated that in its opinion the case is closed. But in our minds it is still open; and the individual members of the various organizations which cooperated to bring Hume to justice find it hard to stop talking it over. The features of the murderer behind Hume are so mysterious. For one thing they are so trustful. It may be that Hume himself never met him face to face, but he knew the identity of his agents, and whether they were Maxie, The Boy, and Greenie, or anybody else, they left a trail which could have been followed back by Hume himself or by the police. Who was the man who could devise a cunning and intricate murder that but for the whimsical pull of the moon on certain tides would have gone for ever undetected, and confided the execution of it to a flying man who could only by a miracle have performed the flying essential to the plan, and who habitually gossiped and lied and boasted? Nobody could do anything so mad. But somebody had done it; and the behaviour of the witnesses was to give, before the case slipped down into the depths of memory, evidence that no course of action is so mad that some human being will not adopt it.

One day the crime reporter who had been haled before the court because of his letter and telegram to Mrs Hume was sitting in his office when there came in, with that shy smile which told of such a strong desire to be liked, Philip. He carried a telegram which he said he had received at his London lodgings. It was from the gang, and it threatened him with revenge. What gang? And why did anybody want to revenge themselves on him? Why, Philip explained, the gang in Paris. They were angry with him because he had gone into the witness box and told how he knew Maxie, The Boy, and Greenie. The crime reporter was nonplussed by the reappearance of these characters. Pulling himself together, he expressed sympathy, regretted that he could do nothing about it, and advised Philip to go to Scotland Yard and tell them about it there. They went out and had some coffee and a chat, and Philip went off into London with a charming wave of the hand. The crime reporter never expected to hear anything more of the matter. But Philip took his advice. He went to Scotland Yard, where they took little interest in the telegram but looked at him sadly. Now he had come back to see them they could not help arresting him for a new charge that had been brought up against him since he forced his way into the limelight by giving evidence in the Hume case. He had been committing bigamy, and he got two years for it.

Up in Golders Green, Mrs Hume was still living in the apartment, not because she was insensitive to the tragedy which had taken place there (whatever that had been) but because of the times. The apartment was under the Rent Restriction Act, so she got it for just over three dollars a week; and even if she had been financially justified in going out and looking for a more expensive one, the housing shortage was still so acute that it would have been difficult to find one. No fine feelings can disregard such solid facts. Now her sister and her little niece were living with her, but otherwise her domestic arrangements were much as before. The charwoman, Mrs Stride, had presented herself on her usual day and had said that, if Mrs Hume did not mind her working for her after she had given evidence against Mr Hume, she would be pleased to continue to give her every Wednesday. When Mrs Stride was asked by any of her other employers or in any of the local shops whether it was true that she was still working for Mrs Hume, she was accustomed to reply with dignity, borrowing locutions used only in old-fashioned and majestic establishments of a sort not now found in Golders Green, that she was proud to do her best for Madam and Miss Margaret. By Miss Margaret she meant the six-months-old baby. But it would be unsafe to draw from this manner of speech any conclusion regarding Mrs Stride's view of social problems. It is her moral nature which is asserting itself. She will have no cruelty practised on the innocent and the unfortunate.

In that household also the Hume case is not closed. But it is not the same case that continues to perplex the outer world. What puzzled Mrs Hume was not the identity of the man who sent the parcels to her husband: that was just somebody male doing something unusually silly and horrid. It was the identity of her husband, the identity of her home. Nothing in her life was what she had believed it to be, not even the dog. A short time after the trial she found herself telling a visitor how this cheerful mongrel, part Alsatian, part collie-dog, had come to belong to her husband. When he was in Europe with the RAF in 1945 his squadron took over an airport which the Germans had abandoned, and found a paddock in which the German airmen had left their dogs; and he and this mongrel had taken an instant fancy to each other, so he smuggled him back to England in his plane next time he flew home. That was the story she repeated, as she had heard him tell it again and again, to her, to their friends, to strangers, to anybody who was moved by the dog's jolly character to ask where he had got it. Now it suddenly struck her that the story could not be true. Her husband had not been an RAF pilot, he had taken no part in the liberation of Europe, he had been by then a civilian. This made the dog a double mongrel, part Alsatian and part collie, part real and part phantom. She looked at it doubt-fully, fearing that if she patted it her hand would go through it.

She felt a like amazement about her husband. Not, it must be emphasized, about his involvement in the murder. Women of her type resemble artists in their failure to feel surprise at the exceptional event. What amazed her was the incongruity between the facts which the police told her about her husband and what she herself knew about him. Of her own knowledge she was for the most part silent; she has a great faculty for silence. But sometimes she spoke of merits that he had, such as his great kindness, not merely warm and impulsive, but responsible and enduring, towards the men he had employed in his radio business. She did not deny that what the police said was true, she simply made a claim that what she knew was also true. It was a pity for her sake that she was not more sentimental and bemused, that she would have to go in a state of stone-cold emotional sobriety to all the prison visits which lay ahead of her; and indeed those visits went worse than could have been imagined,

318

and later, because of them, she was granted a divorce. But these matters did not, of course, touch on the really important point. The baby upstairs was putting on the right amount of weight now. It was everything that a baby should be. Her mother would bring her up so that she was an attractive girl, very like any other attractive girl. The snarl in Hume's genetic line would be disentangled.

The mystery which involved him with Mr Setty will be written about as long as there is a literature of crime; but it will exist only on the printed page. Day by day, through the years, somewhere in the outer suburbs of London, its practical effects will have been quietly smoothed away, and it will be as if it had never happened.

FROM The New Meaning of Treason (1964)

(Revised and expanded from *The Meaning of Treason*, 1949)

From I. The Revolutionary

1

The idea of a traitor first became real to the British of our time when they heard the voice of William Joyce on the radio during the war. The conception of treachery first became real to them when he was brought to trial as a radio traitor. For he was something new in the history of the world. Never before have people known the voice of one they had never seen as well as if he had been a husband or a brother or a close friend; and had they foreseen such a miracle they could not have imagined that this familiar unknown would speak to them only to prophesy their death and ruin. A great many people had experienced this hideous novelty, for it was easy to chance on Joyce's wave length when one was tuning in on the English stations, and there was a rasping yet rich quality about his voice which made it difficult not to go on listening; and he was nearly convincing in his assurance. It seemed as if one had better hearken and take warning when he suggested that the destiny of the people he had left in England was death, and the destiny of his new masters in Germany life and conquest, and that, therefore, his listeners had better change sides and submit; and he had the advantage that the news in the papers confirmed what he said. He was not only alarming, he was ugly. He opened a vista into a mean life. He always spoke as if he was better fed and better clothed than we were, and so, we now know, he was. He went farther than that mockery of his own people's plight. He sinned that sin which travesties legitimate hatred because it is felt for kindred, as incest is the travesty of legitimate love. When the U-boats were sinking so many of our ships that to open the newspapers was to see the faces of drowned sailors, he rolled the figures of our lost tonnage on his tongue. When we were facing the hazard of D-day, he rejoiced in the thought of the English dead which would soon lie under the West Wall.

So all the curious went off to the Central Criminal Court on September 17, 1945, when he came up for trial. The Old Bailey was as it had not been before the war and is not now. Because of the blitz it stood in a beautiful desert of charred stone. Churches stood blackened but apparently intact; birds, however, flew through the empty sockets of the windows, and long grass grew around their altars. A red brick Georgian mansion, hidden for a century by sordid warehouses, looked at the dome of Saint Paul's, now astonishingly great, across acres where willow-herb, its last purple flowers passing into silver clouds of seed dust, and yellow ragwort grew from the ground plan of a city drawn in rubble. The grey stone of the Old Bailey itself had been gashed by a bomb. Its solidarity had been sliced as if it were a cake, and the walls of the slice were crude new red brick. Inside the building, because there was not yet the labour to take down the heavy black-out, the halls and passages and stairs were in perpetual dusk. The courtroom—the Court No. 1, where all the most famous criminal trials of modern times have taken place—was lit by electric light, for the shattered glass dome had not yet been rebuilt. Bare boards filled it in, giving an odd-come-short look to what had been a fine room in its austere way.

The strong light was merciless to William Joyce, whose appearance was a shock to all of us who knew him only over the air. His voice had suggested a large and flashy handsomeness, but he was a tiny little creature and not handsome at all. His hair was mouse-coloured and sparse, particularly above his ears, and his pinched and mis-shapen nose was joined to his face at an odd angle. His eyes were hard and shiny, and above them his thick eyebrows were pale and irregular. His neck was long, his shoulders narrow and sloping, his arms very short and thick. His body looked flimsy and coarse. There was nothing individual about him except a deep scar running across his right cheek from his ear to the corner of his mouth. But this did not create the savage and marred distinction that it might suggest, for it gave a mincing immobility to his small mouth. He was dressed with a dandyish preciosity which gave no impression of well-being, only of nervousness. He was like an ugly version of Scott Fitzgerald, but more nervous. He moved with a jerky formality and, when he bowed to the judge, his bow seemed sincerely respectful but entirely inappropriate to the occasion, and it was difficult to think of any occasion to which it would have been appropriate.

He had been defying us all. Yet there was nobody in the court who did not look superior to him. The men and women in the jury box were all middle-aged, since the armies had not yet come home, and, like everybody else in England at that date, they were puffy and haggard. But they were all more pleasant to look at and more obviously trustworthy than the homely and eccentric little man in the dock; and compared with the judicial bench which he faced he was, of course, at an immense disadvantage, as we all should be, for its dignity is authentic. The judge sat in a high-backed chair, the sword of justice in its jewelled scabbard affixed to the oak panel behind him, splendid in his scarlet robe, with its neckband of fine white linen and its deep cuffs and sash of purplish-black taffeta. Beside him, their chairs set farther back as a sign of their inferiority to him, sat the Lord Mayor of London and two aldermen, wearing antique robes of black silk with flowing white cravats and gold chains with pendant badges of office worked in precious metals and enamel. It sometimes happens, and it happened then, that these pompous trappings are given real significance by the faces of men who wear them. Judges are chosen for intellect and character, and city honours must be won by intellect combined with competence at the least, and men in both positions must have the patience to carry out tedious routines over decades, and the story is often written on their features.

Looking from the bench to the dock, it could be seen that not in any sane community would William Joyce have had the ghost of a chance of holding such offices as these. This was tragic, as appeared when he was asked to plead and he said, "Not guilty." Those two words were the most impressive uttered during the trial. The famous voice was let loose. For a fraction of a second we heard its familiar quality. It was as it had sounded for six years, reverberating with the desire for power. Never was there a more perfect voice for a demagogue, for its reverberations were certain to awake echoes in every heart tumid with the same desire. Given this passionate ambition to exercise authority, which as this scene showed could not be gratified, what could he ever have done but use his trick of gathering together other poor fellows luckless in the same way, so that they might overturn the sane community that was bound to reject them, and substitute a mad one that would regard them kindly?

That was the reason why he was in the dock; that, and Irish history. For it was at once apparent that this trial, like the great treason trial of the First World War, which sent Sir Roger Casement to the gallows, had started on the other side of the Saint George's Channel.

There had been rumours that Joyce was Irish, but they had never been officially confirmed, and his accent was difficult to identify. But there was no doubt about it when one saw him in the dock. He had the real Donnybrook air. He was not a very fortunate example of the small, nippy, jig-dancing kind of Irish peasant, and the appearance of his brother, who attended the court every day in a state of great suffering, proved the family's origin. Quentin Joyce, who was then twenty-eight, was eleven years William's junior. He was the better-looking of the two, with a sturdy body, a fresh colour, thick lustrous brown hair, and the soft eyes of a cow. Nobody could mistake him for anything but a country-bred Irishman, and there were as clear traces of Irish origins in many of the followers of Joyce, who watched the trial. True, his best friend was visibly a Scot: a black Highlander, with fierce black eyes blazing behind thick glasses, a tiny fuzz of black hair fancifully arranged on his prematurely bald head, and wrists and ankles as thin as lead piping. He was Angus MacNab, the editor of a Fascist paper. He was plainly foredoomed to follow odd bypaths, and a variation in circumstances might have found him just as happily a spiritualist medium or a believer in the lost ten tribes of Israel. As it was, he was wholly committed to Joyce. So too were the rank and file of the faithful, who were for the most part men of violent and unhappy appearance, with a look of animal shyness and ferocity, and, in some cases, a measure of animal beauty. They were on the whole rather darker than one would expect in subscribers to the Aryan theory. One, especially, looked like a true gipsy. Many of them had an Irish cast of feature, and some bore Irish names. It was to be remembered that Joyce had seceded from Mosley's movement some years before the war and had started his own. These were not at all like Mosleyites, who were as a rule of a more varied and more cheerfully brutal type.

The case was tinged with irony from the start because the prosecuting counsel for the Crown was Sir Hartley Shawcross, the Attorney-General appointed by the new Labour Government. People in court were anxious to see what he was like, for when the Labour Party had previously held office it had experienced some difficulty in getting law officers of the quality the Tories could provide; and it was a relief to find that he was a winning personality with a gift for setting out a lucid argument in the manner of a great advocate. He was, in fact, certain to enjoy just that success which the man he was prosecuting had desired so much as to put himself in danger of a capital charge; a capital charge of which he was sure, it seemed in the earlier parts of the case, to be convicted.

There were three counts in the indictment brought against him. He had offended, it seemed, against the root of the law against treason: a statute in which Edward III, in the year 1351, "at the request of the lords and commons" declared that "if a man do levy war against our Lord the King in his realm or be adherent to the King's enemies in his realm, giving them aid and comfort in the realm or elsewhere," he was guilty of treason. So the Clerk of the Court, Sir Wilfred Knops, said: "William Joyce, you are charged in an indictment containing three counts with high treason. The particulars in the first count are that on the 18th September, 1939, and on other days between that day and the 29th May, 1945, you, being a person owing allegiance to our Lord the King, and when a war was being carried on by the German realm against our King, did traitorously adhere to the King's enemies, in parts beyond the seas, that is to say in Germany, by broadcasting propaganda. In a second count of the same indictment, it is charged that you, on the 26th September, 1940, being a person owing allegiance as in the other count, adhered to the King's enemies by purporting to become naturalized as a subject of Germany. And in the third count, the particulars are the same as in the first count, that is to say, you are charged with broadcasting propaganda, but the dates are different, and the dates in this case are the eighteenth day of September, 1939, and on days between that day and the second day of July, 1940, being then to wit, on the said several days, a person owing allegiance to our Lord the King." Later the first two counts were amended, for reasons emerging during the trial, and he was described in them as "a British subject," but, significantly, no such change was made in the third.

It seemed as if William Joyce must be found guilty on the first two of these counts. What was first told of his life in court showed it as an open-and-shut case. William Joyce's dead father had been a Galway man named Michael Joyce, who had worked as a builder and contractor in America during the nineties; he married in May 1902 a Lancashire girl named Gertrude Emily Brooke in New York at the Roman Catholic Church of All Saints on Madison Avenue and 129th Street, and had settled down with her in Brooklyn, where William had been born in 1906. Later inquiry into the story behind the evidence showed their life to have been very pleasant. The Joyces must have been quite prosperous. They lived in a very agreeable house, now a realtor's office, on a corner lot in a broad street planted with trees, charming with the square, substantial, moderate charm of old Brooklyn. Now that street is occupied at one end by Negroes and at the other by Italians, but then it was a centre of the staider Irish, and the solid petty-bourgeois German quarter was not far off.

In 1909 he took his family back to Ireland, a decision he must often have regretted. But at the time he must still have been very happy. By the time the First World War broke out he was the owner of considerable house property in County Mayo and County Galway, and he was manager of the horse-tramway system in Galway.

In 1922 he left Ireland, because it had become Eire. He was one of those native Irish who were against their own kind and on the side of the English oppressor. Nowadays we recognize the existence of such people, but fancy them quislings, which is quite often unjust. Doubtless some of them were seduced by bribery dispensed by Dublin Castle, but many, and amongst those we must include Michael Joyce, were people who honestly loved law and order and preferred the smart uniforms and soldierly bearing of the English garrisons and the Royal Irish Constabulary to the furtive slouching of a peasantry distracted by poverty and revolutionary fever. The error of such people was insufficient inquiry into first causes, but for simple natures who went by surface indications the choice was natural enough.

In any case Michael Joyce paid the price of his convictions, and it was not light. He came to England for three very good reasons. The first was that the horse-tramways in Galway were abolished. One may deduce that he was a man of courage because he apparently ranked that reason as equal in importance to the other two, which were that his neighbours had been so revolted by his British sympathies that they burned down his house, and that he had been confused in many people's minds with an informer, also called Michael Joyce, who had denounced a priest to the Black and Tans. (It must be noted that William Joyce's father was indeed innocent of this crime, and, so far as is known, of any other; the identity of the other Michael Joyce was well established.)

On arriving in England the Joyces settled in Lancashire, and William alone made his way to London, where he enrolled as a science student at Battersea Polytechnic. In August 1922 he, being sixteen years of age, sent a letter of application to the London University Officers' Training Corps, in which he said he wanted to study with a view to being nominated by the university for a commission in the Regular Army. This letter was read in court, and it is very touching. It must have startled the recipient. It would not (nor would the note Joyce's father wrote later in support of the application) have convinced him that by the still snobbish standards of 1922 this was a likely candidate for the officers' mess, but it had another point of interest. "I have served with the irregular forces of the Crown in an Intelligence capacity, against the Irish guerrillas. In command of a squad of sub-agents I was subordinate to the late Captain P. W. Keating, 2nd RUR, who was drowned in the *Egypt* accident. I have a knowledge of the rudiments of Musketry, Bayonet Fighting, and Squad Drill." The *Egypt* was sunk off Ushant in May 1922; which meant that, if this story was true, the boy was engaged in guerrilla fighting with the Black and Tans when he was fifteen years old. The story was true. A photograph of him taken at that time shows him in a battle dress, and a number of people remembered this phase of his life. Later, on an official form, he gave the duration of his service as four months, named the regiment with which he had been associated as the Worcestershires. Further confirmation was given during his trial by an old man from County Galway who stood in the crowd outside and expressed to bystanders his hearty desire that William Joyce should be hanged for treason against the King of England, on the ground that he had worked with the Black and Tans in persecuting the Irish when they were revolting against the English. The crowd, with that toleration which foreigners possibly correctly suspect of being a form of smugness, was amused by the inconsistency.

But there was something in the letter more relevant to his trial. "I must now," wrote Joyce, "mention a point which I hope will not give rise to difficulties. I was born in America but of British parents. I left America when two years of age, have not returned since, and do not propose to return. I was informed, at the brigade headquarters of the district in which I was stationed in Ireland, that I possessed the same rights and privileges as I would if of natural British birth. I can obtain testimonials as to my loyalty to the Crown. I am in no way connected with the United States of America, against which, as against all other nations, I am prepared to draw the sword in British interests. As a young man of pure British descent, some of whose forefathers have held high position in the British army, I have always been desirous of devoting what little capability and energy I may possess to the country which I love so dearly. I ask that you may inform me if the accident of my birth, to which I refer above, will affect my position. I shall be in London for the September Matriculation Examination and I hope to commence studies at the London University at the beginning of the next academic year. I trust that you will reply as soon as possible, and that your reply will be favourable to my aspirations." At an interview with an official of the OTC he conveyed that he was "in doubt as to whether he was a 'British subject of pure European descent,'" a doubt which must have been honest if he expressed it all in view of the ardent hope expressed in his letter; but he asserted that his father had never been naturalized. This the father confirmed when the official wrote to him for further particulars. "Dear Sir, your letter of the 23rd October received. Would have replied sooner, but have been away from home. With regard to my son William. He was born in America, I was born in Ireland. His mother was born in England. We are all British and not American citizens."

Now, there was some doubt in William Joyce's mind about his status. Throughout his life when he was filling in official forms he was apt to give his birthplace as Ireland or England, although he had a birth certificate which gave it as Brooklyn. But his disquiet was vague. In the statement he made to the Intelligence officers on his arrest he expressed himself uncertainly. "I understand, though I have no documents to prove my statement, that my father was American by naturalization at the time of my birth, and I believe he lost his American citizenship later through failing to renew it, because we left America in 1909 when I was three years old. We were generally treated as British subjects during our stay in Ireland and England. I was in Ireland from 1909 till 1921 when I came to England. We were always treated as British during the period of my stay in England whether we were or not." But when his defence counsel began to outline his case, there was not the faintest doubt about it: William Joyce had not been born a British subject. Documents were brought into court which showed that Michael Joyce had become an American citizen in 1894, twelve years before the birth of William at 1377 Herkimer Street, Brooklyn. In 1909 he had travelled back to England on an American passport. When he and his wife had oscillated between Lancashire and Galway during the First World War they had had to register under the Aliens Act 1915. An old man gave evidence, who had known Michael Joyce all his life. On Joyce's advice this witness had gone to America, worked as a civil engineer, and taken American citizenship, but he had returned to Great Britain during the First World War and had been greatly inconvenienced by his alien status. He spoke of a visit to Mrs Joyce, who was known as Queenie, and who seems to have been very well liked, at her house in a Lancashire town. They had exchanged commiserations because they both had to report all their movements to the police. His cracked old voice evoked a picture of two people cosily grumbling together over their cups of good strong tea thirty years ago.

William's brother Quentin went into the witness box. There passed between him and the man in the dock a nod and a smile of pure love. One realized that life in this strange family must sometimes have been great fun. But it evidently had not been fun lately. Quentin told the court that his father had died in 1941, shortly after the house in which he had lived for eighteen years had been destroyed by a bomb, and his mother had died in 1944. Out of the wreckage of the house there had been recovered a few boxes full of papers, but none had any bearing on the question of the family's nationality, and there was a reason for that. Michael Joyce had told young Quentin, when he was ten years old, that he and all the family were American citizens but had bade him never to speak of it, and had in later years often reiterated this warning. Finally, in 1934, the boy, who was then sixteen, had seen him burn a number of papers, including what appeared to be an American passport. He had given a reason for what he was doing, but the witness was not required to repeat it. The date suggests what that reason may have been. By that time the police knew William Joyce as a troublesome instigator of street fighting and attacks on Communists and Jews, and in November 1934 Joyce was prosecuted, together with Sir Oswald Mosely and two other Fascists, on a charge of riotous assembly at Worthing; and though this prosecution failed, it indicated a serious attempt by the authorities to rid themselves of the nuisance of Fascist-planned disorder. Michael Joyce had every reason to fear that, if the police ever got an inkling of his secret, they would deport his son and, not improbably, the whole family.

Now it seemed as impossible to convict William Joyce as it had been, when the prosecution was opening its case, to imagine his acquittal. The child of a naturalized American citizen, born after his father's naturalization, is an American citizen by birth. Therefore William Joyce owed the King of England no allegiance such as arises out of British nationality. It seemed he must go scot free. He had committed no offence whatsoever in becoming a naturalized German subject on September 26, 1940. That would have been high treason had he been a British subject, for a British subject is forbidden by law to become the naturalized subject of an enemy country in wartime. But when he took out his naturalization papers in Germany he was an American citizen, and even the American government could not have questioned his action, being then at peace with Germany, which did not declare war on the United States until December 11, 1941. It followed, then, that his broadcasting was, if only his nationality had to be considered, an offence against nobody. After September 26, 1940, he had been a good German working for the fatherland. But our law is not really as arbitrary as all that. Allegiance is not exacted by the Crown from a subject simply because the Crown is the Crown. The idea of the divine right of kings is a comparatively modern vulgarity. According to tradition and logic, the state gives protection to all men within its confines, and in return exacts their obedience to its laws; and the process is reciprocal. When men within the confines of the state are obedient to its laws they have a right to claim its protection. It is a maxim of the law, quoted by Coke in the sixteenth century, that "protection draws allegiance, and allegiance draws protection" (*protectio trahit subjectionem, et subjectio protectionem*). It was laid down in 1608, by reference to the case of Sherley, a Frenchman who had come to England and joined in a conspiracy against the King and Queen, that such a man "owed to the King obedience, that is, so long as he was within the King's protection." That is fair enough; and indeed very fair, if the limitations which were applied to this proposition are considered. For in Hale's *History of the Pleas of the Crown*, in the seventeenth century, it was written: "Because as the subject hath his protection from the King and his laws, so on the other side the subject is bound by his allegiance to be true and faithful to the King. And hence it is, that if an alien enemy comes into this kingdom hostilely to invade it, if he be taken, he shall be dealt with as an enemy, but not as a traitor, because he violates no trust nor allegiance. But if an alien, the subject of a foreign prince in amity with the King, live here, and enjoy the benefit of the King's protection, and commit a treason, he shall be judged and executed, as a traitor, for he owes a local allegiance."

There could be no doubt whatsoever that William Joyce owed that kind of allegiance. He had certainly enjoyed the protection of the English law for some thirty years preceding his departure to Germany. The lawyers for the defence, in proving that he did not owe the natural kind of allegiance which springs from British birth, had found themselves under the necessity of disproving beyond all doubt that he owed this other acquired kind; and there were the two damning sentences in his statement: "We were generally counted as British subjects during our stay in Ireland and England. . . . We were always treated as British during the period of my stay in England whether we were or not." Thus, though an alien, William Joyce owed the Crown allegiance and was capable of committing treason against it. Again he was heading for conviction. But not for certain. There was a definition of the law which was likely to help him.

In 1707 an assembly of judges laid it down that "if such alien seeking the Protection of the Crown having a Family and Effects here should during a War with his Native Country go thither and there Adhere to the King's Enemies for the purpose of Hostility, He might be dealt with as a Traitor. For he came and settled here under the Protection of the Crown. And though his Person was removed for a time, his Effects and Family continued still under the same Protection."

Now, the letter of this judgement did not apply to William Joyce. He had taken his wife with him to Germany, and by that marriage he was childless. He had two children by a former marriage, but they were in the care of their mother and did not enter into this case. The effects he possessed when he quitted England were of such a trifling nature that it would be fairer to regard them as abandoned rather than as left under the protection of the Crown. Had he retained any substantial property in the country he would not have had to avail himself of the provisions of the Poor Prisoners' Defence Act. But he was within the sphere of the spirit of the judgement. Joyce disappeared from England at some time between August 29, 1939—when he issued an order dissolving the National Socialist League, the Fascist organization of which he was the head—and September 18, when he entered the service of the German radio. He was the holder of a British passport; it was part of his lifelong masquerade as a British subject. He had declared on the application papers that he had been born in Galway and had not "lost the status of British subject thus acquired." He obtained his passport on July 6, 1933, and there is perhaps some significance in that date. He had become a member of the British Fascists in 1923, when he was seventeen, but had left this organization after two years, to become later an active member of the

Conservative Party. In January 1933 Hitler seized power, and later in the year Mosley formed the British Union of Fascists, which William Joyce joined. This passport was, like all British passports, valid for five years. When July 1938 came round he let it lapse, but applied on September 24, 1938, for a renewal for the customary period of one year; and there is, perhaps, some significance in that date also, for the Munich Agreement was signed on September 29. The next year he was careful not to let it lapse. He made an application for renewal over a month before its expiry, on August 24, 1939, and there was certainly some significance in that date, for war broke out on September 3. Each of these renewals was dated as if the application had been made when the passport expired. So when William Joyce went to Germany he was the holder of a British passport which was valid until the beginning of July 1940. That was why the third count of the indictment charged him with committing high treason by broadcasting between "the eighteenth day of September, 1939, and on divers other days thereafter, and between that day and the second day of July, 1940, being then to wit, on the said several days, a person owing allegiance to our Lord the King." It was, in fact, the case for the prosecution that a person obtaining a passport placed himself thereby under the protection of the Crown and owed it allegiance until the passport expired.

No ruling on the point existed, because no case of treason involving temporary allegiance had been tried during the comparatively recent period when passports, in their modern sense, have been in use, so the judge had to make a new ruling; and for one sultry afternoon and a sultrier morning the prosecuting and defending counsel bobbed up and down in front of the bench, putting the arguments for and against the broadening of the law by inclusion of this modern circumstance. People with legal minds were entranced, and others slept. Joyce enjoyed this part of the trial very much, and frequently passed down to his counsel notes that were characteristically odd. Like all prisoners in the dock, he had been given octavo sheets to write on, and could certainly have had as many as he wanted. But when he wrote a note he tore off irregularly shaped pieces and covered them with grotesquely large handwriting; so large that it could be read by people sitting in the gallery. One ended with the words, "but it is not important." His enjoyment of the argument was not unnatural in one who loved complications, for no stage of it was simple. Much depended on the nature of a passport, and this had never been defined by the law, for a passport has been different things at different times and has never been merely one thing at a time. It was originally a licence given by the Crown to a subject who wished to leave the realm, an act as a rule prohibited because it deprived the King of a man's military services; but it was also a licence given to an alien to travel through the realm; and it was a pass given to soldiers going home on leave, or paupers discharged from a hospital. Through the ages it changed its character to a demand by the issuing state that the person and property of one of its subjects shall be respected by other states when he travels in their realms; a voucher of his respectability, demanded by the states he intends to visit, as a precaution against crime and political conspiracy; and a source of revenue to the states, which charged heavily for such permits. Of its protective nature in our day there can be little doubt, since the preamble on every British passport announces that "we," the Foreign Secretary of the day, "request and require in the Name of His Majesty all those whom it may concern to allow the bearer to pass freely without let or hindrance, and to afford him or her every assistance and protection of which he or she may stand in need." In 1905 the Lord Chief Justice of that day, Lord Alverstone, defined a passport as "a document issued in the name of a Sovereign, on the responsibility of a Minister of the Crown, to a named individual, intended to be presented to the governments of foreign nations and to be used for that individual's protection as a British subject in foreign countries."

It is a strange thing that many people found something distasteful in this argument that William Joyce, alien by birth, who had acquired a temporary and local allegiance, did not lose it when he left England to take service with the Nazis because he took his British passport with him. They did not reflect on what would have followed from the rejection of this argument. If it had been established that a temporary allegiance could not be carried over by an alien to the Continent, that he divested himself of it by the mere act of passing beyond the three-mile territorial limits, then an alien who was resident in England and for some reason had been given a British passport (as sometimes happens in the case of one who has rendered special services to England) could pop across the Channel, conspire with an enemy of England at Calais, and pop back again, not only once but hundreds of times, and never be tried for treason, because at three miles from Dover he lost his duty of allegiance.

Joyce's counsel also argued that his client's passport could give him no protection because he had acquired it by a false statement; yet it was hard to see how it could fail to protect him until the fraud was discovered and the passport was withdrawn. Supposing that William Joyce had fallen out with the Germans during 1940 and had become a civil internee; he could have called on the assistance of the Swiss Embassy in Berlin, as Switzerland was "the protective power" appointed to safeguard the interests of Britons in hostile territory during wartime.

All this filigree work delighted the little man in the dock, who watched his lawyers with a cynical brightness, as if he were interested in seeing whether they could get away with all this nonsense but had no warmer concern with the proceedings. He showed no special excitement, only a continuance of amused curiosity, when on the third day of the trial, at the end of the morning, the judge announced that he would give his ruling on these legal submissions after the luncheon interval; and at two o'clock he returned to the dock with his usual eccentric excess of military smartness and his sustained tight-lipped derisiveness. The judge announced that "beyond a shadow of doubt" William Joyce had owed allegiance to the Crown of this country when he applied for his passport, and that nothing had happened to put an end to that allegiance during the period when the passport was valid. In other words, he ruled that a person holding a British passport owed allegiance to the Crown even when he was outside the realm. This ruling made it quite certain that William Joyce was going to be sentenced to death.

If the sentence was carried out he would die the most completely unnecessary death that any criminal has ever died on the gallows. He was the victim of his own and his father's lifelong determination to lie about their nationality. For had he not renewed his English passport, and had he left England for Germany on the American passport which was rightfully his, no power on earth could have touched him. As he became a German citizen by naturalization before America came into the war, he could never have been the subject of prosecution under the American laws of treason.

It is not easy to understand why the family practised this imposture; Michael Joyce is an enigmatic figure. Since he loved England it would have been more natural for him to emigrate to England than to America. There were, of course, some pro-English Irish who went to America to act as informers on the anti-English Irish, who were at that time fomenting the Fenian and other separatist movements. It is said that Michael Joyce was a candid and honourable man, but even such could, even against their own wish, be entangled in the fierce intrigues and counter-intrigues of those days. It is very difficult to see why, when Michael Joyce returned to England and found his American citizenship such a burden that he warned his children to keep it a deadly secret, he never took the simple steps which would have readmitted him to British nationality. It would have cost him only a few pounds, and he was in those years well-to-do. It cannot have been the legal technicalities which baffled him; his wife's brother was a solicitor. The official resistance to the process was not great. Can Michael Joyce have feared to remind either the British or the American government of his existence? Had he once been involved in some imbroglio and got a black mark against his name? Was he working his passage home when he gained the good opinion of the Royal Irish Constabulary? There is probably nobody alive now who knows. All that we can be sure of is that the story was probably incredibly complicated. Nothing was simple in that world of espionage and counter-espionage.

William Joyce was being sentenced to death because his father had tried to save him from what must have been a lesser danger; and sentence was passed on him in a terrible way, because nobody in court felt any emotion at all. People wanted Joyce to pay the proper legal penalty for his treason, but not because they felt any personal hatred against him. They wanted to be sure that in any other war this peculiarly odious form of treachery, which invaded the ears of frightened people, would be discouraged before it began, and that was about the limit of their interest in the matter. At no other such trial have the spectators, as soon as the jury went out to consider their verdict and the judge retired from the bench and the prisoner was taken down to the cells, got up from their seats and strolled about and chattered as if they were at a theatre between the acts. At no other such trial have the jury come back from considering the verdict looking as if they had been out for a cup of tea. And at no other such trial has the judge assumed the black cap—which is not a cap at all but a piece of black cloth that an attendant lays across his wig—as if it were in fact just a piece of black cloth laid across his wig. He spoke the words of the sentence of death reverently, and they were awful, as they always must be: "William Joyce, the sentence of the Court upon you is, that you be taken from this place to a lawful prison, and thence to a place of execution, and that you be there hanged by the neck until you are dead; and that your body be afterwards buried within the precincts of the prison in which you shall have been confined before your execution. And may the Lord have mercy on your soul."

But the effect of these words was, on this uniquely shallow occasion, soon dissipated. It was indeed pitiful when Joyce was asked if he wanted to make a statement before sentence was passed on him, and he shook his head, the hungry and inordinate voice in him at last defeated. He had been even more pitiful earlier in the trial, when the judge had warned the jury to consider very carefully their verdict because a person found guilty must be sentenced to death, for he had put up his hand and touched his neck with a look of wonder. That he deserved pity was noted by the intellect; pity was not felt. Nor was anybody in the court very much moved by the extreme courage with which he bore himself, though that was remarkable. He listened to the sentence with his head high, gave one of his absurd stiff bows, and ran down to the cells, smiling and waving to his brother and his friends, acting gaiety without a flaw. Such a performance would once have moved us, but not then. All had changed. Even a trial for a capital offence was then quite different from what it had been before the war, when the spectators were living in a state of security, and the prisoner was an exceptionally unfortunate person who had strayed into a district not generally visited, perhaps for lack of boldness. But every man and woman who attended Joyce's trial had at some time during the last six years been in danger of undeserved death or pain, and had shown, or seen others showing, great courage. William Joyce could not make any claim on them by being pitiful and brave. He could not arouse their interest because it was exceptional to meet violent death, since he was in the dock by reason of failure to acquit himself well when that had been their common destiny. So they turned away from him and left the court as if it had been a cinema or concert. But in the dark corridor a woman said, "I am glad his mother's dead. She lived near us in Dulwich. She was a sweet little lady, a tiny little woman. I often used to stand with her in the fish queue. In fact, that's how I met her. One day after the blitz had been very bad I said something about that blasted Lord Haw-Haw, and someone said, 'Hush, that's his mother right beside you,' and I felt dreadful. But she only said—but she was ever so Irish, and I can't speak like she did—'Never mind, my dear, I'm sure you didn't mean it unkindly.' " This story recalled the lilt of affection of the old man in the witness box when he had spoken of having tea with Queenie.

The dark corridor passed to a twilit landing. Down a shadowed staircase the band of Fascists were descending, tears shining on their astonished faces. Joyce's brother walked slowly, his eyes that were soft and brown like a cow's now narrowed and wet, and the slight blond solicitor just behind him. There was a block, and for a minute the crowd all stood still. The solicitor plucked at Quentin Joyce's jacket and said kindly, "This is just what he expected, you know." "Yes," said his brother, "I know it's just what he expected." The crowd moved on, but after it had gone down a few steps the solicitor plucked at the young man's jacket again and said, "It's the appeal that matters, you know," and Quentin said, "Yes, I know. The appeal's everything."

At the counter where the spectators had to collect their umbrellas and coats, a jurywoman was saying good-bye to one of her colleagues. They were shaking hands warmly and expressing hopes that they would meet again. They might have been people parting at the end of a cruise. Jostling them were the Fascists, waiting for their raincoats, garments which those of their kind affect in all weathers, in imitation of Hitler. The young man who looked like a gipsy held his head down. Heavy tears were hanging on his long black lashes. He and his friends still looked amazed. They had wanted people to die by violence, but they had not expected the lot to fall on any of their own number. Another dark and passionate young man was accosted by a reporter, and he cried out in rage that he had been four years in Brixton Jail under Security Regulation 18B, all for patriotism, and he had come out to see the persecution of the finest patriot of all. His black eyes rolled and blazed about him. It did not do. About him were standing people who had been in the Dieppe expedition, at Arnhem, in submarines, in prison camps; even the women knew about fear, had been, perhaps, on the Gestapo list of persons to be arrested immediately after the Germans conquered England. There was this new universality of horrible experience, this vast common martyrdom which made it no use to play execution as if it were a trump card.

The little band of Fascists gathered together in a knot by the door, and after they had wiped their faces, and composed themselves, they went into the street. In the open space in front of the building was a

336

line of parked cars, and behind them stood a crowd, down a street that narrowed and lost itself in a network of alleys. Nobody followed them, but they began to hurry. By the time they got into the shelter of the alleys, they were almost running. ◇ ◇ ◇

9

But there remains a mystery about William Joyce and all his kind of Fascist leader. Why is it so important to them that they should stand on the political platform, hold office, give commands with their own voices, and be personally feared? A man who is not acceptable as a national leader is given by our system the opportunity to exercise as much political power as is necessary for his self-respect and the protection of his right. He can vote in Parliamentary and local elections; and he can serve his country as a private Member of Parliament or as a member of a local authority or as a member of a special committee. Why should William Joyce and his kind howl after impossible eminence when in the common run they had no occasion for humiliation? There are other means of establishing exceptional value. If Joyce was not loved by the mass he was loved well by some near to him, and to some was a good lover; to his brother Quentin and to his second wife he was light and warmth. He was also a very good teacher. Happily he transmitted knowledge, and was happy to see it happily received. That surely should have been enough for him: to be a good brother, to be a good husband, to be a good teacher. Many are given less. Yet he hungered for the mere audience, for the wordless cheering, the executive power which, if it be not refined to nothing by restraint, is less than nothing.

Perhaps right was on his side. Perhaps it is not enough to be a good brother, or to be a good husband, or to be a good teacher. For human relationships are always qualified by questioning. A brother, and a wife, and pupils have their own selves to maintain, so they must sometimes defend themselves and keep back their secrets. They will sometimes pass over to the attack and seek out the secrets of the brother, the husband, and the teacher, and often time changes them so that there is no acceptance, only this questioning. It would be better for a man to have a relationship with a person who knew all about him and therefore had no need to question him, who recognized that he was unique and precious and therefore withheld no confidence from him, who could not be changed by time, though by his steadfastness he might change time and make it kind and stable. Those who believe in God enjoy such a relationship. It would be impertinent to speculate about Joyce's relationship with God, about which we know nothing relevant save that he left the Church in which he was born, returned to it before his death, and in the meantime had inscribed himself on the Nazi records as a "believer." But it can be taken that his mind had been trained over the trellis erected round him by society, and that that trellis was cut in a non-Christian or even anti-Christian pattern. Whether he enjoyed his relationship with God or not, he must often have believed that it did not exist.

Those who have discarded the idea of a super-personal God and still desire an enduring friendship must look for it in those fields of life farthest removed from ordinary personal relationship, because human personality lacks endurance in any form of love. The most obvious of these is politics. There a leader can excite love in followers who know nothing of him save his public appearances. That love is unqualified; for no party can cause its enemies to rejoice by admitting that its leader has any faults, and what parties profess they soon sincerely feel, especially in crowded halls. That love swears itself undying, too; for no party can afford to let itself be overheard contemplating the exchange of its leader for another.

Therefore many men who would have been happy in the practice of religion during the ages of faith have in these modern times a need for participation in politics which is strong as the need for food, for shelter, for sex. Such persons never speak of the real motives which impel them to their pursuit of politics, but continually refer, in accents of assumed passion, to motives which do indeed preoccupy some politicians, but not them. The chief of these is the desire to end poverty. But William Joyce had never in his life known what it was to be hungry or cold or workless, and he did not belong to the altruistic type which torments itself over the plight of others; and indeed there was probably no callousness in this, for surely if he himself had been destitute he would have been too completely absorbed in his rages and his books to notice it. His was another hunger, another chill, another kind of unemployment. But the only people in the generation before him who attacked the governing class had been poor or altruist, and since their attack had been successful their vocabulary held a tang of victory, and William Joyce and his kind borrowed it.

338

Therefore they spoke of economics when they were thinking of religion; and thus they became the third wing of a certain triptych. In the third and fourth centuries of this era Europe and North Africa and Nearer Asia were racked by economic problems caused by the impending dissolution of the Western Roman Empire. The study of economics was then barely begun; there was as yet no language in which the people could analyse their insecurity and design their security. But several men of genius and many of talent had been excited by the personality of Christ and excited by the bearings of his gospel on the discoveries made by the ancient philosophers. Hence the science of theology was developed to a stage where intelligent people could grasp the outlines with which it delineated universal experiences and applied its phraseology to their particular experiences. Therefore those suffering economic distress complained of it in theological terms. They cried out to society that its structure was wrong, in terms which, taken literally, meant that the orthodox Christian faith was mistaken; they rushed from the derelict estates where they starved as peons and sought the desert, where they could eat better on brigandage, and said that they did this because they had had a peculiar revelation concerning the Trinity. The hungry disguised themselves as heretics. Now, in our day, those suffering from religious distress reverse the process and complain of it in economic terms. Those who desire salvation pretend that they are seeking a plan to feed the hungry. Between the two wings of the triptych shone the rich panel of European civilization, created during a happy interim when, for various reasons, man found it easy to say what he meant.

It is undignified for any human being to be the victim of a historical predicament. It is a confession that one has been worsted, not by a conspiracy of enemies, nor by the hostility of nature, but by one's environment, by the medium in which one's genius, had one possessed such a thing, should have expressed itself; as harsh as it is for an actor to admit that he cannot speak on a stage, for an artist to admit that he cannot put paint on canvas. So the victims of historical predicaments are tempted to pretend that they sacrificed themselves for an eternal principle which their contemporaries had forgotten, instead of owning that one of time's gables was in the way of their window and barred their view of eternity. But William Joyce pretended nothing at his trials. His faint smile said simply, "I am what I am." He did not defend the faith which he had held, for he had doubted it; he did not attack it, for he had believed in it. It is possible that in these last days Fascism had passed out of the field of his close attention, that what absorbed him was the satisfaction which he felt at being, for the first time in his life, taken seriously. It had at last been conceded that what he was and what he did were matters of supreme importance. It was recognized that he had been involved by his birth in a war between the forces in the community which desired to live and those which desired to die, a war between the forces in himself which desired to live and those which desired to die. It was an end to mediocrity.

He said that he had had a fair trial; but he had had two trials. On the floor of the courts where he was put in the dock there was tested an issue of how far the letter is divorced from the spirit, an issue which must have come up again and again since the birth of law. Centuries ago, or in the part of the world least visited by civilization, it might be debated whether a man can live all his life among a tribe and eat its salt and in the hour of its danger sharpen the spears that its enemies intend for their attack on it, and go free because he has not undergone the right ceremonies which would have made him a member of that tribe. But in the upper air above the courts it was argued whether the God with whom man can have a perfect relationship is the dream of disappointed sons imagining a perfect Father who shall be better than all fathers, or is more real than reality. This other trial was not concluded, for it began with some remote birth and will not now end till the last death. It is this uncertainty which gives life its sickening and exquisite tension, and under that tension the fragility of William Joyce was as impressive as his strength. He sat in the dock, quietly wondering at time as it streamed away from him; and his silence had the petitioning quality we had heard in his voice over the air during the war. He had his satisfactions. He had wanted glory, and his trial gave him the chance to wrestle with reality, to argue with the universe, to defend the revelations which he believed had been made to him; and that is about as much glory as comes to any man. But treason took to itself others not so fortunate.

From III. Decline and Fall of Treason

5

◇ ◇ ◇ In the early part of 1963 a girl named Christine Keeler appeared in the news as certainly involved in prostitution and possibly in espionage. She was at once desired and hated more than her deserts.

It was not unreasonable that she should have excited desire, for she was beautiful in a nostalgically unfashionable style. She was not at all unlike the Virgin Mary in Dante Gabriel Rossetti's "Annunciation." She had a remote distinction of bearing and manner unexpected in one who had been brought up on a riverbank near the Slough desert (a district comparable in charm to the New Jersey flats) in a converted railway carriage. As for hatred, she might have been spared the full blast of what she got, for she had hardly had the benefit of the protection we profess to give the young. Admittedly by the time she got into the news, at the age of twenty, it would have been difficult to protect her save by some such drastic technique as bricking her up in a wall, according to the practice which the cruder kind of Protestant used to believe prevalent in convents. But earlier she had had bad luck. She had been seduced by an American sergeant at a tender age and went off to earn a living in London in her middle teens. Eventually she found herself in the cabaret show of a famous London night club, and there she might have found a way out of the dust, for this club looks after its girls well and a fair number make good marriages or break into the entertainment world. But she was committed to a less fortunate destiny when she met a man thirty years older than herself, named Stephen Ward, and went to live with him. They apparently remained throughout their association on brother-and-sister terms, but she joined the long line of girls who had lived under his control during the years since the end of the war, most of whom he handed over to various rich men of his acquaintance, most commonly as mistresses though sometimes as wives.

Attempts have been made to represent Stephen Ward as a glamorous rebel and sexual deviate. But to the experienced eye he was a not unfamiliar type of daffy. He struck some people as mildly insane, and indeed he had the shining eyes and effusiveness of a manic-depressive on the upswing, and something of the single-minded mindlessness which Harpo Marx used to affect. Other people who met him at the houses of his wealthy patrons regarded him as a quite gifted court jester, with a flow of amusing gossip. Other people again regarded him as brilliant, but it must be admitted that they were themselves not so much brilliant as loyal and affectionate. They were apparently much impressed by a kind of diluted Nietzscheanism which had filtered into his brains through smoky night sessions with his more literate (but still not very literate) friends. As a witness at his own trial and as an interviewee on television he seemed ingenious rather than intelligent, and curiously blind to the effect he was creating on his audience. His memoirs were poorly written and trivial.

But he was a man of many and marked gifts. He was a born professional: he was capable of acquiring all the skills necessary to the successful pursuit of an exciting occupation, and using them continuously at a high level. It was not for him to claim much originality or individuality; he joined the ranks of those who find it enjoyable and profitable to march along the paths traced out by original individuals of the past. His first profession was osteopathy. It is not clear how he came to adopt it. His father, a clergyman, a handsome man, only slightly handicapped by a malformation of the spine which just stopped short of making him a hunchback, was a noted preacher and ended his days as a Canon of Rochester Cathedral. The Wards were certainly prosperous and by all accounts were a united and affectionate family, and one would have expected all the sons to have an orthodox education. But after a number of experiments (which included a term or two at the Sorbonne) Ward went to America at the age of twenty-two and took a degree at a well-known osteopathic college in Missouri. It is beyond question that he became a master of his craft. Other osteopaths, even those who thought him mad and bad, admired him for both his manipulative powers and his acuteness in diagnosis.

But he also played bridge like a professional and could hardly have encumbered his time more heavily with fixtures had he been a bridge-player by profession; and there was nothing amateurish about the portrait drawings he was ceaselessly producing. They were of limited artistic value. Some of the faithful (whose devotion recalls the spaniel) compared them to the work of Michelangelo, but a juster comparison would have referred to Miss Olive Snell and Miss Molly Bishop, the charming and industrious chroniclers of English society beauties in this and the last generation. Stephen Ward was less gifted than either of these ladies and not nearly so well schooled, but he possessed something of their expertise, the power to pick out the sweeter aspects of an image and put them down on the right part of the paper with just the right weight of line to make looking at the things as easy as swallowing cream. As time went on he marketed to advantage the products of his emollient art, and when his career came to an end he was drawing £1500 a year from a contract with an illustrated weekly.

His three professions worked in well together. If a prominent man came to him in his capacity as an osteopath, he would offer to draw him or her and would then ask for introductions to other prominent people in the same field, on the plea that he wished to draw them too. He would then, if the signs were favourable, invite them to his bridge parties or to his country cottage, and familiarity would be established. This process sometimes developed so far as to land the prominent person in the field of Ward's fourth profession, which was pimping.

The general public hesitated to believe that Ward was a pimp. He was tried and found guilty of living on the immoral earnings of Christine Keeler and another and still younger girl, Mandy Rice-Davies, but the average man was inclined to think him the victim of a technicality, for the reason that there was little evidence of money having passed from them to him. He could hardly have been convicted had it not been that a man who is habitually in the company of prostitutes is presumed by the law to be living on their earnings, though it accepts a disproof. But his innocence cannot be established by criticism of that presumption, which is in fact a realistic recognition of the shyness of pimps to confide their financial affairs to paper. The situation is discussed in a curious passage in Lord Denning's report on Ward's affairs and their consequences. "In money matters," Lord Denning oddly states, "he was improvident." He goes on to explain:

He did not keep a banking account. He got a firm of solicitors to keep a sort of banking account for him, paying in cheques occasionally to them and getting them to pay his rent. More often he cashed his incoming cheques through other people; or paid his bills with the incoming cheques. He had many cash transactions which left no trace.

But these practices do not indicate improvidence. On the contrary, as the Inland Revenue would testify, they are devices practised by persons so excessively provident that they grudge wasting money on the payment of income tax. Here in England the improvident have no aversion from banking accounts, which they open optimistically and which offer them their own peculiar food in the English conception of the overdraft. Neither is there any special feature attractive to improvidence in the act of paying in cheques to a firm of solicitors rather than to a bank manager; the excessively provident might find the solicitors preferable, particularly if they did not tell them absolutely everything. Moreover, we must dismiss any picture of Stephen Ward running across the road to ask his greengrocer to cash a patient's cheque for five guineas. An organization which was sued for libel by Stephen Ward made its own inquiries and discovered that he was in the habit of cashing cheques for both small and large amounts at gambling-houses which performed this service for their clients and charged quite a heavy commission.

There is much evidence that Stephen Ward was capable of great generosity. True, he was close-fisted with his girls. When they lived under his roof the housekeeping was frugal, and they had to pay their share of the overheads. But he gave free treatment to many needy patients and on some hard cases he bestowed not only his skill and his time but considerable sums of money. Yet there is much evidence that he loved money and that he pimped for gain. There was really, from his point of view, no reason why he should not be a procurer. He liked, as some people like teaching and others like nursing, to bring together two human beings in order that they might have sexual relations on a mercenary basis. This conception existed in his mind in a strange, diagrammatic isolation. The public in its daydreams saw him as surrounded by beautiful girls, and so he often was, but some of his chosen companions were ill-favoured in face and in figure, and were repellent or pitiful in personality. It was as if he wished his women to incarnate the idea of prostitution in its impure purity, without making allusion to the agreeable in any form. Pimping was thus to him a mission, and many missionaries accept payment for their labours. It would take unusual credulity to hold, on the evidence given at the trial, that Ward did not do that very thing. The only thing it did not show was where the money went.

The pattern had been glaring enough before the trial. In the late fifties the wife of an MP called on Ward to arrange for osteopathic treatment and never went back to have it. She saw enough to make her certain that some sort of call-girl racket was being conducted from his house. Again, he treated as friends and colleagues various

well-known vice-racketeers, including the two most celebrated dis-
seminators of pornography in our day, and an internationally known
organizer of flagellationist orgies. Again, Ward was careful to profess
great hatred for Peter Rachman, the slum-landlord and club-owner,
but two of his girls, one of them being Mandy Rice-Davies, became
Rachman's mistresses, and he himself was Rachman's tenant. Again,
it was his habit to give frequent bridge parties, and some of these
were that and nothing more; but others ended in the sudden incur-
sion of a troupe of young women, lightly clad and brandishing whips,
who performed a bizarre cabaret turn. Our story has now strayed so
far from normal territory that the pattern may be so surprising as to
be virtually unacceptable. It appears to be true, but could never be
credible, that many of these young women were quite respectable,
and amongst themselves alluded to the elderly gentlemen who formed
the larger part of the audience in derisive and even hostile terms.
Nevertheless, even if allowance is made for these singular facts, it
appears unlikely that such a party should be given, not now and
again, but again and again, by a man far from lavish in his expenditure, from motives of hospitable altruism.

Ward's four professions worked together to give him yet a fifth,
which is hard to define. He was not a traitor and not a spy. Let us
say he mucked about with security in the shadow of the Soviet Union.
This, like his pimping, would not strike him as morally wrong. A
highly intelligent woman, who was his patient and was also involved
with him through her husband's association with one of his close
friends, asserts that he had been a convinced Communist for about
seven years, from about 1955 or 1956. This was not at all rare in his
social ambience. On the more slippery slopes of the entertainment
world, where it shelves abruptly to the vice racket and the unortho-
dox financial complexity, there is a great deal of revolutionary
enthusiasm. Some of this wells up from deep sources. A man who
wants to destroy sexual taboos or to make money in socially forbidden ways may be moved to take these particular actions by a general
desire to overturn all existing institutions. But the motive may be
more naïve and less ferocious; there may be a belief that under communism everything is divided up and everybody is equal, so social
prohibitions will be less stringent; and if one got on the right side
of the machine, one might have the benefit of all this new simplicity
while fiddling a bit on the side for oneself in the good old way.
Among Stephen Ward's friends were several men and women who

had made large sums out of various bizarre enterprises and were closely connected with Communist underground activities.

Round about the end of 1960 Ward told a patient of his, the editor of a newspaper, that he wished to go to Moscow and draw various people there, including Khrushchev, and would like to get in touch with some Soviet officials in London who could help him to realize this ambition. The editor knew an assistant naval attaché at the Soviet embassy, called Captain Eugene Ivanov, and introduced the two men at a large luncheon-party he was giving at a London club on January 20, 1961. At this early stage the story is already odd. Ward had for a long time known a number of people, some highly respectable and some not so greatly that, who could have helped him to contact the Soviet Embassy.

The two men immediately struck up a warm friendship. Ivanov was a Soviet Intelligence officer, and he was very much the same sort of operator as Gordon Lonsdale.* He was superficially expansive, vulgar, jolly, sociable, a cheerful womanizer, and good-natured. He spoke English fluently and was allowed by his embassy to go here, there, and everywhere wherever he was invited, which is not the case with Soviet diplomats as a general rule. He ingratiated himself with his hosts by playing a good game of bridge, eating and drinking with naïve enjoyment, telling funny stories, and chattering and laughing in the character of a simple child of nature. He shared with Lonsdale a curious readiness to be photographed when engaged in amorous horseplay. It was as if both men were looking for certificates of frivolity.

Meanwhile Ward was acting as if he meant to be to Ivanov what Houghton was to Lonsdale. How completely he had moved into the classic role of the agent is shown by an unpleasing episode concerning Madame Furtseva, the Soviet Minister of Culture, who paid a visit to London in 1961. He asked if he might draw her and through Ivanov this was arranged. The sitting took place in a drawing-room at the chief Soviet Embassy building in Kensington Palace Gardens and lasted for an hour. Madame Furtseva sat on the sofa under the huge picture of a Soviet peasant woman and in excellent English chatted away on such subjects as Pasternak, the Hungarian rising, the hopes and fears of her country, and the problem of the Russian immigrant

* A Canadian-born half-Finnish Soviet agent who assumed the name of an actual deceased Canadian, as told in a chapter omitted here.

groups. She talked with unusual candour, and Ward thought the conversation so interesting that when he went home he wrote down what he could remember of it. Then it struck him, he said, that the editor who had introduced him to Ivanov might like to publish it. He realized that he could not publish the notes without permission, so he sent them, not to Madame Furtseva, but to the Soviet Embassy officials.

They were, he reported afterwards, horrified. Madame Furtseva had spoken so very openly. They refused him permission to publish the notes, and he thought this a great pity. That is his account of it. But it can hardly be doubted that he was performing with professional skill a well-known technique of a profession he had only just adopted. It could be objected that Madame Furtseva may have left London by the time his notes were finished and that he could not send them to her to be passed, so he had sent them to the Soviet Embassy officials as the next best thing. But he could, on learning of her departure, have decided to drop the whole idea of publication, lest he should find himself informing on her to her own security system.

The most conspicuous service Ward rendered to Ivanov, however, was of a far less chaste nature, and it was also complex. It showed Ward performing another professional trick, indeed two of them. His association with Ivanov did not go unremarked. On June 8, 1961, a representative of security met Stephen Ward at a restaurant in Marylebone in order to question him about this involvement, and was taken by him to his mews flat, where he met a girl who was living there, possibly Christine Keeler. At the end of the interview Ward asked the security officer whether it was all right for him to continue his friendship with Ivanov, was told that it was, said that he was very ready to help in any way he could, and was instructed to get in touch with security should Ivanov make any propositions to him. To his superiors the security officer reported that he thought Ward's political ideas were probably exploitable by the Russians, but that he himself was not a "security risk," and that the appearance of the young woman in the mews could be considered "corroborative evidence that he had been involved in the call-girl racket." He also added that "he is obviously not a person we can use."

The result of such a visit would be, in most cases, the visited person's instant resolve to break off the association which had been the subject of inquiry. It was not so with Ward. Exactly a month later, in the evening of Saturday, July 8, Ward was bathing with some of his girls at the swimming pool at Lord Astor's house, Cliveden. Lord Astor had been a patient of Ward's for thirteen years and was on familiar terms with him, often treating his needier friends to courses of Ward's osteopathic ministrations; and Ward's country cottage was on the Cliveden estate. One of the girls was Christine Keeler, who had been separated from her bathing dress and was swimming naked when Lord Astor came down with his guests from a dinner party. They included Mr Profumo, the Minister of War. For Ward there can have been no element of surprise in the situation. He knew very well at what time Lord Astor was accustomed to bring down his guests to the swimming pool, and he knew what guests were staying at the house. He also knew Mr Profumo. Miss Keeler dressed herself, Ward and his girls spent some time with the Astor party round the pool, and they went up to the house for a short time. The next day, Sunday, July 9, the Ward party joined the Astor party down at the pool again, and this time Ward brought with him Ivanov, who thus made the acquaintance of Mr Profumo. Ivanov took Christine Keeler back with him to Ward's house in the early evening, where they were reported to have drunk a great deal of whisky and to have had sexual relations. Whether these relations actually occurred we can never know for certain, and it is an aspect of truth we can well suffer to elude us.

On the day after that, Monday, July 10, Ward telephoned to the security officer who had visited him and asked if he might see him; and when the security officer arrived two days later, he told him that he had summoned him in obedience to the instructions he had been given to report any propositions Ivanov might make to him. Ivanov had, he said, asked him to find out why the Americans were going to arm Western Germany with atomic weapons. He also made a peculiar communication regarding Christine. It is obvious that during the week-end she was making a play for Mr Profumo, and by the time Ward saw the security officer there had probably been a telephone call from Mr Profumo which showed that the play had succeeded. Ward, however, told the security officer that Ivanov "was undoubtedly attracted by Christine." It is very doubtful if he ever was. Lord Denning thinks he was not. All that is certain is that for a time Christine seems to have felt it obligatory to say that he was, and presumably she was coached to say this by Ward.

The security officer reported the matter to his superiors in terms which inspired them to follow two lines. First, they asked the Special

Branch to make inquiries about Ward's character, which they thought might be not all it should be, and to identify Miss Keeler. It must make us all blush to learn that the Special Branch could not trace Christine Keeler, who could have been found by some simple inquiries at certain photographers', coffee bars, and shops in the Marylebone district; and we must blush again to hear that the Special Branch was of the opinion that nothing was known to Ward's discredit. His address, it claimed, "was in a respectable neighbourhood where any openly unseemly conduct would come to police notice." The security organization's second line was to explore the possibilities of getting at Ivanov, possibly through Mr Profumo, and persuading him to be a defector. These deliberations were simplified by the failure of any of them to notice that Mr Profumo was spending hours alone with Miss Keeler in Ward's flat and other places and driving her around London.

The head of the security service then suggested to Sir Norman Brook (now Lord Normanbrook), the Secretary of the Cabinet, that he should speak to Mr Profumo on the subject, which he did on August 9. Sir Norman then put it to him that he should be careful in his dealings with Ward, since any information he might drop would be passed on to Ivanov by this master of indiscretion, and asked him if he thought that Ivanov could be persuaded to defect. Mr Profumo said he felt no enthusiasm for the project and went away, sweating at every pore. As Lord Denning was afterwards to learn, he thought that the security service had discovered his relations with Miss Keeler and that Sir Norman's conversation was a tactful way of warning him. He had an assignation with Miss Keeler the very next night, but wrote a letter to her calling it off. Lord Denning cautiously says, "I am satisfied that the letter, if not the end, was the beginning of the end of the association between Mr Profumo and Christine Keeler." In March 1963, Mr Profumo told the House of Commons that he had gone on seeing her till December. But he afterwards explained that this was only because Sir Norman had said, "I thought I should see you before we go away for the recess," and when he recollected this he thought it was the December recess, but realized later it was the August recess. In other words, he could not, in March 1963, remember whether an affair he had had in 1961 with an exceptionally beautiful girl had lasted one month or six. This fact should be put before all young girls over the age of twelve as an important part of their education.

349

The longer the affair lasted, the better for Stephen Ward in his capacity of Soviet dogsbody. It was not that there was much hope, or any at all, of Christine Keeler's getting from Mr Profumo the date of the American delivery of atom bombs to West Germany, and imparting it to Ivanov. Not only would Mr Profumo never have told her, she would never have asked him. The girl had a vigorous if sombre and joyless intelligence. But there was another purpose served by her relationship with the Minister of War. Lord Denning states:

It has been suggested to me that Ivanov filled a new role in Russian technique. It was to divide the United Kingdom from the United States by these devious means. If Ministers or prominent people can be placed in compromising situations, or made the subject of damaging rumour, or the Security Service can be made to appear incompetent, it may weaken the confidence of the United States in our integrity and reliability. So a man like Captain Ivanov may take every opportunity of getting to know Ministers or prominent people—not so much to obtain information from them (though this would be a useful by-product) but so as to work towards destroying confidence. If this were the object of Captain Ivanov, with Stephen Ward as his tool he succeeded only too well.

Unfortunately, Lord Denning is wrong in thinking the technique new. It has been in use for many years and practice has brought it to the pitch of perfection. It is to be noted that during the next two years the story was plugged throughout London that Christine Keeler was having an affair with both Mr Profumo and Ivanov. In late July 1962 a glossy magazine published an allusion to it. Yet by that time Mr Profumo had not seen Miss Keeler for at least six months, and Lord Denning is of the opinion that she had never had a love-affair with Ivanov at all. The story must have been circulated by Ward. People might have remembered seeing Mr Profumo with Miss Keeler in compromising circumstances, but they could not have had a glimpse of an affair with Ivanov which had never happened.

Ward would naturally have liked to satisfy his Soviet masters; but perhaps he felt this a special urgency just then, for it looks as if he was attempting to perform an operation only possible to agents who are valued employees. Throughout 1961 and 1962 he advertised himself more and more blatantly as a Communist sympathizer, particularly to his patients. A number of reports were made to the security services, and again the same officer was sent to interview him and made a mildly unfavourable report. He described Ward as "basically a quite decent fellow," whose only fault was that he "accepted as true much of the propaganda Ivanov has pumped into him." Again he did not think him a security risk. Significantly he wrote: "More than once Ward assured me that if Ivanov ever attempted to make use of him for any illegal purpose, or *if he showed any inclination to defect* he would get in touch with me immediately."

Meanwhile Ward and Ivanov carried on a campaign of ingratiation with the official world of London. As soon as Mr Profumo had begun his process of disengagement from Miss Keeler, Ward, as if trying a new tack, offered his services to the Foreign Office as an intermediary with the Soviet Embassy through Ivanov and got a chilly dismissal. He got a credulous MP to involve the Foreign Office in some twitterings about the Berlin problem and the Oder-Neisse line, and he succeeded in introducing Ivanov to Sir Harold Caccia, permanent Under-Secretary of State at the Foreign Office, who recoiled vigorously. When the Cuban crisis blew up in October 1962, the activities of the pair became frenetic. On October 24 Ward telephoned to the Foreign Office and alleged that Lord Astor had recommended him to contact Sir Harold Caccia, as Ivanov wished to tell him that the Soviet government was looking to the United Kingdom as the only hope of mediation in this crisis, and that the United Kingdom should call a summit conference immediately. The Foreign Office remained impassive, and the next day Ward got the credulous MP to meet Ivanov and go to the Foreign Office with this proposal, about which Ward telephoned to it himself later. On the same day he got Lord Astor to speak to Lord Arran, a newspaper director, and tell him, as Lord Denning puts it, that there was a Russian official who was trying to pass information of an urgent nature to the British government. Two days later, on October 27, 1962, Ward took Ivanov to Lord Arran's house, where he repeated the suggestion of the summit conference, adding that Khrushchev would accept the invitation with alacrity. Lord Arran suspected that this was an attempt to drive a wedge between the United Kingdom and the Americans and reported it in an unfavourable light to the Foreign Office and the Admiralty. Lord Arran has a notorious sense of humour, and these proceedings must be thought of as punctuated by his robust laughter.

The next day, Sunday, October 28, Ward and Ivanov went up to Cliveden, where there was the usual week-end party, and while they were there it was announced on the radio that the Russian ships had turned back from Cuba. Ivanov gave way to his surprise and rage, and all the guests noticed it. But three days later they were at it again. Ward accidentally picked up an MP in a restaurant and took him back to his house, where they found Ivanov and Christine Keeler and Mandy Rice-Davies. This peculiar assemblage discussed the Cuban crisis with passion, the two young ladies occasionally breaking in with support of Ivanov. This must have been an entrancing spectacle. In appearance they were like the strange women against whom King Solomon warned us, but the voices were those of good readers of the left-wing weeklies. When the Tory MP got up to go Ward said, referring to Ivanov and himself, "that they too must go, for they had to dine with Mr Iain Macleod." This statement froze the blood of the Tory MP, Mr Macleod being then Minister for Commonwealth Affairs, and in view of the company present this can well be understood. In fact they did not know Mr Macleod. Ward had persuaded a young man to ask Mrs Macleod if he might bring him and Ivanov to a party the Macleods were giving for their young son and daughter and their friends. On finding that Mr Macleod was not there, the pair stayed only a few minutes and left.

The MP who had been inveigled into this astonishing visit compared notes with Mr Macleod, who reported the matter to the Foreign Office, with the result that on November 2 that body entered into further exasperated correspondence with the security service about Ward. It is to be noted that by now the security service had very strong suspicions indeed that Ward was (the security officer put it in a letter to the Foreign Office) "providing some of his influential friends with highly satisfactory mistresses," or (as he put it more tersely in his report to his own department) was "a provider of popsies for rich people." This knowledge undoubtedly lowered the temperature in which Ivanov and Ward were working.

But they were indefatigable. On November 7 Ward wrote to Mr Harold Wilson about his activities, telling him that the Russians had made an offer to the Foreign Office for a summit conference. "I can vouch for the authenticity of this," he declared, "since I was the intermediary." But Mr Wilson was unimpressed. A veil then drops but is lifted for a moment on Boxing Night to show us a dinner party given by a peer and his wife, who had been a close friend of Ward before her marriage, to which Ward and Ivanov had been invited to meet a highly placed Foreign Office official and his wife. It seems that they brought up in conversation the Nassau Conference and the American delivery of nuclear weapons to the Germans, but the Foreign Office official preserved silence. It is to be doubted, however, that

Ward and Ivanov hoped to extract any information. It is much more likely that they came to give rather than to receive. That had certainly been the role Ward had been trying to play for the previous eighteen months. If we trace the story from the beginning, we find something which looks very like the attempt of an agent, who was perhaps not quite an agent, to become a double agent. Ward showed himself very obliging to the British security service. A security officer had only to tell him that his friendship with Ivanov had been remarked upon, and instruct him to report any propositions made to him by Ivanov, for him to come back within a month with the story that Ivanov had indeed made him a proposition, and the further (and false) story that Ivanov had taken a mistress who was under his own control. From then on, in the communications of the security service, there are references to the possibility of Ivanov's defecting: a possibility which must have been conjured up by Ward. During the Cuban crisis Ivanov was presented to Lord Arran as "a Russian official seeking to pass information of an urgent nature to the British government" behind the back of his ambassador: that is, as next door to a defector.

In fact, Ward was trying to insinuate himself into the British security service with the high prestige of a double agent who brings to his second employer a valuable agent recruited from the security service which was his first employer. He may have been inspired by genuine patriotism of a cracked sort; he may have been, knowingly or unknowingly, acting at the instigation of the Soviet authorities who wanted to plant Ivanov on the British in order to supply them with misleading information; or he may simply have been gratifying an unassuageable appetite for complications. Which motive impelled him we shall never now learn, but we do know that Ivanov had no intention of becoming a defector, straight or crooked. Some time late in January, Ward had to tell Ivanov that their joint effort had been wrecked by a disregarded human element, and the whole story of their connection might be published at any moment. Then was the moment when, had Ivanov desired to forsake his own people, and had his proceedings not been known and approved by his own superiors throughout, he would have applied to the British for political asylum. Instead, he returned to his country on January 29.

It was Christine Keeler who, for reasons partly to her credit and partly to her discredit, had wrecked Ward's venture into the field of security. She and Mandy Rice-Davies were growing resentful of the control Ward exercised on their lives. Both had had some taste of luxury, but not much. Though Peter Rachman was still living with Mandy at the time of his death in 1962, he had made no provision for her in his will. There was no ill feeling. He merely suffered from the same testamentary difficulties which must have vexed King Solomon if he had a grateful disposition. After that, times had gone badly with them. Neither of them was really framed for success in the terms Ward could provide it. The courtesan who satisfies the rich and great must have a woman's body and a yes-man's soul; and Christine had an uneasy, donnish intelligence, while Mandy's wit and humour were untamed and formidable. Under Ward's direction they were frittering away their lives on prostitution only occasionally mitigated by affection and friendship, and they were most meagrely rewarded in money or comfort. They wanted to get away from him, and it was a sign of character that they did.

But Christine had gone downhill rapidly in the last few months. About the time of her parting from Mr Profumo, Ward had introduced her to the use of marijuana cigarettes, which he smoked himself. This had involved her with two West Indians, Lucky Gordon and John Edgecombe, both convicted criminals. She lived with both of them in turn and left them, and they engaged in a barbaric fight for possession of her. When she sought refuge with Ward, Lucky Gordon perpetually raised riot round the house, banging on the door and shouting, at all hours of the day and night; Edgecombe was even more to be feared. On October 27, 1962, he inflicted serious wounds on Lucky Gordon in a brawl over Christine, but he eluded arrest. Discontented with Ward's regime as she was, she was forced by this sort of mishap to take refuge with him, but he received her with some acrimony. He could not approve of one of his girls' abandoning her appointed duties and going off on her own; and it is possible that his conscience told him he had led her too far away from the normal. It must be admitted also that, at a time when he was trying to impose himself on the Foreign Office and the security service as a discreet and responsible person, it was awkward to have his home besieged by West Indians whose conduct might well attract the attention of the police and who, if questioned, would declare themselves in search of a young prostitute, under his roof for reasons hard for him to explain.

On December 14, 1962, the crisis broke. Edgecombe came to Ward's house when Christine was paying a visit to Mandy, and on being refused admission shot the place up, whereupon he was arrested. Christine was badly shaken. She had had reason to fear for her life. At all times she suffered from a neurotic garrulity, but now she became a cascade of reminiscence. She talked to everybody she met, about everything which had ever happened to her, whether it concerned Edgecombe or not. Nine days later she happened to meet a former Labour Member of Parliament, a technologist and inventor of some note in his younger days and more recently a financier. He encouraged Christine to talk, and soon he heard the whole story of Mr Profumo and Ivanov and the request for information about the American delivery of nuclear weapons to Germany. He did in fact give the distraught waif some good advice, telling her that to protect her own interests in these matters she must go to a solicitor. But he also passed on the Profumo story to the Labour Party security expert, Mr George Wigg, a soldier who had risen from ranker to colonel. He was appalled by it. The campaign Mr Wigg then started was to his party's advantage, but he is a man of integrity, and it is fair to say that in all his reactions he was moved by honest disgust at the twilit world which the story revealed. He has that peculiarly intense primness which is found in that rare breed, a prim soldier.

But Christine's loquacity had found another outlet. She was in a deplorable state. Edgecombe's shooting affray had led to a bitter quarrel between her and Ward, and she could no longer find a room in his house. She had no money. At a time when prostitutes are prosperous as never before, she had no banking account; a curious fact. It was not surprising that Ward had none; but the same considerations did not apply to her. She was unlikely to earn more money at the moment, for she was ill and overwrought and cannot have been any real recreation for the warrior. Some friends suggested that she should sell her story to the press, and she immediately started hawking it round Fleet Street, presently concluding an arrangement with a newspaper, the first of a series, which, among other benefits, set her up in a comfortable apartment of her own. It is hard to see any other way by which this poor little waif could have got a home at that moment. What is strange, in a girl who appeared to her friends as scatterbrained and inconsiderate but not ill-natured, is the ruthlessness with which she pursued a course certain to bring ruin on Mr Profumo. But it is the case against prostitution that it puts people in the power of others who have no affection for them, and Mr Profumo had taken the risk with his eyes open.

But Christine continued to talk, involving him in another sphere.

355

On January 26 a police sergeant called on her to serve her notice to attend the trial of John Edgecombe, and she gave him a reward which must have been far beyond his expectations with a statement in which she told once again the whole Profumo-Ivanov-nuclear-arms story. Meanwhile there were repercussions from her disclosures in Fleet Street. They had come to Stephen Ward's ears, and on January 28 his counsel brought her proposal to publish memoirs involving Mr Profumo to the attention of the law officers of the Crown. They had already heard the rumours, possibly much earlier. They sent for Mr Profumo and questioned him on the matter, and he denied having committed any sexual impropriety with Christine. On February 1, a senior executive of a newspaper telephoned Admiralty House and, as the Prime Minister was abroad, was given an appointment with a secretary, to whom he reported the sale of Christine Keeler's memoirs to a certain newspaper (which in the event never published them) and indicated the extent to which they compromised the Minister of War. Therefore the security services were immediately alerted, though not, it proved, to any very good purpose.

On February 4, Ward tried one last professional trick. He reported to Marylebone police court that two photographs had been stolen from him. They were taken at the Cliveden swimming pool and one showed Ward and three of his girls and bore a quite innocuous inscription by Mr Profumo on the back, and the other showed Mr Profumo with two girls, one of whom was Christine. Later Ward made a statement alleging that the photographs had been stolen by a friend of Christine's who meant to sell them. Then, to quote the police officer's note as given by Lord Denning:

Dr Ward said that if this matter, including the association between Mr Profumo and Miss Keeler, became public, it might very well "bring down" the Government. He also added that he had no personal liking for this Government but would not like to see it go out of office in this way.

He then indicated quite clearly that Miss Keeler's memoirs would mention many well-known names, and that he himself had connections with MI5 and was involved with a Soviet diplomat. This was blackmail, quite unpunishable as such, since it was made in the course of a complaint about a theft made to the police, but also quite certain to reach its mark. This should be remembered when attempts are made to present Ward as an artless and sincere deviate.

It would be pleasant to report that this nefarious effort was unsuccessful, but in point of fact it attained its ends, though indirectly, through a grotesque official decision. The security service, and also the Special Branch, and the Criminal Investigation Department alike came to the conclusion that Ward and Christine Keeler were low persons and they wanted to have nothing to do with them. This fastidiousness, which seems peculiarly misplaced in the police, was not the result of political pressure. On the contrary, the government was clamouring for all possible assistance in getting at the truth. The action of these organizations was entirely spontaneous, and it was responsible for all the subsequent scandal which makes 1963 a black date in Parliamentary history. If Christine Keeler had been questioned by the police then, she could have furnished many proofs (as she did some weeks later) that her story of an affair with Mr Profumo was true. He would thus have had no temptation to deny his relationship with her.

Ward had only six months to live, and he spent them trying to repeat this success. He was inspired by an intense anxiety regarding his association with Ivanov. He explained his own innocence of espionage on television; and after Mr Wigg had appeared on "Panorama" and spoken of Ivanov as a slick and competent Intelligence officer, Ward called on Mr Wigg at the House of Commons in a dithering condition and for three hours protested that he and Ivanov had been just friends, that Ivanov had nothing to do with Intelligence, and that there had been nothing whatsoever between Miss Keeler and Mr Profumo which Ivanov could have exploited. He seems to have spent much of the twenty-four hours in making such confidences to anyone who would listen to him. When Mr Profumo had untruthfully denied his guilt to the House of Commons and an uneasy hush had fallen, Ward seemed to be relieved and to grow more confident.

But almost at once there were threats of another sort of trouble. The CID received a number of communications alleging that Ward was living on the immoral earnings of his girls, and that he was being protected from prosecution by his influential friends, and in April it started taking statements from a number of persons connected with him, including some of his patients. When this reached his ears in May, he tried to defend himself again by blackmail. For this purpose he had deliberately to assume again the contacts he had taken such pains to abandon: he had to become again a security risk. Making use of Mr Profumo quite as ruthlessly as Christine, he sent a letter confessing the truth of the Profumo-Ivanov-nuclear-arms story to the Prime Minister, Mr Harold Wilson, his Member of Parliament, the national newspapers (which did not publish it), and the Home Secretary. There could be no mistaking the purport of this last letter: unless the police stopped their inquiries, the truth about Mr Profumo would be published. He took the opportunity to involve his friend and patient Lord Astor, who had lent him £500 three months before and had consented to guarantee his overdraft up to £1500 a few days before. "It was by accident," Ward wrote of Christine, "that she met Mr Profumo and through Lord Astor that she met him again. I intend to take the blame no longer."

The blackmail failed. The government made up its mind to set up an inquiry, and when Mr Profumo realized this he confessed the truth. Ward found himself adrift in a world which had become much more dangerous for him in the last few weeks. Christine Keeler had suffered a complete collapse. On the tide of her own hysteria she had been swept up and down Fleet Street, out to Spain and back again, in and out of solicitors' offices, on a continual merry-go-round swinging between Marylebone police court and the Old Bailey, in and out of the witness box, in and out of expensive flats rented by eccentrics with no visible means of support, into motor crashes, back and forth through booing, jeering, leering crowds. She was a pitiful sight. She remained beautiful, but her beauty was now a thin veil worn by a sick and grubby child. Her one salient characteristic was the desire for respect; she would have enjoyed being the head of a women's college. But external circumstances and her own will, which seemed as indifferent to her well-being as if it too were external to her, conspired without end to annul any possibility that she should be respected. The same enmity between the will and the self was visible in Ward. Considered as a sexual being, he was the incarnation of a chemist's window in the Charing Cross Road. Not merely did he offend the god of love; he insulted Silenus. The bare catalogue of his efforts to degrade sensuality below the level of charm would have been enough to alienate the court. Yet though he bore himself as if he were born on the side of authority, unalterably among those who passed judgment rather than among the judged, the unfortunate man kept on strengthening the case for his exclusion from honour. He actually handed himself over to his prosecutors. Yes, he had had relations with one of the prostitutes who had given evidence, a poor puny little waif who looked like a photograph of an Indian famine-relief poster. But that was natural, indeed it was inevitable. He had gone out late at night to buy cigarettes, and there, beside a cigarette machine, this waif had been standing. Well, that was enough, wasn't it? The two machines had been standing side by side, waiting for custom; of course he had taken the mobile one home. *Of course* he had, he insisted, though the judge, as a flash of gold had reminded us from time to time, was one of the few Englishmen who wear a wedding ring. It was no use for Ward to try to disguise what he was. The poor demented man, in spite of all his kindness, all his gifts, had committed himself to be a pimp. In him disloyalty had gone on the streets.

A little less than a quarter of a century had passed since Joyce had sat where Ward was sitting in the Old Bailey dock. The only similar quality in the men was their willingness to deal too obediently with another country, to their country's danger; otherwise the differences were extreme. Joyce was the apotheosis of the amateur, who was sustained only by his ideals and unsupported by any technique. He had broken out of England and fled to Germany as artlessly as a boy breaking out of an approved school; he had forced himself on the insufficiently organized propaganda system in Berlin as he might have joined the gipsies; when the end came he had to go out alone to flee the armies. Ward was the apotheosis of the professional: since there was a technique for helping foreign powers, he had acquired it, and when there had been a technical hitch he had met the technique of the police with the technique of legality. Joyce would never have been a pimp, nor would most of the traitors of World War II who had followed him into the dock; the nineteenth-century political dissenter practised innocence as a defence from conformist criticism. Ward was so much of a pimp that the charges which got him into the dock related to pimping, and when he died by his own hand after the sixth day of his trial, his death shocked into protest everyone who in his heart of hearts would have liked to be a pander.

Supposing, a surprisingly large number of people asked, that Ward had been procuring young women for rich men, was there anything so shocking about that? Surely it was archaic to regard with disfavour any action which promoted sexual intercourse? That was loudly asked, but in the overtones of the inquiry could be heard a rider: "particularly if there is money in it." Through the memory of those who had attended the Joyce trials there rang the voice of the Scotsman who had raised a disturbance in the lobby of the House of Lords when the last appeal was lost, urging that when Joyce had left England to broadcast for the Nazis he had simply gone abroad to better himself, and there could be nothing wrong about that. "He had a fine position waiting for him, and he just took it." In 1945 this had been the cry of a lone eccentric. In 1963 he could have spoken for a considerable and not undistinguished part of England.

The Ward case had many ugly consequences. The crowds round the courts were uncommonly nasty. The witnesses had to walk through a vast leer, a huge concupiscent exposure of cheap dentures. The children were grown up who had been brought by their mothers to wait outside Wandsworth Jail while Joyce was being hanged; they were now bringing their own children to see these poor sluts on their way to humiliation. The show was perhaps at its grimmest in the Dickensian streets round the Marylebone police court. Christine Keeler was every afternoon led out by the police and put in her car, which was covered by a tent of photographers, who climbed on the footboards, the bonnet, and the roof. Then they fell away and their place was taken by a mob of women, mostly old or middle-aged, without exception ill-favoured and unkempt, and shabby elderly men. Inside the car Christine Keeler sat in terrified dignity, her face covered with the pancake make-up which levels the natural toning of the skin, and her determination not to show her fear ironing out her features to the flatness of a mask. The cries and boos of the crowd expressed the purest envy. It was disagreeable to see a number of women candidly confessing that at the end of their days they bitterly resented not having enjoyed the happiness of being prostitutes, and a number of men in the same situation wishing they had been able to afford the company of prostitutes.

The passion of the mob was rushing in to fill a vacuum. It is natural for a community to think and feel and express itself when anything threatens its accustomed habit, so that it can explain the significance of the threat and take appropriate action. But the community did not know what to think or feel about the Ward-Profumo affair; it could not understand its significance and it most certainly could not promise itself that it could guard against the recurrence of just such a scandal. Obviously the ordinary penal mechanism did not work in this case. Mr Profumo had had an affair with a young woman deeply involved in the disreputable; he had thus involved himself in the sphere of security; he had lied to the House of Commons, which is indeed a comprehensive insult to the English present and the English past. But none of these are punishable offences. The public would probably have felt better if the Foreign Office had been able to ask for the withdrawal of Ivanov from the Soviet Embassy as a *persona non grata*. But, alerted by Ward, he had already gone back to Russia. Ward himself had been pursued by the law, but not for the offences which the community was so bitterly resenting, which led to the suspicion (fanned by the special character of the law under which he was charged) that he was being prosecuted out of revenge by an Establishment jealous of its own. Even Peter Rachman, the slum-landlord and club-owner who had kept Christine Keeler and Mandy Rice-Davies, could not be prosecuted, for the good reason that he was dead.

The fear caused by recognition that the law was not able to prevent or punish such gross misbehaviour was transmuted, for the sake of the community's self-respect, into a fear that the law was doing too much. Miss Keeler had had a series of long legal involvements with the West Indians, John Edgecombe and Lucky Gordon, who had both been sent to prison. Lucky Gordon appealed, and the Court of Criminal Appeal quashed his conviction in nine minutes. But it did not disclose the evidence which led it to this decision. There were three reasons which made this reticence inevitable. The Court of Appeal had received the evidence in a form difficult to discuss within its own limitations, which are crippling. The evidence must have referred to matters alluded to at the trial of Ward, which was still progressing. And as the Director of Public Prosecutions was not resisting the appeal, there was no case to be disproved by the judgement. But the public, by now thoroughly confused, misinterpreted the action of the court as an attempt to cover the derelictions of other branches of the law. The men in high places who had assumed the burden of responsibility became suspect, and so did their brothers whose irresponsibility had caused this crisis. It was felt that Ward's rich patrons had shown shocking disloyalty by not giving evidence at his trial. This was unjust; the defence would have called these men, and they could not have resisted the summons, if their evidence would have disproved the charges against Ward instead of confirming it. These public attitudes were absurd, yet they were founded on a vigilance of which England had need. Scepticism was necessary. The administration of the law had grown slipshod; there were to be several police scandals to prove it. It was true too that if Ward had gone too far out of the course prescribed by society, he had been paid to run the extra distance, and his wealthy paymasters were worse than he was, not being as daft as he was and capable enough to exercise considerable responsibility in other fields. But all the same, circumstances had intensified the natural reactions of the public to a paranoiac extreme. ◇ ◇ ◇

CONCLUSION

There is a case for the traitor. He is a sport from a necessary type. The relationship between a man and his fatherland is always disturbed if either man or fatherland be highly developed. A man's demands for liberty must at some point challenge the limitations the state imposes on the individual for the sake of the masses; and if he is to carry on the national tradition he must wrestle with those who, claiming to be traditionalists, desire to crystallize it at the point reached by the previous generation. It is our duty to readjust constantly the balance between public and private liberties. Men must be capable of imagining and executing and insisting on social change, if they are to reform or even maintain civilization, and capable too of furnishing the rebellion which is sometimes necessary if society is not to perish of immobility. Therefore all men should have a drop of treason in their veins, if the nations are not to go soft like so many sleepy pears.

But, all the same, there is a case against the traitor. The law states it with simple logic: if a state gives a citizen protection it has a claim to his allegiance, and if he gives it his allegiance it is bound to give him protection. But there are now other reasons for regarding treachery with disfavour, which grow stronger every year.

We are not yet within sight of disarmament. Our total population increases, and with it our population of scientists and industrialists, who continue to present the state with more and more intricate and terrible weapons, each arousing the curiosity of our neighbours. This curiosity can be satisfied partially by such devices as the monitoring which gives confirmation of the discharge of nuclear weapons on alien territories, and these are fair enough uses of scientific technique. But the other forms of espionage, such as are grouped under the title of "cloak and dagger," are becoming more and more objectionable.

The stories told in these pages have behind them a second story of huge unproductive expenditure, of lifelong labours which do not add one single grain to the world's resources. Lonsdale and [some of the others], the grimy small fry* ◇◇◇, were maintained by the honest people who teach, doctor the sick, till the soil, work in factories, and are scholars and poets and scientists. Only one-eighth of an iceberg, they say, appears above the water; the proportion of detected espionage to the whole is probably considerably less. Facing the spies are the security officers, probably as numerous, unproductively engaged in catching the unproductive. The size of the bill is the more lamentable when it is considered that when a spy expensively succeeds in stealing a secret document and security officers expensively succeed in catching him, the document is probably obsolete by the time he has served half his term in prison; and that probably both spy and security officers are sufficiently gifted to have been capable of much sound productive work.

In this situation, as Vassall showed us, we are threatened by collaboration between the primary form of overpopulation and its secondary form: the excessive production of objects by an excessive number of people. The vast population excretes a number of documents so vast that a vast number of people have to be employed to work on them, so vast that it becomes impossible to buy their honesty by high wages and impossible to employ enough security officers to see that they keep their filing cupboards locked and take nothing secret home. The existence of a huge accumulation of unguarded secret documents extends the same invitation to thievery as the huge number of automobiles which have to be left in the street because their owners cannot buy garage-space. Treachery and allied misdemeanours thus cease to have the connection with idealism of which they could boast when the Fascists and the first Communist offenders stood in the dock against the Official Secrets Act. That idealism was never not disputable. But such men were all certainly interested in ideas, and that is to be interested in ideals at one remove. The kind of offences for which they were sentenced are, however, now committed by people who have no ideological interests at all but who have rejected all moral taboos and will pursue any prohibited activity, provided it brings them sufficient reward in money, power, or security.

This alters the whole character of the security field, partly because these purloiners of secrets have now to satisfy technical demands which make it possible to class the traitors of the past as amateurs and traitors of the present as professionals. Andronnikov could play

*[Described in earlier chapters, omitted here.]

his part by chattering to ministers and Rasputin, and Joyce could utter generalizations over the radio, but Vassall had to practise the advanced technique of photography as he learned it in the RAF. But there is a difference which goes deeper than that. When the spy becomes a man who has made a sweeping rejection of taboos and pursues other prohibited activities as well as espionage, his detection opens the door to a general suspicion of society. He will of necessity have found the paymasters for his illegal activities among the wealthy, and some of them are likely to be identified with one or other of our social institutions. It will also be difficult for the public not to believe that he was aided in his attack on national safety by the influence of these powerful persons for whose unsanctioned tastes he had catered. It can never be easy to prove or disprove these suspicions, for the reason that when such connivance exists it functions in secrecy, and that very often no such connivance exists, and it is still impossible to prove a negative. The public therefore suffers a sense of impotence, and in despair engages in the devaluation of values at a moment peculiarly unfavourable to the creation of new ones. The march towards civilization is interrupted, and on that journey, though we have eternity before us, we are always short of time.

At least we have large and able security organizations to protect us from our spies; and it is impossible not to applaud the courageous, shrewd, and patient men who work to preserve our national safety. Yet they too are a source of danger to the state. The essential conditions of their being work out badly for themselves and everybody else. They can find the infinitesimally small proportion of the population which takes to spying only by subjecting large numbers of persons to restrictions on their freedom against which it is a good citizen's duty to protest, unless he is told the reason for them; and such explanation is often inadvisable from a security point of view. The officers are obliged to work in the strictest secrecy, and this is unhealthy. No organization working under cover can remain fully efficient, least of all one which is perpetually in danger of infiltration by the forces which it is fighting. Yet it is necessary for the security organizations to work behind a veil, so necessary that the habit of secrecy has to be cultivated until it becomes a monomania. The Denning Report tells us that the head of the Special Branch decided not to interview Christine Keeler, for fear she might inform the press that she had been interviewed by the Special Branch. This was a calamity, for the whole Profumo scandal would have been short-circuited by what she had to say; and it is impossible to imagine that that highly desirable state of affairs would have been discounted by any disadvantage arising out of the fact that the public knew the interview had taken place.

This is but one example of the conflict between the secrecy practised by the security organizations and the public good. A more striking example, indeed, happened later in the summer of 1963. In March 1963, Harold Philby, who had been named "the third man" in the Burgess and Maclean case, disappeared from Lebanon, where he had been representing *The Observer* and *The Economist*, and in July it was known that he had gone behind the Iron Curtain. There was perhaps no immediate political implication in his flight at all. He was a close friend of Guy Burgess, who had fallen ill with a mortal sickness, and was to die later in the year. Mr Heath, Lord Privy Seal, was obliged to admit to the House of Commons that at the time of the disappearance of Burgess and Maclean it had become known that Mr Philby had had Communistic associations and that he had been asked to resign from the Foreign Service in July 1951, which he did; but that now, twelve years later, he had admitted that he had worked for the Soviet authorities before 1946 and that he had in fact warned Maclean through Burgess that the security services were about to take action against him. Again it must be noted that this is an incomprehensible statement. It does not explain why a Soviet agent in England, certainly in touch with local agents, could be warned that he was being watched by English security agents only by another Soviet agent in America who sent a third all the way to England to tell him so. Soviet intelligence has better communications than that. This cannot be the story.

But let that rest. Mr Philby was now officially recognized as part of a Soviet apparatus, which had long been known to many persons on both sides of the Atlantic. This exasperated Mr Marcus Lipton, the MP for Brixton, who in the year 1955 had said the very same things about Mr Philby that Mr Heath was now saying, had received no end of a dressing-down from government spokesmen, and had made a very handsome apology to Mr Philby. It shows the moral degradation of the Soviet agent's life that Mr Philby could accept that apology. This revelation of Mr Lipton's wrong exasperated the public, and their rage mounted when the editors of *The Observer* and *The Economist* disclosed that they had employed Mr Philby as their correspondent at the direct suggestion of an official of the Foreign Office. It was then stated, and generally believed, that even in the Middle East Mr Philby had continued to have connections with British Intelligence. This was not a helpful contribution to our national well-being in the summer of 1963.

The government would have been well advised to specify the reasons which had made the security organizations so long nourish this viper in their bosoms, and to announce the resignation of some of the bosoms. But this was not done, and the Philby affair is an un-healed sore in the public mind. Doubtless there were sound reasons for this failure to solve the mystery, but all the same the sore did not heal. If we try to solve the mystery by speculation, we are forced to recall that persons who work in a self-contained unit are apt to develop theories which develop none the better for never being sub-jected to open discussion. The security organizations have shown a disposition to believe that by skilful manipulation they can persuade Communists that communism is not incompatible with patriotism, and they will be drawing the Soviet Union and the West closer together if they act as British agents. This is a preposterous theory. A Communist might collaborate with an England which had gone Fascist, because Fascists and Communists share the doctrine of totali-tarianism, and what Stalin and Hitler once did, men could do again. But a Communist could not collaborate with a democratic England because he is in love with its opposite. Failure to recognize this truth led the security organizations to load themselves up with some ter-rible material in the Second World War; and it is possible that for the same reason they acquired Mr Philby. If they had to air their theories they would have been laughed out of this one; but obviously security organizations can air neither their theories nor their practice.

This situation is not static. It will develop, and a melodramatic pessimism might envisage its development as hideous. The world might be dotted with huge weapon-making installations and huge bureaucratic office buildings in which all the workers would be degraded by inhibiting controls, and distracted by suspicion of their fellows, owing to the operations of espionage coldly organized by professional criminals. These would be found in mass, with their talents highly trained, and their powers of expenditure a menace to society, since such espionage would go on the budgets of foreign powers who could pay them highly because they would buy secrets as a cheaper alternative to researches and experimental constructions on the monstrous scale necessitated by modern scientific discovery. In such a vicious world a government could not form a respectable image of itself or its functions. It would toil on, perhaps sustained only by memories of our age (which might look quite agreeable, seen from an angle of such a future), nervously cultivating distrustful and joyless alliances, and giving up any hope of not being a police state. The security organizations would be no help. They would have to operate in more stringent secrecy than ever. They would be therefore even more subject to infiltration, which would reinforce the endemic distrust and might even lead to conquest by alien powers. If they resisted that temptation, they might form peculiar and too simple political theories which would lead them to perpetrate those nasty events known as "palace revolutions" or exercise a tyranny by threatening such uprisings, in the tiresome manner of the Praetorian Guard.

This will not happen. Though men draw many straight lines, they are not, except in fantasy, prolonged into infinity. Here and there our kind has gone on doing what it ought not to do till it nearly died of it, but there would not be so many of us alive today if our forefathers had not obeyed a deep-seated instinct to stop before it was too late. But we may go a very long way to that nightmare future if we do not regard espionage with a realistic eye. If nuclear weapons were used they would inflict the most hideous damage on the human kind; such as would survive might find survival not worth while. But nuclear weapons have not been used since the error born of ignorance which was committed in Japan eighteen years ago, and it is to be doubted whether they will ever be used again. But in modern espionage there is being used, day in and day out, a weapon which inflicts on society considerable spiritual and material devastation. Let anyone who does not consider the life of George Blake as horrible consider the poor rats who, fawning, brought him titbits of lethal gossip out of the maimed city of Berlin. It makes civilization impossible if the government has to suspect the governed of participation in such squalor and tease them with constricting routines, which the governed cannot accept with a sense of necessity because they know that the government is itself involved in that squalor. The expenditure of wealth on munitions has many times been denounced; but it is not less disgusting to pour it out on the promotion of theft and deceit.

There is no immediate remedy. The unilateral abandonment of

espionage is the only real remedy, and this is as unpractical as unilateral disarmament; and obviously multilateral disarmament must
precede the multilateral abandonment of espionage. Nevertheless
there are some holes which can be stopped up. The cutting down of
our embassies behind the Iron Curtain to a skeleton staff is obviously
advisable; and in the opinion of experts such as Commander Anthony
Courtney, MP, it is feasible. If it is not, the modern development of
communication is a mockery. There is also the proposal, espoused by
the Tory government and apparently favoured by the Labour Party,
to set up a standing commission on security. This would have a judicial chairman and be composed of retired civil servants and officers of
the armed services experienced in security matters, and the Prime
Minister would decide when it was to be brought into use, having
consulted the leader of the Opposition. If ever the commission found
it desirable to have powers to compel evidence, then it would be converted into a tribunal of inquiry under the 1921 act; and again
before this could be done there would have to be consultation between
the Prime Minister and the leader of the Opposition, though the
Labour Party seems more likely to have recourse to the appointment
of select committees of the House on such occasions.

The intention behind the creation of this new body is to lift
security matters out of party politics, and this is indeed necessary.
Security is literally concerned with security: with safety: with the
survival of this country and, indeed, this globe. It is disgusting that
at least a third of any Parliamentary debate on security consists of
partisan jabber. The commission would also for the first time give
security a voice of its own. The public knows nothing of treachery
and espionage except what it hears from the lips of ministers in the
Houses of Parliament, or from counsel and judges at the trials of
persons charged with offences against the Treason or Official Secrets
Acts, or from the press. Of these three sources the last has been much
the most reliable. The press is often vulgar, because, like all commercial enterprises, it tends to adapt itself to the tastes of its customers,
and large numbers of these demand vulgarity. But, vulgar or not, it
has brought striking ability and courage to this particular duty of
telling the public what is happening to national security in our times.
The work done on the Burgess and Maclean case by the *Daily
Express*, for example, informed the community of a series of gross
administrative blunders indicative of a degree of eccentricity in the
standards of permanent officials which required correction. But the

press works under severe handicaps. One of these may be its own sensationalism; but that there are others, and those not to its discredit, will be realized if it be considered just how a conscientious editor could have discharged his duty of telling his readers the truth about Mr Harold Philby. It is to be hoped that the standing commission would prevent such unfortunate happenings.

But once security is given a public voice, that is to say a public identity, it is certain to become the object of a Communist assault such as has not been previously experienced in Great Britain. If the United States had been the venue of the achievements of Fuchs, Nunn May, the Portland spy ring, Vassall, or Blake, or Barbara Fell, their innocence would have been maintained day in day out from the moment of their arrest till long after their trial, and attacks would have been made on all persons concerned with their trials. The probity of the prosecuting counsel, magistrates, and judges alike would be attacked, and every witness giving evidence against them would be denounced as a Titus Oates. Hence a large number of Americans form the opinion that there is no such thing as a Communist spy and never has been, and against this another large section of the population reacts by coming to believe that everybody is a Communist spy and always will be. An American who considers an espionage case with the same balance and detachment that he would bring to a case of robbery with violence or grave larceny has to exercise unusual independence of judgement. In Great Britain the public is protected from a like situation because of our laws, which prevent comment on cases *sub judice* and protect the bench from criticism. But it can hardly be doubted that, if British security were given a public personality in the standing committee, this would become a target for dishonest attack in the Communist interests. This will face the public with a new challenge.

Treachery is a problem we will have to live with for a long time, and the nearest we can come to a solution is to recognize the problem for what it is. The man tempted to become a traitor will be helped if public opinion keeps it clear before him that treachery is a sordid and undignified form of crime. It is not necessary to hate him. Few of us spend much time hating burglars, but the community has established that burglary is not in its opinion an honourable or humanitarian profession, and this ill repute, coupled with our penal laws, constitutes a useful deterrent. Even so we should abandon all sentimentality in our views of the traitor, and recognize him as a thief and a liar. He may be other things; a criminal is very rarely simply a criminal. But to a marked degree the traitor is also a thief and a liar.

But beyond that we must be quick to detect and frustrate the effect of treachery. The traitor can change the community into a desert haunted by fear, and it is our business to realize what force is at work and change it back again. Loyalty has always had its undramatic but effective answer to treason, insisting on its preference for truth instead of deceit, and good faith instead of bad. But on occasion the answer has to be framed more cleverly than at other times, and ours is a period when it becomes no answer at all, but a pact with treachery, if it be not dictated by caution and fastidiousness. We must keep our clear sight; we must not, for example, blind ourselves to the knowledge that the Rosenbergs faced death with magnificent courage. We must reject evil and dispel suspicion without falling into the error of confusing unpopular forms of virtue with evil. We must remember that quite noble attempts to defeat evil may, in sufficiently perverse circumstances, be mistaken for evil; and unfounded suspicions may be engendered. Since the traitor's offence is that he conspires against the liberty of his fellow countrymen to choose their way of life, we ally ourselves with him if we try to circumvent him by imposing restrictions on the liberty of the individual which interfere with the legitimate business of his soul. It is true that such issues do not often arise. The story told in these pages shows that we would have been spared a great deal of trouble if we had simply kept our cupboards locked and had removed from our public service officials who were habitually blind drunk. But if we do not keep before us the necessity for uniting care for security with determination to preserve our liberties, we may lose our cause because we have fought too hard. Our task is equivalent to walking on a tightrope over an abyss, but the continued survival of our species through the ages shows that, if we human beings have a talent, it is for tightrope-walking.

IV. LITERARY CRITICISM

FROM The Strange Necessity

FROM Battlefield and Sky
From The Strange Necessity: Essays and Reviews (1928)

Elegy [D. H. LAWRENCE]
From Ending in Earnest: A Literary Log (1931)

FROM The Court and the Castle:
SOME TREATMENTS OF A RECURRENT THEME (1957)
Part III.: The Castle of God

Uncollected Articles:
Charlotte Brontë (1932)
Rudyard Kipling (1936)
A Visit to a Godmother (1964)
A Grave and Reverend Book (1966)
And They All Lived Unhappily Ever After (1974)

FROM The Strange Necessity

From I

◇◇◇ This is not to say that Joyce does not write beautiful prose. The description of the young man bathing in the first part of *Ulysses*, blue seas engulfing clean white limbs which because of their youth and beauty seem like the waters, not as dense as earth, while from Buck Mulligan there come slow indolent shouts of lewdness, like the roaring of a bull far down under the waters, far down under the earth, waiting for the hour when it may hammer its hoofs up some highway into that foolish thing, so extravagantly much less dense than earth, the light, and trample down to the earth all fair bloodless things like grass and flowers, and all things that having blood within them are disloyal to their corruptible content and seem ethereal, like these clean white limbs; the description of the Dublin summer afternoon, threaded with creeping bodies, with creeping minds, that do not know quite what they do, that do not do quite what they know, that are like ants, over which men express respectful wonder at the creative powers of nature, but on which they tread without compunction; the description of Marion Bloom, the great mother who needs not trouble to trace her descent from the primeval age whence all things come, who lies in a bed yeasty with her warmth and her sweat, and sends forth in a fountain from her strong, idea-less mind thoughts of generation and recollection of sunshine, and the two are one, twisting and turning, the two are seen to be one: these are outside the sphere and beyond the power of any other writer alive or dead. ◇◇◇

In the course of the Clark lectures Mr E. M. Forster delivered on "Aspects of the Novel," he discusses whether any but the simplest rhythms, those that consist of repetition plus variation, have ever been created in fiction. "Is there any effect in novels," he asks, "comparable to the effects of the Fifth Symphony as a whole, where, when the orchestra stops, we hear something that has never actually been played? The opening movement, the andante, and the trio-scherzo-

373

trio-finale-trio-finale that composes the third block, all enter the mind at once and extend one another into a common entity. This common entity, this new thing, is the symphony as a whole, and it has been achieved mainly (though not entirely) by the relation between the three big blocks of sound which the orchestra has been playing." I should have said that the monologue of Marion Bloom which is the end of *Ulysses* perfectly achieved just such an effect: just such a unified beauty. ◇-◇-◇

There is that in her reverie which sets before one the image of a recumbent woman. The air above her, that is to say the air above our mother earth, seems to become full of men, whom she calls into existence by her desirousness. Men and men and men crowd the air of the universe, with vague faces, with defined bodies. Surely there is no air left to breathe, it is all full of men. One thinks of the art of many countries, of many ages, of times and spaces which have nothing in common but this business of engenderment: of Demeter, shaped like a ship built for cargo, moving on the earth as a ship moves on the water; of a stone arch in India carved with more than computable figures emblematic of fertility, more figures than can ever have been carved, that must surely have multiplied by fission under the artist's fingers, surely now multiplying so under the beholder's eyes, and surely to be trusted to multiply still more when his back is turned; of the Chinese goddess that is called of mercy but has no particular interest in mercy, who looks down on city squares where passers-by do not wait long enough to watch the executioner's sword fall on all the fourteen bared napes and on dark rivers where the bodies of children float in tiny fleets, and is not disturbed, knowing that however far death throws the ball, she can throw it further; ◇-◇-◇ of Raphael's Madonna, drooping her cheek to the hapless child whom she has borne that He may be crucified.

All these attitudes arising out of reproduction that have ringed history and the globe are to be found in this dingy little room in Dublin, in the innocent and depraved, the tender and callous musings of Marion Bloom. They move, these creations of her need to be fertile: this one serves her youth and goes, that one serves her maturity and goes, even she throws the noose of desire round Stephen Dedalus and draws him near to her. The Mother is going to draw the Son back into her body, by his consent he will become the Father, who will beget a son. By observing the rhythm of Marion Bloom we have been given knowledge, not otherwise stated, of the rhythms of Leopold Bloom and Stephen Dedalus. Surely it might be said that "all enter the mind at once, and extend one another into a common entity." It is not the philosophy which gives the book beauty. That eternally Leopold Bloom and Simon Dedalus will kill Rudy Bloom and Stephen Dedalus, but that that will be no victory, since eternally Marion Bloom and May Dedalus will raise up their enemies against them, is not a happy ending on the facts. Personally I would prefer man to draw a better design, even if it was drawn but once and was not repeated like the pattern on a wall-paper. But I claim that the interweaving rhythms of Leopold Bloom and Stephen Dedalus and Marion Bloom make beauty, beauty of the sort whose recognition is an experience as real as the most intense personal experiences we can have, which gives a sense of reassurance, of exultant confidence in the universe, which no personal experience can give. ◇ ◇ ◇

◇◇◇As I continued on my way along the Rue de Rivoli; still full of that sense of peace and satisfaction and reassurance which rested on me like a pencil of brightness, proceeding from the rhapsodic figure of Marion—from meeting any of whose equivalents in the real world may the merciful Powers preserve me!—I was conscious of another pencil of brightness searching for my breast, whose beneficence also I could receive if I would but stand in the way of it. It proceeded almost visibly from certain grey walls, garlanded with stone that has taken on the variegation of living matter, being pearly above, where the rain falls, and soot-black, black-cat-black, beneath, on the other side of the street; from the Museum of the Louvre. I said to myself, "Ingres!" Greedily I promised myself another deep draught of just such peace, just such satisfaction, just such reassurance, as I had been receiving from James Joyce. Now, how could that be? How in the world could two artists so entirely unlike in every way as Ingres and James Joyce conceivably cause a like emotion? To begin with, there is no reason why objects so utterly different as a book and a picture, whose approach to the spectator is along such different sensory avenues, should have anything like the same effect. But there is even more reason why a mind furnished as Ingres' (in the manner of the drawing-room Empire style of a silly but beautiful and competent woman) should create the same impression as a mind furnished like James Joyce (which is furnished like a room in a Westland Row tenement in which there are a bedstead and a broken chair,

375

on which there sits a great scholar and genius who falls over the bedstead whenever he gets up). Ingres must have been a perfect idiot. When he committed allegorical pictures of nude ladies being rescued from dragons, it is as if Time had turned over in his sleep and been vexed by a prevision of disinfectant advertisements; and in his representation of the harem having its Turkish bath he gets the effect of crowded merriment that has often rewarded the efforts of Mr Fred Karno. One is certain that his taste in literature and music was all for the momentary and the worst of that. Only he knew how to handle a brush so that it was a part of his will; astoundingly his medium seemed a friend and not the enemy—which it is to nearly all artists. He had the innocence of the eye that all the rest of the world has lost long ago, so that he looks on flesh as Adam might have looked on Eve before lust rose in him, and lets its values be manifest in their purity, and on the Rivière family as if they were the first human beings ever created and his soul rushed forward on the tide of a new dispensation to greet them and apprehend all their qualities.

Hardly to be prognosticated as the fruit of the same earth is James Joyce, good Latinist, good Aquinist, master of tradition, who can pour his story into the mould of the Odyssey and do it with such scholarship that the ineptitude of the proceedings escapes notice, who pushes his pen about noisily and aimlessly as if it were a carpet-sweeper, whose technique is a tin can tied to the tail of the dog of his genius, who is constantly obscuring by the application of arbitrary values those vast and valid figures in which his titanic imagination incarnates phases of human destiny. It would not seem possible that two people of such different sorts, progressing along such divergent paths and arriving at the two points, surely as nearly unrelated as any two points in the universe, of painting a bright-eyed young man with dark hair curling damp on his forehead and a snuff-coloured coat, and of writing the reveries of a slut between blankets in a Dublin back bedroom and should thereby cause in a total stranger to the world of both, in whose life there is nothing which either a young man with dark damp curls and a snuff-coloured coat or a Dublin slut recalls or symbolizes, the most intense and happy emotion. And this emotion is not merely an isolated incident, not merely a discharge of psychic energy caused by an unusual stimulus. It is part of a system; it refers to one of the rhythms of which we are the syntheses. For I was saying to myself, "If you go to Versailles tomorrow you will not have time to see the Ingres," and although Versailles is one of the places in which of all the world I like most to be, I decided to stay and see the Ingres: and then I remembered that when I had been in Paris four months before I had had to make the same choice and that then I had chosen to go to Versailles, but that the time before the choice had been as it was now; and I recognized that in noting those alterations of attitude I had detected my organism recognizing its necessities by the state of its appetite, as it does when it feels hunger acute half an hour before dinner and not at all half an hour after it. But what is the necessity that is served in me by the contemplation alike of a young man with damp dark curls and a snuff-coloured coat and of a Dublin slut? What is the meaning of this mystery of mysteries? Why does art matter? And why does it matter so much? What is this strange necessity?

From III

◇◇◇To doubt that painting and music are just as capable as literature of giving us information about the universe is to show ourselves hag-ridden by the intellect. It is true that literature alone presents us with information in a form on which the intellect can use her accomplishments of logic and the like; but painting presents us with material which does not wait for completion by the intellect, which rounds itself off in the present, which does not need to be treated as a premise because it is itself a complete syllogism, and music presents us with material on which the intellect has already done all the work it can, on the effects produced by a multitude of syllogisms. When Michelangelo carved the waking woman on the Medici tomb he was recording the behaviour of a certain mass at a certain instant which was a complete event in itself. When Shakespeare wrote the sonnet beginning, "Let me not to the marriage of true minds Admit impediments," he was recording a certain event of a much more complicated kind (largely owing to the much more untidy position it occupies in regard to time) which offers the intellect just the job it can do in its need for clarification. When Beethoven wrote the Quartet in C sharp minor he recorded an event of still greater complication that was precipitated as the result of a series of experiences of the simple kind that are the subject of the plastic arts and those of the not so simple kind that are the subject

377

of literature: in fact, he recorded what happens after a thing has happened, what life amounts to after it has been lived. It seems to be true that all the arts are on a perfect equality regarding this necessity to collect information of one sort or another about the universe. ◇◇◇

VII

I have run after myself like an excited *douanier* and insisted on searching myself because I have observed myself behaving in a suspicious manner. I find that I seem to be a quite sane and respectable person, and to have a perfect right to all the emotional goods that are found on me. But . . . what about this? This blazing jewel that I have at the bottom of my pocket, this crystalline concentration of glory, this deep and serene and intense emotion that I feel before the greatest works of art. You know, what Roger Fry means when he says somewhere, "That is just how I felt when I first saw Michelangelo's frescoes in the Sistine Chapel." I get it myself most powerfully from *King Lear*. It overflows the confines of the mind and becomes an important physical event. The blood leaves the hands, the feet, the limbs, and flows back to the heart, which for the time seems to have become an immensely high temple whose pillars are several sorts of illumination, returning to the numb flesh diluted with some substance swifter and lighter and more electric than itself. Unlike that other pleasure one feels at less climactic contacts with art it does not call to any action other than complete experience of it. Rather one rests in its lap. Now, what in the world is this emotion? What is the bearing of supremely great works of art on my life which makes me feel so glad?

It might be, of course, that in such works there are references to the conditions of another world which would be more friendly to us than this. There, most often, are these colours, these forms; there sounds sound most often like this music; there experience most often takes this turn. This universe must be real as ours, since it is weakening to brood on what is wholly fictitious (as apart from imaginary, and I have suggested that imagination is a function created by the organism to deal as specifically as the digestion with purely mundane experiences, and consequently could play no part here) and the effect of this contemplation is strengthening. It must therefore lie parallel

378

with this, our paradise from which we are exiled by some cosmic misadventure, and which we can re-enter at times by participating in the experience of those artists who are supposed by some mystical process to have gained the power to reproduce in this universe the conditions of that other. But the overwhelming argument against this theory is that the people who prefer science to art appear to get precisely the same emotion out of contact with achievements, say in the sphere of mathematics or physics, which relate beyond all doubt to the universe of which we are a part and no other. One must look for another explanation of our good fortune in possessing this blazing jewel of emotion, this priceless treasure.

An analogy strikes me. Is it possible that the intense exaltation which comes to our knowledge of the greatest works of art and the milder pleasure that comes of our more everyday dealings with art, are phases of the same emotion, as passion and gentle affection are phases of love between a man and a woman? Is this exaltation the orgasm, as it were, of the artistic instinct, stimulated to its height by a work of art which through its analysis and synthesis of some experience enormously important to humanity (though not necessarily demonstrable as such by the use of the intellect) creates a proportionately powerful excitatory complex, which, in other words, halts in front of some experience which if left in a crude state would probably make one feel that life was too difficult, and transform it into something that helps one to go on living? I believe that is the explanation. It is the feeling of realized potency, of might perpetuating itself. But . . . do I really love life so much that I derive this really glorious pleasure from something that merely helps me to go on living? That is incredible, considering that life has treated me as all the children of man like a dog from the day I was born. It is incredible, that is, if things are what they seem, if there is not a secret hidden somewhere. . . . I can't justify it, I can't answer half the questions I ask myself. I can just gape and wonder and turn over in my hands this marvellous jewel which, there's no question, I certainly do possess. "There's a whole lot of things I'd like to know about you, my lad!" exclaims the exasperated *douanier*, dashing off to peer into a peasant woman's basket, or touch his hat to an automobile, or somehow to deal with the respectably objective. I want him to come back and bully me, for I too would like to know a lot of things about myself. Not only am I wandering in the universe without visible means of support, I have a sort of amnesia, I do not clearly know

379

who I am . . . what I am. . . . And that I should feel this transcendent joy simply because I have been helped to go on living suggests that I know something I have not yet told my mind, that within me, I hold some assurance regarding the value of life, which makes my fate different from what it appears, different, not lamentable, grandiose.

FROM Battlefield and Sky

◇ ◇ ◇ A work of art may be simple, though that is not necessary. There is no logical reason why the camel of great art should pass through the needle of mob intelligence; to consider the matter from the purely utilitarian point of view, an artist might do humanity more good than any other has ever done by work so complex that only the six cleverest men in his country could understand it, provided it was powerful enough to affect them. In any case, the poems of John Donne exist to prove that a poem can be as complicated as a telephone exchange switchboard and yet indubitably great. But whatever a work of art may be, the artist certainly cannot dare to be simple. He must have a nature as complicated and as violent, as totally unsuggestive of the word innocence, as a modern war.

If one looks back at the Victorian novelists one sees that in each case their art was lifted out of their nature by the force of internal conflicts just as islands are lifted out of the waters by subaqueous earthquakes. Charles Dickens wrote because he was a snob, who, when he was the world's darling, could blush if he was reminded that a kind old gentleman had given him a half-crown tip twenty years before. He found he could escape from the loathed circumstances of his being by exercising his faculty of impersonation; by pouring his vitality into the creation of character after character, with which for the time being he could identify himself. That was the secret of his virtue as an artist; just as the secret of his vice was his determination to use every device of overloading his books with diffuse, incomprehensible, mutually destructive plots so that his imagined world never would crystallize into coherence, lest it should reveal itself as governed by the same laws as the real coherent world, and he should be born again into obscurity and contempt.

Thackeray also used impersonation for escape from a world he found intolerable for different reasons. It was his nature to inquire without fear into the nature of things; but just how much he feared what Victorian society would do if he gave his nature liberty may be judged from the paper in which he bickers at Dean Swift in a voice raucous with envy of a man with a similar temperament who had had the luck to be born in a century that was admiring of satire. He was also vexed by his married life. His wife had been taken from him by an illness of a tragic sort which necessitated a separation, and he was obliged to live a celibate life, which he could correct only by temperate friendships with his wife's friends or furtive loves with women grossly his inferior. So he scattered his soul among the Crawleys and the Newcomes and the Esmonds, allowing his work to assume a nearer approach to coherence than Dickens could because his youthful nerves had not been frayed to cowardice by a sense of social inferiority. And Anthony Trollope was in a more acidulated state of fury than any of them, for he hated his spirited, roving, financially unstable mother with that unsurpassable hatred that a man deficient in virility feels for a woman who is the better man. He fled from his loathing of his being and its origin into an endless round of impersonations all having their being in that world of respectability from which he felt his angularly raffish mother had debarred him.

These were not men, they were battlefields. And over them, like the sky, arched their sense of harmony, their sense of the beauty and rest against which their misery and their struggles were an offence, to which their misery and their struggles were the only approaches they could make, of which their misery and their struggles were an integral part. Over the battlefield that was Anthony Trollope there was not enough sky. He was so absorbed in the conflict arising out of his hatred for his mother that he had no energy left for sensitiveness to the flux of life in general. That is why, though he wrote better than Dickens and Thackeray, though the passages concerning the parson suspected of theft in *The Last Chronicles of Barsetshire* beat Flaubert and Maupassant at their own game, he does not rank as such a considerable artist. It is necessary to have both things, the battlefield and the sky.◇-◇-◇

Elegy

It is difficult to describe accurately the effect that D. H. Lawrence's death had on London. If one says that the effect was tremendous, one makes a suggestion of a capital in mourning, which is ludicrous. Not even among his own caste was he honoured as he should have been. I myself realized with a shock how much of what I had always put down as Lawrence's persecution mania had a solid basis, in fact, when I read obituaries in which not only was the homage due from the living to dead genius meanly denied, but the courtesy paid to any corpse was so far as possible withheld. "Messy stuff," was the delicate phrase bestowed by one of our greatest dailies on his poetry. He might, judging from another of them, have been a lunatic of the same sort as those who, though normal and even exceptionally gifted at most times, every now and then embarrass their friends by suddenly removing their clothes in public places. Less crass than these but just as infuriating were the articles by mediocrities whom we cannot blame for having stayed in safety, since they plainly lacked the vitality to push on the long journey to the edge of danger. They made excuses for Lawrence. It appeared to them that he saw life as a flaming mystery because he suffered from tuberculosis, though nothing seemed plainer to those who knew him best than that this malady gained its hold only because his intense perceptions had exhausted his body. It appeared to them that he wanted to crack the crust which society has allowed to form on the surface of its existence and look underneath, because he was a miner's son and had an inferiority complex about the respectable. If that were true, it were still not to be sneered at, for if a creature of such quality as Lawrence found himself in a world that by its social ordinances ignored that quality, he had a right to question those ordinances. But there was so much more than that in the spiritual drama of Lawrence's life that it is not true. Those traits in Lawrence could hardly have emerged save to those who were regarding their subject very oddly because they were looking at it through the wrong end of field glasses, wishing to see that which is much greater than themselves as much less.

383

The most sympathetic obituary I have yet seen was an affectionate note on him as a man which appeared in *The Times Literary Supplement*.

> I desire (if I can) [says the anonymous writer] to correct the impression, which is widespread, that D. H. Lawrence was a madman of genius, savagely bent on violating sanctuaries, and bruising the finer conscience of his fellow men. To defend Lawrence's passionate convictions is no part of my hasty undertaking. These do not need to be defended, only to be understood, and understood in the light of an experience extraordinary in its depths and comprehensiveness. And again I am not invoking the beauty of his personality to excuse his work. It is right that I should make it clear that I do not consider his work needs any excuse.

It is true that the unknown goes on to say:

> If it was wrong, it was passionately wrong; and to be passionately wrong is far better than to be coldly right,

a sentence which I find it impossible to record without expressing my dissent.

> If it was not right, it was not right with attendant conditions that have no demonstrable connection with values, and to be not right with these attendant conditions that have no demonstrable connection with values is to be more right than to be right with other attendant conditions that also have no demonstrable connection with values.

Such a statement seems to me wrong in itself, and unnecessary as a defence of Lawrence, since he was passionately right. But we can follow this anonymous writer without question when he says:

> Lawrence was the most remarkable and the most lovable man I have ever known. Contact with him was immediate, intimate and rich. When he was gay, and he was often gay—my dominant memory of him is of a blithe and joyful man—he seemed to spread a sensuous enchantment about him. By a natural magic he unsealed the eyes of those in his company; birds and beasts and flowers became new-minted as in Paradise; they stood revealed as what they were, and not the poor objects of our dull and common seeing. The most ordinary domestic act—the roasting of a joint of meat, the washing up of crockery, the painting of a cottage room—in his doing became a gay sacrament.

This is the poet; and this was Lawrence.

This article is just in its estimation of his wonder: and so too was

384

an obituary in the *Manchester Guardian*. But, considering the sowing, this is a meagre harvest that his genius reaps from contemporary fame; and it might be supposed that the *Frankfurter Zeitung* was right in the leader it published the other day, which claimed with a sneer that Lawrence was better appreciated in Germany than in England. Yet it is not so. The grief caused by his death proves far otherwise. I do not speak of his friends and his intimates. They had all cause to regret him for purely selfish reasons. Such a gay companion as the article in *The Times Literary Supplement* delineates is not easily replaced; nor such a friend.

He was completely generous. At a moment when there were not ten pounds between him and destitution he thrust five of them upon a friend and because the friend refused them, flew into a transport of high-pitched rage.

It was not only with his money he was generous. He had *caritas*. That which was needed had to be given. These traits in him would explain the grief of his friends; but another explanation, which can only lie in his genius, must be found for the effect of his death on those who had never set eyes on him. I know nobody of middle age or less, above a certain standard of intellectual integrity or imaginative vigour, who is not stricken by his loss. The prevalent feeling was well described by a young man, a critic and a poet, who said to me the other day, "I've felt rather ill ever since Lawrence died." There is the general malaise one feels after a severe shock, after a loss that cannot be made good.

How deep the experience goes can be measured by the attempts the mind made to refuse it; for everybody I know, and myself also, refused to believe the news when it came. The first threat of trouble came to me between the acts of *This Way to Paradise*, a dramatization of Aldous Huxley's *Point Counter Point*. It is not so good as a play as it was as a novel. Curiously enough, although one usually thinks at a non-Shavian play that its intellectual content is pitiably below that of most novels, the dialectic stuff of this novel, which was far above the level of current fiction, seemed poor and unsatisfying when one heard it recited over the footlights. This was perhaps because Aldous Huxley's novels are, for all their simulation of realism, half way to poetry. The characters, and the rhythm of their appearance, give an account of the phenomena in their creator's spiritual universe. Young Quarles, the intellectual who cannot satisfy his wife Elinor's need for emotion, so that she turns to Webley, the brainless man of action, represents the fantasy that vexes man with a nightmare vision in which his environment assumes a thousand forms to take his potency away from him. If he thinks, surely the power is draining away from him in a thin flood; if he turns to action, he does but bleed from a different vein; and there are always women. Old Quarles, with his perturbed tootings, "A babah? Surely not a babah?" was the picture of the father the son makes in rebellion, the symbol of humanity that the individual invents when he desires to make the gesture of power that is his alone. These, and all the other figures of *Point Counter Point*, were real events in Aldous Huxley's mind, and the sequence in which they appeared and reappeared revealed how his argument with himself about its values was going. It was therefore acceptable by all readers who had reached a certain level of self-consciousness, by reason of the comparison and contrasts they could find between his universe and theirs.

But when these same characters and events were presented in the terribly material medium of the stage, without any disguise of poetry, one had to judge them as if they were taking place on the plane of everyday life. Then one watched the young Quarles household only to imagine how Elinor would react to the torture, hardly to be described in the humanitarian pages of an Occidental publication, though the *Chinese Police Gazette* might like it, which one has long devised for all wives who interrupt their husbands when they are working to ask them if they remember those summer evenings in the garden at Wherever eight years ago. Old Quarles was exactly as significant in comparison with all the other senile libertines the stage has seen as his lines enable him to be, and no more. The dialectic speeches, put into the mouth of those who had diminished from real poetic creations to stage types, seemed irrelevant and papery. But certain things still emerged as important. Profound meaning rang out through lines that bore relation to matters not transplanted from the novel into the play, like bells heard across a lake from a church hidden in the hills on the other side. One was conscious of this whenever Mark Rampion, in whom Aldous Huxley has very obviously depicted Lawrence, came on the stage. One thought, "Even Aldous Huxley, who is so far above the rest of us, feels that he has to look up to Lawrence." When the curtain fell I said as much to my companion, who answered, "You know Lawrence is dangerously ill." For no reason at all I replied, "Oh, I don't believe that, it's quite impossible," just as lots of people, equally without reason, felt confidently, "There's some mistake," when they read in the newspapers about his death at Vence. What would Aldous Huxley or anybody who had seen *This Way to Paradise* have done if they had suddenly heard that the producers of the play had decided to cut out the character of Mark Rampion? All alike would have cried out that the best thing would then be gone, that the producers could not meditate such a folly. Even so did those of us who heard of Lawrence's death feel that from the spectacle of the universe, by the incredible stupidity of a destroying angel, the best thing had gone. Since we see nothing in the universe outside us which we cannot identify with what we see in the universe within us, this means that the forces which moved Lawrence seem to us the best part of our human equipment.

What were these forces? I can find an answer most easily, I find, by referring not to his work, but to my personal acquaintanceship with him, though that was slight. One spring day about ten years ago I was lunching in Florence with Reggie Turner and Norman Douglas. Reggie Turner has been described by Max Beerbohm as Artemus in his paper on wits in *And Even Now*, and there is no need to add a line save to commemorate a supremely imaginative act of charity. When Oscar Wilde came out of prison, Reggie Turner sent him one of the most expensive and completely useless fitted dressing cases that Bond Street has ever achieved. There is need to tell over again the tale of Norman Douglas' accomplishments, because the mind finds them so incredible that it has a disposition to forget them. Besides being a master of English prose, he is one of the finest classical scholars in Europe, a great linguist (he can even speak and write Russian), a pianist, a composer, a caricaturist, a botanist, and a landscape gardener—all to the highest degree of accomplishment. By one of those ironies which forbids us to believe that nature is neutral, even when one has been forced to give up one's faith that she is kindly, Reggie Turner, in whose heart is innocence, wears the winking face of a devil off a quattrocento choir stall; and Norman Douglas, whose heart, so far as innocence is concerned, is as the Gobi Desert, looks as one who has never seen Dr Cadman would imagine him to look. There are what one has been led to believe are the stigmata of moral earnestness: the penetrating eyes under level brows, compressed lips, head set sturdily between the shoulders, as if here reason were firmly rooted in the moral law, and hair white as if the scalp itself had renounced all such vanity as colour. And indeed there is here some of the quality suggested. There is in him an austere loyalty to an interpretation of life that might, if need pushed him to it, not baulk at renunciation. Less than paganism is his religion. Things are what they are. If the landscape seems to form a pattern and the figure of a god to emerge, then that does but prove that a god is but a landscape seeming to form a pattern. That being so, all things are equal and unrelated, perpetually dissolvent back to their point of least significance. Believing this he will not forswear his belief. That day at lunch his conversation perpetually made and unmade the world till late in the afternoon; and then, though there would have seemed to an observer no reason why we should ever move, we were entertaining each other so well, we rose to our feet. Lawrence was coming in by some slow train that crawled up from Rome laden with poor folks that could not pay for speed, and would by now be installed in his hotel. To each of us, different though we were in type, it appeared of paramount importance that we should go and pay him our respects at the first possible moment.

He was staying in a poorish hotel overlooking what seems to me, since I am one of those who are so enamoured of Rome that they will not submit themselves to the magic of Florence, to be a trench of drab and turbid water wholly undeserving of the romantic prestige we have given the Arno. Make no mistake, it was the hotel that overlooked the Arno, not Lawrence. His room was one of the cheaper ones at the back. His sense of guilt which scourged him perpetually, which was the motive power of his genius, since it made him inquire what sin it was which he and all mankind have on their conscience, forbade him either enjoying comfort or having the money to pay for it, lest he should weaken. So it was a small, mean room in which he sat tapping away at a typewriter. Norman Douglas burst out in a great laugh as we went in and asked him if he were already writing an article about the present state of Florence; and Lawrence answered seriously that he was. This was faintly embarrassing, because on the doorstep Douglas had described how on arrival in a town Lawrence used to go straight from the railway station to his hotel and immediately sit down and hammer out articles about the place, vehemently and exhaustively describing the temperament of the people. This seemed obviously a silly thing to do, and here he was doing it. Douglas' laughter rang out louder than ever, and malicious as a satyr's.

But we forgot all that when Lawrence set his work aside and laid himself out to be a good host to us. He was one of the most polite people I have ever met, in both naïve and subtle ways. The other two knew him well, but I had never seen him before. He made friends as a child might do, by shyly handing me funny little boxes he had brought from some strange place he had recently visited; and he made friends too as if he were a wise old philosopher at the end of his days, by taking notice of one's personality, showing that he recognized its quality and giving it his blessing. Also there was a promise that a shy wild thing might well give and exact from its fellows, that he would live if one would let him live. Presently he settled down to give, in a curious hollow voice, like the soft hoot of an owl, an account of the journey he had made, up from Sicily to Capri, from Capri to Rome, from Rome to Florence. There seemed no reason why he should have made these journeys, which were all as uncomfortable as cheap travelling is in Italy; nor did there seem any reason why he was presently going to Baden-Baden. Yet, if every word he said disclosed less and less reason for this journeying, it also disclosed a very definite purpose. These were the journeys that the mystics of a certain type have always found necessary. The Russian saint goes to the head of his family and says good-bye and takes his stick and walks out with no objective but the truth. The Indian fakir draws lines with his bare feet across the dust of his peninsula which describe a diagram, meaningless to the uninitiated, but significant of holiness. Lawrence travelled, it seemed, to get a certain Apocalyptic vision of mankind that he registered again and again and again, always rising to a pitch of ecstatic agony. Norman Douglas, Reggie Turner, and I, none of whom would have moved from one place to another except in the greatest comfort procurable and with a definite purpose, or have endured a disagreeable experience twice if we could possibly help it, sat in a row on the bed and nodded. We knew that what he was doing was right. We nodded and were entranced.

The next day Norman Douglas and I went for a walk with Lawrence far out into the country, past the Certosa. It was a joy for me to leave the city, for I cannot abide trams and Florence is congested with them. Impossible to pass through the streets without feeling that one is being dogged by a moaning tram one had betrayed in one's reckless youth; and it had been raining so hard that there had for long been no opportunity to walk in the country. Now there had been a day's sunshine, and the whole world was new. Irises thrust out of the wet earth like weapons suddenly brought into action. The cypresses, instead of being lank funereal plumes commemorating a foundered landscape, were exclamation marks drawn in Chinese ink, crying out at the beauty of the reborn countryside. About the grassy borders of the road there was much fine enamelwork in little flowers and weeds as one has seen it on the swards of Botticelli. Of the renascent quality of the day Lawrence became an embodiment. He was made in the angelic colours. His skin, though he had lived so much in the Southern countries, was very white, his eyes were light, his hair and beard were a pale luminous red. His body was very thin, and because of the flimsiness of his build it seemed as if a groove ran down the centre of his chest and his spine, so that his shoulder blades stood out in a pair of almost winglike projections. He moved quickly and joyously. One could imagine him as a forerunner, speeding faster than spring can go from bud to bud on the bushes, to tell the world of the season that was coming to save it from winter. Beside him Norman Douglas lumbered along stockily. Because he knew what emperor had built this road and set that city on a hill, and how the Etruscans had been like minded in their buildings before him, he made one feel that there have been so many springs that in effect there is no spring, but that that is of no great moment. Bending over a filemot-coloured flower that he had not seen since he found it on Mount Olympus, his face grew nearly as tender as a mother bending over her child. When a child tumbled at his feet from the terrace of an olive orchard, his face became neither more nor less tender than before. They moved in unison of pace along the road, these two, and chatted. They were on good terms then, Ormuzd and Ahriman.

We stopped for lunch at a place that was called the Bridge of Something: an inn that looked across a green meadow to a whitish river. We ate at a table on which a trellis of wistaria painted a shadow far more substantial than the blue mist that was its substance. The two men talked for long of a poor waif, a bastard sprig of royalty, that had recently killed himself after a life divided between conflicting passions for monastic life, unlawful pleasures, and financial fraud. He had sought refuge at the monastery of Monte Cassino, that nursery of European culture, where St Thomas Aquinas himself was educated; but soon was obliged to flee down one side of the sugar loaf mountain while the carabinieri climbed up the other with a warrant for his arrest on charges connected with the Italian law of credit. Then he had gone to Malta, and played more fantasia on the

theme of debt, till his invention was exhausted. This was the man*
whose recollections of service in the French Foreign Legion were published with a preface by Lawrence which provoked Norman Douglas
to a savage retort that stands high among the dog fights of literary
men. But then they were joined in amity while they talked of him
with that grave and brotherly pitifulness that men who have found
it difficult to accommodate themselves to their fellow men feel for
those who have found it impossible. They broke off, I remember, to
look at some lads who made their way across the meadow and began
to strip by the river bank. "The water will be icy," said Douglas, "it
won't be warm till the snow goes off the mountains." He began to
chuckle at the thought of the shock that was coming to the boys who
had been tempted by the first hot day. Lawrence let his breath hiss
out through his teeth at the thought of their agony; but he seemed to
find pleasure in it, as he would in any intense feeling.

Presently we rose and went on our way. Norman Douglas took
the landlord's hand and wrung it heartily, saying a fervid good-bye.
Lawrence exclaimed, "Douglas, how can you shake hands with these
people!" He meant by this that the antipathy between the Northern
and the Southern peoples was so great that there could be no sincere
attempt at friendship with them. Douglas answered with a grin, "Oh,
it takes something off the bill next time." He did not mean that. It
was simply the first way that came to hand of saying that he would
not get excited about these fine points, that in his universe every
phenomenon was of equal value. We walked away. After a minute or
two I looked back through the olive trees and saw the landlord standing where we had left him, sending after us a hard black Italian stare.
"Do you know, Douglas," said Lawrence suddenly, though he had
not looked back, "I can't help thinking that the man understood
English." "Oh, no," I said falsely, "I'm sure he didn't." But Douglas,
laughing more deeply than ever, said, "I got that too." We all
walked along without speaking, ill at ease, though Douglas kept his
eyes crinkled as if he were still laughing. Ormuzd and Ahriman alike
did not want unnecessary explosions of the forces they well knew to
be latent in their universe.

Later Lawrence began to talk of the Sicilian peasants and how full
of hatred and malice he had found them. There was a great tale about
some old crones who had come up at twilight to his house in Taor-
mina with some jars of honey they had wanted him to buy, and had

* [Maurice Magnus.]

391

crouched down on his terrace while he tested their goods with malignity in their eyes, in their squatting bodies. They had meant to cheat him, for it was last year's honey and ill preserved. He detected the fraud in an instant, with his sturdy wisdom about household matters, and bade them be gone. Silently they rose and filed out through his olive trees with their jars on their shoulders, with increased malignity in their eyes and in their prowling bodies, because they had not been able to cheat him. "Such hatred!" he cried in effect. "Such black loathing." Again I felt embarrassed, as I did when we discovered him pounding out articles on the momentary state of Florence with nothing more to go on than a glimpse at it. Surely he was now being almost too flatly silly, even a little mad? Of course peasants try to cheat one over honey or anything else, in Italy or anywhere else, and very natural it is, considering how meagrely the earth gives up its fruits. But as for hatred and black loathing, surely this is persecution mania? I was a little unhappy about it, which was a pity, for that made an unsatisfactory ending to what was to be my last meeting with Lawrence, though mercifully not my last contact with him. For a few months ago I received a letter from him thanking me for some little tribute I had paid him during the trouble about his pictures in London. This letter showed the utmost humility in him to take notice of such a small courtesy; and it showed more than that. With marvellous sensitiveness he had deduced from a phrase or two in my article that I was troubled by a certain problem, and he said words that in their affectionate encouragement and exquisite appositeness could not have been bettered if we had spent the ten years that had intervened since our meeting in the closest friendship.

The point about Lawrence's work that I have been unable to explain save by resorting to my personal acquaintance with him is this: that it was founded on the same basis as those of his mental movements which then seemed to me ridiculous, and which, now that I have had more experience, I see as proceeding in a straight line to the distant goal of wisdom. He was tapping out an article on the state of Florence at that moment without knowing enough about it to make his views of real value. Is that the way I looked at it? Then I was naïve. I know now that he was writing about the state of his own soul at that moment, which, since our self-consciousness is incomplete, and since in consequence our vocabulary also is incomplete, he could only render in symbolic terms; and the city of Florence was as good a symbol as any other. If he was foolish in taking the material universe and making allegations about it that were true only of the universe within his own soul, then Rimbaud was a great fool also. Or to go further back, so too was Dante, who made a new Heaven and Hell and Purgatory as a symbol for the geography within his own breast, and so too was St Augustine, when in *The City of God* he writes an attack on the pagan world, which is unjust so long as it is regarded as an account of events on the material plane, but which is beyond price as an account of the conflict in his soul between that which tended to death and that which tended to life. Lawrence was in fact no different from any other great artist who has felt the urgency to describe the unseen so keenly that he has rifled the seen of its vocabulary and diverted it to that purpose; and it took courage to do that in a land swamped with naturalism as England was when Lawrence began to write.

When he cried out at Douglas for shaking hands with the inn-keeper because the North and the South were enemies, and when he saw the old crones who had come to cheat him out of an odd lira or two over the honey as mænads too venomous even to be flamboyant, I thought he was seeing lurid colours that were in his eye and not in the universe he looked on. Now I think he was doing justice to the seriousness of life, and had been rewarded with a deeper insight into its nature than most of us have. If one has the dislike of any proof that the universe has structure which is the mark of an incoherent mind, then one will find something very distasteful in his assumption that John Smith and Giovanni Grimaldi are not merely individuals, but are parts of two systems of life so fundamentally opposed that their minutest constituents must also be in opposition. If one has no purpose and therefore does not need to know the relationship between the forces of the mind and events in the external world, then it is as well to say that old women out for liras were simply old women out for liras, and leave it at that. But if one hopes that some day the mind shall govern life, then it is of value that one shall be shown a small instance of the sadism that makes the human being rejoice in killing, hurting, robbing its neighbour, and one shall be told that this is as horrible as war, since war also is the fruit of this sadism; and that therefore the mind must walk proudly and always armed, that it shall not be robbed of its power. There is nothing disconcerting about these or any other of Lawrence's attitudes, if one is a true inheritor of tradition and realizes that the greatest sons of man have always recognized that the mind which is his house is ablaze and that if the fire is not put out he will perish. Then one will rejoice that our age produced one artist who had the earnestness of the patristic writers, who like them could know no peace till he had discovered what made men lust after death. He laboured under a disadvantage compared with the fathers, in his lack of a vocabulary of symbolic terms such as was given them by theology; in the allegory of the death of the soul which ends with the death of Gerald among the mountains in *Women in Love,* he cannot tell his story save by the clumsy creation of images that do not give up their meaning till the book has been read many times. But even these struggles are of value, since they recall to one the symbolic nature of all thought. Knowledge is but a translation of reality into terms comprehensible by the human mind, a grappling with a mystery. None undertake it with the courage of Lawrence unless they very greatly care.

His claim to our reverence and gratitude was not in the least part diminished by *Lady Chatterley's Lover.* It is an appalling fact that man should speak of the functions on which depend the continued existence of his species and the tender life of the heart in words that cause shame and ugly laughter when they are spoken. When Lawrence's pity was aroused by this wound in the side of life he did what saints do: he asked for a miracle. He laid sex and those base words for it on the salver of his art and held them up before the consciousness of the world, which was his way of approaching creation, and prayed that both might be transmuted to the highest that man could use. There are many people like myself who feel that his prayer was in vain: that those words were nothing but the expressions of hatred felt by the will to die for the will to live, and they could never be converted to anything else. But people like myself are infinitely lesser than Lawrence. The presumption is that if he did not reach the truth he at least came nearer it than we did. In any case, it was the special merit of this and all his other works, as I can see by looking back at our meeting and measuring the change in my attitude towards his characteristic traits, that in no way did he underrate the gravity of the human situation.

As I write there comes to me this week's issue of *Time and Tide,* and I find in it a letter about Lawrence, from Catherine Carswell, an infrequent but gifted writer—her note on Duse in the *Adelphi* was one of the finest pieces of dramatic criticism I have ever read. Her letter is worth reprinting.

SIR:

The Picture of D. H. Lawrence suggested by the obituary notices of "competent critics" is of a man morose, frustrated, tortured, even a sinister failure. Perhaps this is because any other view would make his critics look rather silly. Anyhow, to those who knew him, and I knew him since 1914 as friend, hostess and guest in varying circumstances, often of the most trying kind, at home and abroad, that picture would be comic if it were not in the circumstances disgraceful.

Lawrence was as little morose as an open clematis flower, as little tortured or sinister or hysterical as a humming bird. Gay, skilful, clever at everything, furious when he felt like it but never grieved or upset, intensely amusing, without sentimenality or affectation, almost always right in his touch for the content of things or persons, he was at once the most harmonious and the most vital person I ever saw.

As to frustration, consider his achievements. In the face of formidable initial disadvantages and lifelong delicacy, poverty that lasted for three-quarters of his life and hostility that survives his death, he did nothing that he did not really want to do, and all that he most wanted to do he did. He went all over the world, he owned a ranch, he lived in the most beautiful corners of Europe, and met whom he wanted to meet and told them that they were wrong and that he was right. He painted and made things and sang and rode. He wrote something like three dozen books, of which even the worst pages dance with life that could be mistaken for no other man's, while the best are admitted, even by those who hate him, to be unsurpassed. Without vices, with most human virtues, the husband of one wife, scrupulously honest, this estimable citizen yet managed to keep free from the shackles of civilization and the cant of literary cliques. He would have laughed lightly and cursed venomously in passing at the solemn owls—each one secretly chained by the leg—who now conduct his inquest. To do his work and lead his life in spite of them took some doing, but he did it, and long after they are forgotten, sensitive and innocent people—if any are left—will turn Lawrence's pages and know from them what sort of a rare man Lawrence was.

CATHERINE CARSWELL

We must ourselves be grievously defeated if we do not regard the life of D. H. Lawrence as a spiritual victory.

FROM The Court and the Castle

Part III "The Castle of God"

1. NONCONFORMIST ASSENTERS AND INDEPENDENT INTROVERTS

Among the novelists writing in English at this period there were some resistant personalities unaffected by the Rousseauist influences of their time; but the greatest among them were not English. There was Henry James, who had come to England from his native America perhaps because his parents were affected by a Pelagian belief that a well-ordered court could save its courtiers by ceremonial which tamed the blood and developed the taste, and there were as yet few traces of a like discipline in his native land. In 1880 he wrote, in his study of Hawthorne (ch. II, p. 43):

... one might enumerate the items of high civilization, as it exists in other countries, which are absent from the texture of American life, until it should become a wonder to know what was left. No State, in the European sense of the word, and indeed barely a specific national name. No sovereign, no court, no personal loyalty, no aristocracy, no church, no clergy, no army, no diplomatic service, no country gentlemen, no palaces, no castles, nor manors, nor old country-houses, nor parsonages, nor thatched cottages, nor ivied ruins; no cathedrals, nor abbeys, nor little Norman churches; no great Universities nor public schools—no Oxford, nor Eton, nor Harrow; no literature, no novels, no museums, no pictures, no political society, no sporting class—no Epsom nor Ascot! Some such list as that might be drawn up of the absent things in American life—especially in the American life of forty years ago, the effect of which, upon an English or a French imagination, would probably, as a general thing, be appalling. The natural remark, in the almost lurid light of such an indictment, would be that if these things are left out, everything is left out. The American knows that a good deal remains; what it is that remains—that is his secret, his joke, as one may say. It would be cruel, in this terrible denudation, to deny him the consolation of his natural gift, that "American humor" of which of late years we have heard so much.

Henry James' work was largely an ironic criticism of this attitude; and he began his researches when he went to Europe as a boy of twelve in 1855, a year in which Thackeray was lecturing on "The Four Georges," Dickens was writing *Little Dorritt*, and Trollope published *The Warden*. He himself published his first book in 1875, the year in which Meredith's *Beauchamp's Career* was running as a serial in *The Fortnightly Review*. and Hardy was writing *The Hand of Ethelberta*; he published his last book in 1914, the year in which the First World War broke out, a year after Shaw's *Pygmalion* had been produced, and three years after Wells had published *The New Machiavelli*. He liked few of the changes that took place in this long span of years, and he would have liked to travel backward through time to avoid them, passing the eightenth century, passing the seventeenth century, avoiding the huge serene effort of Fielding, to the Shakespearean days when the formality of a palace had a visible connection with salvation and damnation. But he could not write his books about the contemporary English court, for it hardly existed. The historical process, of which the beginnings were described by Shakespeare, had detached the crown from politics, and though that hardly mattered to him, for he was truly apolitical, it mattered to him that the widowhood of Queen Victoria had left the court a vacuum in the midst of English social life. But he took the English aristocratic life as the next best thing, and his novels assume that it should have been, and sometimes was, a school of virtue. His work consists largely of descriptions of the conflict which was bound to break out when those who were teachers and pupils in this school came in contact with those who lacked this education. That conflict took many forms: sometimes the untutored showed a simple virtue which put to shame those who had been schooled too well and had gone stale like overtrained athletes; sometimes the untutored showed a presumptuous incapacity to understand what it was they had to learn; sometimes the teachers had become so immersed in cultivating the refinements of their study that they forgot its elements and let some situation be stained by the presence of evil, which James, with a simplicity alien from his age, firmly believed to be a reality; and always the custodians of this redeeming cult were threatened by the eternal enemy, the usurper, in the shape of people who had not the right credentials, who had not a clear title, who were parvenus.

The extent to which Henry James identifies evil with vulgarity was extreme. Nearly all his works, with the exception of his lamentable plays, are impressive, and none more immediately so than *The Turn of the Screw*. That masterpiece conveys a sense of evil with which we are all familiar from childhood, since it lurks in fairy tales, in the person of the bad fairy or the dwarf or the talking crow, as dreadfully as it does in the doorways of cities depraved since the beginning of time: a sense of evil which is terrifying because it defies the dimensions, and is at once deeply entrenched in the flesh yet is half way to another and immaterial world. The incarnation of that evil, Peter Quint, who has come back from hell with the true Lucifer light about him, was a gentleman's gentleman, as valets called themselves in Victorian days, who would have been scorned by other gentlemen's gentlemen, for he stole his master's shirts. The converse of this argument is expressed in that great humanist version of the cry of hunger and thirst for righteousness, *The Wings of the Dove*. That story of a dying girl who finds herself the victim of a cruel and mercenary fraud and contrives to deal with this hideous situation so that it flowers in beauty is so told that her moral triumph seems to be vitally connected with the taste that takes her to die in a Venetian palace. This made Henry James' meliorist contemporaries regard him as lacking in seriousness, but they did him an injustice.

Henry James could not have been more earnest regarding the salvation of the soul, but he was historically unfortunate, as appears if his prefaces to the collected editions of his novels (published together under the title *The Art of the Novel*) are compared with Fielding's essays on the same subject in *Tom Jones*. Henry James shows agreement with Fielding in all essentials. He certainly held that genius lay in "that power, or rather those powers, of the mind which are capable of penetrating into all things within our reach and knowledge, and of distinguishing their essential difference," and that the novelist must have "the sort of knowledge beyond the power of learning to bestow and this is to be had by conversation"; and that imagination must be controlled by observation. But Henry James lays a peculiar stress, which Fielding would hardly have understood, on the need for a "lens," for the presence of a clear, balanced intelligence among the characters of a novel which, by its obvious authority, should impose on the reader a proper estimate of what is happening. He insisted on numerous occasions that the need for that unifying intelligence was really desperate; and so it was, for he had to guide complicated themes through a world which was not only complicated but confused, and thus inimical to the definiteness which he always sought. It is obvious that Henry James started at a disadvantage compared to Shakespeare, when we consider that no action in the world he described could give such radical information about the character who performed it as the withholding of the last sacrament from men about to die. But that disadvantage Henry James could overcome by his subtlety. A disadvantage far less easy to overcome was his lack of a framework for belief in the good, which Fielding found in his world of honest parsons and classical scholars. Henry James' gospel had to be passed by word of mouth from drawing room to drawing room in the London squares; and there was a curious insubstantiality about the guarantees which could be given in those mansions. He seems to have pinned his faith to the wrong society and got that wrong too. It seems conjectural, in the style of the models of brontosauri and pterodactyls which are constructed in plaster of Paris according to theories derived from the study of fossils. We cannot doubt his thesis that the court saves the courtiers, for the courtiers he shows us are living and are saved, but it is not quite possible to believe in the court.

There was Rudyard Kipling, who was almost as foreign as Henry James, though he was of English blood, for the reason that he was Indian born. Curiously enough, there was a strong element of Rousseauism in him, for he embraced those parts of the faith which are rejected by his meliorist contemporaries. He was with the philosopher, where Shaw and Wells and Galsworthy left him, in his enthusiasm for the training Sparta gave its youth, armouring them with courage and loyalty and asceticism, and teaching them contempt for self-interest, and in his belief that ancient laws must be the best, since it must be their excellence which has made them survive so long. There is of course a great deal to be said for both Spartan discipline and ancient laws, but unfortunately Kipling gave the impression that he was ready to go still further with Rousseau on this line of thought, and to agree with him that the development of the arts and sciences had destroyed the primitive virtues, and therefore ought to be destroyed in the form that we know them; and the ancient laws which he most admired seemed to be those which placed India under the tutelage of England, though these date back no further than the seventeenth century, and already in the eighteenth century Warren Hastings and many another had made it clear that they must be regarded as temporary expedients. But it has to be noted that Kipling expressed his admiration for Spartan discipline and the

English occupation of India with a fire which would probably have burned less fiercely had it not happened that his contemporaries were so loudly denying the need for any discipline, whether Spartan or of any other kind, and so loudly affirming that the English were in India only for purposes of spoliation. Kipling was placed in time even less fortunately than Henry James, for in some respects he lagged behind his age and in others he was far in advance of it. He was the first important writer to feel the romantic charm of machinery, and this was taken as a mark of the permanent adolescence of his extrovert nature, though the same emotion was later to be held natural and laudable when the Americans rejoiced in their maturing industry and the Russians in their nascent industry.

But it is also true that one of the reasons why Kipling looked odd in his time was his acceptance of the institutions of Church and State. In fact most of the English people were of his way of thinking in this matter, but the rest of contemporary literature was proclaiming that these institutions were now held in contempt by all save a few financially interested reactionaries. He was, from the point of view of other writers, a dissenter from the current faith in his wholehearted acceptance of the English tradition, but he was an assenter from the point of view of the general public. He could have fairly claimed that everybody was out of step but our Jamie. Yet in his application of the English tradition he came to offend even the general public in his later years, by his inability to understand that for many of them the Labour and the Liberal parties were the new form taken by that tradition. It is a matter for wonder that a man who had such uneasy relations with his time won such colossal success, and even now he is not comfortable in his immortality. The books of his which establish his claim most firmly are those concerning children, who live in partial agreement and partial disagreement with the several worlds which exist in the period traversed between infancy and childhood. It would be strange to think of a future when children would not read *The Jungle Books* and *The Just-So Stories*, and when adults would not read *Kim*, in which a child acts as the central unifying intelligence in a confused scene, the need for which Henry James defined.

Neither of these writers, though their greatness abides no one's question, has any seminal quality. An author of another age who worked on the same material in the same style as either of them would be a copyist, for the two men were made by historical imbroglios, one in each hemisphere, hardly likely to recur for centuries. But their great contemporary, Joseph Conrad, writes of a situation which perpetually recurs. He was, though it was not then foreseen, an earnest of the things to come. He had the kind of wisdom that was to disconcert many of us when it reappeared among displaced persons; and he had come by it honestly. His father and mother were Poles of the landowning class, who, by their protest against the Russian occupation of their country, brought on themselves envenomed persecution which sent them to their graves before their time. Their son went to France and became a seaman, and by chance joined the crew of an English freighter, which was the first step towards his curious integration with England and English literature. He was a religious man and his life fostered his religion, and he strongly believed that the courtiers would be saved by the action of grace bestowed by God. The court was an instrument of grace, as it reconstituted itself wherever there was a group of men threatened by danger, which was the constant condition of sailors at sea. There time ran back to simplicity. It became necessary, in order to confront the storm, or fire, or the human enemy, that there should be one person chosen to command the others. Kingship was once more brought to birth. There was, in effect, an oath taken by which this selected person, the captain, swore to protect them, and another oath taken by the other persons involved, the crew, to give obedience in return for this protection. The safety of the ship and each human being on the ship depended on the keeping of these oaths; and it became more and more plain to Conrad that this was the type of all human situations, that in relations between human beings, and between states and citizens, nothing could go well if all persons did not take fidelity as their guiding principle.

This has some resemblance to what Kipling thought, but there is a fundamental difference. Kipling also was a religious man and he believed that a man could be saved by grace, which would be granted if he were loyal to some organization of high authority, such as the British Army or the Indian Civil Service. But he seems to think that grace is granted to the man because of that obedience. It is as if grace had been bestowed on the organization (secular though it be), as is conceived to be the case of the Churches. Conrad evidently thought that grace is granted to the man who can lend it to the organization by an effort of his will, which has been made innocent by the action of grace, and then the organization can reflect an atmosphere which is favourable to grace, though not identical with it. While Henry James believed that man kept the moral atmosphere in being by the constant exercise of refined discrimination, Kipling believed that man could keep it in being by the constant practice of obedience to the highest moral authorities; but Conrad regarded the moral universe as being constantly in danger of annulment by the weakness of man, and as constantly confirmed in being by cooperation between man and God. This belief gives *Lord Jim* its meaning and it pervades all his books.

He was in a sense nearer Shakespeare than any other modern novelist, because he was thinking of power in the same terms, and this has now made him seem one of the most modern of writers; for many of us have seen danger rebuild Shakespeare's court round us during the last forty years, as Conrad saw it rebuilt round him on board ship or in far tropical places. It is to be noted that Herman Wouk's *The Caine Mutiny*, which was a best-seller after the Second World War, dealt with material which was common to Shakespeare and Conrad: with a question of keeping or breaking an oath taken to meet a danger. The treatment is more Shakespearean than Conradian, for Keefer belongs to Shakespeare's company of usurpers, who may end a wrong but cannot themselves be right; but the author's sense of an operation of the spirit which is more creative and discriminating than mere obedience, though respectful to it, is exactly what Conrad meant by fidelity. But indeed this same situation, wherein the necessity for government is suddenly made visible in a confined and threatened area, is the better part of the material of most 'war novels, of widely differing degrees of merit though its significance is often obscure in the author's own eyes and resented when it is perceived.

There were, of course, many works being written in the first fifty years of this century which did not concern themselves with the problem of power, the parallel between the public and the private life, the riddle as to whether either or both of these two lives can run to a good end: which take no part in the argument which, for the present purpose, has been taken as beginning with, or rather, so far as the English are concerned, as having its grandest early statement in, *Hamlet*. If nineteenth-century writers were below a certain merit, they simply followed the practice of spawning characters, which, once the exploration of character was limited to superficialities, became easy and was often entertaining, though quite often not entertaining at all. If later writers were above a certain level, they turned aside and engaged in a respectable research of their own. Instead of trying to find out where humanity was going, they tried to find out what humanity was. They refused to make any attempt to find a prose equivalent for the soliloquy, which should expose the essentials of a man or woman in pregnant but selective phrases. They wanted the whole of their men and women down on the page, and selection means exclusion. So they evolved the "stream of consciousness" method, they set about spinning "the interior monologue," which should give an account of the day-to-day, hour-to-hour, moment-to-moment impressions life made on their subjects. This was something which Fielding had not had in his mind. "One day this young couple accidentally met in the garden, at the end of the two walks which were both bounded by that canal in which Jones had formerly risked drowning to retrieve the little bird that Sophia had there lost." (*Tom Jones*, Bk. V, ch. 6.) And that was what he remembered: falling into the canal out of the tree where he had recaptured the little bird. The gardener may have had a little white dog, but Tom Jones saw no reason to recall it.

Trollope worked a little closer to his characters' impressions, but not much so; here is poor Plantagenet Palliser, standing on the portico of his hated grand house, which Lady Glencora has been pompifying to add to his glory as a prime minister:

And now as he stood there he could already see that men were at work about the place, that ground had been moved here, and grass laid down there, and a new gravel road constructed in another place. Was it not possible that his friends should be entertained without all these changes in the gardens? Then he perceived the tents, and descending from the terrace and turning to the left towards the end of the house he came on a new conservatory. The exotics with which it was to be filled were at this moment being brought in on great barrows. (*The Prime Minister*, ch. 19.)

There is still not a word about the gardener's little white dog. It is sometimes supposed that Henry James came so near to rendering the stream of consciousness that he could claim to have been the first explorer of its course, but though he describes a stream of something which is passing through his characters' minds, it is very far from being the whole flow of their consciousness:

It was quite for the Prince after this as if the view had further cleared;

so that the half-hour during which he strolled on the terrace and smoked
—the day being lovely—overflowed with the plenitude of its particular
quality. Its general brightness was composed doubtless of many elements, but what shone out of it as if the whole place and time had
been a great picture, from the hand of genius, presented to him as a
prime ornament for his collection and all varnished and framed to hang
up—what marked it especially for the highest appreciation was his
extraordinarily unchallenged, his absolutely appointed and enhanced
possession of it. Poor Fanny Assingham's challenge amounted to nothing :
one of the things he thought of while he leaned on the old marble
balustrade—so like others that he knew in still more nobly-terraced Italy
—was that she was squared, all-conveniently even to herself, and that,
rumbling toward London with this contentment, she had become an
image irrelevant to the scene. (*The Golden Bowl*, Bk. III, ch. 9.)

There is no chance at all for the gardener's little white dog to make
itself seen across this broad river of comment by the self on itself,
which is an artistic convention made by James to suit his hand, for
few selves are capable of giving themselves such undivided attention.
This is not because their egotism is weak, but because their faculty
of attention is insufficiently strong. In fact the mind see-saws between broodings on its special situation and surrender to whatever
sights or sounds or odours address it through the senses; and we get
a deliberate effort to give a faithful representation of that see-saw
when we come to Dorothy Richardson, who can fairly claim to be
the originator of the method:

The strange shock of the bedroom, the strange new thing springing out
from it . . . the clear soft bright tones, the bright white light streaming
through the clear muslin, the freshness of the walls . . . the flattened
dumpy shapes of dark green bedroom crockery gleaming in a corner; the
little green bowl standing in the middle of the white spread of the
dressing-table cover . . . wild violets with green leaves and tendrils put
there by someone with each leaf and blossom standing separate . . .
touching your heart; joy, looking from the speaking pale mauve little
flowers to the curved rim of the green bowl and away to the green
crockery in the corner; again and again the fresh shock of the violets . . .
the little cold change in the room after the books, strange fresh findings
and fascinating odd shapes and sizes, gave out their names . . . The
White Boat—Praxiter—King Chance—Mrs Prendergast's Palings . . .
the promise of them in their titled wooden case by the bedside table from
every part of the room their unchanged names, the chill of the strange
sentences inside—like a sort of code written for people who understood,
written at something, clever raised voices in a cold world. In Mrs

Prendergast's Palings there were cockney conversations spelt as they were spoken. None of the books were about ordinary people . . . three men, seamen, alone, getting swamped in a boat in shallow water in sight of land . . . a man and a girl he had no right to be with wandering on the sand, the cold wash and sob of the sea; her sudden cold sad tears, the warmth of her shuddering body. Praxiter beginning without telling you anything, about the thoughts of an irritating contemptuous superior man, talking at the expense of everybody. Nothing in any of them about anything one knew or felt, casting you off . . . giving a chill ache to the room. To sit . . . alone, reading in the white light, amongst the fresh colours—but not these books . . . to go downstairs was a sacrifice: coming back there should be the lighting of the copper candlestick, twisting beautifully up from its stout stem. What made it different to ordinary candlesticks? What? It was like . . . a gesture. (*The Tunnel*, ch. 6, sec. 4.)

It is obvious that if the gardener's little white dog is not on the page it is only because it was not in Miriam's bedroom. But a lot of other things were. This passage describes the state of being of an educated and gifted woman, still young, who is friendless and poor and follows the occupation, far below her talents, of a dentist's receptionist; she has written to an old school friend reviving their acquaintance, and her friend has answered at once, telling her that she has married a well-known writer, and giving her a warm invitation to stay with them. When she arrives she is delighted at the welcome they give her and by the comfort and charm of their house, but at the same time she feels hostility to the world of intellectuals to which they belong, suspecting it of coldness and arrogance, and also fearing that she will not measure up to its standards, while at the same time she is honest enough to admire some of their achievements. The extreme skill of the presentation is to be admired: the tide flows, and changes channel as it flows, and changes back again, "I see this, I like it; I see that, I do not like it; I see this, I like it." The presentation breaks down at one point, as writing is bound to break down if it tries too hard to do the work of painting: the reader is not clear about the promise given by Praxiter's books in their tilted wooden case. This is a pitfall which has engulfed many of Dorothy Richardson's imitators; but she herself failed in her later book for quite another reason. Miriam's interior monologue went deeper and deeper, and in the end Dorothy Richardson would not interrupt it to record such external facts as the going out and coming in of other characters, with the result that it is never certain who is speaking to whom. But even then the per-

sonality of Miriam is not breached; and the series is still worth reading for the sake of the solidity of Miriam and such minor characters
as Alma and Eleanor Dear, as well as for its stud-farm interest as the
progenitor of hundreds of later novels. It has a further interest in the
realistic portraits it paints of English intellectuals at the beginning of
the century in the circle that gathers round Alma and Hypo, and in
the confirmatory material it furnishes regarding the educated and
lonely and dispossessed city-dwellers which Gissing had taken as his
subject.

Virginia Woolf can have been influenced but slightly by Dorothy
Richardson, for they began writing about the same time; and indeed
Virginia Woolf is recognizable as a child of Meredith, who cheerfully
accepted her spiritual father's legacy of tropes, but rebelled against
his love of well-made plots and chose to have no theme but character.
Originally, and most notably in *Jacob's Room*, she concentrated on a
patchwork of sensory impressions which gave clues to the preoccupations of her characters. But by the time she wrote *To the Lighthouse*
she had given a depth to the streams of consciousness she traced, by
giving not only the sensory impression of her characters, but the
associations evoked by those impressions (Pt. I, sec. 17.):

"Andrew," she said, "hold your plate lower, or I shall spill it." (The
Boeuf en Daube was a perfect triumph.) Here, she felt, putting the
spoon down, was the still space that lies about the heart of things, where
one could move or rest; could wait now (they were all helped,) listening:
could then, like a hawk which lapses suddenly from its high station,
flaunt and sink on laughter easily, resting her whole weight upon
what at the other end of the table her husband was saying about the
square root of one thousand two hundred and fifty-three. That was the
number, it seemed, on his watch.

What did it all mean? To this date she had no notion. A square
root? What was that? Her sons knew. She leant on them; on cubes and
square roots; that was what they were talking about now; on Voltaire
and Madame de Staël; on the character of Napoleon; on the French
system of land tenure; on Lord Rosebery; on Creevey's Memoirs; she let
it uphold and sustain her, this admirable fabric of the masculine intelligence, which ran up and down, crossed this way and that, like iron
girders spanning the swaying fabric, upholding the world, so that she
could trust herself to it utterly, even shut her eyes, or flicker them for
a moment, as a child staring up from its pillow winks at the myriad
layers of the leaves of a tree. Then she woke up. It was still being
fabricated. William Bankes was praising the Waverley Novels.

It is worth while turning back to Henry James and seeing how widely this method differs from his. If Adam and Maggie Verver had ever heard of Voltaire and Madame de Staël, we were not told of it. We are simply given what they felt under the harrow of an intense personal experience during a limited period of time. Mrs Woolf gave us how her character lived, not necessarily under any acute strain, during a limited period of time, which seems unlimited, because the impressions she ascribes to her characters arouse associations which lead inward to their hidden natures and backward through time to their formative years. Certainly Mrs Woolf conveys much more of the selves of her characters than Henry James does, and though this does not mean that she tells more about the essential principle of each character than he does, it does mean that she by implication tells us more about the nature of the self. But her effort is sometimes impaired by a certain weakness which arises out of a trait which she freely confessed in conversation. Only the familiar gave up its secrets to her. She was, as *The Common Reader* shows, the most sensitive of critics; but, as she often said, she really did not know what to think of a contemporary work unless it bore an obvious relationship to some predecessor which she already understood. She often annoyed her friends, when they told her enthusiastically that some new book was really good, by telling them that she could not trouble to read it until they had told her what to look for in it. Once she was told what she ought to see in it, she could tell them with exquisite discrimination whether it was there or not, but she had to be given the clue. This is not an uncommon trait, though it is far from common to confess it, and it has a bearing on her novels. The best are those which deal with material familiar to her because she had lived with it. *To the Lighthouse, Mrs Dalloway*, and *Between the Acts* were descriptions of people and events not only known but well known to her; and *Orlando*, the only successfully invented myth in English literature of our time, incarnates the development of the poetic genius in England, a subject with which she was deeply familiar. Where she dealt with material more remote, she became tame. *Jacob's Room* is gracefully written, but though Virginia Woolf knows her subject, the life of a young man about to lose it in the First World War, to be of great tragic importance, she is at such a distance from it that she makes no discoveries. The content of the book could be predicted by anybody who was informed of the subject and was acquainted with Virginia Woolf's work.

The Waves is open to the same objection. It is an ambitious book, her most ambitious effort, composed of a series of interior monologues delivered by a set of characters on their way from birth to death, and the intention is to show us the very flux of life. But the interior monologues turn out to be essays, not original in any way and not unlike those written by the Victorian writer Alice Meynell, and they are uncomfortable to read because they seem to be damming back some force which, had nature been allowed to take its course, would have flowed through them. This was perhaps merely a plot. It is right and proper for a novelist to take character as his starting point, and not a planned sequence of events; but characters, once created, enter into conflicts and alliances, and events follow, and the governing necessity forms them into a pattern. The most delicate novelist, loving plot no better than any lyric poet, could not create Mr Plantagenet Palliser and Lady Glencora, the old Duke and Madame Goesler, Mr Lopez and Mr Sexty Parker, without finding a complicated plot on his hands, for the reason that these were people who dealt with complicated matters in the visible world. This failure of Virginia Woolf would hardly be worth noting, so much does her success outweigh it, were it not that the two writers who went further than she did in their exploration of the self made use of the plot.

D. H. Lawrence was to reject all modern technique, and after some straightforward writing, held to realism by its autobiographical character, he invented a new kind of novel which appeared to be realistic but was actually an exercise on symbolism. The characters in *The Rainbow* and *Women in Love* act and speak as real people would be unlikely to do, even if they possessed the attributes ascribed to the characters by their author and were enlaced in the same circumstances. Fielding's injunction that the novelist should always keep within the bounds of probability is disregarded, but for a purpose: these incredible actions and speeches declare the progress of the characters' inner lives with the clarity of poetry. In all his later exploitation of this new vehicle Lawrence never hesitated to display intricate plots. And he was not alone. James Joyce was to pursue quite a different path from Lawrence, and was to outdo every previous practitioner of the stream of consciousness technique by a procedure which demanded titanic genius. When he wrote *Ulysses*, he was able to choose the two protagonists who would best serve him as material for vivisection; his intelligence was mighty enough to grasp the totality of the Catholic Ireland which was their environment, it was refined enough to trace the network of association which ran from their sensory impressions inward to their obscurest infantile fantasy or outward to the furthest limit of their living or reading. This network thickens to a changing, heaving pulp of self, now solid, now translucent, now rigid, now fluid. The two selves, Bloom and Dedalus, are sometimes the same, sometimes a world apart; sometimes they are of today, sometimes they run back to the beginning of consciousness, to the threshhold of the species. But from this pulp there emerges constantly the primeval intermingling of joy and fear, the myth, the legend: the plot.

But these two great writers, like their predecessors, were not concerned directly with the problem of power; they drew no analogy between the public and the private life. They were both (though Lawrence did not know it) prepolitical. They were both of them too busily engaged in finding out what the self had been before modern culture repressed and prettified it to follow any line of thought not concerned with those relationships which could be traced back to the primitive. If Lawrence's empty irritation with the modern world be contrasted with Shakespeare's firm grasp of history or Fielding's response to it, it is to be seen that he really cannot be considered as joining in this argument. His lack of feeling for developed society can be detected in his book on American literature, where nothing seems to him really important which is not on the pioneer level; when he describes the American individual as subjected to the pressure of environment, he thinks of the wildness of the virgin forest, the attack by enemies of another race, the inconveniences of having neighbours after living alone in the free lands. It would be absurd to try to gather from Lawrence's writings what it is like to live in a capitalist democracy, in either of the hemispheres; and it is as absurd to accuse him, as some have done, of sympathy with fascism on the basis of *The Plumed Serpent*. That book represents not support of Hitler but hostility to Rousseau. Lawrence too thought that man was born free and was everywhere in chains, but he considered this to be the source of all man's sorrows; and he was proposing a new sort of social contract in which the individual would not be forced to alienate his right to passionate being, A useful analogy can be traced, particularly by those who care to note how often artists get into trouble by projecting their inner conflicts into the visible world, between the accusations made against Lawrence and those made against the German poet Stefan George, who was even more patently innocent than

Lawrence, since he lived to see Hitler and reject him. There is as little political matter in the works of James Joyce, though he knew the world about him better than Lawrence had done, being a man of greater intellectual stature. Yet he teaches the apt political lesson that there is a great part of humanity which can never be tamed by the statesman. But there we are back with *Hamlet* again, for it is part of the attraction of Hamlet that he cannot be tamed by the court; he proudly claims that there is a part of him which is outside its power. ◇ ◇ ◇

4. THE TWENTIETH-CENTURY BUREAUCRAT

They were given the choice of becoming kings or the king's messengers. As is the way with children, they all wanted to be messengers. That is why there are only messengers racing through the world, and since there are no kings, calling out to each other the messages that have now become meaningless. They would willingly put an end to this miserable existence, but they cannot because they are bound by an oath of loyalty.

This saying is apposite to the work of Proust,* but it was written by another writer, who also lived in a world where power was diffused, where there was no longer a king, but who believed in God and therefore came to another conclusion about the condition of man : Franz Kafka.

—R.W.

We are constrained to study Kafka for the same reason which constrains us to study Proust in connection with a theme that first attracts the attention of most of us when we read *Hamlet*. Proust and Kafka are not English writers but most English readers read Proust and Kafka, and literature is a reciprocal process. But it is an uncomfortable inclusion, for it is almost impossible to study Kafka as a great writer should be studied. His production is too incoherent. He was for most of his life ill and often in pain; he died at the age of forty-one in 1924, which meant that he had lived through a hideous historical crisis; he was terrified by intimation that another and more hideous crisis was to come; he was exposed to a disintegrat-

*[The subject of the preceding chapter. "The Dissolution of the Court." This quotation and the author's comment that concludes it serve as an epigraph for the final chapter.]

ing intellectual climate. Hence his writings are in themselves disorderly, most of them mere sketches and beginnings, and he handled them with the carelessness of a sick man; and even the major works are so feverishly taken up and set aside that the actual sequence of chapters in one of his two masterpieces, *The Trial*, is uncertain. When he died he took no measures for the preservation of his writings, but on the contrary ordered their destruction, and it is only to the disobedience of his friend Max Brod that we owe our knowledge of them. Of the papers he left, many were seized by the Nazis, long after his death, and are lost. It is therefore necessary, in considering his work, to abandon sometimes the simple duty of the reader to attend to what he wrote, and take it that that is what he meant, and instead to guess at his meaning, often by reference to his personal life.

The ground should be cleared by recognition that a great deal of what Kafka wrote is not worth studying. There are a number of short stories and unfinished stories which have been treated by his admirers as holy writ with little or no justification. *The Judgement* is an absurd *avant garde* story of a kind that was being published all over the world in the Little Reviews at that time, about a young man with a friend in Russia and a bedridden father, who makes incoherent and disparaging remarks about the friend in Russia, with the result that the young man runs out of the house and throws himself into a river, remarking that he loved both his parents. One of his interpreters finds a special significance in the fact that when he passed the servant on the stairs in this flight, he was running downstairs, while she was running upstairs. There is another absurd *avant garde* story called *The Metamorphosis* about a man who was changed into a monstrous louse, which is greatly admired by the faithful but has no merits except its discovery of a striking symbol for an inferiority complex. Kafka was well acquainted with the theory of psychoanalysis, as was the circle of young intellectuals which surrounded him, and a number of his stories, such as *The Dog, The Giant Mole*, and *The Burrow*, are more or less mechanical attempts to make a literary formula out of the symbolic system which Freud had detected in dreams. These, and a number of fragments which amount to little more than the opening paragraphs of abandoned stories, please by their masterly handling of language, particularly by their presentation of visual images. We may here remember Proust's address to Albertine on the consistent universe which is the private property of every great

411

writer: just as Hardy always shows us the same stony and angular Wessex, so Kafka always shows us the same solid, three-dimensional, sharply defined, yet ambiguous landscape that is Czechoslovakia, and perhaps somewhere else as well. But much that Kafka wrote has little interest. Kafka's title to immortality lies in his two long works, *The Trial* and *The Castle*, his short story *In a Penal Settlement*, many short passages which (though they are sometimes embedded in short stories) present a thought or impression complete in itself, and a number of aphorisms. His novel *Amerika* and some other short stories are entertaining, but they are not of great moment.

Both *The Trial* and *The Castle* present us with a chain of mysterious events which are never explained in rational terms. *The Trial* describes the last days of a bank clerk who was suddenly visited by some warders and told that he was charged with a crime, never defined, by a court of which he has never heard, which has no recognized courtroom, and of which people seem to have only a sort of folkloric knowledge. K. more and more clearly realizes that by all standards of human justice, he is the victim of injustice, and that the court's dealings with him are clumsy, inefficient, and cruel, above all in its refusal to give him the least hint of the charge that is being made against him. Yet the whole pattern of events makes him feel more and more that he is indeed guilty, and that there is a way of looking at this injustice which would reveal it as absolute justice. In the end he is executed for his crime, without the pretence of a fair trial. *The Castle* is the story of a land surveyor, who is also called by the initial of Kafka's own surname, who arrives in a village to take up a position to which he believes he has been appointed by an authority housed in a great castle which overlooks the village. But he cannot himself get in touch with the castle, for any attempts he makes to communicate with it are rebuffed; and all that happens is that various officials send down messages suggesting that the appointment has not really been made, and that anyway there is no need for the services of any land surveyor in the neighbourhood. The wretched man drags on his days, surrounded by hostile or at least derisive villagers, his hopes occasionally stimulated by messages from the castle which suggest that perhaps he was appointed after all, perhaps his services would be valuable, and had the book ever been finished we were to see him die in this state of uncertainty, which is the more bewildered because he comes toward the end to feel that perhaps the castle has reason for its attitude.

It is important to understand that these fantastic stories are not fantasies. They have a realistic basis, and they strain belief only because Kafka was looking at an institution about which he knew more than most people and about which he had a completely objective but ardent feeling, so that he set down the best and the worst about it with an intensity usually associated with prejudice. For these books are on one level about bureaucracy, as *Hamlet* is on one level about the affairs of the royal family of Elsinore, though on a deeper level they are, like *Hamlet*, about the soul of man and his prospects of salvation and damnation. Kafka knew a very great deal about bureaucracy. He was brought up under the highly bureaucratic political system of the Habsburg Empire, and he lived his mature life under the democratized bureaucracy of Czechoslovakia. It is to be noted that the bureaucracy of Europe is an impressive institution, particularly in Eastern Europe. It is said that the civil service in that area enjoys a special prestige because the fathers of that service were the scribes who acted as intermediaries between the kings and princes of the aboriginal peoples in their dealings with the barbarian invaders. The civil service had also, in more recent ages, a special value to the population, for when a peasant or artisan family produced an intellectual, he could go into the priesthood, or take up a profession, or, if he wanted to avoid the limitations of the ecclesiastical life and the insecurity of professional life, become a civil servant. This became an even more useful social resource when Maria Theresa opened the civil service to her Jewish subjects. The consumer also was in favour of the institution, for it operated efficiently enough in spite of the many jests at its *Schlamperei*, and it covered a large territory with a network of social services which did in fact protect the interests of most of the population, and met nearly all eventualities. The inhabitant of the Habsburg Empire had great reason to feel gratitude to its bureaucracy. But that it was reasonable to feel such gratitude provoked a conflict of a complicated nature in any man placed as Kafka was.

He was a Jew living in the Czech division of the Empire, then called Bohemia. The Czechs did not wish to be part of the Empire, which was dominated by Austrian Germans and Magyars, whereas they were Slavs, with all the Slav passion for independence. Therefore they resented the Habsburg law and bureaucracy, even when these worked well; but the German inhabitants rejoiced in them. The Jews ranged themselves with the Germans, because the Habsburgs had treated the Jews well on the whole, and also because they were suspicious of the Czechs, precisely because they were anti-German, and because they were Slavs and kin to the great Slav power Russia, which was then the most anti-Semitic power in existence. The Jews' relation to Russia was not only hostile but shamefaced. Russia was the promoter of pogroms and the maintainer of ghettos, and it had succeeded in oppressing its Jews till they had become nightmare figures which the Western Jews did not like to recognize as brethren, since, isolated and terrorized, shut up with their religion in a state of tension which revived all their primitive fantasies, they had become at once barbaric and pedantic. Inevitably the Jews of Prague were driven over to the side of the Germans. But the Germans were often anti-Semitic.

Kafka was acutely conscious of this dilemma. He related to Gustav Janouch, a Gentile who was for a brief period his Eckermann, how the Prague Jewish poet Oskar Baum had as a little boy attended the German primary school where there were frequent fights between the German and Czech pupils. During one of these, little Baum was hit over the head with a pencil-box by a Czech child, so hard that he sustained a detached retina and ultimately lost his sight. Kafka said: "The Jew Oskar Baum lost his sight as a German, although in fact he never was one, and no Germans would have accepted him as one. Perhaps Oskar is merely a melancholy symbol of the so-called German Jews of Prague" (*Conversations with Kafka*, p. 67). There was therefore the paradox that Jews, by the mere fact of acting as loyal Austrian citizens and upholding the Habsburg law, might cause outbreaks of lawlessness; and it must be remembered that this was not a merely local predicament, for the heart of the Empire had been profoundly influenced at that time by the demagogics of its famous burgomaster Karl Lueger, who was an apostle of anti-Semitism. The Habsburg law that the Jews respected was therefore hostile to the Jewish law, to which they paid more than respect. To many people this would have meant that they had to choose which of the two laws they would uphold and which they would repudiate or consider of secondary importance. But Kafka was not a rebel. It was part of his doctrine that the time had come to conform. However much that the Habsburg law and the Jewish law might conflict, he meant to uphold them both. The reconciliation of opposites, of making consistency out of inconsistencies, was therefore, a familiar idea to him.

When he grew up he became a member of the staff of the Workmen's Accident Assurance Association, and, irritable though he was, and artist though he was, he did not rebel even at the actual routine of bureaucracy. He lamented that it left him so little time for his own writing, but he bowed to the social importance of his work; and in time he came to write the following letter to a woman he loved, who had begged him to tell a lie and get leave of absence to spend some time with her (*Letters to Milena*, pp. 127–8):

I can't come because I can't tell a lie to the office. I can lie to the office, but only for two reasons, out of fear (it's actually an office privilege, it belongs to it, there I tell lies unprepared, by heart, inspired) or out of dire necessity (for instance, supposing it were "Elsa ill," Elsa, Elsa—not you, Milena, you don't fall ill, that would be direct necessity, of this I won't even talk) thus out of necessity I could lie at once, then no telegram would be needed. Necessity can get by in the office. In this case I leave either with or without permission. But in all cases where, among the reasons that I would have for lying, happiness the necessity for happiness, is the main reason, there I cannot lie, can do it as little as I can lift two Kg. dumb-bells. If I came to the Director with the Elsa-telegram, it would certainly drop out of my hand, and if it fell I would certainly step on it, on the lie, and having done that, I would certainly run away from the Director without having asked for anything. You must realize, Milena, that the office is not just any old stupid institution (though it is this too, and superabundantly, but that is not the point, as a matter of fact, it is more fantastic than stupid) but it has been my life up to now, I cannot tear myself away from it, though perhaps this wouldn't be so bad, but up to now it has been my life, I can treat it shabbily, work less than anyone else (which I do), botch the work (which I do), can in spite of it make myself important (which I do) can calmly accept as due to me the most considerate treatment imaginable in an office—but lie, in order to travel suddenly as a free man, being after all only an employed official, to a place where "nothing else" but my natural heart-beat drives me—well, in this way I cannot lie. But one thing I wanted to tell you even before I received your letter—that right away this week I'll try to get my passport renewed or otherwise made valid so that I can come at once if it has to be.

. . . Perhaps it's more difficult for me to tell lies in the office than for someone (and most officials are like this) who is convinced he is unfairly treated, that he works beyond his capacity—if only I had this conviction it would almost mean an express train to Vienna—someone who considers the office to be a stupidly run machine—which he would run much better—a machine in which, owing to the management's stupidity, he is employed in the wrong place—according to his abilities he should be an upper-upper-wheel and here he has to work as an upper-under-wheel and so on, but to me the office—and so was elementary school, grammar school, university, family, everything—to me the office is a living person who looks at me wherever I am with his innocent eyes, a person with whom I'm connected in some way unknown to myself, although he's stranger to me than the people whom at this moment I hear crossing the Ring in their automobiles. He is strange to me to the point of absurdity, but just this requires consideration, I make hardly any effort to conceal my being a stranger, but when does such innocence recognize this—in a word : I cannot lie.

This is, of course, a modern version of "I could not love thee, Dear, so much Loved I not honor more." But it is more than that. Here was a man who was feeling for the bureaucratic system in which he lived something like the emotion which Shakespeare felt for the monarchy; and like Shakespeare he was clear-eyed for all his loyalty, and he knew the worst about the object of his loyalty. A storm of blood and misery has raged over Eastern Europe since his time; but these two letters have survived.

To Herr Dr Franz Kafka, clerk in Prague V, Mikulasska str 36. You are required to answer the communication from this office, dated 25th September 1922, Rp 38/21, within eight days. In the event of your failure to do so the matter will be referred to District Finance Headquarters, Prague, and you will become liable to payment of a fine.

To the Revenue Department, Zizhov, Prague. Your enquiry of the . . . has already been answered by me, not verbally, because I am seriously ill, but on a postcard and immediately. The card was certainly delivered, for some time later I received from your Department an enquiry as to what I was referring to on that card, there being no record at your office of any summons dated 25th September 1922 Rp 38/21. In order to avoid complicating this matter, as completely unimportant to the Revenue Department as to myself, I did not answer this second enquiry, incidentally wishing to save postage; if the original letter of the . . . , was no longer on your files, I was quite justified in letting it go at that. But since the matter has now been revived by your communication of the 3rd November and I am now, in spite of having long ago answered in a correct manner, even being threatened with a fine, I should like to inform you again that since Paul Hermann's entry into the firm of First Prague Asbestos Works no further investments have been made by the partners and that the firm ceased to exist in March 1917. I hope that this time my answer will reach the department concerned.*

* *Wedding Preparations.* The first letter is in the Notes, p. 445; the second is in "Paralipomena," pp. 428-29.—R. W.

We see here the confusion of the overcomplex modern state of which Proust complained: but Proust saw it from the consumer's point of view. Kafka saw it as a producer. The product was more innocent than it had been in the past. The State did not cut off people's heads any more; it might send a sick man to hospital but it might suddenly and by error cut off an old man's pension and let him starve. It is therefore possible for Kafka to see the bureaucracy of which he was a part as beneficent, comic, absolutely necessary and murderously cruel. (This is, of course, what Shakespeare thought about the monarchy.) That vision of the bureaucracy undoubtedly inspires both *The Trial* and *The Castle*, which must be read as being satires on the subject. But there are three reasons for considering them as having another and more important significance.

The first reason is objective: both books contain material impossible to relate to bureaucratic affairs. The most devoted civil servant would admit that the atmosphere of Whitehall or the Pentagon does not accord with the solemnity of the cathedral chapter in *The Trial*; and indeed the execution scene at the end of the book does not correspond with any part of normal office routine. Nor is there anything in any known bureaucratic system which exactly corresponds with the strange collection of women found in the village in *The Castle*. Frieda and Olga and Amalia and Pepi might conceivably be members of a typists' pool, but the two landladies of the inns resist classification. The second reason is also objective: Kafka was deeply concerned with religion, and it would be odd if he wrote two books in which he dealt with ideas so closely associated with religious thought as guilt and punishment and redemption, and kept his mind exclusively on bureaucracy. The third reason is subjective: many persons who read these books find that they awaken associations of a philosophical and religious nature. But this might be a protective device put up by posterity against a masterpiece, like the misreading of *Hamlet*.

Both books can be interpreted as religious allegories. It is possible to regard K. in *The Trial* as not only a bank clerk who gets involved with a piece of state machinery which he does not understand, but a soul labouring under the conviction of having sinned against God. His rational self asks what sin it is that he has committed, because he has kept the laws of man faithfully, and longs to seek God and ask Him how He dares find him, or any other man, guilty of sin when He created the sinner and gave him the opportunity to sin. It is also possible to regard K. in *The Castle* not simply as a land surveyor who cannot do this work because the authority which employs him has got into a muddle, but as a soul who is anxious to serve God but who cannot find out what it is that God wills him to do, nor even how to conceive God. In both books K. wants to look upon the face of God and fails; and there is here a correspondence with the lot of modern man, who when he looks at the social power which shapes his material destiny, looks not at a king but at a faceless democracy. But it is not to be taken for granted that Kafka justifies the ways of God to man, that he accepts either the spiritual or social world. The end of *The Trial* describes how K. is taken from his home by his two executioners, in a state of consent to his own death. He knows that in some sense he is not innocent. The executioners take him to a place outside the town where there is an abandoned quarry with a house standing beside it, they lay him down on the ground, they take out a long butcher's knife. As he is stabbed the casements of a window in the top story of the house fly open, someone leans over the sill and stretches out his arms. There is a sense of someone watching who is on his side; and the executioners have folded up K.'s clothes "as if they were likely to be used again at some time, though perhaps not immediately." There is thus a promise of resurrection, but the last words of the book are bitter beyond any sweetening. " 'Like a dog!' he said; it was as if the shame of it must outlive him." Could eternity ever wipe out the humiliation of time? Could man ever be at peace with a God who had forced him to endure life?

The Castle contains a like admission of man's guilt followed by a counterattack on God. When the land surveyor arrives in the village to take up the post to which the Castle has appointed him, the Castle takes up an equivocal position, sometimes denying this and sometimes admitting it, and doing nothing whatsoever to protect him from the villagers' hostility. It is to be noted that Kafka suggests sometimes that K. has in fact been appointed and sometimes that he is an able but unscrupulous man who wants this appointment and hopes he may get it by pretending he has got it. Thus he is shown as both the king and the usurper; and as the spiritual parallels of the king and the usurper are different phases of the same man, this is apparent nonsense and real sense. The king is man at any given moment; the usurper is that same man when, discontented with his state, he performs an act of will, and changes himself. But in the end K. admits that the castle was in any case right. He says to Pepi the chambermaid (p. 378):

It is as if we had both striven too intensely, too noisily, too childishly, with too little experience, to get something that for instance with Frieda's calm and Frieda's matter-of-factness can be got easily and without much ado. We have tried to get it by crying, by scratching, by tugging—just as a child tugs at the tablecloth, gaining nothing, but only bringing all the splendid things down on the floor and putting them out of its reach for ever.

He means, surely, that they had lacked what Keats called "Negative capability, that is, when a man is capable of being in uncertainties, mysteries, doubts, without any irritable reaching after fact and reason." To that degree K. is shown to be at fault. Yet the village women in *The Castle* make an accusation against God. All of them are involved in love affairs with the officials in the castle, principally with the very important Herr Klamm, who seems to be the permanent under-secretary; and so much is this approved that one woman, Amalia, is universally scorned because, on receiving a brutally indecent summons from an official who had seen her at a festival, she tore it up and closed her window on the messenger. To understand this curious situation, it must be realized that Kafka had a great distaste for sex, even greater than Shakespeare's. "Love," he once remarked, "always appears hand in hand with filth," and he was therefore forced to regard women as involved in evil, although he recognized that the material world could not survive without sex and women. Here we may look back at *Hamlet* and remember that Hamlet thought Fortinbras as a king was murderous but was necessary because he was a good king. Women were seen by Kafka as Shakespeare saw soldier-kings, so he had to face the fact that God had committed Himself to a scheme for the human race which involved imperfection, and of a peculiarly gross kind. Kafka was willing to admit that God must be right, and that explains the episode of Amalia. She is considered a sinner for refusing the indecent summons of the official because she was thereby refusing to cooperate with the Divine Will on the grounds that it did not conform with human standards of decorum. Frieda, on the other hand, who has been Klamm's mistress, enjoys the peace of acceptance, which for Kafka was a paradox. But it is not certain that Kafka ever found a way of reconciling himself to the strange degree of God that such impurity should be necessary. That may be why he left the book unfinished.

Kafka was not with Shakespeare in the permanent argument which we have traced. He was not with Fielding; it is almost comic to think of him in conjunction with that serene Pelagian. He was not with any of their successors whom we have discussed.* He thought of the will of man as corrupt with a corruption even fouler than Shakespeare ever ascribed to it; and he thought a little better of the court than Shakespeare did, for though it reeked of corrupting humanity it was also part of a divine plan which oriented it, corruption and all, toward salvation. But this was not of final consequence, for God would redeem the soul of man and gather it to Him in eternity, and the court would pass away, as all things which belong to time. This is a not unusual religious opinion, and it illustrates the curious dislocation of modern thought that many people find it astonishing that a major imaginative writer should have been inspired by it, and can hardly believe that that is what Kafka meant. It is also true that Kafka makes his point obscurely, because of a conscious decision he made regarding method. He rebelled against the spawning of characters which was choking the brooks of fiction with fish not worth the taking; and he would have liked to write a novel so far as possible without the use of character, concentrating on the development of a theme. Janouch says that he asked Kafka if the characters of Rosman and the Stoker, in the story named *The Stoker*, which was afterward incorporated in *Amerika*, were drawn from life, and Kafka answered impatiently, "I was not describing people, I was telling a story, these characters are only images, symbols." Obviously he handled this method successfully; the distress of K. in both volumes is clearly etched on a not too cluttered background. But it was not without its perils. It made his critical judgements absurd; he thought Balzac a poor author, for no other reason than that he created many characters, and would have liked Dickens better (though he liked him well enough to write *Amerika* in imitation of him) had he created fewer characters. But there are grounds for suspecting that this was not a purely aesthetic decision; it seems to have been in part the result of a personal defect.

Kafka seems to have lacked the power to perceive and appreciate character. This is not to say he was unsociable or uninterested in his kind. From an early age he was an object of veneration to a number

*[Among many of the other successors to Shakespeare and Fielding, the author devoted herself specially to Richardson, Emily Brontë, Jane Austen, Thackeray, Meredith, Hardy, Rousseau, and, in the chapter included above, Henry James et al. She then gave two significant sessions to Proust before reaching this final chapter.]

of his contemporaries and his juniors, and he gave them and the people he met through his work genuine guidance and help. But his benevolence was impersonal; it flowed.out to people in whose idiosyncrasies he was not interested. This is exactly the sort of kindness which is to be expected in a born bureaucrat. But in his closer relationships he might even be called insensitive. When he was well on in his thirties, he wrote a letter to his father, many pages long, and gave it to his mother in order that she should pass it on to his father, though happily she had the good sense to withhold it. It is an extremely cruel document, which shows a smattering of psychoanalytic knowledge, and is an early example of the painful truth that Freud gave sadists a new weapon by enabling them to disguise themselves as hurt children. It is also significant that Kafka was engaged to two girls, and constantly writes about his engagements and their dissolution in terms which give absolutely no clue to the girls' personalities or even to their appearances.

There is an even more striking example of his failure to register the facts of others' being in his love affair with a Czech girl named Milena Yeshenka, a young writer. She kept his letters and gave them up after his death for publication, and they are love letters of a certain austere beauty and undoubted sincerity. He has one playful sentence which convinces: "Today I saw a map of Vienna, for an instant it seemed to me incomprehensible that they built such a big city when all you need is just one room." He writes to her as if she were a beautiful and gifted person, but shows no sign that she was a person of any remarkable moral worth. Indeed, when he turns from her he seems to feel that he is turning from levity to seriousness. Yet she was, as the future was to prove, a very great woman. We have a detailed picture of her end in a book written by Margarete Buber-Neumann, who was a prisoner in the Nazi concentration camp of Ravensbrück, to which Milena was sent for her anti-Nazi activities. Milena, who was by then a middle-aged woman and crippled by arthritis, worked in the medical post, and she saved many lives by deliberately falsifying the reports, by such tricks as representing a sputum test as negative when it was positive, in order to save a patient from instant consignment to the gas chamber. Each time she did this she risked her own life, as she did when she smuggled rations to prisoners who were on starvation diet in the punishment cells. She also kept her mind intact, and wrestled for the sanity of those not so fortunate, and preserved her grace and humour until she died, after great suffering, in 1944. It is almost as disconcerting to discover that the Milena of the Kafka letters is the Milena of Ravensbrück as it would be to find that the Dark Lady of the Sonnets was a saint and martyr of the order of Joan of Arc.

It can hardly be doubted that Kafka's renunciation of the novelist's power to create character sprang from a defective perception of character, but for all that it might not affect him disadvantageously as an artist. There is the diagrammatic clarity of the theme of *The Trial*, the almost as impressive emphases of *The Castle*. Yet there is cause for regretting this defect and this decision. The exact point at which many of his fragments break off is of some significance. To take one example (*Wedding Preparations*, p. 276): Kafka's room opens and a green dragon slides round the door and Kafka asks him to come in, and the dragon smiles and says, half in embarrassment, half in shyness, "Drawn here by your longing, I have pushed myself here over quite a distance, and I have scraped my underparts quite raw, but I am glad to do it, gladly do I come, gladly do I offer myself to you—" the fragment ends. There is a shop full of people doing incomprehensible things; at the back of the shop there is a door, which opens and everybody is surprised—the fragment ends. A woman sitting with her husband at the opera is importuned by a stranger who lies along the velvet balustrade in front of them, and she hands her husband a little mother-of-pearl knife—the fragment ends. All these fantasies break down at the same point, when the motive behind some action must be explained; and motive can only completely be explained by reference to the character which conceives it. This may account for the large number of unfinished works which Kafka left; it may even account for his failure to finish *The Castle*. As he came to the end of the book, he was attempting to prove the necessity that human beings should accept the impure conditions of this life, by contrasting Frieda, who had bowed her neck to the yoke of matter and, in the words of Keats, "was capable of being in uncertainties, mysteries, and doubts," with Amalia, who sulked at them and Pepi, who was full of "irritable reaching after fact and reason." But Kafka's exposition fails by reason of his failure to give Frieda, the most important figure of the three, any recognizable character. We learn from K. that she struck him as serene and disciplined but nothing she says or does makes that impression on the reader. She simply seems more voluble than Amalia, and her volubility is cast in a style not too easily distinguishable from Pepi's despised crotchetings. It does not matter that

Kafka hurries on to the landlady of the Herrenhof, the lady of many dark dresses, who is perhaps the angel of death; the failure to convince us of the different effects of obedience and resistance to the demands of the castle lies like a barricade across the book. The refusal to create character has here seriously interfered with the development of the theme.

That so much of his work was unfinished seems part of his excellence to the kind of mind which likes to play with literature but does not wish to commit himself to what may be the harsh pain of listening to what literature has to say. When Hannah Godwin wrote to her brother William recommending Miss Gay as a possible bride, she included among her attractive attributes that she had "about as much religion as my William likes." There is also such a thing as about as much literature as my William likes; and it is possible to find that in Kafka's work, to ignore everything in it except the satire of Swift (who in fact influenced him) and the grotesquerie of Hieronymus Bosch and an enigmatic pictorial beauty which recalls certain of Rembrandt's work, notably *The Polish Rider*. But Kafka also presents the real and insoluble problems of man's nature so truly and so cruelly that he is one of the few authors who can keep pace with the cruelty of history. His work even seems to show a certain foreknowledge of the fate which was to befall his world through the establishment of the totalitarian governments. Many passages might be read as prophetic visions of the occupation of his country, of the deportations, of the concentration camps. Though the unjustified arrests, the irregular trials, the murderous executions are symbols chosen to illustrate his themes, they also come oddly close (even to the details of the uniforms worn by some of the more sinister officials) to the forms in which destiny was to destroy his world with a completeness which recalls some of his own ravaged landscapes; for his three sisters were all to be murdered by the Nazis, and so were many of his friends, while others died in exile, some by suicide. But there is no need to look to clairvoyance for an explanation. Kafka had lived through the First World War and the starvation and uncertainty that followed the collapse of the Habsburg Empire, and if Czechoslovakia enjoyed a favoured position, there was the threat of what might happen in Germany, which nearly happened even then, in the early twenties, since the Hitler Putsch and the unrest of the Ruhr had the germ of the pestilence in them; and there were enough manifestations in his own Prague to make him know that if the pestilence were to spread, his fellow countrymen would not be immune. In one of his letters to Milena he describes how he looked out of the window and saw a Jew-baiting riot (*Letters to Milena*, p. 213): "mounted police, *gendarmerie* ready for a bayonet charge, a screaming crowd dispersing, and up here in the window the loathsome disgrace of living all the time under protection." Since it was his fellow countrymen who were to fall sick, it was impossible for him to guess what visions they would see in their fever, what acts of violence they would commit in their delirium. His greatness lies not in magic but in his exceptional courage, which enabled him to explore the most dangerous areas of the mind, where familiar objects display an unfamiliar significance which leaves nothing sure.

He is at his bravest in *In a Penal Settlement*. Here he shows us how punishment, an age-old and accepted feature of all civilizations, can be extended to include the most bloody tortures, which no man should inflict on another. When we read the description of the officer proudly explaining the operation of the lethal machine to the explorer, within earshot of the man who is condemned to die in its embrace, we are aware that a human being could behave like that, human ideas are of a nature which would permit it; and history was to prove that this was so not very many years after Kafka wrote this story. But as we contemplate the disturbing identification of punishment and obscene ritual cruelty of a sort that civilized humanity would like to disown, we are confronted with a still more disturbing identification between such obscene cruelty and a sacred self-dedicated sacrifice; for the officer takes the place of the condemned man and himself lies down in the lethal machine. This action is apparently regarded by Kafka as a truly sacred sacrifice, for when the officer gives himself to the lethal machine it breaks itself as it kills him, and can do no harm to the condemned man or to any other. But at the same time there is no mysticism about the sacrifice. The officer does not rise again, but lies, with a spike through his forehead, as dead as any other slaughtered animal, nor does his death start a procession of events which might lead to a reign of mercy in the penal settlement. All we know that promises a counteraction to the cruelty is that the other officials of the settlement and their ladies feel vaguely humanitarian impulses which made them refuse to attend the execution of the condemned man. But we are given to understand that these officials and their ladies were poor things, who could think of nothing better to do for the condemned man than give him some fine handkerchiefs, whereas the officer who was inhumane and admired the lethal machine actually saved the life of the condemned man by taking his place in the machine, though he did it for no humane reason, but to vindicate the authority of the machine and its originator, which had been impugned by the explorer.

He died, indeed, a strangely legalistic death, for he was inspired by the injunction "Be just!" which was contained in the script that gave instructions regarding the use of the machine; and when the explorer questioned that in giving the machine the condemned man to kill, justice was being done, then the officer was correcting the situation by offering himself as a substitute victim, for to Kafka (as to Kierkegaard) it is self-evident to every thinking man that he is guilty before God. The whole story indeed recalls Kierkegaard, for it is relevant to his belief that the Incarnation and the Atonement are realized to be facts by the thinking man, but cannot be reconciled with any kindly or logical system of thought. The truth that has to be embraced by the man who desires to be saved is cruel, unreasonable, and incomprehensible. But among Kafka's own aphorisms there is one which is also highly relevant. "The German word *Sein* has two meanings; it means to exist, and it means to belong to Him" (*Wedding Preparations*, "Reflections on Sin, Suffering, Hope, and the True Way," No. 46). This aphorism in its turn has two meanings. It may mean, "The world is full of many things, and some of them are beautiful, and all of them will at the end of time be revealed to be so, since they belong to God." It may also mean, "The world is full of many things and some of them are foul and shameful, yet they are all the work of God, and therefore our conception of beauty, and all our thought is a delusion due to our imperfection."

But the force of this aphorism is weakened by our uncertainty as to what Kafka saw when he wrote the word "Him," as the story *In a Penal Settlement* is weakened by our uncertainty about the character of the officer who gave himself to the lethal machine. After all, the point of the Crucifixion lies in who it was that gave himself to be crucified. We are back again at Kafka's indifference to character; and we have again to consider the effect of man's social environment on his view of the inner life. A man who lived under a monarchy belonged to a more or less rigid caste system, which restricted his knowledge of the effects of government, but made him able to visualize the head of the government easily enough. It also made him able to think of God as the centre of the universe as easily as he could think of the king standing at the centre of the state. But a man who is part of the bureaucratic democracy has a far greater chance of learning the effects of government on different classes of human being, yet he has no model before his eyes to give him the idea of a single source of power. Kafka, who was so specially interested in the bureaucratic system, gives us half the religious story. We see in his pages what it is to be set down in the desert by God and picked up by Him and set down at another point in aridity, or raised to some unmapped peak of salvation; but we receive no intimation of God Himself.

This is not to say that Kafka had no intimation of God; God is the context of his work. But the temporal model of his being hampered him in expressing what he knew. Included in the volume entitled *A Country Doctor* he has represented the difficulty under which the artist labours when he seeks to tell his revelation (*In a Penal Settlement*, p. 155):

The Emperor—so the story goes, has sent a message to you, the lone individual, the meanest of his subjects, the shadow that has fled before the Imperial sun until it is microscopic in the remotest distance, just to you has the Emperor sent a message from his deathbed. He made the messenger kneel by his bed and whispered the message into his ear; he felt it to be so important that he made the man repeat it into his own ear. With a nod of the head he confirmed that the repetition was accurate. And then, before the whole retinue gathered to witness his death—all the walls blocking the view had been broken down and on the wide high curve of the open stairway stood the notables of the Empire in a circle—before them all he empowered the messenger to go. The messenger set off at once; a robust, an indefatigable man; thrusting out now one arm, now the other, he forces his way through the crowd; where he finds obstacles he points to the sign of the sun on his breast; he gets through easily too, as no one else could. Yet the throng is so numerous; there is no end to their dwelling-places. If he only had a free field before him, how he would run, and soon enough you would hear the glorious tattoo of his fists on your door. But instead of that, how vain are his efforts; he is still forcing his way through the chambers of the innermost palace; he will never get to the end of them; and even if he did, he would be no better off; he would have to fight his way down the stairs; and even if he did that, he would be no better off; he would still have to get through the courtyards; and after the courtyards, the second outer palace enclosing the first; and more stairways and more courtyards; and still another palace; and so on for thousands of years; and did he finally dash through the outermost gate—but that will never, never happen—he would still have the capital city before him, the centre of the world, overflowing with the dregs of humanity. No one can force a way through that, least of all with a message from a dead man. But you might receive that message as you sit by your window and drowse, while evening falls.

This is an event which one can imagine as meat for a number of writers. Shakespeare might have seen it as what happened at the deathbed of an English king; one noble would have forced his way through the crowd, his passage made possible by the magic of his belief that the dead king had been truly anointed and had been faithful to his coronation oath. Fielding would have trusted Tom Jones and Amelia to perform the errand by virtue of the magic of good sense and sound instincts. In later hands the accounts of the messengers might have been too circumstantial for deep interest, until we came to Proust, who might hold us by writing the passage as an account of the last hours of a president at Rambouillet: some festivity was being given by a Guermantes in the district, and all the roads were blocked by his guests' cars, while Monsieur de Norpois' friends in the ministries and in the press were monopolizing all the telephone lines, but the lone integrity of Swann saw that the message was delivered. It was, however, Kafka who wrote the passage, and according to him the messenger never started. Yet what he had to deliver was of the greatest importance, for it came from the lips of the emperor before he died, from God at some time when He was not veiling Himself from the gaze of humanity, when He was willing to communicate with him otherwise than by the operations of an incomprehensible law, when He was not hiding Himself in the castle. Nevertheless the message could not be delivered, because of the courtiers who blocked the staircase, the lesser officials who thronged the courtyards, the rabble in the streets of the capital city. These have many names. They are the circumstances of family life, the terrifying father, the embarrassing sister; the disabling sicknesses; the love which one is not strong enough to achieve and which is therefore a painful distraction, the interruptions of history, the wars, the inflationary crises, the Jew-baiting in the streets. They may be purely internal and not really discreditable; a man may be so intellectually vigorous that he cannot let the message remain as it was given by the emperor, he must seize it as it goes by him and improve it by debate, injecting into it ideas that are perhaps really brilliant, though not those conveyed by the words which actually passed the emperor's lips. It may also happen that the intervention is more remote; that the world will do to the message what it has done to *Hamlet,* and will dislike its meaning so much that it will pretend that it means something else.

But Kafka tells us that what happens to the messenger does not really matter, because the message will be delivered in any case, "as you sit by your window and drowse, while evening falls." There are two things which he might mean by this. He might mean that the artistic process is so sure, though unpredictable, that in spite of all forms of external and internal pressure it will discover the truth and convey it, and there is a hint that Keats' "negative capability" is the means of resisting such pressures. But it might also mean that if the artist should fail to discover the truth and convey it to his readers, they might themselves receive it by direct mystical experience. The first meaning emphasizes the dependence of society on the artist and his special gift; and the second lays stress on the deeper solidarity of the artist and society. The experiences which the artist celebrates are not peculiar to him, they are common to all human beings, his only peculiarity lies in his power to analyse these experiences and synthesize the findings of his analyses. That being so, it is not surprising that the artist should deviate from his straight aesthetic course and occupy himself with the interests which preoccupy the society of which he is a member. He still has his particular grace, to which William Blake referred when he wrote: "If Homer's merit was only in these Historical combinations and rival sentiment he would be no better than Clarissa." Nevertheless it is a tendency of creative literature, when it rises above a certain level, to involve itself with statecraft and with religion: to exist and to belong to Him.

Charlotte Brontë

From *The Great Victorians*, ed. H. J. and Hugh Massingham (London, 1932).

This generation knows that Charlotte Brontë's own generation gave her too high a place in the artistic hierarchy when it exalted her above her sister Emily, but is itself tempted to place her too low because of the too easily recognizable *naïveté* of her material.

It is true that the subject-matter of all her work is, under one disguise or another, the Cinderella theme which is the stand-by of the sub-artist in fiction and the theatre, all the world over and in any age. She treats it in the form it takes in the hands of those who have moved just one degree away from complete *naïveté*: instead of it being supposed that Cinderella has the advantage of physical beauty over the Ugly Sisters, it is supposed (as an absolute and more magical compensation to the sense of inferiority which weaves and needs the story) that it is they who are beautiful, and she who is ugly, though possessed of an invisible talisman of spiritual quality which wholly annuls that disadvantage. This is the theme of *Jane Eyre* and *Villette*, and, with certain elaborations and feints, of *Shirley* also; and it cannot be denied that we have grave reason to associate it with work which is not artistic at all, which sets out not to explore reality, but to nourish the neurotic fantasies with which feebler brains defend themselves from reality.

Charlotte Brontë also uses material which many people denounce as naïve with, I think, less foundation. She records oppressions practised by the dowered on the dowerless, and by adults on children, and seems to many of her readers absurd and unpleasant when she does so; but that is perhaps not because such incidents never happen, but because we dislike admitting that they happen. There is hardly a more curious example of the gap we leave between life and literature than the surprise and incredulity recorded by successive generations of Brontëan commentators at the passages in the sisters' works which suggest that the well-to-do are sometimes uncivil to their employees. In actual fact, all of us, even today, if we were connected with a young girl who was going out into the world as a governess, would feel an anxiety that she should be with "nice people," which would imply a lively fear of what nasty people are capable of doing to governesses; but these commentators write as if Charlotte and Anne must have been the victims of hysterical morbidity when they implied that governesses were sometimes treated rudely, although the idea then prevalent, that one was divinely appointed to one's social station, cannot have improved the manners of employers. It has been the opinion of all moral teachers from the days of the Psalmist that riches lead to haughtiness and froward bearing; yet when Miss Blanche Ingram tells the footman, "Cease that chatter, blockhead," the commentators shake their heads and smile, without reflecting that she was supposed to have made that remark in the year preceding Queen Victoria's accession to the throne, when much of the eighteenth-century coarseness of manners still lingered, and that even today women can be found who have the tiresome habit of being rude to waiters and menservants.

We may suspect, then, that the common objection to this material is not that it has no correspondence with reality, but that it is intensely embarrassing for us to contemplate. The feeling of inferiority, under which we all labour, may find a gratifying opportunity for self-pity in the accounts of the suffering which superiors can unjustly inflict on their inferiors, but only if they are not too vivid; for if they are, then we feel terror at the quality of the universe. And if that be so when the accounts refer to the relatively remote symbolism of social matters, which we all of us can discount by reference to some other system of values which we have devised to suit our special case, how much more will it be so when they refer to the actual and agonizing experiences of our childhood! In these days one is weaker than nearly all the world. However kindly one is treated, one is frustrated and humiliated, one's natural habits are corrected, and one's free speech censored; and if one is not kindly treated, one can take no revenge, one is without means of protecting one's dignity. There must be something shameful in such a phase to an organism as much in love with the idea of its own free will as the human being. Thus the descriptions of Jane Eyre's ill-treatment at the hands of the Reeds, and the sufferings of the pupils at Lowood, revive a whole series of associations in the readers' minds which the more imaginative and intellectually developed among them will hate to recall. They will turn from Charlotte Brontë's work with the accusation that it is infantile; but what they mean is that she exposes her own and their infantilism. She lifts a curtain, and reveals what the world usually keeps hidden. In her pictures of these oppressions she demonstrates the workings of our universal sense that we are worms; as in her use of the Cinderella theme she demonstrates our universal hope that, though we are but worms, a miracle will happen, and we shall be made kings of the world. It may be objected that any hack writer of penny dreadfuls does as much; but that is untrue. The hack writer spins the consoling fantasy, and so does Charlotte Brontë; but she also depicts the hunger that goads the spinner to the task. Her work, considered as a whole, is as powerful an analysis of the working of the sense of inferiority and its part in creating romanticism as the mind of man has ever made.

But colour is lent to the suspicion that Charlotte Brontë is not an artist but a sub-artist, that she does not analyse experience, but weaves fantasies to hang between man and his painful experience, by her frequent use of the sub-artist's chosen weapon, sentimental writing. This also is a feature of her work which is specially repugnant to the present generation's hyper-sensitiveness to the superficial decorum of literature; and it remains an indefensible defect. But it adds to Charlotte Brontë's power over our attentions, because in so far as she discloses it with her unequalled ardour and honesty, she gives us a picture of the eternal artist experiencing an eternally recurrent misadventure.

For Charlotte Brontë's tendency to sentimental writing was not due to an innate inaptitude for the artistic process, but to the pressure of external circumstance. In one important respect her life was unfavourable to the practice of art. This was not loneliness and privation: Emily Brontë, suffering the same portion of these ills, was the complete artist. It was not the misconduct of her brother Branwell, though that was a contributing factor to it. It was her specially acute need to make, by separate and violent acts of the will, the place in the world for herself and her two younger sisters which should have been made for them by their elders. Her realization of this need must have been panic-stricken and desperate, for the whole of her life was ravaged by a series of progressively bitter disappointments in the protection which children expect from adults and which women expect from men.

Mrs Brontë died of cancer when Charlotte was five years old, and for some time before her death the progress of her malady and her regular confinements prevented her from giving her children much attention. Mr Brontë was an eccentric recluse whose capacity for parenthood seems to have been purely physical. Even before he had taken to the bottle, he took no trouble to provide his children with either his own sympathy or proper companionship, or any but the barest preparation for adult life. Mrs Brontë's sister, who came North from Cornwall to take charge of the orphaned children, disliked Yorkshire, retired to her bedroom, and cared for none of them except Branwell. From the terrible matter-of-factness with which Emily and Charlotte Brontë draw (in Nelly Deans and in Bessie) the servant whose unimaginative cruelty changes to a not very reliable kindness, one sees that there was no steady comfort for the children in the kitchen. It was in her sister Maria, the oldest of the family, that Charlotte found a substitute for her mother: we know that from the portrait of Helen Burns in *Jane Eyre*. But Maria died at the age of twelve, when Charlotte was eight; and her only other older sister, Elizabeth, died two months later.

About the time of Charlotte's ninth birthday, then, the negligence and death of her elders left her with her own way to make in the world. But that is an understatement, for it supposes her burdenless. It would be more accurate to say that she became the head of the family, with one brother and two sisters, all deeply loved, dependent on her for everything above the bare physical necessities of life. The records of the Brontës' childhood show her eagerly answering the call to leadership; but she was not then altogether to be pitied. She was still supported by her penultimate hope. Whatever the defections of Mr Brontë, they would not be without a man to look after them as soon as their brother grew up. It is confessed honestly and radiantly in Charlotte Brontë's books how she craved for the support that the child-bearing faculty of woman logically entitles her to expect from man, and there was a special factor in her environment to give intensity to that craving.

Victorian England was a man's country. She might well have hoped that with Branwell Brontë's fine natural endowment he would easily find a place in it, and that she would see herself and her sisters decently maintained or helped to decent employment. But she was still a girl when it became apparent that Branwell, in spite of all his brilliant promise, was growing up, not into a man, but into a pathetic nuisance, who would not even decently maintain himself. For the sixth time natural supports had failed her. She knew the terrible fear felt by the young who begin to suspect that they are going to be cheated out of the fullness of life; and she was not fearful for herself alone, but also for Anne and Emily, in whose gifts she had faith, and for whose health she had every reason to fear. She had seen her two elder sisters die, and she had probably forebodings that she was to see the other two die also. It is known that she had such forebodings about Anne.

During the years when it was becoming plain that Branwell was going to be of no help to them, but "a drain on every source," Charlotte became more and more desperate. By this time, it is interesting to note, she was half-blind. But if no one would give her and her sisters their fair share of life, she herself would see that they got what she could snatch; and she snatched far more than one would think possible. The astounding thing about the Brontës' life is not its emptiness but—considering the bareness of Haworth Parsonage—its fullness. There were several friends; there was a good deal of employment, including the Brussels expedition; there was the literary adventure. And it was Charlotte who made the friends, Charlotte who found the teaching posts, Charlotte who wrote the letters to the publishers. Now, it is easy to sneer at these achievements, on the ground that the greatest of the three sisters, Emily, found them purely vexatious, since she was shy of strangers, loathed leaving the moors of Haworth, and would rather have kept her poems to herself. Nevertheless, Charlotte's actions followed the natural direction of sanity. Like all living things, she strove for the survival of herself and her belongings with the balance of her impulses. It was hardly to be expected that reverence of Emily's genius should oust the desire to keep her alive, and any change which removed her from the rigours of the Parsonage must have at first seemed favourable to that end. There is nothing to be said against Charlotte's frenzied efforts to counter the nihilism of her surroundings, unless one is among those who would find amusement in the sight of the starving fighting for food.

In the sphere of life they were unquestionably noble; but it unfortunately happened—and here lies the disconcerting value of Charlotte as a revelation of the artist-type—that in the sphere of art they had a disintegrating effect. They committed her to a habit of activism which was the very antithesis of the quietism demanded from the artist. In her desire to make a place in the world for herself and her family against time, she could let nothing establish itself by slow growth, she had to force the pace of every intimacy and every action, which means that she had constantly to work upon people with the aim of immediately provoking them to certain emotions. Sprightly or touching letters had to be written to the friends to keep them near in spite of distance; Miss Branwell had to be induced to finance the Brussels expedition, and Mrs Wooler had to have her interest in the new school kept warm; Southey, Wordsworth, Tennyson, Lockhart, and de Quincey had to be addressed in the vain attempt to rouse their interest in Currer, Ellis, and Acton Bell. In fact, she was forced to a passionate participation in a business of working on people's feelings exclusive of the true business of art, and the root of the evil that we call sentimentality.

This, therefore, was Charlotte's special temptation: she was so used to manipulating people's feelings in life that she could not lose the habit in her art, and was apt to fall into sentimentality. All her novels are defaced to varying degrees by passages which have nothing to do with the organic growth of the story, and are inspired simply by guess-work as to the state of the reader's feelings. An extreme example of this is the scene where the Yorkes call on Miss Moore and find Caroline Helstone in her parlour, in the twenty-third chapter of *Shirley*. The same error is committed in an earlier scene of the book, but it is here more noteworthy and disastrous, because here there is promise of high poetic value. Caroline is sick with love for Robert Moore, and faint with despair. Mrs Yorke looms over her like a personification of the cruelty that must govern the world if it is true that she is not to have her love; the Yorke children have the fantastic, unclassical quality that all objects not the beloved assume under the lover's eye. When Caroline's veins are flushed with quicksilver rage against that cruelty, the scene should end, and she should be left still waiting for Robert at the jessamined window. But Miss Brontë's habit of bustling was too strong for her then. She could not trust her slow magic to make the reader's interest slowly mount. She felt she must put them under a swiftly growing debt to her for entertainment. She remembered how Martha Taylor, who was the original of little Jessy Yorke, had often entertained her with her precocious tirades; so she reproduced one there and then. She also remembered what a poignant effect had been made by this child's early death; so she inserted a description of her funeral. The continuity of the scene is broken, the author's and the reader's contacts with Caroline are lost, and whatever emotion is felt is diverted from the real theme.

It would be easy to point to many other pages in Charlotte Brontë's novels where sentimental writing has been allowed to destroy the

434

structure of the work; and there is one case where sentimentality has been allowed to plan such a structure faultily. The melodramatic plot of *Jane Eyre* is not a symbol honestly conceived by extreme *naïveté*, but was invented, in her own admission, to suit a supposed popular demand for sensationalism. That was a pity, for there are pages in the book, such as the scene where the lovers walk in the orchard under the rising moon, which deserve the best of settings. But great as is the harm done to the valuable content of Charlotte Brontë's work by her choice of certain episodes and series of episodes simply for their immediate effect on her readers, still greater is the harm done by the diffusion of sentimentality through her style. It is crammed with direct appeals to the emotions, which make it tediously repetitive, explosive, and irrelevant to the deeper themes discussed.

That this defect was not inborn in Charlotte, but was the product of her circumstances, can be proved by a reference to a letter quoted by Mrs Gaskell from *The Little Magazine*, which the Brontës composed in their childhood. It begins: "SIR,—It is well known that the Genii have declared that unless they perform certain arduous duties every year, of a mysterious nature, all the worlds in the firmament will be burnt up and gathered together in one mighty globe," and no style could be more decorous and more sincere. But she wrote it at the age of thirteen, before she had become a panic-stricken adept in the art of negotiation. She was never to write such prose again until her passion for M. Héger made her forget all her schemes and anxieties, and changed her to the insanely honest instrument of one intention and one need.

The obviousness with which what was a virtue in Charlotte Brontë's life became a vice in her art makes her one of the most disconcerting among great writers to contemplate. She is suspended between the two spheres of art and life, and not in a state of rest. She is torn between them. But where this generation will probably err is in supposing that her plight is unique. There is sentimentality in every age, even in our own; and we swallow it whole if its subject-matter is not of a sort that arouses suspicion. That was where Charlotte Brontë erred. All of us not actually illiterate or imbecile feel that something is wrong when a writer attempts to compel his readers' feelings by the exploitation of early deaths, handsome sinners with lunatic wives, and ecstatic dithyrambs. The march of culture has forced such knowledge on the least of us.

But let us examine the current attitude to the great Russians. A great many readers, and some of these drawn from the professionally fastidious, place Tolstoy above Turgenev and Dostoevski. Yet Turgenev was, as Mr George Moore has said in that incomparable book of criticism, *Avowals*, "a sort of Jesus of Nazareth in art," who gave himself to the artistic process with so little reservation for his personal ends, that there is no conflict in his work, only serenity; and though it is true, as Mr Moore says in the same book, that, before we can admire Dostoevski's novels, "modern life must wring all the Greek out of us," he also, albeit with constant cries of protest at the pain it cost him, forced himself to the honest analysis of experience. But Tolstoy is fully as sentimental a writer as Charlotte Brontë. In *War and Peace, Anna Karenina,* and *Resurrection,* he pushes his characters about with the greatest conceivable brusqueness in order to prove his thesis, and exhorts his readers to accept his interpretations of their movements. He even admits in *What Is Art?* that he thinks this the proper way for the artist to behave. Nevertheless, Tolstoy arouses no repugnance in this generation, although this use of art to prove what man already knows is a shameful betrayal of the mission of art to tell man more than he knows. This is only because the subject-matter of his sentimentality is unfamiliar. He attempts to influence his readers in favour of a thesis dependent on the primitive sense of guilt, and the need for expiation by the endurance and infliction of suffering, which had been forbidden expression above a certain cultural level in the rationalist nineteenth century. We are not on our guard against it as we are against Charlotte Brontë's Cinderella theme; and we succumb to what must be an eternally recurrent temptation.

Yet if Charlotte Brontë represents an eternally recurrent defeat of the artist, she also represents his eternally recurrent triumph. She told the truth even about matters concerning which the whole civilization round her had conspired to create a fiction; and her telling of it is not an argument, but an affirmation, that comes and is, like the light of the sun and the moon. It is not only true that, as Swinburne said, again and again she shows the

power to make us feel in every nerve, at every step forward which our imagination is compelled to take under the guidance of another's, that thus and not otherwise, but in all things altogether even as we are told and shown, it was, and must have been, with the human figures set before us in their action and their suffering; that thus, and not otherwise, they absolutely must and would have felt and thought and spoken under the proposed conditions.

436

It is not only true that she abounds in touches of that kind of strange beauty which, dealing solely with the visible world, nevertheless persuades us that the visible world is going to swing open as if it were a gate and disclose a further view: like the description of the stable-yard in Thornfield at dawn, with the blinds still drawn in the windows, and the birds twittering in the blossom-laden orchard, when the mysterious stranger drives away with the surgeon after his mysterious wounding. She does more than that, she makes a deeper revelation of the soul.

In an age which set itself to multiply the material wants of mankind (with what results we see today) and to whittle down its spiritual wants to an ethical anxiety that was often mean, Charlotte Brontë serenely lifted up her voice, and testified to the existence of the desires which are the buds of all human thoughts and actions. Her candid and clairvoyant vision of such things is displayed again and again throughout her works, but never more notably than in the two instances which make *Villette* one of the most interesting of English novels. The first is the description of the innocent but passionate love of the little girl Polly for the schoolboy John. The second is the description of how Lucy Snowe's love passed without a break from John Bretton to Paul Emanuel; never before has there been such a frank admission of the subtle truth that the romantic temperament writes a lover's part, and then casts an actor to play it, and that nevertheless there is more there than make-believe. To realize how rare a spirit it required to make and record such observations at the time one must turn to Miss Harriet Martineau's comments on the book as given in Mrs Gaskell's *Life*; though one should remember that Miss Martineau was herself to suffer from the age's affectation of wantlessness. For when, as an elderly lady, she received a present of money from her admirers, the subscribers were greatly incensed when she proposed to spend an undue proportion of it on a silver tea equipage; yet surely any earlier age would have understood this belated desire for a little handsomeness.

But Charlotte Brontë did more than unconsciously correct the error of her age; she saw as deeply as poets do. There are surely two scenes which have the dignity and significance of great poetry. One is the scene in *Villette*, where the fevered girl wanders by night out of the silent school, with the intention of seeking a certain stone basin that she remembers to have seen, brimming with cool water, in a glade of the park; and finds the city ablaze with light, thronged with a tide of happy people, which bears up to the park that is now fantastic with coloured lights and pasteboard palaces, a phantasmagoria in which she walks and sees her friends, her foes, her beloved, but is not seen. There has never before been found a more vivid symbolic representation of the state of passion in which the whole universe, lacking the condition of union with the beloved, seems a highly coloured but insubstantial illusion, objective counterpart to delirium. Yet even finer is the scene in *Shirley* called "A Summer Night," when Shirley and Caroline creep across the moonlit fields to warn Moore of the approach of rioters, and are too late. There, when the two girls stand "alone with the friendly night, the mute stars, and these whispering trees," listening to the shouts and watching the fires of masculine dissension (which is their opposite and what they live by), and while what is male in woman speaks with the voice of Shirley, and what is female speaks with the voice of Caroline, one perceives that a statement is being found for that which the intellect has not yet stated in direct terms.

Charlotte Brontë was a supreme artist; and yet she was very nearly not an artist at all. That will make her an unsympathetic figure to many in these days, when a school of criticism, determined to exert authority but without the intellectual power to evolve an authoritative doctrine, has imported into this country its own puerile version of the debate between romanticism and classicism which has cut up the French world of letters into sterile sectionalism, and trots about frivolously inventing categories on insufficient bases, rejecting works of art that do not fit into them, and attaching certificates to those that do. But she will inspire and console those who realize that art is a spiritual process committed to imperfection by the flesh, which is its medium; that though there are artists who seem to transcend the limitations of that medium, like Bach and Mozart and Emily Brontë, they are rare as the saints, and like them, sublime but not final in their achievements; and that the complete knowledge and mastery of experience which would be attained in a perfect world of art is like the *summum bonum* of the theologians, the vision of God which is to reward the pure in heart, and cannot be realized until time is changed to eternity.

Rudyard Kipling

From *New Statesman* (London, January 25, 1936).

The chief tragedy of Rudyard Kipling's life was summed up in two of the tributes published in the newspaper the morning after his death. Major-General Dunsterville, the original of Stalky, boasted: "In three-score years and ten no man's outlook on life could have changed less than that of Rudyard Kipling." Sir Ian Hamilton wrote precisely and powerfully: "As one who must surely be about Kipling's oldest friend, I express my deep sorrow. His death seems to me to place a full stop to the period when war was a romance and the expansion of the Empire a duty." Those two sentences indicate the theme of that tremendous and futile drama in which a man, loving everything in life but reality, spent his days loathing intellectuals as soft and craven theorists, and yet himself never had the courage to face a single fact that disproved the fairy-tales he had invented about the world in youth; and who, nevertheless, was so courageous in defending this uncouragcous position that he had to be respected as one respects a fighting bull making its last stand. That drama explains why the public regards Rudyard Kipling as one of the most interesting men of our time. He stands among those Laocoön figures who in pride and strength are treading the road to the highest honours, when they are assailed by passions, which seem not to be a part of the victim's individualities, but to have crawled out of the dark uncharted sea of our common humanity. Such men are judged not by their achievements in action or the arts but by the intensity of the conflict between them and their assailants. Such judgement had to recognize Rudyard Kipling as a memorable man.

That, in part, explains his fame on the Continent. His warmest admirers would have to admit that that is extravagantly inflated. A short time ago I was present when one of the greatest figures in European literature explained to our most subtle living novelist that it could only be political prejudice which prevented him from recognizing *Soldiers Three* and *They* as permanent glories of English literature, very near its apex. "You think them very much better

439

than anything Shaw and Wells have written?" "Oh much!" "Better than anything Dickens and Thackeray have written?" "Of course! Much better than anything else in your modern English literature— except Oscar Wilde and Lord Byron!" The just cataloguing of Rudyard Kipling with two other Laocoön figures suggests that an imperfect knowledge of a language may permit a reader to see the main pattern of a fabric, which a reader of great linguistic accomplishment might lose because of absorption in fine verbal touches. But it does not explain the curious progress of his fame in this country. That followed a course which it is hard to explain to a post-war generation.

Those of us who were born in the first half of the nineties remember a childhood shadowed by certain historical facts: the gathering trouble in South Africa, the Home Rule question, the Dreyfus Case, the Diamond Jubilee, and the fame of Mr Kipling. These were of not easily differentiated importance; and it must be remembered that Kipling was not thirty-five till the turn of the century. He enjoyed the celebrity and rewards of Mr Noel Coward and Mr Priestley put together, at less than Mr Noel Coward's present age, with something of the more than merely political, almost priestly, aureole of Mr Baldwin. He had laid the foundations of this fame principally with his volumes of short stories, *Plain Tales from the Hills*, *Soldiers Three* and *Life's Handicap*, his novel, *The Light That Failed*, and his volumes of poetry, *Barrack Room Ballads* and *The Seven Seas*.

It will seem to anyone who now takes up these volumes for the first time, or can read them in a state of detachment, that their fame was not deserved. Those books are the work of a preternaturally clever boy in his early twenties, of odd and exciting, but limited experience, and they are just as good as could be expected, and just as bad. *Plain Tales from the Hills* are just the stories a young writer of parts will write when he is mastering the bare elements of the story-teller's craft; when he is teaching himself to get down on paper the crude sequence of events, the mere mechanical movements of people in and out of rooms and up and down stairs. *Soldiers Three*, for all they have stamped the imagination of a people, are anecdotes told with too much gusto and too little invention. *Life's Handicap* are better stories, for in them Kipling has perfected the art of hooking a reader's attention as neatly as an accomplished salmon-fisher casting a fly. I cannot believe that a young officer and his Hindu mistress would converse so exclusively in the manner of conscientious members of the Chelsea Babies' Club as is represented in *Without Benefit of Clergy*, but I shall not forget that story till I die. As for *The Light That Failed*, it is a neat, bright, tightly painted canvas but it falls far short of deserving to cause a sensation. Dick Heldar is a boy's idea of an artist and a man; Maisie is a boy's idea of a woman; Bessie Broke is a boy's idea of a drab; Torp is a boy's idea of an adventurer. The verse is naturally better. Poetic genius makes a qualitative demand on experience; fiction makes a quantitative test as well. And indeed all his life long Kipling was a better poet than he was a prose-writer, though an unequal one. In his verse he was a fusion of Ella Wheeler Wilcox, Adelaide Procter, Alfred Noyes, George R. Sims (*Gunga Din* is as bad as that), with a militarist A. P. Herbert, one of the grander Scottish hymnal-writers and a pure and perfect lyrist, who could distil a day of alien weather in a verse as bright and clear as a dewdrop. But it must be doubted whether an age that recited *Gunga Din* and *The Absent-minded Beggar* at the top of its voice was really swayed by admiration for that shy and delicate lyrist in its estimate of Kipling's genius.

Yet there was nothing at all fortuitous about Kipling's success. It could not be called a fluke. To begin with, his work then and all through his life had the curious property of seeming better than it disclosed itself after a few years. Some of his work was gold; and the rest was faery gold. Moreover, it had rare qualities which made it superbly relevant to its time. The first two were the emphasis on colour in his style, and the vast geographical scope of his subject-matter, which made his work just the nourishment the English-speaking world required in the period surrounding the Jubilee and the Diamond Jubilee. I do not find that the post-war generation realizes what marvellous shows these were, or how they enfranchised the taste for gorgeousness in a population that wore dark clothes, partly from a morbid conception of decorum and partly because cleaning was so expensive, and lived in drab and smoky times. Of the Jubilee I cannot speak; but of the Diamond Jubilee I have enchanting memories of such feasts for the eye as I do not think I knew again until the Russian Ballet came to dip the textiles of Western Europe in bright dyes. London was full of dark men from the ends of the earth who wore glorious colours and carried strange weapons, and who were all fond of small children and smiled at them in the streets. I remember still with a pang of ecstasy the gleaming teeth of a tall bearded warrior wearing a high head-dress, gold ear-rings and necklaces, a richly multi-coloured uniform, and embroidered soft leather boots. There were also the Indian troops in Bushey Park, their officers exquisitely brown and still, and coiffed with delicately bright turbans, the men washing their clothes at some stretch of water, small and precise and beautiful. They came from remote places and spoke unknown tongues. They belonged to an infinite number of varied races. They were amiable, they belonged to our Empire, we had helped them to become amiable by conquering them and civilizing them. It was an intoxicating thought; and it was mirrored in the work of Rudyard Kipling and nowhere else, for nobody could match his gift of reflecting visual impressions in his prose, and he alone among professional writers had travelled widely, and had the trick of condensing his travels into evocative runes which are almost as much magic as poetry. Hence he could restore confidence to a population that had slowly lost touch with their traditional assurances throughout the nineteenth century and give them a new sense of religious destiny. Since they were subjects of the British Empire they were members of a vast redemptory force.

And, indeed, that belief produced some not at all poisonous fruits. One night, when I was some years older, my mother returned from an expedition to town, and with flashing eyes described how she had come on a vast crowd standing round a hotel and raising cheer after cheer. Presently there appeared at the lighted window the stiff head and beard of Botha, woodenly bowing acknowledgements. The crowd had gathered to cheer the South African Generals, come to London to settle the peace, not (as one of the post-war generation startled me by assuming the other day on hearing this anecdote) because they were pro-Boer, but because they were full of the spirit of *parcere subjectis*. Uglier things have happened in history.

The third quality which made Kipling the presiding genius of his time was his passion for machinery. He assured the slaves of a mechanized world that what they tended were civilizing forces; that the task of tending them was a discipline and high achievement, and that the humblest who performed that task worthily could hold up his head among kings. Again, he brought a sense of religious destiny back into a disorganized world. He was able, in fact, to render an immense service to his age, and it is no wonder that in his later years, when it became apparent that that age had passed for ever, he refused to recognize the change, and raised a disgruntled pretence that nothing was happening save an outburst of misconduct on the part of the intellectuals and the lower classes. It is no wonder that he should want to do so, human nature being as frail as it is; but it is surprising that the writer of the masterpiece *Kim* should have found himself able to do so.

It was partly the consequence of a real incapacity for handling general ideas and grasping the structure of the world in which he lived. He was full of contempt for Pagett, M P, the radical English politician who came out to India for a few months and then laid down the law to administrators who had known the country for a lifetime. But Sir Edmund Gosse, that wavering convert to the conventional, who could never be trusted not to lapse into dangerous penetration and sincerity, once pointed out that whenever Kipling wrote about England or any place but India he was simply a Pagett M P turned inside out. This was partly due to his Indian childhood, but it must also be laid to the charge of the kind of education which England provides for its governing classes. It is interesting to turn back to his very early travel book, *From Sea to Sea*, if only to see how carefully he hammered out that descriptive style which has had even more influence in France than here, since it is the foundation of the best in *le grand reportage*; but it is interesting also as an indication of just how well Stalky & Co. were taught. It begins with a chapter of jeers at a wretched young man from Manchester on a trip through India, who had bought some silly sham antiques and failed to understand the working of some wells on the plains. But in the later chapters Kipling himself travels through the Western States, only fifty years after the forty-niners, with not the faintest appreciation of what the settlement of the country meant. He gets off the train at Salt Lake City and has no word of reverence for that miracle of statesmanship which set a noble city and a stable State on a trackless and waterless desert. Merely he complains that the *Book of Mormon* is illiterate, that the Tabernacle is not pretty, and that polygamy is shocking. Could any young man from Manchester do worse? Surely the United Services College should have taught him better than that?

But the same wonder regarding the value of our English system of education arises when we look round at Kipling's admirers among the rich and great. He was their literary fetish; they treated him as the classic writer of our time; as an oracle of wisdom; as Shakespeare touched with grace and elevated to a kind of mezzanine rank just below the Archbishop of Canterbury. But he was nothing of the sort. He interpreted the mind of an age. He was a sweet singer to the last. He could bring home the colours and savours of many distant places.

He liked the workmanship of many kinds of workers, and could love them as long as they kept their noses to their work. He honoured courage and steadfastness as they must be honoured. But he was not a fabulous writer. His style was marred by a recurrent liability to a kind of two-fold vulgarity, a rolling over-emphasis on the more obviously picturesque elements of a situation, whether material or spiritual, and an immediate betrayal of the satisfaction felt in making that emphasis. It is not a vice that is peculiar to him—perhaps the supreme example of it is Mr Chesterton's *Lepanto*—but he committed it often and grossly. Furthermore, his fiction and his verse were tainted by a moral fault which one recognizes most painfully when one sees it copied in French books which are written under his influence, such as M. de St Exupéry's *Vol de Nuit*, with its strong, silent, self-gratulatory airmen, since the French are usually an honest people. He habitually claimed that any member of the governing classes who does this work adequately was to be regarded as a martyr who sacrificed himself for the sake of the people; whereas an administrator who fulfils his duties creditably does it for exactly the same reason that a musician gives a masterly performance on his fiddle or a house-painter gives a wall a good coat of varnish, because it is his job and he enjoys doing things well. But the worst of all was the mood of black exasperation in which Kipling thought and wrote during his later years. He had before him a people who had passed the test he had named in his youth—the test of war; and they had passed it with a courage that transcended anything he can have expected as far as war transcended in awfulness anything he can have expected. Yet they had only to stretch out a hand towards bread or peace or power or any of the goods that none could grudge them in this hour when all their governors' plans had broken down, for Kipling to break out in ravings against the greed and impudence of the age. Was this a tragedy to deplore or a pattern to copy?

But perhaps the rich and great admired Kipling for retiring into rage and shutting his eyes against his times, because they were obscurely conscious of the dilemma that must have faced him had he left them open. Supposing that one has pledged one's imagination before the war to the ideal of a great Power which would ruthlessly spread its pattern of civilization over all conquerable lands so far as it could reach, without tenderness for its executives or the conquered peoples; which would count the slaves of the machines as the equal of kings, provided they performed their tasks with competence, and far superior to the intellectuals who are infatuated with the notion of freedom; which asked of its children discipline, and discipline, and then discipline, and stood proudly to meet the force of the world with force—what power would claim one's allegiance after the war, every year more surely? It has often seemed fantastic that the author of *MacAndrew's Hymn* should have feared and loathed the aeroplane. Perhaps he felt that, had he given his passion for machinery its head, that and the rest of his creed might have led him straight to Dneprostroi.

A Visit to a Godmother

BBC talk, reprinted in *Writers on Themselves*, ed. Norman Nicholson (London, 1964).

What I chiefly want to do when I write is to contemplate character: either by inventing my own characters in novels and short stories based on my own experience, or by studying characters in history, ancient or, by preference, modern. This is an inborn tendency in me, I am sure, but various events have stimulated it, and one among them was a visit to my godmother which I paid more than half a century ago. When I was thirteen my godmother invited me and my elder sister Winifred to stay with her. The prospect filled me with excitement. I had never met her since I was a very small child, but I had reason to have more grateful and romantic feelings for her than most god-children feel for their sponsors. She had a picturesque connection with my mother's early life. When my mother was in her late twenties she had had a nervous breakdown caused by her grief at the loss of a brother, and she had given up her career as a musician and had become for two or three years what was then known as "a musical governess." It was a pleasant post such as this age, so mistakenly called affluent, could never afford. She was engaged by a rich city banker, whom we may call Mr Kastner, to live with his family and give piano lessons to his two daughters, Amanda and Charlotte, who were in their late teens and had finished their general education; she had also to take them to concerts and the opera and talk French, German, and Italian with them. It was perhaps the most tranquil time in my mother's life.

445

The family had a house in Belgravia and a country place in the South Downs with a great park full of splendid trees and far views, which my mother always remembered with delight.

It happened that the mother of her pupils was a very unhappy woman. She came from the southern states of America. She was thus three thousand miles from her own relatives, and her husband suffered from an internal malady which made him irritable and morose; and he had alienated most of his family by his temper. The arrival of my mother, gifted, witty, full of vitality, and kind, was a godsend to her. Mrs Kastner was very sad indeed when after three years or so my mother's own family reclaimed her, and the two women never lost touch with each other. When my mother was left a penniless widow with three children, Mrs Kastner immediately made her an allowance, not a large one, for she had little money of her own, but it was all she could do and it meant a great deal to us.

But only a short time afterwards she died. My mother had wept for the loss of a friend, and later had been chilled by the thought that in the future she was going to be poorer. But then the elder Kastner daughter, Amanda, who had been my godmother, wrote and announced her intention of continuing the allowance. This was remarkably kind. She had married late, a man not at all rich, whom I shall call Bolton, who was working as a not very successful cattle-breeder in South America. She had inherited no great fortune from her father, whose fortunes had declined in his last years. My mother exclaimed at Amanda's generosity and refused it, but resolutely Amanda had sent the allowance as before through a London solicitor.

Now, when I was thirteen, my godmother and her family had returned from South America and had settled in the Midlands, and I was eager to see her.

I had so often between sleeping and waking seen these four women, dressed in the be-bustled fashions of the eighties, pacing a lawn under great cedars or resting on the seat under the beech tree at the turn of the high path where a break in the downs showed a blue triangle of distant sea. Mrs Kastner I saw as a melancholy and graceful woman, an ageing Mariana in the Moated Grange. Charlotte was faceless for me because I knew nothing about her, she was an invalid who lived in Switzerland, but Amanda was very visible. I saw her bland as her name, like a Jane Austen character, but with a Brontëan nobility, which I imputed to her because it had been impressed on me that to continue our allowance after her mother's death she must be making sacrifices. I knew that when my sister and I visited her in the Midlands we would see her in a very different setting. But I expected some of the glory of that setting to have clung to her.

My sister and I were nervous as we travelled down from Edinburgh towards the Midlands. We knew the Boltons would be poor, but they certainly would not be as poor as we were. We never came across anybody who was as poor as we were. We therefore had to take it for granted that they would think our clothes were awful. But we also took it for granted that my godmother's family would be too nice to mind about them. But if there were visitors they might not be so nice. This, I must explain, was a real point. In those days there were no attractive cheap ready-made clothes. If you were poor you had to wear clothes run up by sewing-women, and you looked terrible. But on the other hand I was aware we had a trump card to play. My sister Winifred was very beautiful, in the style of an early Victorian beauty, with smooth chestnut hair and an oval face and regular features. It seemed to me that if people asked two girls they had never seen to stay with them they would be bound to be pleased if one of them turned up looking like Winifred.

For the rest, we wondered what the talk would be about; we had grown up in air thick with conversation about literature, politics, music, painting. I took it for granted that we would step into a house where people were discussing their pet ideas, and imagined that, as we would arrive in the evening, they would be engaged in an argument, probably with the reference books got out.

It was not at all like that. To begin with, we were disconcerted by the landscape. We knew London, we knew Edinburgh, we knew the superb hill ranges of Lowland Scotland and the lochs and mountains of the Highlands. But we had never before been in country which, no matter in what direction one looked, one saw nothing but flat fields and hedges. We could not think why my godmother and her husband should have chosen to live in such a god-forsaken corner of the country, as the dog-cart carried us along five flat miles to the house.

This was pleasant. It was one of those comfortable rectories that were built in the second half of the eighteenth century. But once we entered the house we received a shock. We were met by a big, bouncing woman in dull clothes who uttered words of mechanical welcome without taking the smallest trouble to pretend that she meant them.

We wondered why the godmother we imagined should have such a dreary person in her house, and then the authority in her voice as she spoke to the groom warned us that this was Amanda. Her eyes ran over us and did not seem to notice anything special about my sister's appearance. She asked us how our mother was and before we could answer turned away and told a housemaid to take us to our rooms. My sister insisted on delaying for a moment to give her the presents my mother had sent her, the classic Edinburgh presents, shortbread and Edinburgh rock. Mrs Bolton made the proper acknowledgements but her manner expressed a conviction that whatever it was that we had brought her it could not interest her.

Our visit lasted a fortnight and at no time was my godmother much more gracious to us, nor was her husband, nor were her children. Two guests arrived, two young women in their late twenties, daughters of relatives. I realize now, from my recollection of remarks which my godmother and her husband exchanged over our heads that these girls were in the miserable plight which befell Edwardian young women who failed to marry in their first youth and were not very well off. They would never have married at all if they had gone out to work, so they either sat at home doing nothing or bumping round the country staying with friends who were doing nothing, quite simply waiting and hoping. I then felt no pity for their humiliating lot. We had hoped they would give us some companionship, but when they arrived they whispered together in corners and glowered at us, particularly at my poor pretty sister. They quite rudely stared at our clothes, they were indeed sometimes rude in words, so rude that my sister and I did not like to speak to each other about it. But once my sister said to me, when we had taken refuge in our bedrooms, "Well, it's probably true, that bit about Lady Blanche being so rude to Jane Eyre."

Nobody in the whole house was agreeable to us except the nursery governess, a gay little creature. Everybody seemed in favour of our alliance with her, and we understood why when we took some flowers down to the church and the vicar's wife said, "Ah, yes, you're the old governess' children, aren't you." This put us in a psychologically difficult position. From a snobbish point of view, my sister and I were at least as well-born as my godmother. But we couldn't resent this classification of us because our whole disposition was to consider such a distinction absurd, and we hadn't the slightest wish to dissociate ourselves from the dear little nursery governess.

It was not only such incivilities which irked us. One day a newcomer to the district, the wife of an engineer employed on some large construction near by, a reservoir, came to return my godmother's call. She was amazingly beautiful. I am not wrong about that, for I was to come across her a few years later in circumstances which proved it. She went on the stage and George Bernard Shaw and Granville-Barker put her into the first production of *Androcles and the Lion* as a flower-seller who was to go to and fro at the back of the stage offering her wares to a crowd while the actors talked to each other in the front of the stage. Shaw and Barker had to take her out of the part because as long as she was on the stage the audience paid no attention to the actors.

My sister and I were fascinated, and sat with our eyes and our ears open, for she was a delightful talker. When she left my sister and I were deputed to go and help her get her little donkey-cart out into the road, and once out of the house my sister dared to say to her, "You're not English, are you?"

"No, I'm Russian." This was something tremendous. Then, not less than now, Russia was the country of mysterious enchantment. But she did better than that. She added, "Before I married I was Vera Tchaikovsky." "Not ...?" "His niece." We chattered until the donkey brayed with impatience and she had to go. Was St Petersburg as marvellously beautiful as people said? Did she know the wonderful people at the Conservatory of Music in St Petersburg? Did she know Rubinstein? Had she read Gorky? He was just then bursting on the world of the young in England. When she had finally left we hurried back to the drawing-room to make known our marvellous discovery. Dead faces looked at us and not a word was spoken. I have recalled that moment every time I have come across the lines, "Like a party in a parlour, all silent and all damned." Then my godmother said, "Well, whoever she may be, she was returning a first call; she should have stayed only twenty minutes, and she stayed forty."

Sometimes the household mollified me by amusing me. Once, when my godmother's husband seemed less surly than usual, I tried, delicately, to find out why they lived in that particular flat and unexciting part of England. He explained that he and his wife had chosen to live there because it was hunting country. "Oh, do you hunt?" I asked. "But where are the horses?" No, he didn't hunt. He had long ago suffered an injury to his leg which prevented him from doing more than sit a horse. "I see. You like to be with people who hunt." No, the hunting set round there had not much use for people who didn't hunt. He didn't see much of them. "But you like to be where

449

hunting is going on?" Yes, that was it. This tickled me; so might a devout old lady who was bedridden choose to live near a cathedral so that she could hear the chimes. To keep the conversation going I went on, "But I suppose you hunted a great deal at one time." No. He had injured his leg at his preparatory school. He had never hunted at all. I still think that such abstract piety, such reverence for the mere idea of hunting, was very funny.

They were sometimes funny and they were good. I realized that, for it became clear that the allowance they made my mother did inconvenience them to some extent. They were able to live in a comfortable house with a cook, a butler, a housemaid, a knife-boy, a groom, and a gardener. But on the other hand they were not even able to go and stay in London as often as they would have liked, much less go abroad. And I was so deeply familiar with the technique of poverty in my own home that I recognized it elsewhere. The carpets here and the curtains and the loose covers all needed replacing. I felt guilty and grateful.

But they would not let me feel just that. They were, as it proved, too rude. One morning they were going to a neighbouring town to conclude some business with a solicitor, and had to take an early train. They had left the breakfast room when I came down. When they were all ready to leave in the dog-cart they sent in a message to ask me if I would care to drive with them to the station. I put on my coat and hat and hurried out and took my place on the high seat beside the groom, and immediately passed into an unexpected ecstasy. It was quite early in the morning. The rabbits were still out in the fields. There had been rain in the night and now there was sun, and the grass was shining like wet paint and the flooded dykes were like blue crystal. Above us there was a tremendous sky-battle of what we at home called clouds-of-war, and the wind was fresh as if it had come straight off the sea. The horse was a lovely little cob a rich relative had given my godmother, and it brought down its hooves on the roadway as if it thought it was playing a percussion instrument in a band. I had never enjoyed anything much more in my life, and I remember regretting that my sister was not there.

When we got to the station the groom slipped off the seat and ran to open the dog-cart door, and I hastened to clamber down so that I could thank my godmother for the treat. But before I got to the ground they had walked past me towards the platform, as if I were not there. I had opened my mouth to thank them, and it remained open. I stared at them to see if I had offended them, but it was not that. Their faces were not tense. They simply could not be bothered to say good-bye to me, they could not be bothered to recognize the presence of someone who meant nothing to them, who was both a child and the child of an unimportant person. I told myself that I must have made a mistake. Perhaps people didn't say good-bye to each other in such circumstances. But the groom sucked in his breath through his teeth, and I had the final shame of knowing that he thought they were being very rude to me and had probably seen that I was having hard work not to cry.

Through tears of rage I stared at the two square, unyielding, un-genial figures standing on the platform beside a cluster of milk churns, with hatred in my heart. But it was soon displaced. I found there was something more interesting to do than hate my godmother. I remember my mind sliding out towards her, palpating her character with my mind as a surgeon's hand palpates his patient's body. What was the pattern of this curious woman's attributes? She was a boor and she had behaved boorishly to me; she behaved boorishly to every-body not in her family, so far as I could see; she was so unresponsive to human beings that she remained unmoved when a beautiful niece of Tchaikovsky strayed in sparkling from the Leicestershire lanes. How on earth did it happen that she was giving my mother an allowance she could ill afford? She was even, I perceived, trying to do more than that. She certainly had planned no pleasure for herself when she invited my sister and myself to stay with her.

She must have been moved by benevolence. But what could be the nature of the benevolent impulse which took the curious form of inviting children to her house to insult their powerlessness? I felt, I remember, excited at the spectacle of such inconsistencies, I felt greedy for some revelation which would make me able to account for them. Of course I never did. I was to learn later that though she seemed incapable of emotion, she had deeply cared for her children; she broke her heart when one of them died. There was also a moving explanation for her generosity to my mother. It seemed that she had passionately loved her mother, and had resented her father's treat-ment of her, with such warmth that years afterwards, she was willing to impose sacrifices on herself in order to give my mother some reward for having given *her* mother two or three years of happiness. She was in fact far more loving than the bland Amanda I had visual-ized walking on the lawn. But how could she love a woman as gracious as Mrs Kastner must have been, from all accounts, without absorbing any of her graciousness? How could such love exist without creating some loveliness? But even in her ungraciousness, she had charm, for she had her own mystery, as each human being does. My writing is about that.

A Grave and Reverend Book

From *Harper's Magazine* (New York, February 1966).

"In Cold Blood" by Truman Capote.
Random House, New York.

It is to Mr Capote's disadvantage that every book he writes turns into what our great grandmothers used to call "a pretty book." He knows that ours is a bloodstained planet but he knows also that it turns on its axis and moves round the sun with a dancer's grace, and his style defines the dancer as ballet-trained. For this reason Mr Capote is often not taken as seriously as he should be, and it is possible that his new book, *In Cold Blood*, may be regarded simply as a literary *tour de force* instead of the formidable statement about reality which it is.

In six long years Mr Capote crawled like an ant of genius over the landscape where, on a November night in 1959, a prosperous Kansas farmer, his wife, his daughter of sixteen, and his son of fifteen were murdered by two ex-convicts, who gained only forty or fifty dollars by the slaughter. That Mr Capote has invented nothing and recorded with a true ear and utter honesty is proved by the conversations in the book. The inhabitants of Holcomb, Kansas, do not on any page engage in the subtle and economical dialogue Mr Capote ascribes to the characters in his novels. They speak the words which reporters hear when they interview the participants in prodigious events, and listen to with embarrassed ears. The stuff is corny, yet not just corny. The corn is celestial. Even the cleverest writer who tries to invent it achieves an obvious fakery, which is quite absent from this book.

If there be one point in this book more admirable than another, it is its treatment of a certain technical difficulty. Some years ago I wrote for *The New Yorker* an account of a peculiarly sordid murder in which a man dropped a dismembered corpse from a plane onto a sea marsh, where it was discovered by a fisherman.* When I went to see the fisherman, I found that he and his family were people of acute intelligence, so acute that they could, had they chosen, have been as aggressive and complicated and self-seeking as the worst of us. But they had made another choice. They did one a great kindness by talking to one, they gave one a share in a strong, unpriggish, gracious sort of peace they had made for themselves. I could not get these people down on paper as I got the man who had thrown the corpse out of the plane. I perceived that for me, at any rate, it was not so easy to write about the dynamically good as about the dynamically bad. Immodestly, I did not leave it there. Thinking it over, I reflected that the schizophrenic character of *Paradise Lost*, its fundamental unease, is due to Milton's surprise at finding that throughout his epic Satan kept on coming up as more interesting than God. As Milton was 90 per cent pure writer and a raging egotist he imagined that this aesthetic situation had moral implications. I also reflected that since Bach's "Sheep May Safely Graze" hardly anybody had written music so serene without toppling over into *schmaltz*. I thought I had discovered a limitation likely to apply to the writers of our time.

But Mr Capote represents the victims of the murder as brilliant, powerful, and important in their goodness. Mr Clutter was a gifted and able man, an expert in the elaborate techniques of modern farming, his vision of the material world so clear and his mastery over it so assured that it might well have been his sole interest. But he was a just man, who knew that the only true justice is mercy, and a kind, unstinting man to whom giving people a fair chance was a quiet kind of pleasure. True, he had his chilling aspects. His contracts with his employees were voidable if they were "harboring alcohol" as one might say "harboring vermin" or "harboring diseases." But Mr Capote convinces us that the dead man's puritanism was a long-term scheme for enjoyment. If he kept a rein on his daughter Nancy, it was only because he wanted a future for her which would match her perfection.

As for Nancy, it took great courage on the part of Mr Capote to set down the fact of her angelic radiance. Deliciously pretty, she was president of her class and a leader of the 4-H program, she won prizes at the county fair for pastry and preserves and needlework, and in

*[*Mr Setty and Mr Hume*, See p. 260 in this volume.]

the last hours of her life she taught little Jolene how to make cherry pie in her incomparable way, coached little Roxie Lee at her trumpet solo for the school concert, got on with her bridesmaids' dresses for her absent sister's approaching wedding, and, as always, got on with the family chores. Worse still, for the playroom she shared with her brother she embroidered cushions with the legends "Happy?" and "You Don't Have To Be Crazy To Live Here But It Helps." She did not cross herself and murmur the words, "Pop Art," before committing this dreadful act. She did it cold.

Nevertheless, when the community lost the Clutters it was as if there had suddenly vanished from the district some natural feature which also served a practical purpose, say a mountain lake which had also provided a water supply. Yet the family labored under a handicap. Mrs Clutter was a melancholic, a weeping wraith, given to periods of inassuageable grief and delusions of intense cold which persisted throughout sweltering summers. Mr Clutter and his daughter and son were joined together to protect the poor woman from her misery, to protect each other from this invasion of the abnormal, and to go on giving the community what it needed from them, in spite of this drain on their resources. All this Mr Capote does not merely tell the reader, he proves it, and without a shade of *schmaltz*.

The two murderers were drawn to the Clutters' home because its beneficence had so impressed the twilit mind of a convict that he made a symbol for it in a wholly imaginary safe stuffed with dollars. He had babbled of this to Richard Hickock, whom he had known in prison, the younger of the two murderers, and the simpler character. Hickock had only two serious cases against his life. First, he had been born into the grinding poverty of a poor farm; but his parents were affectionate and agreeable, and he had ample intelligence to work himself up to a good level of living. Second, at nineteen an automobile accident had spoiled what had been considerable good looks. But there was an abnormality in him which predated his accident. When he was a boy, a neighbor's son had come back from a holiday on the Gulf Coast with a collection of shells. These he had stolen, and hammered one by one into dust. "Envy," writes Mr Capote, "was constantly with him; the Enemy was anyone who was someone he wanted to be or who had anything he wanted to have." As he appears in *In Cold Blood* he is the most complete study I can remember of the spite which makes a certain sort of criminal, such as the men whose entries in the card index of burglars of Scotland Yard are of a special color, because they make a practice, when they have neatly packed up their loot, of defecating on the best carpet on the premises.

The other murderer, Perry Smith, was worse because he was better. He was a physical oddity, with the torso of an athlete and stunted legs, so that he stood no taller than a twelve-year-old child. He had a hideous life, being born into a family disrupted by misfortune, and subjected during his childhood to institutional experiences which, whether they were as he recalled them, filled him with resentment. He spent some time in the merchant marine, and went with the Army to Korea and Japan, where he piled up a crime sheet, returned to the United States, and was injured in an automobile accident far worse than Hickock's, which seven years after left him with agonizing pains in his legs and made him an aspirin addict. He drifted into crime, and was soon in a penitentiary. His only brother and one of his two sisters committed suicide.

He was half-Cherokee and had a dark charm; he was literate, read verse, was musical, loved his guitar, cultivated his sensitiveness, and bore himself according to the rumor of the romantic tradition which had reached him from far-off. And his woe was real. He had, Mr Capote tells us, "the aura of an exiled animal, a creative walking wounded." He excites pity as Hickock does not. Yet he was far more dreadful, as Mr Capote admits with heroically honest detachment. If one asks why he was so dreadful, the answer seems to be that he was guilty of a sin which is the spiritual equivalent of usury. He exploited all his misfortunes to the full; he laid them out with cool prudence to bring in the heaviest possible yield of pity: he came to love pity too much. He coveted the precious substance more and more, he could not bear anyone else to get any, he wanted all there was in the world. He became infinitely cruel, as was shown in his relations with his father.

That poor wretch had had as sad a life as his son. He was a rodeo performer who had married a Cherokee Bronco rider in the same show. They were both cut down by illness when the family were still little children, and both had to leave the show. Smith had nothing to fall back on in the waning West during the Depression but such obsolete arts as bear-skinning; and at the same time his wife had become a drunkard, a prostitute, a maniac, and died a disgusting death. He loved his children and was horrified when two of them committed suicide, and he finally became eccentric. Perry could not

455

forgive him. It was his father's duty to be happy, so that he could provide his son with happiness.

Perry's inhumanity was exhibited also in his relations with his one surviving sister, Barbara, who had burrowed her way out of the family hell and made a good life out of a modest marriage. She understood her brother well, and uttered a very competent analysis of one of his characteristics, the generalized sensitiveness of the romantic:

He can seem so warm-hearted and sympathetic. Gentle. He cries so easily. Sometimes music sets him off and when he was a little boy he used to cry because he thought a sunset was beautiful. Or the moon. Oh, he can fool you. He can make you feel so sorry for him.

She might have said worse, for he had committed a considerable offence against her. He had sent her a young girl, with a letter saying that this was his twenty-year-old wife, and asking that she be looked after as he was in trouble. After a day or two the girl (who was in fact fourteen and nobody's wife) departed with her hosts' suitcases, crammed with their clothes, their silver, and the kitchen clock. Nevertheless when Perry was in prison Barbara wrote him a long, clumsy, touching, unhappy, loving letter, asking him not to blame his father for his misfortunes and to get on with his life. He kept it only because of the "very sensitive" commentary on it which was written in pidgin psychologese by a fellow prisoner, an Irish tenor who had spent twenty years in prison for dismal little thefts, and thought nothing of Barbara. Perry loved jargon; he kept a little notebook, full of rare words, such as "thanatoid" and "amerce." Also he loved contempt. He was an inveterate moralizer. Almost any act committed by any person other than himself provoked him to sneering condemnation on high ethical grounds.

Perry was to exhibit this holier-than-thou attitude very strongly in the death house. To an Army buddy, a saintly young man, who visited him out of Christian charity, he explained he felt no remorse for murdering the Clutters:

It's easy to kill—a lot easier than passing a bad check. Just remember, I only knew the Clutters maybe an hour. If I'd really known them, I guess I'd feel different. I don't think I could live with myself. But the way it was, it was like picking off targets in a shooting gallery.

But he had prefaced these blank and icy words by a brief exercise of his talent for moralizing on a subject which never ceased to shock him.

Soldiers don't lose much sleep. They murder, and get medals for doing it. The good people of Kansas want to murder me and some hangman will be glad to get the work.

He could not get over the disgusting barbarism which made the inhabitants of the State of Kansas retain capital punishment on their statute book and voluntarily incur the blood guilt of hanging him. Yet it was he who had killed all four Clutters. Hickock had conspired with him to kill them, but Perry confessed that it was he who had cut Mr Clutter's throat and shot the others. Before Perry got to the death house he had reason to know that he had not been attacked by a unique and unrepeated impulse. Twice after the murder he and Hickock had stood in the highway and thumbed a lift from prosperous drivers, meaning to rob and murder them. The first stopped, gave them a look over, did not like what he saw, and drove on. The second, when the rock was already neatly packed in the handkerchief to crash down on his skull, was saved by his own good nature. With two hitchhikers in his automobile, he suddenly stopped for a third, a Negro soldier. Yet to the end Perry looked down on the citizens of Kansas because they found themselves capable of killing him. "I don't believe in capital punishment, morally or legally," he said on the gallows. What bourgeois today could achieve such a fine flower of hypocrisy? Tartuffe still lives, but has changed his address.

In Cold Blood leaves us asking whether the waste of these six lives could have been avoided by a society which had the wits and was willing to take the pains. Some elements in the tragedy are beyond our control. Nothing in Hickock's origin or upbringing explains his spite, and Perry Smith's situation explains his all too well. It is one of the few notable omissions in the book that Mr Capote does not tell us if he found any material in the California child-welfare files to throw any light on the degree to which Perry was helped or abandoned in his childhood. One can imagine that he would have been as hard to help as a trapped animal. For the rest, the trial of the two was consonant with the law. Hickock was hanged for murder which he had not committed, when he should have been sentenced to a term of imprisonment as an accessory, but this was his own fault. The truth could only be established if both he and Perry chose to give evidence, but this, for a reason Mr Capote does not explain, they did not do.

This curious abstinence is a proof of the irrelevance of capital punishment. The prospect of hanging could never have acted as a deterrent to these two men who were, to use a word from Perry Smith's little book, obstinately thanatoid. They were obsessed with death.

Yet society had its blame to carry. As companions in the death house Hickock and Perry had two very handsome boys, one eighteen, one nineteen, one with a background like Perry's, the other from a home in every way fortunate. They had gone on a ten days' murder jag round the South, killing four men and three women, one a little motel waitress of eighteen. None of these people had done anything against them, one man had stopped to ask if their automobile had broken down and if he could help them; the little girl had let them sleep with her. When the boys were asked why they had butchered these people, they explained the world was rotten and to kill people was to do them a favor. "We hate the world," they smiled from the local television screen. One is aware of a process which Mr Capote has constantly demonstrated during his superb exposition of the doom shared by Hickock and Perry Smith: the seeping of a certain literary tradition through society from the top to the bottom.

It is within the knowledge of all of us that life is often hard to bear. But it has oddly happened that our society, which is, if not perfect, at least more generally comfortable than any society has succeeded in being before, has produced a literature quite often taking as its basis the pretence that life is quite unbearable. This pretence is behind some good plays and novels and some bad ones. A work of art does not have to be completely valid either in its facts or in its philosophy, so it may share imperfection with books and plays which cannot be classed as works of art at all. This pretence that life is unbearable is not accepted as literally true by any but a minute number of readers or writers; very few people commit suicide. However it is widely adopted as an intellectual counter, not an opinion which one sincerely holds and would act upon, but which one uses as a substitute for opinion when talking or writing, like the chips one uses when gambling at casinos. It then passes into general currency, in films, on television, in chatter, and so it happens that one day a naïve person with stronger dramatic instincts than most, and less sense of self-preservation, comes to believe that sophisticated people believe life to be unbearable, and therefore it is not terrible to carry the belief to its logical conclusion and to deprive his fellow-men of their lives. When society shows its horror the murderer feels himself lifted into the distinction so difficult to attain in our vast societies: he is one of the few strong and logical people in a community of weaklings afraid to act up to their beliefs.

What air do these people breathe not permeated with the culture we have made? Where else could they have caught this infection but from us? There is a hateful continuity between the world of literature and the world of Mr Capote's criminals. Hickock bought an expensive gun on credit from the store beside his parents' home, took it with him to the Clutters' house, where it did its work, took it back to his parents' home, and abandoned it there. They, thinking he had used it only once on a pheasant shoot, tried to get the storekeeper to take it back, but he refused, and they had to pay for it. At all times they were poverty-stricken and his father was dying of cancer. It is depressing to recognize how easily this episode would find a home in fiction. It would work in nicely to a certain kind of Roman Catholic novel, in which God would find the ripe sinnerhood of Hickock far preferable to the insipid Pelagian virtue of his parents. It would be warmly welcomed in a violence cult novel, which would maintain that the murder of the Clutters would extend the experience of the murderers so far beyond ordinary limits that they would rank as supermen, and the parents could be regarded as serfs justly paying tribute to their lords. It would also find a place in the physical-horror type of novel, which would revel in Hickock's father's cancer and Perry's habit of bed-wetting. Literature must go its own way, sometimes a blessing to its age, sometimes a curse: for no soothsayer can ever predict when it is going to be the one or the other. All the same, there are occasions when it is comprehensible why Plato felt fear lest the poets corrupt the minds of the people. But at any rate nothing but blessing can flow from Mr Capote's grave and reverend book.

And They All Lived Unhappily Ever After

From *The Times Literary Supplement* (London, July 26, 1974):
Women and Literature—1

Mutual understanding has never been the strong point of the sexes—an opinion it would be advisable to check by reference to the work of women imaginative writers. The restriction is necessary, for non-fiction always tends to become fiction; only the dream compels honesty. We have an elegant sufficiency of women novelists, and they give us a great deal of evidence which will enable us to make up our minds whether the feminist pioneers have been disappointed in their hope that, if women were admitted to the universities and the professions and commerce and industry, and exercised the vote and were eligible for both Houses of Parliament, they would not only be able to earn their own livings and develop their minds and live candidly, but might also be luckier in love than their mothers and grandmothers, and would take it better if they were unlucky. But this evidence is not forthcoming. After a course of study in Contemporary Women Novelists it is as if one heard a massed female choir singing, "Early one morning, just as the sun was rising, I heard a maid sing in the valley below, 'Oh, don't deceive me, oh, never leave me, how could you use a poor maiden so?' "

The deception is of all sorts and degrees. Consider the characters of Edna O'Brien, May Queens whose May Days are always rainy. Their misadventures are not trivial and they leave bitterness because they are a breach of faith. It was a waste of time for all these convent girls to spend years throwing off their inhibitions in order to plunge into the permissive society, if men were not going to avail themselves of it. They thought that the men who had imposed the inhibitions were different from the ones who had joined the permissive society. But they were the same men, with the same cold streak in them, and that cold streak was still getting all the fun it used to get out of imposing inhibitions; only now the mechanism involved teasing, ill-nature, and speedy desertion. A cell is more honest than a forsaken bedroom; it always made it clear that one would sleep alone.

It might be that Miss O'Brien's rural background explains why her gay and pretty girls were such easy marks for deceiving and leaving; but Margaret Drabble's academic and urban environment has produced much the same results. Her Cinderella is led by her fairy godmother through the prams in the hall and out to the pumpkin coach and on to the castle, where Prince Charming obliges with the classic reaction, makes her his shining bride, and then baulks at the end, which surely is the real point of the story. He does not want to live happily ever after. Yet not only did he say that that was what he wanted, it is impossible to imagine a sane man not wanting it; but there he is, running away, as if what he was escaping was eternal misery.

It would be wrong to write down Miss Drabble's case against the world as anything like as simple as that. She is too rich-minded to harp monotonously on one theme. But all through her books it can be seen that she recognizes and sympathizes with (though she would not approve) the peculiar mathematics which apply to many cases of desertion. A woman who loses her husband or lover often seems to lose more by his absence than she ever gained by his presence. Perhaps it is that before such women lived in the company of men they did not recognize their own loneliness because they had never known anything else, and on meeting it a second time they realized its nature down to the primal root.

This process can be seen in Penelope Mortimer's *Long Distance*, which puts its main character into a clinic, after she has been thrown off balance by the break-up of her marriage and her home. One finds oneself muttering as one reads, "Come now, it cannot have made all that difference to you that he is not around." But that is what the book is about, excessive grief, and Mrs Mortimer has an interesting view of it. If the pain left by an experience is so great that it destroys the coherence of the mind which suffered it, then that pain and incoherence are a judgement on the experience, delivered by the only person qualified to judge it. Normality, resumed at the request of a community which simply wants not to be bothered, enters a false judgement; and such compliances build up an immense lie about life.

This is possibly true; but what a relief it is that we do not have to consider this problem in the world of Doris Lessing. This splendid figure may be styled the English George Sand. Like her, Mrs Lessing would try anything twice, and her strength is as the strength of ten— she would certainly object if it were claimed that this was because her heart was pure in any mawkish sense. She is not as elegant a writer as her counterpart; she could not write any equivalent of that passage in *La Comtesse de Rudolstadt* which the fastidious critic Alain pronounced to be the crystallization of the romantic view of love. But both women have the same Mississippian flow of being, which it is hardly possible to separate into the intellectual and the physical; this forceful tide bears with it whatever useful material happens to be lying about on the territory it washes, and bears it on to the wide estuary and shoreless sea of our general culture. Should one wish to know how the French intellectuals of the early nineteenth century regarded the movement of the Slav states of the Austro-Hungarian Empire, one has to read George Sand's *Consuelo* and its sequel. Should one wish to learn the nature of the Compagnons de la Route, the organization which bridged the time-gulf between the medieval guilds and the modern trade unions, George Sand wrote a novel on the subject. As for Mrs Lessing, social historians of the future will be grateful to her for her case-histories of the effect on the average man, who picks up his thoughts when and where he can, of ideas—such as psychoanalysis and Marxism—worked out by specialist scholars of intelligence much superior to his own, often in totally different environments, and, what is more, at a time long past. She can throw light on the byways of history, telling us how the dissident European intellectuals, forced out to Africa by the wartime fragmentation of the Continent, practised a routine which exasperated the indigenous population by continuing to hold pedantic study circles, as if they were still in Amsterdam or Geneva, very much as colonists of another sort used to change for dinner.

It is a culminating disappointment that such a formidable woman, who can carry about with her such a heavy intellectual satchel and has conquered the difficulties of self-support, plainly cannot believe that women can hope for satisfactory sexual lives. That, indeed, she seems to regard as the most depressing feature of the modern world. The general impression given in most of her books is that men reject women for reasons they cannot understand, terminating sexual relationships which appeared to be satisfactory and companionship which they appeared to enjoy. It is not that all of these women expected to be given financial support or a place in society, for many could provide those requirements for themselves, and it might be apparent to all of them that some men could provide neither. It is not even that all of the women expected the commitment of the man to a per-

462

manent relationship. Rather is it that a certain scene is re-enacted, which might take this form: The man comes into the kitchen, suffused for her by a delightful atmosphere caused by recent embraces and continuing friendship, and says, "Please cut me some bread and butter, remembering that I like the bread very thin and the butter very thick." But he gives her no time to sharpen the bread-knife, so the bread is rather thick, and he comments on this though he is silent about the abundance of butter. The only explanation of this behaviour (irrational if only because of his declared liking for butter) is that men do not like women. But perhaps that last phrase should be written "that men do not like." It is possible that men are deficient in the capacity for love, and that women too suffer from the same deficiency, but had to hide it in the days of their subordination, and would in any case be least likely to exercise it in their times of sexual flowering, when things were going best for them. But these are account-books which can never be balanced. All we can do to dam this source of suffering is to love more and hate less; and this leads me to Iris Murdoch and her preoccupation with goodness.

Miss Murdoch exercises a unique fascination on the reading public of today, because she has formed an ambitious plan, which many would find rebarbative if they were not prepared for it, and she has devised a brilliant technique for preparing them. The standard beginning of a Murdoch novel might show a deplorable house in a deplorable street in a deplorable suburb; on the first floor, two middle-aged people, worse than plain, are engaged in copulation (though the physical defects their creator has lavished on them deprive their embraces of any erotic significance and recall rather the problems topologists deal with, such as the one about the possibility of turning a doughnut inside out); on the second floor is someone also plain, wearing repulsive underclothes, who has either just succeeded or failed in committing suicide; and on the third floor an adolescent boy, deaf and dumb (but, as is shown later in the book, extraordinarily attractive to homosexuals), is skinning a goat.

This fantasy gets the reader nicely off the fish-hook of naturalism. One is transported into a world which is not our world but an interpretation of it, and one watches events that are a commentary, inspired by a sense of eternity, on actions performed in time. To facilitate the presentation, Miss Murdoch often builds her stories round happenings the like of which can be found in Russian novels and which are known as "scandals." A group of people is shown in a

463

state of rest, which is suddenly terminated by the setting-up of an action, unexpected and probably of arguable legitimacy, by members of the group. Once the group is in a state of motion it suffers irreversible moral and intellectual changes so that when it settles into a state of rest again it is new in substance and it can be said that, by little or by much, the universe is not the same.

The "scandals" in Miss Murdoch's work are sometimes regarded as an attempt to rectify the disorder of human affairs by imposing on it the order dreamt of by the philosophers; and it is not to be doubted that they have a spiritual significance for Miss Murdoch in the satisfaction with which she chronicles the diminution of the riot and the restoration of a peace more peaceful than before. But care has to be taken in recognizing this feature of Miss Murdoch's work not to do injustice to the past. The philosophic search for order was not unconnected with the "happy ending," which novelists have used since the beginning of their art, and is sometimes wishful thinking of the crudest sort and sometimes a real celebration of harmony. Miss Murdoch's lectures on philosophy, published under the title *The Sovereignty of Good*, show that she feels the same personal affection for the idea of goodness that Conrad, who was no great philosopher, felt for the idea of honour. This dedication gives her an authority that does not often come to novelists who will not trouble to be lucid.

Yet that same volume contains a passage which makes one doubt if Miss Murdoch possesses the ultimate virtue of the novelist. She writes in convincing style about goodness, but about good men she writes:

We realize that on reflection we know little about good men. There are men in history who are traditionally thought of as having been good (Christ, Socrates, certain saints), but if we try to contemplate them we find that the information about them is scanty and vague, and that, their great moments apart, it is the simplicity and directness of their diction which chiefly colours our conception of them as good. And if we consider contemporary candidates for goodness, if we know of any, we are likely to find them obscure, or else on closer inspection full of frailty. Goodness appears to be both rare and hard to picture. It is perhaps most convincingly met with in simple people—inarticulate, unselfish mothers of large families—but these cases are also the least illuminating.

Now this is most alarming. Even if the passage is written with irony, it is still alarming, for the irony would be wasted: few people's observations are so poor. From the time we are children we know that the

464

people round about us are good or bad. Cousin Jessie is good, Aunt Sophie is bad. We go on making judgements throughout life. It is our first source of self-help and self-defence of a psychological kind, and as we grow older and like ourselves less and less we apply our critical experience as a basis for criticizing our consciences. And surely we set store by life largely because of the good, or partially good, men and women we have known.

There is a remarkable novel published recently by A. L. Barker called A *Source of Embarrassment*, a novel as good perhaps as any of the novels written by the contemporaries here noted. It is a book about a good woman whose goodness is an embarrassment to her and her family, and becomes more so when it enables her to accept her approaching death from inoperable cancer. The book is written drily, without partisanship; the vulgar are allowed to speak their piece. It is also a completely acceptable book; the cultures of the world have not laboured without success in restating the need for more love and less hate. What is true is worth saying over and over again.

It is the time-scales of the universe which put us all wrong. A baby takes nine months to bring to birth, and a woman can have a baby a year; yet it will take centuries before the sexual life of a woman, which produced these babies with such speed, becomes guaranteed against the humiliation and insecurity described by contemporary women novelists. But we were never promised otherwise.

V. LATER FICTION

Parthenope

My Uncle Arthur had red hair that lay close to his head in flat, circular curls, and a pointed red beard, and his blue-green eyes were at once penetrating and bemused. He was the object of mingled derision and respect in our family. He was a civil servant who had early attracted attention by his brilliance; but the chief of his department, like so many English civil servants, was an author in his spare time, and when he published a history of European literature, my uncle reviewed it in the leading weekly of the day, pointing out that large as was the number of works in the less familiar languages that his chief supposed to be written in prose, though in fact they were written in verse, it was not so large as the number of such works that he supposed to be written in verse, though in fact they were written in prose. He wrote without malice, simply thinking his chief would be glad to know. My uncle never connected this review with his subsequent failure to gain a promotion that had seemed certain, or to have the day as snug as civil servants usually had it in the nineteenth century. But in the course of time his chief died, and my uncle rose to be an important official. However, he did a Cabinet Minister much the same service he had rendered his chief, and he never received the title that normally went with his post.

So he seesawed through life, and I liked his company very much when he was an old man and I was a young girl, for it was full of surprises. When I asked him a question, I never knew if his answer would show that he knew far less than I did or far more; and though he was really quite old, for he was my father's elder by many years, he often made discoveries such as a schoolchild might make, and shared them with an enthusiasm as little adult. One day he gave me no peace till I had come with him to see the brightest field of buttercups he had ever found near London; it lay, solid gold, beside the great Jacobean mansion Ham House, by the river Thames. After we had admired it he took me to nearby Petersham Church, to see another treasure, the tomb of Captain Vancouver, who gave his name to the island; my uncle liked this tomb because he had spent some years of his boyhood in Canada and had been to Vancouver Island when it was hardly inhabited. Then we had tea in an inn garden and it happened that the girl who waited on us was called away by the landlord as she set the china on the table. His voice came from the kitchen: "Parthenope! Parthenope!" My uncle started, for no very good reason that I could see. There had been a time when many ships in the British Navy were called after characters in Greek history and mythology, male and female, and therefore many sailors' daughters had been given the names of nymphs and goddesses and Homeric princesses and heroines of Greek tragedy. The only strange thing was that it was a long time since British ships had been christened so poetically, and most of the women who had acquired these classical names by this secondary interest were by now old or middle-aged, while our little waitress was very young. She had, as she told us when she came back, been called after a grandmother. But my uncle was plainly shaken by hearing those four syllables suddenly borne on the afternoon air. His thin hand plucked at the edge of the tablecloth, he cast down his eyes, his head began to nod and shake. He asked me if he had ever told me the story of the Admiral and his seven daughters, in a tone that suggested that he knew he had not and was still trying to make up his mind whether he wanted to tell it now. Indeed, he told me very little that day, though I was to hear the whole of it before he died.

The story began at the house of my grandmother's sister, Alice Darrell, and it could hardly have happened anywhere else. When her husband, an officer in the Indian Army, died of fever, her father-in-law had given her a house that he had recently and reluctantly inherited and could not sell because it was part of an entailed estate. He apologized for the gift, pleading justly that he could not afford to buy her another, and she accepted it bravely. But the house lay in a district that would strain anybody's bravery. To reach it, one travelled about eight miles out of London along the main Hammersmith Road, the dullest of highways, and then turned left and found something worse. For some forgotten reason, there had sprung up at this point a Hogarthian slum, as bad as anything in the East End, which turned into a brawling hell every Saturday night. Beyond this web of filthy hovels lay flatlands covered by orchards and farmlands and market gardens, among which there had been set down three or four large houses. There was nothing to recommend the site. The Thames was not far distant, and it was comprehensible enough that along its bank there had been built a line of fine houses. But at Alice Darrell's there was no view of the river, though it lay near enough to shroud the region in mist during the winter months. It was true that the gardens had an alluvial fertility, but even they did not give the pleasure they should have done, for the slum dwellers carried out periodical raids on the strawberry beds and raspberry canes and orchards.

These stranded houses had been built in Regency times and were beautiful, though disconcerting, because there was no reason why they should be there, and they were so oddly placed in relation to each other. They all opened off the same narrow road, and Aunt Alice's house, Currivel Lodge, which was the smallest of them, lay at the end of a drive, and there faced sideways, so that its upper windows looked straight down on the garden of the much bigger house beside it, as that had been built nearer the road. This meant that my grandaunt could not sit on the pretty balcony outside her bedroom window without seeming to spy on her neighbours, so she never used it. But when my Uncle Arthur went to stay with her as a little boy, which was about a hundred years ago, nothing delighted him more than to shut himself in his bedroom and kneel on his window and do what his Aunt Alice could not bear to be suspected of doing.

Currivel Lodge should have been a dreary place for the child. There was nowhere to walk and nowhere to ride. There was no village where one could watch the blacksmith at his forge and the carpenter at his bench. In those days, nobody rowed on the Thames anywhere but at Oxford, unless they were watermen earning their living. There was little visiting, for it took a good hour to an hour and a half to drive to London, and my needy grandaunt's horses were old crocks. Her children were all older than little Arthur. But he enjoyed his visit simply because of the hours he spent on that window seat. I know the setting of the scene on which he looked, since I often stayed in that house many years later; for of course my grandaunt's family never left it. When the entail came to an end and the property could have been sold, there were the Zulu Wars, the South African War, the First World War, and all meant that the occupants were too busy or too troubled to move; and they were still living there when the house was swept away in a town-planning scheme during the twenties. What Arthur in his day and I in mine looked down on was a croquet lawn framed by trees, very tall trees—so tall and strong, my uncle said with approval, that though one could not see the river, one knew that there must be one not far away. Born and reared in one of the wettest parts of Ireland, he regarded dry weather and a dry soil as the rest of us regard dry bread.

To the left of this lawn, seen through foliage, was a stone terrace overgrown with crimson and white roses. Behind the terrace rose the mellow red rectangle of a handsome Regency house with a green copper cupola rising from its roof. What my uncle saw there that was not there for me to see was a spectacle that gave him the same sort of enjoyment I was to get from the ballet "Les Sylphides." When the weather was fine, it often happened that there would come down the broad stone steps of the terrace a number of princesses out of a fairy tale, each dressed in a different pale but bright colour. Sometimes there were as few as four of these princesses; occasionally there were as many as seven. Among the colours that my uncle thought he remembered them wearing were hyacinth blue, the green of the leaves of lilies of the valley, a silvery lilac that was almost grey, a transparent red that was like one's hand when one holds it up to a strong light, primrose yellow, a watery jade green, and a gentle orange. The dresses were made of muslin, and billowed in loops and swinging circles as their wearers' little feet carried them about in what was neither a dance nor the everyday motion of ordinary people. It was as if these lovely creatures were all parts of a brave and sensitive and melancholy being, and were at once confiding in each other about their griefs, which were their common grief, and giving each other reassurance.

Some carried croquet mallets and went on to the lawn and started to play, while the others sat down on benches to watch them. But sooner or later the players would pause and forget to make the next stroke, move toward each other and stand in a group, resting their mallets on the ground, and presently forget them and let them fall, as the spectators rose from their seats to join them in their exchange of confidences. Though they appeared in the garden as often as three times a week, they always seemed to have as much to say to one another as if they met but once a year; and they were always grave as they talked. There was a wildness about them, it was impossible to tell what they would do next, one might suddenly break away from the others and waltz round the lawn in the almost visible arms of an invisible partner; but when they talked, they showed restraint, they did not weep, though what they said was so plainly sad, and they rarely laughed. What was true of one of them was true of all, for

472

there seemed very little difference between them. All were golden-headed. The only one who could be told apart was the wearer of the lilac-grey dress. She was taller than the rest, and often stood aloof while they clustered together and swayed and spoke. Sometimes a woman in a black gown came down from the terrace and talked to this separate one.

The girls in the coloured dresses were the seven daughters of the Admiral who owned the house. My uncle saw him once, when he called on Alice Darrell to discuss with her arrangements for repairing the wall between their properties: a tall and handsome man with iron-grey hair, a probing, defensive gaze, and a mouth so sternly compressed that it was a straight line across his face. The call would never have been made had there not been business to discuss. The Admiral would have no social relations with his neighbours; nobody had ever been invited to his house. Nor, had such an invitation been sent, would Aunt Alice have accepted it, for she thought he treated his daughters abominably. She could not help smiling when she told her nephew their names, for they came straight off the Navy List: Andromeda, Cassandra, Clytie, Hera, Parthenope, Arethusa, and Persephone. But that was the only time she smiled when she spoke of them, for she thought they had been treated with actual cruelty, though not in the way that might have been supposed. They were not immured in this lonely house by a father who wanted to keep them to himself; their case was the very opposite.

The Admiral's daughters were, in effect, motherless. By Aunt Alice my Uncle Arthur was told that the Admiral's wife was an invalid and had to live in a mild climate in the West of England, but from the servants he learned that she was mad. Without a wife to soften him, the Admiral dealt with his daughters summarily by sending each of them, as she passed her seventeenth birthday, to be guided through the London season by his only sister, a wealthy woman with a house in Berkeley Square, and by giving each to the first man of reasonably respectable character who made her an offer of marriage. He would permit no delay, though his daughters, who had inheritances from a wealthy grandfather, as well as their beauty, would obviously have many suitors. These precipitate marriages were always against the brides' inclinations, for they had, strangely enough, no desire but to go on living in their lonely home.

"They are," Aunt Alice told her nephew, hesitating and looking troubled, "oddly young for their ages. I know they are not old, and that they have lived a great deal alone, since their mother cannot be with them. But they are really very young for what they are." They had yielded, it was said, only to the most brutal pressure exercised by their father. It astonished my uncle that all this was spoken of as something that had happened in the past. They did not look like grown-up ladies as they wandered in the garden, yet all but two were wives, and those two were betrothed, and some of them were already mothers. Parthenope, the one with most character, the one who had charge of the house in her father's absence, had married a North Country landowner who was reputed to be a millionaire. It was a pity that he was twice her age and had, by a dead wife, a son almost as old as she was, but such a fortune is a great comfort; and none of her sisters was without some measure of that same kind of consolation. Nevertheless, their discontent could be measured by the frequency with which they returned to the home of their childhood.

The first time my uncle visited Currivel Lodge, the Admiral's seven daughters were only a spectacle for his distant enjoyment. But one day during his second visit, a year later, his aunt asked him to deliver a note for Miss Parthenope at the house next door. Another section of the wall between the properties was in need of buttresses, and the builder had to have his orders. My uncle went up to his bedroom and smoothed his hair and washed his face, a thing he had never done before between morning and night of his own accord, and when he got to the Admiral's house, he told the butler, falsely but without a tremor, that he had been told to give the note into Miss Parthenope's own hands. It did not matter to him that the butler looked annoyed at hearing this: too much was at stake. He followed the butler's offended back through several rooms full of fine furniture, which were very much like the rooms to which he was accustomed, but had a sleepy air, as if the windows were closed, though they were not. In one there were some dolls thrown down on the floor, though he had never heard that there were any children living in the house. In the last room, which opened on the stone terrace and its white and crimson roses, a woman in a black dress with a suggestion of a uniform about it was sitting at an embroidery frame. She stared at him as if he presented a greater problem than schoolboys usually do, and he recognized her as the dark figure he had seen talking with the tallest of the daughters in the garden.

She took the letter from him, and he saw that the opportunity he had seized was slipping out of his grasp, so he pretended to be younger and simpler than he was, and put on the Irish brogue, which he never used at home except when he was talking to the servants or the people on the farms, but which he had found charmed the English. "May I not go out into the garden and see the young ladies?" he asked. "I have watched them from my window, and they look so pretty."

It worked. The woman smiled and said, "You're from Ireland, aren't you?" and before he could answer she exclaimed, as if defying prohibitions of which she had long been weary, "What is the harm? Yes, go out and give the note to Miss Parthenope yourself. You will know her—she is wearing grey and is the tallest." When he got out on the terrace, he saw that all seven of the Admiral's daughters were on the lawn, and his heart was like a turning windmill as he went down the stone steps. Then one of the croquet players caught sight of him—the one who was wearing a red dress, just nearer flame colour than flesh. She dropped her mallet and cried, "Oh, look, a little boy! A little red-haired boy!" and danced toward him, sometimes pausing and twirling right round, so that her skirts billowed out round her. Other voices took up the cry, and, cooing like pigeons, the croquet players closed in on him in a circle of unbelievable beauty. It was their complexions that he remembered in later life as the marvel that made them, among all the women he was ever to see, the nonpareils. Light lay on their skin as it lies on the petals of flowers, but it promised that it would never fade, that it would last forever, like the pearl. Yet even while he remarked their loveliness and was awed by it, he was disconcerted. They came so close, and it seemed as if they might do more than look at him and speak to him. It was as if a flock of birds had come down on him, and were fluttering and pecking about him; and they asked so many questions, in voices that chirped indefatigably and were sharper than the human note. "Who are you?" "You are Mrs Darrell's nephew?" "Her brother's child or her sister's?" "How old are you?" "What is your name?" "Why is your middle name Greatorex?" "Oh, what lovely hair he has—true Titian! And those round curls like coins!" "Have you sisters?" "Have they hair like yours?" Their little hands darted out and touched his hands, his cheeks, his shoulders, briefly but not pleasantly. His flesh rose in goose pimples, as it did when a moth's wing brushed his face as he lay in bed in the dark. And while their feathery restlessness poked and cheeped at him, they looked at him with eyes almost as fixed as

475

if they were blind and could not see him at all. Their eyes were immense and very bright and shaded by lashes longer than he had ever seen; but they were so light a grey that they were as colourless as clear water running over a bed of pebbles. He was glad when the woman in the black dress called from the terrace, "Leave the boy alone!" He did not like anything about the Admiral's daughters, now he saw them at close range. Even their dresses, which had looked beautiful from a distance, repelled him. If a lady had been sitting to a portrait painter in the character of a wood nymph, she might have worn such draperies, but it was foolish to wear them in a garden, when there was nobody to see them. "Leave the boy alone!" the woman in black called again. "He has come with a letter for Parthenope."

She had not been one of the circle. Now that the others fell back, my uncle saw her standing a little way off, biting her lip and knitting her brows, as if the scene disturbed her. There were other differences, beyond her height, that distinguished her from her sisters. While they were all that was most feminine, with tiny waists and hands and feet, she might have been a handsome and athletic boy dressed in woman's clothes for a school play. Only, of course, one knew quite well that she was not a boy. She stood erect, her arms hanging by her sides, smoothing back the muslin billows of her skirt, as if they were foolishness she would be glad to put behind her; and indeed, she would have looked better in Greek dress. Like her sisters, she had golden hair, but hers was a whiter gold. As my uncle and she went toward each other, she smiled, and he was glad to see that her eyes were a darker grey than her sisters', and were quick and glancing. He told her who he was, speaking honestly, not putting on a brogue to win her, and she smiled and held out her hand. It took her a little time to read the letter, and she frowned over it and held her forefinger to her lips, and bade him tell his aunt that she would send over an answer later in the day, after she had consulted her gardeners, and then she asked him if he would care to come into the house and drink some raspberry vinegar. As she led him across the lawn to the terrace, walking with long strides, he saw that her sisters were clustered in a group, staring up at a gutter high on the house, where a rook had perched, as if the bird were a great marvel. "Should I say good-bye to the ladies?" he asked nervously, and Parthenope answered, "No, they have forgotten you already." However, one had not. The sister who wore the light-red dress ran after him, crying, "Come back soon, little boy. Nobody ever comes into this garden except to steal our strawberries."

Parthenope took him through the silent house, pausing in the room where the dolls lay on the floor to lift them up and shut them in a drawer, and they came to a dining room, lined with pictures of great ships at war with stormy seas. There was no raspberry vinegar on the top of the sideboard—only decanters wearing labels marked with the names of adult drinks he was allowed only at Christmas and on his birthday, and then but one glass, and he always chose claret. So they opened the cupboard below, and sat down together on the carpet and peered into the darkness while he told her that he did not really want any but if it had gone astray he would be pleased to help her find it. But when the decanter turned up at the very back of the shelf (and they agreed that that was what always happened when one lost any-thing, and that there was no doubt that objects can move), they both had a glass, talking meanwhile of what they liked to eat and drink. Like him, she hated boiled mutton, and she, too, liked goose better than turkey. When he had finished and the talk had slowed down, he rose and put his glass on the sideboard, and offered her a hand to help her up from the floor, but she did not need it; and he gave a last look round the room, so that he would not forget it. He asked her, "Why is your chandelier tied up in a canvas bag? At home that only happens when the family is away." She answered, "Our family is away," speaking so grimly that he said, "I did not mean to ask a rude question." She told him, "You have not asked a rude question. What I meant was that all but two of us have our own homes, and those two will be leaving here soon." It would not have been right to say that she spoke sadly. But her tone was empty of all it had held when they had talked about how much better chicken tastes when you eat it with your fingers when you are out shooting. He remembered all the sad things he had heard his aunt say about her family, the sadder things he had heard from the servants. He said, "Why don't you come back with me and have tea with my aunt?" She said, smiling, "She has not asked me." And he said, "Never think of that. We are not proper English, you know; we are from Ireland, and friends come in any time." But she thanked him, sighing, so that he knew she would really have liked to come, and said that she must go back to her sisters. As the butler held the front door open for my uncle, she gave him a friendly slap across the shoulders, as an older boy might have done.

After that, my uncle never watched the Admiral's daughters again. If a glance told him that they were in the garden, he turned his back on the window. He had not liked those staring eyes that were colourless as water, and it troubled him that though some of them had children, none had said, "I have a boy, too, but he is much younger than you," for mothers always said that. He remembered Parthenope so well that he could summon her to his mind when he wished, and he could not bear to see her with these women who made him feel uneasy, because he was sure that he and she felt alike, and therefore she must be in a perpetual state of unease. So when, the very day before he was to go back to Ireland, he looked out of his bedroom window and saw her alone on the lawn, he threw up the sash and called to her; but she did not hear him.

She was absorbed in playing a game by herself, a game that he knew well. She was throwing a ball high into the air, then letting her arms drop by her sides, and waiting to the last, the very last moment, before stretching out a hand to catch it. It was a strange thing for a grown-up lady to be doing, but it did not distress him like the playground gambolling and chattering of her sisters. They had been like children as grownups like to think of them, silly and meaningless and mischievous. But she was being a child as children really are, sobered by all they have to put up with and glad to forget it in play. There was currently some danger that his own father was going to get a post in some foreign place and that the whole family would have to leave County Kerry for years and years; and when he and his brothers and sisters thought of this, they would go and, each one apart, would play this very same game that Parthenope was playing.

He did not want to raise his voice in a shout, in case he was overheard by his aunt or his mother. They would not understand that although Parthenope and he had met only once, they knew each other quite well. He got up from the window seat and went out of his room and down through the house and out into the garden. There was a ladder in the coach house, and he dragged it to the right part of the wall and propped it up and stopped it with stones, and climbed to the top and called "Miss Parthenope!" When she saw him, she smiled and waved at him as if she really were glad to see him again.

"Where are your sisters?" he asked cautiously.

"They have all gone away. I am going home tomorrow."

"So am I."

478

"Are you glad?"

"Papa will be there," he said, "and my brothers and sisters, and Garrity the groom, and my pony."

She asked him the names of his brothers and sisters, and how old they were, and where his home was; and he told her all these things and told her, too, that his father was always being sent all over the world, and that of late he and his brothers and sisters had heard talk that someday, and it might be soon, he would be sent to some foreign place for so long that they would have to go with him, and they didn't want this to happen; for though they loved him and wanted to be near him, they loved County Kerry, too. At that, she stopped smiling and nodded her head, as if to say she knew how he must feel. "But perhaps it won't happen," he said, "and then you must come and stay with us for the hunting."

He thought of her in a riding habit, and at that he noticed that she was wearing a dress such as his own mother might have worn— a dress of grey cloth, with a tight bodice and a stiffened skirt, ornamented with braid. He said, "How funny to see you dressed like other ladies. Don't you usually wear that lilac-grey muslin dress?"

She shook her head. "No. My sisters and I only wear those muslin dresses when we are together here. My sisters like them."

"Don't you?" he said, for her tone had gone blank again.

"No," she answered, "not at all."

He was glad to hear it, but it seemed horribly unfair that she should have to wear clothes she did not like, just because her sisters did; nothing of the sort happened in his own family. "Then don't wear them!" he said passionately. "You mustn't wear them! Not if you don't like them!"

"You're making your ladder wobble," she said, laughing at him, "and if you fall down, I can't climb over the wall and pick you up." She started across the lawn toward the house.

"Garrity says that you're lost if you let yourself be put upon," he cried after her, his brogue coming back to him, but honestly, because he spoke to Garrity as Garrity spoke to him. He would have liked to have the power to make her do what she ought to do, and save her from all this foolishness.

"Good-bye, good-bye," she called across the growing distance. "Be a good boy, and come back to see us next year."

"You will be here for sure?" he asked eagerly.

"Oh, yes," she promised. "We will always be back here for some time in the summer. My sisters would rather be here than anywhere in the world."

"But do you like it yourself?" he asked angrily.

It was no use. She had run up the steps to the terrace.

My uncle did not come back the next year, because his fears were realized and his father was appointed to a post in Canada. But from his aunt's letters to his mother he learned that even if he had returned to Currivel Lodge, he would not have seen Parthenope, for the Admiral sold the house later that year, as soon as his two remaining daughters went to the altar, which they did with even greater reluctance than their elder sisters. Alice Darrell's maid happened to be at the window one winter day and saw the two of them walking up and down the lawn, dressed in those strange, bright muslin gowns and wearing no mantles, though the river mist was thick, while they wept and wrung their hands. Aunt Alice felt that even if the Admiral had felt obliged to bundle all his daughters into matrimony, he should at least not have sold the house, which was the one place where they could meet and have a little nursery happiness again.

In the course of time, Uncle Arthur came back to Ireland, and went to Trinity College, Dublin, and passed into the English Civil Service, and was sent to London. The first time he went back to Currivel Lodge, he stood at his bedroom window and stared out at the croquet lawn of the house next door, and it looked very much like other croquet lawns. Under the trees two men and two women were sitting round a tea table, all of them presenting the kind of appearance, more common then than now, that suggests that nothing untoward happens to the human race. It occurred to him that perhaps his boyish imagination had made a story out of nothing, but Aunt Alice gave him back his version intact. The Admiral had really hectored his daughters into early and undesired marriages, with the most brutal disregard for their feelings, and the daughters had really been very strange girls, given to running about the garden in a sort of fancy dress and behaving like children—all except Parthenope, who was quite remarkable. She had made her mark in society since then. Well, so they all had, in a way. Their photographs were always in the papers, at one time, and no wonder, they were so very pretty. But that seemed over now, and, indeed, they must all be out of their twenties by now, even the youngest. Parthenope's triumphs, however, had been more durable. It was said that Queen Victoria greatly approved of her, and she was often at Court.

My uncle always thought of Parthenope when he was dressing for any of the grander parties to which he was invited, and he soon found his way to the opera and ascertained which was her box, but she was never at the parties, and, unless she had changed out of all recognition, never in her box at Covent Garden, either. My uncle did not wish to approach her, for he was a poor young man, far below her grandeur, and they belonged to different generations; at the least, she was twelve years older than he was. But he would have liked to see her again. Soon, however, he received an intimation that that would not be possible. One morning at breakfast he unfolded his newspaper and folded it again almost immediately, having read a single paragraph, which told him that Parthenope had met a violent death.

He had failed to meet her at parties and to see her in her opera box because she had been spending the winter abroad, taking care of two of her sisters who had both been the victims of prolonged illness. Originally, they had settled at Nice, but had found it too urban, and had moved to a hotel at Grasse, where they spent some weeks. Then a friend had found them a pleasant villa at Hyères, and the party had started off from Grasse in two carriages. Parthenope and her sisters and a lady's maid had travelled in the first, and another maid and a courier had followed in the second. The second carriage had dropped far behind. Afterwards, the coachman remembered that he had been oddly delayed in leaving the inn where they had stopped for a midday meal; he had been told that a man was looking for him with a letter for his employers, and failing to find him had gone to a house some way down the village street. The coachman sought him but there was nobody there; and on his return to his horses he discovered that a harness strap was broken, and he had to mend it before they could resume their journey. After a sharp turn in the road, he had found himself driving into a felled tree trunk, and when the courier and the maid and the coachman got out, they could see no sign of the first carriage. It was found some hours later, abandoned on a cart track running through a wood to a river. There was no trace of any of its occupants. Later that same day the maid crawled up to a farmhouse door. Before she collapsed she was able to tell the story of an attack by masked men, who had, she thought, killed the three sisters outright because they refused to tell in which trunk their jewel cases were packed. She had escaped during the struggle, and while she was running away through the woods, she had heard terrible prolonged screaming from the riverbank. As the river was in flood, there was no hope of recovering the bodies.

After my uncle had read all the accounts of the crime that appeared in the newspapers, and had listened to all he could hear from gossiping friends, there hung, framed on the wall of his mind, a romantic picture of a highway robbery, in the style of Salvator Rosa, with coal-black shadows and highlights white on hands lifted in imploration, and he felt no emotion whatsoever. When he had opened *The Times* at breakfast, his heart had stopped. But now he felt as if he had been stopped before an outmoded and conventional picture in a private gallery by a host who valued it too highly.

A year or so later, Alice Darrell mentioned to him an odd story she had heard. It appeared that Parthenope had been carrying a great deal more jewelry than would seem necessary for a woman travelling quietly with two invalid sisters. To be sure, she had not taken all the jewelry she possessed, but she had taken enough for the value to be estimated at fifty thousand pounds; and of this not a penny could be recovered, for it was uninsured. Her husband had left the matter for her to handle, because she had sold some old jewelry and had bought some to replace it just about the time that the policy should have been renewed, but she had failed to write the necessary letter to her lawyers till the very night before the journey to Hyéres, and it was found, unposted, at the hotel in Grasse.

"Parthenope!" my uncle said. "Let an insurance policy lapse! Parthenope! I'll not believe it."

"That's just what I said," Alice Darrell exclaimed. "Any of the others, but not Parthenope. She had her hand on everything. Yet, of course, she may have changed. They are a queer family. There was the other one, you know—the one who disappeared. That was after the accident."

It seemed that another sister—Hera, Aunt Alice thought it was—had also suffered ill health, and had gone to France with a nurse, and one day her cloak and bonnet were found on the bank of a river.

"I wish that things turned out better," Aunt Alice remarked sadly. "They do sometimes, but not often enough."

This was the only criticism of life he had ever heard her utter, though she had had a sad life, constantly losing the people she loved, to tropical diseases or to wars against obscure tribes that lacked even the interest of enmity. What she uttered now made him realize that she had indeed thought Parthenope remarkable, and he said, smiling, "Why, we are making ourselves quite miserable about her, though all we know for sure is that she let an insurance policy lapse."

He did not hear of the Admiral's daughters again until after a long space of time, during which he had many other things to think about: his career, which was alternately advanced by his brilliance and retarded by his abstracted candour; a long affair with a married woman older than himself, some others that were briefer; and his marriage, which, like his career, and for much the same reason, was neither a success nor a failure. One day when he was reading the papers at his club, he heard two men speaking of a friend who was distressed about his mother, whose behaviour had been strange since she had been left a widow. She had rejected the dower house and gone off to the Continent to travel by herself, and now refused to come back to see her family or to meet them abroad. The mother had an old Greek name, and so had a sister, who had got herself murdered for her jewels in the South of France. My uncle went on staring at his newspaper, but it was as if a door in his mind were swinging backward and forward on a broken hinge.

Many years later, when Aunt Alice was dead and my uncle was a middle-aged man, with children who were no longer children, he broke his journey home from a conference in Spain at a certain town in the southwest of France, for no other reason than that its name had always charmed him. But it proved to be a dull place, and as he sat down to breakfast at a café in the large and featureless station square, it occurred to him to ask the waiter if there were not some smaller and pleasanter place in the neighbourhood where he could spend the rest of the day and night. The waiter said that if Monsieur would take the horse-bus that started from the other side of the square in half an hour, it would take him to the village where he, the waiter, was born, and there he would find a good inn and a church that people came all the way from Paris to see. My uncle took his advice; and because his night had been wakeful, he fell asleep almost as soon as the bus started. He woke suddenly to find that the journey had ended and he was in a village which was all that he had hoped it would be.

A broad, deliberate river, winding among low wooded hills, spread its blessings at this point through a circular patch of plain, a couple of miles or so across, which was studded with farmhouses, each standing beside its deep green orchard. In the centre of this circle was a village that was no more than one long street, which looked very clean. The houses were built of stone that had been washed by the hill rains, and beside the road a brook flowed over a paved bed. There were bursts of red valerian growing from the cracks in the walls and in the yard-long bridges that crossed the brook. The street ended in a little square, where the church and the inn looked across cobblestones, shaded by pollarded limes, at the *mairie* and the post office. At the inn, my uncle took a room and slept for an hour or two in a bed smelling of the herbs with which the sheets had been washed. Then, as it was past noon, he went down to lunch, and ate some potato soup, a trout, some wood strawberries, and a slice of cheese. Afterwards, he asked the landlord how soon the church would be open, and was told that he could open it himself when he chose. The priest and his housekeeper were away until vespers, and had left the church keys at the inn.

When he went to the church, it was a long time before he unlocked the door, for there was a beautiful tympanum in the porch, representing the Last Judgement. It was clear-cut in more than one sense. There was no doubt who was saved and who was damned: there was a beatific smile on the faces of those walking in Paradise, which made it seem as if just there a shaft of sunlight had struck the dark stone. Also the edges of the carving, though the centuries had rubbed them down, showed a definition more positive than mere sharpness. Often my uncle played games when he was alone, and now he climbed on a wooden stool which was in the porch, and shut his eyes and felt the faces of the blessed, and pretended that he had been blind for a long time, and that the smiles of the blessed were striking into his darkness through his fingertips.

When he went into the church, he found, behind an oaken door, the steps that led to the top of the tower. He climbed up through darkness that was transfixed every few steps by thin shafts of light, dancing with dust, coming through the eyelet windows, and he found that though the tower was not very high, it gave a fine view of an amphitheatre of hills, green on their lower slopes with chestnut groves, banded higher with fir woods and bare turf, and crowned with shining rock. He marked some likely paths on the nearest hills, and then dropped his eyes to the village below, and looked down into the oblong garden of a house that seemed larger than the rest. At the farther end was the usual, pedantically neat French vegetable garden; then there was a screen of espaliered fruit trees; then there was a lawn framed in trees so tall and strong that it could have been guessed from them alone that not far away there was a river. The lawn was set with croquet hoops, and about them were wandering four figures in bright dresses—one hyacinth blue, one primrose yellow, one jade green, one clear light red. They all had croquet mallets in their hands, but they had turned from the game, and as my uncle watched them they drew together, resting their mallets on the ground. Some distance away, a woman in black, taller than the others, stood watching them.

When one of the croquet players let her mallet fall on the grass, and used her free hands in a fluttering gesture, my uncle left the top of the tower and went down through the darkness and shafts of light and locked the church door behind him. In the corner of the square he found what might have been the château of the village—one of those square and solid dwellings, noble out of proportion to their size, which many provincial French architects achieved in the seventeenth century. My uncle went through an iron gateway into a paved garden and found that the broad door of the house was open. He walked into the vestibule and paused, looking up the curved staircase. The pictures were as old as the house, and two had been framed to fit the recessed panels in which they hung. The place must have been bought as it stood. On the threshold of the corridor beyond, he paused again, for it smelled of damp stone, as all the back parts of his father's house in County Kerry did, at any time of the year but high summer. It struck him as a piece of good fortune for which he had never before been sufficiently grateful that he could go back to that house any time he pleased; he would be there again in a few weeks' time. He passed the open door of a kitchen, where two women were rattling dishes and pans and singing softly, and came to a closed door, which he stared at for a second before he turned the handle.

He found himself in a salon that ran across the whole breadth of the house, with three French windows opening on a stone terrace overlooking the garden. As he crossed it to the steps that led down to the lawn, he came close to a bird cage on a pole, and the scarlet parrot inside broke into screams. All the women on the lawn turned and saw him, and the tall woman in black called, "*Que voulez-vous, Monsieur?*" She had put her hand to her heart, and he was eager to reassure her, but could not think how, across that distance, to explain why he had come. So he continued to walk toward her, but could not reach her because the four others suddenly scampered toward him, crying "Go away! Go away!" Their arms flapped like bats' wings, and their voices were cracked, but, under their white hair, their faces were unlined and their eyes were colourless as water. "Go away!" shrilled the one in light red. "We know you have come to steal our strawberries. Why may we not keep our own strawberries?" But the figure in black had come forward with long strides, and told them to go on with their game, and asked again, "*Que voulez-vous, Monsieur?*"

Her hair was grey now, and her mouth so sternly compressed that it was a straight line across her face. She reminded my uncle of a particular man—her father, the Admiral—but she was not like a man, she was still a handsome and athletic boy, though a frost had fallen on him; and still it was strange that she should look like a boy, since she was also not male at all. My uncle found that now he was face to face with her, it was just as difficult to explain to her why he had come. He said, "I came to this village by chance this morning, and after I had luncheon at the inn I went to the top of the church tower, and looked down on this garden, and recognized you all. I came to tell you that if there is anything I can do for you I will do it. I am a civil servant who has quite a respectable career, and so I can hope that I might be efficient enough to help you, if you need it."

"That is very kind," she said, and paused, and it was as if she were holding a shell to her ear and listening to the voice of a distant sea. "Very kind," she repeated. "But who are you?"

"I am the nephew of your neighbour, Mrs Darrell," said my uncle. "I brought you a letter from her, many years ago, when you were all in your garden."

Her smile broke slowly. "I remember you," she said. "You were a fatherly little boy. You gave me good advice from the top of a ladder. Why should you have found me here, I wonder? It can't be that, after all, there is some meaning in the things that happen. You had better come into the house and drink some of the cherry brandy we make here. I will get the cook to come out and watch them. I never leave them alone now."

While she went to the kitchen, my uncle sat in the salon and noted that, for all its fine furniture and all its space and light, there was a feeling that the place was dusty, the same feeling that he had noticed in the Admiral's house long ago. It is the dust of another world, he thought with horror, and the housemaids of this world are helpless against it. It settles wherever these women live, and Parthenope must live with them.

When she came back, she was carrying a tray with a slender decanter and very tiny glasses. They sat sipping the cherry brandy in silence until she said, "I did nothing wrong." He looked at her in astonishment. Of course she had done nothing wrong. Wrong was what she did not do. But she continued gravely, "When we all die, it will be found that the sum I got for the jewelry is intact. My stepson will not be a penny the worse off. Indeed, he is better off, for my husband has had my small inheritance long before it would have come to him if I had not done this."

"I knew you would have done it honestly," said my uncle. He hesitated. "This is very strange. You see, I knew things about you which I had no reason to know. I knew you had not been murdered."

Then my uncle had to think carefully. They were united by eternal bonds, but hardly knew each other, which was the reverse of what usually happened to men and women. But they might lapse into being strangers and nothing else if he showed disrespect to the faith by which she lived. He said only, "Also I knew that what you were doing in looking after your family was terrible."

She answered, "Yes. How good it is to hear somebody say that it is terrible, and to be able to answer that it is. But I had to do it. I had to get my sisters away from their husbands. They were ashamed of them. They locked them up in the care of strangers. I saw their bruises." My uncle caught his breath. "Oh," she said, desperately just, "the people who looked after them did not mean to be cruel. But they were strangers; they did not know the way to handle my sisters. And their husbands were not bad men, either. And even if they had been, I could not say a word against them, for they were cheated; my father cheated them. They were never told the truth about my mother. About my mother and half her family." She raised her little glass of cherry brandy to her lips and nodded, to intimate that that was all she had to say, but words rushed out and she brought her glass down to her lap. "I am not telling the truth. Their husbands cheated, too. . . . No, I am wrong. They did not cheat. But they failed to keep their bond. Still, there is no use talking about that."

"What bond did your sisters' husbands not keep?" my uncle asked.

"They married my sisters because they were beautiful, and laughed

487

easily, and could not understand figures. They might have considered that women who laugh easily might scream easily, and that if figures meant nothing to them, words might mean nothing, either, and that if figures and words meant nothing to them, thoughts and feelings might mean nothing, too. But these men had the impudence to feel a horror of my sisters."

She rose, trembling, and told him that he must have a sweet biscuit with his cherry brandy, and that she would get him some; they were in a cupboard in the corner of the room. Over her shoulder, she cried, "I cannot imagine you marrying a woman who was horrible because she was horrible, and then turning against her because she was horrible." She went on setting some wafers out on a plate, and he stared at the back of her head, unable to imagine what was inside it, saying to himself, "She realizes that they are horrible; there is no mitigation of her state."

When she sat down again, she said, "But it was my father's fault."

"What was your father's fault?" he asked gently, when she did not go on.

"Why, he should not have made us marry; he should not have sold our house. My sisters were happy there, and all they asked was to be allowed to go on living there, like children."

"Your father wanted his daughters to marry so that they would have someone to look after them when he was dead," my uncle told her.

"I could have looked after them."

"Come now," said my uncle, "you are not being fair. You are the same sort of person as your father. And you know quite well that if you were a man you would regard all women as incapable. You see, men of the better kind want to protect the women they love, and there is so much stupidity in the male nature and the circumstances of life are generally so confused that they end up thinking they must look after women because women cannot look after themselves. It is only very seldom that a man meets a woman so strong and wise that he cannot doubt her strength and wisdom, and realizes that his desire to protect her is really the same as his desire to gather her into his arms and partake of her glory."

Moving slowly and precisely, he took out his cardcase and was about to give her one of his cards when a thought struck him. She must have the name of his family's house in County Kerry as well as his London address, and know that he went there at Christmas and at

Easter, and in the summer, too. She would be able to find him whenever she wanted him, since such bootblack service was all he could render her.

She read the card and said in an astonished whisper, "Oh, how kind, how kind." Then she rose and put it in a drawer in a *secrétaire*, which she locked with a key she took from a bag swinging from the belt of her hateful black gown. "I have to lock up everything," she said, wearily. "They mean no harm, but sometimes they get at papers and tear them up."

"What I have written on that card is for an emergency," said my uncle. "But what is there I can do now? I do not like the thought of you sitting here in exile, among things that mean nothing to you. Can I not send you out something English—a piece of furniture, a picture, some china or glass? If I were in your place, I would long for something that reminded me of the houses where I had spent my childhood."

"If you were in my place, you would not," she said. "You are very kind, but the thing that has happened to my family makes me not at all anxious to remember my childhood. We were all such pretty children. Everybody always spoke as if we were bound to be happy. And in those days nobody was frightened of Mamma—they only laughed at her, because she was such a goose. Then one thing followed another, and it became quite certain about Mamma, and then it became quite certain about the others; and now I cannot bear to think of the good times that went before. It is as if someone had known and was mocking us. But you may believe that it is wonderful for me to know that there is someone I can call on at any time. You see, I had supports, which are being taken away from me. You really have no idea how I got my sisters out here?"

My uncle shook his head. "I only read what was in the newspapers and knew it was not true."

"But you must have guessed I had helpers," she said. "There was the highway robbery to be arranged. All that was done by somebody who was English but had many connections in France, a man who was very fond of Arethusa. Arethusa is the one who spoke to you in the garden; she always wears red. This man was not like her husband; when she got worse and worse, he felt no horror for her, only pity. He has always been behind me, but he was far older than we were, and he died three years ago; and since then his lawyer in Paris has been a good friend, but now he is old, too, and I must expect him to

489

go soon. I have made all arrangements for what is to happen to my sisters after my death. They will go to a convent near here, where the nuns are really kind, and we are preparing them for it. One or other of the nuns comes here every day to see my sisters, so that they will never have to be frightened by strange faces; and I think that if my sisters go on getting worse at the same rate as at present, they will by then believe the nuns when they say that I have been obliged to go away and will come back presently. But till that time comes, I will be very glad to have someone I can ask for advice. I can see that you are to be trusted. You are like the man who loved Arethusa. My poor Arethusa! Sometimes I think," she said absently, "that she might have been all right if it had been that man whom she had married. But no," she cried, shaking herself awake, "none of us should have married, not even me."

"Why should you not have married?" asked my uncle. "That the others should not I understand. But why not you? There is nothing wrong with you."

"Is there not?" she asked. "To leave my family and my home, to stage a sham highway robbery, and later to plot and lie, and lie and plot, in order to get my mad sisters to a garden I had once noted, in my travels, as something like the garden taken from them when they were young. There is an extravagance in the means my sanity took to rescue their madness that makes the one uncommonly like the other."

"You must not think that," my uncle told her. "Your strange life forced strangeness on your actions, but you are not strange. You were moved by love, you had seen their bruises."

"Yes, I had seen their bruises," she agreed. "But," she added, hesitantly, "you are so kind that I must be honest with you. It was not only for the love of my sisters that I arranged this flight. It is also true that I could not bear my life. I was not wholly unselfish. You do not know what it is like to be a character in a tragedy. Something has happened which can only be explained by supposing that God hates you with merciless hatred, and nobody will admit it. The people nearest you stand round you saying that you must ignore this extraordinary event, you must—what were the words I was always hearing?—'keep your sense of proportion,' 'not brood on things.' They do not understand that they are asking you to deny your experiences, which is to pretend that you do not exist and never have existed. And as for the people who do not love you, they laugh. Our tragedy was so ridiculous that the laughter was quite loud. There were all sorts of really funny stories about the things my mother and sisters did before they were shut up. That is another terrible thing about being a character in a tragedy; at the same time you become a character in a farce. Do not deceive yourself," she said, looking at him kindly and sadly. "I am not a classical heroine, I am not Iphigenia or Electra or Alcestis, I am the absurd Parthenope. There is no dignity in my life. For one thing, too much has happened to me. One calamity evokes sympathy; when two calamities call for it, some still comes, but less. Three calamities are felt to be too many, and when four are reported, or five, the thing is ludicrous. God has only to strike one again and again for one to become a clown. There is nothing about me which is not comical. Even my flight with my sisters has become a joke." She sipped at her glass. "My sisters' husbands and their families must by now have found out where we are. I do not think my husband ever did, or he would have come to see me. But there are many little indications that the others know, and keep their knowledge secret, rather than let loose so monstrous a scandal."

"You say your husband would have come to see you?" asked my uncle, wanting to make sure. "But that must mean he loved you."

At last the tears stood in her eyes. She said, her voice breaking, "Oh, things might have gone very well with my husband and myself, if love had been possible for me. But of course it never was."

"How wrong you are," said my uncle. "There could be nothing better for any man than to have you as his wife. If you did not know that, your husband should have made you understand it."

"No, no," she said. "The fault was not in my husband or myself. It was in love, which cannot do all that is claimed for it. Oh, I can see that it can work miracles, some miracles, but not all the miracles that are required before life can be tolerable. Listen: I love my sisters, but I dare not love them thoroughly. To love them as much as one can love would be to go to the edge of an abyss and lean over the edge, farther and farther, till one was bound to lose one's balance and fall into the blackness of that other world where they live. That is why I never dared let my husband love me fully. I was so much afraid that I might be an abyss, and if he understood me, if we lived in each other, he would be drawn down into my darkness."

"But there is no darkness in you," said my uncle, "you are not an abyss, you are the solid rock."

"Why do you think so well of me?" she wondered. "Of course, you are right to some extent—I am not the deep abyss I might be. But how could I be sure of that when I was young? Every night when I lay down in bed I examined my day for signs of folly. If I had lost my temper, if I had felt more joy than was reasonable, I was like one of a tuberculous family who has just heard herself cough. Only the years that had not then passed made me sure that I was unlike my sisters, and until I knew, I had to hold myself back. I could not let the fine man who was my husband be tempted into my father's fault."

"What was your father's fault?" asked my uncle, for the second time since he had entered that room.

Again her disapproval was absolute, her eyes were like steel. But this time she answered at once, without a moment's hesitation: "Why, he should not have loved my mother."

"But you are talking like a child!" he exclaimed. "You cannot blame anyone for loving anyone."

"Did you ever see him?" she asked, her eyes blank because they were filled with a distant sight. "Yes? You must have been only a boy, but surely you saw that he was remarkable. And he had a mind, he was a mathematician, he wrote a book on navigation that was thought brilliant; they asked him to lecture to the Royal Society. And one would have thought from his face that he was a giant of goodness and strength. How could such a man love such a woman as my mother? It was quite mad, the way he made us marry. How could he lean over the abyss of her mind and let himself be drawn down into that darkness?"

"Do not let your voice sink to a whisper like that," my uncle begged her. "It—it—"

"It frightens you," she supplied.

"But have you," he pressed her, "no feeling for your mother?"

"Oh, yes," she said, her voice breaking. "I loved my mother very much. But when she went down into the darkness, I had to say good-bye to her or I could not have looked after my sisters." It seemed as if she was going to weep, but she clung to her harshness and asked again, "How could my father love such a woman?"

My uncle got up and knelt in front of her chair and took her trembling hands in his. "There is no answer, so do not ask the question."

"I must ask it," she said. "Surely it is blasphemy to admit that one

492

can ask questions to which there are no answers. I must ask why my father leaned over the abyss of my mother's mind and threw himself into it, and dragged down victim after victim with him—not only dragging them down but manufacturing them for that sole purpose, calling them out of nothingness simply so that they could fall and fall. How could he do it? If there is not an answer—"

He put his hand over her lips. "He cannot have known that she was mad when he begot his children."

Her passion had spent itself in her question. She faintly smiled as she said, "No, but I never liked the excuse that he and my sisters' husbands made for themselves. They all said that at first they had simply thought their wives were rather silly. I could not have loved someone whom I thought rather silly. Could you?"

"It is not what I have done," said my uncle. "May I have some more cherry brandy?"

"I am so glad that you like it," she said, suddenly happy. "But you have given me the wrong glass to fill. This is mine."

"I knew that," he told her. "I wanted to drink from your glass."

"I would like to drink from yours," she said, and for a little time they were silent. "Tell me," she asked meekly, as if now she had put herself in his hands, "do you think it has been wrong for me to talk about what has happened to me? When I was at home they always said it was bad to brood over it."

"What nonsense," said my uncle. "I am sure that it was one of the major misfortunes of Phèdre and Bérénice that they were unable to read Racine's clear-headed discussions of their miseries."

"You are right," said Parthenope. "Oh, how kind Racine was to tragic people! He would not allow for a moment that they were comic. People at those courts must have giggled behind their hands at poor Bérénice, at poor Phèdre. But he ignored them. You are kind like Racine." There was a tapping on the glass of the French window, and her face went grey. "What has happened now? Oh, what has happened now?" she murmured to herself. It was the cook who had tapped, and she was looking grave.

Parthenope went out and spoke with her for a minute, and then came back, and again the tears were standing in her eyes. "I thought I might ask you to stay all day with me," she said. "I thought we might dine together. But my sisters cannot bear it that there is a stranger here. They are hiding in the raspberry canes, and you must have heard them screaming. Part of that noise comes from the parrot,

493

but part from them. It sometimes takes hours to get them quiet. I cannot help it; you must go."

He took both her hands and pressed them against his throat, and felt it swell as she muttered, "Good-bye."

But as he was going through the paved garden to the gateway he heard her call "Stop! Stop!" and she was just behind him, her skirts lifted over her ankles so that she could take her long strides. "The strangest thing," she said, laughing. "I have not told you the name by which I am known here." She spelled it out to him as he wrote it down in his diary, and turned back toward the house, exclaiming, "What a thing to forget!" But then she swung back again, suddenly pale, and said, "But do not write to me. I am only giving you the name so that if I send you a message you will be able to answer it. But do not write to me."

"Why not?" he asked indignantly. "Why not?"

"You must not be involved in my life," she said. "There is a force outside the world that hates me and all my family. If you wrote to me too often it might hate you, too."

"I would risk that," he said, but she cried, covering her eyes, "No, no, by being courageous you are threatening my last crumb of happiness. If you stay a stranger, I may be allowed to keep what I have of you. So do as I say."

He made a resigned gesture, and they parted once more. But as she got to her door, he called to her to stop and hurried back. "I will not send you anything that will remind you of your home," he said, "but may I not send you a present from time to time—some stupid little thing that will not mean much but might amuse you for a minute or two?"

She hesitated but in the end nodded. "A little present, a very little present," she conceded. "And not too often." She smiled like the saved in the sculpture in the church, and slowly closed the door on him.

But when he was out in the square and walking toward the inn, he heard her voice crying again, "Stop! Stop!" This time she came quite close to him and said, as if she were a child ashamed to admit to a fault, "There is another thing that I would like to ask of you. You said that I might write to you if I wanted anything, and I know that you meant business things—the sort of advice men give women. But I wonder if your kindness goes beyond that; you are so very kind. I know all about most dreadful things in life, but I know nothing about

494

death. Usually I think I will not mind leaving this world, but just now and then, if I wake up in the night, particularly in winter, when it is very cold, I am afraid that I may be frightened when I die."

"I fear that, too, sometimes," he said.

"It seems a pity, too, to leave this world, in spite of the dreadful things that happen in it," she went on. "There are things that nothing can spoil—the spring and the summer and the autumn.

"And, indeed, the winter, too," he said.

"Yes, the winter, too," she said and looked up at the amphitheatre of hills round the village. "You cannot think how beautiful it is here when the snow has fallen. But, of course, death may be just what one has been waiting for; it may explain everything. But still, I may be frightened when it comes. So if I do not die suddenly, if I have warning of my death, would it be a great trouble for you to come and be with me for a little?"

"As I would like to be with you always, I would certainly want to be with you then," he said. "And if I have notice of my death and you are free to travel, I will ask you to come to me."

My uncle found that he did not want to go back to the inn just then, and he followed a road leading up to the foothills. There he climbed one of the paths he had remarked from the top of the church tower, and when he got to the bare rock, he sat down and looked at the village beneath him till the twilight fell. On his return to London, he painted a water-colour of the view of the valley as he recollected it, and pasted it in a book, which he kept by his bedside. From time to time, some object in the window of an antique shop or a jeweller's would bring Parthenope to his mind, and he would send it to her. The one that pleased him as most fitting was a gold ring in the form of two leaves, which was perhaps Saxon. She acknowledged these presents in brief letters; and it delighted him that often her solemn purpose of brevity broke down and she added an unnecessary sentence or two, telling him of something that had brightened her day—of a strayed fawn she had found in her garden, or a prodigious crop of cherries, which had made her trees quite red. But after some years these letters stopped. When he took into account how old she was, and by how many years she had been the elder, he realized that probably she had died. He told himself that at least she had enjoyed the mercy of sudden death, and presently ceased to think of her. It was as if the memory of her were too large to fit inside his head; he felt actual physical pain when he tried to recollect her. This was the time when such things as the finest buttercup field near London and the tomb of Captain Vancouver seemed to be all that mattered to him. But from the day when he heard the girl at the inn called by the name of his Parthenope, he again found it easy to think of her; and he told me about her very often during the five years that passed before his death.

FROM The Birds Fall Down

FOREWORD

This novel is founded on a historical event: perhaps the most momentous conversation ever to take place on a moving railway train. Students of modern history will recognize the necessity for specifying that it was moving. The Armistice which ended the First World War was signed in a stationary train. The conversation in this book takes place on a slow train making its way up through Northern France at the very beginning of the twentieth century, just after the close of the South African War; the conversation which historians have recorded took place nearly ten years later, on the Eastern Express between its departure from Berlin and its arrival at Cologne. The real participants differed from my characters in many respects, but not in their interests and emotions; and their exchange of information had the same effect on the Russian political scene. There were certainly other factors at work. But it is true that because of this conversation the morale of the powerful terrorist wing of the revolutionary party crumbled, and the cool-headed Lenin found the reins in his hands. It is also true that the Russian bureaucracy found the affair gravely disillusioning.

Most of the characters in these pages are portraits of people who were living at this period and were seriously involved in this situation, though they bore other names, and I have drawn heavily on their recorded sayings and their writings. I think I can claim to have told a true story, as it may have happened on a parallel universe, differing from ours only by a time-system which every now and then gets out of true with our own. Sometimes my story may surprise only because the changes in our society have been so rapid and so fundamental. It would have been inevitable in 1900 that a girl like Laura would speak and understand, as a matter of course, Russian, the Old Slavonic of the liturgy, French, and English; and she would probably have been a fair German and Italian scholar as well. And it would not have been surprising at that time that a French professor in a medical college was an enthusiastic Latinist. It is also to be noted that

I have exaggerated neither the bloody score of the terrorists, nor the number of executions and imprisonments for which the Tsarist government must bear responsibility, as well as its interferences with liberty, such as the violation of the mails, known as perlustration. *◇ ◇ ◇

---

* [The 125-page conversation in the railroad train, referred to in the author's Foreword, concerns a fictional Russian statesman named Nikolai who, though honourably devoted to Tsar Nicholas II, had been exiled to Paris for unproven charges. In Chapters IV through VIII, after the scene has been set, he is travelling from Paris to the seacoast with his granddaughter, Laura. (Her father is a British Member of Parliament separated from her Russian mother.) The two travellers are accosted by a "shabby stranger" who unfolds a circumstantial tale of plots and counterplots between the Tsarist secret police and the terrorist underground. In brief, he asserts that the grandfather's faithful and attractive factotum in Paris is also, under another name, chief counterspy of the terrorist extremists.

The grandfather, stricken by the revelations, has had to leave the train, and a doctor has found him a hotel room. Chapter X, which follows complete, represents only a fraction of this long novel; it was characteristically chosen by the author as a favourite single scene from her own fiction.]

X

The doctor touched Laura on the shoulder. She had fallen asleep while she was praying for a miracle which would bring her father to her at once, faster than the railway could do it. Looking up at the doctor, she asked, "How ill is my grandfather?"

"It's not easy to say." He had lost all his affectation. His fine head was less like a plaster cast, he was blinking and polishing his pince-nez. The gesture sent a shudder running through her. The lenses might be clear glass. He might be on the other side, one of Kamensky's men. True, his eyes, which were singularly beautiful, violet-blue and set far apart, had grown soft with concern for her grandfather, and even seemed to be a little moist as they met hers. That meant nothing: Kamensky would choose his lieutenants from people who could look like that when they did not mean it. But her suspicions left her, for he began to speak with a bewilderment which could not be pretence. It had the prick of hurt pride, and deceivers, she had noticed at school, were always proud of themselves.

He was saying that he could not understand her grandfather's case. The Count ought to be very ill, to go by his pulse, his blood-pressure, his respiration. "Yet he's fully conscious, he's talking vigorously, and he grasped my hand a minute or two ago—thinking we were saying good-bye, though of course I'll be looking in every couple of hours or so—quite firmly, indeed, quite painfully. I understand he had a shock?"

"A shock?"

"Yes, I understand there was a man on the train—"

How could he know that? He must be one of them.

"A Russian, wasn't it?" She could not speak. "Did I make a mistake then? Didn't Professor Saint-Gratien tell me that you and your grandfather had been bothered by some Russian on the train?"

"Oh, that. Yes, of course. There was a tiresome Russian on the train. I'd forgotten that. But it was nothing."

"Odd, I understood from my colleague that he thought you had been quite upset over it."

"No. Not really. To tell you the truth, I didn't quite understand what was going on, but it was nothing my grandfather couldn't have dealt with ordinarily, in spite of his age. They're wonderful people, his family," she told him, her voice shrill, as if she were lodging a complaint. "I can say it without being conceited, for I'm half-English. What they are is diluted in me. But the whole strength, it's something tremendous. And for the family, he's not very old. My mother says most of their relatives live into the eighties. Oh, you don't know what the Slavs are like. They're not like us, those people at the other end of Europe." At the thought of the power of some of them, and how it might be exercised, she went over to a chair at the other side of the room and sat down with her head in her hands. "They're not Europeans at all."

The Professor murmured, "Yes, everybody knows that the Russians are formidable, formidable. But all the same," he objected sadly, "even Russians don't live for ever."

"No," she agreed bleakly. "We don't live for ever. We haven't the prescription for that."

"Not even for long, with such a pulse, such blood-pressure, such respiration rate. No, really, that he can't do. Whoever he is. Is it really impossible, as Professor Saint-Gratien says you feel it is, for your mother to come from Paris? You're quite sure?"

As she shook her head she thought, "Will they never leave me alone?" It appeared the only sensible thing that she would have to tell them the truth, but that was impossible. "No, I'm sorry, if my mother was told, she might tell a man who would come and kill my

499

grandfather and me. Who is he? Well, he's two people. Gorin and Kamensky." But it sounded sheer madness.

"I'm sorry to hear it. For this is going to be a very harrowing sick-bed. Your grandfather, he's in a highly emotional state. He cried out to me that he must go back to Russia, and that at once. I've never heard anything like the passion behind his cries. I avoid dishonesty in dealing with my patients, what happens to them is the will of the good God and it is my duty to acquaint them with it, but I felt obliged to assure him that he would be able to start on the journey after a few days' rest, may God pardon me for the falsehood."

His eyes lay on her with a certain fixity. It might have been that he was racking his brains to think of a way to help her, it might have been that he did not believe her. But in any case, he was not being annoyed with her for being in a difficult position, making him feel he ought to do something about it. Gratefully, she said, "But don't worry about me. My father's coming. He'll start from London the very moment he can. I'll be all right."

"But have you heard definitely that he's on his way? I understood from my colleague that—"

"No. But he'll come."

"I wish you had heard from him. A telegram or a telephone mes-sage. I know from experience how difficult it can be to get in touch with relatives in cases of emergency. There seems to be a malignant fate at work—"

"But it'll be easy to find my father. He'll be either at home or at the House of Commons. There's nowhere else he could be. He's sure to come."

"All the same," sighed the Professor, "I wish you'd had an answer." There was a knock at the door and he grew calmer. "This may be some message. Come in, come in."

Something had gone wrong. The chambermaid Catherine came in slowly, her mouth a little open, her pale eyes wide, plainly the bearer of news so bad, and yet not so very bad, that they were enjoyable. "Professor," she said, "Monsieur Saint-Gratien has sent along Madame Verrier to nurse the Duke."

"Madame Verrier!" repeated the Professor. "Not Madame—" his voice cracked—"Verrier?"

A little woman with clear-cut features pushed past Catherine, dark and pale and slight, wearing a severe coat and skirt and hat, like a man's, and carrying a black bag. Lowering her head as if about to butt, she said, "I am a qualified nurse as well as a midwife. And there's someone ill here, isn't there? So why are you surprised to see me, Monsieur the Professor?"

"My grandfather is your patient," said Laura, going into an impersonation of her mother, and holding out her hand. "I'm so glad you have come. I am Laura Rowan. How do you do?"

The woman made a truce with the world just long enough to return the greeting, then said, "Now perhaps I might be taken to the patient, Professor." They went into the bedroom and Laura was left with Catherine, who was still breathing heavily. "You know Madame Verrier?" asked Laura. "Why are you surprised to see her? Doesn't she nurse as a regular thing?"

"Oh, yes, she's a regular nurse. But it's not suitable," said Catherine. "It's funny of Professor Saint-Gratien to have sent her. That's all."

"Isn't she a good nurse?"

"Oh, yes," said Catherine, looking this way and that in embarrassment. "She's a good nurse all right. She never has an accident. Not like the others. But it's not suitable."

"Lots of things that aren't suitable are happening today," said Laura. Then she caught her breath. "Madame Verrier isn't connected with Russia in any way, is she?"

"With Russia? No. Whatever made you think that? We've no Russians here in Grissaint except some students at the medical college, and a doctor or two, and she's nothing to do with them. She's the daughter of Brunois the watchmaker down by the Prefecture."

"She isn't mixed up with politics? She isn't a revolutionary, you know what I mean, a nihilist, someone who would throw bombs?"

"Heavens, no. I never heard her worst enemies say that about her. She's not a Catholic, of course, that she couldn't be, doing what she does. That's why Professor Barrault doesn't like her. He's a very good Catholic, the President of all our Catholic societies."

"But what is that this Madame Verrier does, then?" asked Laura. "Could she hurt my grandfather?" Catherine clapped her hand over her mouth to hide her laughter, and Laura shook with sudden rage. "Please go and get me some Evian or Vichy water."

"Yes, Mademoiselle," said Catherine. trying to smooth out the amusement on her face, and she turned at the door to say timidly, "I didn't mean any harm, but it's not suitable, not at all."

The Professor hardly spoke when he left. He simply kissed

Laura's hand and said, "I'll be back before long, and in the meantime you will find Madame Verrier—" he almost moaned it—"very competent." She did not dare ask him what it was that Madame Verrier did which showed her to be a bad Catholic, and the mystery became greater when the nurse came back into the salon. It seemed impossible she should have been a bad anything, and she even might have been uncomfortably good. She had clear grey eyes which probed and might easily accuse. She had taken off her coat and had discovered some speck adhering to the cuff of her very clean, slightly starched white blouse, and she scratched at it constantly with her exquisitely kept hands, frowning deeply. She was thin, not merely slender, but thin, as if she ate too frugally. At first she spoke in an argumentative tone, but this was evidently habit, her voice softened as she told Laura that her grandfather was sleeping and that she would call her when he woke.

It was not long before she did. Through the shadows of the bedroom the old man was weakly complaining: "I long to receive Holy Unction, not only for the sake of the anointment, but for the sake of hearing the priests chant the hymns of the rite, which are of a special beauty. I hunger and thirst to hear them, and not a word will come back to me. Some of the prayers, yes, they are with me. 'O Holy Father, Physician of Souls and Bodies, who didst send Thy only begotten Son, our Lord Jesus Christ, which healeth every infirmity and delivereth from death.' Yet is that right? It seems to me I'm making some mistake, but what? At any rate, the hymns are much dearer to me, they would give me back my lost power over myself, and of them I've forgotten every phrase."

"Please, dear, dear Grandfather," said Laura, "you're forgetting the hymns simply because you're tired. Rest, and in the morning you will remember them."

"It isn't entirely because I'm tired that I can't remember the hymns," said Nikolai. "It's partly because my mind is in an impure state. I keep on thinking about Kamensky and wondering why he did not love me. Also the real reason I'm tired is because I can't remember the hymns, not the other way round. Each of the services the Church appoints for an ordeal common to mankind is appropriate to that particular ordeal, to it and no other, and it alone can make that ordeal tolerable. Oh, God, give me back my memory of those dear hymns and take away my fatigue. Which is enormous. I feel as if I were about to fall through the mattress."

"When I can't remember poetry at school," said Laura, "I shut my eyes and don't think of anything at all, and sometimes it comes back to me."

"I'll try that," said Nikolai, "but I am afraid I will think of Kamensky."

"No, you don't think of anything if you do something funny with the front part of your head."

"Why, I knew that also when I was very young." He grew still, so still that she sat back in her chair so that the bed curtain was between her and the sight of his stony whiteness, which could not have been more like stone or whiter, unless he died.

His cry was happy. "I've remembered one hymn! How the words comfort me as they flow on to my tongue. Where are you, Laura? Listen, listen! This is the hymn to the Mother of God. 'Like drops of rain dried up by the summer sun, my days which are evil and few, gently vanish into nothingness. O Lady, save me . . .' But, Laura, my memory hasn't come back. Not altogether. For this is beautiful, but it is not quite right. Ah, but now I remember. 'Through thy tenderness of heart and the many bounties of thy nature, O Lady, intervene for me in this dread hour, O Invincible Helper.' Strange, it's not right. 'Great terror imprisoneth my soul, trembling unutterable and grievous, because it must go forth from the body.' It must go forth from my body. It must go forth from my body. Ah, now I understand."

He lifted up his voice in a shout which became a weak howl. The nurse opened the folding-doors and stood at the end of the bed, looking down at him with bent head and scrutinizing brows.

"My memory is perfect. Of course it is perfect. We Diakonovs never lose our memories. My memory has simply more common sense than my foolish heart, which makes me desire the consolation of Holy Unction, which is no longer for me. The prayer and the hymns which are coming into my mind are those appropriate to my state. They come from the Office for the Parting of the Soul from the Body."

Laura cried out, "No!" The idea that he was dying shocked her as if it had never occurred to her before, as if she had not thought him dead at the station, as if she had not discussed his death first with Chubinov and then with the doctors. Until this moment some part of her had not believed that anybody could really die. "You're ill," she argued, "very ill, but you're not dying."

"Allow your elders to know their own business best. I am on the point of death." He began to pray again. " 'O our Lady, Holy Birthgiver, O Conqueror and Tormentor of the Fierce Prince of the Air, O Guardian of the Dread Path, help thou me to pass over unhindered, as I depart from earth. Lo, terror is come to meet me, O Lady, and I fear it.' "

She sat quite still, covering her eyes, while the wild prayers flew about the room like bats.

" 'Vouchsafe that I may escape the hordes of bodiless barbarians and rise through the abysses of the air, and enter into Heaven, and I will glorify thee forever, O Holy Birthgiver of God. O thou who didst bear the Lord God Almighty, banish thou far from me in my dying hours the Chieftain of Bitter Torments who ruleth the universe, and I will glorify Thee forever.' " The nurse was standing at the end of the bed, crushing a tablet with a spoon in a glassful of water. "Who is she?" asked Nikolai. "But that I don't really want to know. How vast is the number of people who exist, who even serve one, and whom one doesn't want to know about. But I would like to know who that man was who told us that long story in the train. A senior police official, I suppose. Trust no one of his occupation. Do not trust me. Do not trust any of us, from the greatest man of state to the last lowest simpleton, who aid our Tsar in the sacred task of taking on the guilt of power in order that the common man may remain innocent. All, all of us are saved and tainted. But this man knew his business. You didn't happen to hear his name?"

"He was Vassili Iulievitch Chubinov."

"Really? I'm surprised at that. I knew him as a boy. He never showed any promise of being as good as that. All one could say in his favour was that he was a good revolver shot, and there are not many of them. Someone must have worked hard to raise him to that level. I wonder who it was." He lay staring through the wall beyond the end of his bed. The nurse held the glass to his lips and he drank the water without looking at her. "If only I had a secretary who could take down my thoughts as I dictated them. If only Kamensky was here."

"You shouldn't think of doing anything tiring like that," said Laura. "Try and go to sleep and tomorrow you can do everything you want."

"You don't understand the obligations inherent in this event—my death, I mean. It actually is written in the rite, 'Arise, O my soul! O my soul, why sleepest thou? The end draweth near and thou must speak.' Go into the other room, dear child, while I think what words they are that I ought to speak. It's not easy. For one thing, I should speak of my own sins, and though I know I'm a very sinful man, I've never been able to see what my sins are. They don't seem comparable to the sins which have been committed against me. But I understand that before I die I must really convince myself that I also have been in the wrong. I will have to work hard on this during my last hours, I will have to concentrate, for up till now I cannot see how I have ever been anything but in the right. Also, little one, if I rave of the deceptions and injustices which have been practised on me, you might feel that the world was too horrible for you to bear, not realizing that though these afflictions should by logic be unbearable, God gives you strength to bear them. I have really been enjoying myself all the time. But my agonies also have been stupendous, and my groans over them might mislead you, so go away, my dear little girl, my dear little Tania's dear little daughter. It is not because I don't love you that I wish you to leave me, it is because I do."

She leaned over him to give him a kiss, and he said, "Tell the lacemakers not to sing so loud. I approve of them singing hymns while they work, but they are disturbing me."

She went back to the salon and found that Catherine had brought in a bottle of Vichy water, which was standing in a bowl of ice. She filled a glass and went back to the window. The street was busier now. More customers than before were going in and out of the lit shops and stopping to gossip with the women and old men who were sitting on cane chairs beside the doorways, while the younger men leaned against the walls. Nearly all the women were sewing or knitting as they sat, and some of the old ones were bending their white linen caps over little pillows on which their lace was pinned, but their real occupation was the talk, which by jerked hands, shrugged shoulders, hands flung out palm upwards, wove the French fairy-tale about other people having shown an extraordinary lack of common sense. In the middle of the paved causeway children in blue overalls played gentle games. If a wrangle turned rough, parents started forward in their chairs and shot out jets of scolding, but the mellowness set in again at once. As the street darkened the sky grew brighter. The red roofs glowed terracotta, and in one of them, some distance off, a high sky-light blazed scarlet and diamond. There must be a magnificent sunset. Red sky at morning the shepherd's warning, red sky at night the shepherd's delight. The Channel would be smooth for her father.

When it was nearly night all the children ran to one end of the street and escorted back a boy and girl of eleven or nine or so, dressed in party clothes, carrying toys and leading between them a little girl, not more than five, golden-haired and dressed in a white frock with a blue sash low on her hips, who was clasping in her arms a doll dressed in white like herself. They all bore themselves like celebrities, and the occasion from which they had returned had evidently been recognized by everybody in the neighbourhood as quite out of the ordinary. As they went along the causeway, bright figures at the head of their blue-clad companions, the people sitting outside the houses eagerly called on them to stop, questioned them, examined their toys, admired their clothes, rubbing the hems of the little girls' dresses between finger and thumb, kissed them all, and waved them on with congratulating gestures. After they had gone, the other children lost interest in their play and by twos and threes went indoors. Now the roofs were darkening to brown, and the sky-light might just have been a hole, the glass gave back no light. Above, across a crystal blue-green sky pricked with the first stars, there raced black clouds, sometimes mounting up into great cliffs fissured with gulfs and staying so, sometimes marching like armies, substanceless but full of purpose. Up towards this aerial confusion the smoke rose from the chimney-pots in tight blue spirals, and swallows descended from the higher air to the eaves and up again, in flight as quick as cries. Her fear was like a dark arch over the lit stage where these things happened. She drank the cool water and put her forehead against the cool glass and prayed that her father would come soon.

Madame Verrier came out and said, "Your grandfather wants you. That sedative hardly worked at all. But the Professor will be coming back."

Though the nurse had lit the gas and the bedroom was not dark, Nikolai asked Laura, "Who are you?" and then said to himself, "Yes, it's her voice. And her slight accent. You would know she was not born in Russia." Then he told her, without tenderness, as if giving instructions to a clerk, "Well, now I know what it was all about, and you must listen."

"And what was it all about?"

"Why, nothing at all. When I say, nothing at all, I mean that that Kamensky business was of no importance."

"What, you mean that what Chubinov said wasn't true, was nonsense?"

506

"No, nothing he said was nonsense. He was one of us. He was one of the Russian nobility. Not a great family, but noble. If our sort talked nonsense, it was only because the occasion made it useless to talk sense. There have been many such occasions in Russian history. This was not one of them. The story Chubinov told us about Kamensky was perfectly true. But it meant nothing. Had no significance. Neither had the story of which it was a part, including my disgrace. That had no significance either. All that has happened is simply a consequence of the law that if opposites exist and meet they must destroy each other. To me the Tsar's power is the point at which historical being meets the will of God. But it seems to Kamensky and his imbeciles that the Tsar debauched history and that there is no God. If we could have remained separate, Kamensky and I, we might have done each other no harm. But we were drawn together by the existence of the Tsar, by the existence of God, they forced us two to confront each other. So all that was he rushed out to destroy me, so all that was I rushed out to destroy him. It is an accident, that is all, like a collision between two railway trains."

"But you aren't destroyed."

"In an earthly sense, I am. Utterly destroyed. First my honour, then my life. I would have lived years longer if I had not learned this morning that little Sasha was my Judas. I felt the sword coming out at the other side of my thick body. And Kamensky will die too. Chubinov will kill him."

She breathed, "You're sure of that?"

"Quite sure. To begin with, Chubinov is not such a fool as he looks. And consider his education. I took quite a lot of pains to make him a good revolver shot. My reason was that it was the sort of thing his father thought he would not be able to do, and he despised him for it. But whether I went to all this trouble out of Christian charity, because I was sorry for poor young Vassili, or because I wanted to keep his father in his place as inferior to me, I really cannot say. Well, there was I training him to kill Kamensky, without knowing it, and on the other side there was Kamensky training him to kill Kamensky, without knowing it either, by rubbing into him through the years the tactics and strategy of assassination. But, Laura, I hope you understand that you must do everything you can to prevent Chubinov killing Kamensky."

"Of course, Grandfather."

"Don't say 'of course.' It is your Christian duty, but nobody can say 'of course' with any appositeness about a Christian duty, which is always forced and extravagant and the last thing any sensible person would choose to undertake. I feel more certain that it is your duty to attempt to stop Chubinov killing Kamensky because it is so very unlikely that a young girl will be able to avert this crime. Oh, Laura, my little Laura, I grieve for you. Kamensky is very low. I had to raise him up to a great height before we could speak together and form a mutual affection, form what I believed to be a mutual affection. But through his lowness a great force travelled. Oh, my little one, dear child of my dear child, it may destroy you, it must certainly alter your world. The universe is full of great forces which manifest themselves in disgusting ways through our fallen humanity. O Lord, when I am dead, explain to me the folly of Thy creation, for the wisdom Thou Thyself has given me faints with bewilderment."

Professor Barrault and Madame Verrier had stolen in quietly through the folding-doors. "What are those two shuffling about for? Do they think I cannot see and hear? Till the last moment of my life my senses will be sharper than theirs have ever been. Ask the woman to leave. The man can stay, but not the woman. Yes, I know she is a nurse, but she affects me disagreeably, like the women students in our Russian universities. Thank you, my dear. Now give the man a chair. I am sure he knows his business so well that he will notice when I give signs of actually dying and will come forward and do what is necessary. Convey to him my respect for his skill and my gratitude that I should be the object of it. Now let me get on with what I must tell you, Laura. It's fortunate for you that you have inherited the Diakonov intelligence and will understand at least part of my story. You see, I have discovered what my sins are, or rather what my great sin is. What is extraordinary is that, though nobody could call me a vain man, it proceeds from vanity. Some time ago you left the room—what did you do?"

"I sat at a window and looked down at the street."

"What did you see?"

"Old people sitting at the doors, people going in and out of the shops, children playing, three children coming back from a party. It was quite pretty."

"It may have been pretty but it can't have been of the slightest importance. Whatever you did when you left the room can't have meant anything at all. You see, when you went away I tried to imagine what it will be like when I am dead and come into the presence of God, and it wasn't very hard, for I am no longer with you in my entirety. Half of me has already left my body and this world. So I could see how it will be when I meet God. And it will be a meeting between two beings who are different, more different than a man from a woman, more different than a white man from a Negro, totally different. It was like that"—he could still snap his fingers—"I saw the difference between God and Man running through the universe as a flash of lightning runs through the sky. I say that because that difference is a thing in itself. Other differences are comparisons. Not this, which is unique."

He wept and impatiently dried his eyes with the sheet. Laura wiped away his tears with her own handkerchief and called him softly the tender names her nannie used to call her when she was ill, knowing that he would not understand them and could not blast them away with his scorn. He could not argue off-hand that he was not a cocker-nonny. Choking, he went on: "I've been wrong all the time. O my God, when I have done my best to serve Thee, why didst Thou not inform my ignorance and keep me from this sin? When we are face to face explain to me the mystery of Thy lack of candour. Almost before Thou dost anything else. Well, I have always known that God is good and the maker of all things good, the sower who broadcasts good seed and reaps the good harvest, and I have known too that Man is not good, he is a chaos in which evil mingles with good and is always preferred by its host, he is the bad land in which the good seed can grow but poorly, and then only by grace. But I thought Man was a lesser member of God's family, even as I have relatives who are drunkards and adulterers and many things that I am not. I saw God as a man divinely free of Man's evil, with no human qualities save when he clothed Himself with Jesus, and I saw Man as a God with the divinity extracted and the human qualities grossly proliferating into perpetual sin. On the contrary, God is God and Man is Man, and there is no bridge between them but grace, and that does not change Man into God, it simply saves him from damnation. In the same way, I could not make Kamensky my kinsman simply by making him my friend."

"Well, then, that's settled, you're not God, you're Man," said Laura. "But we all loved you as a man. Of course God will forgive you. Now lie back and rest, dear, dear Grandfather."

He sobbed a little longer and said, as soon as he could, "I would be glad if you would see that Kamensky and Chubinov are each given some little possession of mine as a souvenir. An object of some value but with no family associations. Neither is related to me."

"Yes, Grandfather," said Laura. She turned aside and muttered into her wet handkerchief, "I'll see them damned first."

Professor Barrault said, "But this must stop. He is exhausting himself. Another tablet, I think, Mademoiselle—"

"He's being quite happy in his way," said Laura.

"You grasp the appalling consequences of my mistake. Since I didn't understand that God and His Son are unique, I didn't grasp that His suffering was unique and unlike that of any human being. Therefore I was led into the blasphemy of supposing that because His suffering has meaning, so has mine. Pretentious idiot that I was! I thought that in suffering I was buying something at a great price, carrying out a costly sacrifice which in time would be hailed in heaven and on earth as glorious. So I have lived in anguish. I've been tormented by the itch to inquire into the mechanism of my disgrace, for a martyr can't help, I imagine, but have some curiosity about the details of his martyrdom. Sebastian must have wondered why all those pagan arrows did not harm him, though later the pagan rods beat him to death. Without dignity I panted like a thirsty dog, waiting for the day when my persecutors would be routed and my martyrdom acclaimed by men and angels. So I howled and caterwauled and made the lives of those around me a misery because I impudently expected my agony to be a sacrament, to be the symbol in this material world of an event in the spiritual world. I've been no better than a peasant who goes mad and believes himself heir to an immense fortune, to an estate in the Crimea and mines in the Urals, so that he refuses to work and lets his wife and children and old parents starve. I have wasted my life because I have not seen that my pains are of no more significance than my pleasures, and they have none, and that my only worth lies in my love of God, and all that I did and was on earth is without meaning, because I am a man."

He was in agony. She said, "This isn't true. I love you, my mother loves you, my grandmother loves you, many people love you, for all sorts of reasons which matter. Oh, for one thing, you were so brave when you were hounded down."

In a small voice he said, "Above the window."

She turned about and looked.

"That blotch on the wall, running towards the corner of the room. The rain's seeped in from a gutter on the outside. A workman's

510

scamped his work. My suffering means only that. I am evil because I am human, my evil heritage called to those cursed by the same heritage, and together we laid out our portion so that it increased. I am repenting. God will forgive me. But that doesn't make my sufferings any more interesting. If you remember my misfortunes and your kind heart and your family loyalty make you pity me, remember that blotch on the wall. My whole life is as important as that blotch, no less and no more."

Laura prayed aloud, "Oh, God, don't let him think anything so awful. Do some sort of miracle."

Nikolai said, "Ah, I've broken your heart. But I had to tell you, and it's of no importance that anybody's heart is broken. Conquer your pride and your respect for the emotions, which should be despised with all you can muster of contempt, which I hope is not much, since you are a woman, and remember what I say: 'Man is not God, God is not Man,' and repeat it often to yourself. You will have children, all women in our family marry, they never lack great attractions, and you must repeat it to those children of yours also. You may think it isn't necessary, for the difference between the human and the divine is stated in every book of the Bible and in every office of our liturgy. But there's a treacherous paradox here. There's no better guide than custom, but on all that's customary there settles the thick dust of material time, so that the mind turns away from it in distaste. For me that message of the Scriptures and the Church was dimmed with many readings and many hearings, so only in this last bitter hour did I learn what they had been trying to tell me. What a mistake, what frustration, but it does not matter, I know now I am a man."

She prayed silently, "God, let him die now, God, let him die now." Surely God could see the foam on his lips.

"I hope you go back to Russia, Laura. Oh, God, grant me this, since I am penitent, send my little Laura back to Russia. Our Russian society is the society which is precious to Thee, all the others are chance coagulations of pagan mobs. Russian society alone serves God, but not strenuously enough. It prays but it does not fast. At present it simply tells each of its members to spare himself the trouble of deciding what he shall be and do here on earth, since the Tsar makes all such decisions for him and takes on himself the guilt of earthly power. How beautiful, how very beautiful is our system. As time goes on it will be admired as the most merciful and fatherly form of government the world has ever known. Yet it has its faults. It is insufficiently rigid. There are occasions when it permits a man to use his own will. Even I, who have given my utter loyalty to the system, can look back to moments when I have made my own choice, God forgive me."

Laura's eyes and mouth opened wide. Was he really unaware that from his birth he had done exactly as he pleased?

"At many moments our Russian State turns to water. It often does not stand four-square. These weaker moments are speciously attractive. My own doctor is the son of one of my father's serfs, and in my folly I have rejoiced in this as admirable. But now I see I was wrong, for such liberty leads straight to the sin I have committed. If a man can change his place in the world and the conditions of the world, he must construct for himself some philosophical belief which will teach him what changes to make, and since he is vain he will attach great importance to this belief, since it is the work of his own mind. Then he is bound to sin with me and forget that God is God and Man is Man. He will become a rival to God and pretend that he understands life as well as God does and can control the direction of history. Then he must become a miserable and grieving rebel against God, and will insist that his suffering has a meaning, though the whole of existence will prove to him that it has not, and he will waste his life in useless lamentations as I have wasted mine, or in murderous conspiracies like my poor little Sasha and that idiot Vassili Iulievitch. A small man has come into the room, my eyes are failing, I can only see that he is small. How curious it must be to be small. I am glad I was spared that humiliation. Who is he?"

"He's the doctor who was so kind to us at the station."

"Tell him he may stay if he does not interrupt. Oh, Laura, we Russians have been too lax. Let Russians build up a citadel of goodness, where everybody realizes that his highest destiny, his only respectable destiny is to obey. Let each Russian offer up the dear wayward son of his soul, his will, as God the Father offered up His dear obedient son, Christ. For the sake of the world we must surrender our souls to God and our bodies to His servant the ruler of Russia. This is not even very much to ask of ourselves, for it is not a sacrifice which need be made for ever. When Holy Russia has been anointed for centuries by the blessed oil of its children's abnegated will, all Russians will be born committed to innocence. The State is only an instrument of man's moral struggle, so then, all men being moral, there will be no need for the State. It will wither away. Grace will replace the law. The kingdom of Heaven will be established on earth. Laura, go back to Russia and await that day."

He threw himself back on his bed and closed his eyes violently, as if to kill his sight. Professor Barrault came forward and put his fingers on his wrist and said to the nurse, "Quick, the syringe." But Nikolai flung off his hand and said, "Remember, Laura, to give my love to my dear wife and all my family, the women as well. I realize how much I must have tried their patience by my preoccupation with my griefs. But I suppose I made it up to them in quite a number of ways."

"Nurse," said Professor Barrault, "let's try again. He really ought to have the injection."

"I shouldn't bother," said Professor Saint-Gratien.

Nikolai heaved himself up in bed again. Shuddering, he said, "In the desert place I may see a giant hand or foot. I must try to keep my self-command though I will be dead and remember that it's an illusion of the Devil. Why has nobody lit the gas? I saw a gas-jet when I came into the room."

"The gas is on," said Professor Barrault.

"Then get candles," said Nikolai, turning his face about so that everybody present got the full force of his displeasure. "Must we talk in the dark like gipsies?"

It was as if he himself were a candle: a lit candle which was then blown out.

When the doctors sent Laura out of the bedroom, she went back to the window and looked out through the lenses of her tears. The shops were still bright and had some customers, but there were no children in the causeway, except a few who were leaning against the walls and eating sandwiches or supping out of bowls, with an air of discontent and abandonment. All the chairs had been taken in from the doorways. Most of the upper rooms were lit and it was there life was being carried on now: dark figures moved backwards and forwards against the wavering blow of lamplight. The hours were passing, it could not be so long before her father would be with her. She did not know how she could bear this sharp pain without him. For as she had found earlier that fear is an affliction of the body, gliding about in the bowels, so she was now finding out that grief was a wound in the chest. Presently the doctors came in and drew up two chairs beside her. Now that she had seen a dead person, the living seemed more strange. How did one move and feel? While she listened to the doctor she surreptitiously looked down at her hand, spread out the fingers, brought them together again, and wondered at the miracle.

It seemed that she must not go back to the bedroom for a time, the nurse had various things to do to Nikolai. She nodded, accepting that there were yet more mysteries, and told them that it was important his icon must be put on his breast. The doctors went on to say that her grandfather must have been a very great man. A man of state, said Professor Barrault, drawing himself up, broadening his shoulders, impersonating unassailability. She wanted to deny it, to disclose that Nikolai had been oppressed and deceived and persecuted and pitiful, but was not sure that he would have liked them to know it. Then Professor Barrault asked if she would care to spend the night at his house, Professor Saint-Gratien breaking in to explain that he could not make such an offer, since his was a bachelor establishment. Professor Barrault hastily mentioned, as if to clear a colleague from a suspicion of light-mindedness, that Professor Saint-Gratien had the misfortune to be a widower. He himself enjoyed the happiness of having a wife and three daughters, and his eldest girl would be glad to give up her room to Laura. True, he and his family would be out all evening, for they were going to the ball which was to be held downstairs, so heartless, he added, was circumstance. But his servants would give her supper and help her to retire early.

She was shocked. They should not think her capable of leaving her grandfather alone. While she was talking to them she was also talking to him, in her mind, assuring him again and again that the giant head or foot would be an illusion of the Devil, and letting her left hand hang over the arm of her chair so that his spirit hand could grasp it if he wanted. As soon as the nurse had finished whatever it was she was doing, she would go and pray beside him. But it turned out that Professor Saint-Gratien and Madame Verrier had known that she should want to keep Nikolai company during his first night of death, for they had already arranged for a camp-bed to be put in the salon, and Madame Verrier was to stay with her till the morning. Then the two doctors said good-bye, promising to come in later, when they were at the ball, and Laura said she would be glad, but that her father would be here soon, and would want to meet them. When the door had closed she knelt by the window and again put her forehead against the glass and let the tears run down her face, and repeated all the prayers she could remember from the Orthodox service, sometimes speaking to Nikolai. Now there was true night above the roofs, and the street was empty. Most of the shops were shuttered, though the windows above still glowed with lamplight and were crossed by silhouettes. Down below the ball had begun. She could hear the band.

Madame Verrier came out of the bedroom and stood beside her at the window, patted her shoulder, and gave her a clean handkerchief. Two dogs chased a cat down the causeway, a door opened, the cat shot in, the dogs yapped and sauntered on. The half-hour struck on a distant clock. Then a woman, her cloak drawn high about her head, ran in a soft helter-skelter along the causeway.

"Madame Gallet," said the nurse. "I'd know her anywhere, wrap up as she likes."

"Is she one of your patients?"

"She's been to me twice."

The woman down in the causeway came to a halt, let the cloak fall on her shoulders, smoothed her hair, shook out her skirts, and went at a sober pace into a house.

"Thoughtless girl," said Madame Verrier. "'I wonder where she's gone. But she's no worse than thoughtless. Life's very hard." Staring out into the darkness, she raised her small clean hand and beat out the rhythm of the quadrille which was bumpety-bumping through the walls and floor. "Your grandfather," she said, with hostility, "must have been a very handsome man." But then, as if an extenuating circumstance had crossed her mind, she exclaimed, "The poor old gentleman. It's hard on a man when he comes to die. Harder than it is for women. For many dying men, it's the first time that anything's gone against them, the first time they find their bodies not doing just what they're told. Women are used to that, which of us would choose what happens to us every month? That's an idiotic business. And as for children, it's the women who want them who don't have them, and the poor women who don't want them, God help them, nobody else does, who get them. In either case, it's a great injustice, indeed one might call it the great injustice. But men, everything goes as they want it till the last moment and then they aren't able to credit it that their luck's turning. One can't," she said in a grudging tone, "help feeling sorry for them."

515

FROM This Real Night

1

The day was so delightful that I wished one could live slowly as one can play music slowly. I was sitting with my two sisters, Cordelia and Mary, my twin, and our cousin, Rosamund, in the drawing-room of our house in Lovegrove, which is a suburb of South London, on a warm Saturday afternoon in late May, nearly fifty years ago. It was warm as high summer, and bars of sunshine lay honey-coloured across the floor, the air above them shimmering with motes; and bees droned about a purple branch of viburnum in a vase on the mantel-piece. We four girls were bathed in a sense of leisure we had never enjoyed before and were never to enjoy again, for we were going to leave school at the end of term, and we had passed all the examinations which were to give us the run of the adult world. We were as happy as escaped prisoners, for we had all hated being children. A pretence already existed in those days, and has grown stronger every year since then, that children do not belong to the same species as adults and have different kinds of perception and intelligence, which enable them to live a separate and satisfying life. This seemed to me then, and seems to me now, great nonsense. A child is an adult temporarily enduring conditions which exclude the possibility of happiness. When one is quite little one labours under just such physical and mental disabilities as might be inflicted by some dreadful accident or disease; but while the maimed and paralysed are pitied because they cannot walk and have to be carried about and cannot explain their needs or think clearly, nobody is sorry for babies, though they are always crying aloud their frustration and hurt pride. It is true that every year betters one's position and gives one more command over oneself, but that only leads to a trap. One has to live in the adult world at a disadvantage, as member of a subject race who has to admit that there is some reason for his subjection. For grown-ups do know more than children, that cannot be denied; but that is not due to any real superiority, they simply know the lie of the land better, for no other reason than that they have lived longer. It is as

516

if a number of people were set down in a desert, and some had compasses and some had not; and those who had compasses treated those who had not as their inferiors, scolding and mocking them with no regard for the injustice of the conditions, and at the same time guiding them, often kindly, to safety. I still believe childhood to be a horrible state of disequilibrium, and I think we four girls were not foolish in feeling a vast relief because we had reached the edge of the desert. ◇ ◇ ◇

2

The large square room of Mr Morpurgo's car trundled us* across the Thames and past the Houses of Parliament into the part of London south of Hyde Park, where the squares are faced with stucco and the tall houses are white cliffs round the green gardens; and he grew very cheerful. "Now we are near home," he said, "and I am quite looking forward to meeting my wife at luncheon. Though she has been back for two days I have hardly seen her. Unhappily her journey has given her one of those agonizing headaches which are the curse of her life. They make it absolutely impossible for her to talk to anybody, and while they last she simply has to shut herself up in her bedroom and pull down the blinds, and that's what she has been doing ever since she came back. We had a long talk together on her arrival, and suddenly the old pain started. No, no, there was no question of putting you off. I would have been quite ruthless in asking you to come another day if it had been necessary. But I asked her yesterday evening, and she said that if she dined in bed and took a sleeping draught she would be quite fit for the party today."

"Travel has been unlucky for you both lately," said Mamma. "You really looked quite ill when you came back from that Continental journey which you said you hadn't enjoyed."

"Ah, yes," he sighed, sobered by the memory. "But that, as you realized, was because of all the cooking in oil. See, this is where I live, the big house, the very big house, lying crossways at the corner of

*[Cordelia and Rose (the narrator), two of the three Aubrey sisters of chapter 1, with their mother, Clare, and their younger brother, Richard Quin. They and their host, Mr Morpurgo, have been introduced in chapter 1. All of them appeared also in *The Fountain Overflows* (1956), to which this as yet unfinished novel is to be a sequel.]

the square, and not at all in keeping. There is nothing one can do about that. As the Almighty pointed out to Job, nothing can be done about behemoth and leviathan. No, do not get out yet, the footman will open the door."

At those last words I was stricken with terror. Like all people brought up in households destitute of menservants, we regarded them as implacable enemies of the human kind, who could implement their ill-will by means of supernatural powers which enabled them to see through a guest's pretensions as soon as they let him into the house and to denounce him to the rest of the company without the use of speech. We hurried past the footman with our eyes on the ground and thus were unaware till we had entered the hall that this was not just a large house, such as we had expected Mr Morpurgo to possess, it was large like a theatre or a concert-hall. We stood washed by the strong light that poured from a glass dome far above us, on a shining floor set with a geometric pattern of black and white marble squares and triangles and crescents; a staircase swept down with the curve of a broad, slow waterfall; the walls were so wide that one took a tapestry where two armies fought it out on land round a disputed city in the foreground, and in the background two navies fought it out among an archipelago lying where a sea and estuary met; and on the facing wall a towering Renaissance chimneypiece rose into a stone forest honeycombed by several hunts. When Mr Morpurgo had had his hat and coat taken from him, he wheeled round and faced us, his little arms spread out, his little legs wide apart.

"Of course," he said gravely, "we have no need for a house as large as this, there are only five of us. But a man must have a house he can turn round in." We remained silent, and he went to Mamma and took her hand and kissed it. "Clare, you have brought up your children beautifully. Not one of them laughed. So I will tell you about this house, and why you must not laugh at it."

The butler and the footmen all suddenly looked as remote as if they had taken a drug, and shifted on their feet. They did not look like the devils I had expected; rather they recalled Shakespearean courtiers dealing with what must have been the chief problems of their lives, how to stand within earshot of their loquacious betters and seem not to be listening, and how to find a stance which would carry them comfortably through soliloquies. "The truth is," said Mr Morpurgo, "I have too much house, as I am apt to have too much everything. But there is reason to be kind about the excess of this place. My father built it, because he was a Jew, one of a persecuted people, and he was entertained by King Edward the Seventh, on an occasion which really deserves to be remembered. Nobody said anything about it the other day when he died, I suppose it was impossible because we want to keep the peace among the nations. But it may in the future be remembered as an example of a thing that only a king could do, and a thing that you would not expect to be within the range of a Hanoverian king, for it had wit. As you are sure to know, the Tsar of Russia hates his Jewish subjects. He has been furiously anti-Semitic ever since the time when he was a young man travelling in Japan and a waiter who had gone mad hit him on the head with a heavy tray; and it does not merely happen that there are pogroms in Russia, they are promoted by the government, that is to say, by the Tsar. Well, when the Tsar came to England in 1894 the Prince of Wales administered a rebuke to his niece's young husband. He invited him to spend a weekend at Sandringham, and when the Tsar got there he found that nearly all his fellow-guests were Jews. One of them was my father, and he was profoundly impressed. It is true that many people, on hearing this story, are less impressed, and point out that the Prince of Wales had borrowed a great deal of money from those Jews which he had never repaid. But such people are always Gentiles. We Jews know that there are many people who borrow money from us and do not repay it, and that it is not really very usual for such borrowers to make beautiful and courteous gestures in defence of our race. So my father, having been asked to Sandringham on this auspicious occasion, built this house, because he felt exalted and wanted to make a visible symbol that our race is honoured on earth as we have always been perhaps a little too certain that it is honoured in heaven. Therefore, children, think gently of this house, and forget, as I try to forget, that my father should really have understood that it is ridiculous to build in the Renaissance style with machine-cut stone—"

He suddenly came to a halt and his smile faded. "Manning," he said, and the butler came forward. Mr Morpurgo pointed to a Homburg hat that was lying on the hall-table, and asked, "Does that mean that we have another guest for luncheon?"

"Yes, sir," said the butler. "Mr Weissbach is in the drawing-room."

Mr Morpurgo repeated, "Mr Weissbach? But why has he come? I did not ask him." He passed his hand across his forehead. "There

519

must be some mistake. I must have asked him for another day. Yet I can't remember doing anything of the sort."

The butler licked his lips. "Mr Weissbach rang up this morning just after you left, sir, and said that he had just come back from abroad, and was very anxious to see you, and I put him through to Madam, who spoke to him and then told me there would be another guest for luncheon."

He spoke with gloating discretion. Mr Morpurgo seemed stupefied by what he heard. There was the same atmosphere that there used to be at school when there was trouble between the teachers. Only Mamma did not realize that something had gone wrong. Her eyes were wandering among the handsome valour of the lances and pennants on the armies in the tapestries, the compressed churches and palaces in the city they disputed; she was softly humming some music that seemed to her appropriate.

Mr Morpurgo continued to stare at the Homburg hat. At last he said, in the voice of a reasonable and unperturbed man, "It seems that my wife has arranged for you to meet Mr Mortimer Weissbach. An art-dealer, a famous art-dealer. Not one of the dealers I took you to see, Clare, when we had your pictures to sell. He specializes in Italian art. God has thought fit to take the Holy Land away from my people, but of late years He has done much to compensate for this by giving some of them the Quattrocento to cultivate instead. Come, let us go up my staircase, my enormous staircase."

He halted us on the landing. A single picture hung between two doors, presented with pomp, set in a gilt panel carved with pilasters and adjoining arch: a Madonna and Child painted in flat, bright colours with much gold. "My Simone Martini," he said tenderly. As he gazed on it he might have been sucking toffee. Shyly he added, "Hardly a painting, I've often thought, more a mosaic made of tiles taken up from the floor of heaven. New tiles. I've got another picture, my Gentile da Fabriano, who did the trick with some of the worn tiles from the same place. I don't know which I like better."

"Beautiful, beautiful," Mamma murmured and passed into a trance. She opened her mouth, and Mr Morpurgo drew nearer to hear what comment his treasure had drawn from her. She said, "I wish Piers had been more interested in pictures. It would have given him such a nice rest from politics, and he would have enjoyed painting had he turned his mind to it, he had quite a feeling for painting."

"Indeed he had," said Richard Quin. "We have lots of sketch-books of his, you know, with water-colours he did in Ireland and Ceylon and South Africa."

"Where are those sketch-books now?" asked Cordelia in sudden panic. "We must not lose them, we lose everything."

"I have them, dear," said Mamma, and continued, "He had no ear for music, and anyway music would not have been right for him. But painting is a calm art, and he needs calm."

"Well, calm can come to a man in many ways," said Mr Morpurgo. "And what a family it is!" he groaned. "You look at a picture, and you appreciate it, I can see by the way you keep your eyes on this one that you get its form and its colours, yet they all turn into thoughts of Piers. But for you everything, absolutely everything, turns into thoughts of Piers, doesn't it?"

"You must forgive us," said Mamma, "we cannot help it. And really—" she added impatiently, and then checked herself and smiled. For an instant she had supposed Mr Morpurgo was being silly, but of course he was so nice that it was wrong to admit that, even when it was true. "And really it isn't a fault. Even if it wasn't Piers we're talking about, and of course he stands head and shoulders above anyone else, isn't it natural for a wife to think of her husband, for children to think of their father?"

"Yes," agreed Mr Morpurgo, "it is natural. One might go further and say it is nearly the whole of nature." The idea seemed to please him. He warmed himself at it for a moment, then said gravely, "And now, come and meet the people of whom I naturally think. Come and meet my wife and daughter."

Now the butler, who had maintained his character as a Shakespearean courtier by moving a couple of paces away from us with an air of withdrawing to another part of the forest, came forward and opened a door at a blank verse pace. We found ourselves in a large room which seemed to us glittering and confused. The light that streamed in from high windows was given back by chandeliers, brocaded hangings, the glass on pictures and in display cabinets, and a number of crystal and silver objects; and among the buhl chairs and tables there stood several great screens of flowers, four or five feet high. At the end of the room, dark against a window, stood a group of people, from which, after too long a pause, a tall and rounded figure detached itself. It was Mrs Morpurgo, and she was extremely surprised. She wore a hat; at that time all women of position wore hats when they entertained their friends to luncheon. Her hat was huge, and under it her thick ginger-gold hair was piled up in the shape of a Phrygian cap, and this gave her a preternaturally massive head, so it could clearly be seen that she had drawn it back, as people do when faced with something they simply cannot understand. Her body too was magnified by her puffed sleeves and her rich, self-supporting, flounced skirt, and so the questioning shrug of her shoulders, the hesitation of her gait, were magnified too. It was nothing about us which startled her; her glance had not examined us. She seemed not to have expected anybody, anybody at all, to have come in by that particular door; and as there were two other doors in the room, and as the three young girls behind her were smiling as if they were witnessing a ridiculously familiar scene, I supposed that Mr Morpurgo obstinately entered this room by a door which for some reason should not be used, just as Papa always left the gas burning in his study when he went to bed. But it was odd of Mrs Morpurgo to make a fuss about so small a matter at this moment, for her husband was caught up in solemn exaltation. If his eyes had met mine I would not have dared to smile. He said, "Herminie, this is my old friend, Clare Aubrey." His voice wavered, and he cleared his throat. "The wife," he explained, "of Piers Aubrey, whom I so much admire. And here are her Cordelia, and Rose and Richard Quin." As he slowly spoke our names he spread out his arms around us in a patriarchal gesture which announced his hope that his family and ours should be welded together for ever in the shelter of his affection. But he immediately curbed his gesture. Had it been completed, it must have included within its scope Mr Weissbach, who at that moment stepped from behind a pyramid of gladioli and roses and took up a position beside the young girls. The manner in which Mr Morpurgo exclaimed, "Ah, Weissbach!" conveyed too brutally just where the project of adoption he had declared left off. Though Mr Weissbach plainly did not need to be adopted since he was an elegantly dressed gentleman in middle life, silver-haired and neatly bearded and closely resembling King Edward the Seventh, he might well have felt hurt. Mr Morpurgo began again, "You remember, Herminie, I have so often talked of these young people," but the remark broke against the hard surfaces of his wife's total bewilderment. His voice cracked, his hands made fluttering, coaxing movements, and then were still. He sighed something kind which could hardly be heard.

I had mistaken the cause of Mrs Morpurgo's surprise. We had not come into the room by the wrong door. But her husband had come into the room, and had brought us with him, and she was surprised by that, because everything her husband did struck her as inexplicable. This I realized very soon, for Mrs Morpurgo had no secrets. She controlled her words well enough, saying the same sort of things that the mothers of our school-fellows said when we went to tea with them, but as she spoke, the truth was blared aloud by the intonations of her commanding voice, the expressions which passed over her face, legible as the words on a poster, and her vigorous movements. "This is Marguerite," she told my mother, "and this is Marie Louise, nearly grown-up, just grown-up, which should I say? Just like your Cordelia and Rose. Oh, yes, terribly dignified, aren't you, my pets? And here's our baby, Stephanie. Is your boy as young?" But her clear, protruding, astonishingly bright grey-green eyes were saying, "Well, I am doing what he wants, but why should he want me to do it? Who can these people be that he thrusts them on me?" She went on, "Ah, then there are three months between them, but he is inches taller," and her accents asked, "What can possibly come of it if I am as nice to them as he insists? We have nothing in common with them; how am I to carry on a relationship even if I begin it?" In the midst of a pleasant remark about Cordelia and myself, she bit her lip in annoyance and shuddered. "It is always the same," she might as well have said aloud, "he never stops doing this sort of thing, it is insupportable."

Then her eyes flashed, she turned aside from us. "Edgar, my dear," she said, with the air of clearing up at least one tangle in this disordered world that was being created about her against her will, and seeing to it that he should not make one of his absurd accusations that she was the one who muddled things, "you may be surprised to see Mr Weissbach here, but he rang up just after you went out, and specially wanted to see you, because he's just this minute come back from Italy, where he's been picking up all sorts of lovely things, and I thought that as we were having Mrs Aubrey and her family to lunch, we would be delighted to see Mr Weissbach, too."

A coldness came into the genial smile that lived brilliantly and all the time between Mr Weissbach's neatly clipped moustache and pointed beard, and Mr Morpurgo put down his head as if his wife's speech had had an echo and he were listening to it with scientific interest. The extreme fatigue with which Mrs Morpurgo had uttered the last phrase could not have more clearly intimated that as her husband had insisted she should waste time to luncheon, Mr Weissbach, who also wanted to waste her time, might as well waste the same piece of time. Mamma regarded her with the pity she always extended to people under a special handicap, one of the daughters giggled, the tick of the ormolu clock on the mantelpiece sounded very loud. Mrs Morpurgo looked at her husband with the expression which could have been foretold. "Again you are behaving incomprehensibly," she wondered silently, running a firm finger over her lips in affected doubt. "Why on earth could what I have just said have annoyed anybody?" Furiously she addressed my mother, "Will you not sit down?" and drew her to a chair beside the fireplace, and remained standing beside her, sometimes rocking back on her heels, as if the strangeness of what was happening to her had actually thrown her off her balance, while she impatiently engaged her in light conversation. She was splendid under the light from the high windows. Her face was unlined. Her skin was smooth and radiant like the surface of fine porcelain. It seemed to have something to do with her difficulty in apprehension.

I was left with her two elder daughters, at whom I smiled, for they had aroused my respect. They had escaped the ugliness of their father but they had not achieved the handsomeness of their mother; for she was handsome. Though she made war on ease by every word she said, she promised ease by the cushioned firmness of her flesh, the brilliance of her flesh, her eyes, and skin and hair. But the girls were exquisitely neat in their blouses and belling skirts, even neater than Cordelia. It did not occur to me that this was because they were dressed by a lady's maid, so I imagined them to be deft and fastidious and precise. I saw them preparing for the day in miraculously tidy bedrooms cleaned by the cool morning light, standing in front of cheval glasses and stroking their blouses into the right flutings at their waists, their narrow beds smooth behind them, almost undisturbed by the night. I was disconcerted when they answered me with smiles which were certainly reserved and perhaps mocking. Cordelia was having better luck, for Mr Weissbach was talking to her as politely as if she were a grown-up; I had expected this in Mr Morpurgo's house, I had supposed that there people would take it for granted that they should make much of everybody they met. Richard Quin had asked Mr Morpurgo about a miniature on one of the tables, and Mr Morpurgo was answering, "It is interesting that you should

want to know who that is. My little Stephanie here is always fascinated by him. He was a Bavarian Marshal of Irish origin. Come
here, Stephanie, and tell Richard Quin all you know about him."
That, too, I had expected here, his happy, harmless pedantry, his
enjoyment of knowledge which was as purely ornamental as flowers,
unlike my father's kind of knowledge, which was a stock of fuel for
crusades. But Marguerite and Marie Louise, who continued to be
silent and look as if I amused them, were not what I had expected. I
had to own that Mary might be right. The world might have its
resemblances to school.

Mrs Morpurgo suddenly broke off her conversation with Mamma
to remark in the voice of desperation itself, "Surely luncheon is very
late!"

"No," said Mr Morpurgo coldly. "It is now three minutes before
our usual hour."

"I could not have believed it," said Mrs Morpurgo. "But it is
strange, time seems to pass so quickly at times, and so slowly at
others. Well, at luncheon," she said, with an air of clinging to a
plank, "we will be able to listen to Mr Weissbach telling us of all
the treasures he found in Italy. Treasures," she explained to us with
a light laugh, "to Mr Weissbach and to my husband, not to me. Can
you bear these stupid-looking stiff Madonnas and these ugly little
Christs? And no perspective! What's a picture," her upturned eyes
asked not only her family and her guests but the gilded and painted
ceilings, "without perspective? I tell my husband that my Marie
Louise can paint a better picture than all his Florentines and Sienese.
But he won't believe me. He follows the fashion," she told Mamma.
"I believe that some things are beautiful and other things are ugly,
and that nothing can alter that. Nightingales and roses," she said to
her husband, in accents suddenly sharp with hatred, "you'll be telling
me next there's no beauty in them."

"Here is Manning to tell us that luncheon is ready two minutes
early," said Mr Morpurgo softly and sadly.

When we left the room we were led across the landing to a room
on the same floor, and he spoke from behind us, "Are we not to have
luncheon in the dining-room?"

We all paused. The butler again reminded me of a Shakespearean
courtier. Mrs Morpurgo replied, exercising again her faculty for surprise, "It never occurred to me that you would wish to lunch down
there today."

"I should have liked to show Mrs Aubrey and the children the room and the Claudes and the Poussin," said Mr Morpurgo.

"The Claudes and the Poussin, perhaps, but why the room? Is there anything special about the room, except that it's very large?" asked Mrs Morpurgo, wrinkling her nose. "But, oh, dear, oh, dear. Shall we all go back to the drawing-room and wait till they move luncheon down to the dining-room? It could," she said, as if inviting the headsman to use his axe, "be done. If, of course, you do not mind waiting."

"Our company includes six people below the age of nineteen," said Mr Morpurgo, pleasantly, "and there must be something wrong with them if they are not so hungry that snatching luncheon from under their noses would be sheer cruelty." Stephanie was hanging on his arm, and he suddenly drew her to him. He seemed to think she was the nicest of his daughters. Perhaps she was. She had been all right with Richard Quin. "Even this skinny little thing eats like a wolf. And Mr Weissbach and I have come to an age when we are fussy about our food and would prefer not to eat luncheon that has been kept waiting for twenty minutes. But next time the Aubreys come we must have luncheon in the dining-room. Will you remember, Manning?"

The room where we lunched was not suitable for our party. Evidently the Morpurgos lunched there with their children when they had no guests, and it was pretty enough; and it interested Cordelia and Richard Quin and me to see that the walls were covered with photographs and pictures which were not only of people. There were many horses and bulls and cows and dogs as well. The table was too small, for we now numbered eleven, having been joined by the daughters' French governess, a woman in a black dress, who had the same look of gloating discretion as the butler. She sat with her head bowed, and this might have been partly because it was weighed down by a large chignon of chestnut hair; but she had also the air of hoping to evade attention lest she be brought into the conversation and say too much. This was so little subtle a method of avoiding notice that it appeared possible that she was not very clever. But this was not a clever household. Mrs Morpurgo had certainly chosen to have luncheon in these cramped quarters to express her impatience at having to entertain Mr Weissbach and us; yet she was astonished at the inconvenience she had brought on herself. She looked about her in annoyance and said, "How crowded we are! It is quite uncomfortable.

Mrs Aubrey, I must apologize. Stephanie and your boy might have had luncheon together in the schoolroom, but I did not think."

"No, indeed, that would not have done," said Mr Morpurgo, "see, I have put Richard Quin at my left instead of Cordelia, because I have put Stephanie on his other side, so that she can learn how clever someone of her own age can be, and every now and then I am going to lean across him and tell her how shocked I am at the difference."

Mrs Morpurgo took no notice but continued, "I must really apologize, everything went out of my head, I have had such migraine." Abruptly she fell into a reverie and only answered in monosyllables when Mr Weissbach spoke to her, and she might have remained sealed in a surly dream had she not been aroused by the odd consequences of his interest in Cordelia. He was sitting on Mrs Morpurgo's right and faced Cordelia across the table; and he kept on speaking to Mrs Morpurgo of her possessions and her interests but shifting his gaze from her to Cordelia before the end of each remark, so that the possessions and interests seemed transferred to my sister. "I was only one day in Padua," he told Mrs Morpurgo, "but I took the opportunity to call on your charming cousin, the Marchesa Allegrini." His eyes had gone to Cordelia long before the Italian name was pronounced, so that it was as if my sister had suddenly acquired a Marchesa for a cousin. "Are you still breeding those charming little French poodles?" Even in the course of so short a sentence the ownership of the dogs passed from Mrs Morpurgo to Cordelia. Mr Weissbach's absorption in my sister was so extreme that it was soon noticed by Marguerite and Marie Louise, who raised eyebrows at each other across the table and giggled; and the French governess raised her head and hissed a rebuke. She was not a woman with a light hand. Mrs Morpurgo was drawn from her abstraction by the sound, and looked about her with an expression of fear lest something to her disadvantage might have happened while she had laid down her defences. She raised her head, confident that she had only to capture the attention of the room for all to be well. She said so loudly that everybody stopped talking, "Well, let us hear what treasures Mr Weissbach found in Italy to delight my husband, and not me."

"A Lorenzetti panel," Mr Weissbach said to Mr Morpurgo.

"Which Lorenzetti?" asked Mr Morpurgo.

"Ambrogio," answered Mr Weissbach. "You are not a Pietro man."

"You blackguard, you, "said Mr Morpurgo, "you would have thought me one if you had found a Pietro."

"Do you never think," said Mr Weissbach, "how painful it is for me to do business with someone who understands me as well as you do? But anyway, this is an Ambrogio, and the attribution is quite firm."

"To the dickens with the attribution," said Mr Morpurgo. "Does it look like an Ambrogio? The two things should be the same, but with all you rascals getting so scholarly they often aren't. An Ambrogio Lorenzetti! Well, anyway, it will be too dear for me."

"I would certainly think it too dear," Mrs Morpurgo told the table. "But my husband can have it his own way—the house," she said with distaste, "is his. All but my drawing-room. That drawing-room we were in," she informed my mother, as if to indicate that differences of rank mattered nothing, one woman could understand the other, "is mine, the pictures are mine. I might say that the century is mine, for everything in it is eighteenth century, and that was the age in which," she said, lifting her glass with a gesture which made too broad an attempt at refinement, "I should have been born. It was then that everything was perfect, and my pictures are nearly as perfect as pictures ought to be. You must look at them, Mrs Aubrey. A couple of Chardins. Three delightful Greuzes. An Oudry. A Largillière. A Fragonard. A too delicious Vigée le Brun, of my great-grandmother. And though, of course, that's late, a Prud-homme. My husband and Mr Weissbach can fill the rest of the house with heir wooden-faced saints and madonnas, their cardboard landscapes with the trees coming straight out of the ground like telegraph poles. They don't seem to care that anyway they are wrong in this house, which is, so far as it's anything, in the Renaissance style."

"More or less," agreed Mr Morpurgo, smiling.

"Oh, more," said Mrs Morpurgo, "there's nothing less in this house; everywhere there's more, and more, and more, and in fact too much. But why should I grumble? I can always go and shut myself up among the real pictures in my drawing-room, which I have known all my life. For I brought the whole room as it stands from my home in Frankfurt when my father died."

"From Frankfurt!" exclaimed my mother happily. "You are a Rhinelander! That explains why you and your daughters are called by charming French names. You are, of course, bi-lingual. That is what struck me when I was in Frankfurt, it is a meeting-place for French and German culture."

"You have been to Frankfurt then?" asked Mrs Morpurgo.

"I have played there several times," said Mamma.

"Played there? What did you play," asked Mrs Morpurgo, in a tone of bewilderment, as if she suspected Mamma of being a footballer.

"I told you, my dear," said Mr Morpurgo, "Mrs Aubrey was Clare Keith, the pianist."

"You must forgive me," said Mrs Morpurgo. "I never remember the names of musicians except the ones like Paderewski. But you were saying you knew Frankfurt?"

"I had several very good concerts there," said Mamma, quite at ease, supposing that Mrs Morpurgo would like to hear pleasant reports of her native town, "and one most agreeable private engagement. I was engaged, secretly, to play a piano quintet at the golden wedding of a banker and his wife, and the composer was the banker himself, who had been a fine musician in his youth, and had given it up for banking. His sons and daughters had the charming thought of having his favourite composition played by professionals after the family banquet, and the old man was delighted. I have never forgotten the lovely room, yes, very like your drawing-room, and all lit by candles in great silver sconces, and everything reflected in great mirrors. And such nice people. I grew very friendly with one of the daughters and stayed with her once when I had played in Bonn. Oh, I envy you coming from Frankfurt! It was a world which was infinitely distinguished without being aristocratic."

Looking back, I see that my mother was speaking with the utmost simplicity of a society as she had seen it; but it was not unnatural that the remark should fail to please Mrs Morpurgo. Mamma did not perceive this and continued happily, "My children will tell you that I have often told them about Frankfurt. There was such lovely eighteenth century everywhere, and not only in the houses, it seems to me that I remember a most beautiful bank, with a wonderful wrought-iron staircase."

"The Bethman bank," said Mr Morpurgo. "The first Rothschild started there, working as a runner. My wife's family bank was beautiful, too. She was a Krossmayer."

"Oh, but I knew the Krossmayers well," said Mamma. "I visited them every time I was there; they lived in ＿＿."

"No," said Mrs Morpurgo.

"Those were my wife's cousins," said Mr Morpurgo. "The house from which I abstracted my bride was in the ____."

"Well, then I knew your parents, too," said Mamma. "The Krossmayers took me to their cousin's home for a party, to drink that lovely kind of punch called the *Maibowle*. How strange, I must have seen there all those beautiful things we have just seen in your drawing-room. Dear me, I played a duet among those pictures and that china with your cousin, Ella Krossmayer. She would be your cousin? She was older than you, she might have been an aunt."

"My cousin," said Mrs Morpurgo.

"I knew her best of the whole family," Mamma said in a tone of tender reminiscence. "We had a special sympathy because she loved music. Indeed, she hoped for quite a time that she might play professionally."

"Oh, surely not professionally," said Mrs Morpurgo, smiling.

"Yes, though that may surprise you," said Mama, missing the point. "But it is very easy for an amateur to be deceived by the politeness of relatives and friends." Cordelia moved her head sharply. "But Ella was a charming girl, and as I say, I have always remembered Frankfurt as one of the most civilized places in Europe."

"It may have been so," said Mrs Morpurgo. "I left it," she added, with discontent, "so young. But at any rate we had pictures that looked like pictures. I am sure," she said, turning to Mr Weissbach, "that you know in your heart of hearts that pictures should look like mine and not like yours." But he did not reply. His eyes were set on Cordelia's red-gold curls, her candid sea-coloured gaze, her small straight nose with the tiny flat triangle just under the point, her soft but dogged pink mouth, her round chin, pure in line as a cup. Mrs Morpurgo followed the line of his eye and was arrested. Till then she had turned on us only vague, unfocussed, sweeping glances, but she stared at Cordelia intensely and then grew sad; she might have been spreading out cards to read her fortune and come on the ace of spades. Suddenly humble, she looked round the table, as if begging someone to say something that would distract her. The sight of her daughters recalled her usual exasperation, and she looked again at my flawless and collected sister, and muttered to the governess, "Can you really do nothing to make the girls sit up straight?" The governess raised her massive head with an air of resignation which was not meant to go unperceived. A silence fell, and as it grew oppressive Mrs Morpurgo flung at Mamma the questions, "So you have travelled? And your husband is a great traveller, too, isn't he? What was it that Edgar was telling me about him, that he's gone on a journey?"

Mamma's eyes grew large, she opened her mouth but no word came out of it. I could not say anything, because I so vehemently wanted to kill Mrs Morpurgo.

Cordelia spoke, her white brows creased with a gentle frown. "Yes, Papa has gone away to write a book."

Cordelia could say no more. She made a movement of her little hand, and looked about as if for mercy. Richard Quin leaned forward from his place at the end of the table, and said, "My father has gone to Tartary."

Mr Morpurgo said, "Yes, he has gone to Tartary," and laid his hand for a second on my brother's wrist.

"To Tartary," repeated Mrs Morpurgo, busy with her lamb cutlet. "Is that," she asked, as if she were saying something clever, "a good place to write a book?"

Nobody answered her, and she looked up and saw that her husband was staring at her in open rage. She recoiled as if his hatred had a definite range and she wished to retreat beyond it, and sat turning from side to side her large, blunt, handsome head. She had gone further than she had wished; she had meant to be nearly, but not quite, intolerable. Again we could see her telling herself that she had not the slightest idea how she had overstepped the mark. Had she said something so very tactless? And if she had, how could it matter, when there was only this obscure woman, this unknown Mrs Aubrey, these tiresome girls, this schoolboy, to be offended? All this was just more of her husband's nonsense. Her contempt for him re-established itself. She shook her head to disembarrass herself of all these absurdities, and went on eating. But her hands were trembling.

The silence that had fallen once more was broken by a peal of bells, and another, and another.

"Someone's getting married," said Mr Weissbach, bravely jovial, "and making no end of fuss about it."

"I did not know we had a church so near," said Mr Morpurgo.

"Did you never happen to notice," asked Mrs Morpurgo, "that St James' was just round the corner?"

The bells rang on. A remark bubbled in laughter on Marguerite's lips. Finally, she had to say it. "Why, these might be the bells at Captain Ware's wedding."

She had said it. Her two sisters covered their smiling mouths. They looked just like the worst girls at school. "Why should they be that?" said Mr Morpurgo, absently.

"Marguerite is talking nonsense," said Mrs Morpurgo, "she is talking about someone who is getting married in Pau, not in London."

"Yes," said Marguerite, "but this is the very day, isn't it?"

"Who is Captain Ware?" asked Mr Morpurgo. He was like that. If he heard a name, any time, he liked to know all about the person who bore it.

Marguerite hesitated. Her sisters' shining eyes dared her to go on. Her own answered, "Oh, then, if you think I won't, I will!" She continued with the blandness of malice, "Why, he's the handsome captain who's been teaching us riding all the time we've been at Pau. We made great friends with him," she finished artlessly, "we were so surprised a fortnight ago, when he told us he was going to marry the daughter of the rich old man who owned our hotel. He hadn't said a word about it, not till the invitations went out. We were asked," she said, as if that had been the cream of the jest.

The governess jerked up her head. She had ceased to look a hum-bug; and she uttered a sound that was not, "Hush," but a noble and vulgar ejaculation of disgust, such as I had once heard from a woman in the street who saw a drunken man lurch against a frightened child. The three girls had been staring down on their plates, the corners of their mouths twitching, not merely enjoying their victim's pain, but acting their enjoyment so that she should feel a second pain. They were very like the worst girls at school. But the governess' expression of contempt, which wounded as if she had just checked herself from spitting, frightened the girls into a second's rigidity. They turned to their father almost as if they were expecting him to protect them from her rage, but his eyes were set on Stephanie's face. I think he felt horror because she had not shown herself different from her sisters. Then he looked at Mrs Morpurgo, who had been in an instant changed from persecutor to persecuted. She was not terrible any longer. She tried to go on eating, but found it hard to swallow, and soon laid down her knife and fork and sat quite still, her chin high and her lids lowered as people do, when they are keeping themselves from shedding tears.

"I wish," he said to my mother, "that you could see my wife on horse-back. I have never seen a woman look better in a riding-habit. Not even the Empress of Austria. My dear Herminie, I am so very glad that you have come home, so that when I boast of you my friends can see that I am not exaggerating. Now, Weissbach, tell us about your Lorenzetti."

After luncheon it seemed as if we were going to have a good time after all. We crossed the landing and went into a library, the first of a line of small rooms that ran along the side of the house. There Mr Morpurgo said to Richard Quin, "You would like to stay here and look at the books, wouldn't you?" Richard Quin nodded. He was quite white, which was strange, for usually when anything disagreeable happened, he did a conjuring trick in his mind and it vanished. But of course it would have been hard to annul Mrs Morpurgo and her daughters. "On that stand," said Mr Morpurgo, "there is a Book of the Hours with very lovely pictures in it. Sit on that stool and look at it. Or take anything you want from the shelves, and ring if it is too heavy for you to handle by yourself." He laid his arm round my brother's shoulders and for a second I saw them as men together, men in over-womened families, who found comfort in each other. Then the rest of us went on through another room lined with cabinets full of porcelain figures, into a corner room, flooded with light from windows in the two outside walls, and hung with silk neither quite grey nor quite blue. There were some very comfortable chairs there, and we sat down and drank black coffee, which I did not think nice at all, out of little ruby red cups encrusted with gold which were very nice indeed. The three girls sat at the other side of the room in sallow and restless silence. Their governess was not with them. She had broken away on the landing, and we had seen her hurrying up the staircase to a higher floor, her elbows held well out from her body as she lifted her skirts to clear the steps, a kind of fish-wife vigour and freedom about her which she had not seemed to possess when she had first glided into the dining-room. Mrs Morpurgo took her coffee and drank it by the window, moving her head as if to see something in the street below.

Mr Morpurgo put down his cup and said to the footman, "Please set up the easel but first ask Mr Kessel to be kind enough to come here," and told us with happy smugness: "You may think this a dull room, but it is designed to fulfil a special purpose. There is a cold light from the north and from the east, and the walls and the carpet are of no particular colour, so that an object can be seen quite clearly, without any reflected colours spoiling its own. And I brought you here because I want you to see some things from the collections my father and mother started. But I will not be the showman for some of the things you might like best, for Herminie knows more about them than I do. My dear, you had better show them my mother's collection of Chelsea and Bow, you have far more feeling for that sort of thing than I have."

Mrs Morpurgo whirled round. "Alas, there's no question of that!" she exclaimed. To my astonishment she was no longer pitiful, she was once more a brass band; she had not been abandoned to grief as she stood hiding her face by the window, she had been recovering her faculty for insolent surprise. "No, indeed! How I wish there were! But the girls and I have to go to a charity fête at Gunnersbury Park. The Rothschilds, you know," she explained to Mamma, meaning that she was sure Mamma did not know. "It's in aid of all those poor horses somewhere. The Rothchilds are very fond of horses. I said I'd go so long ago that I can't possibly not keep my promise." It appeared then that she was no more able to keep her private thoughts when they were to her own disadvantage than when they assailed other people. Her expression now made it plain that what she had just said was not true, that she thought her husband would perceive this, and that now she was improvising. "To tell the truth," she said, "I'm being punished for my dishonesty. I wrote from Pau saying I would be pleased to come to this wretched fête, thinking I hadn't a ghost of a chance of being back here for months, because of Mamma's illness, so that I'd seem good-natured, and have a perfect excuse when the time came, because I'd be out there in the Pyrénées, hundreds, or is it thousands, of miles away. But here I am, and Lady Rothschild's telephoned twice since she saw in *The Times* that I was back again. I can't, I really can't, disappoint her." She paused, quite relaxed. But as Mr Morpurgo said nothing to break the silence, her handsome features broke their ranks again, she looked disturbed. "I suppose you're not going to maintain," she said bitterly, "that we're in a position to snub the Rothschilds? And we have to start early, it takes hours and hours to get out to Gunnersbury." She appealed to my mother for sympathy. "Isn't it tiresome when one's friends live neither in town nor in the country? One has to set out in one's car for a journey one should go by train, but trains don't go to such suburban places. Well, we must go now. I know you will understand, Mrs Aubrey. And so should you, Edgar." Again it was apparent that she was a little frightened by her husband's continued silence. "I told you all this. Long ago. I really did. I told you that I had an engagement early this afternoon. Always, from the first, I said, 'Luncheon, luncheon I can just manage, but I will have to leave immediately afterwards.' "

"I do not remember that," Mr Morpurgo answered pleasantly enough. "But very well, go. We will get on very well by ourselves. I have sent for Mr Kessel and he will look after us, and Mr Weissbach," he said, smiling, "can fill in the gaps. So you and the girls can say good-bye, and go off to give the poor horses what you might have given to us."

"I need not go this minute," said Mrs Morpurgo, suddenly timid.

"Oh, you had better not wait any longer," her husband told her. "Gunnersbury Park is certainly a long way off, as you say, and if you leave later you may disturb the Aubreys when they have settled down to looking at the things."

When she and her daughters had left, the time and the place came to their own. We became aware of a fine day looking in at the windows, and of the great ugly, competently capacious house which pretended to be a palace, but was something better, a complex of store cupboards stocked with celestial sorts of jam. "My father and mother collected all sorts of things, but hardly any pictures except what they brought back from the Continent when they'd been travelling; the rest I've found," said Mr Morpurgo comfortably. "But I keep up the original collections; I even add to them, I like to keep things going. One must," he sighed, "keep things going. There are the bronzes, I'm fond of the bronzes. They're all over the house. When you see a bronze about, Rose, go up and look at it, it's probably good. There's a copy of a classical Andromeda by a man called Bonacolsi Antico who worked at Mantua, and that's something more than the original. And I've got a room full of prints, but I don't believe you'd care for them, though probably that's because I don't care for them myself. My father loved them, but then he loved technicalities and I hate them. The first impression, the second impression, the third impression, it puts one in touch with the artist's troubles. I like objects which pretend to have been laid like an egg. Don't you agree, Weissbach?"

"I do indeed," said Mr Weissbach. But he was in a state to agree to anything. As soon as he had been given his coffee-cup he had sat down next Cordelia, and had minute by minute grown more rosy and contented, while she had assumed the character which had been hers on the concert platform, and became a remote and dreaming child, unaware of her own loveliness, and terrified lest someone should be unkind to her, since, so far as she knew, she had no claim on the world's kindness. He rose and said to Mamma, "With your permission I am going to take Miss Cordelia—what a lovely name!—into the next room and show her the English porcelain." Mamma assented without enthusiasm and indeed uttered a faint moan when he turned as he led Cordelia over the threshold and said richly, "I feel I'm doing something most appropriate; there are at least two charming figures here which are quite in Miss Cordelia's style."

Then the footman returned with Mr Kessel, who was a little old man in a black suit, who bowed obsequiously to Mr Morpurgo and then fixed him with a small tyrannical eye. No, he had not brought the Gentile da Fabriano, he had not been sure that that was really the picture which was wanted. He was sullen as a child asked to share his toys. As he turned to go back for it, the footman began to put up the easel and Mr Morpurgo asked if it could be set nearer Mamma so that she would not have to leave the sofa when the picture came. Mr Kessel paused on the threshold to say that the footman had been placing the easel on the very spot at which, as had been established by experiments he had carried on during the first five years after the house was built, a picture could be shown to best advantage, and if Mr Morpurgo had any reason to think that there was a better spot he would be glad to know it. Mr Morpurgo said quickly that it did not matter where the easel was, and Mamma said she could easily move, but the young footman was annoyed, he clicked his tongue before he could stop himself.

As soon as Mr Kessel had gone, Mr Morpurgo said in an undertone to the footman, "Ah, Lawrence, you must remember that you will be old some day," and when we were alone he sighed, "What am I to do with Kessel? He is a pest about the house, and I do not know what to do with him. It is an odd story. He is a Russian of German descent, the great-great-grandson of a Dresden silversmith who went to Russia in a party of craftsmen imported by Peter the Great. But I cannot send him back to Russia, for it is forty years since he left it and nobody he knew will be alive. He worked at his hereditary craft at Fabergé's, and then was sent over here to bring the Russian Embassy a new set of table silver Fabergé had made for it, and to do some repairs to a famous silver table equipage they had, a glorious thing with elephants. He liked England so well that he decided to stay here, and worked for Spink's for a time, and got interested in all sorts of works of art outside his own line, and presently came to my father and mother to look after their collections. That was while we still had our old house in Portman Square. I wish we had never left it. I have told you why my father built this barrack, and it has to be respected, yet I have never felt life to be very lucky here. But what has amused me always about Kessel's story is that he decided to stay in England after a fortnight spent in Stoke Newington, where the Russian Embassy boarded him out so that he could be near some special workshop. I think this must be the sole occasion when the charms of Stoke Newington have detached a single soul from its allegiance to its native land. But what a fool I am! Kessel probably stayed here not because he liked London, but because something had happened to him which made him dislike St Petersburg. Clare, why are you tearing yourself in two by trying to listen to what I say and at the same time give the most frenzied attention to what you can see in that mirror?"

"Edgar, you must forgive me," breathed Mamma, "I am sorry for that poor old Russian and it is wonderful to hear how careful you are for all your people, but the door to the next room is open, and I can see the reflection of Cordelia and Mr Weissbach, and I feel I ought not to take my eyes off them; he may be very nice, I am sure he is very nice, but he is so remarkably like King Edward."

"Clare, Clare," laughed Mr Morpurgo, "you don't understand your children. You know that Cordelia is a very proper little girl, but I don't think that she is also a little prizefighter in disguise, who would knock Mr Weissbach into the ropes if he offended her sense of propriety, and would have done the same by King Edward if he had earned it. But Mr Weissbach won't do anything he shouldn't because he hopes to sell me a great many more pictures. Cordelia's virtue is being safeguarded not only by her own ferocity, but by a number of long dead Florentines and Sienese, who might not have been on that side had they been still alive. But I'll sit beside you and watch them, just in case poor Weissbach should forget himself and have two ribs and a collar-bone broken."

He poured himself out another cup of coffee and sat down on the sofa, still laughing. "Clare, it is so pleasant to be with you, I forget all my troubles. This is just like the very first day I met your mother, Rose. She cheered me up then when I was feeling very sad. Has she ever told you about it?"

"No, please tell me now," I answered with avidity, and Mamma

537

leaned forward eagerly. He was constantly alluding to his first meeting with her, and she retained no recollection of it whatsoever.
But we were never to be enlightened. Mrs Morpurgo was with us
again.

"Sit down, my dear," said her husband.

She remained standing. "I wanted," she said hesitantly, "to explain
something that may have puzzled you at luncheon."

"I don't remember anything happening at luncheon which I didn't
perfectly understand," said Mr Morpurgo.

"The girls were giggling," said Mrs Morpurgo, sadly.

"Why, Herminie, you should not have bothered to come back to
talk of this!" He looked up at her tenderly. He could not bear her to
be sad. "Yes, the girls were giggling, and I did not like it. They had
some private joke, and I suspected it was an unkind one. But there
was no reason for you to give it another thought."

"But I wanted to explain what it was all about," said his wife.
"I knew you would be annoyed; who wouldn't have been? But it was
just a piece of schoolgirlish nonsense. Marguerite and Marie Louise
have been teasing Stephanie for months because they said she had
fallen in love with this Captain Ware. He was a handsome fellow.
In his way. And they pretended that she was upset when he suddenly
announced that he was getting married. But of course there was
nothing in it at all. Nothing."

Mr Morpurgo made no reply, and Mrs Morpurgo continued to
stand beside us, swaying backwards and forwards on her high heels.
"I thought I had better tell you what was behind it all," she said.

"Will you not sit down, Herminie, my dear?" said Mr Morpurgo
at last. "I am sorry you have vexed yourself about this business.
You are wrong, quite wrong, in thinking that I had not grasped what
had happened. Handsome riding masters have always existed and
will always exist, and they have a right to existence, because they
redress the balance of nature, which swings too much the other way.
There are so many men like me who are not handsome, and do not
become any better-looking when they get on a horse. I assure you
that I am not angry with Stephanie for her flight of fancy. It was
most natural. I am only sorry that she should have suffered some
distress. For I know quite well that you are not telling me the truth."

Mrs Morpurgo stared at him with protruding eyes.

"I think Stephanie was in love with Captain Ware," said Mr
Morpurgo.

"There was nothing in it," repeated Mrs Morpurgo.

"That is what I think, too," said Mr Morpurgo, smiling. "There was nothing in it. But my poor girl was in love with her riding-master. And such things are nothing."

She continued to look at him doubtfully, swaying backwards and forwards.

"Herminie," said Mr Morpurgo, speaking slowly, with spaces between the words, in much the same manner that our mathematics mistress used towards her most backward pupils, "I assure you, there is no need to concern yourself with this business any longer, so far as I am concerned. There are some things so sad that when they happen to people one cares for one cannot be angry about them. I mean to forget that I ever heard Captain Ware's name, and I hope Stephanie will soon forget it too. My only sorrow is that she will take longer to forget him than I will. For I know that such disappointments take their own time to heal."

His wife still said nothing, and he sighed and went on, "Now come and sit down with us. I will send Manning to ask Mademoiselle to take the girls to Gunnersbury House without you, and I shall have the pleasure of your company, which I missed so much when you were at Pau."

"I cannot do that," said Mrs Morpurgo. She was perplexed. Surely there was a second meaning in what he was saying? She had better leave him as quickly as possible before she got caught up in his incomprehensibility. She bounced back into the part of a woman of the world. "Lady Rothschild will be expecting me; what's the use of offending people, one's got to live with them."

"People will eat strawberries and cream off glass plates in a marquee as well without you as with you," said Mr Morpurgo. "But Mrs Aubrey and Rose and I will not be nearly as happy sitting here unless you are with us."

Mrs Morpurgo resorted again to her affectation of surprise. "I'm charmed," she told Mamma, "that my husband should have this passion for my company. But I wonder why it should choose to burn so fiercely just this afternoon of all afternoons, when my friends are waiting for me miles away."

"The point is," said Mr Morpurgo drily, "that this is indeed an afternoon of afternoons."

She was the dull pupil again, staring at the blackboard.

"Not," he said, more drily still, "that anything has happened which has not happened before. But we are going to behave as if nothing had happened, and as if Stephanie had not been more foolish than I have a right to expect."

"I have told you that there was nothing in it," she said again, perplexed.

"Yes. Yes. I accept that," he said. "And now sit down, my dear. First I want to show the Aubreys some of our things, and then it would be kind of you to show them your pictures and your drawing-room, which I know they did not have the time to look at before luncheon. Then they will be going home to Lovegrove, and you and I can have the end of the afternoon to spend together."

A look of fear passed over her face. "I have told you," she said, "Lady Rothschild telephoned to me more than once. She wants me to do something special, at this wretched fête."

"The end of the afternoon is always pleasant," said Mr Morpurgo, "and we will talk of nothing troublesome. We will be beautifully vacant, like two horses in a meadow."

"Two horses!" said Mrs Morpurgo. "That would be delightful, no doubt. And the Rothschilds would love us all the better for it. But we're not horses, my dear Edgar, and we have duties horses haven't got."

"You will not stay with me though I particularly want you to?" asked her husband.

"If I may talk of my plans," said Mamma, while Mrs Morpurgo shook her head, "I think that, lovely as your house is, and much as we are enjoying being here, we will not take up so much of your husband's time as he proposes." Her face lit up with amusement. "I resemble Lady Rothschild in one respect, and in one respect only. I also live a long way off. I think we should be going home at once."

"No, not at once," said Mr Morpurgo. "Your home is quite a distance away, but you have plenty of time, Clare. It is Herminie who is running short of that."

"Yes, I spend my days hurrying from pillar to post," said Mrs Morpurgo. "That is what I am always complaining about, and I will not make things any better by breaking engagements."

"You have less time at your disposal than you realize," said Mr Morpurgo. "Will you stay with me this afternoon or will you not?"

He had till then been speaking in quiet and even tones, but now his voice was thin and strained, an odd voice to come from so fat a little man. Now Mrs Morpurgo lost her perplexity, now she was sure of her ground. Requests coming from the bottom of the heart were things one refused. "I've already made it clear, dear Edgar," she said triumphantly, "that Gunnersbury House is where I've promised I'll be this afternoon, and like all good women, I keep my promises."

She turned away from us as if the pleasure she felt at denying her husband what he wanted were so strong that she herself recognized it as gross, and wished to hide it. She went towards the door, just as Mr Kessel shuffled back, faintly smiling, and holding a panel wrapped in a cloth, with an air of consequence. Mrs Morpurgo recoiled, crying archly, "What's this? One of my husband's treasures brought out for your special delectation, Mrs Aubrey? I hope you'll find the right thing to say about it, or he won't continue to adore you." As he so unaccountably does, her tone added. "Now, which of them is it, I wonder?" she demanded. "I can't wait to see!" But that she could not do at once. The old man halted and hugged the panel closer, like a child whose game has been interrupted by a stronger and rougher child, and fears for his toys.

"You've been very quick, Mr Kessel," said Mr Morpurgo, and rose and took the panel from him, and put it on the easel and drew the cloth away. He was no taller than the easel, and as his little arms spread out and settled the panel on the ledge he looked comically like an up-ended tortoise. Mrs Morpurgo shuddered in sudden rage. "Oh, your Florentines, your Sienese, your Umbrians!" she exclaimed. She had cast away her affectations. This was honest hatred, eager to destroy everything that was dear to the object of its loathing. But the moment passed. She stood raising and lowering her eyebrows while Mr Morpurgo spoke of his picture. "Not a great masterpiece, I'll admit it, though Weissbach wouldn't. Not as great as the Simone Martini I showed you on the landing. Too much a piece of happy story-telling. But it's lovely. Isn't it, Clare? Look at that pale gilding I was speaking about. Those men in their gilded crowns, their horses champing beside them in their gilded harness, the woman and the child sitting in the broken house with gilded circles round their heads. And above the hills at the back there's the night sky, and beyond it another firmament, that's faintly gilded. It's an exquisite way of underlining what one knows to be really important in the story, the power, the trappings, the real thing above it all."

But we were interrupted by a cry from Mrs Morpurgo. Her hands were fluttering in a gesture expressing violated refinement, so wide that it included in its complaint the picture, her husband, and the ornate house about us. "I believe," she told her husband, "I really do believe that you only like these pictures because there is so much gold on them."

"No, you must go," said Mr Morpurgo. "You really must go now. You must be off to Gunnersbury Park."

"Why?" asked his wife. This time she was really surprised.

"In pursuit of holy poverty, I suppose," he answered.

She could make nothing of that. "How you change!" she said, in a teasing tone. "A minute ago you seemed about to go on your knees to me in your anxiety that I should stay here."

"But you have let your time run out," he said. "Now you must go."

She repeated his words to herself several times; one saw her lips moving. True, he had not said that he was angry with her; but she could not help suspecting that he was not pleased. She made herself gentle for his benefit, compliance soft on her face like the bloom on a peach. But he had set his eyes on the picture. She shook her head and shrugged her shoulders, said a second and absent-minded good-bye to my mother and myself, and left us. The doors of the rooms were all open, and I watched her walking away through the room where the porcelains were, through the library where Richard Quin was reading, through the ante-chamber beyond. Before she went out to the landing she stopped and looked back, small at the end of a long strip of shining parquet. All that could be grasped of her at that distance was her huge hat, her bright hair beneath it, and her forth-right womanly figure. Even so, her appearance seemed to promise melting ease and the forgetfulness of care; it was hard to believe that spending an hour with her had not been as agreeable as sailing under a cloudless sky on a calm sea. But she made a slight but ugly and argumentative movement of her head and shoulders, and swung about, her full skirts turning more slowly than her hips, and was gone across the threshold. I was sure that I would never see her again. My mother and Mr Morpurgo and Mr Kessel were contemplating the Italian picture in silence. We could hear Mr Weissbach and Cordelia talking in the next room: his quick questioning murmurs and full-bodied chuckles, the crisp yesses and noes with which she began each of her answers. Outside in the street the horses' hooves clattered, the motor-horns hooted, the more distant traffic was a blur on the ear. I was sad as I had thought I would never be outside my own home.

Presently Mr Weissbach and Cordelia joined us. Bowing voluptuously from the waist he told Mamma that he thought her charming daughter possessed a real feeling for art, while Cordelia stood by and primly put on her gloves. "And about that Lorenzetti?" he asked Mr Morpurgo. "I've kept the gallery open, on the off chance you cared to look in this afternoon."

"That was good of you," said Mr Morpurgo. "I hate to wait, once I've heard of a picture. But I can't look at it now."

"Why not go, Edgar?" said Mamma. "You might enjoy it, and you need not think of us. We are going home."

"It isn't that," said Mr Morpurgo. "The fact is, I do not feel very well."

"Quite so, quite so," said Mr Weissbach, nodding. "Next week, perhaps. I'll let nobody else look at it," he added, obviously wanting to be specially nice.

"You always treat me well, Weissbach," said Mr Morpurgo, "And I'm very grateful for the wonderful things you bring me. But today I'm feeling ill, and I have a great many things to attend to." They shook hands, and Mr Weissbach said something pleasant in German to Mr Kessel, and went away.

"Sit down and look at my Gentile a minute longer, Clare," said Mr Morpurgo, and we all sat down again. But Mr Kessel said contentiously, "He is civil, Mr Weissbach. Always he is civil. And it is not every art-dealer who troubles to be civil to wretched old Kessel. Never a word from Mr Merkowitz, never a word from Mr Leyden."

Mr Morpurgo groaned, and then said, "I know, I know. But they are busy men, and they forget; they do not mean to be rude. I assure you they do not mean to be rude."

"Maybe yes, maybe no," grumbled the old man, and Mamma cried out in German, "Oh, Mr Kessel, Mr Morpurgo has a dreadful headache."

"Ach, so," breathed the old man. "Yes, they are busy men," he said a moment later, and then was quiet. We all stared at the picture: at the people who were dead tired at the end of a journey but so excited at what they found there that their fatigue did not matter to them. An unnatural and ecstatic wakefulness was painted into the night itself. Then Mr Morpurgo told Mr Kessel to take the picture away, gently and affectionately, telling the old child that playtime

543

was over and it was time he took away his toys. Mamma stood up and thanked them both and said that now we must really go. We went out into the room where the porcelain shepherds and shepherdesses, nymphs and fauns in leopard-skins, teapots and vases and tureens, stood in the white over-garment of their glaze on the lit shelves, and Mr Morpurgo said, "Nobody will be looking at them again today," and touched the switch, and the things lost their glory and were dull among the shadows. In the library we found that Richard Quin had tired of the Book of Hours, and had taken another great book over to the window-seat, but had tired of that too, and had laid it down and was staring out on the treetops in the square. He turned a sad face towards us and Mr Morpurgo said, "Take the girls downstairs, Clare, Richard Quin and I will follow, we must close the cases." Though it was the afternoon, it was as if he were shutting up the house for the night.

As we came to the head of the stairs we looked down on the butler and the footmen in the hall below, whispering together in a knot. They dispersed and stood a little apart from each other on the black and white tiles, like chessmen on the board as the game comes to an end. While we sat on a Renaissance bench, rich but hard, waiting for the others, I could hear the quick and shallow breathing of the younger footman, who was standing nearest me. I wondered if he were still angry with old Mr Kessel or if the whole household knew that Mr Morpurgo was angry with Mrs Morpurgo. Of course the servants had been in the room during luncheon, and what had happened since she had probably conveyed to them by an expressive departure, by coming down the staircase with her huge hat bobbing on her large contemptuous head, by sweeping through the bronze doors as if they had not been opened widely enough to let pass her swelling indignation, her great sense of wrong. The menservants had some knowledge of the crisis, for they stirred sharply and then became rigid when Mr Morpurgo and my brother appeared on the landing. It was horrible that this poor little man should have to endure his sorrows before so many people; at least Mamma had not had to bear her troubles over Papa's gambling in front of a crowd. I looked up at him in pity, but immediately my heart closed in the spasm of jealousy. At the turn of the staircase Mr Morpurgo and my brother had paused and exchanged a few words and nodded, as if they were confirming an agreement, smiled as if they liked each other the better for it, and made their faces blank as they continued their way down.

My heart contracted. I loved Richard Quin, and I loved Rosamund, and I was beginning to love Mr Morpurgo as I had not thought I would ever love anybody outside the family, and I was glad that these three should love each other. But at the thought that Richard Quin had compacts with both Rosamund and Mr Morpurgo from which I was excluded I felt as if I were exiled to a distant place where love could not reach me.

My mother uttered an exclamation of surprise. "Why, Richard Quin is taller than Mr Morpurgo," she said. "How strange it is that a boy shall be taller than a grown man. But of course," she added, speaking quite stupidly, "it often happens." I thought this was an odd remark for her to make, since it was usually the fault of her conversation that it left the obvious too far behind. I put it down to her distress, which increased when Mr Morpurgo came towards us, and the butler, evidently thinking his master might be going back to Lovegrove with us, approached him and said to him in an undertone, "Mademoiselle wishes to see you as soon as possible." He looked up at the landing, and all our eyes followed his. There a figure had taken up its stand, with her head bowed and her hands clasped before her dark flowing skirts, and a threat in every line of pent-up emotion about to burst its dam. "Oh, no!" groaned Mr Morpurgo, "Oh, No!" Recovering himself, he told us, "She is an excellent creature."

As soon as the Daimler had rolled us out into the square Mamma cried out, "Oh, children, and I thought this was going to be such a treat for you," and took off her hat. This was an extraordinary act for a respectable woman to perform outside her own house in those days and I expected Cordelia to protest, but when she said, "Mamma," it was with the air of one who wants to make an important announcement on her own behalf. "Not now, dear, not now," said Mamma faintly, grasping the speaking-tube. She made such a poor business of using it that the chauffeur stopped the car and asked, smiling, what he could do for her. It was Brown, the younger of Mr Morpurgo's two chauffeurs. We preferred old McIver, who had been a coachman and used to click his tongue to encourage or check the Daimler, but Brown was nice too. He had thick brown curls and bright blue eyes and strong white teeth, and would have been handsome if he had not had a thick neck and a look of being full of blood.

"Please do not drive us home," my mother begged. "Put us down anywhere. Anywhere! St James' Park, that is near here, isn't it? Put us down in St James' Park."

"Yes, madam," said Brown. "But whereabouts?"

"Near a flower-bed," sighed Mamma.

He drove us down Birdcage Walk, but we stopped him before we got to the flower-beds because we saw the lake lying silver behind the trees, and cool waters seemed an answer to Mrs Morpurgo. We thanked Brown and bade him good-bye and walked along the path, Mamma uttering little cries of relief and appalled recollection, until we found some little green chairs near the edge of the lake, just as some people were rising from them. "How lucky, when the place is crowded," said Mamma, sinking down, "and what peace, what calm! Oh, children, I would not have chosen to expose you to that! But I could not tell that such extraordinary things were going to happen, and perhaps it served a purpose. I suppose that sooner or later you had to learn that there are husbands and wives who do not get on together." ◇ ◇ ◇

VI. HISTORY AND TRAVEL

FROM Black Lamb and Grey Falcon

A JOURNEY THROUGH YUGOSLAVIA
(1941)

GERMANY (AUSTRIA)   HUNGA

FROM Munich   TO Budapest

R. Drava

Lyublyana

Zagreb

Trieste   R. Dra

Karlovats   R. Sava   Sha

Fiume Sushak   Brod

KRK   Senj   Banjaluka   R. Bos

Plitvitse Lakes

RAB   YUGOSLA

Yezero Yaitse   Travnik

Vakuf   Vi

Zara (It.)   Kiselyak

Yablanitsa   Ilidzh

Shiberiik   MT.TR

Trogir Salonæ

Split   Mostar

Hvar HVAR   Metkovit

Korchula   Grush

LAGOSTA   Dubrovnik
(It.)   Hertseg Nov

TO SUSHAK

A D R I A T I C

ITALY

0   50   100
Miles

The spelling of Yugoslavian names presents a serious problem. The Serbo-Croat language is spoken in all parts of Yugoslavia described in this book; but to write it the Serbs use the Cyrillic alphabet (which is much the same as the Russian, but simpler) and the Croats use the Latin alphabet. Most foreign writers on Yugoslavia follow the Croatian spelling, but this is not satisfactory. The Cyrillic alphabet is designed to give a perfect phonetic rendering of the Slav group of languages, and provides characters for several consonants which other groups lack. The Latin alphabet can only represent these consonants by clapping accents on other consonants which bear some resemblance to them; and the Croatian usage still further confuses the English eye by using "c" to represent not "s" and "k" but "ts," and "j" for "y." I have found that in practice the casual English reader is baffled by this unfamiliar use of what looks familiar and is apt to pass over names without grasping them clearly. I have therefore done my best to transliterate all Yugoslavian names into forms most likely to convey the sound of them to English ears. Cetinje is written here as Tsetinye, Jajce as Yaitse, Peč as Petch, Sestinje as Shestine. Kosovo I have written Kossovo, though the Serbo-Croat language uses no double consonants, because we take them as a sign that the preceding vowel is short.

This is a rough and ready method, and at certain points it has broken down. The Cyrillic alphabet provides special characters for representing liquid consonants; the Latin alphabet can only indicate these by adding "j" to the consonant, and this is extremely confusing at the end of a word. In pronouncing "Senj" the speaker says "Sen," then starts to say a "y" sound, and stops half-way. The English reader, seeing "Senj," pronounces it "Senge" to rhyme with "Penge." I have therefore regarded the problem as insoluble, and have left such words spelt in the Croatian fashion, with the hope that readers will take the presence of the letter "j" as warning that there are dark phonetic doings afoot.

I have also given up any attempt to transliterate "Sarajevo" or "Skoplje." For one thing "Sarajevo" is a tragically familiar form; and for another, it is not a pure Slav word, and has the Turkish word "sarai," a fortress, embedded in it, with the result hardly to be conveyed by any but a most uncouth spelling. It is pronounced something like "Sa-raï-ye-vo," with a faint accent on the second syllable, and a short "e." I have committed another irregularity by putting an "e" into the word "Tsrna," so often found in place-names. This makes it easier for the English reader to grasp that the vowel sound in the rolled "r" comes before it and not after.

R. W.

Black Lamb and Grey Falcon

FROM Prologue

I raised myself on my elbow and called through the open door into the other wagon-lit:

"My dear, I know I have inconvenienced you terribly by making you take your holiday now, and I know you did not really want to come to Yugoslavia at all. But when you get there you will see why it was so important that we should make this journey, and that we should make it now, at Easter. It will all be quite clear, once we are in Yugoslavia."

There was, however, no reply. My husband had gone to sleep. It was perhaps as well. I could not have gone on to justify my certainty that this train was taking us to a land where everything was comprehensible, where the mode of life was so honest that it put an end to perplexity. I lay back in the darkness and marvelled that I should be feeling about Yugoslavia as if it were my mother country, for this was 1937, and I had never seen the place till 1936. Indeed, I could remember the first time I ever spoke the name "Yugoslavia" and that was only two and a half years before, on October the ninth, 1934.

It was in a London nursing-home. I had had an operation, in the new miraculous way. ◇ ◇ ◇ I had been told beforehand that it would all be quite easy; but before an operation the unconscious, which is really a shocking old fool, envisages surgery as it was in the Stone Age, and I had been very much afraid. I rebuked myself for not having observed that the universe was becoming beneficent at a great rate. But it was not yet wholly so. My operation wound left me an illusion that I had a load of ice strapped to my body. So to distract me, I had a radio brought into my room, and for the first time I realized how uninteresting life could be and how perverse human appetite. After I had listened to some talks and variety programmes, I would not have been surprised to hear that there are householders who make arrangements with the local authorities not to empty dustbins but

551

to fill them. Nevertheless there was always good music provided by some station or other at any time in the day, and I learned to swing like a trapeze artist from programme to programme in search of it.

But one evening I turned the wrong knob and found music of a kind other than I sought, the music that is above earth, that lives in the thunderclouds and rolls in human ears and sometimes deafens them without betraying the path of its melodic line. I heard the announcer relate how the King of Yugoslavia had been assassinated in the streets of Marseille that morning. We had passed into another phase of the mystery we are enacting here on earth, and I knew that it might be agonizing. The rags and tags of knowledge that we all have about us told me what foreign power had done this thing. It appeared to me inevitable that war must follow, and indeed it must have done, had not the Yugoslavian Government exercised an iron control on its population, then and thereafter, and abstained from the smallest provocative action against its enemies. That forbearance, which is one of the most extraordinary feats of statesmanship performed in post-war Europe, I could not be expected to foresee. ◇ ◇ ◇ So I rang for my nurse, and when she came I cried to her, "Switch on the telephone! I must speak to my husband at once. A most terrible thing has happened. The King of Yugoslavia has been assassinated." "Oh dear!" she replied. "Did you know him?" "No," I said "Then why," she asked, "do you think it's so terrible?"

Her question made me remember that the word "idiot" comes from a Greek root meaning private person. Idiocy is the female defect: intent on their private lives, women follow their fate through a darkness deep as that cast by malformed cells in the brain. It is no worse than the male defect, which is lunacy: they are so obsessed by public affairs that they see the world as by moonlight, which shows the outlines of every object but not the details indicative of their nature. I said, "Well, you know, assassinations lead to other things!" "Do they?" she asked. "Do they not!" I sighed, for when I came to look back on it my life had been punctuated by the slaughter of royalties, by the shouting of newsboys who have run down the streets to tell me that someone has used a lethal weapon to turn over a new leaf in the book of history. I remember when I was five years old looking upward at my mother and her cousin, who were standing side by side and looking down at a newspaper laid on a table in a circle of gaslight, the folds in their white pouched blouses and long black skirts kept as still by their consternation as if they were carved in stone. "There was the Empress Elizabeth of Austria," I said to the nurse, thirty-six years later. "She was very beautiful, wasn't she?" she asked. "One of the most beautiful women who ever lived," I said. "But wasn't she mad?" she asked. "Perhaps," I said, "perhaps, but only a little, and at the end. She was certainly brilliantly clever. Before she was thirty she had given proof of greatness." "How?" she asked. To her increasing distress I told her, for I know quite a lot of Habsburg history, until I saw how bored she was and let her go and leave me in darkness that was now patterned by the lovely triangle of Elizabeth's face.

How great she was! In her early pictures she wears the same look of fiery sullenness we see in the young Napoleon: she knows that within her there is a spring of life and she is afraid that the world will not let it flow forth and do its fructifying work. In her later pictures she wears a look that was never on the face of Napoleon. The world had not let the spring flow forth and it had turned to bitterness. But she was not without achievements of the finest sort, of a sort, indeed, that Napoleon never equalled. When she was sixteen she came, a Wittelsbach from the country bumpkin court of Munich, to marry the young Emperor of Austria and be the governing prisoner of the court of Vienna, which was the court of courts since the French Revolution had annulled the Tuileries and Versailles. The change would have made many women into nothing. But five years later she made a tour of Lombardy and Venetia at Franz Josef's side which was in many ways a miracle. It was, in the first place, a miracle of courage, because he and his officials had made these provinces loathe them for their brutality and inefficiency. The young girl sat with unbowed head in theatres that became silent as the grave at her coming, that were black with mourning worn to insult her, and she walked unperturbed through streets that emptied before her as if she were the plague. But when she came face to face with any Italians there occurred to her always the right word and gesture by which she uncovered her nature and pled: "Look, I am the Empress, but I am not evil. Forgive me and my husband and Austria for the evil we have done you, and let us love one another and work for peace between us."

It was useless, of course. Her successes were immediately annulled by the arrests and floggings carried out by the Habsburg officials. It was inevitable that the two provinces should be absorbed in the new kingdom of Italy. But Elizabeth's sweetness had not been merely automatic, she had been thinking like a liberal and like an Empress. She knew there was a real link between Austria and Hungary, and that it was being strained by misgovernment. So the next year she made a journey through Hungary, which was also a matter of courage, for it was almost as gravely disaffected as Lombardy and Venetia, and afterwards she learned Hungarian, though it is one of the most difficult of languages, cultivated the friendship of many important Hungarians, and acquainted herself with the nature of the concession desired by Hungary. Her plans fell into abeyance when she parted from Franz Josef and travelled for five years. But in 1866 Austria was defeated by the Prussians, and she came back to console her husband, and then she induced him to create the Dual Monarchy and give autonomy to Hungary. It was by this device alone that the Austro-Hungarian Empire was able to survive into the twentieth century, and both the idea and the driving force behind the execution belonged to Elizabeth. That was statesmanship. Nothing of Napoleon's making lasted so long, nor was made so nobly.

Elizabeth should have gone on and medicined some of the other sores that were poisoning the Empire. She should have solved the problem of the Slav populations under Habsburg rule. The Slavs were a people, quarrelsome, courageous, artistic, intellectual, and profoundly perplexing to all other peoples, who came from Asia into the Balkan Peninsula early in the Christian era and were Christianized by Byzantine influence. Thereafter they founded violent and magnificent kingdoms of infinite promise in Bulgaria, Serbia, and Bosnia, but these were overthrown when the Turks invaded Europe in the fourteenth century, and all were enslaved except the Slavs on the western borders of the Peninsula. These lived under the wing of the great powers, of Venice and Austria and Hungary, which was a doubtful privilege, since they were used as helots and as man-power to be spent without thrift against the Turks. Now all of these were under the Austro-Hungarian Empire, the Czechs and the Croats, and the Slovenes and the Slovaks and the Dalmatians; and they were alike treated oppressively, largely because the German-Austrians felt a violent, instinctive loathing of all Slavs and particularly of the Czechs, whose great intelligence and ability made them dangerous competitors in the labour market. Moreover, Serbia and Bulgaria had thrown off the Turkish yoke during the nineteenth century and had established themselves as free states, and the reactionary parties in Austria and Hungary feared that if their Slav populations were given liberty they would seek union with Serbia under Russian protection. Therefore they harried the Slavs as much as they could, by all possible economic and social penalties, tried with especial venom to destroy their languages, and created for themselves an increasing amount of internal disorder which all sane men saw to carry a threat of disruption. It might have saved the Empire altogether, it might have averted the war of 1914, if Elizabeth had dealt with the Slavs as she dealt with the Hungarians. But after thirty she did no more work for the Empire.

Her work stopped because her marriage, which was the medium for her work, ceased to be tolerable. It appears probable, from the evidence we have, that Elizabeth could not reconcile herself to a certain paradox which often appears in the lives of very feminine women. She knew that certain virtues are understood to be desirable in women: beauty, tenderness, grace, house-pride, the power to bear and rear children. She believed that she possessed some of these virtues and that her husband loved her for it. Indeed, he seemed to have given definite proof that he loved her by marrying her against the will of his mother, the Archduchess Sophie. And she thought that because he loved her he must be her friend. In that she was artless. Her husband, like many other human beings, was divided between the love of life and the love of death. His love of life made him love Elizabeth. His love of death made him love his abominable mother, and give her an authority over Elizabeth which she horribly misused.

The Archduchess Sophie is a figure of universal significance. She was the kind of woman whom men respect for no other reason than that she is lethal, whom a male committee will appoint to the post of hospital matron. She had none of the womanly virtues. Especially did she lack tenderness. There is no record of her ever having said a gentle word to the girl of sixteen whom her son brought home to endure this troublesome greatness, and she arranged for the Archbishop who performed their marriage ceremony to address an insulting homily to the bride, bidding her remember that she was a nobody who had been called to a great position, and try to do her best. In politics she was practised in every kind of folly that most affronted the girl's instinctive wisdom. She was always thrusting the blunt muzzle of her stupidity into conclaves of state, treading down intelligent debate as a beast treads down the grass at a gate into mud, undermining the foundations of the Empire by insisting that everybody possible should be opposed and hurt. She was personally respon-

555

sible for some very ugly persecutions: one of her victims was the peasant philosopher Konrad Deubler. She was also a great slut. She had done nothing to reform the medievalism of the Austrian Palaces. It was the middle of the nineteenth century when Elizabeth came to Vienna, but both at the Winter Palace and the Summer Palace, at the Hofburg and Schönbrunn, she was expected to perform her excretory functions at a commode behind a screen in a passage which was patrolled by a sentry. The Archduchess Sophie saw to it that the evil she did should live after her by snatching Elizabeth's children away from her and allowing her no part in their upbringing. One little girl died in her care, attended by a doctor whom Elizabeth thought old-fashioned and incompetent; and the unhappy character of the Crown Prince Rudolf, restless, undisciplined, tactless, and insatiable, bears witness to her inability to look after their minds.

After Franz Josef had lost Elizabeth by putting this inferior over her and proving that love is not necessarily kind, he showed her endless kindness and indulgence, financing her wanderings and her castle-buildings with great good temper and receiving her gladly when she came home; and it seems she had no ill-feeling against him. She introduced the actress, Katherina Schratt, into his life very much as a woman might put flowers into a room she felt to be dreary. But she must have hated him as the Habsburg of Habsburgs, the centre of the imbecile system, when on January the thirtieth, 1889, Rudolf was found dead in his shooting-box at Mayerling beside the body of a girl of seventeen named Marie Vetsera. This event still remains a mystery. Marie Vetsera had been his mistress for a year and it is usually supposed that he and she had agreed to die together because Franz Josef had demanded they should part. But this is very hard to believe. Marie Vetsera was a very fat and plain little girl, bouncing with a vulgar ardour stimulated by improper French novels, which had already led her into an affair with an English officer in Egypt; and it seems unlikely that Rudolf, who was a man of many love-affairs, should have thought her of supreme value after a year's possession, particularly considering that he had spent the night before he went to Mayerling with an actress to whom he had long been attached. It would seem much more probable that he had taken his life or (which is possible if his farewell notes were forged) been murdered as a result of troubles arising from his political opinions.

Of these we know a great deal, because he wrote a great number of articles for anonymous publication in the *Neues Wiener Tageblatt* and an even greater number of letters to its editor, a gifted Jew named Moritz Szeps. These show that he was a fervent liberal and loathed the Habsburg system. He loathed the expanding militarism of Germany, and prophesied that a German alliance would mean the destruction of Austria, body and soul; and he revered France with its deeply rooted culture and democratic tradition. He was enraged by anti-Semitism and wrote one of his most forcible articles against a gang of aristocrats who after a drunken orgy had gone round the Ghetto of Prague smashing windows, and had been let off scot free by the police. He was scandalized by the corruption of the banks and law-courts, and by the lack of integrity among high officials and politicians, and most of all by the Austro-Hungarian Empire. "As a simple onlooker," he wrote, "I am curious to know how such an old and tough organism as the Austrian Empire can last so long without cracking at the joints and breaking into pieces." Particularly was he eager to deal with the Slav problem, which had now grown even more complicated. Bosnia and Herzegovina had driven out the Turks and had been cheated of the freedom they had thus won by the Treaty of Berlin, which had given the Austro-Hungarian Empire the right to occupy and administer them. This had enraged the Slavs and given Serbia a grievance, so it was held by reactionaries to be all the more necessary to defend Austrian and Hungarian privileges. Rudolf had shown what he felt early in his career; when Franz Josef had appointed him colonel he had chosen to be attached to a Czech regiment with middle-class officers which was then stationed in Prague.

Whatever the explanation of Mayerling it must have raised Elizabeth's impatience with Vienna to loathing. The situation was unmitigated waste and ruin. She had never achieved a happy relationship with her son, although there was a strong intellectual sympathy between them, because of the early alienating influence of the Archduchess Sophie, and the Habsburgs had spoiled what they had not let her save. Rudolf had been forced for dynastic reasons into a marriage with a tedious Belgian princess, an acidulated child with golden hair, small eyes, and the conservative opinions one would expect from a very old member of the Carlton Club. She was literally a child; at the time of her wedding she had not yet shown the signs of womanhood. Owing to a slip in the enormously complicated domestic machinery of the Habsburgs she and her young bridegroom, who was only twenty-two, had been sent for their honeymoon to a remote castle which had been left servantless and unprepared. This ill-begun

557

marriage had gone from bad to worse, and both husband and wife tortured and were tortured in turn. But it was the Habsburg situation, not merely the specific wrongs the Habsburgs brought on Rudolf, that was his ruin. Chamberlains fussed, spies scribbled, the police bullied and nagged, everybody knew where everybody else was at every moment of the day; Franz Josef rose at four each morning and worked on official papers for twelve or fourteen hours; and not a minute's thought was given to correcting the evils that were undermining the foundations of the Empire. Rudolf, as any intelligent member of the family must have done, tried to remedy this. Either he made some too ambitious plan and was detected and killed himself or was killed, or from discouragement he soused himself with brandy till it seemed proper to die for a plump little hoyden of seventeen. Now he lay dead, and the Austro-Hungarian Empire was without a direct or satisfactory heir.

Elizabeth lived nine years after her son's death, as drearily as any other of the unemployed. Then, perhaps as a punishment for having turned her back on the Slav problem, the key to Eastern Europe, a Western problem slew her. For the newspaper my mother and her cousin spread in the gaslight was wrong when it said that the man who killed her, Luccheni, was a madman. It is true that he said that he had killed Elizabeth because he had vowed to kill the first royal person he could find, and that he had gone to Évian to stab the Duke of Orléans but had missed him and had come back to Geneva to get Elizabeth instead; and this is an insane avowal, for no benefit whatsoever could be derived by anybody from the death of either of these people. But for all that Luccheni was not mad. Many people are unable to say what they mean only because they have not been given an adequate vocabulary by their environment; and their apparently meaningless remarks may be inspired by a sane enough consciousness of real facts.

There is a phase of ancient history which ought never to be forgotten by those who wish to understand their fellow-men. In Africa during the fourth century a great many Christians joined a body of schismatics known as the Donatists who were wrecking the Church by maintaining that only sacraments administered by a righteous priest were valid, and that a number of contemporary priests had proved themselves unrighteous by showing cowardice during the persecutions of Diocletian. They raved: for according to the Church, Christ is the real dispenser of the sacraments, and it is inconceivable that a relationship prescribed by Him could break down through the personality of the mediator, and in many cases the tales were scandal-mongering. But though these people raved they were not mad. They were making the only noises they knew to express the misery inflicted on them by the economic collapse of the Western Roman Empire. Since there was no economic literature there was no vocabulary suitable to their misery, so they had to use the vocabulary given them by the Church; and they screamed nonsense about the sacraments because they very sensibly recognized that the Western Roman Empire was going to die, and so were they.

It was so with Luccheni. He performed his meaningless act out of his consciousness of what is perhaps the most real distress of our age. He was an Italian born in Paris of parents forced to emigrate by their poverty and trodden down into an alien criminal class: that is to say, he belonged to an urban population for which the existing forms of government made no provision, which wandered often workless and always traditionless, without power to control its destiny. It was indeed most appropriate that he should register his discontent by killing Elizabeth, for Vienna is the archetype of the great city which breeds such a population. Its luxury was financed by an exploited peasant class bled so white that it was ready to send its boys into the factories and the girls into service on any terms. The beggars in the streets of Vienna, who, the innocent suppose, were put there by the Treaty of St Germain, are descendants of an army as old as the nineteenth century. Luccheni said with his stiletto to the symbol of power, "Hey, what are you going to do with me?" He made no suggestions, but cannot be blamed for it. It was the essence of his case against society that it had left him unfit to offer suggestions, unable to form thoughts or design actions other than the crudest and most violent. He lived many years in prison, almost until his like had found a vocabulary and a name for themselves and had astonished the world with the farce of Fascism.

So Elizabeth died, with a terrible ease. All her life her corsets had deformed and impeded her beautiful body, but they did not protect her from the assassin's stiletto. That cut clean through to her heart. Even so her imperial rank had insulated her from emotional and intellectual achievement, but freely admitted sorrow. And it would not leave her alone after her death. She had expressed in her will a solemn desire to be buried in the Isle of Corfu, but for all that Franz Josef had her laid in the Habsburg vault at the Capuchin church of

Vienna, fifteenth in the row of Empresses. The Habsburgs did not restrict themselves to the fields of the living in the exercise of their passion for preventing people from doing what they liked. Rudolf also asked that he might not be buried among his ancestors, but he had to yield up his skeleton; and the Prime Minister himself, Count Taaffe, called on Marie Vetsera's mother and asked her not to pray beside her daughter's grave, and received many police reports on her refusal to abandon this practice, which seems innocent enough even from the point of view of the court, since the whole of Vienna already knew how the girl had died. This was the kind of matter the Austrian Secret Police could handle. In the more important matter of keeping royal personages alive they were not nearly so successful.

After that Austria became a quiet place in Western eyes. Proust has pointed out that if one goes on performing any action, however banal, long enough, it automatically becomes "wonderful": a simple walk down a hundred yards of village street is "wonderful" if it is made every Sunday by an old lady of eighty. Franz Josef had for so long risen from his camp bed at four o'clock in the morning and worked twelve or fourteen hours on his official papers that he was recognized as one of the most "wonderful" of sovereigns, almost as "wonderful" as Queen Victoria, though he had shown no signs of losing in age the obstinacy and lack of imagination that made him see it as his duty to preserve his court as a morgue of etiquette and his Empire as a top-heavy anachronism. He was certain of universal acclamation not only during his life but after his death, for it is the habit of the people, whenever an old man mismanages his business so that it falls to pieces as soon as he dies, to say, "Ah, So-and-so was a marvel! He kept things together so long as he was alive, and look what happens now he has gone!" It was true that there was already shaping in his court a disaster that was to consume us all; but this did not appear to English eyes, largely because Austria was visited before the war only by our upper classes, who in no country noticed anything but horses, and Austrian horses were good.

The next time the red light of violence shone out it seemed of no importance, an irrelevant horror. When I was ten years old, on June the eleventh, 1903, Alexander Obrenovitch, King of Serbia, and his wife Draga were murdered in the Palace at Belgrade, and their naked bodies thrown out of their bedroom into the garden. The Queen's two brothers and two Ministers were also killed. The murder was the work of a number of Army officers, none of whom was then known outside

Serbia, and the main characters were not interesting. Alexander was a flabby young man with pince-nez who had a taste for clumsy experiments in absolutism, and his wife, who strangely enough belonged to the same type as Marie Vetsera, though she had in her youth been far more beautiful, was understood to have the disadvantages of being disreputable, having an ambitious family, and lying under the suspicion of having tried to palm off a borrowed baby as an heir to the throne. There can be no question that these people were regarded with terrified apprehension by the Serbians, who had freed themselves from the Turk not a hundred years before and knew that their independence was perpetually threatened by the great powers. The crime lingered in my mind only because of its nightmare touches. The conspirators blew open the door of the Palace with a dynamite cartridge which fused the electric lights, and they stumbled about blaspheming in the darkness, passing into a frenzy of cruelty that was half terror. The King and Queen hid in a secret cupboard in their bedroom for two hours, listening to the searchers grow cold, then warm, then cold again, then warm, and at last hot, and burning hot. The weakly King was hard to kill: when they threw him from the balcony they thought him doubly dead from bullet wounds and sword slashes, but the fingers of his right hand clasped the railing and had to be cut off before he fell to the ground, where the fingers of his left hand clutched the grass. Though it was June, rain fell on the naked bodies in the early morning as they lay among the flowers. The whole of Europe was revolted. Edward VII withdrew his Minister and most of the great powers followed his example.

That murder was just a half-tone square, dimly figured with horror, at the back of my mind: a Police News poster or the front page of a tabloid, seen years ago. But now I realize that when Alexander and Draga fell from that balcony the whole of the modern world fell with them. It took some time to reach the ground and break its neck, but its fall started then. For this is not a strictly moral universe, and it is not true that it is useless to kill a tyrant because a worse man takes his place. It has never been more effectively disproved than by the successor of Alexander Obrenovitch. Peter Karageorgevitch came to the throne under every possible disadvantage. He was close on sixty and had never seen Serbia since he left it with his exiled father at the age of fourteen; he had been brought up at Geneva under the influence of Swiss liberalism and had later become an officer in the French Army; he had no experience of statecraft, and he was a man of modest and retiring personality and simple manners, who had settled down happily at Geneva, to supervise the education of his three motherless children and pursue mildly bookish interests. It appears to be true that though he had told the conspirators of his readiness to accept the Serbian throne if Alexander Obrenovitch vacated it, he had had no idea that they proposed to do anything more violent than force an abdication; after all, his favourite author was John Stuart Mill. The Karageorgevitch belief in the sacredness of the dynasty brought him back to Belgrade, but it might have been safely wagered that he would need all the support he could get to stay there. He was entirely surrounded by the conspirators whose crime he abhorred, and he could not dismiss them, because in sober fact they numbered amongst them some of the ablest and most public-spirited men in Serbia; and with these fierce critics all about him perfectly capable of doing what they had done before, he had to keep order in a new and expanding country, vexed with innumerable internal and external difficulties.

But Peter Karageorgevitch was a great king. Slowly and soberly he proved himself one of the finest liberal statesmen in Europe, and later, in the Balkan wars which drove the Turk out of Macedonia and Old Serbia, he proved himself a magnificent soldier. Never was there worse luck for Europe. Austria, with far more territory than she could properly administer, wanted more and had formed her Drang nach Osten, her Hasten to the East policy. Now the formidable new military state of Serbia was in her way, and might even join with Russia to attack her. Now, too, all the Slav peoples of the Empire were seething with discontent because the free Serbians were doing so well, and the German-Austrians hated them more than ever. The situation had been further complicated by giving up the pretence that Bosnia and Herzegovina were provinces which she merely occupied and administered, and formally annexing them. This made many Slavs address appeals to Serbia, which, as was natural in a young country, sometimes answered boastfully.

The situation was further complicated by the character of the man who had succeeded Rudolf as the heir to the Imperial Crown, the Archduke Franz Ferdinand of Este. This unlovable melancholic had upset all sections of the people by his proposals, drafted and expressed without the slightest trace of statesmanship, to make a tripartite monarchy of the Empire, by forming the Slavs into a separate kingdom. The reactionaries felt this was merely an expression of his bitter hostility towards the Emperor and his conservatism; the Slavs were unimpressed and declared they would rather be free, like Serbia. The reaction of Austria to this new situation was extravagant fear. The Austrian Chief of General Staff, Conrad von Hötzendorf, was speaking for many of his countrymen and most of his class when he ceaselessly urged that a preventive war should be waged against Serbia before she became more capable of self-defence. He and his kind would not have felt this if Alexander Obrenovitch had not been murdered and given place to a better man, who made a strong and orderly Serbia.

Then on June the twenty-eighth, 1914, the Austro-Hungarian Government allowed Franz Ferdinand to go to Bosnia in his capacity of Inspector-General of the Army to conduct manœuvres on the Serbian frontier. It was strange that he should wish to do this, and they should allow him, for that is St Vitus' Day, the anniversary of the battle of Kossovo in 1389, the defeat of the Serbs by the Turks which meant five hundred years of enslavement. That defeat had been wiped out in the Balkan War by the recapture of Kossovo, and it was not tactful to remind the Serbs that some of their people were still enslaved by a foreign power. But Franz Ferdinand had his wish and then paid a visit to Sarajevo, the Bosnian capital, where the police gave him quite insufficient protection, though they had been warned that attempts were to be made on his life. A Bosnian Serb named Princip, who deeply resented Austro-Hungarian misrule, was able without any difficulty to shoot him as he drove along the street, and accidentally killed his wife as well. It must be noted that he was a Serb and not a Serbian. A Croat is a Catholic member and a Serb an Orthodox member of a Slav people that lies widely distributed south of the Danube, between the Adriatic and Bulgaria, and north of the Greek mountains. A Serbian is a subject of the kingdom of Serbia, and might be a Croat, just as a Croatian-born inhabitant of the old Austrian province of Croatia might be a Serb. But Princip had brought his revolver from Belgrade, and though he had been given it by a private individual and not by the Government, the Austro-Hungarian Empire used this as a pretext to declare war on Serbia. Other powers took sides and the Great War started.

Of that assassination I remember nothing at all. Every detail of Elizabeth's death is clear in my mind, of the Belgrade massacre I keep a blurred image, but I cannot recall reading anything about the Sarajevo *attentat* or hearing anyone speak of it. I was then very busy being an idiot, being a private person, and I had enough on my hands.

But my idiocy was like my anæsthetic. During the blankness it dispensed I was cut about and felt nothing, but it could not annul the consequences. The pain came afterwards.

So, that evening in 1934, I lay in bed and looked at my radio fearfully, though it had nothing more to say that was relevant, and later on the telephone talked to my husband, as one does in times of crisis if one is happily married, asking him questions which one knows quite well neither he nor anyone else can answer and deriving great comfort from what he says. I was really frightened, for all these earlier killings had either hastened doom towards me or prefigured it. If Rudolf had not died he might have solved the Slav problem of the Austro-Hungarian Empire and restrained its imperialist ambition, and there might have been no war. If Alexander Obrenovitch had not been killed Serbia might never have been strong enough to excite the Empire's jealousy and fear, and there might have been no war. The killing of Franz Ferdinand was war itself. And the death of Elizabeth had shown me the scourge of the world after the war, Luccheni, Fascism, the rule of the dispossessed class that claims its rights and cannot conceive them save in terms of empty violence, of killing, taking, suppressing.

And now there was another killing. Again it was in the South-East of Europe, where was the source of all the other deaths. That seemed to me strange, in 1934, because the Slav problem then seemed to have been satisfactorily settled by the war. The Czechs and the Slovaks had their pleasant democratic state, which was working well enough except for the complaints of the Sudeten Germans who under the Habsburgs had been pampered with privileges paid for by their Slav neighbours. The Slovenes and the Croats and the Dalmatians and the Montenegrins were now united in the kingdom of the South Slavs, which is what Yugoslavia means; and though the Slovenes and Croats and the Dalmatians were separated in spirit from the Serbs by their Catholicism and the Montenegrins hankered after their lost independence, the state had seemed to be finding its balance. But here was another murder, another threat that man was going to deliver himself up to pain, was going to serve death instead of life.

A few days later my husband told me that he had seen a news film which had shown with extraordinary detail the actual death of the King of Yugoslavia, and as soon as I could leave the nursing-home I went and saw it. I had to go to a private projection room, for by that time it had been withdrawn from the ordinary cinemas, and I took the opportunity to have it run over several times, while I peered at it like an old woman reading the tea-leaves in her cup. First there was the Yugoslavian warship sliding into the harbour of Marseilles, which I know very well. Behind it was that vast suspension bridge which always troubles me because it reminds me that in this mechanized age I am as little able to understand my environment as any primitive woman who thinks that a waterfall is inhabited by a spirit, and indeed less so, for her opinion might from a poetical point of view be correct. I know enough to be aware that this bridge cannot have been spun by a vast steel spider out of its entrails, but no other explanation seems to me as plausible, and I have not the faintest notion of its use. But the man who comes down the gangway of the ship and travels on the tender to the quay, him I can understand, for he is something that is not new. Always the people have had the idea of the leader, and sometimes a man is born who embodies this idea.

His face is sucked too close to the bone by sickness to be tranquil or even handsome, and it would at any time have suggested a dry pedantry, unnatural in a man not far advanced in the forties. But he looks like a great man, which is not to say that he is a good man or a wise man, but is to say that he has that historic quality which comes from intense concentration on an important subject. What he is thinking of is noble, to judge from the homage he pays it with his eyes, and it governs him entirely. He does not relapse into it when the other world fails to interest him; rather does he relapse into noticing what is about him when for a moment his interior communion fails him. But he is not abstracted, he is paying due respect to the meeting between France and Yugoslavia. Indeed he is bringing to the official occasion a naïve earnestness. When Monsieur Barthou, the French Foreign Minister, comes and greets him, it is as if a jolly priest, fully at ease in his orders, stands before the altar beside a tortured mystical layman. Sometimes, too, he shows by a turn of the head, by a dilation of the pinched nostrils, that some aspect of the scene has pleased him.

About all his reactions there is that jerky quickness which comes of long vigilance. It was natural. He had been a soldier from boyhood, and since the Great War he had perpetually been threatened with death from within, by tuberculosis, and with death from without, by assassination at the hand of Croats or Macedonians who wanted independence instead of union with Serbia. But it is not fear that is his preoccupation. That, certainly, is Yugoslavia. He has the look of

565

one of those men who claim that they rule by divine right whether they be kings or presidents, because their minds curve protectively over their countries with the inclusiveness of the sky. When one sees President Roosevelt one is sure that he is thinking about America; sometimes his thought may be soft and loose, but it is always dedicated to the same service. Those who saw Lenin say that he was always thinking of Russia; even when his thought was hard and tight it knew the same dedication. In our own King George V we recognized that piety.

Now King Alexander is driving down the familiar streets, curiously unguarded, in a curiously antique car. It can be seen from his attempt to make his stiff hand supple, from a careless flash of his careful black eyes, it can be seen that he is taking the cheers of the crowd with a childish seriousness. It is touching, like a girl putting full faith in the compliments that are paid to her at a ball. Then his preoccupation veils his brows and desiccates his lips. He is thinking of Yugoslavia again, with the nostalgia of an author who has been interrupted in writing his new book. He might be thinking, "*Heureux qui, comme Ulysse, a fait un beau voyage. . . .*"* But then the camera leaves him. It recedes. The sound-track records a change, a swelling astonishment, in the voice of the crowd. We see a man jumping on the footboard of the car, a soldier swinging a sword, a revolver in the hand of another, a straw hat lying on the ground, a crowd that jumps up and down, up and down, smashing something flat with its arms, kicking something flat with its feet, till there is seen on the pavement a pulp covered with garments. A lad in a sweater dodges before his captors, his defiant face unmarked by fear, although his body expresses the very last extreme of fear by a creeping, writhing motion. A view of the whole street shows people dashed about as by a tangible wind of death.

The camera returns to the car and we see the King. He is lying almost flat on his back on the seat, and he is as I was after the anæsthetic. He does not know that anything has happened, he is still half rooted in the pleasure of his own nostalgia. He might be asking, "*Et en quelle saison Revoiray-je le clos de ma pauvre maison, Qui m'est une province, et beaucoup d'avantage?*" It is certain that he is dying, because he is the centre of a manifestation which would not happen unless the living had been shocked out of their reserve by the presence

*[From the sonnet by Joachim du Bellay, which the author calls elsewhere "one of the most beautiful poems in the world."]

of death. Innumerable hands are caressing him. Hands are coming from everywhere, over the back of the car, over the sides, through the windows, to caress the dying King, and they are supremely kind. They are far kinder than faces can be, for faces are Marthas, burdened with many cares because of their close connection with the mind, but these hands express the mindless sympathy of living flesh for flesh that is about to die, the pure physical basis for pity. They are men's hands, but they move tenderly as the hands of women fondling their babies, they stroke his cheeks as if they were washing it with kindness. Suddenly his nostalgia goes from him. His pedantry relaxes. He is at peace, he need not guard against death any more.

Then the camera shows an official running wildly down a street in top hat and frock-coat, demonstrating the special ridiculousness of middle-aged men, who have the sagging, anxious faces and protruding bellies appropriate to pregnancies, but bring forth nothing. It would be a superb ending for a comic film. Then we see again the warship and the harbour, where the President of the Republic stands with many men around him, who are all as naïvely earnest as only one man was when that ship first came into the harbour. Now there is no jolly priest confident that he has the sacred mysteries well in hand: Barthou by now was also dead. All these men look as the King looked at his coming, as if there lay behind the surface of things a reality which at any moment might manifest itself as a eucharist to be partaken of not by individuals, but by nations. The coffin containing the man through which this terrible sacrament has been dispensed to France is carried on board, and the warship takes it away from these people, who stand in a vast circle, rigid with horror and reverence. They are intensely surprised that the eucharist was of this nature, but the King of Yugoslavia had always thought it might be so.

I could not understand this event, no matter how often I saw this picture. I knew, of course, how and why the murder had happened. Luccheni has got on well in the world. When he killed Elizabeth, over forty years ago, he had to do his own work in the world, he had to travel humbly about Switzerland in search of his victims, he had but one little two-edged dagger as tool for his crime, and he had to pay the penalty. But now Luccheni is Mussolini, and the improvement in his circumstances can be measured by the increase in the magnitude of his crime. In Elizabeth the insecure and traditionless town-dweller struck down the symbol of power, but his modern representative has struck down power itself by assuming itself and degrading its essence. His offence is not that he has virtually deposed his king, for kings and presidents who cannot hold their office lose thereby the title to their kingdoms and republics. His offence is that he made himself dictator without binding himself by any of the contractual obligations which civilized man has imposed on his rulers in all credible phases of history and which give power a soul to be saved. This cancellation of process in government leaves it an empty violence that must perpetually and at any cost outdo itself, for it has no alternative idea and hence no alternative activity. The long servitude in the slums has left this kind of barbarian without any knowledge of what man does when he ceases to be violent, except for a few uncomprehending glimpses of material prosperity. He therefore can conceive of no outlet for his energies other than the creation of social services which artificially and unnaturally spread this material prosperity among the population, in small doses that keep them happy and dependent; and, for his second string, there is the performance of fantasias on the single theme of brute force. All forms of compulsion are practised on any element within the state that is resistant or is even suspected of retaining consciousness of its difference from the dominating party; and all living beings outside the state are conceived as enemies, to be hated and abused, and in ideal conditions to be robbed and murdered. This aggressiveness leads obviously to the establishment of immense armed forces, and furtively to incessant experimentation with methods of injuring the outer world other than the traditional procedure of warfare.

These methods, as time went on and Mussolini developed his foreign policy, included camps where Croats and Macedonians who objected to incorporation with Yugoslavia, or who were simply rogues, were trained as terrorists in the use of bombs and small arms and financed to use the results of that training in raids on Yugoslavia in the alleged service of their separatist campaigns. There could be no more convincing proof of the evil wrought on our civilization by the great cities and their spawn, for in not one state in pre-war Europe could there have been found any such example of an institution designed to teach the citizens of another state to murder their rulers. The existence of these camps and the necessity felt by human beings to practise any art they have learned explain the assassination of King Alexander without properly conveying its indecency. For Italy instructed her satellite, Hungary, to follow her example, and a notor-

ious camp was established near the Yugoslav–Hungarian border at
Yanka Puszta. Honour often seems a highly artificial convention, but
life in any level of society where it has been abandoned astonishes by
its tortuousness. When the Italians sent assassins from their training
camps to murder the King, they went to great pains to make it
appear that his murderers came from Yanka Puszta, even inducing
a Macedonian assassin who had been associated with the Hungarian
camp to come to Marseille and be killed, so that his dead body could
be exhibited as proof of the conspirators' origin. It is a measure of the
inevitable frivolity of a state governed by Fascist philosophy that the
crime was entirely wasted and was committed only because of a
monstrous miscalculation. Mussolini had believed that with the
King's death the country would fall to pieces and be an easy prey to
a foreign invader. But if Croat discontent had been a thousand times
more bitter than it was, it would have remained true that people prefer to kill their tyrants for themselves; and actually the murder
shocked Yugoslavia into a unity it had not known before. So there
was not war; there was nothing except the accomplishment of a further stage in the infiltration of peace with the depravity of war, which
threatens now to make the two hardly distinguishable.

But the other participator in the event remained profoundly mysterious. At each showing of the film it could be seen more plainly
that he had not been surprised by his own murder. He had not merely
known of it as a factual possibility, he had realized it imaginatively
in its full force as an event. But in this matter he seemed more intelligent than his own intelligence. Men of action often take an obstinate
pride in their own limitations, and so, too, do invalids; and his face
hinted that he, being both sick and soldierly, had combined the two
forms of fault. All that I could read of his reign confirmed this indication and showed him as inflexible and slow. Yet there was in him this
great wisdom, which brought him to the hour of his death sustained
by a just estimate of what it is to die, and by certain magnificent conceptions such as kingliness and patriotism. It would be an enigma
were it not that an individual had other ways of acquiring wisdom
than through his own intellectual equipment. He can derive it, as it
were, through the pores from the culture of his race. Perhaps this
peculiar wisdom, which appeared on the screen as definitely as the
peculiar sanity of Françoise Rosay or the peculiar narcissism of Garbo,
was drawn by the King of Yugoslavia from the kingdom of Yugoslavia, from the South Slavs.

As to that I could form no opinion, for I knew nothing about the South Slavs, nor had I come across anybody who was acquainted with them. I was only aware that they formed part of the Balkan people, who had played a curious role in the history of British benevolence before the war and for some time after it. They had been, till they severally won their independences at various times in the nineteenth and twentieth centuries, the Christian subjects of the Turkish or Ottoman Empire, which had kept them in the greatest misery by incompetent administration and very cunningly set each section of them at odds with all the others, so that they could never rise in united rebellion. Hence each people was perpetually making charges of inhumanity against all its neighbours. The Serb, for example, raised his bitterest complaint against the Turk, but was also ready to accuse the Greeks, the Bulgarians, the Vlachs, and the Albanians of every crime under the sun. English persons, therefore of humanitarian and reformist disposition constantly went out to the Balkan Peninsula to see who was in fact ill-treating whom, and, being by the very nature of their perfectionist faith unable to accept the horrid hypothesis that everybody was ill-treating everybody else, all came back with a pet Balkan people established in their hearts as suffering and innocent, eternally the massacree and never the massacrer. The same sort of person, devoted to good works and austerities, who is traditionally supposed to keep a cat and a parrot, often set up on the hearth the image of the Albanian or the Bulgarian or the Serbian or the Macedonian Greek people, which had all the force and blandness of pious fantasy. ◇ ◇ ◇

Violence was, indeed, all I knew of the Balkans: all I knew of the South Slavs. I derived the knowledge from memories of my earliest interest in Liberalism, of leaves fallen from this jungle of pamphlets, tied up with string in the dustiest corners of junk-shops, and later from the prejudices of the French, who use the word *"Balkan"* as a term of abuse, meaning a *rastaquouère* type of barbarian. In Paris, awakened in a hotel bedroom by the insufficiently private life of my neighbours, I have heard the sound of three slashing slaps and a woman's voice crying through sobs, *"Balkan! Balkan!"* Once in Nice, as I sat eating langouste outside a little restaurant down by the harbour, there were some shots, a sailor lurched out of the next-door bar, and the proprietress ran after him, shouting, *"Balkan! Balkan!"* He had emptied his revolver into the mirror behind the bar. And now I was faced with the immense nobility of the King in the film, who was certainly *Balkan, Balkan,* but who met violence with an imaginative realization which is its very opposite, which absorbs it into the experience it aims at destroying. But I must have been wholly mistaken in my acceptance of the popular legend regarding the Balkans, for if the South Slavs had been truly violent they would not have been hated first by the Austrians, who worshipped violence in an imperialist form, and later by the Fascists, who worship violence in a totalitarian form. Yet it was impossible to think of the Balkans for one moment as gentle and lamblike, for assuredly Alexander and Draga Obrenovitch and Franz Ferdinand and his wife had none of them died in their beds. I had to admit that I quite simply and flatly knew nothing at all about the south-eastern corner of Europe; and since there proceeds steadily from that place a stream of events which are a source of danger to me, which indeed for four years threatened my safety and during that time deprived me for ever of many benefits, that is to say I know nothing of my own destiny.

That is a calamity. Pascal wrote: "Man is but a reed, the most feeble thing in nature; but he is a thinking reed. The entire universe need not arm itself to crush him. A vapour, a drop of water, suffices to kill him. But if the universe were to crush him, man would still be more noble than that which killed him, because he knows that he dies and the advantage which the universe has over him; the universe knows nothing of this." In these words he writes the sole prescription for a distinguished humanity. We must learn to know the nature of the advantage which the universe has over us, which in my case seems to lie in the Balkan Peninsula. It was only two or three days distant, yet I had never troubled to go that short journey which might explain to me how I shall die, and why. While I was marvelling at my inertia, I was asked to go to Yugoslavia to give some lectures in different towns before universities and English clubs, and this I did in the spring of 1936.

It was unfortunate that at the end of my journey I went to Greece and was stung by a sand-fly and got dengue fever, which is also known, and justly so, as breakbone fever. On the way back I had to rest in a *Kurhaus* outside Vienna, and there they thought me so ill that my husband came out to fetch me home. He found me weeping in my bedroom, though this is a town governed by its flowers, and as it was May the purple and white lilacs were as thick along the streets as people watching for a procession, and the chestnut trees were holding their candles to the windows of the upper rooms. I was well enough to be out, but I was sitting in a chair with a heap of coarse linen dresses flung over my knees and feet. I showed them to my husband one by one, saying in remorse, "Look what I have let them do!" They were dresses which I had bought from the peasants in Macedonia, and the Austrian doctor who was treating me had made me have them disinfected, though they were quite clean. But the nurse who took them away had forgotten what was to be done with them, and instead of putting them under the lamp she had given them to the washerwoman, who had put them in strong soak. They were ruined. Dyes that had been fixed for twenty years had run and now defiled the good grain of the stuff; stitches that had made a clean-cut austere design were now sordid smears. Even if I could have gone back immediately and bought new ones, which in my weakness I wanted to do, I would have it on my conscience that I had not properly protected the work of these women which should have been kept as a testimony, which was a part of what the King had known as he lay dying.

"You must not think me stupid," I said to my husband; "you cannot understand why I think these dresses important; you have not been there." "Is it so wonderful there?" he asked. "It is more wonderful than I can tell you," I answered. "But how?" he said. I could not tell him at all clearly. I said, "Well, there is everything there. Except what we have. But that seems very little." "Do you mean that the English have very little," he asked, "or the whole of the West?" "The whole of the West," I said, "here too." He looked at the butter-yellow baroque houses between the chestnut trees and laughed. "Beethoven and Mozart and Schubert wrote quite a lot of music in this town," he said. "But they were none of them happy," I objected. "In Yugoslavia," suggested my husband, smiling, "everybody is happy." "No, no," I said, "not at all, but . . ." The thing I wanted to tell him could not be told, however, because it was manifold and nothing like what one is accustomed to communicate by words. I stumbled on, "Really, we are not as rich in the West as we think we are. Or, rather, there is much we have not got which the people in the Balkans have got in quantity. To look at them you would think they had nothing. The people who had made these dresses looked as if they had nothing at all. But if these imbeciles here had not spoiled this embroidery you would see that whoever did it had more than we have." I saw the blue lake of Ochrid, the mosques of Sarajevo, the walled town of Korchula, and it appeared possible that I was unable to find words for what I wanted to say because it was not true. I am never sure of the reality of what I see, if I have seen it only once; I know that until it has firmly established its objective existence by impressing my senses and my memory, I am capable of conscripting it into the service of a private dream. In a panic I said, "I must go back to Yugoslavia, this time next year, in the spring, for Easter." ◇ ◇ ◇

Croatia

They were waiting in the rain on the platform of the real Zagreb, our three friends. There was Constantine, the poet, a Serb, that is to say a Slav member of the Orthodox Church, from Serbia. There was Valetta, a lecturer in mathematics at Zagreb University, a Croat, that is to say a Slav member of the Roman Catholic Church, from Dalmatia. There was Marko Gregorievitch, the critic and journalist, a Croat from Croatia. They were all different sizes and shapes, in body and mind.

Constantine is short and fat, with a head like the best-known satyr in the Louvre, and an air of vine-leaves about the brow, though he drinks little. He is perpetually drunk on what comes out of his mouth, not what goes into it. He talks incessantly. In the morning he comes out of his bedroom in the middle of a sentence; and at night he backs into it, so that he can just finish one more sentence. Automatically he makes silencing gestures while he speaks, just in case somebody should take it into his head to interrupt. Nearly all his talk is good, and sometimes it runs along in a coloured shadow show, like Heine's *Florentine Nights*, and sometimes it crystallizes into a little story the essence of hope or love or regret, like a Heine lyric. Of all human beings I have ever met he is the most like Heine: and since Heine was the most Jewish of writers it follows that Constantine is Jew as well as Serb. His father was a Jewish doctor of revolutionary sympathies, who fled from Russian Poland about fifty years ago and settled in a rich provincial town in Serbia and became one of the leaders of the medical profession, which has always been more advanced there than one might have supposed. His mother was also Polish Jewish, and was a famous musician. He is by adoption only, yet quite completely, a Serb. He fought in the Great War very gallantly, for he is a man of great physical courage, and to him Serbian history is his history, his life is a part of the life of the Serbian people. He is now a Government official; but that is not the reason why he believes in Yugoslavia. To him a state of Serbs, Slovenes, and Croats, controlled by a central government in Belgrade, is a necessity if these peoples are to maintain themselves against Italian and Central European pressure on the west, and Bulgarian pressure, which might become in effect Central European pressure, on the east.

Valetta comes from a Dalmatian town which was settled by the Greeks some hundreds of years before Christ, and he has the strong delicacy and the morning freshness of an archaic statue. They like him everywhere he goes, Paris and London and Berlin and Vienna, but he is hall-marked as a Slav, because his charm is not associated with any of those defects that commonly go with it in other races. He might suddenly stop smiling and clench his long hands, and offer himself up to martyrdom for an idea. He is anti-Yugoslavian; he is a federalist and believes in an autonomous Croatia.

Gregorievitch looks like Pluto in the Mickey Mouse films. His face is grooved with grief at the trouble and lack of gratitude he has encountered while defending certain fixed and noble standards in a chaotic world. His long body is like Pluto's in its extensibility. As he sits in his armchair, resentment at what he conceives to be a remediable injustice will draw him inches nearer to the ceiling, despair at an inevitable wrong will crumple him up like a concertina. Yugoslavia is the Mickey Mouse this Pluto serves. He is ten years older than Constantine, who is forty-six, and thirty years older than Valetta. This means that for sixteen years before the war he was an active revolutionary, fighting against the Hungarians for the right of Croats to govern themselves and to use their own language. In order that the Croats might be united with their free brother Slavs the Serbs, he endured poverty and imprisonment and exile. Therefore Yugoslavia is to him the Kingdom of Heaven on earth. Who speaks more lightly of it spits on those sixteen years of sorrow, who raises his hand against it violates the Slav sacrament. So to him Constantine, who was still a student in Paris when the Great War broke out, and who had been born a free Serb, seems impious in the way he takes Yugoslavia for granted. There is the difference between them that there was between the Christians of the first three centuries, who fought for their faith when it seemed a lost cause, and the Christians of the fourth century, who fought for it when it was victorious.

And to Gregorievitch, Valetta is quite simply a traitor. He is more than an individual who has gone astray, he is the very essence of treachery incarnate. Youth should uphold the banner of the right against unjust authority, and should practise that form of obedience to God which is rebellion against tyranny; and it seems to Gregorievitch that Valetta is betraying that ideal, for to him Yugoslavia represents a supreme gesture of defiance against the tyranny of the Austro-Hungarian Empire. Only a sorcerer could make him realize that the Austro-Hungarian Empire ceased to be when Valetta was six years old, and that he has never known any other symbol of unjust authority except Yugoslavia.* ◇ ◇ ◇

From SHESTINE

"This is a very delightful place," said my husband the next morning. It was Easter Sunday, and the waiter had brought in on the breakfast-tray dyed Easter eggs as a present from the management. ◇ ◇ ◇

We drove through a landscape I have often seen in Chinese pictures: wooded hills under snow looked like hedgehogs drenched in icing sugar. On a hill stood a little church, full to the doors, bright inside as a garden, glowing with scarlet and gold and blue and the unique, rough, warm white of homespun, and shaking with song. On the women's heads were red handkerchiefs printed with yellow leaves and peacocks' feathers, their jackets were solidly embroidered with flowers, and under their white skirts were thick red or white woollen stockings. Their men were just as splendid in sheepskin leather jackets with appliqué designs in dyed leathers, linen shirts with fronts embroidered in cross-stitch and fastened with buttons of Maria Theresa dollars or lumps of turquoise matrix, and homespun trousers gathered into elaborate boots. The splendour of these dresses was more impressive because it was not summer. The brocade of a rajah's costume or the silks of an Ascot crowd are within the confines of prudence, because the rajah is going to have a golden umbrella held over him and the Ascot crowd is not far from shelter, but these costumes were made for the winter in a land of unmetalled roads, where snow lay till it melted and mud might be knee-deep, and showed a gorgeous lavishness, for hours and days, and even years had been spent in the stuffs and skins and embroideries which were thus put at the mercy of the bad weather. There was lavishness also in the

* [These three men, especially Constantine, were to companion the author and her husband off and on through their travels in Yugoslavia.]

singing that poured out of these magnificently clad bodies, which indeed transformed the very service. Western church music is almost commonly petitioning and infantile, a sentiment cozening for remedy against sickness or misfortue, combined with a masochist enjoyment in the malady, but this singing spoke of health and fullness.

The men stood on the right of the church and the women on the left. This is the custom also in the Orthodox Church, and it is reasonable enough. At a ceremony which sets out to be the most intense of all contacts with reality, men and women, who see totally different aspects of reality, might as well stand apart. It is inappropriate for them to be mixed as in the unit of the family, where men and women attempt with such notorious difficulty to share their views of reality for social purposes. From this divided congregation came a flood of song which asked for absolutely nothing, which did not ape childhood, which did not pretend that sour is sweet and pain wholesome, but which simply adored. If there be a God who is fount of all goodness, this is the tribute that should logically be paid to Him; if there be only goodness, it is still a logical tribute. And again, the worship, like their costume, was made astonishing by their circumstances. These people, who had neither wealth nor security, nor ever had them, stood before the Creator, and thought not what they might ask for but what they might give. To be among them was like seeing an orchard laden with apples or a field of ripe wheat, endowed with a human will and using it in accordance with its own richness.

This was not simply due to these people's faith. There are people who hold precisely the same faith whose worship produces an effect of poverty. When Heine said that Amiens Cathedral could have been built only in the past, because the men of the day had convictions, whereas we moderns have only opinions, and something more than opinions are needed for building a cathedral, he put into circulation a half-truth which has done a great deal of harm. It matters supremely what kind of men hold these convictions. This service was impressive because the congregation was composed of people with a unique sort of healthy intensity. At the end we went out and stood at the churchyard gate, and watched the men and women clumping down a lane to the village through the deep snow, with a zest that was the generalized form of the special passion they had exhibited in the church. I had not been wrong about what I had found among the Yugoslavs.

"Are they not beautiful, the costumes of Croatia?" asked Gregorievitch, his very spectacles beaming, his whole appearance made unfamiliar by joy. "Are they not lovely, the girls who wear them, and are not the young men handsome? And they are very pious." "Yes," I said, "I have never heard a mass sung more fervently." "I do not mean that," he said irritably, "I meant pious in their Croat patriotism." It appeared that the inhabitants of Shestine wore these wonderful clothes not from custom but from a positive and virile choice. They would naturally wear ordinary Western European clothes, as most other peasants round Zagreb do, but they are conscious that the great patriot Anton Starchevitch is buried in the graveyard of their church, and they know that to him everything Croatian was precious. We went and stood by his tomb in the snow, while Gregorievitch, taller than ever before though not erect, hung over its railings like a weeping willow and told us how Starchevitch had founded the Party of the Right, which defied both Austria and Hungary and attempted to negotiate his country back to the position of independence it had enjoyed eight hundred years before. "It was Starchevitch's motto, 'Croatia only needs God and the Croats,'" said Gregorievitch. "For thirty years when the glamour and wealth and triumphant cruelty of nineteenth-century Hungary might have tempted us young Croats to forget our country, he made us understand that if we forgot the tradition of our race we lost our souls as if by sin." We were conscious of the second coat that lies about a snow-covered world, the layer of silence; we smelt the wood-smoke from the village below. "As a child I was taken to see him," said Gregorievitch, his voice tense as if he were a Welsh evangelist; "we all drew strength from him." Constantine, looking very plump and cosy, announced, "His mother was a Serb." "But she had been received at the time of her marriage into the True Church," said Gregorievitch, frowning.

We moved away, and as Constantine and I stepped into the snow-drifts of the lane we passed three men, dark as any Hindu, carrying drums and trumpets. "Ohé! Here are the gipsies," said Constantine, and we smiled at them, seeing pictures of some farm kitchen crammed with people in dresses brighter than springtime, all preparing with huge laughter to eat mountains of lamb and pig and drink wells of wine. But the men looked at us sullenly, and one said with hatred, "Yes, we are gipsies." Both Constantine and I were so startled that we stopped in the snow and gaped at each other, and then walked on in silence. In the eastern parts of Yugoslavia, in Serbia and in Macedonia, the gipsies are proud of being gipsies, and other people, which is to say the peasants, for there are practically none other, honour them for their qualities, for their power of making beautiful music and dancing, which the peasant lacks, and envy them for being exempt from the necessities of toil and order which lie so heavily on the peasant; and this has always been my natural attitude to those who can please as I cannot. It was inconceivable to both Constantine and myself that the gipsies should have thought we held them in contempt or that we should have expressed contempt aloud if we had felt it.

The whole world was less delightful. The snow seemed simply weather, the smell of the wood-smoke gave no pleasure. "I tell you, Central Europe is too near the Croats," said Constantine. "They are good people, very good people, but they are possessed by the West. In Germany and Austria they despise the gipsies. They have several very good reasons. The art of the gipsies commands no respect, for the capitalist system has discredited popular art, and only exploits virtuosos. If I go and play Liszt's scaramoucheries very fast, thump-thump-thump and tweedle-tweedle-tweedle, they will think more of it than the music those three men play, though it is perfectly adapted to certain occasions. Also the gipsies are poor, and the capitalist system despises people who do not acquire goods. Also the West is mad about cleanliness, and the gipsies give dirt its rights, perhaps too liberally. We Serbs are not bourgeois, so none of the reasons make us hate the gipsies, and, believe me, our world is more comfortable."

I looked back at the gipsies, who were now breasting the hill, huddled under the harsh wind that combed its crest. Life had become infinitely poorer since we left church. The richness of the service had been consonant with an order of society in which peasants and gipsies were on an equal footing and there was therefore no sense of deprivation and need; but here was the threat of a world where everybody was needy, since the moneyed people had no art and the people with art had no money. Something alien and murderous had intruded here into the Slav pattern, and its virtue had gone out of it.

From TWO CASTLES

Yes, the German influence was like a shadow on the Croat world. We were to learn that again the next day. Gregorievitch had arranged to take us on Easter Monday into the country. ◇ ◇ ◇

It is of the highest importance that the reader should understand Gregorievitch. If it were not for a small number of Gregorievitches the eastern half of Europe (and perhaps the other half as well) would have been Islamized, the tradition of liberty would have died for ever under the Habsburgs, the Romanoffs, and the Ottoman Empire, and Bolshevism would have become anarchy and not a system which may yet be turned to many uses. His kind has profoundly affected history, and always for the better. Reproachfully his present manifestation said to us, "Are you not ready yet?" We stared at him, and my husband asked, "But is not the weather far too bad?" He answered, "The sun is not shining, but the countryside will be there all the same, will it not? And the snow is not too deep." "Are you sure?" my husband asked doubtfully. "I am quite sure," answered Gregorievitch. "I have rung up a friend of mine, a general who has specialized in mechanical transport, and I have told him the make of our automobiles, and he is of the opinion that we will be able to visit both castles."

There, as often before and after, Gregorievitch proved that the essential quality of Slavs is not, as might be thought, imagination. He is characteristically, and in an endearing way, a Slav, but he has no imagination at all. He cannot see that the factual elements in an experience combine into more than themselves. He would not, for example, let us go to the theatre at Zagreb. "No, I will not get you tickets," he said with a repressed indignation, like a brawl in a crypt, "I will not let you waste your money in that way. Since you cannot follow Serbo-Croat easily even when it is spoken slowly, and your husband does not understand it at all, what profit can it be for you to go to our theatre?" He envisaged attendance at a play as an attempt to obtain the information which the author has arranged for the characters to impart to the audience by their words and actions; and that the actions could be used as a basis for guesswork to the words, that the appearance of the actors, the inflections of their voices, and the reactions they elicited from the audience could throw light not only on the play but the culture of which it was a part was beyond his comprehension. So now he conceived of an expedition to the country as being undertaken for the purpose of observing the physical and political geography of the district, and this could obviously be pursued in any climatic conditions save those involving actual physical discomfort. Nevertheless the Slav quality of passion was there, to disconcert the English or American witness, for it existed in a degree which is found among Westerners only in highly imaginative people. As he stood over us, grey and grooved and Plutoish, he palpitated with the violence of his thought, "These people will go away without seeing the Croatian countryside, and some day they may fail Croatia for the lack of that knowledge." His love of Croatia was of volcanic ardour; and its fire was not affected by his knowledge that most of the other people who loved Croatia were quite prepared, because he favoured union with the Serbs, to kill him without mercy in any time of crisis. ◇ ◇ ◇

"What can have happened to them all?" asked Gregorievitch. He went and pounded on the door* of the porter's lodge, and when an astonished face apeared at the upper windows he demanded, "And where is Nikolai? Why is Nikolai not here to meet us?" "He is up at the castle," said the porter; "he did not think you would be coming." "Thought we were not coming!" exclaimed Gregorievitch. "What made him think we were not coming?" It had distressed him very much to find that Valetta and the Croats and my husband and I seemed unable to grasp the common-sense point of view that if one wanted to see a castle one went and saw it, no matter what the weather, since the castle would certainly be there, no matter what the weather; but he had excused it because we were by way of being intellectuals and therefore might be expected to be a little fanciful. Here, however, were quite simple people who were talking the same sort of nonsense. He said testily, "Well, we will go up and find him for ourselves." We climbed the sugar-loaf hill by whimsically contrived paths and stone steps, among fir trees that were striped black and white like zebras, because of the branches and the layer of white snow that lay on each of them, while the porter, who was now invisible to us through the snow, cried up to the castle, "Nikolai! Nikolai! They have come!" I was warm because I was wearing a squirrel coat, but all the men were shaking with cold, and we were all up to our knees in snow. At last we came to a walk running round some ramparts, and Nikolai, who was a very handsome young peasant with golden hair and blue eyes framed by long lashes, dropped the broom with which he had been trying to clear a path for us and ran towards Gregorievitch, crying, "How brave you are to make such a journey in this weather!" "Lord above us," said Gregorievitch, "what does everybody mean? Open the door, open the door!"

* [At the first Austrian castle, after a wintry drive.]

When the door was opened the point of this fierce Arctic journey proved to be its pointlessness. For indeed there was nothing in the castle to match the wildness of the season, of the distraught horses and the wavering birds, of Gregorievitch and his people. A fortress six hundred years old had been encased in a vast building executed in that baronial style which owed so much more to literary than to architectural inspiration, having been begotten by Sir Walter Scott; and though the family which owned it had been unusually intelligent, and free-minded to the point of being Croatian patriots, their riches had brought them under the cultural influence of the Austro-Hungarian Empire. So there were acres of walls covered from floor to ceiling with hunting trophies. These never, in any context, give an impression of fullness. I remembered the story of the old Hungarian count who was heard to mutter as he lay dying, "And then the Lord will say, 'Count, what have you done with your life?' and I shall have to say, 'Lord, I have shot a great many animals.' Oh, dear! Oh, dear! It doesn't seem enough." Nobody but the fool despises hunting, which is not only a pleasure of a high degree, but a most valuable form of education in any but a completely mechanized state. Marmont, who was one of Napoleon's most intelligent marshals, explains in his memoirs that he was forced to hunt every day from two o'clock to nightfall from the time he was twelve, and this put him into such perfect training that no ordeal to which he was subjected in all his military career ever disconcerted him. But as a sole offering to the Lord it was not enough, and it might be doubted if this was the right kind of hunting. These trophies spoke of nineteenth-century sport, which was artificial, a matter of reared beasts procured for the guns by peasants, and so essentially sedentary that the characteristic sportsman of the age, commemorated in photographs, had a remarkable paunch.

There was also a clutterment of the most hideous furniture of the sort that was popular in the Austro-Hungarian Empire in the second half of the nineteenth century, walloping stuff bigger than any calculations of use could have suggested, big in accordance with a vulgar idea that bigness is splendid, and afflicted with carving that made even the noble and austere substance of wood ignoble as fluff. It would have been interesting to know where they had put the old furniture that must have been displaced by these horrors. One of the most beautiful exhibitions in Vienna, the Mobiliendepot, in the Mariahilfestrasse, was composed chiefly of the Maria Theresa and

Empire furniture which the Emperor Franz Josef and the Empress Elizabeth banished to their attics when they had refurnished their palaces from the best firms in the Tottenham Court Road.

There were also a great many bad pictures of the same era: enormous flushed nudes which would have set a cannibal's mouth watering; immense and static pictures showing what historical events would have looked like if all the personages had been stuffed first; and one of the family had over-indulged in the pleasures of amateur art. She herself had been a woman of enormous energy; a fashionable portrait painter had represented her, full of the uproarious shire-horse vitality common to the women admired by Edward VII, standing in a pink satin ball dress and lustily smelling a large bouquet of fat roses in a massive crystal vase, apparently about to draw the flowers actually out of the water by her powerful inhalations. This enormous energy had covered yards of the castle walls with pictures of Italian peasant girls holding tambourines, lemon branches, or amphoræ, which exactly represented what is meant by the French word "*niaiserie.*"

There were also some portraits of male members of the family, physically superb, in the white-and-gold uniform of Hungarian generals, solemnized and uplifted by the belief that they had mastered a ritual that served the double purpose of establishing their personal superiority and preserving civilization as they knew it; it was as pathetic to see them here as it would be to go into the garret of a starving family to see the picture of some of its members who had been renowned on the stage as players of kings and emperors. It might be said that though all these things were poor in themselves, they represented a state superior to the barbaric origins of Croatian society. But it was not so, for the family portraits which depicted the generations of the late sixteenth and seventeenth centuries showed people with their heads held high by pride and their features organized by intelligence, set on canvas by artists at least as accomplished and coherent in vision as the painters of our Tudor portraits. They gave documentary proof that German influence had meant nothing but corruption.

The corruption was profound. I left my companions at one point and turned back to a bedroom, to look again from its windows on an enchanting view of a little lake, now a pure sheet of snow, which lay among some groves below the sugar-loaf hill. I found Gregorievitch sitting on the window-sill, with his back to the view, looking about him at the hideous pictures and furniture with a dreamy and absorbed expression. "It would be very pleasant to live this way," he said, without envy, but with considerable appetite. This was the first time I had heard him say anything indicating that he had ever conceived living any life other than his own, which had been dedicated to pain and danger and austerity; and I could be sure that it was not the money of the people who lived in the castle, not the great fires that warmed them or the ample meals they ate, it was their refinement that he envied, their access to culture. I had never thought before what mischief a people can suffer from domination by their enemies. This man had lived his whole life to free Croatia from Hungarian rule; he had been seduced into exalting Hungarian values above Croatian values by what was an essential part of his rebellion. He had had to tell himself and other people over and over again that the Hungarians were taking the best of everything and leaving the worst to the Croats, which was indeed true so far as material matters were concerned. But the human mind, if it is framing a life of action, cannot draw fine distinctions. He had ended by believing that the Hungarians had had the best of everything in all respects, and that this world of musty antlers and second-rate pictures and third-rate furniture was superior to the world where peasants sang in church with the extreme discriminating fervour which our poets envy, knowing themselves lost without it, and wore costumes splendid in their obedience to those principles of design which our painters envy, knowing themselves lost without instinctive knowledge of them. ◇ ◇ ◇

My attention was caught by a crack that had suddenly begun to fissure the occasion. The superintendent* had been telling my husband and me what pleasure he had in welcoming us to Croatia, when Gregorievitch had leaned across the table and corrected him. "To Yugoslavia," he said in the accents of a tutor anxious to recall his pupil to truth and accuracy. There fell a silence. "To Yugoslavia," he repeated. Severity still lived in his brows, which he brought together by habit. But his eyes were stricken; so does an old dog look when it hopes against hope that the young master will take him out on a walk. After another silence, the superintendent said, "Yes, I will say that I welcome them to Yugoslavia. Who am I, being a Serb, to refuse this favour to a Croat?" They all laughed kindly at

*[The next castle was now a sanatorium.]

584

Gregorievitch after that; but there had sounded for an instant the authentic wail of poverty, in its dire extreme, that is caused by a certain kind of politics. Such politics we know very well in Ireland. They grow on a basis of past injustice. A proud people acquire a habit of resistance to foreign oppression, and by the time they have driven out their oppressors they have forgotten that agreement is a pleasure and that a society which has attained tranquillity will be able to pursue many delightful ends. There they continue to wrangle, finding abundant material in the odds and ends of injustices that are left over from the period of tyranny and need to be tidied up in one way or another. Such politics are a leak in the community. Generous passion, pure art, abstract thought, run through it and are lost. There remain only the obstinate solids which cannot be dissolved by argument or love, the rubble of hate and prejudice and malice, which are of no price. The process is never absolute, since in all lands some people are born with the inherent sweetness which closes that leak, but it can exist to a degree that alarms by the threat of privation affecting all the most essential goods of life; and in Croatia I had from time to time felt very poor.

Dalmatia

From SENJ

The next morning* we woke early, prodigiously early, so that before we embarked on our little steamer we could cross the bridge over the river that leads from Sushak to Fiume. There we found a town that has the quality of a dream, a bad headachy dream. Its original character is rotund and sunburnt and solid, like any pompous southern port, but it has been hacked by treaties into a surrealist form. On a ground plan laid out plainly by sensible architects for sensible people, there is imposed another, quite imbecile, which drives high walls across streets and thereby sets contiguous houses half an hour apart by detour and formality. And at places where no frontiers could possibly be, in the middle of a square, or on a bridge linking the parts of a quay, men in uniform step forward and demand passports, minatory as figures projected into sleep by an uneasy conscience.

"This has meant," said my husband as we wandered through the impeded city, "infinite suffering to a lot of people," and it is true. Because of it many old men have said to their sons, "We are ruined," many lawyers have said to widows, "I am afraid there will be nothing, nothing at all." All this suffering is due, to a large part, to English inefficiency. The Treaty of London, signed by the Allies and Italy in 1915, was intended as a bribe to induce the Italians to come into the war on the Allied side, and it promised them practically the whole Adriatic seaboard of the Austro-Hungarian Empire and all but one of the Adriatic islands. It was made by Lord Oxford and Lord Grey, and it reflected the greatest discredit on them and on the officials of the Foreign Office. For it handed over to a new foreign yoke the Slav inhabitants of this territory, who were longing to rise in revolt against the Central Powers in support of the Allies; and an Italian occupation of the Adriatic coast was a threat to the safety of Serbia, who of all the Allies had made the most sacrifices. These were good reasons why the Italians should not have Dalmatia, and there were no reasons why they should, for the Italian population was negligible.

*[in Sushak.]

586

Mercifully the Treaty of London was annulled at Versailles, largely through the efforts of Lloyd George and President Wilson. But it had done its work. It had given Italian greed a cue for inordinacy; it started her wheedling and demanding and snatching. So she claimed Fiume on the ground that the inhabitants were Italian, and proved it by taking a census of the town, excluding one part which housed twenty-five per cent of the population. The Italian Government was discouraged by European opinion from acting on that peculiar proof, but thereafter d'Annunzio marched his volunteers into Fiume, in an adventure which in mindlessness, violence, and futility exactly matched his deplorable literary works, and plunged it into anarchy and bloodshed. He was made to leave it, but the blackmail had been started. Yugoslavia had to buy peace, and in 1920 she conceded Italy the capital of Dalmatia, Zara, three Dalmatian islands, and the hinterland behind Trieste, and she entered into arrangements concerning Fiume which, in the end, left the port as it is.

All this is embittering history for a woman to contemplate. I will believe that the battle of feminism is over, and that the female has reached a position of equality with the male, when I hear that a country has allowed itself to be turned upside-down and led to the brink of war by its passion for a totally bald woman writer. Years ago, in Florence, I had marvelled over the singular example of male privilege afforded by d'Annunzio. Leaning from a balcony in the Lung'arno I had looked down on a triumphal procession. Bells rang, flags were waved; flowers were thrown, voices swelled in ecstasy; and far below an egg reflected the rays of the May sunshine. Here in Fiume the bald author had been allowed to ruin a city: a bald-headed authoress would never be allowed to build one. Scowling, I went on the little steamer that was taking us and twenty other passengers and as many cattle and sheep southwards to the island of Rab, and we set off in a cold dither of spray.

The bare hills shone like picked bones. I fell asleep, for we had risen at six. Then my husband shook me by the shoulder and said, "You must come up on deck. This is Senj." I followed him and stared at the port, which was like many others in Spain and Italy: from the quayside high buttoned-up houses washed in warm colours and two or three campaniles struggled up a hill towards a ruined fortress, the climbing mass girt in by city walls. I groaned, remembering that the climbing mass certified man to be not only incompetent but beastly, that here the great powers had mocked out of their own fullness at another's misery and had shown neither gratitude nor mercy.

Senj was the home of Uskoks. These are not animals invented by Edward Lear. They were refugees. They were refugees like the Jews and Roman Catholics and liberals driven out by Hitler. They found, as these have done, that when one door closed on them others that should have been open suddenly were not. These were driven out of their homes, out of the fellowship of Christendom, out of the world of virtue, into an accursed microcosm where there was only sin. They were originally Slavs of blameless character who fled before the Turks as they swept over Bulgaria and Serbia and Bosnia, and formed a strange domestic army, consisting of men, women, and children, that fought many effective rearguard actions over a period of many years. Finally they halted at the pass over the Dalmatian mountains, behind the great port of Split, and for five years from 1532 they held back the Turks single-handed. Then suddenly they were told by their Christian neighbours to abandon the position. Venice, which had just signed a pact with Turkey, and was a better friend to her than Christian historians like to remember, convinced Austria that it would be wise to let Turkey have the pass as a measure of appeasement.

Then the Uskoks came down to the coast and settled in this little town of Senj, and performed a remarkable feat. Up till then they had displayed courage and resolution of an unusual order. But they now showed signs of genius. Some of them were from the southern coast of Dalmatia, down by Albania, but most of them were inland men. In any case they can have had few marine officers. But in a short time they had raised themselves to the position of a naval power.

This was not a simple matter of savage daring. The Uskoks had unusual talent for boat-building. They devised special craft to suit the special needs of the Dalmatian coast, which resembled those with which the ancient Illyrians used to vex the Roman fleet: light boats that could navigate the creeks and be drawn up on the beach where there was no harbour. They also developed extraordinary powers of seamanship which enabled them to take advantage of the situation of Senj. Just here the channel between the mainland and the island of Krk widens to ten miles or so, which makes a fairway for the north wind, and it meets another channel that runs past the tail of the island to the open sea, so the seas roar rougher here than elsewhere on the coast. It was so when we came into Senj; a wave larger than

588

any we had met before slapped against the quay. The Uskoks developed a technique of using this hard weather as a shield against their enemies, while they ran through it unperturbed. Therefore they chased the Turkish ships up and down the Adriatic, stripped them, and sank them; and year by year they grew cleverer at the game. This success was amazing, considering they numbered at most two thousand souls. If the Venetian fleet had been directed by men of the quality of the Uskoks the Turks might have been driven out of European waters, which would have meant out of Europe, in the middle of the sixteenth century.

Venice, however, was in her decline, which was really more spiritual than economic. Her tragedies were due to maladministration and indecisive politics rather than to actual lack of means.

She tried to placate Turkey in another way. She stopped attacking her at sea. To the Uskoks this capitulation of the great Christian powers must have seemed the last word in treachery. They had, within the memory of all those among them who were middle-aged or over, been driven from their homes by the Turks in atrocious circumstances; and they had believed that in harrying the Turks they were not only avenging their wrongs but were serving God and His Son. They had often been blessed by the Church for their labours, and Gregory XIII had even given them a large subsidy. But now they were treated as enemies of Christendom, for no other crime than attacking its enemies. And not only were they betrayed in the spirit, they were betrayed in the body. How were they to live? Till then they had provided for themselves, quite legitimately, since the Turks had dispossessed them of all their homes, by booty from Turkish ships. But now all that was over. The Christian powers had no suggestions to make. The plight of a refugee, then as now, provoked the feeling that surely he could get along somehow. There was nothing for the Uskoks to do except defy Venice and Austria, and attack their ships and the Turks' alike.

It seems certain that to see the story of the Uskoks thus is not to flatter them. For nearly thirty years they lived in such a state of legitimate and disciplined warfare that they attacked only Turkish ships. It is not until 1566 that there is the first record of an Uskok attack on a Christian ship. Thereafter, of course, the story is very different. They became gangsters of the sea. They developed all the characteristics of gunmen: a loyalty that went unbroken to the death, unsurpassable courage, brutality, greed, and, oddly enough, thriftlessness.

Just as a Chicago racketeer who has made an income of five figures for many years will leave his widow penniless, so the Uskoks, who helped themselves to the richest loot the sea ever carried, always fell into penury if they survived to old age. Also they were looted, as thieves often are, by the honest. It is said that they bribed the very highest Austrian officials, even in the seat of government itself at Graz; and that a Jewish merchant might recognize there on a great lady's breast a jewel which he had seen snatched by a robber's hand on the Adriatic. Because of this traffic, it is alleged, the Austrians did little to restrain the Uskoks after they had become pirates. In any case it is certain that Venetian officials often bought the Uskoks' prizes from them and marketed them at a profit in Venice.

In a very short time the moral confusion of these people was complete. At Christmas and Easter every year there were expeditions financed by the whole of Senj. Everybody, the officials, the soldiers, the private families, the priests and monks, paid their share of the expenses and drew a proportionate share of the booty. The Church received its tithe. This would be funny if murder had not been a necessary part of such expeditions, and if barbarity did not spread from heart to heart as fire runs from tree to tree in a forest in summer. Some of the later exploits of the Uskoks turn the stomach; they would knife a living enemy, tear out his heart, and eat it. Not only did the perpetrators of these acts lose their own souls, but the whole level of Slav morality was debased, for the Dalmatian peasant knew the Uskok's origin and could not blame him. And the infection spread more widely. All the villains of Europe heard that there was good sport to be had in the Adriatic, and the hardier hurried to Senj. It testifies to the unwholesomeness of Renaissance Europe that some of these belonged to the moneyed classes. When a party of Uskoks were hanged in Venice in 1618 nine of them were Englishmen, of whom five were gentlemen in the heraldic sense of the word, and another was a member of one of the noblest families in Great Britain.

It is sometimes very hard to tell the difference between history and the smell of skunk. Both Venice and Austria used the degradation of these men as extra aces in their cheating game. The Austrians pretended to want to suppress them, but rather liked to have them harrying Venice. Venice sacrificed them to her friendship with Turkey, but that friendship was a sham; she never really wept over those Turkish ships. Also she liked to have a legitimate source of grievance against Austria. The insincerity of both parties was proven by their refusal to grant the Uskoks' demand, which was constantly presented during a period of fifty years, that they should be transported to some inland place and given a chance to maintain themselves either by tilling the soil or by performing military duties. Again and again the poor wretches explained that they had no means of living except by piracy, and that they would abandon it at once if they were shown any other way of getting food. But Venice and Austria, though one was still wealthy and the other was becoming wealthier every day, haggled over the terms of each settlement and let it go. Once there was put forward a scheme of selling the forests of pine and beech that in those days still grew round Senj, and using the proceeds to build fortresses on the Austrian frontiers which would be manned by Uskoks. It fell through because neither power would agree to make an initial payment amounting to something like fifty pounds. At the same time the Uskoks were not allowed to go to any country which was prepared to make room for them. They were strictly forbidden to enlist in foreign service. They were shut up in piracy as in jail by powers that affected to feel horror at their crimes.

In the end their problem was settled in the course of an odd war between Austria and Venice, in which the Uskoks were used as a pretext by several people who wanted a fight. This war, which was almost nothing and led to nothing, lasted three years and must have brought an infinity of suffering to the wretched Dalmatian peasant. But, mercifully, as it was supposed to be about the Uskoks, the Peace Treaty had to deal with them. A good many were hanged and beheaded and the rest were transported, as they themselves had requested for fifty years, to the interior. But the method of their transport was apparently unkind. There were no stout fortresses built for them, or hopeful villages, for no certain trace of them can be found. Some say their descendants are to be found on the Alps at the very southern end of Austria; others have thought to recognize them on the slopes of a mountain in North Italy. It is to be feared that their seed was scattered on stony ground. That is sad, for the seed was precious.

We went down to the little dining-saloon and had a good, simple, coarse, well-flavoured luncheon. Opposite us sat a young man, handsome and angry: ◇ ◇ ◇ He thrust away his plate as soon as it was brought to him with a gesture of fury. "This soup is cold!" he shouted, his brows a thick straight line. "This soup is as cold as the sea!" But he was not shouting at the soup. He was shouting at the

Turks, at the Venetians, at the Austrians, at the French, and at the Serbs (if he was a Croat) or at the Croats (if he was a Serb). It was good that he shouted. I respected him for it. In a world where during all time giants had clustered to cheat his race out of all their goods, his forefathers had survived because they had the power to shout, to reject cold soup, death, sentence to piracy, exile on far mountain slopes. ◇ ◇ ◇

DUBROVNIK (RAGUSA) I

"Let us wire to Constantine and ask him to meet us earlier in Sarajevo," I said, lying on the bed in our hotel room. "I can't bear Dubrovnik." "Perhaps you would have liked it better if we had been able to get into one of the hotels nearer the town," said my husband. "Indeed I would not," I said. "I stayed in one of those hotels for a night last year. They are filled with people who either are on their honeymoon or never had one. And at dinner I looked about me at the tables and saw everywhere half-empty bottles of wine with room-numbers scrawled on the labels, which I think one of the dreariest sights in the world." "Yes, indeed," said my husband, "it seems to me always when I see them that there has been disobedience of Gottfried Keller's injunction, 'Lass die Augen fassen, was die Wimper hält von dem goldnen Ueberfluss der Welt,' 'Let the eyes hold what the eyelids can contain from the golden overflow of the world.' But you might have liked it better if we were nearer the town." "No," I said, "nothing could be lovelier than this."

We were staying in a hotel down by the harbour of Gruzh, which is two or three miles out of Dubrovnik, or Ragusa as it used to be called until it became part of Yugoslavia. The name was changed, although it is pure Illyrian, because it sounded Italian: not, perhaps, a very good reason. Under the windows were the rigging and funnels of the harbour, and beyond the crowded waters was a hillside covered with villas, which lie among their gardens with an effect of richness not quite explicable by their architecture. The landscape is in fact a palimpsest. This was a suburb of Dubrovnik where the nobles had their summer palaces, buildings in the Venetian Gothic style furnished with treasures from the West and the East, surrounded by terraced flower-gardens and groves and orchards, as lovely as Fiesole or Vallombrosa, for here the Dalmatian coast utterly loses the barrenness which the traveller from the North might have thought its essential quality. These palaces were destroyed in the Napoleonic wars, looted and then burned; and on their foundations, in the nineteenth and twentieth centuries, have been built agreeable but undistinguished villas. But that is not the only confusion left by history on the view. The rounded slope immediately above the harbour is covered by an immense honey-coloured villa, with arcades and terraces and balconies hung with wistaria, and tier upon tier of orange trees and cypresses and chestnuts and olives and palms rising to the crest. It makes the claim of solidity that all Austrian architecture made, but it should have been put up in stucco, like our follies at Bath and Twickenham; for it was built for the Empress Elizabeth, who, of course, in her restlessness and Habsburg terror of the Slavs, went there only once or twice for a few days.

"I like this," I said, "as well as anything in Dubrovnik." "That can't be true," said my husband, "for Dubrovnik is exquisite, perhaps the most exquisite town I have ever seen." "Yes," I said, "but all the same I don't like it, I find it a unique experiment on the part of the Slav, unique in its nature and unique in its success, and I do not like it. It reminds me of the worst of England." "Yes," said my husband, "I see that, when one thinks of its history. But let us give credit for what it looks like, and that too is unique." He was right indeed, for it is as precious as Venice, and deserves comparison with the Venice of Carpaccio and Bellini, though not of Titian and Tintoretto. It should be visited for the first time when the twilight is about to fall, when it is already dusk under the tall trees that make an avenue to the city walls, though the day is only blanched in the open spaces, on the bridge that runs across the moat to the gate. There, on the threshold, one is arrested by another example of the complexity of history. Over the gate is a bas-relief by Mestrovitch, a figure of a king on a horse, which is a memorial to and a stylized representation of King Peter of Serbia, the father of the assassinated King Alexander, he who succeeded to the throne after the assassination of Draga and her husband. It is an admirable piece of work. It would surprise those who knew Mestrovitch's work only from international exhibitions to see how good it can be when it is produced under nationalist inspiration for a local setting. This relief expresses to perfection the ideal ruler of a peasant state. Its stylization makes, indeed, some reference to the legendary King Marko, who is the hero of all Serbian peasants. This king could groom the horse he rides on, and had bought it for himself at a fair, making no bad bargain; yet he is a true king, for no man would daunt him from doing his duty to his people, either by strength or by riches. It is enormously ironic that this should be set on the walls of a city that was the antithesis of the peasant state, that maintained for centuries the most rigid system of aristocracy and the most narrowly bourgeois ethos imaginable. The incongruity will account for a certain coldness shown towards the Yugoslavian ideal in Dubrovnik; which itself appears ironical when it is considered that after Dubrovnik was destroyed by the great powers no force on earth could have come to its rescue except the peasant state of Serbia.

For an ideal first visit the traveller should go into the city and find the light just faintly blue with dusk in the open space that lies inside the gate, and has for its centre the famous fountain by the fifteenth-century Neapolitan architect Onofrio de la Cava. This is a master-piece, the size of a small chapel, a domed piece of masonry with fourteen jets of water, each leaping from a sculptured plaque set in the middle of a panel divided by two slender pilasters, into a continuous trough that runs all round the fountain: as useful as any horse-trough, and as lovely and elevating as an altar. On the two steps that raise it from the pavement there always lie some carpets with their sellers gossiping beside them. At this hour all cats are grey and all carpets are beautiful; the colours, fused by the evening, acquire rich-ness. On one side of this square is another of the bland little churches which Dalmatians built so often and so well, a town sister of that we had seen in the village where the retired sea captains lived. At this hour its golden stone gives it an air of enjoying its own private sun-set, prolonged after the common one. It has a pretty and secular rose-window which might be the brooch for a bride's bosom. Beside it is a Franciscan convent, with a most definite and sensible Pietà over a late Gothic portal. The Madonna looks as if, had it been in her hands, she would have stopped the whole affair; she is in no degree gloating over the spectacular fate of her son. She is not peasant, she is noble; it is hardly possible to consider her as seducible by the most exalted destiny. Facing these across the square is the old arsenal, its façade pierced by an arch; people walk through it to a garden beyond, where lamps shine among trees, and there is a sound of music. For background there are the huge city walls, good as strength, good as honesty.

Ahead runs the main street of the town, a paved fairway, forbidden to wheeled traffic, lined with comely seventeenth-century houses that have shops on their ground floor. At this time it is the scene of the Corso, an institution which is the heart of social life in every Yugoslavian town, and indeed of nearly all towns and villages in the Balkans. All of the population who have clothing up to the general standard—I have never seen a person in rags and patches join a Corso in a town where good homespun or manufactured textiles are the usual wear, though in poverty-stricken districts I have seen an entire Corso bearing itself with dignity in tatters—join in a procession which walks up and down the main street for an hour or so about sunset. At one moment there is nobody there, just a few people going about the shops or sitting outside cafés; at the next the street is full of all the human beings in the town that feel able to take part in the life of their kind, each one holding up the head and bearing the body so that it may be seen, each one chattering and being a little gayer than in private, each one attempting to establish its individuality. Yet the attempt defeats itself, for this mass of people, moving up and down the length of the street and slowly becoming more and more like each other because of the settling darkness, makes a human being seem no more than a drop of water in a stream. In a stream, moreover, that does not run for ever. The Corso ends as suddenly as it begins. At one instant the vital essence of the town chokes the street with its coursing; the next, the empty pavement is left to the night.

But while it lasts the Corso is life, for what that is worth in this particular corner of the earth; and here, in Dubrovnik, life still has something of the value it must have had in Venice when she was young. A city that had made good bread had learned to make good cake also. A city that had built itself up by good sense and industry had formed a powerful secondary intention of elegance. It is a hundred and thirty years ago that Dubrovnik ceased to exist as a republic, but its buildings are the unaltered cast of its magnificence, its people have still the vivacity of those who possess and can enjoy. Here the urbanity of the Dalmatian cities becomes metropolitan. Follow this Corso and you will find yourself in the same dream that is dreamed by London and Paris and New York; the dream that there is no limit to the distance which man can travel from his base, the cabbage-patch, that there is no pleasure too delicate to be bought by all of us, if the world will but go on getting richer. This is not a dream to be despised; it comes from man's more amiable parts, it is untainted by cruelty, it springs simply from a desire to escape from the horror that is indeed implicit in all man's simpler relationships with the earth. It cannot be realized in a city so great as London or Paris or New York, or even the later Venice; it was perhaps possible to realize it in a city no larger than Dubrovnik, which indeed neither was nor is very far from the cabbage-patches. For on any fine night there are some peasants from the countryside outside the walls who have come to walk in the Corso.

To taste the flavour of this Corso and this city, it is good to turn for a minute from the main street into one of the side streets. They mount steep and narrow to the walls which outline the squarish peninsula on which the city stands; close-pressed lines of houses— left at this hour to sleeping children, the old, and servant-maids— which are rich in carved portals and balconies, and perfumed with the spring. For it took the Industrial Revolution to make man conceive the obscene idea of a town as nothing but houses. These carved portals and balconies are twined with flowers that are black because of the evening but would be scarlet by day, and behind high walls countless little gardens send out their sweetness. Back in the main street the people from these houses and gardens sweep down towards their piazza, past a certain statue which you may have seen in other towns, perhaps in front of the Rathaus at Bremen. Such statues are said to represent the hero Orlando or Roland who defeated the Saracens: they are the sign that a city is part of liberal and lawful Christendom. To the left of the crowd is the Custom House and Mint, in which the history of their forebears for three centuries is written in three stories. In the fourteenth century the citizens of the Republic built themselves a Custom House, just somewhere to take in the parcels; in that age the hand of man worked right, and the courtyard is perfection. A hundred years later so many parcels had come in that the citizens were refined folk and could build a second story for literary gatherings and social assemblies, as lovely as Venetian Gothic could make it. Prosperity became complicated and lush, the next hundred years brought the necessity of establishing a handsome Mint on the top floor, in the Renaissance style; and for sheer lavishness they faced the Custom House with a loggia. Because the people who did this were of the same blood, working in a civilization that their blood and none other had made, these different styles are made one by an inner coherence. The building has a light, fresh, simple charm.

They mill there darkly, the people of Dubrovnik, the buildings running up above them into that whiteness which hangs above the earth

596

the instant before the fall of the night, which is disturbed and dispersed by the coarser whiteness of the electric standards. The Custom House is faced by the Church of St Blaise, a great baroque mass standing on a balustraded platform, like a captive balloon filled with infinity. In front is an old tower with a huge toy clock: at the hour, two giant bronze figures of men come out and beat a bell. The crowd will lift their heads to see them, as their fathers have done for some hundreds of years. Next to that is the town café, a noble building, where one eats well, looking on to the harbour; for we have reached the other side of the peninsula now, the wind that blows in through the archways is salt. Then to the right is the Rector's palace, that incomparable building, the special glory of Dubrovnik, and even of Dalmatia, the work of Michelozzo Michelozzi the Florentine and George the Dalmatian, known as Orsini. Simply it consists of a two-storied building, the ground floor shielded by a loggia of six arches, the upper floor showing eight Gothic windows. It is imperfect: it once had a tower at each end, and these have gone. Nevertheless, its effect is complete and delightful, and, like all masterpieces of architecture, it expresses an opinion about the activities which are going to be carried on under its roof. Chartres is a speculation concerning the nature of God and of holiness. The Belvedere in Vienna is a speculation concerning political power. With its balanced treatment of its masses and the suggestion of fecundity in its springing arches and proliferating capitals, the Rector's palace puts forward an ideal of an ordered and creative society. It is the most explicit building in an amazingly explicit town, that has also an explicit history, with a beginning and an end. It is another example of the visibility of life which is the special character of Yugoslavia, at least so far as those territories which have not been affected by the Teutonic confusion are concerned.

The Corso says, "This is the city our fathers made." The city says, "These are the men and women we have made." If you should turn aside and go into the café to eat an evening meal, which here should be preferably the *Englische Platte*, an anthology of cold meats chosen by a real scholar of the subject, the implications of this display will keep you busy for the night. There is, of course, the obvious meaning of Dubrovnik. It was quite truly a republic: not a protectorate, but an independent power, the only patch of territory on the whole Dalmatian coast, save for a few unimportant acres near Split, that never fell under the rule of either Hungary or Venice. It was a republic that was a miracle: on this tiny peninsula, which is perhaps half a mile across, was based a great economic empire. From Dubrovnik the caravans started for the overland journey to Constantinople. This was the gateway to the East; and it exploited its position with such commercial and financial and naval genius that its ships were familiar all over the known world, while it owned factories and warehouses in every considerable port of Southern Europe and in some ports of the North, and held huge investments such as mines and quarries in the Balkans. Its history is illuminated by our word "argosy," which means nothing more than a vessel from Ragusa. It is as extraordinary as if the city of London were to have carried out the major part of the commercial achievements of the British Empire up to, say, the reign of Henry VII, with no more territory than itself and about three or four hundred square miles in the home counties which it had gradually acquired by conquest and purchase. That is the primary miracle of Dubrovnik; that and its resistance to Turkey, which for century after century coveted the port as the key to the Adriatic and the invasion of Italy, yet could never dare to seize it because of the diplomatic genius of its defenders.

But as one contemplates the town other issues crowd on the mind. First, the appalling lack of accumulation observable in history, the perpetual cancellation of human achievement, which is the work of careless and violent nature. This place owes its foundation to the ferocity of mankind towards its own kind. For Dubrovnik was first settled by fugitives from the Greek city of Epidaurus, which is ten miles farther south down the coast, and from the Roman city of Salonæ, when these were destroyed by the barbarians, and was later augmented by Slavs who had come to these parts as members of the barbarian forces. It was then monstrously harried by the still greater ferocity of fire and earthquake. Some of the fires might be ascribed to human agency, for the prosperity of the group—which was due to its fusion of Greek and Roman culture with Slav virility—meant that they were well worth attacking and therefore they had to make their rocky peninsula into a fortress with abundant stores of munitions. They were, therefore, peculiarly subject to fires arising out of gunpowder explosions. The Rector's palace was twice burned down for this reason during twenty-seven years. But such damage was trifling compared to the devastation wrought by earthquakes.

The bland little church beside the domed fountain at the City Gate was built in the sixteenth century as a thanksgiving by those who had been spared from an earthquake which, in a first convulsion, shook down houses that were then valued at five thousand pounds, and then continued as a series of shocks for over eighteen months; and there was apparently an earthquake of some degree in this district every twenty years. But the worst was the catastrophe of 1667. The sea was tilted back from the harbour four times, each time leaving it bone dry, and each time rushing back in a flood-wave which pounded many vessels to pieces against the docks and cliffs. The greater part of the public buildings and many private houses were in ruins, and the Rector of the Republic and five thousand citizens were buried underneath them. Then fire broke out; and later still bands of wolfish peasants from the mountain areas devastated by Venetian misrule and Turkish warfare came down and plundered what was left.

We know, by a curious chance, exactly what we lost in the way of architecture on that occasion. In the baroque church opposite the Rector's palace there is a two-foot-high silver statuette of St Blaise, who is the patron saint of the city, and he holds in his hand a silver model of Dubrovnik as it was before the earthquake. It shows us the setting for a fairy-tale. In particular it shows the Cathedral, which was built by Richard Cœur de Lion as a thanksgiving for his escape from shipwreck on this coast, as a thirteenth-century building of great beauty and idiosyncrasy, and the main street as a unique expression of commercial pride, a line of houses that were true palaces in their upper parts and shops and offices below. We can deduce also that there was an immense loss of pictures, sculptures, textiles, jewels, and books, which had been drawn by the Republic from West and East during her centuries of successful trading. Indeed, we know of one irreparable loss, so great that we cannot imagine what its marvellous content may have been. There existed in Bosnia a society that was at once barbarous and civilized, an indirect heir to Byzantine civilization and able to fight Rome on doctrinal points as a logic-chopping equal, but savage and murderous. This society was destroyed by the Turk. At the end of the fifteenth century, Catherine, the widow of the last King of Bosnia, murdered by his illegitimate son, who was later himself flayed alive by Mahomet I, fled to Dubrovnik and lived there till she went to Rome to die. Before she left she gave some choral books, richly illustrated and bound, to the monks of the Franciscan monastery, who had a famous library. If these books had survived they would have been a glimpse of a world about which we can now only guess: but the whole library perished.

What is the use of ascribing any catastrophe to nature? Nearly always man's inherent malignity comes in and uses the opportunities it offers to create a graver catastrophe. At this moment the Turks came down on the Republic to plunder its helplessness, though their relationship had till then been friendly. Kara Mustapha, the Turkish Grand Vizier, a demented alcoholic, pretended that the armed resistance the citizens had been forced to put up against the wretched looters from the mountains was in some obscure way an offence against Turkish nationals, and on this pretext and on confused allegations of breach of tariff agreements he demanded the payment of a million ducats, or nearly half a million pounds. He also demanded that the goods of every citizen who had been killed in the earthquake should be handed to the Sublime Porte, the Republic being (he suddenly claimed) a Turkish possession. For fifteen years the Republic had to fight for its rights and keep the aggressors at bay, which it was able to do by using its commercial potency and its diplomatic genius against the Turks when they were already rocking on their feet under the blows of Austria and Hungary. Those were its sole weapons. France, as professed defender of Christianity and order in Europe, should have aided the Republic. But Louis XIV would not lift his little finger to help her, partly because she had been an ally of Spain, partly because the dreary piece of death-in-life, Madame de Maintenon, supreme type of the she-alligator whom men often like and admire, had so inflamed him with pro-Jesuit passion that a mere rumour that the Republican envoy was a Jansenist was enough to make him cancel his mission.

The story of what happened to the four ambassadors who left to plead with the Turkish Government is one of the classic justifications of the human race: almost a promise that there is something to balance its malignity. Caboga and Bucchia were sent to Constantinople to state the independence of the Republic. They were, by a technique familiar to us today, faced with documents admitting that the Republic was a Turkish possession and told with threats and curses that they must sign them. They refused. Dazed and wearied from hours of bullying they still refused, and were thrown into a plague-stricken prison. There they lay for years, sometimes smuggling home dispatches written in their excrement on packing paper. Their colleagues, Bona and Gozzi, went to Sarajevo to make the same statement of independence to the Pasha of Bosnia, and were likewise thrown into captivity. They were dragged behind the Turkish Army on a war it was conducting with Russia on the Danube, and there thrown in irons into the dungeons of a fortress in a malarial district, and told they must remain prisoners until they had signed the documents which Caboga and Bucchia had refused to sign in Constantinople. There Bona died. A Ragusan priest who had settled in the district stood by to give him the last sacrament, but was prevented by the jailers. There is no knowing how many such martyrs might have been demanded of Dubrovnik and furnished by her, had not the Turks then been defeated outside Vienna by John Sobieski, King of Poland. Kara Mustapha was executed, and there was lifted from the Republic a fear as black as any we have felt today.

It is a glorious story, yet a sad one. What humanity could do if it could but have a fair course to run, if fire and pestilence did not gird our steps and earthquakes engulf them, if man did not match his creativeness with evil that casts down and destroys! It can at least be said that Dubrovnik ran well in this obstacle race. But there is not such exaltation in the spectacle when it is considered how she had to train for that victory, both so far as it was commercial and diplomatic in origin. Everywhere in the Dalmatian cities the class struggle was intense. The constitution of the cities provided for the impartial administration of justice, legal and economic, to persons arranged in castes and made to remain there, irrespective of their merits, with the utmost rigid injustice. This was at first due to historical necessity. The first-comers in a settlement, who had the pick of the economic findings and whatever culture was going, might really be acting in the public interest as well as defending their own private ends, when they insisted on reserving to themselves all possible social power and not sharing it with later-comers, who might be barbarians or refugees demoralized by years of savage warfare. But it led to abuses which can be measured by the continual rebellions and the horrible massacres which happened in every city on the coast. In Hvar, for instance, the island where the air is so sweet, the plebeians took oath on a crucifix held by a priest that they would slaughter all the nobles. The Christ on the crucifix bled at the nose, the priest fell dead. Nevertheless the plebeians carried out their plans, and massacred many of the nobles in the Hall of Justice in the presence of the Rector, but were overcome by a punitive expedition of the Venetian fleet and themselves put to death or mutilated.

This caste system never led to such rebellions in Dubrovnik, partly because the economic well-being of the community choked all discontent with cream, partly because they had little chance of succeeding; but it existed in a more stringent form than anywhere else. The population was divided into three classes: the nobles, the commoners, and the workers. The last were utterly without say in the government. They did not vote and they could hold no office. The commoners also had no votes, but might hold certain unimportant offices, though only if appointed by the nobles. The actual power of government was entirely in the hands of the nobles. The body in which sovereignty finally rested was the Grand Council, which consisted of all males over eighteen belonging to families confirmed as noble in the register known as the Golden Book. This Council deputed its executive powers to a Senate of forty-five members who met four times a week and at times of emergency; and they again deputed their powers to a Council of Seven (this had numbered eleven until the earthquake) who exercised judicial power and performed all diplomatic functions, a Council of Three, who acted as a tribune of constitutional law, and a Council of Six, who administered the Exchequer. There were other executive bodies, but this is a rough idea of the anatomy of the Republic. It must be remembered that these classes were separated in all departments of their lives as rigidly as the Hindu castes. No member of any class was permitted to marry into either of the other two classes; if he did so he lost his position in his own class and his children had to take the rank of the inferior parent. Social relations between the classes were unthinkable.

It is interesting that this system should have survived when all real differences in the quality of classes had been levelled by general prosperity, when there might be commoners and even workers who were as rich and as cultured as any noble. It is interesting, too, that it should have survived even when the classes were cleft from within by disputes. When Marmont went to Dubrovnik in 1808 he found that the nobles were divided into two parties, one called the Salamancans and the other the Sorbonnais. These names referred to some controversy arising out of the wars between Charles V of Spain and Francis I of France, a mere matter of two hundred and fifty years before. It had happened that in the earthquake of 1667 a very large proportion of the noble class was destroyed, and it was necessary to restore it to strength by including a number of commoners. These the Salamancans, sympathizers with Spanish absolutism, would not treat as equals; but the Sorbonnais, Francophil and inclined to a comparative liberalism, accepted them fully. It is also a possible factor in the situation that the Sorbonnais had been specially depleted by the earthquake casualties and wanted to keep up their numbers. Be that as it may, the two parties were exactly equal in status and sat together on the Councils, but they had no social relations and did not even greet each other on the streets; and a misalliance between members of the two parties was as serious in its consequences as a misalliance between classes.

But this was far from being the only sop offered by the Republic to that disagreeable appetite, the desire of a human being to feel contempt for another not in fact very different from himself. The commoners in their turn were divided into the confraternities of St Anthony and St Lazarus, who were as rancorous in their relationship as the Salamancans and the Sorbonnais. The survival of this three-class system in spite of these dissensions suggests that it was actually a fusion of long-standing customs, native to the different races which composed the Republic: say a variation of the classical system of aristocracy grafted on some ancient Illyrian organization of which we now know nothing, which pleased the Slav late-comers, though themselves democratic in tendency, because of the solid framework it gave to internal bickerings. "Whether they agree or do not agree," an exasperated Roman emperor wrote of the first Slav tribes to appear within the Empire's ken, "very soon they fall into disturbances among themselves, because they feel a mutual loathing and cannot bear to accommodate one another."

The system, of course, was far from being merely silly. One may wonder how it survived; one cannot question the benefits it conferred by surviving. The Republic was surrounded by greedy empires whom she had to keep at arm's length by negotiation lest she perish: first Hungary, then Venice, then Turkey. Foreign affairs were her domestic affairs; and it was necessary that they should be conducted in complete secrecy with enormous discretion. It must never be learned by one empire what had been promised by or to another empire, and none of the greedy pack could be allowed to know the precise amount of the Republic's resources. There was therefore every reason to found a class of governors who were so highly privileged that they would protect the status quo of the community at all costs, who could hand on training in the art of diplomacy from father to son, and who were so few in number that it would be easy to detect a case of blabbing. They were very few indeed. In the fifteenth century, when the whole population was certainly to be counted by tens of thousands, there were only thirty-three noble families. These could easily be supervised in all their goings and comings by those who lived in the same confined area.

But it is curious that this ultra-conservative aristocratic government should develop a tendency which is often held to be a characteristic vice of democracy. Dubrovnik dreaded above all things the emergence of dominant personalities. The provisions by which this dread is expressed in the constitution are the chief differences which distinguish it from its obvious Venetian model. The Senate was elected for life, and there you had your small group of hereditary diplomats. But these elections had to be confirmed annually, and infinite precautions were taken lest any Senator should seize excessive power and attempt dictatorship. The Rector wore a superb toga of red silk with a stole of black velvet over the left shoulder, and was preceded in his comings and goings by musicians and twenty palace guards; but he held his office for just one month, and could be re-elected only after intervals of two years; and this brevity of tenure was the result of ever-anxious revisions, for the term had originally been three months, had been reduced to two, and was finally brought down to the single month. He was also held prisoner within the palace while he held office, and could leave it only for state appearances, such as his obligatory solemn visit to the Cathedral.

The lesser offices were as subject to restriction. The judiciary and diplomatic Council of Seven was elected afresh every year, and could not be re-elected for another year. The Council of Three, who settled all questions of constitutional law, was also elected for but one year. The Council of Six, who administered the state finances, was elected for three years. There were also certain regulations which prevented the dominance of people of any particular age. The Council of Seven might be of any adult age, but the youngest had to act as Foreign Secretary; but the Council of Three had all to be over fifty. These devices were entirely justified by their success. Only once, and that very early in the history of Dubrovnik, did a noble try to become a dictator; and then he received no support, save from the wholly unrepresented workers, and was forced to suicide. Later, in the seventeenth century, some nobles were seduced by the Duke of Savoy into a conspiracy to seize power, but they were arrested at a masked ball on the last day of Carnival, and executed by general consent of the community.

That terror of the emergent personality is not the only trait of this aristocratic society which recalls its contrary. There is a great deal in the history of Dubrovnik which had its counterpart among our Puritan capitalists. The nobles believed in education even more seriously than was the custom of their kind in other Dalmatian towns, though even there the standard was high: the Venetian Governor of Split is found complaining of young men who came back from their studies at Oxford filled with subversive notions. But they did not, as might have been expected, try to keep learning as a class prerogative. As well as sending their own sons to universities in Italy and France and Spain and England, they built public schools which were open to the children of all three classes. They also created a hospital system which included the first foundling hospital in the whole civilized world, and they were as advanced in their treatment of housing problems. After one of the earlier earthquakes they put in hand a town-planning scheme which considered the interests of the whole community, and their arrangements for a water supply were not only ahead of the time as an engineering project but made an attempt to serve every home.

They also anticipated philanthropists of a much later date and a wholly different social setting in their attitude to the slave-trade. In 1417 they passed what was the first anti-slavery legislation except for our own English laws discouraging the export of human cargo from Bristol. This was no case of damning a sin for which they had no mind, since a great deal of money could be made in the Mediterranean slave-trade, a considerable amount of which had come to certain Republican merchants living farther north on the coast; and it must be remembered that, owing to the survival of the feudal system in the Balkans long after it had passed away from the rest of Europe, the state of serfdom was taken for granted by many of the peoples under the Republic's rule or in relationship with her. But the Grand Council passed a law providing that anybody selling a slave should be liable to a heavy fine and six months' imprisonment, "since it must be held to be base, wicked, and abominable, and contrary to all humanity, and to redound to the great disgrace of our city, that the human form, made after the image and similitude of our Creator, should be turned to mercenary profit, and sold as if it were brute beast." Fifty years later they tightened up this law and made the punishment harsher, adding the proviso that if a slave-trader could not recover his victims from captivity within a certain period after he had been directed to do so by the authorities, he was to be hanged.

All through the next three centuries, until the Mediterranean slave-trade became wholly extinct, it was a favourite form of philanthropy among the wealthy Republicans to buy slaves their freedom.

There were other Whig preferences in Dubrovnik: the right of asylum, for instance, was strictly maintained. When the Turks beat the Serbs at Kossovo in 1389 one of the defeated princes, the despot George Brankovitch, took refuge in Dubrovnik and was hospitably received, though the Republic was an ally of Turkey. When the Sultan Murad II protested and demanded that he should be delivered up, the Senate answered, "We, men of Ragusa, live only by our faith, and according to that faith we would have sheltered you also, had you fled hither." But there is a quality familiar to us Westerners not only in the political but in the social life of the Republic. The citizens kept extremely comfortable establishments, with the best of food and drink and furniture, but their luxury was strictly curbed in certain directions. There was never any theatre in Dubrovnik till fifty years after the destruction of the Republic, when one was built by the Austrians. In the fifteenth century, which was a gay enough season for the rest of Europe, Palladius writes: "To make manifest how great is the severity and diligence of the Ragusans in the bringing up of their children, one thing I will not pass over, that they suffer no artistic exercises to exist in the city but those of literature. And if jousters or acrobats approach they are forthwith cast out lest the youth (which they would keep open for letters or for merchandising) be corrupted by such low exhibitions."

There must have been many an English family of wealthy bankers and manufacturers in Victorian days who ate vast meals and slept in the best Irish linen and were surrounded by the finest mahogany and the most distinguished works of Mr Leader and Mr Sidney Cooper (and, perhaps, thanks to John Ruskin, some really good Italian pictures), but who never set foot in a theatre or music-hall or circus. But an even more significant parallel between the Republic and England is to be found in the hobbies of the wealthier citizens. English science owes a great deal to the discoveries of business men, particularly among the Quakers, who took to some form of research as an amusement to fill in their spare time. So was it also in Dubrovnik. The citizens had a certain taste for letters, though chiefly for those exercises which are to literature as topiary is to gardening, such as the composition of classical or Italian verses in an extremely formal style; but their real passion was for mathematics and the physical

sciences. They produced many amateurs of these, and some professionals, of whom the most notable was Roger Joseph Boscovitch, a
wild Slav version of the French encyclopædists, a mystic, a mathematician and physicist, a poet and diplomat. In his writings and those of
his compatriots who followed the same passion, there are pæans to
science as the illuminator of the works of God, which have countless
analogues in the writings of Englishmen of the same class in the
eighteenth and early nineteenth centuries.

But the resemblance does not stop there. There is a certain case to
be made against the bourgeois class of Englishmen that developed
into the nonconformist liberals who followed Mr Gladstone through
his triumphs, and reared their sons to follow Lord Oxford and Mr
Lloyd George to the twilight hour of their faith. It might be charged
against them that their philanthropy consisted of giving sops to the
populace which would make it forget that their masters had seized all
the means of production and distribution, and therefore held them in
a state of complete economic subjection. It might be charged against
them also that they were virtuous only when it suited their pockets,
and that while they would welcome Kossuth or Mazzini or any other
defender of oppressed people outside the British Empire, they were
indifferent to what happened inside it. It might be charged against
them that they cared little how much truth there was in the bitter
description of our exports to the coloured races, "Bibles, rum, and
rifles," so long as there was truth in the other saying, "Trade follows
the flag." There is enough testimony to the virtue of this class to
make such charges not worth discussing with any heat of spirit; but
there was enough truth in them to make it impossible to regard the
accused as an ideal group, and the society which produced them as
paradisaical. It is even so with Dubrovnik.

The Republic was extremely pious. She spoke of her Christianity at
all times, and in her Golden Book there is a prayer for the magistrates
of the Republic which runs: "O Lord, Father Almighty, who hast
chosen this Republic to serve Thee, choose, we beseech Thee, our
governors, according to Thy Will and our necessity: that so, fearing
Thee and keeping Thy Holy Commandments, they may cherish and
direct us in true charity. Amen." Never was there a city so full of
churches and chapels, never was there a people who submitted more
loyally to the discipline of the Church. But there was a certain incongruity with this in their foreign policy. Had Dubrovnik the right to
pose with proud and fastidious Catholic power considering her rela-

tions with the Ottoman Empire, the devouring enemy of Christendom? The other Dalmatian towns were less complaisant than Venice in their attitude to the Turks, the Republic far more. She never fought the Turk. She paid them tribute, and again tribute.

Every year two envoys left the city for Constantinople with their load of golden ducats, which amounted, after several increases, to fifteen thousand. They wore a special dress, known as the uniform of the divan, and had their beards well grown. They placed their affairs in order, embraced their families, attended mass at the Cathedral, and were bidden godspeed by the Rector under the arches of his palace. Then, with their cashier, their barber, numerous secretaries and interpreters, a troop of armed guards, and a priest with a portable altar, they set forth on the fifteen days' journey to the Bosporus. It was not a very dangerous journey, for the caravans of the Republic made it an established trade route. But the envoys had to stay there for twelve months, till the next two envoys arrived and took their place, and the negotiation of subtle business with tyrants of an alien and undecipherable race, while physically at their mercy, was a dangerous task, which was usually performed competently and heroically. This was not, however, the only business they transacted with the Turks. The envoys to Constantinople had also to do a great deal of bribery, for there was a sliding scale of tips which covered every official at the Porte from the lowest to the highest. This burden increased yearly as the Turkish Empire increased in size to the point of unwieldiness, and the local officials became more and more important. As time went on it was almost as necessary to bribe the Sandjakbeg of Herzegovina and the Pasha of Bosnia and their staffs as it was to make the proper payments to the Sublime Porte.

All this would be very well, if Dubrovnik had avowed that she was an independent commercial power in a disadvantageous military and naval position, and that she valued her commerce and independence so highly that she would pay the Turks a great ransom for them. But it is not so pleasing in a power that boasts of being fervent and fastidious in its Christianity. Of course it can be claimed that Dubrovnik was enabled by her relations with the Porte to render enormous services to the Christians within the territories conquered by the Turks; that wherever her mercantile colonies were established—and that included towns all over Bosnia and Serbia and Bulgaria and Wallachia and even Turkey itself—the Christians enjoyed a certain degree of legal protection and religious freedom. But on the other hand the Republic won for herself the right to pay only two or sometimes one and a half per cent on her imports and exports into and out of the Ottoman Empire, while all the rest of the world had to pay five per cent. It is no use. Nothing can make this situation smell quite like the rose. If Dickens had known the facts he might have felt about Dubrovnik as he felt about Mr Chadband; and if Chesterton had attended to them he might have loathed it as much as he loathed cocoa.

Especially is this readiness to rub along with the Turks displeasing in a power which professed to be so fervent and fastidious in its Christianity that it could not let the Orthodox Church set foot within its gates. Theoretically, the Republic upheld religious tolerance. But in practice she treated it as a fair flower that was more admirable if it blossomed on foreign soil. Though Dubrovnik had many visitors, and even some natives, who were members of the Orthodox Church, they were not allowed to have any place of worship within the Republic. It curiously happened that in the eighteenth century this led to serious difficulties with Catherine the Great, when her fleet came to the Mediterranean and Adriatic to tidy up the remains of Turkish sea-power. Her lover Orloff was the Admiral in charge, and he presented the Republic with an agreement defining her neutrality, which included demands for the opening of an Orthodox church for public use in Dubrovnik, and the establishment of a Russian consulate in the city, to protect not only Russians but all members of the Orthodox Church. The second request was granted, the first refused. Jesuit influence, and the Pope himself, were again illustrating the unfailing disposition of the Roman Catholic Church to fight the Orthodox Church with a vehemence which could not have been exceeded if the enemy had represented paganism instead of schism, whatever suffering this campaign might bring to the unhappy peoples of the Balkan Peninsula.

The agreement Russia offered the Republic was in every other regard satisfactory; but for three years an envoy from Dubrovnik argued the point in St Petersburg, and in the end won it, by using the influence of Austria and Poland, and the personal affection that the Prussian Ambassador to Russia happened to feel for the beauty of the city. It is pathetic how these Northerners love the South. In the end, after two more years, Orloff had to sign a treaty with Dubrovnik, by which she exchanged the right to trade in Russian waters for her sanction of the appointment of a Russian consul, who was to protect only Russian subjects, and who might build in his house a private chapel at which his own nationals might worship according to the Orthodox rite. History is looked at through the wrong end of the opera-glasses when it is recorded that the Republican envoy signed the treaty, went straight to Rome, and was given the warmest thanks for the services he and the Republic had rendered the Holy Catholic religion by "forbidding the construction of a Greek chapel." Such pettiness is almost grand. Owing to a change in Russia's foreign policy the consul was never appointed, and the Republic permitted instead the building of a tiny chapel in a deserted spot over a mile from the city walls. When, in 1804, the Republic was again asked to grant its Orthodox citizens the free practice of their religion it absolutely refused.

This intolerance led ultimately to the extinction of the Republic. At the Congress of Vienna the Tsar Alexander could have saved it, and the cause of this small defenceless state might well have appealed to his mystic liberalism; but he remembered that the Republic had obstinately affronted his grandmother, and that in order to persecute his own religion, and he withheld his protection. But it would be a mistake to suppose that in the defence of the Papacy the Republic acted out of fidelity to its religious principles and contempt for its worldly interests. It found—and here we find it achieving a feat of economy that has brought on its English prototypes many a reproach —that in serving the one it served the other. When an Austrian commissioner was taking over Dubrovnik after it had been abandoned by the French, he remarked to one of the nobles that he was amazed by the number of religious establishments in the city. The answer was given, "There is no cause for amazement there. Every one of them was as much good to us as a round-house." And indeed this was true. The Roman Catholic fervour of this state that lay on the very border of the Orthodox territory guaranteed her the protection of two great powers, Spain and the Papacy. Again there is a smell not of the rose.

This equivocal character of the Republic is worth considering, because it affects an argument frequently used in the course of that soft modern propaganda in favour of Roman Catholicism which gives testimony, not to the merits or demerits of that faith, but to the woolliness of modern education. It is sometimes put forward that it is right to join the Roman Catholic Church because it produces pleasanter and more mellow characters than Protestantism. This, of course, is a claim that the Church itself would regard with contempt. The state of mind demanded from a Roman Catholic is belief that certain historic events occurred in fact as they are stated to have occurred by the teachers of the Church, and that the interpretation of life contained in their teachings is literally and invariably true. If membership in the Church inevitably produced personalities intolerable to all other human beings, that would have no bearing on the validity of the faith. But those who do not understand this make their bad argument worse by an allegation that Roman Catholicism discourages two undesirable types, the Puritan and his complicated brother, the hypocritical reformist capitalist, and that Protestantism encourages them. Yet the Puritan appears throughout the ages under any form of religion or none, under paganism and Christianity, orthodox and heretical alike, under Catholicism and Protestantism, under deism and rationalism, and in each case the authorities have sometimes encouraged and sometimes discouraged him. There is indeed some excuse for the pretence that Protestantism has had a special affection for the reformist capitalist, because geographical rather than psychological conditions have made him a conspicuous figure in the Northern countries which resisted the Counter-Reformation. But here in Dubrovnik, here in the Republic of Ragusa, is a complete chapter of history, with a beginning and an end, which shows that this type can spring up in a soil completely free from any contamination of Protestantism, and can enjoy century after century the unqualified approbation of Rome.

Herzegovina

From TREBINYE

All tourists at Dubrovnik go on Wednesdays or Saturdays to the market at Trebinye. It is over the border in Herzegovina, and it was under a Turkish governor until the Bosnians and Herzegovinian rebels took it and had their prize snatched from them by the Austrians in 1878. It is the nearest town to the Dalmatian coast which exhibits what life was like for the Slavs who were conquered by the Turks. The route follows the Tsavtat road for a time, along the slopes that carry their olive terraces and cypress groves and tiny fields down to the sea with the order of an English garden. Then it strikes left and mounts to a gorgeous bleakness, golden with broom and gorse, then to sheer bleakness, sometimes furrowed by valleys which keep in their very trough a walled field, preserving what could not be called even a dell, but rather a dimple, of cultivable earth. On such bare rock the summer sun must be a hypnotic horror. We were to learn as we mounted that a rainstorm was there a searching, threshing assault.

When the sky cleared we found ourselves slipping down the side of a broad and fertile valley, that lay voluptuously under the guard of a closed circle of mountains, the plump grey-green body of a substantial river running its whole length between poplars and birches. We saw the town suddenly in a parting between showers, handsome and couchant, and like all Turkish towns green with trees and refined by the minarets of many mosques. These are among the most pleasing architectural gestures ever made by urbanity. They do not publicly declare the relationship of man to God like a Christian tower or spire. They raise a white finger and say only, "This is a community of human beings and, look you, we are not beasts of the field." ◇ ◇ ◇

I said, looking down the slopes towards the sea,* "It was odd a Moslem should be living there. But it is a place that has only recently

---

*[Back near Dubrovnik, after stopping at Moslem homes near Trebinye.]

been resettled. Until the Great War this district was largely left as it was after it had been devastated in the Napoleonic wars. Ah, what a disgusting story that is! See, all day long we have seen evidences of the crimes and follies of empires, and here is evidence of how murderous and imbecile a man can become when he is possessed by the imperial idea." "Yes," said my husband, "the end of Dubrovnik is one of the worst of stories."

When France and Russia started fighting after the peace of Pressburg in 1805 Dubrovnik found itself in a pincer between the two armies. The Republic had developed a genius for neutrality throughout the ages, but this was a situation which no negotiation could resolve. The Russians were in Montenegro, and the French were well south of Split. At this point Count Caboga proposed that the inhabitants of Dubrovnik should ask the Sultan to grant them Turkish nationality and to allow them to settle on a Greek island where they would carry on their traditions. The plan was abandoned, because Napoleon's promises of handsome treatment induced them to open their gates. This meant their commercial ruin, for the time, at least, since after that ships from Dubrovnik were laid under an embargo in the ports of all countries which were at war with France. It also meant that the Russian and Montenegrin armies invaded their territory and sacked and burned all the summer palaces in the exquisite suburbs of Larpad and Gruzh, hammering down the wrought-iron gates and marble terraces, beating to earth the rose gardens and oleander groves and orchards, firing the houses themselves and the treasures their owners had accumulated in the last thousand years from the best of East and West. The Russians and Montenegrins acted with special fervour because they believed, owing to a time-lag in popular communication and ignorance of geography, that they were thus defending Christianity against the atheism of the French Revolution.

When Napoleon was victorious the inhabitants of Dubrovnik expected that since they had been his allies they would be compensated for the disasters the alliance had brought on them. But he sent Marshal Marmont to read a decree to the Senate in the Rector's palace, and its first article declared: "The Republic of Ragusa has ceased to exist." This action shows that Napoleon was not, as is sometimes pretended, morally superior to the dictators of today. It was an act of Judas. He had won the support of Dubrovnik by promising to recognize its independence. He had proclaimed when he founded the Illyrian provinces that the cause of Slav liberation was dear to him; he now annulled the only independent Slav community in Balkan territory. He defended his wars and aggressions on the ground that he desired to make Europe stable; but when he found a masterpiece of stability under his hand he threw it away and stamped it into the mud.

There is no redeeming feature in this betrayal. Napoleon gave the Republic nothing in exchange for its independence. He abolished its constitution, which turned against him the nobles, from which he should have drawn his administrators, as the Venetians had always done in the other Adriatic cities. Hence, unadvised, he committed blunder after blunder in Dalmatia. In a hasty effort at reform he repealed the law that a peasant could never own his land but held it as a hereditary tenant, and therefore could never sell it. In this poverty-stricken land this was a catastrophe, for thereafter a peasant's land could be seized for debt. He also applied to the territory the Concordat he had bullied Pius VII into signing, which bribed the Church into becoming an agent of French imperialism, and caused a passionately devout population to feel that its faith was being tampered with for political purposes. This last decree was not made more popular because its execution was in the hands of a civil governor, one Dandolo, a Venetian who was not a member of the patrician family of that name, but the descendant of a Jew who had had a Dandolo as a sponsor at his baptism and had, as was the custom of the time, adopted his name. These errors, combined with the brutal indifference which discouraged Marmont's efforts to develop the country, make it impossible to believe that Napoleon was a genius in 1808. Yet without doubt he was a genius till the turn of the century. It would seem that empire degrades those it uplifts as much as those it holds down in subjection.

ROAD

Because there was a wire from Constantine announcing that he would arrive at Sarajevo the next day, we had to leave Dubrovnik, although it was raining so extravagantly that we saw only little vignettes of the road. An Irish friend went with us part of the way, for we were able to drop him at a farmhouse fifteen miles or so along the coast, where he was lodging. Sometimes he made us jump from the car and peer at a marvel through the downward streams. So we saw the source of the Ombla, which is a real jaw-dropping wonder, a river-mouth without any river. It is one of the outlets of the grey-green waters we had seen running through Trebinye, which suddenly disappear into the earth near that town and reach here after twenty miles of uncharted adventure under the limestone. There is a cliff and a green tree, and between them a gush of water. It stops below a bridge and becomes instantly, without a minute's prepara-tion, a river as wide as the Thames at Kingston, which flows glori-ously out to sea between a marge of palaces and churches standing among trees and flowers, in a scene sumptuously, incredibly, oper-atically romantic.

Our sightseeing made us dripping wet, and we were glad to take shelter for a minute or two in our friend's lodgings and warm ourselves at the fire and meet his very agreeable landlady. While we were there two of her friends dropped in, a man from a village high up on the hills, a woman from a nearer village a good deal lower down the slopes. They had called to pay their respects after the funeral of the landlady's aunt, which had happened a few days before. Our Irish friend told us that the interment had seemed very strange to his eyes, because wood is so scarce and dear there that the old lady had had no coffin at all, and had been bundled up in the best table-cloth. But because stone is so cheap the family vault which received her was like a ducal mausoleum. The man from the upland village went away first, and as the landlady took him out to the door our Irish friend said to the woman from the foothills, "He seems very nice." "Do you think so?" said the woman. Her nose seemed literally to turn up. "Well, don't you?" asked our friend. "We-e-e-ell," said the woman, "round about here we don't care much for people from that village." "Why not?" asked our friend. "We-e-e-ell, for one thing, you sometimes go up there and you smell cabbage soup, and you say, 'That smells good,' and they say, 'Oh, we're just having cabbage soup.'" A pause fell, and our friend inquired, "Then don't they offer you any?" "Oh, yes." "And isn't it good?" "It's very good. But, you see, we grow cabbages down here and they can't up there, and they never buy any from us, and we're always missing ours. So, really, we don't know what to think."

Bosnia

A Moslem woman walking black-faced in white robes among the terraces of a blossoming orchard, her arms full of irises, was the last we saw of the Herzegovinian plains; and our road took us into mountains, at first so gruffly barren, so coarsely rocky that they were almost squalid. Then we followed a lovely rushing river, and the heights were mitigated by spring woods, reddish here with the foliage of young oaks, that ran up to snow peaks. This river received tributaries, after the astonishing custom of this limestone country, as unpolluted gifts straight from the rock face. One strong flood burst into the river at right angles, flush with the surface, an astonishing disturbance. Over the boulders ranged the exuberant hellebore with its pale-green flowers.

But soon the country softened, and the mountains were tamed and bridled by their woodlands and posed as background to sweet small compositions of waterfalls, fruit trees, and green lawns. The expression "sylvan dell" seemed again to mean something. We looked across a valley to Yablanitsa, the Town of Poplars, which was the pleasure resort of Mostar when the Austrians were here, where their officers went in the heat of the summer for a little gambling and horse-racing. Before its minarets was a plateau covered with fields of young corn in their first pale, strong green, vibrant as a high C from a celestial soprano, and orchards white with cherry and plum. We drove up an avenue of bronze and gold budding ash trees and lovely children dashed out of a school and saluted us as a sign and wonder. We saw other lovely children later, outside a gipsy encampment of tents made with extreme simplicity of pieces of black canvas hung over a bar and tethered to the ground on each side. Our Swabian chauffeur drove at a pace incredible for him, lest we should give them pennies.

A neat village called Little Horse ran like a looped whip round a bridged valley, and we wondered to see in the heart of the country so many urban-looking little cafés where men sat and drank coffee.

The road mounted and spring ran backwards like a reversed film; we were among trees that had not yet put out a bud, and from a high pass we looked back at a tremendous circle of snow peaks about whose feet we had run unwitting. We fell again through Swissish country, between banks blond with primroses, into richer country full of stranger people. Gipsies, supple and golden creatures whom the window-curtains of Golders Green had clothed in the colours of the sunrise and the sunset, gave us greetings and laughter; Moslem women walking unveiled towards the road turned their backs until we passed, or if there was a wall near by sought it and flattened their faces against it. We came to a wide valley, flanked with hills that, according to the curious conformation, run not east and west nor north and south but in all directions, so that the view changed every instant and the earth seemed as fluid and restless as the ocean.

"We are quite near Sarajevo," I said; "it is at the end of this valley." Though I was right, we did not arrive there for some time. The main road was under repair and we had to make a detour along a road so bad that the mud spouted higher than the car, and after a mile or so our faces and topcoats were covered with it. This is really an undeveloped country, one cannot come and go yet as one chooses.

SARAJEVO I

"Look," I said,"the river at Sarajevo runs red. That I think a bit too much. The pathetic fallacy really ought not to play with such painful matters." "Yes, it is as blatant as a propagandist poster," said my husband. We were standing on the bridge over which the Archduke Franz Ferdinand and his wife would have driven on the morning of June the twenty-eighth, 1914, if they had not been shot by a Bosnian named Gavrilo Princip, just as their car was turning off the embankment.

We shuddered and crossed to the other bank, where there was a little park with a café in it. We sat and drank coffee, looking at the *Pyrus Japonica* and the white lilacs that grew all round us, and the people, who were almost as decorative as flowers. At the next table sat a Moslem woman wearing a silk overall striped in lilac and purple and dull blue. Her long narrow hand shot out of its folds to spoon a drop from a glass of water into her coffee-cup; here there is Turkish coffee, which carries its grounds in suspension, and the cold drop precipitates them. Her hand shot out again to hold her veil just high enough to let her other hand carry the cup to her lips. When she was not drinking she sat quite still, the light breeze pressing her black veil against her features. Her stillness was more than the habit of a Western woman, yet the uncovering of her mouth and chin had shown her completely un-Oriental, as luminously fair as any Scandinavian. Further away two Moslem men sat on a bench and talked politics, beating with their fingers on the headlines of a newspaper. Both were tall, raw-boned, bronze-haired, with eyes crackling with sheer blueness: Danish sea captains, perhaps, had they not been wearing the fez.

We noted then, and were to note it again and again as we went about the city, that such sights gave it a special appearance. The costumes which we regard as the distinguishing badge of an Oriental race, proof positive that the European frontier has been crossed, are worn by people far less Oriental in aspect than, say, the Latins; and this makes Sarajevo look like a fancy-dress ball. There is also an air of immense luxury about the town, of unwavering dedication to pleasure, which makes it credible that it would hold a festivity on so extensive and costly a scale. This air is, strictly speaking, a deception, since Sarajevo is stuffed with poverty of a most denuded kind. The standard of living among the working classes is lower than even in our great Western cities. But there is also a solid foundation of moderate wealth. The Moslems here scorned trade but they were landowners, and their descendants hold the remnants of their fortunes and are now functionaries and professional men. The trade they rejected fell into the hands of the Christians, who therefore grew in the towns to be a wealthy and privileged class, completely out of touch with the oppressed Christian peasants outside the city walls. There is also a Jewish colony here, descended from a group who came here from Spain after the expulsory decrees of Ferdinand and Isabella, and grafted itself on an older group which had been in the Balkans from time immemorial; it has acquired wealth and culture. So the town lies full-fed in the trough by the red river, and rises up the bowl of the blunt-ended valley in happy, open suburbs where handsome houses stand among their fruit trees. There one may live very pleasantly, looking down on the minarets of the hundred mosques of Sarajevo, and the tall poplars that march the course of the red-running river. The dead here also make for handsomeness, for acres and acres above these suburbs are given up to the deliberate care-lessness of the Moslem cemeteries, where the marble posts stick slant-wise among uncorrected grass and flowers and ferns, which grow as cheerfully as in any other meadow.

But the air of luxury in Sarajevo has less to do with material goods than with the people. They greet delight here with unreluctant and sturdy appreciation, they are even prudent about it, they will let no drop of pleasure run to waste. It is good to wear red and gold and blue and green: the women wear them, and in the Moslem bazaar that covers several acres of the town with its open-fronted shops there are handkerchiefs and shawls and printed stuffs which say "Yes" to the idea of brightness as only the very rich, who can go to dressmakers who are conscious specialists in the eccentric, dare to say it in the Western world. Men wash in the marble fountain of the great mosque facing the bazaar and at the appointed hour prostrate themselves in prayer, with the most comfortable enjoyment of coolness and repose and the performance of a routine in good repute. In the Moslem cookshops they sell the great cartwheel tarts made of fat leaf-thin pastry stuffed with spinach which presuppose that no man will be ashamed of his greed and his liking for grease. The looks the men cast on the veiled women, the gait by which the women admit that they know they are being looked upon, speak of a romanticism that can take its time to dream and resolve because it is the flower of the satisfied flesh. This tradition of tranquil sensuality is of Moslem origin, and is perhaps still strongest among Moslems, but here it shines on Jewish and Christian faces also.

Though Sarajevo has so strong a character it is not old as cities go. It was originally a mining town. Up on the heights there is to be seen a Turkish fortress, reconditioned by the Austrians, and behind it are the old workings of a mine that was once exploited by merchants from Dubrovnik. This is not to say that it ever had the casual and reckless character of a modern mining town. In past ages, before it was realized that though minerals seem solid enough their habits make them not more reliable as supports than the rainbow, a mining town would be as sober and confident as any other town built on a hopeful industry. But it was neither big nor powerful when it fell into the hands of the Turks in 1464. The capital of Bosnia was Yaitse, usually but unhelpfully spelt Jajce, about ninety miles or so north in the mountains. But after the conquest Sarajevo became extremely important as a focal point where various human characteristics were demonstrated, one of which was purely a local peculiarity, yet was powerful and appalling on the grandest scale.

It happened that the Manichæan heresy, which sees life as a struggle between supernatural Good and supernatural Evil in very material terms, had struck even deeper roots in Bosnia, where a sect called the Bogomils had attracted a high proportion of the people, including both the feudal lords and the peasants. We do not know much about this sect except from their enemies, who were often blatant liars. It is thought from the name "Bogomil," which means "God have mercy" in old Slavonic, and from the behaviour of the surviving remnants of the sect, that they practised the habit of ecstatic prayer, which comes easy to all Slavs; and they adapted the dualism of this heresy to Slav taste. They rejected its Puritanism and incorporated in it a number of Christian superstitions such as the belief in the haunting of certain places by elemental spirits and the practice of gathering herbs at certain times and using them with incantations. They also gave it a Slav character by introducing a political factor. Modern historians suggest that Bogomilism was not so much a heresy as a schism, that it represented the attempt of a strong national party to form a local church independent of either the Roman or the Orthodox Church.

Whatever Bogomilism was, it satisfied the religious necessities of the mass of Bosnians for nearly two hundred and fifty years, notwithstanding the savage attacks of both the Roman Catholic and the Orthodox Churches. The Roman Catholic Church was the more dangerous to them. This was not because the Orthodox Church had the advantage in tolerance: the Council of Constantinople laid it down that Bogomils must be burned alive. It was because the political situation in the East became more and more unfavourable to the Orthodox Church, until finally the coming of the Turks ranged them among the objects rather than the inflictors of persecution. The Latin Church had no such mellowing misfortunes; and though for a time it lost its harshness towards heretics, and was, for example, most merciful towards Jews and Arians under the Carlovingians, it was finally urged by popular bigotry and adventurous monarchs to take up the sword against the enemies of the faith.

At the end of the twelfth century we find a King of Dalmatia who wanted to seize Bosnia complaining to the Pope that the province was full of heretics, and appealing to him to get the King of Hungary to expel them. This began a system of interference which was for long wholly unavailing. In 1221 there were none but Bogomil priests in Bosnia, under whom the country was extremely devout. But the zeal of the Church had been fired, and in 1247 the Pope endeavoured to inspire the Archbishop of Bosnia by describing to him how his predecessors had tried to redeem their see by devastating the greater part of it and by killing or carrying away in captivity many thousands of Bosnians. The people, however, remained obstinately Bogomil, and as soon as the attention of the Papacy was diverted elsewhere, as it was during the Waldensian persecutions and the Great Schism, they stood firm in their faith again. Finally it was adopted as the official state religion.

But the Papacy had staked a great deal on Bosnia. It had preached crusade after crusade against the land, with full indulgences, as in the case of crusades to Palestine. It had sent out brigades of missionaries, who had behaved with glorious heroism and had in many cases suffered martyrdom. It had used every form of political pressure on neighbouring monarchs to induce them to invade Bosnia and put it to fire and the sword. It had, by backing Catholic usurpers to the Bosnian throne, caused perpetual disorder within the kingdom and destroyed all possibility of dynastic unity. Now it made one last supreme effort. It supported the Emperor Sigismund of Hungary, who held Croatia and Dalmatia, and who wished to add Bosnia to his kingdom. This was not a step at all likely to promote the cause of order. Sigismund was a flighty adventurer whose indifference to Slav interests was later shown by his surrender of Dalmatia to Venice. But the Pope issued a Bull calling Christendom to a crusade against the Turks, the apostate Arians, and the heretic Bosnians, and the Emperor embarked on a campaign and scored the success of capturing the Bosnian king. The Bosnians were unimpressed and replaced him by another, also a staunch Bogomil. Later Sigismund sent back the first king, whose claim to the throne was naturally resented by the second. The wretched country was again precipitated into civil war.

This was in 1415. In 1389 the battle of Kossovo had been lost by the Christian Serbs. For twenty-six years the Turks had been digging themselves in over the border of Bosnia. They had already some foothold in the southern part of the kingdom. A child could have seen what was bound to happen. The Turks offered the Bogomils military protection, secure possession of their lands, and full liberty to practise their religion provided they counted themselves as Moslems and not as Christians, and did not attack the forces of the Ottoman

Empire. The Bogomils, having been named in a Papal Bull with the Turks as common enemies of Christendom and having suffered invasion in consequence, naturally accepted the offer. Had it not been for the intolerance of the Papacy we would not have had Turkey in Europe for five hundred years. Fifty years later, the folly had been consummated. Bosnia was wholly Turkish, and the Turks had passed on towards Hungary and Central Europe. ◇ ◇ ◇

But the story does not stop there. It was only then that a certain peculiar and awful characteristic of human nature showed itself, as it has since shown itself on one other occasion in history. There is a kind of human being, terrifying above all others, who resist by yielding. Let it be supposed that it is a woman. A man is pleased by her, he makes advances to her, he finds that no woman was ever more compliant. He marvels at the way she allows him to take possession of her and perhaps despises her for it. Then suddenly he finds that his whole life has been conditioned to her, that he has become bodily dependent on her, that he has acquired the habit of living in a house with her, that food is not food unless he eats it with her.

It is at this point that he suddenly realizes that he has not conquered her mind, and that he is not sure if she loves him, or even likes him, or even considers him of great moment. Then it occurs to him as a possibility that she failed to resist him in the first place because simply nothing he could do seemed of the slightest importance. He may even suspect that she let him come into her life because she hated him, and wanted him to expose himself before her so that she could despise him for his weakness. This, since man is a hating rather than a loving animal, may not impossibly be the truth of the situation. There will be an agonizing period when he attempts to find out the truth. But that he will not be able to do, for it is the essence of this woman's character not to uncover her face. He will therefore have to withdraw from the frozen waste in which he finds himself, where there is neither heat nor light nor food nor shelter, but only the fear of an unknown enemy, and he will have to endure the pain of living alone till he can love someone else; or he will have to translate himself into another person, who will be accepted by her, a process that means falsification of the soul. Whichever step he takes, the woman will grow stronger and more serene, though not so strong and serene as she will if he tries the third course of attempting to coerce her.

Twice the Slavs have played the part of this woman in the history of Europe. Once, on the simpler occasion, when the Russians let

Napoleon into the core of their country, where he found himself among snow and ashes, his destiny dead. The second time it happened here in Sarajevo. The heretic Bosnian nobles surrendered their country to the Turks in exchange for freedom to keep their religion and their lands, but they were aware that these people were their enemies. There could be no two races more antipathetic than the Slavs, with their infinite capacity for inquiry and speculation, and the Turks, who had no word in their language to explain the idea of being interested in anything, not because they were unintelligent but because they were abandoned to the tropism of a militarist system. This antipathy grew stronger as the Turks began to apply to Bosnia the same severe methods of raising revenue with which they drained all their conquered territories, and the same system of recruiting. For some time after the conquest they began to draw from Bosnia, as from Serbia and Bulgaria and Macedonia, the pick of all the Slav boys, to act as Janizaries, as the Prætorian Guard of the Ottoman Empire. It was the fate of these boys to be brought up ignorant of the names of their families or their birth-places, to be denied later the right to marry or own property, to be nothing but instruments of warfare for the Sultan's use, as inhuman as lances or bombs.

To these exactions the Bosnians submitted. They could do nothing else. But the two Bosnian nobles who had been the first to submit to the Turks came to this mining town and founded a city which was called Bosnia Sarai, from the fortress, the *Sarai*, on the heights above it. Here they lived in a pride undiminished by conquest, but adapted to it. It must be remembered that these people would not see themselves as renegades in any shocking sense. The followers of a heresy itself strongly Oriental in tone would not feel that they were abandoning Christianity in practising their worship under Moslem protection, since Mohammed acknowledged the sanctity of Christ, and Moslems had no objection to worshipping in Christian churches. To this day in Sarajevo Moslems make a special point of attending the Church of St Anthony of Padua every Tuesday evening. The Bosnian Moslems felt that they had won their independence by a concession no greater than they would have made had they submitted to the Roman Catholic Church. So they sat down in their new town, firm in self-respect, and profited by the expanding wealth of their conquerors.

It was then, no doubt, that the town acquired its air of pleasure, for among the Turks at that time voluptuousness knew its splendid holiday. An insight into what its wealth came to be is given us by a catastrophe. When Kara Mustapha, the Vizier who tormented Dubrovnik, was beaten outside Vienna his camp dazzled Europe with a vision of luxury such as it had never seen, such as perhaps it has never known since. His stores were immense; he travelled with twenty thousand head apiece of buffaloes, oxen, camels, and mules, a flock of ten thousand sheep, and a country's crop of corn and sugar and coffee and honey and fat. His camp was the girth of Warsaw, wrote John Sobieski to his wife, and not imaginable by humble Poles. The Vizier's tent—this I know, for I once saw it in Vienna—was a masterpiece of delicate embroidery in many colours. There were also bathrooms flowing with scented waters, gardens with fountains, superb beds, glittering lamps and chandeliers and priceless carpets, and a menagerie containing all manner of birds and beasts and fishes. Before Kara Mustapha fled he decapitated two of his possessions which he thought so beautiful he could not bear the Christian dogs to enjoy them. One was a specially beautiful wife, the other was an ostrich. The scent of that world, luxurious and inclusive, still hangs about the mosques and latticed windows and walled gardens of Sarajevo.

But however sensuous that population might be, it was never supine. Sarajevo, as the seat of the new Moslem nobility, was made the headquarters of the Bosnian Janizaries. These Janizaries, however, singularly failed to carry out the intention of their founders. Their education proved unable to make them forget they were Slavs. They insisted on speaking Serbian, they made no effort to conceal a racial patriotism, and what was more they insisted on taking wives and acquiring property. Far from inhumanly representing the Ottoman power in opposition to the Bosnian nobles, they were their friends and allies. The Porte found itself unable to alter this state of affairs, because the Janizaries of Constantinople, who were also Slavs, had a lively liking for them and could not be trusted to act against them. It had no other resources, for it had exterminated the leaders of the Bosnian Christians and in any case could hardly raise them up to fight for their oppressors.

Hence there grew up, well within the frontiers of the Ottoman Empire, a Free City, in which the Slavs lived as they liked, according to a constitution they based on Slav law and custom, and defied all interference. It even passed a law by which the Pasha of Bosnia was forbidden to stay more than a night at a time within the city walls.

For that one night he was treated as an honoured guest, but the next morning he found himself escorted to the city gates. It was out of the question that the Ottoman Empire should ever make Sarajevo its seat of government. That had to be the smaller town of Travnik, fifty miles away, and even there the Pasha was not his own master. If the Janizaries of Sarajevo complained of him to the Sublime Porte, he was removed. Fantastically, the only right that the Porte insisted on maintaining to prove its power was the appointment of two officials to see that justice was done in disputes between Christians and Moslems; and even then the Commune of Sarajevo could dismiss them once they were appointed. Often the sultans and viziers must have wondered, "But when did we conquer these people? Alas, how can we have thought we had conquered these people? What would we do not to have conquered these people?"

Things went very well with this mutinous city for centuries. Its independence enabled it to withstand the shock of the blows inflicted on the Turks at Vienna and Belgrade, which meant that they must abandon their intention of dominating Europe. There came a bad day at the end of the seventeenth century, when Prince Eugène of Savoy rode down from Hungary with his cavalry and looked down on the city from a foothill at the end of the valley. Then the Slavs proved their unity in space and time, and the Bosnians rehearsed the trick that the Russians were later to play on Napoleon. The town, Prince Eugène was told, had been abandoned. It lay there, empty, to be taken. Prince Eugène grew thoughtful and advanced no further, though he had been eager to see this outpost of the East, whose atmosphere must have been pleasing to his own type of voluptuousness. He turned round and went back to the Danube at the head of a vast column of Christian refugees whom he took to Austrian territory. Perhaps that retreat made the difference between the fates of Prince Eugène and Napoleon.

After that a century passed and left Sarajevo much as it was, plump in insubordination. Then came the great reforming sultans, Selim III and Mahmud II, who saw that they must rebuild their house if it were not to tumble about their ears. They resolved to reorganize the Janizaries and, when that proved impossible, to disband them. These were by now a completely lawless body exercising supreme authority over all lawfully constituted administrative units. Also the sultans resolved to reform the land and taxation system which made hungry slaves of the peasants. Nothing would have been less pleasing to Sarajevo. The Janizaries and the Bosnian nobility had worked together to maintain unaltered the feudal system which had perished in nearly all other parts of Europe, and the proposal to remove the disabilities of the Christian peasants reawakened a historic feud. The Bosnian Moslem city-dwelling nobles hated these Christian peasants, because they were the descendants of the Catholic and Orthodox barons and their followers who had opened the door to the invader by their intolerance of Bogomilism.

Therefore the Janizaries and the Moslem nobles fought the sultans. The Janizaries refused to be disbanded and when their brothers had been exterminated in Constantinople the prohibited uniform was still to be seen in Sarajevo: the blue pelisse, the embroidered under-coat, the huge towering turban, decorated when the wearer was of the higher ranks with bird-of-paradise plumes, the high leather boots, red and yellow and black according to rank. In time they had to retreat from the town to the fortress on the heights above it, and that too fell later to the troops of the central authority; Bosnian nobles were beheaded, and the Pasha entered into full possession of the city where for four centuries he had been received on sufferance. But after a few months, in July 1828, the Sarajevans took their revenge and, aided by the citizens of a neighbouring town called Visok, broke in and for three days massacred their conquerors. Their victory was so terrible that they were left undisturbed till 1850, and then they were defeated by a Turkish Empire which itself was near to defeat, and was to be drummed out of Bosnia by peasants not thirty years later. At last the two lovers had destroyed each other. But they were famous lovers. This beautiful city speaks always of their preoccupation with one another, of what the Slav, not to be won by any gift, took from the Turk, and still was never won, of the unappeasable hunger with which the Turk longed throughout the centuries to make the Slav subject to him, although the Slav is never subject, not even to himself.

From SARAJEVO II

We knew we should try to get some sleep before the evening, because Constantine was coming from Belgrade and would want to sit up late and talk. But we hung about too late in the bazaar, watching a queue of men who had lined up to have their fezes ironed. It is an amusing process. In a steamy shop two Moslems were working, each clapping a fez down on a fez-shaped cone heated inside like an old-fashioned flat-iron and then clapping down another cone on it and screwing that down very tight, then releasing the fez with a motherly expression. "What extremely tidy people the Moslems must be," said my husband; but added, "This cannot be normal, however. If it were there would be more shops of this sort. There must be some festival tomorrow. We will ask the people at the hotel." But we were so tired that we forgot, and slept so late that Constantine had to send up a message saying he had arrived and was eager to go out to dinner.

When we came downstairs Constantine was standing in the hall, talking to two men, tall and dark and dignified, with the sallow, long-lashed dignity of Sephardim. "I tell you I have friends everywhere," he said. "These are two of my friends, they like me very much. They are Jews from Spain, and they speak beautiful soft Spanish of the time of Ferdinand and Isabella, not the Spanish of today, which is hard and guttural as German. This is Dr Lachan, who is a banker, and Dr Marigan, who is a judge."

The men greeted us with beautiful and formal manners, and we went down the street to the café. ◇—◇ But at the door they began to think of us and wonder if they should take us to such a place. "For us and our wives it is nice," they said, "but we are used to it. Perhaps for an English lady it will seem rather strange. There are sometimes dancers . . . well, there is one now." A stout woman clad in sequined pink muslin trousers and brassière was standing on a platform revolving her stomach in time to the music of a piano and violin, and as we entered she changed her subject-matter and began to revolve her large firm breasts in opposite directions. This gave an effect of hard, mechanical magic; it was as if two cannon-balls were rolling away from each other but were for ever kept contingent by some invisible power of attraction. "Your wife does not mind?" asked the judge and the banker. "I think not," said my husband. As we went down the aisle one of the cannon-balls ceased to revolve, though the other went on rolling quicker than ever, while the woman cried out my name in tones of familiarity and welcome. The judge and the banker showed no signs of having witnessed this greeting. As we sat down I felt embarrassed by their silence and said, in explanation, "How extraordinary I should come across this woman again." "I beg your pardon?" said the judge. "How extraordinary it is" I repeated, "that I should come across this woman again. I met her last year in Macedonia." "Oh, it is you that she knows!" exclaimed the judge and the banker, and I perceived that they had thought she was a friend of my husband's.

I was really very glad to see her again. When Constantine and I had been in Skoplje the previous Easter he had taken me to a night club in the Moslem quarter. That form of entertainment which we think of as peculiarly modern Western and profligate was actually far more at home in the ancient and poverty-stricken Near East. In any sizeable village in Macedonia I think one would find at least one café where a girl sang and there was music. In Skoplje, which has under seventy thousand inhabitants, there are many such, including a night club almost on a Trocadéro scale. In the little Moslem cabaret we visited there was nobody more opulent than a small shopkeeper, but the performers numbered a male gipsy who sang and played the gusla, a very beautiful Serbian singer, a still more beautiful gipsy girl who sang and danced, and this *danseuse de ventre*, who was called Astra. When Astra came round and rattled the plate at our table I found she was a Salonika Jewess, member of another colony of refugees from Ferdinand and Isabella who still speak Spanish, and I asked her to come and see me the next day at my hotel and give me a lesson in the *danse de ventre*.

She was with me earlier than I had expected, at ten o'clock, wearing a curious coat-frock, of a pattern and inexpert make which at once suggested she had hardly any occasion to be fully dressed, and that she would have liked to be a housewife in a row of houses all exactly alike. The lesson in the *danse de ventre* was not a success. I picked up the movement wonderfully, she said; I had it perfectly, but I could not produce the right effect. "Voyez-vous, Madame," she said, in the slow French she had picked up in a single term at a mission school, "*vous n'avez pas de quoi.*" It is the only time in my life that I have been reproached with undue slenderness; but I suppose Astra herself weighed a hundred and sixty pounds, though she carried no loose flesh like a fat Western woman, but was solid and elastic. After the lesson had failed we sat and talked. She came of a family of musicians. She had a sister who had married an Englishman employed in Salonika, and now lived in Ealing and had two pretty little girls, like dolls they were so pretty, Milly and Lily. It was terrible they were so far away. She herself was a widow, her husband had been a Greek lorry driver who was killed in a road accident after three years of marriage. She had one son, a boy of ten. It was her ambition that he should go to a French school, in her experience there was nothing like French education *"pour faire libre l'esprit."* In the meantime he was at a Yugoslavian school and doing well. Now, she told me, she was much happier in Sarajevo than in Skoplje, and remarked, *"Ici les gens sont beaucoup plus intelligents."* ◇ ◇ ◇

But my attention was immediately diverted. A very handsome young man had come up to our table in a state of extreme anger; he was even angrier than any of the angry young men in Dalmatia. He evidently knew Constantine and the judge and the banker, but he did not give them any formal greeting. Though his hair was bronze and his eyes crackled with blueness, and he might have been brother to the two Moslems we had seen talking politics in the park that afternoon, he cried out, "What about the accursed Turks?" The judge and the banker made no reply, but Constantine said, "Well, it was not I who made them." The young man insisted, "But you serve our precious Government, don't you?" "Yes," said Constantine, "for the sake of my country, and perhaps a little for the sake of my soul, I have given up the deep peace of being in opposition." "Then perhaps you can explain why your Belgrade gangster politicians have devised this method of insulting us Bosnians," said the young man, "We are used," he said, stretching his arms wide and shouting, "to their iniquities. We have seen them insulting our brothers the Croats, we have seen them sitting in the faces of all those who love liberty. But usually there is some sense in what they do, they either put money in their pockets or they consolidate their tyranny. But this crazy burlesque can bring them no profit. It can be done for no purpose but to wound the pride of us Bosnians. Will you be polite enough to explain a little why your horde of thugs and thieves have formed this curious intention of paying this unprovoked insult to a people whose part it should be to insult rather than be insulted?"

The judge leaned over to me and whispered, "It is all right, Madame, they are just talking a little about politics." "But what has the Government done to insult Bosnia?" I asked. "It has arranged," said the banker, "that the Turkish Prime Minister and Minister of War, who are in Belgrade discussing our military alliance with them, are to come here to be received by the Moslem population tomorrow." "Ah," said my husband, "that accounts for all the fezes being ironed. Well, do many people take the visit like this young man?" "No," said the banker, "he is a very extreme young man." "I would not say so," said the judge sadly.

629

At that moment the young man smashed his fist down on the table and cried into Constantine's face, "Judas Iscariot! Judas Iscariot!" "No," said poor Constantine to his retreating back, "I am not Judas Iscariot. I have indeed never been quite sure which of the disciples I do resemble, but it is a very sweet little one, the most *mignon* of them all." He applied himself to the business of eating a line of little pieces of strongly seasoned meat that had been broiled on a skewer; and when he set it down wistfulness was wet in his round black eyes. "All the same I do not like it, what that young man said. It was not agreeable. Dear God, I wish the young would be more agreeable to my generation, for we suffered very much in the war, and if it were not for us they would still be slaves under the Austrians."

Cautiously the banker said, "Do you think it is really wise, this visit?" Constantine answered wearily, "I think it is wise, for our Prime Minister, Mr Stoyadinovitch, does not do foolish things." "But why is it objected to at all?" said my husband. "That even I understand a little," said Constantine, "for the Turks were our oppressors and we drove them out, so that we Christians should be free. And now the heads of the Turkish state are coming by the consent of our Christian state to see the Moslems who upheld the oppressors. I see that it must seem a little odd." "But how is it possible," said my husband, "that there should be so much feeling against the Turks when nobody who is not very old can possibly have had any personal experience of their oppressions?"

The three men looked at my husband as if he were talking great nonsense. "Well," said my husband, "were not the Turks booted out of here in 1878?" "Ah, no, no!" exclaimed the three men. "You do not understand," said Constantine; "the Turkish Empire went from here in 1878, but the Slav Moslems remained, and when Austria took control it was still their holiday. For they were the favourites of the Austrians, far above the Christians, far above the Serbs or the Croats." "But why was that?" asked my husband. "It was because of the principle, *Divide et impera*," said the banker. It was odd to hear the phrase from the lips of one of its victims. "Look, there were fifty or sixty thousand people in the town," said the banker. "There were us, the Jews, who are of two kinds, the Sephardim, from Spain and Portugal, and the others, the Ashkenazi, who are from Central Europe and the East, and that is a division. Then there were the Christian Slavs, who are Croats and Serbs, and that is a division. But lest we should forget our differences, they raised up the Moslems, who

630

were a third of the population, to be their allies against the Christians and the Jews."

Their faces darkening with the particular sullenness of rebels, they spoke of their youth, shadowed by the double tyranny of Austria and the Moslems. ◇ ◇ ◇ The doctor and the lawyer returned to the sad subject. The banker sighed, "It is not that we do not like the Moslems. Since the war all things have changed, and we are on excellent terms. But it is not nice when they are picked out by the Government and allowed to receive a ceremonial visit from the representative of the power that crushed us and ground us down into the mud." ◇ ◇ ◇

SARAJEVO III

I woke only once from my sleep, and heard the muezzins crying out to the darkness from the hundred minarets of the city that there is but one God and Mohammed His prophet. It is a cry that holds an ultimate sadness, like the hooting of owls and the barking of foxes in night-time. The muezzins are making that plain statement of their cosmogony, and the owls and the foxes are obeying the simplest need for expression; yet their cries, which they intended to mean so little, prove more conclusively than any argument that life is an occasion which justifies the hugest expenditure of pity. I had nearly fallen asleep again when my husband said out of his dreams, "Strange, strange." "What is strange?" I said. "That Jewish banker," he replied, "he said so proudly that when he was a student in Berlin he felt ashamed because he was treated there as an equal when here he was treated as inferior to the Moslems. I wonder what he feels about Germany now."

In the morning we were not late, but Constantine was down before us, breakfasting in the café. ◇ ◇ "Look at all the flags," he said, "it is a great day for Sarajevo. See how I show you all." But he spoke glumly.

I suspected that he was secretly of his friends' mind about the day's doings; and indeed it was not exhilarating to look out of the café windows and see a stream of passing people, and none of the men without fezes, all of the women veiled. ◇ ◇ "We had better go," said Constantine. "The party from Belgrade are not coming to the railway station, they stop the railway train at a special halt in the middle

631

of the boulevards, near the museum, and it is quite a way from here."

For part of the way we took a cab, and then we had to get out and walk. Because Constantine had his Government pass and we were to be present at the reception at the station, we were allowed to go down the middle of the streets, which also were entirely lined with veiled women and men wearing fezes. Only a few Christians were to be seen here and there. "There seem to be a great many Moslems," I said, after the first two or three hundred yards. The crowd was close-packed and unified by a common aspect. The faces of the men were flattened, almost plastered by an expression of dogged adherence to some standard; they were all turned upwards to one hope. The women were as expressive in their waiting, though their faces were hidden. A light rain was falling on their silk and cotton overalls, but they did not move, and only some of them put up umbrellas, though most of them were carrying them. It was as if they thought of themselves already as participants in a sacred rite. Some of the spectators were arranged in processional order and held small, amateurish, neatly inscribed banners, some of them in Turkish script; and a great many of them carried Yugoslavian flags, very tidily, not waving them but letting them droop. There were many children, all standing straight and good under the rain. I looked at my watch, and I saw that we had been walking between these crowds for ten minutes. There are thirty thousand Moslems in Sarajevo, and I think most of them were there. And they were rapt, hallucinated, intoxicated with an old loyalty, and doubtless ready to know the intoxication of an old hatred.

We came to the halt at the right moment, as the train slid in and stopped. There was a little cheering, and the flags were waved, but it is not much fun cheering somebody inside the tin box of a railway carriage. The crowd waited to make sure. The Moslem Mayor of Sarajevo and his party went forward and greeted the tall and jolly Mr Spaho, the Minister of Transport, and the Yugoslavian Minister of War, General Marits, a giant who wore his strength packed round him in solid masses like a bull. <><> There were faint, polite cheers for them; but the great cheers the crowd had had in its hearts for days were never given. For Mr Spaho and the General were followed, so far as the expectations of the crowd were concerned, by nobody. The two little men in bowlers and trim suits, very dapper and well-shaven, might have been Frenchmen darkened in the colonial service. It took some time for the crowd to realize that they were in fact Ismet

632

Ineunue, the Turkish Prime Minister, and Kazim Ozalip, his War Minister.

Even after the recognition had been established the cheers were not given. No great degree of disguise concealed the disfavour with which these two men in bowler hats looked on the thousands they saw before them, all wearing the fez and veil which their leader the Ataturk made it a crime to wear in Turkey. Their faces were blank yet not unexpressive. So might Englishmen look, if, in some corner of the Empire, they had to meet as brothers the inhabitants of a colony that had been miraculously preserved from the action of time and had therefore kept to their road.

The Moslem Mayor read them an address of welcome, of which, naturally, they did not understand one word. This was bound in any case to be a difficult love-affair to conduct, for the Turks knew no Serbian and the Sarajevans knew no Turkish. They had to wait until General Marits had translated it into French; while they were waiting I saw one of them fix his eye on a distant building, wince, and look in the opposite direction. Some past-loving soul had delved in the attics and found the green flag with the crescent, the flag of the old Ottoman Empire, which these men and their leader regarded as the badge of a plague that had been like to destroy their people. The General's translation over, they responded in French better than his, only a little sweeter and more birdlike than the French of France, and stood still, their eyes set on the nearest roof, high enough to save them the sight of this monstrous retrograde profusion of fezes and veils, of red pates and black muzzles, while the General put back into Serbian their all too reasonable remarks. They had told the Moslems of Sarajevo, it seemed, that they felt the utmost enthusiasm for the Yugoslavian idea, and had pointed out that if the South Slavs did not form a unified state the will of the great powers could sweep over the Balkan Peninsula as it chose. They had said not one word of the ancient tie that linked the Bosnian Moslems to the Turks, nor had they made any reference to Islam.

There were civil obeisances, and the two men got into an automobile and drove towards the town. The people did not cheer them. Only those within sight of the railway platform were aware that they were the Turkish Ministers, and even among those were many who could not believe their eyes, who thought that there must have been some breakdown of the arrangements. A little procession of people holding banners that had been ranged behind the crowd at this point wrangled among itself as to whether it should start, delayed too long, and finally tried to force its way into the roadway too late. By that time the crowd had left the pavements and was walking under the drizzle back to the city, slowly and silently, as those who have been sent empty away.

We had seen the end of a story that had taken five hundred years to tell. We had seen the final collapse of the old Ottoman Empire. Under our eyes it had heeled over and fallen to the ground like a lay figure slipping off a chair. But that tragedy was already accomplished. The Ottoman Empire had ceased to suffer long ago. There was a more poignant grief before us. Suppose that such an unconquerable woman as may be compared to the Slav in Bosnia was at last conquered by time, and sent for help to her old lover, and that there answered the call a man bearing her lover's name who was, however, not her lover but his son, and looked on her with cold eyes, seeing her only as the occasion of a shameful passage in his family history; none of us would be able to withhold our pity.

From SARAJEVO IV

◇ ◇ History takes different people differently, even the same history. The Sarajevo market is held on Wednesdays, at the centre of the town near the bazaar, in a straggling open space surrounded by little shops, most of them Moslem pastrycooks', specializing in great cartwheel tarts stuffed with spinach or minced meat. The country folk come in by driblets, beginning as soon as it is fully light, and going on till nine or ten or eleven, for some must walk several hours from their homes: more and more pigeons take refuge on the roofs of the two little kiosks in the market-place. There are sections in the market allotted to various kinds of goods: here there is grain, there wool, more people than one would expect are selling scales, and there are stalls that gratify a medieval appetite for dried fish and meat, which are sold in stinking and sinewy lengths. At one end of the market are stuffs and embroideries which are chiefly horrible machine-made copies of the local needle-work. The Moslem women are always thickest here, but elsewhere you see as many Christians as Moslems, and perhaps more; and these Christians are nearly all of a heroic kind.

The finest are the men, who wear crimson wool scarfs tied round their throats. This means that they have come from villages high in the mountains, where the wind blows down from the snows; and sometimes the scarf serves a double purpose, for in many such villages a kind of goitre is endemic. These men count themselves as descendants of the Haiduks, the Christians who after the Ottoman conquest took refuge in the highlands, and came down to the valleys every year on St George's Day, because by then the trees were green enough to give them cover, and they could harry the Turks by brigandage. They reckon that man can achieve the highest by following the path laid down in the Old Testament. I cannot imagine why Victorian travellers in these regions used to express contempt for the rayas, or Christian peasants, whom they encountered. Any one of these Bosnians could have made a single mouthful of a Victorian traveller, green umbrella and all. They are extremely tall and sinewy, and walk with a rhythmic stride which is not without knowledge of its own grace and power. Their darkness flashes and their cheek-bones are high and their moustaches are long over fierce lips. They wear dark homespun jackets often heavily braided, coloured belts, often crimson like their headgear, the Bosnian breeches that bag between the thighs and outline the hip and flank, and shoes made of leather thongs with upcurving points at the toes. They seem to clang with belligerence as if they wore armour. In every way, I hear, they are formidable. Their women have to wait on them while they eat, must take sound beatings every now and again, work till they drop, even while child-bearing, and walk while their master rides.

Yet, I wonder. Dear God, is nothing ever what it seems? The women of whom this tale is told, and according to all reliable testimony truly told, do not look in the least oppressed. They are handsome and sinewy like their men; but not such handsome women as the men are handsome men. A sheep-breeder of great experience once told me that in no species and variety that he knew were the male and female of equal value in their maleness and femaleness. Where the males were truly male, the females were not so remarkably female, and where the females were truly females the males were not virile. Constantly his theory is confirmed here. The women look heroes rather than heroines, they are raw-boned and their beauty is blocked out too roughly. But I will eat my hat if these women were not free in the spirit. They passed the chief tests I knew. First, they looked happy when they had lost their youth. Here, as in all Balkan markets, there were far more elderly women than girls; and there is one corner of it which is reserved for a line of women all past middle life, who stand on the kerb hawking Bosnian breeches that they have made from their own homespun, and exchange the gossip of their various villages. Among them I did not see any women whose face was marked by hunger or regret. All looked as if they had known a great deal of pain and hardship, but their experience had led none of them to doubt whether it is worth while to live.

It was quite evident as we watched them that these women had been able to gratify their essential desires. I do not mean simply that they looked as if they had been well mated. Many Latin women who have been married at sixteen and have had numbers of children look swollen and tallowy with frustration. Like all other material experiences, sex has no value other than what the spirit assesses; and the spirit is obstinately influenced in its calculation by its preference for freedom. In some sense these women had never been enslaved. They had that mark of freedom, they had wit. This was not mere guffawing and jeering. These were not bumpkins, they could be seen now and then engaging in the prettiest passages of formality. We watched one of the few young women at the market seek out two of her elders: she raised her smooth face to their old lips and they kissed her on the cheek, she bent down and kissed their hands. It could not have been more graciously done at Versailles; and their wit was of the same pointed, noble kind.

We followed at the skirts of one who was evidently the Voltaire of this world. She was almost a giantess; her greyish red hair straggled about her ears in that untidiness which is dearer than any order, since it shows an infatuated interest in the universe which cannot spare one second for the mere mechanics of existence, and it was tied up in a clean white clout under a shawl passed under her chin and knotted on the top of her head. She wore a green velvet jacket over a dark homespun dress and coarse white linen sleeves, all clean but wild, and strode like a man up and down the market, halting every now and then, when some sight struck her as irresistibly comic. We could see the impact of the jest on her face, breaking its stolidity, as a cast stone shatters the surface of water. The wide mouth gaped in laughter, showing a single tooth. Then a ferment worked in her eyes. She would turn and go to the lower end of the market, and she would put her version of what had amused her to every knot of women she met as she passed to the upper end. I cursed myself because I could not understand one word of what she said. But this much I could hear: each time she made her joke it sounded more

636

pointed, more compact, and drew more laughter. When she came to the upper end of the market and her audience was exhausted, a blankness fell on her and she ranged the stalls restlessly till she found another occasion for her wit.

This was not just a white blackbird. She was distinguished not because she was witty but by the degree of her wit. Later on we found a doorway in a street near by where the women who had sold all their goods lounged and waited for a motor bus. We lounged beside them, looking into the distance as if the expectation of a friend made us deaf; and our ears recorded the authentic pattern, still recognizable although the words could not be understood, of witty talk. These people could pass what the French consider the test of a civilized society: they could practise the art of general conversation. Voice dovetailed into voice without impertinent interruption; there was light and shade, sober judgement was corrected by mocking criticism, and another sober judgement established, and every now and then the cards were swept off the table by a gust of laughter, and the game started afresh.

None of these women could read. When a boy passed by carrying an advertisement of Batya's shoes they had to ask a man they knew to read it for them. They did not suffer any great deprivation thereby. Any writer worth his salt knows that only a small proportion of literature does more than partly compensate people for the damage they have suffered by learning to read. These women were their own artists, and had done well with their material. The folk-songs of the country speak, I believe, of a general perception that is subtle and poetic, and one had only to watch any group carefully for it to declare itself. I kept my eyes for some time on two elderly women who had been intercepted on their way to this club in the doorway by a tall old man, who in his day must have been magnificent even in this land of magnificent men. Waving a staff as if it were a sceptre, he was telling them a dramatic story, and because he was absorbed in his own story the women were not troubling to disguise their expressions. There was something a shade too self-gratulatory in his handsomeness; no doubt he had been the *coq du village* in his day. In their smiles that knowledge glinted, but not too harshly. They had known him all their lives: they knew that thirty years ago he had not been so brave as he said he would be in the affair with the gendarmes at the ford, but they knew that later he had been much braver than he need have been when he faced the Turks in the ruined fortress, they

637

BLACK LAMB AND GREY FALCON

remembered him when the good seasons had made him rich and when the snows and winds had made him poor. They had heard the gossip at the village well pronounce him right on this and wrong over that. They judged him with mercy and justice, which is the sign of a free spirit, and when his story was finished broke into the right laughter, and flattered him by smiling at him as if they were all three young again.

I suspect that women such as these are not truly slaves, but have found a fraudulent method of persuading men to give them support and leave them their spiritual freedom. It is certain that men suffer from a certain timidity, a liability to discouragement which makes them reluctant to go on doing anything once it has been proved that women can do it as well. This was most painfully illustrated during the slump in both Europe and America, where wives found to their amazement that if they found jobs when their husbands lost theirs and took on the burden of keeping the family, they were in no luck at all. For their husbands became either their frenzied enemies or relapsed into an infantile state of dependence and never worked again. If women pretend that they are inferior to men and cannot do their work, and abase themselves by picturesque symbolic rites, such as giving men their food first and waiting on them while they eat, men will go on working and developing their powers to the utmost, and will not bother to interfere with what women are saying and thinking with their (dishonestly admittedly) inferior powers.

It is an enormous risk to take. It makes marriage a gamble, since these symbols of abasement always include an abnegation of economic and civil rights, and while a genial husband takes no advantage of them—and that is to say the vast majority of husbands—a malign man will exploit them with the rapacity of the grave. It would also be a futile bargain to make in the modern industrialized world, for it can hold good only where there are no other factors except the equality of women threatening the self-confidence of men. In our own Western civilization man is devitalized by the insecurity of employment and its artificial nature, so he cannot be restored to primitive power by the withdrawal of female rivalry and the woman would not get any reward for her sacrifice. There is in effect no second party to the contract. In the West, moreover, the gambling risks of marriage admit of a greater ruin. A man who is tied to one village and cannot leave his wife without leaving his land is not so dangerous a husband as a man who can step on a train and find

employment in another town. But the greatest objection to this artificial abjection is that it is a conscious fraud on the part of women,
and life will never be easy until human beings can be honest with one
another. Still, in this world of compromises, honour is due to one so
far successful that it produces these grimly happy heroes, these
women who stride and laugh, obeying the instructions of their own
nature and not masculine prescription.

From SARAJEVO V

One morning we walked down to the river, a brightening day shining
down from the skies and up from puddles. A Moslem boy sold us an
armful of wet lilac, a pigeon flew up from a bath in a puddle, its wings
dispersing watery diamonds. "Now it is the spring," said Constantine,
"I think we shall have good weather tomorrow for our trip to Ilidzhe,
and better weather the day after for our trip to Yaitse. Yes, I think it
will be well. All will be very well." When he is pleased with his country
he walks processionally, like an expectant mother, with his stomach
well forward. "But see what we told you the other night," he said as
we came to the embankment and saw the Town Hall. "Under the
Austrians all was for the Moslems. Look at this building, it is as
Moslem as a mosque, yet always since the Turks were driven out of
Bosnia the Christians have been two-thirds of the population. So did
the Catholic Habsburgs deny their faith."

Actually it is the Moslems who have most reason to complain of
this Town Hall, for their architecture in Sarajevo is exquisite in its
restraint and amiability, and even in modern times has been true to
that tradition. The minaret of the mosque beside it has the air of a
cat that watches a dog making a fool of itself.

But once we entered the building we were somewhere else; we were
on the stage where there had been performed one of the scenes—the
tragedy that had determined all our lives. An official said: "It was
over there that I stood with my father. He had been downstairs in
the hall among those who received the Archduke and Archduchess,
and had seen the Archduke come in, red and choking with rage.
Just a little way along the embankment a young man, Chabrinovitch,
had thrown a bomb at him and had wounded his aide-de-camp.
So when the poor Mayor began to read his address of welcome he
shouted out in a thin alto, 'That's all a lot of rot. I come here to pay

you a visit, and you throw bombs at me. It's an outrage.' Then the Archduchess spoke to him softly, and he calmed down and said, 'Oh, well, you can go on.' But at the end of the speech there was another scene, because the Archduke had not got his speech, and for a moment the secretary who had it could not be found. Then when it was brought to him he was like a madman, because the manuscript was all spattered with the aide-de-camp's blood.

"But he read the speech, and then came up here with the Archduchess, into this room. My father followed, in such a state of astonishment that he walked over and took my hand and stood beside me, squeezing it very tightly. We all could not take our eyes off the Archduke, but not as you look at the main person in a court spectacle. We could not think of him as a royalty at all, he was so incredibly strange. He was striding quite grotesquely, he was lifting his legs as high as if he were doing the goosestep. I suppose he was trying to show that he was not afraid."◇ ◇ ◇

It is unjust to say that Franz Ferdinand had no contact with nature. The room behind him was full of poeple who were watching him with the impersonal awe evoked by anybody who is about to die; but it may be imagined also as crammed, how closely can be judged only by those who have decided how many angels can dance on the point of a needle, by the ghosts of the innumerable birds and beasts who had fallen to his gun. He was a superb shot, and that is certainly a fine thing for a man to be, proof that he is a good animal, quick in eye and hand and hardy under weather. But of his gift Franz Ferdinand made a murderous use. He liked to kill and kill and kill, unlike men who shoot to get food or who have kept in touch with the primitive life in which the original purpose of shooting is remembered. Prodigious figures are given of the game that fell to the double-barrelled Mannlicher rifles which were specially made for him. At a boar hunt given by Kaiser Wilhelm sixty boars were let out, and Franz Ferdinand had the first stand: fifty-nine fell dead, the sixtieth limped by on three legs. At a Czech castle in one day's sport he bagged two thousand one hundred and fifty pieces of small game. Not long before his death he expressed satisfaction because he had killed his three thousandth stag.

By this butchery he expressed the hatred which he felt for nearly all the world, which, indeed, it is safe to say, he bore against the whole world, except his wife and his two children. He had that sense of being betrayed by life itself which comes to people who wrestle through long years with a chronic and dangerous malady. During this time the indiscipline of the court had been specially directed towards him. It happened that for some years it looked as if Franz Ferdinand would not recover from his illness, and during the whole of this time the Department of the Lord High Steward, believing that he would soon be dead, cut down his expenses to the quick in order to get the praises of the Emperor Franz Josef for economy. The poor wretch was grudged the most modest allowance, and even his doctor was underpaid and insulted. This maltreatment had ended when it became obvious that he was going to live, but by that time his mind was set in a mould of hatred and resentment, and though he could not shoot his enemies he found some relief in shooting, it did not matter what. ◇ ◇ ◇

When Franz Ferdinand returned from the balcony into the reception room his face became radiant and serene, because he saw before him the final agent of his ruin, the key beater in this battue. His morganatic wife, Sophie Chotek, had been in an upper room of the Town Hall, meeting a number of ladies belonging to the chief Moslem families of the town, in order that she might condescendingly admire their costumes and manners, as is the habit of barbarians who have conquered an ancient culture; and she had now made the proposal that on the return journey she and her husband should alter their programme by going to the hospital to make inquiries about the officer wounded by Chabrinovitch. Nothing can ever be known about the attitude of this woman to that day's events. She was a woman who could not communicate with her fellow-creatures. We know only of her outer appearance and behaviour. We know that she had an anaphrodisiac and pinched yet heavy face, that in a day when women were bred to look like table-birds she took this convention of amplitude and expressed it with the rigidity of the drill sergeant. We know that she impressed those who knew her as absorbed in snobbish ambitions and petty resentments, and that she had as her chief ingratiating attribute a talent for mimicry, which is often the sport of an unloving and derisive soul.

But we also know that she and Franz Ferdinand felt for each other what cannot be denied to have been a great love. Each found in the other a perpetual assurance that the meaning of life is kind; each gave the other that assurance in terms suited to their changing circumstances and with inexhaustible resourcefulness and good will; it is believed by those who knew them best that neither of them ever fell from the heights of their relationship and reproached the other for the hardships that their marriage had brought upon them. That is to say that the boar we know as Franz Ferdinand and the small-minded fury we know as Countess Sophie Chotek are not the ultimate truth about these people. These were the pragmatic conceptions of them that those who met them had to use if they were to escape unhurt, but the whole truth about their natures must certainly have been to some degree beautiful.

Even in this field where Sophie Chotek's beauty lay she was dangerous. Like her husband she could see no point in consistency, which is the very mortar of society. Because of her noble birth, she bitterly resented her position as a morganatic wife. It was infamous, she felt, that a Chotek should be treated in this way. It never occurred to her that Choteks had a value only because they had been accorded it by a system which, for reasons that were perfectly valid at the time, accorded the Habsburgs a greater value; and that if those reasons had ceased to be valid and the Habsburgs should no longer be treated as supreme, then the Choteks also had lost their claim to eminence. ◇ ◇ ◇

There was a conversation about this proposal which can never be understood. It would be comprehensible only if the speakers had been drunk or living through a long fevered night; but they were sober and, though they were facing horror, they were facing it at ten o'clock on a June morning. Franz Ferdinand actually asked Potiorek if he thought any bombs would be thrown at them during their drive away from the Town Hall. This question is incredibly imbecile. If Potiorek had not known enough to regard the first attack as probable, there was no reason to ascribe any value whatsoever to his opinion on the probability of a second attack. There was one obvious suggestion which it would have been natural for either Franz Ferdinand or Potiorek to make. The streets were quite inadequately guarded, otherwise Chabrinovitch could not have made his attack. Therefore it was advisable that Franz Ferdinand and his wife should remain at the Town Hall until adequate numbers of the seventy thousand troops who were within no great distance of the town were sent for to line the streets.

But they never suggested anything like it, and Potiorek gave to Franz Ferdinand's astonishing question the astonishing answer that he was sure no second attack would be made. The startling element in this answer is its imprudence, for he must have known that any investigation would bring to light that he had failed to take for Franz Ferdinand any of the precautions that had been taken for Franz Josef on his visit to Sarajevo seven years before, when all strangers had been evacuated from the town, all anti-Austrians confined to their houses, and the streets lined with a double cordon of troops and peppered with detectives. It would be credible only if one knew that Potiorek had received assurances that if anything happened to Franz Ferdinand there would be no investigation afterwards that he need fear. Indeed, it would be easy to suspect that Potiorek deliberately sent Franz Ferdinand to his death, were it not that it must have looked beforehand as if that death must be shared by Potiorek, as they were both riding in the same carriage. It is of course true that Berchtold was one of those who believed that a war against Serbia was a sacred necessity, and had written to him on one occasion expressing the desperate opinion that, rather than not have war, he would run the risk of provoking a world war and being defeated in it; and throughout the Bosnian manœuvres he had been in the company of Conrad, who was still thoroughly disgruntled by his dismissal by Franz Ferdinand. It must have been quite plain to them both that the assassination of Franz Ferdinand by a Bosnian Serb would be a superb excuse for declaring war on Serbia. Still, it is hard to believe that Potiorek would have risked his own life to take Franz Ferdinand's, for he could easily have arranged for the Archduke's assassination when he was walking in the open country. It is also extremely doubtful if any conspirators would have consented to Potiorek risking his life, for his influence and military skill would have been too useful to them to throw away.

Yet there is an incident arising out of this conversation which can only be explained by the existence of entirely relentless treachery somewhere among Franz Ferdinand's entourage. It was agreed that the royal party should, on leaving the Town Hall, follow the route that had been originally announced for only a few hundred yards: they would drive along the quay to the second bridge, and would then follow a new route by keeping straight along the quay to the hospital, instead of turning to the right and going up a side street which led to the principal shopping centre of the town. This had the prime advantage of disappointing any other conspirators who might be waiting in the crowds, after any but the first few hundred yards of the route, and, as Potiorek had also promised that the automobiles should travel at a faster speed, it might have been thought that the

Archduke and his wife had a reasonable chance of getting out of Sarajevo alive. So they might, if anybody had given orders to the chauffeur on either of these points. But either Potiorek never gave these orders to any subordinate, or the subordinate to whom he entrusted them never handed them on.

Neither hypothesis is easy to accept. Even allowing for Austrian *Schlamperei*, soldiers and persons in attendance on royalty do not make such mistakes. But though this negligence cannot have been accidental, the part it played in contriving the death of Franz Ferdinand cannot have been foreseen. The Archduke, his wife, and Potiorek left the Town Hall, taking no farewell whatsoever of the municipal officers who lined the staircase, and went on to the quay and got into their automobile. Franz Ferdinand and Sophie are said to have looked stunned and stiff with apprehension. Count Harrach, an Austrian general, jumped on the left running-board and crouched there with drawn sword, ready to defend the royal pair with his life. The procession was headed by an automobile containing the Deputy Mayor and a member of the Bosnian Diet; but by another incredible blunder neither these officials nor their chauffeurs were informed of the change in route. When this first automobile came to the bridge it turned to the right and went up the side street. The chauffeur of the royal car saw this and was therefore utterly bewildered when Potiorek struck him on the shoulder and shouted, "What are you doing? We're going the wrong way! We must drive straight along the quay."

Not having been told how supremely important it was to keep going, the puzzled chauffeur stopped dead athwart the corner of the side street and the quay. He came to halt exactly in front of a young Bosnian Serb named Gavrilo Princip, who was one of the members of the same conspiracy as Chabrinovitch. He had failed to draw his revolver on the Archduke during the journey to the Town Hall, and he had come back to make another attempt. As the automobile remained stock-still Princip was able to take steady aim and shoot Franz Ferdinand in the heart. He was not a very good shot, he could never have brought down his quarry if there had not been this failure to give the chauffeur proper instructions. Harrach could do nothing; he was on the left side of the car, Princip on the right. When he saw the stout, stuffed body of the Archduke fall forward he shifted his revolver to take aim at Potiorek. He would have killed him at once had not Sophie thrown herself across the car in one last expression of her great love, and drawn Franz Ferdinand to herself with a movement that brought her across the path of the second bullet. She was already dead when Franz Ferdinand murmured to her, "Sophie, Sophie, live for our children"; and he died a quarter of an hour later. So was your life and my life mortally wounded, but so was not the life of the Bosnians, who were indeed restored to life by this act of death.

Leaning from the balcony, I said, "I shall never be able to understand how it happened." It is not that there are too few facts available, but that there are too many. To begin with, only one murder was committed, yet there were two murders in the story: one was the murder done by Princip, the other was the murder dreamed of by some person or persons in Franz Ferdinand's entourage, and they were not the same. And the character of the event is not stamped with murder but with suicide. Nobody worked to ensure the murder on either side so hard as the people who were murdered. And they, though murdered, are not as pitiable as victims should be. They manifested a mixture of obstinate invocation of disaster and anguished complaint against it which is often associated with unsuccessful crime, with the petty thief in the dock. Yet they were of their time. They could not be blamed for morbidity in a society which adored death, which found joy in contemplating the death of beasts, the death of souls in a rigid social system, the death of peoples under an oppressive empire.

"Many things happened that day," said the head of the tourist bureau, "but most clearly I remember the funny thin voice of the Archduke and his marionette strut." I looked down on the street below and saw one who was not as the Archduke, a tall gaunt man from the mountains with his crimson scarf about his head, walking with a long stride that was the sober dance of strength itself. I said to Constantine, "Did that sort of man have anything to do with the assassination?" "Directly, nothing at all," answered Constantine, "though indirectly he had everything to do with it. But in fact all of the actual conspirators were peculiarly of Sarajevo, a local product. You will understand better when I have shown you where it all happened. But now we must go back to the tourist bureau, for we cannot leave this gentleman until we have drunk black coffee with him."

As we walked out of the Town Hall the sunshine was at last warm and the plum blossom in the distant gardens shone as if it were not still wet with melted snow. "Though the hills rise so sharply," I said, "the contours are so soft, to be in this city is like walking inside an opening flower." "Everything here is perfect," said Constantine; "and think of it, only since I was a grown man has this been my town. Until then its beauty was a heartache and a shame to me, because I was a Serb and Sarajevo was a Slav town in captivity." "Come now, come now," I said, "by that same reckoning should not the beauty of New York and Boston be a heartache and shame to me?" "Not at all, not at all," he said, "for you and the Americans are not the same people. The air of America is utterly different from the air of England, and has made Americans even of pure English blood utterly different from you, even as the air of Russia, which is not the same as Balkan air, has made our Russian brothers not at all as we are. But the air of Bosnia is the same as Serbian air, and these people are almost the same as us, except that they talk less. Besides, your relatives in America are not being governed by another race, wholly antipathetic to you both. If the Germans had taken the United States and you went over there and saw New England villages being governed on Prussian lines, then you would sigh that you and the Americans of your race should be together again." "I see that," I said. I was looking at the great toast-coloured barracks which the Austrians set on a ledge dominating the town. They seemed to say, "All is now known, we can therefore act without any further discussion": a statement idiotic in itself, and more so when addressed to the essentially speculative Slav.

"All, I tell you," said Constantine, "that is Austrian in Sarajevo is false to us. Look at this embankment we are walking upon. It is very nice and straight, but it is nothing like the embankment we Yugoslavs, Christian or Moslem, would make for a river. We are very fond of nature as she is, and we do not want to hold up a ruler and tell her that she must look like that and not stick forward her bosom or back her bottom. And look, here is the corner where Princip killed the Archduke, and you see how appropriate it was. For the young Bosnian came along the little street from the real Sarajevo where all the streets are narrow and many are winding and every house belongs to a person, to this esplanade which the Austrians built, which is one long line and has big houses that look alike, and seeing an Arch-Austrian he made him go away. See, there is a tablet on that corner commemorating the deed."

I had read much abuse of this tablet as a barbarous record of satisfaction in an accomplished crime. Mr Winston Churchill remarks in his book on *The Unknown War* (*The Eastern Front*) that "Princip died in prison, and a monument erected in recent years by his fellow-countrymen records his infamy and their own." It is actually a very modest black tablet, not more than would be necessary to record the exact spot of the assassination for historical purposes, and it is placed so high above the street-level that the casual passer-by would not remark it. The inscription runs, "Here, in this historical place, Gavrilo Princip was the intiator of liberty, on the day of St Vitus, the 28th of June, 1914." These words seem to me remarkable in their restraint, considering the bitter hatred that the rule of Austria had aroused in Bosnia. The expression "initiator of liberty" is justified by its literal truth: the Bosnians and Herzegovinians were in fact enslaved until the end of the war which was provoked by the assassination of the Archduke Franz Ferdinand. To be shocked at a candid statement of this hardly becomes a subject of any of the Western states who connived at the annexation of these territories by Austria.

One must let the person who wears the shoe know where it pinches. It happened that as Constantine and I were looking up at the tablet there passed by one of the most notable men in Yugoslavia, a scholar and a gentleman, known to his peers in all the great cities of Europe. He greeted us and nodded up at the tablet, "A bad business that." "Yes, yes," said Constantine warily, for they were political enemies, and he dreaded what might come. "We must have no more of such things, Constantine," said the other. "No, no," said Constantine. "No more assassinations, Constantine," the other went on. "No, no," said Constantine. "And no more Croats shot down because they are Croats, Constantine," rapped out the other. "But we never do that," wailed Constantine; "it is only that accidents must happen in the disorder that these people provoke!" "Well, there must be no more accidents," said his friend. But as he turned to go he looked again at the tablet, and his eyes grew sad. "But God forgive us all!" he said. "As for that accident, it had to happen."

I said to Constantine, "Would he have known Princip, do you think?" But Constantine answered, "I think not. He was ten years older, and he would only have known a man of Princip's age if their families had been friends, but poor Princip had no family of the sort that had such rich friends. He was just a poor boy come down from the mountains to get his education here in Sarajevo, and he knew nobody but his schoolfellows." That, indeed, is a fact which is of great significance historically: the youth and obscurity of the Sarajevo conspirators. Princip himself was the grandson of an immigrant whose exact origin is unknown, though he was certainly a Slav. This stranger appeared in a village on the borders of Bosnia and Dalmatia at a time when the Moslems of true Turkish stock had been driven out by the Bosnian insurrectionary forces, and occupied one of the houses that had been vacated by the Turks. There must have been something a little odd about this man, for he wore a curious kind of silver jacket with bells on it, which struck the villagers as strange and gorgeous and which cannot be identified by the experts as forming part of any local costume known in the Balkans. Because of this eccentric garment the villagers gave him the nickname of "Princip," which means Prince; and because of that name there sprang up after the assassination a preposterous legend that Princip's father was the illegitimate son of the murdered Prince Rudolf. He was certainly just a peasant, who married a woman of that Homeric people, the Montenegrins, and begot a family in the depths of poverty. When Austria came in and seized Bosnia after it had been cleared of Turks by the Bosnian rebels, it was careful to leave the land tenure system exactly as it had been under the Turks, and the Bosnian peasants continued on starvation level. Of Princip's children one son became a postman, and married a Herzegovinian who seems to have been a woman most remarkable for strength of character. In her barren mountain home she bore nine children, of whom six died, it is believed from maladies arising out of undernourishment. The other three sons she filled with an ambition to do something in life, and sent them down into the towns to get an education and at the same time to earn money to pay for it. The first became a doctor, the second a tradesman who was chosen at an early age mayor of his town. The third was Gavrilo Princip, who started on his journey under two handicaps. He was physically fragile, and he entered a world distracted with thoughts of revolution and preparations for war.

The two most oppressive autocracies in Europe were working full time to supply themselves and all other European countries with the material of revolution. Russia was producing innumerable authors who dealt in revolutionary thought. The Austrian Empire was producing innumerable men who were capable of any revolutionary act, whether in the interests of military tyranny or popular liberty. The Russian influence came into Bosnia through several channels, some of them most unexpected. For political purposes the Russian imperial family maintained a boarding school for girls at the top of the road from Kotor, in Tsetinye, the capital of Montenegro, where many of the aristocratic families of Dalmatia and Bosnia and Herzegovina and even Croatia sent their daughters to be educated. As all familiar with the perversity of youth would expect, the little dears later put to use the Russian they acquired at that institution to read Stepniak and Kropotkin and Tolstoy. This was but a narrow channel, which served only to gain tolerance among the wealthier classes for the movement which swept through practically the whole of the male youth of the Southern Slavs and set them discussing nihilism, anarchism and state socialism, and experimenting with the technique of terrorism which the advocates of those ideas had developed in Russia.

In this last and least attractive part of their activities the Bosnians show at a disadvantage compared to their Russian brothers during the period immediately before the war: they appear more criminal because they were more moral. Among the Russian revolutionaries there had been growing perplexity and disillusionment ever since 1906, when it was discovered that the people's leader, Father Gapon, owing to the emollient effects of a visit to Monte Carlo, had sold himself to the police as a spy. In 1909 they received a further shock. It was proved that Aseff, the head of the largest and most powerful terrorist organization in Russia, had from the very beginning of his career been a police agent, and though he had successfully arranged the assassination of Plehve, the Minister of the Interior, and the Grand Duke Serge, he had committed the first crime partly because he was a Jew and disliked Plehve's anti-Semitism, and partly because he wanted to strengthen his position in revolutionary circles in order to get a higher salary from the police, and he had committed the second to oblige persons in court circles who had wanted to get rid of the Grand Duke. This made all the sincere revolutionaries realize that their ranks were riddled with treachery, and that if they risked their lives it was probably to save the bacon of a police spy or further a palace intrigue. For this reason terrorism was practically extinct in Russia for some years before the war.

But the Southern Slavs were not traitors. It is true that there existed numbers, indeed vast numbers, of Croats and Serbs and Czechs who attempted to raise funds by selling to the Austro-Hungarian Empire forged evidence that their respective political parties were conspiring with the Serbian Government. But their proceedings were always conducted with the utmost publicity, and their forgeries were so clumsy as to be recognized as such by the most prejudiced court; they presented telegrams, which were supposed to have been delivered, on reception forms instead of transmission forms, and they put forward photographs of patriotic societies' minutes which bore evidence that the original documents must have been over three-foot-three by thirteen inches: a nice size for reproduction but not for a society's minutes. Neither the officials of the Empire nor the Slav nationalists ever took any serious measures against these disturbers of the peace, and they seem to have had such a privileged position of misdoing as is given in some villages to a pilferer, so long as he is sufficiently blatant and modest in his exploits so that he can be frustrated by reasonable care, and the community loses not too much when he scores a success.

But the real traitor and *agent provocateur*, who joined in revolutionary activities for the purpose of betraying his comrades to authority, was rare indeed among the South Slavs, and therefore terrorist organizations could function in confidence. They honeycombed the universities and the schools to an extent which seems surprising, till one remembers that, owing to the poverty of the inhabitants and the defective system of education imposed by the Austrian Empire, the age of the pupils at each stage was two or three years above that which would have been customary in a Western community.

The terrorism of these young men was given a new inspiration in 1912 and 1913 by the Balkan wars in which Serbia beat Turkey and Bulgaria. They saw themselves cutting loose from the decaying corpse of an empire and uniting with a young and triumphant democratic state; and by the multiplication of society upon society and patriotic journal upon patriotic journal they cultivated the idea of freeing themselves by acts of violence directed against their rulers. This, however, did not alter that horrible dispensation by which it is provided that those who most thirstily desire to go on the stage shall be those who have the least talent for acting. The Croats and Serbs are magnificent soldiers; they shoot well and they have hearts like lions. But they are deplorable terrorists. Much more individualist than the Russians, the idea of a secret society was more of a toy to them than a binding force. They were apt to go on long journeys to meet fellow-conspirators for the purpose of discussing an outrage, and on the way home to become interested in some other aspect of the revolutionary movement, such as Tolstoyan pacifism, and leave their bombs in the train. When they maintained their purpose, they frequently lost not their courage but their heads at the crucial moment, perhaps because the most convenient place for such *attentats*, to use the Continental word for a crime directed against the representative of a government, was among crowds in a town, and the young Slav was not used to crowds. He felt, as W. H. Davies put it of himself in urban conditions, "like a horse near fire." Such considerations do not operate now. The Great War hardened the nerves of a generation in the dealing out of death, and it trained the following generation with its experience plus the aid of all the money and help certain foreign nations could give them. The Croats and Macedonians trained in Italy and Hungary who killed King Alexander of Yugoslavia represented the highest point of *expertise* in terrorism that man has yet attained.

But in the days before the war the South Slavs were touching and ardent amateurs. Typical of them was young Zheraitch, a handsome Serb boy from a Herzegovinian village, who decided to kill the Emperor Franz Josef when he visited Bosnia and Herzegovina in 1910. With that end in mind he followed the old man from Sarajevo to Mostar, and from Mostar to Ilidzhe, revolver in hand, but never fired a shot. Then he decided to kill the Governor of Bosnia, General Vareshanin, who was specially abhorrent to the Slavs because he was a renegade Croat. He waited on a bridge for the General as he drove to open the Diet of Sarajevo. The boy fired five bullets at him, which all went wide. He kept the sixth to fire at his own forehead. It is said that General Vareshanin got out of his car and walked over to his body and savagely kicked it, a gesture which was bitterly remembered among all young South Slavs. This poor boy was typical of many of his fellows in his failure. In June 1912 another Bosnian tried to kill the Ban of Croatia in the streets of Zagreb, and killed two other people, but not him. In August 1913 a young Croat tried to kill the new Ban of Croatia, but only wounded him. In March 1914 another young Croat was caught in the Opera House at Zagreb just as he was about to shoot the Ban and the Archduke Leopold Salvator. And so on, and so on. The Balkan wars altered this state of affairs to some extent. A great many young Bosnians and Herzegovinians either swam across the river Drina into Serbia, or slipped past the frontier guards on the Montenegrin borders by night, in order to join irregular volunteer bands which served as outposts for the Serbian

Army as it invaded Macedonia. All these young men acquired skill and hardihood in the use of weapons. But those who stayed at home were incurably inefficient as assassins.

Princip was not among the young Bosnians who had gone to the Balkan wars. He had soon become weary of the school life of Sarajevo, which was reduced to chaos by the general political discontent of the pupils and their particular discontents with the tendentious curriculum of the Austro-Hungarian education authorities. He took to shutting himself up in his poor room and read enormously of philosophy and politics, undermining his health and nerves by the severity of these undirected studies. Always, of course, he was short of money and ate but little. Finally he felt he had better emigrate to Serbia and start studies at a secondary school at Belgrade, and he took that step in May 1912, when he was barely seventeen. One of his brothers gave him some money, and he had saved much of what he had earned by teaching some little boys; but it must have been a starveling journey. In Belgrade he was extremely happy in his studies, and might have become a contented scholar had not the Balkan War broken out. He immediately volunteered, and was sent down to a training centre in the South of Serbia, and would have made a first-rate soldier if gallantry had been all that was needed. But his deprived body broke down, and he was discharged from the Army.

Princip's humiliation was increased to a painful degree, it is said, because another soldier with whom he was on bad terms grinned when he saw him walking off with his discharge and said, "Skart," throw-out, bad stuff. Though he went back to Belgrade and studied hard and with great success, he was extremely distressed at his failure to render service to the Slav cause and prove his worth as a hero. It happened that in Serbia he had become a close friend of a young printer from Sarajevo called Chabrinovitch, a boy of his own age, who had been banished from Bosnia for five years for the offence of preaching anarchism. Much has been written about this youth which is not too enthusiastic, though it might be described as querulous rather than unfavourable. His companions found something disquieting and annoying about his high spirits and his garrulity, but it must be remembered that those who are very remarkable people, particularly when they are young, often repel more ordinary people by both their laughter and their grief, which seem excessive by the common measure. It is possible that what was odd about Chabrinovitch was simply incipient greatness. But he was also labouring under the

652

handicap of an extremely hostile relationship to his father. In any case he certainly was acceptable as a friend by Princip, and this speaks well for his brains.

They had a number of Sarajevan friends in common, whom they had met at school or in the cafés. Among these was a young schoolmaster called Danilo Ilitch, a neurotic and irascible and extremely unpopular ascetic. He is said to have served in the Serbian Army during the Balkan War, but only as an orderly. From the beginning of 1914 he was engaged in an attempt to form a terrorist organization for the purpose of committing a desperate deed, though nobody, least of all himself, seemed to know exactly what. Among his disciples was a young man called Pushara, who one day cut out of the newspaper a paragraph announcing the intended visit of Franz Ferdinand to Bosnia, and posted it from Sarajevo to Chabrinovitch in Belgrade. It is said by some that he meant merely to intimate that there would be trouble, not that trouble should be made. It is also to be noted that one of his family was said to be an Austrian police spy. If he or somebody connected with him had been acting as an *agent provocateur* they could not have hoped for better success. Chabrinovitch showed the paragraph to Princip, and they decided to return to Sarajevo and kill Franz Ferdinand.

But they needed help. Most of all they needed weapons. First they thought of applying to the Narodna Obrana, the Society of National Defence, for bombs, but their own good sense told them that was impossible. The Narodna Obrana was a respectable society acting openly under Government protection, and even these children, confused by misgovernment to complete callousness, saw that it would have been asking too much to expect it to commit itself to helping in the assassination of a foreign royalty. Moreover they both had had experience of the personalities directing the Narodna Obrana and they knew they were old-fashioned, pious, conservative Serbs of the medieval Serbian pattern, who were more than a little shocked by these Bosnian children who sat up till all hours in cafés and dabbled in free thought. When Chabrinovitch had gone to the society to ask a favour, an old Serbian captain had been gravely shocked by finding the lad in possession of Maupassant's *Bel Ami* and had confiscated it.

It is unfortunate that at this point they met a Bosnian refugee called Tsiganovitch who had heard rumours of their intention and who offered to put them in the way of getting some bombs. He was a member of the secret society known as the "Black Hand," or was associated with it. This society had already played a sinister part in the history of Serbia. It was the lineal descendant of the group of officers who had killed King Alexander and Queen Draga and thus exchanged the Obrenovitch dynasty for the Karageorgevitch. The Karageorges, who had played no part in this conspiracy, and had had to accept its results passively, had never resigned themselves to the existence of the group, and were continually at odds with them. The "Black Hand" was therefore definitely anti-Karageorgevitch and aimed at war with Austria and the establishment of a federated republic of Balkan Slavs. Their leader was a man of undoubted talent but far too picturesque character called Dragutin Dimitriyevitch, known as "Apis," who had been for some time the head of the Intelligence Bureau of the Serbian General Staff. He had heard of Ilitch and his group through a Bosnian revolutionary living in Lausanne, Gachinovitch, a boy of twenty-two who had an extraordinary power over all his generation among the South Slavs, particularly among the Bosnians; his posthumous works were edited by Trotsky. It was by his direction that Chabrinovitch and Princip had been approached by Tsiganovitch, and were later taken in hand, together with another Bosnian boy of nineteen called Grabezh who had just joined them, by an officer called Tankositch, who had been concerned in the murder of King Alexander and Queen Draga.

Tankositch took the boys into some woods and saw how they shot —which was badly, though Princip was better than the others. Finally he fitted them out with bombs, pistols, and some prussic acid to take when their attempts had been made so that they might be sure not to break down and blab in the presence of the police. Then he sent them off to Sarajevo by what was known as the underground route, a route by which persons who might have found difficulty in crossing the frontier, whether for reasons of politics or of contraband, were helped by friendly pro-Slavs. The boys were smuggled through Bosnia by two guards who were under orders from the "Black Hand," and with the help of a number of Balkan peasants and tradesmen, who one and all were exceedingly discomfited but dared not refuse assistance to members of a revolutionary body, they got their munitions into Sarajevo.

This journey was completed only by a miracle, such was the inefficiency of the conspirators. Chabrinovitch talked too much. Several times the people on whose good will they were dependent took fright and were in two minds to denounce the matter to the police, and take the risk of revolutionary vengeance rather than be hanged for complicity, as indeed some of them were. Ilitch was even less competent. He had arranged to fetch the bombs at a certain railway junction, but he fell into a panic and did not keep the appointment. For hours the sugar-box containing the weapons lay in the public waiting-room covered with a coat. The station cat had a comfortable sleep on it. Unfortunately Ilitch recovered his nerve and brought the bombs to his home, where he kept them under the sofa in his bedroom. He had swelled the ranks of those who were to use their arms by some most unsuitable additions. He had enrolled a Moslem called Mehmedbashitch, a peculiar character who had already shown a divided mind towards terrorism. In January 1913 he had gone to Toulouse with a Moslem friend and had visited the wonderful Gachinovitch, the friend of Trotsky. He had received from the leader weapons and poison for the purpose of attempting the life of General Potiorek, the Military Governor of Bosnia, but on the way he and his friend had thought better of it and dropped them out of the carriage window. Ilitch had also enrolled two schoolboys called Chubrilovitch and Popovitch, and gave them revolvers. Neither had ever fired a shot in his life. The few days before the visit of the Archduke Ilitch spent in alternately exhorting this ill-assorted group to show their patriotism by association and imploring them to forget it and disperse. He was himself at one point so overcome by terror that he got into the train and travelled all the way to the town of Brod, a hundred miles away. But he came back, though to the very end he seems at times to have urged Princip, who was living with him, to abandon the *attentat*, and to have expressed grave distrust of Chabrinovitch on the ground that his temperament was not suited to terrorism. It might have been supposed that Franz Ferdinand would never be more safe in his life than he would be on St Vitus' Day at Sarajevo.

That very nearly came to be true. On the great day Ilitch made up his mind that the assassination should take place after all, and he gave orders for the disposition of the conspirators in the street. They were so naïve that it does not seem to have struck them as odd that he himself proposed to take no part in the *attentat*. They were told to take up their stations at various points on the embankment: first Mehmedbashitch, then Chabrinovitch, then Chubrilovitch, then Popovitch, and after that Princip, at the head of the bridge that now bears his name, with Grabezh facing him across the road. What happened might easily have been foretold. Mehmedbashitch never threw his bomb. Instead he watched the car go by and then ran to the railway station and jumped into a train that was leaving for Montenegro; there he sought the protection of one of the tribes which constituted that nation, with whom his family had friendly connexions, and the tribesmen kept him hidden in their mountain homes. Later he made his way to France, and that was not to be the end of his adventures. He was to be known to Balkan history as a figure hardly less enigmatic than the Man in the Iron Mask. The schoolboy Chubrilovitch had been told that if Mehmedbashitch threw his bomb he was to finish off the work with his revolver, but if Mehmedbashitch failed he was to throw his own bomb. He did nothing. Neither did the other schoolboy, Popovitch. It was impossible for him to use either his bomb or his revolver, for in his excitement he had taken his stand beside a policemen. Chabrinovitch threw his bomb, but high and wide. He then swallowed his dose of prussic acid and jumped off the parapet of the embankment. There, as the prussic acid had no effect on him, he suffered arrest by the police. Princip heard the noise of Chabrinovitch's bomb and thought the work was done, so stood still. When the car went by and he saw that the royal party was still alive, he was dazed with astonishment and walked away to a café, where he sat down and had a cup of coffee and pulled himself together. Grabezh was also deceived by the explosion and let his opportunity go by. Franz Ferdinand would have gone from Sarajevo untouched had it not been for the actions of his staff, who by blunder after blunder contrived that his car should slow down and that he should be presented as a stationary target in front of Princip, the one conspirator of real and mature deliberation, who had finished his cup of coffee and was walking back through the streets, aghast at the failure of himself and his friends, which would expose the country to terrible punishment without having inflicted any loss on authority. At last the bullets had been coaxed out of the reluctant revolver to the bodies of the eager victims.

From SARAJEVO VI

"Do you see," said Constantine, "the last folly of these idiots?" There is a raw edge to the ends of the bridge, an unhemmed look to the masonry on both sides of the road. "They put up a statue of the Archduke Franz Ferdinand and his wife, not in Vienna, where there was a good deal of expiation to be done to those two, but here, where the most pitiful amongst us could not pity them. As soon as we took the town over after the liberation they were carted away." They may still be standing in some backyard, intact or cut into queer sculptural joints cast down among ironically long grass. There was never more convincing proof that we do not make our own destinies, that they are not merely the pattern traced by our characteristics on time as we rush through it, than the way that the destinies of Franz Ferdinand and Sophie Chotek continued to operate after their death. In their lives they had passed from situation to situation which invited ceremonial grandeur and had been insanely deprived of it in a gross ceremonial setting, and it was so when they were in their coffins. They were sent to Vienna, to what might have been hoped was the pure cold cancellation of the tomb. They were, however, immediately caught up and whirled about in a stately and complicated vortex of contumely and hatred that astonished the whole world, even their world, accustomed as it was to hideousness.

The Emperor Franz Josef cannot be blamed for the insolence which was wreaked on the coffins on their arrival in Vienna. A man of eighty-seven whose wife had been assassinated, whose son was either murdered or was a murderer and suicide, cannot be imagined to be other than shattered when he hears of the assassination of his heir and nephew, who was also his enemy, and his wife, who was a shame to his family. The occasion drew from Franz Josef a superb blasphemy: when he heard the news the thought of the morganatic marriage came first to his mind, and he said that God had corrected a wrong which he had been powerless to alter. But the guilt of the funeral arrangements at Vienna must rest on Prince Montenuovo, the Emperor's Chamberlain, who had tormented Franz Ferdinand and his morganatic wife during their lives by the use of etiquette, and found that by the same weapon he could pursue them after their death. ◇-◇-◇

He arranged that the train which brought the bodies home should be delayed so that it arrived at night. It came in horribly spattered by the blood of a railwayman who had been killed at a level crossing. Montenuovo had two initial reverses. He prescribed that the new heir, the Archduke Charles, should not meet the train, but the young man insisted on doing so. He tried also to prevent Sophie Chotek's coffin from lying beside her husband's in the Royal Chapel during the funeral mass, but to that Franz Josef would not consent. But he had several successes. Sophie's coffin was placed on a lower level to signify her lower rank. The full insignia of the Archduke lay on his coffin, on hers were placed the white gloves and black fan of the former lady-in-waiting. No wreath was sent by any member of the imperial family except Stephanie, the widow of the Crown Prince Rudolf, who had long been on atrocious terms with her relatives. The only flowers were a cross of white roses sent by the dead couple's two children, and some wreaths sent by foreign sovereigns. The Emperor Franz Josef attended the service, but immediately afterwards the chapel was closed, in order that the public should have no opportunity to pay their respects to the dead.

Montenuovo attempted to separate the two in their graves. He proposed that Franz Ferdinand should be laid in the Habsburg tomb in the Capuchin church, while his wife's body was sent to the chapel in their castle at Arstetten on the Danube. But to guard against this Franz Ferdinand had left directions that he too was to be buried at Arstetten. Montenuovo bowed to this decision, but announced that his responsibility would end when he had left the coffins at the West Terminus station. The municipal undertaker had to make all arrangements for putting them on the train for Pöchlarn, which was the station for Arstetten, and getting them across the Danube to the castle. But Montenuovo provided that their task was made difficult by holding back the procession from the chapel till late at night. As a protest a hundred members of the highest Hungarian and Austrian nobility in the costumes that would have been the proper wear at an imperial funeral, thrust themselves into the procession, and walked on foot to the station.

The coffins and the mourners travelled on a train that delivered them at Pöchlarn at one o'clock in the morning. They found that the station had not been prepared for the occasion, there were no crape hangings or red carpets. This was extremely shocking to a people obsessed with etiquette and pomp. But they soon had more solid reasons for resentment. The moment when the coffins were laid on the platform was the signal for a blinding and deafening and drenching thunderstorm. The disadvantages of a nocturnal funeral became apparent. Nobody in charge of the proceedings knew the village, so the mourners could not find their way to shelter and had to pack into the little station, impeding the actual business of the funeral. It had been proposed to take the coffins to a neighbouring church for a further part of the religious services, but the hearses could not be loaded

in the heavy rain, and indeed the mourners would not have known
where to follow them in the darkness. So the bewildered priests consecrated the coffins in the crowded little waiting-room among the
time-tables and advertisements of seaside resorts. At last the rain
stopped, and a start was made for the castle. But there was still much
thunder and lightning, and the sixteen horses that drew the hearses
were constantly getting out of control. It was dawn when the caval-
cade was brought safely to a quay on the Danube, and in the quietness the horses were coaxed on to the ferry-boat by attendants who
had water running down round their feet in streams from their
sodden clothing. The mourners, left on the bank to wait their turn,
watched the boat with thankfulness. But when it was in the middle
of the stream there was a last flash of lightning, a last drum-roll of
thunder. The left pole-horse in front of the Archduke's hearse reared,
and the back wheels slipped over the edge of the ferry-boat. Till it
reached the other side it was a shambles of terrified horses, of men
who could hardly muster the strength to cling to the harness, and
cried out in fatigue and horror as they struggled, of coffins slipping
to the water's edge.

It is strange that it was this scene which made it quite certain that
the Sarajevo *attentat* should be followed by a European war. The
funeral was witnessed by a great many soldiers and officials and men
of influence, and their reaction was excited and not logical. If Franz
Ferdinand had been quietly laid to rest according to the custom of his
people, many Austrians would have felt sober pity for him for a day,
and then remembered his many faults. They would surely have
reflected that he had brought his doom on himself by the tactlessness
and aggressiveness of his visit to the Serbian frontier at the time of
a Serbian festival; and they might also have reflected that those qualities were characteristic not only of him but of his family. The proper
sequel to the *Walpurgisnacht* obsequies of Franz Ferdinand would
have been the dismissal of Prince Montenuovo, the drastic revision
of the Austrian constitution and reduction of the influence wielded
by the Habsburgs and their court, and an attempt at the moral reha-
bilitation of Vienna. But to take any of these steps Austria would
have had to look in the mirror. She preferred instead to whip herself
into a fury of loyalty to Franz Ferdinand's memory. It was only
remembered that he was the enemy of Franz Josef, who had now
shown himself sacrilegious to a corpse who, being a Habsburg, must
have been as sacred as an emperor who was sacred because he was a

Habsburg. It was felt that if Franz Ferdinand had been at odds with this old man and his court he had probably been right. Enthusiasm flamed up for the men who had been associated with Franz Ferdinand in urging a policy of imperialist aggression that they had jointly engendered. Again the corpse was outraged; he could not speak from the grave to say that he had cancelled those preferences, to protest when these men he had repudiated put forward the policy he had abandoned and pressed it on the plea of avenging his death. The whole of Vienna demanded that the pacifism of Franz Josef should be flouted as an old man's folly and that Austria should declare war upon Serbia. ◇◇◇

Serbia

We stood in the disordered rooms of some sort of society called "The Serbian Queen Bee," and I had difficulty in fixing my attention on Constantine and the officials of the society as they explained to us precisely what it was. We had started at seven from Belgrade and had travelled for two hours to Novi Sad, a journey which might have been pleasant, for the train ran beside the hallucinatory landscape of the misted Danube floods, but which was not, because it became apparent that Gerda* had decided to detest us. Every word and movement of hers, and even in some mysterious way her complete inaction, implied that she was noble, patient, industrious, modest, and self-effacing, whereas we were materialist, unstable, idle, extravagant, and aggressive. She was at that moment standing in the corner of the room behind the men who were talking to me, silently exuding this libellous charade.

The town, I understood they were telling me, had been founded by the Patriarch Arsenius III at the end of the seventeenth century. When the Serbians revolted against the Turks in 1689 and failed, the Emperor Leopold of Austria offered them asylum on his territories, with full rights of religious worship and a certain degree of self-government. There were already a number of Serb settlers there who had been introduced by the Turks when Hungary was theirs. The Patriarch accepted the offer and led across the Danube thirty thousand Serbian families, from all parts of the land, as far south as Macedonia and Old Serbia. Some of them had settled here in Neue-stadt, as it had been called. A good many of them had fled back to Turkish territory, for the Emperor broke his promises, and the Austrians and Hungarians bled them white with financial and military levies and forbade them the use of the Orthodox rite. Only for a little time, under Maria Theresa's liberal son, the Emperor Joseph, did the refugee Serbs enjoy honest treatment. But they never forgot their language and their culture, and in 1823 they founded this literary

*[Constantine's German wife, who had joined them in Belgrade.]

society, "The Serbian Queen Bee." It was unfortunate that we had come to visit its headquarters just when it had been handed over to the house painter, they said anxiously.

We could get some idea of what the society had preserved, we replied; and pulled out some of the pictures that were stacked against the wall. We came again and again on typical portraits of the sort that pullulated on the whole of nineteenth-century Europe except France, where there were too many good eighteenth-century portrait-painters for artlessness to take the country by storm. Men who were nothing but moustaches and sloping shoulders, women who were nothing but smoothly parted coiffures and stiffly caged bodices, had their Slav characteristics contracted down to a liverish look. "They did not migrate here," murmured my husband, "until three hundred years after the destruction of the Serbo-Byzantine civilization. I expect the continuity was quite thoroughly broken, and that King Alexander was simply a doctrinaire acting on nationalist——" His voice broke. "Theory," he added, uncertainly. He had turned to the light a Byzantine Madonna, vast-eyed, rigid in the climax of an exalted rhythm. The Serbs had, indeed, not lost all their baggage on their way here.

"I will show you all," said Constantine, "all I will show you. Therefore we must hurry, for I will show you the Patriarchate at Karlovtsi, which has been the headquarters of the Serbian Church since the great migration of Arsenius, before we go to the monasteries of the Frushka Gora." So we soon left this town, which was very agreeable and recalled my own Edinburgh in its trim consciousness of its own distinction. Our road took us into pretty country, green and rolling, at the river's edge. Once we paused at a church that had the remarried look of a building that has changed its faith. It had been a mosque during the hundred and fifty years the Turks held Hungary; it has since the early eighteenth century been a Roman Catholic Church. The clublike atmosphere of a mosque still hung round it: it had a wide terrace overlooking the waters, where there should have been sitting impassive and contented men in fezes, drawing on some immense secret fund of leisure. We stood there for a moment, soothed by the miles of water, pale as light itself, on which stranded willows impressed dark emblems, garlands and true-lover's knots and cat's-cradles. We went back to our contest with mud, with the dark Central European ooze that is never completely mastered save by a drought so extreme as to be a still greater affliction, that rose now in thick waves before our wheels, that kept the upper hand even in the main street of Karlovtsi, though that was a handsome little town.

The Patriarchate was a nineteenth-century stone palace, built in the Byzantine style with Austrian solidity, rich in arch and balcony. We went up a flight of steps to the florid entrance and rang the bell, and looked round us at the gardens, which were very ornate in the formal style, with many flower-beds laid out in intricate shapes and surrounded with low box hedges, and numbers of lilac bushes bearing peculiarly heavy purple flowers. The door did not open. We rang the bell again, we knocked with our fists, we went back to the car and sounded the hooter. Nothing happened, so we went into the gardens, Constantine clapping his hands and crying "Holla! Holla!" to the unresponsive palace. The gardens were mystifying; inside the beautifully tended box hedges the flower-beds were choked with weeds, a single garden chair, made of white painted wire in the Victorian fashion, was set quite alone on a wide gravel space, with an air of deluded sociability, as if it had gone mad and thought that there were about it many other garden chairs. Children came in from the street and followed us about. We could find no gardener, and the only door we could find opened into a large room with stone shelves used for storing an immense quantity of jam. We had given up all hope of entering, and had paused to inhale the scent of the prodigious purple lilacs, when an old man carrying an orange came out of a door we had not seen and told us that the Patriarch was in Belgrade, but there were some priests working at the printing-press near by, and he would fetch us one of them.

There came to us a tall monk, nobly beautiful, wearing a cloak of complicated design and majestic effect: all the garments worn in the Eastern Church are inherited from Byzantium and recall its glory. He had perfect manners, and was warm in his greeting to Constantine and Gerda, but his eyes lay on us with a certain coldness and reproach. I was surprised at this, for I had always found Orthodox ecclesiastics disposed to treat English people as if they were members of the same Church; but I supposed that here, at headquarters, they might be stricter in their interpretation of schism and heresy. But he was courteous, and told us that he would take us over the Patriarchate, and would like also to show us the printing-press, in which he took a special interest as he was head of Propaganda.

It lay behind the gardens, in a no-man's-land of alleys and outhouses, countryish and clean, with here and there more of those prodigious lilacs, and little streams running down to the Danube. From a courtyard filled with green light by a gnarled old fruit tree we went into a dusty office, where an old priest and a young one sat at rickety desks furnished with ink-wells and pens and blotting-paper that all belonged to the very dawn of stationery. Pamphlets of artless appearance, incompetently tied up in bales, were lying about not in disarray but in only amateurish array. We went down a step or two to the composing-room, where a man stood before the sloping trays and set up print in the fantastic Old Slavonic type used in Orthodox missals and in no secular writings whatsoever. We went up a step or two into a room where young girls bound the pamphlets, not very skilfully but most devoutly. Then in another room, either two steps up or two steps down but certainly not on the same level, we found a lovely twisted old man, deformed by the upward spiral of his spirit, as El Greco loved to paint his holy kind. He fed the printing machine with sheets as if he had to school himself to remember that the poor mindless thing could do its sacred work only at a certain pace. We might have been visiting the office of some small, fantastic cult carried on by a few pure and obstinate and unworldly people in some English town. Indeed, I know a shop in a Sussex village, owned by a sect which believes that the way to please God is by ritual water-drinking, which was the precise analogue of this modest and fanatic establishment. Yet this was the analogue of a printing-press owned by the Church of England and housed by the Archbishop of Canterbury in the grounds of Lambeth Palace.

We had still to wait for some minutes before the front door of the Patriarchate, though the priest had gone through the kitchen to send up a servant to open it. Then it slowly swung open, and a withered little major-domo looked out at us. It seemed to me that he pursed his lips when he saw my husband and myself. "Good morning," said Constantine, stepping inside, "and how is life going with you?" "*Polako, polako*," answered the little man, that is, "Only so-so." "Why, he speaks like a Russian," said Constantine, and talked to him for a little. "Yes," he said, "he was a Russian officer, and he is very pious and he would like to be a monk, but he has a wife, so they have made him major-domo here." He was at least somewhere which might have reminded him of his home. I have never been to Russia, but I have visited states which formed part of Tsarist Russia, Finland and Estonia and Latvia, and I am familiar with villas that have belonged to rich Russians in France and Italy and Germany, and I can recognize a certain complex of decoration and architecture as Romanoff and nothing else.

It has elements that can be matched in other countries. Something like it can be seen in the older mansions built by the nineteenth-century barons on Riverside Drive and in the Middle West and the West; there is the same profusion of busy and perforate woodwork in the interior. There is a suggestion also of the photograph-frames and boxes made of shells which are to be bought at English seaside towns; and they recall also the presents that people give each other in German provincial shops, such as umbrellas with pink marble tops cut into stags' heads. There is a suggestion, in fact, of every kind of bad taste known to Western civilization, down to the most naïve and the most plebeian; and there is a curious absence of any trace of the classical and moderating influence which France has exercised on the rest of Europe, though it has suffered the gilt infection spread by the Roi Soleil. Yet there is also from time to time the revelation of a taste so superb that it puts the West to shame. There is here a passion which is the root of our love for beauty, and therefore of our effort for art; the passion for beautiful substances, for coloured gems, for shining stone, for silver and gold and crystal. There is not only this basis for art, there is art, there is a creative imagination that conceives vast and simple visions, as a nomad would see them, who, lifting his eyes from the plains, looks on the huge procession of the clouds. There is also a feeling for craft; this nomad was accustomed to pick up soft metal and twist it into the semblance of horses and wild beasts, shapes he could criticize, since he rode the one and hunted the other, so much that he knew their bodies as his own.

We are perhaps looking not at a manifestation of bad taste at all, but at the bewilderment of a powerful person with perfect taste who has been suddenly transported from a world in which there are only a few materials, and those in a pure state, to be shaped by that taste or ignored, into another world, crammed with small manufactured objects, the product of other people's tastes, which are so different from his that he cannot form any just estimate of their value and is bewildered. ❖ ❖ ❖

There was, indeed, one room in the Patriarchate that was magnificent, a conference chamber with a superb throne and crimson curtains which might have been taken from one of the finest Viennese palaces, but was derived from a larger and more dramatic inspiration. The rest was faintly bizarre and sometimes that not faintly. We sat down in a small drawing-room, while Constantine talked to the priest and the major-domo; and I remarked that the furniture was not what would have been found in an English archbishop's palace. It was a suite made from black wood, including chairs and tables and bookcases, all decorated with gilt carvings, three or four inches long, representing women nude to the waist, with their breasts strongly defined. They were placed prominently on the pilasters of the bookcases, on the central legs of the round tables, on the arms of the chairs. They were a proof, of course, of the attitude of the Orthodox Church regarding sexual matters, which it takes without excitement, and I am sure nobody had ever cast on them a pornographic eye. But for all that they were naïvely chosen as ornaments for an ecclesiastical home.

"But why," I said to Constantine, "are both the priest and the major-domo looking at me and my husband as if they hated us?" "Oh, it is nothing personal," said Constantine, "but they both hate the English." "But what do they know about the English?" asked my husband. "The old officer hates very much the English," explained Constantine, "because he says that it was Sir George Buchanan who started the Russian Revolution." We had to think for a minute before we remembered that Sir George Buchanan had been our Ambassador at St Petersburg in 1917. "But does he not think that perhaps Kerensky and Lenin had a little to do with it?" asked my husband. When it was put to him the major-domo shook his head and emitted an impatient flood of liquid consonants. "He says," translated Constantine, " that that is nonsense. How could unimportant people like Kerensky and Lenin do anything like starting a revolution? It must have been someone of real influence like Sir George Buchanan." ◇ ◇ ◇

The Frushka Gora, that is to say the Frankish Hills, which are called by that name for a historical reason incapable of interesting anybody, lie to the south of the Danube; and we had to drive across the range to find the monasteries founded by the seventeenth-century migrants, for they lie scattered on the southern slopes, looking back towards Serbia. Once we were over the crest we found ourselves in the most entrancing rounded hills, clothed with woods now golden rather than green with the springtime, which ran down to vast green and purple plains, patterned with shadows shed by a tremendous cloudscape, slowly sailing now on its way to Asia. We stopped to eat at a hotel high above a valley that fell in a golden spiral to the plains;

and it should have been agreeable, for this is a centre for walking-tours, and we had around us many young people, probably teachers freed from their duty because it was near Easter, and there is nothing so pretty as the enjoyment people get out of simple outings in countries that have been liberated by the Great War. It is so in all the Habsburg succession states, and it is so in the Baltic provinces that once were Russia, Finland and Estonia and Latvia. But we did not enjoy our outing so much as we might have, because Gerda had been on the wrong side of the peace treaties.

Constantine was saying, "And much, much did we Serbs owe to those Serbs who were in Hungary, who were able to bring here the bodies of their kings and their treasure and keep alive their culture," when Gerda crossly interrupted him. "But why were the Serbs allowed to stay here?" "It is not a question of being allowed to stay here," said Constantine, "they were invited here by the Austrian Empire." "Nonsense," said Gerda; "one does not invite people to come and live in one's country." "But sometimes one does," said Constantine; "the Austrian Emperor wanted the Serb soldiers to protect his lands against the Turks, so in exchange he promised them homes." "But if the Austrians gave the Serbs homes then it was most ungrateful for the Yugoslavs to turn the Hungarians out of this part of the country," said Gerda, "it should still be a part of Hungary." "But we owe nothing to Hungary, for they broke all their promises to the Serbs," said Constantine, "and since the Austro–Hungarian Empire has ceased to exist and we reconstituted it according to the principle of self-determination and there were more Slavs here than any other people, this certainly had to become Yugoslavia."

To change the subject Constantine went on, "But there are Slavs everywhere, God help the world. You have the Wends in Germany, many of them and some distinguished ones, for the great Lessing was a Wend. They are Slavs." "But surely none of them remember that," said my husband. "Indeed they do," said Constantine; "there was a Wendish separatist movement before the war and for some time after the war, with its headquarters in Saxony. I know that well, for in 1913 I went with a friend to stay in Dresden, and when we described ourselves as Serbs the hotel porter would not have it at all. He said, 'I know what you mean, and I have sympathy with all who stand with their race, but you will get me into trouble with the police if you say you are Serbs,' and he would hardly believe it when he looked at our passports and saw that there was a country called

Serbia." "But if all the Wends are Slavs," said Gerda, "why do we not send them out of Germany into the Slav countries, and give the land that they are taking up to true Germans?" "Then the Slavs," I said, "might begin to think about sending back into Germany all the German colonists that live in places like Franzstal." "Why, so they might," said Gerda, looking miserable, since an obstacle had arisen in the way of her ideal programme for making Europe clean and pure and Germanic by coercion and expulsion. She said in Serbian to her husband, "How this woman lacks tact." "I know, my dear," he answered gently, "but do not mind it, enjoy the scenery."

She could not. Her eyes filled with angry tears, the lower part of her face became podgy with sullenness. We none of us knew what to say or do, but just at that moment someone turned on the radio and the restaurant was flooded with a symphony by Mozart, and we all forgot Gerda. Constantine began to hum the theme, and his plump little hands followed the flight of Mozart's spirit as at Yaitse they had followed the motion of the bird at the waterfall. We all drew on the comfort which is given out by the major works of Mozart, which is as real and material as the warmth given by a glass of brandy, and I wondered, seeing its efficacy, what its nature might be. It is in part, no doubt, the work of the technical trick by which Mozart eliminates the idea of haste from life. His airs could not lag as they make their journey through the listener's attention; they are not the right shape for loitering. But it is as true that they never rush, they are never headlong or helter-skelter, they splash no mud, they raise no dust. It is, indeed, inadequate to call the means of creating such an effect a mere technical device. For it changes the content of the work in which it is used, it presents a vision of a world where man is no longer the harassed victim of time but accepts its discipline and establishes a harmony with it. This is not a little thing, for our struggle with time is one of the most distressing of our fundamental conflicts, it holds us back from the achievement and comprehension that should be the justification of our life. How heavily this struggle weighs on us may be judged from certain of our preferences. Whatever our belief in the supernatural may be, we all feel that Christ was something that St Paul was not; and it is impossible to imagine Christ hurrying, while it is impossible to imagine St Paul doing anything else.◇ ◇ ◇

At a point on the plains there was now heaped up a drift of dark cloud; and through this there ran a shaft of lightning. A storm was on us, and it was in alternate blackness and greenish crystal light that we began our journey to four of the monasteries of the Frushka Gora, a journey which was astonishing in the directness of its contact with the past. It was as if one should drive along the South Downs, turning off the main road and following by-roads in to the downlands at Sullington and Washington and Steyning, and should find buildings where persons involved in the tragedy of Richard II had but newly cast aside their garments in mourning, where the sound of their weeping was hardly stilled. It made for a strangeness which immediately caught the eye that all these monasteries, so far from Byzantium, are built in the Byzantine fashion, with the quarters for the monks or nuns and pilgrims built in a square round an open space with the church in the middle. Though some have been burned down and rebuilt in the style of the Austrian baroque, they keep to the original ground plan, and cannot be confused with anything of recent or Western inspiration.

The first monastery we visited had been rebuilt in Austrian fashion. It raised above its quadrangle roofs a cupola as ornate as a piece of white coral, dazzling now in the strange stormlight against an inky sky; and it lay among orchards, their tree-trunks ghostly with spray. It might have been in the Helenenthal, an hour from Vienna. But within we found that the Eastern idea was still in government, that a wall had been built before the altar to dam the flow of light, to store up a reservoir of darkness where mystery could engender its sacred power. It possessed some relics of a saint, a Herzegovinian soldier who had wandered hither and thither fighting against the Turk, first under a Serbian despot and then under a Hungarian king. The legend ran that the Turks took the town where he was buried and were terrified because rays of light proceeded from his grave, and went to their emir, who was overcome at finding who the dead man had been and gave his body to the monks of this monastery. For this emir was a renegade who had been taken prisoner by the Turks and had bought his life by renouncing his faith; and he was not only a Herzegovinian, he was actually kin to the dead man. The news of this wonder came to the saint's widow, who was a refugee in Germany, and she sought out this monastery, in defiance of the Turks, and became a hermit near by, till she died and was buried here, near to her husband.

This might have happened yesterday, indeed it might have happened today, for the monastery is in the care of White Russian nuns, wearing a melancholy head-dress of a close black cap fitting over a black veil that falls about the shoulders, and still preoccupied by the distress of their exile. It was hard to keep their misfortunes distinct in our minds from those of the founders of the monastery, and indeed others had failed to do so. Constantine halted by a grave in the quadrangle to tell me that it housed an abbess who had been stricken down during the seventeenth-century migration; and two young novices who were standing by, girls who had been born after their parents' flight from their fatherland and had been drawn here by an inborn Tsarist nostalgia, exclaimed in surprise. They had thought her one of their own community who had died on her way from Russia.

The black sky was pressing lower, the cloisters gleamed at us through an untimely dusk. Constantine thought that if we were to be storm-bound it had better be in a monastery where there was more to see, and we hurried back to the car under the first heavy pennies of rain. Thunder and lightning broke on us as we ran into Krushedol, another monastery which has been burned and given an Austrian exterior while keeping its ancient core. But this was older than the others. When the leader of the Slav forces at the battle of Kossovo, the Tsar Lazar, was killed on the field, the rags of his power were inherited by his kin, and there was one unhappy heir, named Stephen, whose fate was lamentable even for that age. His father, forced to seal a treaty by giving the Sultan Murad his daughter as a bride, sent his son to bear her company; but in time the Sultan fell into war with his wife's father and put out the young man's eyes lest he should take up arms in the fight. In his private darkness he reeled across the Balkan Peninsula, sometimes a captive dragged from prison to prison, then, released, back to his father's camp on the Danube, then away with his father again to wander in exile. His father died; his two brothers, one blinded like himself by the Sultan, engaged in fratricidal war; his mother also died, it is thought of poison; his blind brother fled and became a monk on Mount Athos; his victorious brother died. Though this dead usurper had named an heir, a party of the nobles took Stephen, and, spinning him round as in the game of blind-man's-buff, made him declare himself Despot of Serbia. The Serbians, seeing themselves threatened with civil war in the face of their Hungarian and Turkish enemies, rushed on him and sent him out of their land, bound and under guard. Again he stumbled about the Balkan Peninsula, sometimes pushed back into Serbia by his heartless supporters and beaten out again by his reluctant subjects, always preserving his gentle, patient fortitude. At one time he seemed to find a lasting refuge in Albania, where the great hero Skanderbeg took a great liking to him and gave him his own daughter, the Duchess Angelina, for wife. But the Turks came to Albania also, and the blind man was homeless again, and was in Italy when death took him. Then his widow and his two sons, now penniless, started to wander afresh, and Hungarian charity maintained them here. One of the sons became a priest, and he founded this monastery, and in time all three of them were laid in the same tomb before the altar. In the dark church, that blazed with light because of the profligate but mellow gilding on the iconostasis, we were shown the Duchess Angelina's narrow and elegant hand, black and mummified, loaded with the inalienable rings of her rank.

But there was other royalty here. Under a round red stone on the floor was buried King Milan Obrenovitch, the king who was so little of a success that he was forced to abdicate in 1889, who wandered almost as much as Stephen, but on more comfortable routes, from Belgrade to Vienna and Paris, harried not by the Turks without but by the Turk within. Nor was his grave all we saw of him at Krushedol. There is a memorial to him in the church wall, erected by the Emperor Franz Josef. "Why not?" said Constantine. "Milan was all for Austria, he governed our country as an Austrian dependency." Later, in the treasury, which was not in the church but in the monastery, a flash of lightning dispersed the unnatural dusk and showed us the contorted trees of the wind-flogged woods outside, and inside a medley of Byzantine church vestments, medieval chalices and crosses, ancient manuscripts, and the cups and saucers, prettily painted with pale flowers in the Slav fashion, the silver teapots and coffee-pots, the wine-glasses and decanters, of King Milan's last establishment. These had been sent here by the Emperor Franz Josef, to whom, by an act of testamentary whimsy, King Milan had left the entire contents of his home.

"It would be, quite simply, that he would hardly notice to whom he left them, so long as it was not to his wife, Natalia," said Constantine. "Is she buried here?" I asked. "No, not at all," said Constantine. The negative he used sounded delightful in this connexion. "She is not dead, she is living in Paris, very poor.* Only the other day the Government was obliged to prevent a German company

* Queen Natalia died in a convent in Paris in May 1941.—R.W.

671

from making a film about the Obrenovitches and she wrote a letter about it." "And she will never be buried here," said the Abbot, a grave person who had been a priest and had become a monk ten years ago, after the death of his beloved wife. "That is, unless she is granted the light before she dies, for she was converted to Roman Catholicism about thirty years ago. It was a strange thing to do, for our people had been kind to her, and had taken her part when her husband dealt wickedly with her."

In another room there was arranged all the furniture from King Milan's drawing-room; a salon of the eighties sat there in its stuffy and shiny richness, and from its walls there stared the portraits of the doomed family—King Milan, with the wide cat-grin of a tormented buffoon, the excessively, grossly beautiful Queen Natalia, their fat son Alexander, who was like his father in resembling a cat, though this time the cat had been doctored, and Queen Draga, who was so prosaic that even now, when we can recognize her expression as fear and know what she feared, her face remains completely uninteresting. "Our Mrs Simpson," said Constantine, pointing to her picture. "Yes! yes! Our Mrs Simpson," cried the Abbot, going into fits of laughter. There was also King Milan's bedroom, furnished in rosewood, and more portraits of these unhappy people, preserved in tragedy like flies in amber.

Before we went away I went into the treasury again to take a last look at the embroideries and caught sight of two photographs which showed Serb peasants and soldiers and priests walking through the snow, with expressions of extreme anguish, bringing the body of King Milan to his grave. "But how could they feel so passionately about Milan Obrenovitch?" I asked Constantine. "He had done ill by his country and ill in his personal life. I noticed that even the Abbot spoke of him as behaving wickedly." "It does not matter what Milan Obrenovitch was in himself," said Constantine. "He was our first-crowned king after the Turkish conquest. When we were free our power flamed like a torch in the hands of our Emperor Stephen Dushan, but afterwards it grew dim, and in the poor wretch who was the husband of the Duchess Angelina it guttered and went out. The dead torch was lit again by Karageorge, and it grew bright in the hand of his successor, Prince Michael Obrenovitch, and when Milan made himself King its light grew steady, though his was not the hand that was to bear it, and it was the same torch that our ancient dynasty of the Nemanyas had carried. So why should we care what else he had done? It was not Milan but their king whom these Serbs were following through the snow, it was the incarnation of Serbian power."

When the storm had lifted we drove out again on the plains, now lying under a purged and crystal air, in which all things were more than visible, in which each blade piercing the rich spring earth could be seen for miles in its green sharpness, in which the pools outside the villages carried not reflections but solid paintings of the blue sky and silver clouds. Then we turned back to the range of downs and entered it by a little valley, which presently ran into a cache of apple orchards, a lovely coomb as sweet as anything Devonshire or Normandy can show. Behind a white wall shielded by fruit trees and Judas trees we found a monastery enclosing an astonishing church, that had been built after the emigration had done its work on the migrated craftsmen's imagination; it was a fusion, lovely but misce-genic, of the Byzantine and the baroque styles, of fourteenth-century Eastern and seventeenth-century Western styles. While we gaped there came up to us a Russian monk, a young man who, like the nuns we had seen at the first monastery, must have been born after his parents had left Russia. He was beautiful, with the eyes seen only in Russians so far as I know, which look dangerous as naked lights carried on the stage, by reason of their extraordinary lambency. He told us with smiling remoteness that the Abbot was away; and we were disappointed, for the Abbot is a Pribitchevitch, one of a family that has been dominant in this Serb colony ever since the migration, and is the brother of a famous democratic politician who died in exile during the dictatorship of King Alexander. "That is a pity," said Constantine; "however, we can still show these English people what is interesting here." "But there is nothing interesting here," said the Russian monk, "we have only the body of a Serbian emperor." He spoke without insolence, his remark proceeded from a complete failure to form any sort of relationship with his surroundings, however hospitable they might have been, which is characteristic of a certain kind of White Russian émigré.

We said that we found that interesting enough; and he went with us into the exquisite mongrel church, and we found it glowing and beautiful within. There were two handsome girls on step-ladders cleaning the windows, and they clattered down and followed us, smiling in welcome and at the same time murmuring in piety, as we went towards the sarcophagus of the Emperor. The Russian monk lifted its lid and showed us the body under a square of tarnished cloth of silver, but would not uncover it for us. He shrugged his shoulders and said that it was only done on the Emperor's day; he would have seemed on a par with a girl in a milliner's shop refusing to take a hat out of the window had it not been quite plain that, while he was flagrantly frivolous, religious ecstasy was not only within the range of his experience, it was never very far from him. But the two girls behind us sighed deeply in their disappointment.

"This is Urosh, the son of Stephen Dushan," said Constantine; "he was a poor weakling, and lost all his father's empire in a few years." "Yet he is venerated," I said. "But certainly," said Constantine. "But do the people who venerate him know what he did?" I asked. "Do these girls, for instance, know that he destroyed the Serbian Empire and paved the way to Kossovo?" "Well, I would not say they could pass an examination in the facts," said Constantine, "but certainly they know that he was weak and he failed. That, however, is not of the smallest importance. He was of our ancient dynasty, he was a Nemanya, and the Nemanya were sacred. Not only were they the instruments of our national power, they have a religious significance to us. Some of them are described on their graves as 'saintemente né,' born in sanctity; and this Urosh, though he was quite simply killed by a usurper of his secular power, is called by our Church the martyr. This is not mere nationalist piety. It is due to the historical fact that the Nemanyas simultaneously enforced on us Serbs Christianity and unity. We were Christians before, of course, but we had not a living church of our own. Then this extraordinary family of little, little princelings from an obscure village below Montenegro on the Adriatic came and did in a few years as much as Rome has done for any state in centuries. The first Nemanya to rule Serbia, Stephen Nemanya, became a monk, when he abdicated in favour of his son Stephen, and is known as St Simeon, and he is a true saint: the oil from his grave at Studenitsa does many miracles; and one of his sons became our St Sava, and was a monk on Mount Athos, and left his monastery when his brother's throne seemed insecure and organized Serbia into such a close-knit fabric of church and state that, though the heirs of the throne were incompetent for sixty years afterwards, nothing could unravel it. But as well as a statesman Sava was a saint, and was a pilgrim and visited the monks of the Thebaid. And his brother, too, King Stephen II, he also was a saint. When he lay dying he sent for St Sava to make him a monk, but St Sava came too late; but God vouchsafed that he should be raised from the dead to take his vows as a monk and so his corpse stood up and was consecrated. I tell you no people could be expected to forget the identification between saint and king, between religion and nationalism, which was made by our early history." ◇ ◇ ◇

Vrdnik is larger than the other monasteries, which is natural, since its unique possessions attract many pilgrims; and because of the wealth drawn from these pilgrimages the large two-storied quadrangle is in good repair, handsomely whitewashed, and laid out like a garden with plum trees and Japanese quinces. The church is also different from the others. It seems to reject the Byzantine prescription that magic must be made in darkness. Direct light shines on the gilded iconostasis and on the multicoloured thrones, and shines back amber from the polished marble pavement. It can be so, for there is no need to manufacture magic here. That already exists in the coffin lying before the iconostasis, which contains the body of the Tsar Lazar who fell at Kossovo.

He lies in a robe of faded red and gold brocade. A dark cloth hides his head and the gap between it and his shoulders. His mummified brown hands, nearly black, are crossed above his loins, still wearing the bright rings of his rank. His dwindled feet have been thrust into modern stockings, and over them have been pulled soft medieval boots of blue silk interwoven with a gold thread. He is shrunken beyond belief; his hip-bones and his shoulders raise the brocade in sharp points. He is piteous as a knot of men standing at a street-corner in Jarrow or a Welsh mining town. Like them he means failure, the disappointment of hopes, the waste of powers. He means death also, but that is not so important. Who would resent death if it came when all hopes had been realized and all powers turned to use? There is an ideal point at which the fulfilment of life must pass into the acceptance of death. But defeat is defeat, and bitter; not only for the sake of pride, but because it blunts the sword of the will, which is the sole instrument man has been given to protect himself from the hostile universe and to impose on it his vision of redemption. When this man met defeat it was not only he whose will was frustrated, it was a whole people, a whole faith, a wide movement of the human spirit. This is told by the splendid rings on the Tsar Lazar's black and leathery hands; and the refinement of the pomp which presents him in his death, the beauty and gravity of the enfolding ritual, show the worth of what was destroyed with him. I put out a finger and stroked those hard dry hands, that had been nerveless for five hundred years. It is written here that the lot of man is pitiful, since the odds are against him, and he can command the success he deserves only if an infinite number of circumstances work in his favour; and existence shows no trace of such a bias.

In a dark and cramped treasury are some untidy ancient manuscripts, on which a Tauchnitz edition of *The Hound of the Baskervilles* has curiously intruded, and certain possessions of the Tsar Lazar: the icon on which he swore his nobles to loyalty before the battle, the beaker from which he drank, the model of one of his cities. There is no reason to doubt that any of these are genuine. The Turks let Lazar's widow take his corpse and all his private treasures, and in the course of time she placed them in the monastery of Ravanista, which he himself had founded, in Serbia, far south of Belgrade on the way to Nish. It was often attacked and damaged by the Turks, and the migrants of 1683 took away its relics and built this new monastery, which for this reason is often also called Ravanitsa, to house them. I went down on my knees to peer at the precious objects through the glass case of the cupboard. The icon was damaged but enormously beautiful: in the background was a soaring close-pressed assembly of saints, conceived by an imagination disciplined and formalized by experience of ceremonial. There was also a panel of velvet, once crimson, now maroon, which was embroidered in silver-gilt thread with words, many words, a prayer, a poem.

It was sewn by the Princess Euphemia, the widow of a Serbian prince killed by the Turks, who had found refuge at the court of the Tsar Lazar. After Lazar had fallen at Kossovo she went with his widow Militza to the monastery of Lyubostinya, where they both became nuns. She was an embroideress of great genius. Two of the most famous pieces of early embroidery in Europe are her work: the curtain for the sanctuary doors in the church of Hilandar, the Serbian monastery on Mount Athos, and a cloth for laying on the altar during Lent, now in the monastery of Putna in Roumania. In the silence of the monastery she worked a pall to cover the severed head silence of the monastery she worked a pall to cover the severed head of the Tsar Lazar, and on it she wrote him a letter with her needle.* ◇ ◇ ◇

*[The translation of her embroidered letter of more than 500 words, praising him and asking his help in the hereafter, is omitted here.]

Macedonia (South Serbia)

From ST GEORGE'S EVE: I

When I arrived at the apartment of Mehmed and Militsa* to go with
them on a tour round the country to see the various rites that are
carried on during St George's Eve, I found her receiving a call from
two ladies, and while Mehmed and Constantine and my husband
talked politics I listened to them discussing a friend of theirs who had
roused Skoplje's suspicions by going to Belgrade for a prolonged visit
without her husband. "I think indeed that this is just foolish talk,"
said Militsa. "Yelena has not left her husband for another man, she
is always a little discontented because her husband gives her no
freedom, and she wants a little time to be alone and enjoy the poetry
of life." "That may be so," said one of the ladies, "but if all she
wanted was a little time to be alone and enjoy the poetry of life, it
seems funny that she went all the way out to Mrs Popovitch's new
house a week before she left to borrow a copy of *Die Dame* that had
some pretty nightdresses in it." They soon left and we turned from
tea to rakia, and Militsa stood for a time discussing neo-Thomism
with my husband in an attitude she often adopts when engaged in
intellectual conversation. She stands by the tea-table with her old
wolf-hound some feet away, and a glass of rakia in her hand, and
every now and then she raises the glass and whips it down so that a
lash of liquid flies through the air, and the dog leaps forward and
swallows it in mid-air. "We must start," said Mehmed. "That is not
the philosophic air I breathe easily," said Militsa, "and religion is for
me not there at all. But I have never found it for me anywhere but
in Greece, in the days when God was not considered creator, when
He was allowed to be divine and free from the responsibility of the
universe." "*Whee!*" went the rakia. "Woof, woof!" went the dog.
"We must start," said Mehmed. "I will be ready in a minute," said

*[Friends the author had met here in Skoplje before. The wife, a gifted
linguist and Ph.D., was a true descendant of Byzantine Greeks ("She talks
with the brilliance of a firefly"); the husband, a Herzegovinian Moslem. Both
had been involved in the Bosnian nationalist movement.]

677

Militsa, and took the last drop of rakia herself. She looked at her husband and mine and nodded approvingly. "Alas for poor Yelena," she said, "her husband is very fat, he has always been too fat, and her lover in Belgrade is quite an old man."

At last in a cold grey evening we three* drove off to see St George at work. This was a more diverse spectacle than one would have supposed. St George, who is the very same that is the patron saint of England, is a mysterious and beneficent figure who is trusted to confer fertility for reasons that are now completely hidden. Pope Gelasius, as early as the fifth century, tactfully referred to him as one of those saints "whose names are justly reverenced among men, but whose actions are known only to God." Gibbon's description of him as a villainous Army contractor is nonsense; he was confusing him with a rascally bishop called George of Laodicea. The other story that he was a Roman officer martyred during the persecutions of Diocletian has, in the opinion of scholars, no better foundation. But they believe that he really existed, and that he was probably martyred about forty miles east of Constantinople some time during the third century. He was apparently a virtuous and heroic person who had some extra-ordinary adventure with a wild beast that made him the Christian equivalent of Perseus in the popular mind. Whatever this adventure was, it must have taken the form of a powerful intervention on behalf of life, for his legends represent him as raising the dead, saving cities from destroying armies, making planks burst into leaf, and causing milk instead of blood to run from the severed head of a martyr. He himself was three times put to death, being once cut in pieces, once buried deep in the earth, and once consumed by fire, and was three times brought back to life. In Macedonia he is said to cure barrenness of women and of lands, both by the Christians and the Moslems; for since he had three hundred years' start of Mohammed he was not to be dug out of the popular mind.

We saw some of his work as soon as we left the house. We had crossed the bridge and were driving along the embankment, and Militsa was saying, "In that house with the flowers in the balcony lives the girl who was Miss Yugoslavia some years ago, and it is a great misfortune for her, because to marry well one must be correct and not do such things as enter beauty contests, and she is quite a good girl, so now she is unmarried and very poor," when I saw that a stream of veiled women dressed in black was passing along the

*[The author's husband had had to await a telephone call.]

pavement beside the river. It was as if the string of a black necklace had broken and the beads were all rolling the same way. "Yes," said Mehmed, "always on St George's Eve they come along to this part of the embankment where these poplars are, and they stand and look down into the river." That is all they were doing: standing like flimsy black pillars and looking over the low stone wall at the rushing Vardar. It was the most attenuated rite I have ever seen, the most etiolated ceremony; it was within a hair's breadth of not happening at all. Of course, if one cannot show one's face, if one is swaddled by clothing till free movement is impossible, if negation is presented as one's guiding physical principle, this is the most one can do. The custom obviously bore some relation to the nature worship which is the basic religion of the peoples in this part, with its special preference for water. But it had none of the therapeutic properties of worship, it gave the worshippers none of the release that comes from expressing reverence by a vigorous movement or unusual action, nor did it give any sense of contact with magical forces. They were merely allowed to approach the idea of worship and apprehend it dimly, as they apprehend the outer world through their veils. "Why do they come to this particular part of the embankment?" I asked Mehmed, but he did not know. Yet I think he was fully acquainted with all the local superstitions held by male Moslems.

Soon we took to a bad road that lurched among the bare uplands at the feet of the mountains. It was as if one left the road in the valley that runs from Lewes to Newhaven and tried one's luck over the fields and downs. Beautiful children in fantastic dresses watched us staggering from side to side of the rutted track, courteous old men in white kilts shouted advice over bleak pastures. Someone was leaning against a stunted tree and piping. After two hours or so we came to a great farm that glimmered whitish through the twilight, among the leggy trunks of a young orchard, and Mehmed said, "This is where we are going to stay, though the owner does not yet know it." I felt shy at being an unannounced guest; I strolled nervously in the garden, dipping my nose to the huge flowers of the lilac bushes that were black in the twilight. Then a voice spoke from the house in beautiful English, English that would have been considered remarkably beautiful even if it had been an Englishman who had spoken it, and a handsome man with fair hair, square shoulders, and a narrow waist came out and welcomed me. He looked like a certain type of Russian officer, but his face was more distracted, being aware of all sorts of alternatives to the actions for which his body was so perfectly shaped. In the porch there stood his wife, a lovely girl in her middle twenties, and her mother, a still lovely woman with silver hair, who were talking to Militsa and Mehmed with that candid appreciation of their friends' charm which makes Slav life so agreeable.

The perfect note for a visit had been struck at once; but when our host heard that we had come to see the rites of St George practised in the neighbourhood he started up and said that we must go at once, for if we left the journey till full darkness it would be impossible to make the journey there and back before midnight. We got back into the car, and with him as our guide we bounced along a dirt-track till we came to a cross-roads with some hovels glimmering through the darkness. "It is here, the Tekiya," said our host. "Yes, this is the Bektashi village," said Mehmed, "I recognize it, I have been here before." I had not before shown any great curiosity as to what we were to see that night, for the reason that I had always found it a waste of time to try to imagine beforehand anything that Yugoslavia was going to offer me. But I knew that Tekiya was the Turkish word for a sanctuary and that the Bektashi were an order of dervishes, that is to say monks who exist to supply the element of mysticism which is lacking in Orthodox Islam. This particular order was founded by a native of Bukhara named Haji Bektash about six hundred years ago, and it was the special cult of the Janizaries, who spread it all over the Balkan Peninsula. It is said to preach an ecstatic pantheism, and to pronounce the elect free to follow their own inspirations regarding mortality. I stepped out of the car into the kind of twilight that is as dazzling as brilliant sunshine. The white houses glared through what was otherwise thick darkness, the last light shone like polished steel from pools in a road that could only be deduced. Towards us came some men in fezes, their teeth and the whites of their eyes flashing through the dusk. They greeted us with the easy and indifferent manners of the Moslem villager, always so much more like a city-dweller in his superficial contacts than his Slav neighbour, who is more profoundly hospitable and indomitably inquisitive, and they led us to a little house that looked like any other. It disturbed me, as I stumbled towards it through the palpitating dusk, and made travel seem a vain thing, that I could no more have deduced that it was a Moslem sanctuary by looking at it than I had been able to deduce Militsa and Mehmed by looking at Skoplje.

Within, it was a square room with a wooden vaulted ceiling,

imperfectly lit by a few candles set in iron brackets waist-high on the plastered walls. Our tremendous amazed shadows looked down on a tall black stone standing in the middle of the room, about seven feet high. There was a small flat stone laid across the top of it; it might have been wearing a mortar-board. A string was tied round it, and from this hung flimsy strips of cloth and beside it lay a collection box. Soon our massive, clear-cut, stolid shadows were brushed across by more delicate shades, and four veiled women were among us. Four times there was the fall of a coin in the collecting-box, four times a black body pressed itself against the black stone, four times black sleeves spread widely and arms stretched as far as possible round its cold girth. "Tonight if a woman wishes while she embraces this stone," one of the men explained to us, "and her fingers meet, then her wish shall be granted." "Is that really what they believe?" I asked, and Mehmed and our host confirmed it. Yet it was quite obvious that that was not what the women believed. They were quite unperturbed when their fingers failed to meet, and indeed I do not think I have seen half a dozen women in my life with arms long enough to make the circuit of this stone. The men's mistake was only more evidence of the pitiful furtiveness of the Moslem woman's life, which necessarily defends secrets almost unthreatened by the curiosity of the male.

The women's belief, it could be seen by watching them, lay in the degree of effort they put into the embrace; they must put all their strength, all their passion, into stretching as far as possible, and take to themselves all they could of the stone. Then they must give it their extreme of homage, by raising their veils to bare their lips and kissing it in adoration that makes no reserves. It struck on the mind like a chord and its resolution, this gesture of ultimate greed followed by the gesture of ultimate charity and abnegation. Each woman then receded, fluttering backwards and bringing her whispered prayer to an end by drawing her finger-tips down her face and bosom. They drew tremulously together and then our crasser shadows were along the walls, though none of us actually saw them go. It might be thought that these veiled women who had come to seek from a stone the power to perform a universal animal function for the benefit of those who treated them without honour, who were so repressed that they had to dilute to as near to nothingness as might be even such a negative gesture as leaving a room, would be undifferentiated female stuff, mere specimens of mother ooze. Yet these four had actually disclosed their nature to the room and its shadows, and each of these natures was highly individual; from each pair of sleeves had issued a pair of hands that was unique as souls are. One pair was ageing and had come near to losing hope; one pair was young but grasped the stone desperately, as if in agony lest hope might go; one pair grasped the stone as desperately but with an agony that would last five mintes, or even less, if she saw something to make her laugh; and one pair made the gesture with conscientious exactitude and no urgency, and would, I think, have been happier joining the Orthodox Moslems of Skoplje in their unsubstantial rite down by the river than in this Bektashi traffic with mystery.

As we went out three other veiled women slipped past us into the holy room. They would come all night on this mission, from all villages and towns where the Bektashi order had its adherents, within an orbit of many miles. We drove on through the pulsing and tumbled darkness dispensed by a sky where thick clouds rode under strong star-light. "Now we are going to the tomb of St George," said Militsa. "There too are many women who want children. Tell me, what did you wish for?" For we had both kissed the stone. The Moslems had suggested it with a courtesy which meant, I think, that because this was a woman's rite they did not feel it to be truly sacred. "For myself," said Militsa, "I wished for something really terribly drastic politically." I would not have given a penny for Mr Stoyadinovitch's* life if the stone was functioning according to repute.

On a little hillside we saw a glimmer of murky brightness and headed for it. We stepped out into a patch of Derby Day, and saw what one might see on Epsom Downs on the eve of the race, when the gipsies are settling in. On a grassy common people were sitting about, eating and drinking and talking as if there had not yet been established in their minds the convention that associates night with sleep. If one shut one's eyes the hubble-bubble sounded astonished, as if an elementary form of consciousness were expressing its amazement that it should not be still unconscious. A gipsy band thrummed and snorted; lemonade sellers cried their livid yellow ware; the gallery of a house overlooking the common was filled with white light, and many heads and shoulders showed black against it. We took a path up the hillside to a little chapel and joined the crowd that pressed into it. It was a new little chapel, not interesting. At first nothing

*[Then Yugoslav Premier under King Peter.]

took my eye save a number of very vividly coloured woollen stockings, knitted in elaborate abstract patterns, which were hanging on the icons and on a rope before the altar. But the crowd bore me forward and I saw in the centre of the floor a cross, and about it a thickening of human stuff. "The cross is over the tomb of St George," whispered Militsa, "and look, oh, look! It is not to be believed! This is the Greek rite of incubation, this is how the Greeks lay all night on the altar of Apollo, so that they could dream themselves into the minds of the gods and know their futures."

Round the cross lay a heap of women in ritual trance, their eyes closed, their breasts rising and falling in the long rhythm of sleep. They lay head to heel, athwart and alongside, one with a shoulder on another's knee, another with a foot in someone's face, tangled and still like a knot of snakes under a stone in winter-time. It seemed to me their sleep was real. Their slow breathing, the lumpiness of their bodies, the anguished, concentrated sealing of their eyes by their lids made me myself feel drowsy. I yawned as I looked down on the face of one woman who had devoted herself to sleep, who had dedicated herself to sleep, who had dropped herself into the depths of sleep as a stone might be dropped down a well. She had pillowed her head on her arm; and on the sleeve of her sheepskin jacket beside her roughened brow there was embroidered an arch and a tree, the rustic descendant of a delicate Persian design. We were among the shards of a civilization, the withered husks of a culture. How had this rite contracted! The Greeks had desired to know the future, to acquaint themselves with the majestic minds of the gods. These women's demand on the future was limited to a period of nine months, and the aid they sought lay in a being so remote as to be characterless save for the murmured rumour of beneficence. Nevertheless the rite was splendid even in its ruin. The life that had filled these women was of the wrong sort and did not engender new life, therefore they had poured it forth, they had emptied themselves utterly, and they had lain themselves down in a holy place to be filled again with another sort of life, so strong that it could reproduce itself. This was an act of faith, very commendable in people who had so little reason to feel faith, who had received so little assurance that existence was worthy of continuance.

As we left the chapel we saw an old peasant woman with a group of friends round her, who held out her hands to two younger women and kissed them on both cheeks. "Take a look at her," said our host, "it was she who saw in a dream that there was a coffin buried on this hillside, and that the body inside it was St George." We tried to see her face through the darkness, but the night was too thick, and we could not learn whether she bore the stigmata of the visionary or of the simpleton. As we passed the apse of the chapel on our way downhill a man went by carrying an electric torch, and its beam showed us that one of the windows was barred with strands of wool, wound from side to side and attached to pieces of wood and metal that had been driven into the wall. "That they do too, the women who want children," said our host; "it must be wool they have spun themselves." On the common a large part of the crowd was gathered round some men and women sitting in a ditch who were having a quarrel, which was curiously pedantic in tone, although they had to shout to drown the gipsy bands and the venders. They put their cases in long deliberate speeches, which the others then criticized, often with a peevish joy in their own phrases familiar to those who have visited Oxford. Suddenly one of the women in the party took off her sheepskin jacket, threw it on the ground, flung herself down on it, and began to weep; and the scene lost its intensity and broke into sympathetic movements round her sobbing body. <> <> <>

ST GEORGE'S EVE: II

Because we were going to see a ceremony that took place on a stone at Ovche Polye, that is to say the Sheep's Field, an upland plateau some miles away, we got up at half-past five and set off in a grey morning. A cold wind moved about the hillside, marbling the fields of young wheat; and along the lanes peasants on pack-horses, nodding with drowsiness, jogged back from the chapel of St George's tomb, their cloaks about them. We took to the good road that runs south beside the Vardar down a gorge to Veles, under steep grassy hillsides splashed here and there with fields of deep-blue flowers and thickets of wild roses. As we got nearer the town, we saw that there were people encamped on the brow of each hill, eating and drinking and confronting the morning. Men stood up and drank wine out of bottles, looking at the whiteness above the mountain-tops.

"How beautiful are these rites," said Militsa, "that make people adore the common thing, that say to all, 'You shall have the fresh eye of the poet, you shall never take beauty for granted'!" "Yes." said

Mehmed, "I am down here in an automobile, because I am a lazy fellow, but I am up there with them in spirit, for I know what the morning means. You know, I should be dead. I should have died twenty-three years ago in prison. For on June the twenty-eighth, 1914, I was walking in Vienna with my cousin, who was, like me, a Herzegovinian nationalist, and we came into the Ring, and we saw that everybody was very excited, and we heard something about Serbs and the heir to the throne being killed. We thought it was our Serbian Crown Prince who had been killed, so we were very sad, and we sat down in a café and had a drink. Then a news-boy came by and I bought a paper, and I saw that it was Franz Ferdinand who had been killed by a Serb, and I got up and said, 'Come, we must escape to Serbia, for now the end of all has come. Let us hurry for the train.' But he would not come with me, because he knew how awful the war was going to be and he did not want to admit that it was bound to happen. So I argued with him till I pulled out my watch and saw that I was going to miss the train, so I took to my heels and just caught it. My cousin was arrested that night, and so would I have been if I had stayed; and my cousin died in prison, and I do not think that the Austrians would have been very careful to keep me alive. When I think of that, I feel what those people up there are feeling. Ouf! The day, just as a day, is good."

As we drew towards Veles we passed a gipsy family trudging homewards, the young daughter in immense balloon trousers of bright pink satin; a primitive cart with some people dressed in black and white, profiline and impressive as Egyptians, from a far village, probably in the Bitolj district; a cart of more modern fashion driven by a plump and handsome young woman in Western clothes, who, on seeing Militsa, threw down her reins and shouted for us to stop. She was a Serbian who had been coached by Militsa in Latin for her science preliminary in Belgrade some years before, had later married a Macedonian politician, and now ran a chemist's shop in a hill town above Veles.

"Why did you not tell me you were coming?" she reproached them. "I am going to the *Slava* of a friend who lives on the other side of Skoplje, but heaven knows I would have liked far better to stay at home and entertain you. For today I take a holiday, and indeed I have a right to it. I am always on my feet from morning till night before St George's Day." "Why is that?" asked Militsa. "Oh, all these women who go to the monasteries to ask for children buy powder and rouge and lipstick to get themselves up for the outing," said the chemist, "they come in all day. But where are you going?" "We are going to the stone in the Sheep's Field," said Militsa. "Oh, you will like that, if you are not too late," said the chemist, "but I think you will be late if you do not hurry. It is a very interesting rite, and I think there is something in it, to judge from my own case. I went there two years ago, because it was nearly five years since Marko and I had been married and we had no children, and I did the easiest thing you can do there, which is to climb up on to the stone and throw a jar down on the ground to break it. Three times I threw down my jar, and it would not break, and still I have no children. I will not keep you any longer, for all the people will be gone unless you make haste."

The road then mounted, we saw in the distance Veles lying like a mosaic, cracked across by the gorge of the Vardar, and we left the road for a hillside track that climbed a pass between two summits black with people saluting the morning, and took us into the Sheep's Field. Here we entered quite a new kind of landscape. It is a wide sea of pastures and arable land, rising and falling in gentle waves within a haven of blue-grey mountains. Under a grey sky this place would be featureless, in a Macedonian summer it must be a hardly visible trough of heat. But this was spring, and the morning was pearly, there was a mild wind and soft sunshine, and all forms and colours in the scene were revealed in their essence. The earth on this upland plain is a delicate red, not so crimson as in the lowlands. Young wheat never looks so green as when it grows from such soil, and where it carries no crop it is transparent and nacreous, because of the powdered limestone which sprays it with the insubstantial conspicuousness of a comet's tail. Of the surrounding hills one stood alone, magnificent in sharp austerity of cliff and pyramid; it is called "the witness of God." As the sun rose higher there was manifest in the valley a light that was like Greek light, a steady radiance which stood like a divine person between the earth and the sky, and was the most important content of the horizon, more important than anything on the ground.

The road we followed became a casual assembly of ruts that persisted across the Field for something like ten miles. We saw, near and far, a few bleak white villages, but we touched none of them, save where we crossed a spindly railway by the side of two preposterously large buildings, one a gendarmerie, the other a combined station and post-office. The Sheep's Field was the subject of an unfortunate experiment in land settlement which was among the early mistakes of the new Yugoslav state after the war. It planted some unhappy families from the North on this highly unsuitable site without the necessary equipment and governed them ill, being entirely inexperienced in the arts and sciences of colonization. On the other side of this railway line we began to come on groups of peasants, the women glorious even from far off because of the soft blaze of their multi-coloured aprons. All were walking slowly, and though they looked quite good-humoured it was obvious that they were very tired. Some carts passed us too, and in these people were lying fast asleep. On the sheepskin jacket of one sleeping woman I saw, as we bumped slowly by, the same Persian pattern I had noted on the sleeve of the woman in trance on the tomb of St George.

It became apparent that we were approaching some focal point, which was not a village. The track was running along the crest of one of the land-waves, and though this was not very high it gave us an advantage over the countryside for several miles. We could see a number of people, perhaps twenty in all, who were travelling in every direction away from some spot on the next crest, a spot which was still not to be discovered by the eye. Some of these people were walking, some were in carts, some of them rode on pack-horses; and there passed close by us a party of dark slender young horsemen, galloping over the pastures on better mounts than I had yet seen in Macedonia, with a gay confidence and a legendary quality that showed them to be the elegants of some isolated and archaic community. "But they are all going away!" exclaimed Militsa. Her husband called out to one of the horsemen, "Are we right for the stone, for the Cowherd's Rock, and are we too late?" The young man reined up his horse with a flourish and trotted towards us, making a courteous gesture with a hand gloved in purple. In a flutelike voice, sweeter than is usual among Europeans, he answered, "Yes, go on, you will see it in a minute or two; you cannot be mistaken, for it is the only stone on the Sheep's Field, and there are still some people there."

Our car left the track and struggled up a stretch of pasture till it could go no further. When we got out we were so near the rock that we could see its colour. It was a flat-topped rock, uneven in shape, rising to something like six feet above the ground, and it was red-brown and gleaming, for it was entirely covered with the blood of the beasts that had been sacrificed on it during the night. A dozen men were sitting or lying at the foot of the rock, most of them wearing the fez; and one man was very carefully laying a little child on a rug not far away. The grass we walked on from the car was trodden and muddied and littered with paper, and as we came nearer the rock we had to pick our way among a number of bleeding cocks' heads. The spectacle was extremely disgusting. The colour of spilt blood is not properly a colour, it is in itself discoloured, it is a visible display of putrescence. In every crevice of the red-brown rock there had been stuck wax candles, which now hung down in a limp fringe of greasy yellow tails, smeared with blood. Strands of wool, some of them dyed red or pink, had been wound round the rock and were now daubed with this grease and blood. A great many jars had been thrown down from the rock and lay in shards among the cocks' heads on the trodden grass. Though there was nothing fæcal to be seen, the effect was of an ill-kept earth closet.

It would have been pleasant to turn round and run back to the car and drive away as quickly as possible, but the place had enormous authority. It was the body of our death, it was the seed of the sin that is in us, it was the forge where the sword was wrought that shall slay us. When it had at last been made visible before the eyes as it is —for we are all brought up among disguised presentations of it—it would have been foolish not to stay for a little while and contemplate it. I noticed that the man who had been settling the child on the rug was now walking round the rock with a black lamb struggling in his arms. He was a young gipsy, of the kind called Gunpowder gipsies, because they used to collect saltpetre for the Turkish Army, who are famous for their beauty, their cleanliness, their fine clothes. This young man had the features and bearing of an Indian prince, and a dark golden skin which was dull as if it had been powdered yet exhaled a soft light. His fine linen shirt was snow-white under his close-fitting jacket, his elegant breeches ended in soft leather boots, high to the knee, and he wore a round cap of fine fur which made it probable that his name was Camaralzaman. He made the circle three times and stopped, then bent and kissed the greasy blood-stained rock. Then he lifted up the lamb, and a man standing on the rock took it from him. It looked to me as if this man held the lamb in a grip that anæsthetized it, for it did not struggle any more and lay still at his feet without making a sound or a movement.

Now the gipsy fetched the child from the rug and brought it to the rock. It was a little girl of eighteen months or so, dressed in very clean white clothes. Her white bonnet was embroidered in designs of the Byzantine tradition in deep brown thread, and was tied with a satin bow of a particularly plangent sky-blue. Her father handed her up to another man who was standing on the rock, and then climbed up himself and set her down tenderly on as clean a place as he could find for her among the filth. Now the man who was holding the lamb took it to the edge of the rock and drew a knife across its throat. A jet of blood spurted out and fell red and shining on the browner blood that had been shed before. The gipsy had caught some on his fingers, and with this he made a circle on the child's forehead. Then he got down again and went round the rock another three times, carrying another black lamb. "He is doing this," a bearded Moslem standing by explained, "because his wife got this child by coming here and giving a lamb, and all children that are got from the rock must be brought back and marked with the sign of the rock." The gipsy kissed the rock again and handed up the lamb, and climbed to the sacrificial platform, and again the sacrifice was offered; but this time he not only marked the child with the circle but caught some of the blood in a little glass bottle. Then he carried her back to the rug, and the man with the knife laid the carcasses of the lambs, which were still faintly smoking at the throat, on the grass, among the shards and the cocks' heads. Under the opening glory of the morning the stench from the rock mounted more strongly and became sickening.

The man with the knife and his friends gathered round us and told us of the virtue of the place. Many women had got children by giving cocks and lambs to the rock. One woman who had come all the way from Prilep had had a child after she had lived in barren marriage for fifteen years. But it was foolish to doubt the efficacy of making sacrifices to the rock, for people would not go on doing it if it were not efficacious, and they had done it for a very long time, for hundreds of years. They should, of course, have said thousands. Their proof, which should have been valid if man were a reasonable animal, was therefore stronger than they supposed. The men who told us these things were good animals, with bright eyes and long limbs and good bones. They were also intelligent. Their remarks on the stone were based on insufficient information, but were logical enough, and when they went on to talk of matters less mysterious than fertility, such as their experiences in the last war, they showed considerable good sense and powers of observation. One spoke a little English, another spoke fluent French; two or three seemed to follow skilled trades. But what they were doing at the rock was abominable.

All I had seen the night before was not discreditable to humanity. I had not found anything being done which was likely to give children to women who were barren for physiological reasons; but I had seen ritual actions that were likely to evoke the power of love, which is not irrelevant to these matters. When the Moslem women in the Tekiya put out their arms to embrace the black stone and dropped their heads to kiss it, they made a gesture of the same nature, though not so absolute, as that which men and women make when they bend down to kiss the cloth which lies instead of Christ on the holy table at Easter. Such a gesture is an imitation by the body of the gesture made by the soul in loving. It says, "I will pour myself in devotion to you, I will empty myself without hoping for return, and I can do this serenely, for I know that as I empty I shall be filled again." Human beings cannot remind themselves too often that they are capable of performing this miracle, the existence of which cannot be proved by logic.

The women who lay in ritual sleep on the tomb of St George were working as fitly as the women in the Tekiya for the health of their souls. We prune our minds to fit them into the garden of ordinary life. We exclude from our consciousness all sorts of knowledge that we have acquired because it might distract us from the problems we must solve if we are to go on living, and it might even make us doubt whether it is prudent to live. But sometimes it is necessary for us to know where we are in eternity as well as in time, and we must lift this ban. Then we must let our full knowledge invade our minds, and let our memories of birth crawl like serpents from their cave and our foreknowledge of death spread its wide shadow. There is nothing shameful for women whose senses have been sharpened by the grief of barrenness to lie down on the tomb of one whose life was visible marvel and explore the invisible marvels of their own nature. Their ritual sleep was wholesome as common sleep.

But the rite of the Sheep's Field was purely shameful. It was a huge and dirty lie. There is a possibility that barrenness due to the mind could be aided by a rite that evoked love and broke down peevish desires to be separate and alone, or that animated a fatigued nature by refreshment from its hidden sources. But this could do nothing that it promised. Women do not get children by adding to the normal act of copulation the slaughter of a lamb, the breaking of a jar, the decapitation of a cock, the stretching of wool through blood and grease. If there was a woman whose womb could be unsealed by witnessing a petty and pointless act of violence, by seeing a jet of blood fall from a lamb's throat on a rock wet with stale and stinking blood, her fertility would be the reverse of motherhood, she would have children for the purpose of hating them.

The rite made its false claims not out of delusion: it was a conscious cheat. Those who had invented it and maintained it through the ages were actuated by a beastly retrogression, they wanted again to enjoy the dawn of nastiness as it had first broken over their infant minds. They wanted to put their hands on something weaker than themselves and prod its mechanism to funny tricks by the use of pain, to smash what was whole, to puddle in the warm stickiness of their own secretions. Hence the slaughter of the lambs and the cocks, the breaking of jars, the mess of blood and grease. But the intelligence of man is sound enough to have noticed that if the fully grown try to go back to the infantile they cannot succeed, but must go on to imbecility and mania. Therefore those who wish to indulge in this make the huge pretension for it that it is a secret way of achieving what is good, and that there is a mysterious process at work in the world which has no relation to causality. This process is a penny-in-the-slot machine of idiot character. If one drops in a piece of suffering, a blessing pops out at once. If one squares death by offering him a sacrifice, one will be allowed some share in life for which one has hungered. Thus those who had a letch for violence could gratify it and at the same time gain authority over those who loved peace and life. It could be seen that the slaughterer of the lamb was very well pleased with this importance, and some of the Moslems round the rock smugly hastened to tell us that they had performed his office some time during the night. It was disgusting to think that they enjoyed any prestige, for though they were performing an action that was thousands of years old and sanctified by custom, there was about them a horrid air of whimsicality, of caprice, of instability. For all their pretensions they were doing what was not necessary. They had achieved unsurpassably what Monsieur André Gide licks his lips over, l'acte gratuit. This is the very converse of goodness, which must be stable, since it is a response to the fundamental needs of mankind, which themselves are stable.

I knew this rock well. I had lived under the shadow of it all my life. All our Western thought is founded on this repulsive pretence that pain is the proper price of any good thing. Here it could be seen how the meaning of the Crucifixion had been hidden from us, though it was written clear. A supremely good man was born on earth, a man who was without cruelty, who could have taught mankind to live in perpetual happiness; and because we are infatuated with this idea of sacrifice, of shedding innocent blood to secure innocent advantages, we found nothing better to do with this passport to deliverance than destroy him. There is that in the universe, half inside and half outside our minds, which is wholly adorable; and this it was that men killed when they crucified Jesus Christ. Our shame would be absolute, were it not that the crime we intended cannot in fact be committed. It is not possible to kill goodness. There is always more of it, it does not take flight from our accursed earth, it perpetually asks us to take what we need from it.

Of that lesson we had profited hardly at all, because resourcefulness rises from the rock like the stench of its blood. The cruel spirit which informed it saved itself by a ruse, a theological ruse. So successful has this ruse been that the rock disgusted me with the added loathsomeness of familiarity, as the drunkenness of a man known to be a habitual alcoholic is more offensive than the accidental excess of a temperate man. Its rite, under various disguises, had been recommended to me since my infancy by various religious bodies, by Roman Catholicism, by Anglicanism, by Methodism, by the Salvation Army. Since its earliest days Christianity has been compelled to seem its opposite. This stone, the knife, the filth, the blood, is what many people desire beyond anything else, and they fight to obtain it. There was an enemy of love and Christ called Saul of Tarsus who could not abide this demonstration by the cross that man was vile and cruelty the essence of his vileness, and for that reason persecuted Christians till his honesty could not tolerate his denial of the adorability of goodness and showed it to him under the seeming of a bright light. But the belief of his heart was in force and in pain, and his mind, which was very Jewish in its refusal to accept defeat, tinkered incessantly with the gospel till it found a way of making it appear as if cruelty was the way of salvation. He developed a theory of the Atonement which was pure nonsense yet had the power to convince, for it was spoken quickly in tones of genius to excited people who listened trustfully, knowing the innocence of Christ and assuming that everything said in his name was innocent also, and being tainted, as all human beings are, with the same love of blood as the speaker. This monstrous theory supposes that God was angry with man for his sins and that He wanted to punish him for these, not in any way that might lead to his reformation, but simply by inflicting pain on him; and that He allowed Christ to suffer this pain instead of man and thereafter was willing on certain terms to treat man as if he had not committed these sins. This theory flouts reason at all points, for it is not possible that a just God should forgive people who are wicked because another person who was good endured agony by being nailed to a cross.

There was a gap in the theory which could never be bridged, but those who loved cruelty tried from then on to bridge it. There were many lesser ones of this sort and one great one, Augustine, so curiously called a saint. Genius was his, and warm blood, but his heart was polluted like the rock. He loved love with the hopeless infatuation of one who, like King Lear, cannot love. His mother and he were like dam and cub in the strength of their natural relationship, but his appetite for nastiness made him sully it. Throughout their lives they achieved from time to time an extreme sweetness, but the putrescence gained, and at her death he felt an exaltation as mean as anything recorded in literature, because she died in Italy, far from her African home, and therefore could not be buried, as she had desired, beside her beloved husband. His relationship with God covered as wide a range. He wanted a supreme being sterilized of all that his genius recognized as foul, but he did not want him to be positively good. He hated all the milder aspects of virtue, he despised the spirit that lets all things flower according to their being, for he liked too well to draw the knife across the lamb's throat. In his desire to establish cruelty in a part of holiness he tried to find a logical basis for the abominable doctrine of St Paul, and he adopted a theory that the Devil had acquired a rightful power over man because of his sins, and lost it because he forfeited all rights by cruci-fying Christ, who was sinless. This went far to proving the universe to be as nonsensical as the devotees of the rock wished it to be. It presents us with a Devil who was apparently to a certain degree respectable, at least respectable enough to be allowed by God to exer-cise his legal rights in the universe, until he killed Christ. This robs the wickedness of man of its ultimate importance. His sins were evidently not so bad, just what you might expect from the subjects of a disorderly native prince. It was perhaps that which recom-mended the theory to Augustine, who knew he was wicked.

It was certainly that which recommended Augustine's theory to Martin Luther, who was not even like the rock, who was the rock, with the sullied grass, the cocks' heads, the grease, the stinking blood. He was the ugliest of the great, a hog magnified and with speech. His only virtue was the virtue of the wild boar; he was courageous. But all other merits he lacked, and strove to muddy life into a sty with his ill opinion of it. He howled against man's gift of reason, and in one of his sermons he cried out to his hearers to throw shit in her face, because she was the Devil's whore, rotten with itch and leprosy, who ought to be kept in the privy. He hated reason for a cause: because it exposed the idiocy of Augustine's theory of Atonement which was dear to him in its bloody violence, which was dear to him because it substituted joy in murder for remorse at the murder of goodness. His honesty blurted out that there was no sense whatsoever in the idea of God's acceptance of Christ's death as a sacrifice for man, but all the same he smacked his lips over it, it was good, it was gorgeous, it was eternal life. Because of him Protestantism has bleated ever since of the blood of the lamb, though not more loudly than Roman Catholicism.

So there has been daily won a victory for evil, since so many of the pious give divine honours to the cruelty which Christ came to earth to expose. If God were angry with man and wanted to punish him, and then let him go scot-free because he derived such pleasure from the sufferings of Christ, then the men who inflicted these sufferings must be the instruments of our salvation, the procurers of God's pleasures; they are at least as high as the angels. The grinning and consequential man standing on the rock with a stained knife in his grubby hand is made a personage necessary to the spiritual world; and because cruelty was built into us in our mothers' wombs we are glad of this, while at the same time everything in us that approves of kindness and can love knows that it is an obscene lie. So it has happened that all people who have not been perverted by the West into caring for nothing but machine-made articles (among which a Church designed to be primarily a social organization can fairly be classed) have found Christianity a torturing irritation, since it offers both the good and the evil in us the most supreme satisfaction imaginable and threatens them with the most final frustration. We are continually told to range ourselves with both the crucified and the crucifiers, with innocence and guilt, with kind love and cruel hate. Our breasts echo for ever with the cries "In murdering goodness we sinned" and "By murdering goodness we were saved." "The lamb is innocent and must not be killed," "The dead lamb brings us salvation," so we live in chaos. This state is the less likely to be relieved because those who defend the rock are too cunning to commit their case to terms that could be grasped and disputed. Though the doctrine of the Atonement profoundly affects most public and private devotions, it has never yet been defined in any creed or by any general Council of the Churches.

Nearly all writers dip their pens in ink-wells tainted with this beastliness. Shakespeare was obsessed by it. He was fully aware of the horror of this rock, but he yielded to its authority. He believed that the rite was in accord with reality, which he thought to be perverse in character. He recognized the adorability of goodness, in its simplicity and in its finer shades, as in worsted kingliness or a magician's age. But there filters into his work from the depths of his nature a nostalgia for infantile nastiness, a love of groping for trout in the peculiar rivers of the body, a letch for cruelty which hardly took pleasure in it, but longed sickly for consummation with the disgusting and destructive but just moment, as martyrs long for their doom. He who perfectly understood the nature of love, who knew that "love is not love which alters when it alteration finds, or bends with the remover to remove," felt under an obligation to castrate it by smearing the sexual function which is the means of bringing together most lovers in the world, be they husbands and wives or parents and children. His respect for the rock forced him to write *King Lear* and take up all lambs of the herd one by one and draw his knife across their throats. All kinds of love are in that play presented as worthless: the love of parent for child, of child for parent, of married people and illicit lovers, all impotent or bestial. But at the end the part of Shakespeare that was a grown man cries out that there is no health in the world save through love, that without it life is madness and death. It is not to the credit of mankind that the supreme work of art produced by Western civilization should do nothing more than embody obsession with this rock and revolt against it. Since we have travelled thus far from the speechless and thoughtless roots of our stock we should have travelled further. There must be something vile in us to make us linger, age after age, in this insanitary spot.

But some were not with us at the rock, but with the sunlight which the stench only so faintly disturbed, which shone inviolate

695

above the mountains. That is the special value of Mozart. It is not that he was kind. When he wanted a lamb for food it had to die. But in all his music there is no phrase which consented to anything so lacking in precision as this ritual slaughter, so irrelevant to its professed purpose as this assault on infertility, nor does he ever concur in the belief that the disagreeable is somehow of magical efficacy. He believes that evil works nothing but mischief; otherwise it would not be evil. "Psst! Psst!" says Leporello, beckoning the masked strangers in the garden, and bidding them to a ball; but since wickedness is the host it is no ball but an occasion for rape and bloodshed. After Don Juan is dead the characters of the play who are good, be it in solemnity or in lightness, gather together in a nightingale burst of song, because the departure of cruelty allows their goodness to act as it must according to its own sweet process. The same precision, the same refusal to be humbugged by the hypocritical claims of cruelty, account for the value of Jane Austen's work, which is so much greater than can be accounted for by its apparent content. But suavity of style is not the secret, for William Blake is rough. His rejection of the rock took another form, he searched his mind for belief in its fraud like a terrified woman feeling her breast for a cancer, he gave himself up to prophetic fury that his mind might find its way back to the undefiled sources of its knowledge of goodness. Here on the Sheep's Field it could be seen where the cleavage lies that can be apprehended to run through art and life: on one side are the people who are accomplices of the rock and on the other those who are its enemy. It appeared also where the cleavage lay in our human nature which makes us broken and futile. A part of us is enamoured of the rock and tells us that we should not reject it, that it is solemn and mystical and only the shallow deny the value of sacrifice. Because here a perfect myth had been found for a fundamental but foul disposition of the mind, we were all on an equality with the haggard and grimy peasant, his neckerchief loose about a goitre, who now slouched to the rock, the very man to attend a nocturnal rite late the next morning, and held up a twitching lamb to the fezed executioner, who was scrambling consequentially to the squalid summit.*

*[This discussion is continued in "The Plain of Kossovo II" in Old Serbia, after an interlude at Kossovo.]

696

Old Serbia

THE PLAIN OF KOSSOVO I

Our road from Skoplje to the Kossovo Polye, the Field of the Black-birds, took us towards grey hills patterned with shadows blue as English bluebells by a valley that had the worn look, the ageing air that comes on the southern landscape as soon as the fruit blossom has passed. Soon Dragutin* made us get out because we had come to a famous well, and we found sitting by the waters a couple of old Albanian Moslems, paupers in rags and broken sandals, who were quietly merry as the morning. "Good day to you," said Constantine. What are you doing here?" It was a natural question, for this was far between villages, and they did not look to be persons of independent means. "I am doing nothing," said the older of the two. "What, nothing?" "Yes, nothing," he said, his grin gashing his beard widely. He had received moral instruction somewhere, he had learned enough about the obligation of honest toil to find a conscious joy in idleness. "Shame on you!" mocked Constantine. "And your friend?" "He has come to help me!" said the Albanian; and over our glasses of stinging water, risen virile from mountainy depths, we jeered at industry.

But back in the car Constantine slumped. It was as if he were a very sick man, for he was sleepy, fretful, inferior to himself, and quarrelsome. He could put nothing in a way that was not an affront. Now he said, "We will stop at Grachanitsa, the church I told you of on the edge of Kossovo Plain, but I do not think you will understand it, because it is very personal to us Serbs, and that is something you foreigners can never grasp. It is too difficult for you, we are too rough and too deep for your smoothness and your shallowness. That is why most foreign books about us are insolently wrong. In my department I see all books about us that are published abroad, because I must censor them, and usually I am astonished by their insolence, which for all the pretences made by Western Europe and America to give

*[Their local chauffeur, from Skoplje: "a handsome and passionate young man who had never been denied anything in his life."]

697

our peoples culture is nothing more than the insolence of a nasty peasant who has learned some trick that lifts him up above the other peasants, who lends them money at usury and then lifts his chin at their misery and says, 'Peuh! What a stink!' but who is still ignorant like the worst of peasants. Did you read John Gunther's *Inside Europe*? Well, was it not a disgusting, a stupid book! How glad I was to forbid the sale of this imbecile book!"

"But it was not a bad book," I objected. "It was altogether bad," said Constantine, "it was ill-informed and what he did not know he could not guess." "Yes, I know some of it was not as good as the rest," I said, "but there were two things in it which were quite excellent: the descriptions of Dollfuss' death and the Reichstag trial. And in any case you should not have censored it." "And why not?" screamed Constantine. "And why not?" "Because," I said, "you know perfectly well that you could not censor *Inside Europe* except by applying standards so strict that they would prevent the publication of any sincere book on any subject." "You are wrong," he shrieked, "there is something your English brain does not know that our Serb blood is sure of, and that is that it is right to stamp on books written by such fools. Why should Western cretins drool their spittle on our sacred things?" He had, of course, censored *Inside Europe* in defiance of his own convictions just as Voltaire might, once in a while, have grimaced and put his liberal conscience to the door just for the sake of taking a holiday from his own nature. But Constantine was pretending to be somebody totally unlike himself, a stupid Prussian officer, a truculent Italian clerk, with whom he had so little in common that he could not persist in his imitation very long, and slumped into silence, his chin on his chest and his belly falling forward in a soft heap. He looked years older, and congested. It was as if in his abandonment to Gerda's nihilism he had withdrawn his consent to every integrating process, even to the circulation of his blood.

Nothing interested him on our journey. He did not leave the car with us when we got out to take some meadowsweet and wild roses, though it was his usual custom to follow us while we gathered flowers, relating to our bent behinds stories of his sexual or academic prowess. "And when I closed my bedroom door that night," we would hear as our fingers closed round the innocent stems, "the wife of the Swiss minister jumped out of the wardrobe, quite naked," or "Do you understand truly the theory of prime numbers? It is something that throws a light on history. I will explain it to you, for I am a mathematician, I." But now he sat in the car, neither asleep nor awake, but simply unhappy. We had to laugh alone when we were given a proof, more absolute than could be given by any homing bird, that the year had come to its kind ripeness. In a field outside one of the dullish Moslem villages which dappled these hillsides with poplars and minarets, we saw an old peasant look up into the sunshine and wipe the sweat from his brow, with the air of one observing clinical symptoms, and enact his verdict by changing from his winter to his summer clothes. No process could be simpler. He stepped out of a fine pair of those white serge trousers with allusive embroideries round the loins and the mysterious affixment to the hip-bone, and he took up his hoe again. He was of the opinion that his shirt, which now showed a neat waist and a handsome gathered tail, and his under-pants made as good a summer suit as anybody needed, and he was right. But to the Western eye the publicity of the adjustment was very diverting. It was as if a stockbroker, talking to a client, should mark a patch of brightness on his office wall and should therefore strip off his coat and waistcoat and trousers, continuing his talk the while, serene in a common understanding that from now on all sane men faced a warmer world in their underclothes.

But Constantine came to life again when the car stopped under a little hill surmounted with a new white church. "This is our church that we Serbs built for Kossovo," he said; "from there we will see the plain where the Turks defeated us and enslaved us, where after five hundred years of slavery we showed that we were not slaves." He was red, he was passionate, he panted, he was as he was when he was happy. We followed a path to the church through the long grass, and as our steps brought us higher there spread before us a great plain. Dragutin clenched his fist and shouted down at the earth, where the dead Turks lay. To him the dead Christians were in Heaven or were ghosts, but not under the ground, not scattered lifeless bones; only the Turks perished thus utterly. Then we were stilled by the stillness of Kossovo. It is not one of the plains, like the *vega* of Granada or the English fens, that are flat as a floor, it lacks that sly look of geological aberration, of earth abandoning its essential irregularity. Its prototype is Salisbury Plain: the land lies loosely, like a sleeper, in a cradle of featureless hills. Not by any means is the ground level. There a shoulder rises, here a hand supports the sleeper's head. But it is obviously prostrate and passive, it has none of the active spirit

699

which makes mountain and forest and the picturesque valley. It is active only as a sleeping body is, with that simplest residual activity, without which sleep would be death, without which the plain would be a desert: the grass pricks the sod, the fallow field changes its substances in biding its time, the green corn surpasses its greenness, but there is no excess beyond these simple functions.

It is the character of the skies that overarch plains to be not only wider than is common, but higher; and here one cloudy continent rode above another, under a vault visible yet of no colour except space. Here light lived. Its rays, brassy because it was nearly the summer, mild because it had been a bad spring, travelled slowly, high and low, discovering terraces of snow beyond the cradling hills on peaks of unseen mountains, the white blocks of a new settlement in a fold of falling fields, and the passage over downlands of a flock of sheep, cream-coloured and nigger-brown and slow-footed as stupidity. Those houses and those herds showed that there was here a world of human activity: thousands of men and women, even tens of thousands, lived and worked and sweated on Kossovo. But the plain absorbed them and nullified them by its own indifference, and there was shown before our eyes the first of all our disharmonies, the basis of our later tragedies: the division between man and nature. In childhood, when we fall on the ground we are disappointed that it is hard and hurts us. When we are older we expect a less obvious but perhaps more extravagant impossibility in demanding that there should be a correspondence between our lives and their setting; it seems to all women, and to many men, that destiny should at least once in their lives place them in a moonlit forest glade and send them love to match its beauty. In time we have to accept it that the ground does not care whether we break our noses on it, and that a moonlit forest glade is as often as not empty of anything but moonlight, and we solace ourselves with the love that is the fruit of sober judgement, and the flower of perfectly harmonious chance. We even forget what we were once foolish enough to desire. Then suddenly at some crisis of incongruity, when we see the site of a tragic historical event that ought to be blasted and is green and smiling, or pass a garden in full blossom when we are carrying our dead to burial, we recall our disappointment at this primary incongruity, and feel bitter desolation. The earth is not our mother's bosom. It shows us no special kindness. We cannot trust it to take sides with us. It makes us, its grass is our flesh, it lets us walk about on it, but this is all it will

700

do for us; and since the earth is what is not us, and therefore a symbol of destiny and of God, we are alone and terrified.

Kossovo, more than any other historical site I know, arouses that desolation. It spreads peacefully into its vast, gentle distances, slow winds polishing it like a cloth passing over a mirror, turning the heads of the standing grain to the light. It has a look of innocence which is the extreme of guilt. For it is crowded with the dead, who died in more than their flesh, whose civilization was cast with them into their graves. It is more tragic even than its own legend, which with the dishonesty and obstinacy of a work of art commemorates one out of several battles of Kossovo. That battle which was fought under the leadership of Tsar Lazar in 1389, and placed the Serbs under the yoke of the Turks, was followed by three others of a major character, in which the Serbs stood up before the Turks and had their death demonstrated to them, the complete annihilation of their will established. Fourteen years later the son of Tsar Lazar fought here for the shrunken title of Serbian Despot against another Serb noble, George Brankovitch. They were competitive parasites of the Sultan's court and each led the half of a rent people. Definite victory was impossible, they both lived on in an undignified compromise; only Kossovo was the richer, and that by many graves. Forty-five years later the conditions of defeat had so thickened that though there was another battle of Kossovo, the Serbs could not fight. They, who of all peoples feel the least reluctance to fighting, had to stand inactive on the field where it was natural they should determine their fate. Now another George Brankovitch, nephew of the first, was Despot of a diminished Serbia; he joined with the famous John Hunyadi, a Roumanian in the service of Hungary, and King Vladislav of Poland, and they formed a great expedition to recover Serbia and Bulgaria from the Turks. Bulgaria could not be saved, but Serbia came into full freedom. A solemn treaty was signed by all the belligerents, binding the Hungarians and the Poles to stay on their side of the Danube and the Sultan to stay on his, and giving George Brankovitch the whole of Serbia, as well as returning to him his two sons, who had been captured and blinded by the Turks. But as the Turks were then being attacked in Asia Minor it seemed to the Pope that this was the right time to drive them out of Europe, and he sent an army under the Cardinal Julian Cesarini to urge the Christian forces to take up arms again. When they protested that they had just signed a treaty pledging themselves to peace, the Cardinal told them that it is lawful for Christians to set aside and break an oath made with an infidel.

The peculiar flavour of the Western Church lies strong on the tongue in that declaration. George Brankovitch refused to join the Poles and Hungarians in availing himself of this licence to perfidy. It is easy to explain this by pointing out that he had done better out of the treaty than the other signatories; but the fact remains that, although such a ruling would have been a great advantage to the Christian subjects of Turkey, at no time during their enslavement did the Eastern Church encourage them to cast away their honour. Therefore George Brankovitch stood by while the Catholic armies advanced on the Turks at Varna in Bulgaria, whose Sultan prayed as they came, "O Christ, if thou art God, as thy followers say, punish their perfidy." His prayer was answered. Both the King of Hungary and the Cardinal fell on the field, with most of their soldiers. But the war dragged on with interruptions for another four years, and came to an end here on Kossovo, in a battle that lasted for three days and gave the plain about fifty thousand more dead. By this time the Serbs were demoralized by the division of the Christian world and by comradeship with their pagan enemies, and it is said that they waited on the hills around the plain till the battle ended and they could rob the dead.

So in the first battle of Kossovo the Serbs learned the meaning of defeat, not such defeat as forms a necessary proportion of all effort, for in that they had often been instructed during the course of their history, but of total defeat, annihilation of their corporate will and all their individual wills. The second battle of Kossovo taught them that one may live on such a low level of existence that even defeat cannot be achieved. The third taught them that even that level is not the lowest, and that there is a limbo for subject peoples where there is neither victory nor defeat but abortions which, had they come to birth, would have become such states. There was to be yet a fourth battle which was to prove still another horrible lesson. Very shortly after the third battle, in 1453 Byzantium fell; and the Turks were able to concentrate on the task of mastering the Balkans. The Serbs were constrained not to resist them by their fear of the Roman Catholic powers, who venomously loathed them and the Bulgarians for their fidelity to the Eastern Church and their liability to the Bogomil heresy. The night fell for four centuries, limbo became Hell, and manifested the anarchy that is Hell's essential character.

It happened that the Slavs who had become Janizaries, especially the Bosnian Serbs, who had been taken from their Christian mothers and trained to foreswear Christ and live in the obedience and enforcement of the oppressive yet sluttish Ottoman law, had learned their lesson too well. When the Turks themselves became alarmed by the working of that law and attempted to reform it, the Janizaries rose against the reformation. But because they remembered they were Slavs in spite of all the efforts that had been made to force them to forget it, they felt that in resisting the Turks, even in defence of Turkish law, they were resisting those who had imposed that Turkish law on them in place of their Christian system. So when the rebellious Janizaries defeated the loyal Army of the Sultan in the fourth battle of Kossovo in 1831, and left countless Turkish dead on the field, they held that they had avenged the shame laid on the Christian Slavs in the first battle of Kossovo, although they themselves were Moslems. But their Christian fellow-Slavs gave them no support, for they regarded them simply as co-religionists of the Turkish oppressors and therefore as enemies. So the revolt of the Janizaries failed; and to add the last touch of confusion, they were finally defeated by a Turkish marshal who was neither Turk nor Moslem-born Slav, but a renegade Roman Catholic from Dalmatia. Here was illustrated what is often obscured by historians, that a people can be compelled by misfortune into an existence so confused that it is not life but sheer nonsense, the malignant nonsense of cancerous growth.

Kossovo speaks only of its defeats. It is true that they were nullified by the Serbs of Serbia, who snatched their own liberty from the Turks under the leadership of Karageorge and Milosh Obrenovitch in the early nineteenth century, and pressed on, against the hostility of the great powers, until they gave liberty to Old Serbia and Macedonia in the Balkan wars. But of this trumph Kossovo says nothing, for the battle which gave it to the Serbs in 1912 was fought not there but at Kumanovo, some miles to the south-east; and even after that it knew defeat again, for here the retreating Serbian Army was bombed by the German aeroplanes as they fled towards the Albanian border, and though they pursued their enemies across it when they returned three years later it was without spectacular event. Here is the image of failure, so vast that it fills the eye as failure sometimes fills an individual life, an epoch.

The white church we found had been built to celebrate the recovery of the lost land, by a society of patriotic Serbian women. Inside it many plaques of thanksgiving, ardent beyond the habit of inscriptions, hung on the whitewashed walls, and outside it, darkened by its short noonday shadow, there lay the grave of this society's president who, her headstone said, had worked all her life long to fire her countrymen with the ambition to free their enslaved brothers, and had expressed with her last breath the desire to be buried within sight of Kossovo. As we stood beside the cross two little boys came out of a white house lying under us on the Kossovo side of the hill, caught sight of us, and stalked us, as though it were we who were wild and shy, not they. They moved in circles about us through the long grass and paused at last about ten yards away, their thumbs in their mouths, their eyes like little dark tunnels down to their animal natures.

Constantine called out, "Little ones! Little ones!" and charmed them to him, step by step; and when they were still some feet away they told him that the white house was an ophanage, founded by the same patriotic society, and that they were all alone there, because they were too young to go to school. It would not be in accordance with our Western ideas that two boys, hardly more than babies, should be left in an orphanage for a morning by themselves, or that they should be barefoot; but they looked quite uninstitutionalized and very healthy and serene. Very likely there was here a wise Slav disorder, as in the sanatorium in Croatia,* that allowed human processes to develop according to their unpredictable design. When Constantine's enchantments had brought the children to his side, he asked them, "Why was the orphanage built here?" and they answered him in a tender and infantile version of official oratory, touching as the flags and wreaths used for a patriotic celebration in a very little village. They spoke of the glorious ancient Serbian Empire, of its shameful destruction by the Turks at Kossovo, of the agonizing captivity that lasted five centuries, of the liberation offered through courage by the Serbian people, and the founding of Yugoslavia, that should be as glorious as ancient Serbia. "And do you know," asked Constantine, "the songs that our people have sung about the terrible day of St Vitus?" They began at once, with the inexhaustible, almost rank verbal memory of the Slav child:

> "Musitch Stephen his cool wine was drinking,
> In his palace, rich with purest silver,
> In his beautiful and lordly dwelling;

*[Referred to in "Two Castles," p. 584.]

And his servant Vaistina poured it,
When of his cool wine he had drunk deeply,
Then said Musitch Stephen to his servant:
'Vaistina, thou my child beloved,
I will lay me down a while to slumber.
Drink some wine and eat some supper,
Then walk before my lordly palace,
Look upon the clear night sky and tell me,
If the the silver moon is sinking westward,
If the morning star is shining eastward,
If the time has come for us to travel
To the fair and level Plain of Blackbirds.' "

The little boys looked noble and devout as they recited. Here was the nationalism which the intellectuals of my age agreed to consider a vice and the origin of the world's misfortunes. I cannot imagine why. Every human being is of sublime value, because his experience, which must be in some measure unique, gives him a unique view of reality, and the sum of such views should go far to giving us the complete picture of reality, which the human race must attain if it is ever to comprehend its destiny. Therefore every human being must be encouraged to cultivate his consciousness to the fullest degree. It follows that every nation, being an association of human beings who have been drawn together by common experience, has also its unique view of reality, which must contribute to our deliverance, and should therefore be allowed a like encouragement to its consciousness: Let people, then, hold to their own language, their own customs, their own beliefs, even if this inconveniences the tourist. There is not the smallest reason for confounding nationalism, which is the desire of a people to be itself, with imperialism, which is the desire of a people to prevent other peoples from being themselves. Intense nationalist spirit is often, indeed, an effort by a people to rebuild its character when an imperialist power has worked hard to destroy it. Finnish nationalism, for example, is a blood transfusion given after the weakening wounds inflicted by Tsarist Russia, and it is accompanied by defensive but not aggressive feelings in relation to its neighbours. Here certainly I could look without any reservation on the scene, on the two little boys darkening their brows in imitation of the heroes as they spoke the stern verse, on Constantine, whose Jewish eyes were full of Serbian tears, on my husband, who bent over the children with the hieratic reverence Englishmen feel for boyhood that has put its neck under the yoke of discipline, on the green bed and stone cross of the happy grave, on the domes of the native church, and the hospitable farmlike orphanage. This was as unlikely to beget any ill as the wild roses and meadowsweets we had gathered by the road.

The scene was exquisite; but it was pitifully without weight, without mass, compared to the plain that spread for forty miles before us, thickened by tragedy. If a giant had taken Kossovo in his right hand and us and the church and the farmhouse and the grave in his left hand, his right hand must have fallen to his side because of the heaviness of the load, but it would have seemed to him that in his left hand there was nothing but a little dust. It is flattery of nature to say that it is indifferent to man. It grossly disfavours him in quantity and quality, providing more pain than pleasure, and making that more potent. The simplest and most dramatic example is found in our food: a good oyster cannot please the palate as acutely as a bad one can revolt it, and a good oyster cannot make him who eats it live for ever though a bad one can make him dead for ever. The agony of Kossovo could not be balanced by the joy that was to be derived from it. The transports of the women who built the church must dull themselves in continuance, and even if they generated the steady delight of founding a new nation that itself was dulled by the resistance offered to the will by material objects, and by the conflict between different wills working to the same end, which is often not less envenomed than the conflict between wills working to different ends. But the agony of Kossovo must have been purely itself, pain upon pain, newly born in acuteness for each generation, throughout five centuries. The night of evil had been supreme, it still was supreme on a quantitative basis.

Above the plain were the soft white castles of the clouds and a blank blue wall behind them. Into this world I had been born, and I must resign myself to it; I could not move myself to a fortunate planet, where any rare tear was instantly dried by a benediction. This is my glass, I must drink out of it. In my anxiety to know what was in the glass, I wondered, "The world is tragic, but just how tragic? I wonder if it is finally so, if we can ever counter the catastrophes to which we are liable and give ourselves a workshop of serenity in which we can experiment with that other way of life which is not tragedy, but which is not comedy. Certainly not comedy, for that is merely life before tragedy has fallen upon it, ridiculous as a clown on the films who grins and capers without seeing that there is a police-

OLD SERBIA

man behind him just about to bring down a club on his head. That other way of life must transcend not only comedy but tragedy, must refuse to be impressed by its grandiose quality and frustrate it at every point."

But I found my mind wandering from the subject, which was surely the nature of tragedy and the points at which it attacked man, to indulge in some of that optimism which serves us in the West instead of fortitude. Life, I said to myself, was surely not as tragic as all that, and perhaps the defeat of Kossovo had not been a disaster of supreme magnitude. Perhaps the armies that had stood up before the Turks had been a huddle of barbarians, impressive only after the fashion of a pack of wolves, that in its dying presented the world with only the uninteresting difference between a live pack of wolves and a dead pack of wolves. That is a view held by some historians, notably the person so unfortunately selected by the editors of the *Cambridge Medieval History* to write the chapter on the Serbian Empire; and it seems to receive some support when one drives, as we did after we left the church, along the fringes of the plain. The population of Old Serbia is sunk far deeper in misery than the Macedonians, and at a superficial glance they justify the poor opinion of the Christian rayahs held by nineteenth-century travellers. Their houses turn a dilapidated blankness on the village street; their clothes are often dirty and unornamented by a single stitch of embroidery; and they gape at the stranger with eyes empty of anything but a lethargic fear which is quite unapposite to the present, which is the residue of a deposit left by a past age, never yet drained off by the intelligence.

Actually I knew that there were many reasons why these women should be so, other than the predisposition of their stock. They were not a fair specimen of the Slav population as it had been at the time of the battle of Kossovo, for most of the noble families had died on the field, and the cream of what were left emigrated to Austrian territory within the next three hundred years. Such as were left suffered from all the disadvantages of Turkish rule without enjoying any of the advantages that had made the ruin of Macedonia so far from absolute. It had no rich capital like Bitolj, nor such trading centres as Skoplje, Veles, Tetovo, and Gostivar; and it had no picturesqueness to tempt wealthy Turks to build country houses. It was purely agricultural land. The Turks raped it of its crops and sent them back to Constantinople, and took the peasants' last

707

farthings in taxes, and gave nothing in return. This plain might have blossomed like the rose with civilization and nothing would have remained. It was also probable, in view of the falsity of the face a house and a peasant turn on the world, that these women were not as they seemed. But for this moment I looked on them idiotically, as if I were Gerda, imputing to them worthlessness instead of difference; and I alleged to myself that probably nothing had fallen at Kossovo that was an irreparable loss, that perhaps tragedy draws blood but never lifeblood.*

From THE PLAIN OF KOSSOVO II

◇ My husband, Constantine and I were on a path that ran up a hill. We were on our way to the field where the Serb forces under the command of Prince Lazar were defeated by the Turks in the great battle of Kossovo in 1389. Here Prince Lazar had had his tent, there the Turks had waited. "But no!" interrupted Dragutin. He was shouting slowly and without rage, as he did when moved by patriotic fervour. "How could they wait in the North-West! Not here, but there were they, the dogs! And there, over there, Vuk Brankovitch should have come in with his troops but turned away and left the battle-field!" "Vuk Brankovitch," said Constantine, "is the Judas of our story. He was the specially beloved brother-in-law of the Prince Lazar, and he is supposed to have sold himself to the Turks and to have led his army off the battle-field at a crucial moment, thus exposing Lazar's flank. But now historians do not think there was any treachery, though it seems likely that one of the Serbian princes did not receive a message in time telling him to go forward to Lazar's support, and so failed him. But we all know that it was not treachery that lost us Kossovo, it is that we were all divided among ourselves." "Yes," said Dragutin, "it is so in our songs, that we were betrayed by Brankovitch, but we know that it was not so, that we lost the battle because we were not of one mind." "How do you mean you know it?" I asked. "Do you mean you learned it at school?" "No," he said, "we know it before we go to school. It is something our people remember." I was again checked by the curious honesty of the Slav

*[The next chapter, beginning "But I could not keep that up for long," restored the balance by describing the marvellous Serbo-Byzantine frescoes of nearby Grachanitsa—omitted here.]

mind, by its refusal to dress up its inconsistencies and make them superficially acceptable to the rationalist censor. They had evolved a myth which accounted for their defeat by treachery within their own ranks and thereby took the sting out of it, just as the Germans did after the war; but they did not suppress the critical part of their mind when it pointed out to them that this myth was merely a myth. With an inconsistency that was not dangerous because it was admitted, they let their myth and the criticism of it coexist in their minds.

Constantine and Dragutin waved their arms at the downland, and still I saw nothing. I turned aside and looked at the white building behind us and I said. "What is this place? Can we go in?" "Certainly, certainly," said Constantine, "it is very interesting; this is the mausoleum of Gazi Mestan, a Turkish standard-bearer who was killed in the battle and was buried where he lay." "Yes," shouted Dragutin, "many of us fell at Kossovo, but, praise be to God, so did many of them." As we went into the wooden porch, the veiled woman and her children padded past us. We found ourselves in a room which, though light and clean, had that look of having been long disused by any normal forces which one expects to be completed by stuffed animals; but there was nothing there except two coffins of the Moslem type, with a gabled top, higher at the head than the heels. They were covered with worn green baize, and hung with cheap pieces of stuff, some clumsily embroidered, others printed. On the walls were a few framed scraps of Turkish calligraphy, a copy of a Sultan's seal, and some picture postcards. A man came towards us, smiling sweetly and indecisively. He wore a faded fez and neat but threadbare Western clothes, and his whole appearance made a wistful allusion to a state better than his own; I have seen his like in England, walking through November rain in a summer suit and a straw hat, still mildly cheerful. He told us of the fame and gallantry of Gazi Mestan in a set speech, unnaturally uttered from some brain-cell petrified by memory. "And you? Who are you?" said Constantine. "I am the descendant of Gazi Mestan's servant," the man answered, "the descendant in the sixteenth generation. My forefather was by him as he fell, he closed his dead master's eyes for him, he preserved his body and guarded it after it had been placed in this tomb. So have we all guarded him."

A weak-eyed boy ran into the room and took his stand beside the man, who laid an arm about his shoulder. "My brother," he said tenderly, and laid his face against the boy's lank hair. They looked incredibly fragile. If one had tapped them with a pebble on the paper-thin temples they would have dropped to the ground, still faintly smiling; the bare ankle-bones showing between the boy's brown shoes and frayed trouser-hems were so prominent that the skin stretched across them was bright red, "What do these people live on?" I asked. "Doubtless they receive gifts, this is a kind of shrine," said Constantine, "and there would probably be an allowance from the Vakuf, the Moslem religious endowment fund. In any case they can do nothing else, this is the family's destiny and it is a distinction." "But they are not like human beings at all," I said, "they are to human beings what a ship inside a glass bottle is to a real boat." I saw before me what an empire which spreads beyond its legitimate boundaries must do to its subjects. It cannot spread its own life over the conquered areas, for life cannot travel too far from its source, and it blights the life that is native to those parts. Therefore it imprisons all its subjects in a stale conservatism, in a seedy gentility that celebrates past achievements over and over again. It could be seen what these people had been. With better bones, with more flesh, with unatrophied wills, they would have been Turks as they were in the great days of the past, or as they are in the Ataturk's Turkey, robust and gracious. But there they were sweet-sour phantoms, human wine gone to vinegar.

Outside we found Dragutin lying on the ground, the girl and the boys about him and a field mouse curled in his hand. "You do not want to go inside?" asked Constantine. "No," he said. "That a Turk was alive and is dead is good news. But this one has been dead so long that the news is a bit stale. Hola!" he roared, and opened his hand and the field mouse made a brown streak for safety. "Now I am to take you to the tomb of the Sultan Murad," he said, standing up, "but thank God we stop at a Christian monument first." It was some miles down the main road, a very plain cross set back in a fenced garden where irises and lupins and the first roses grew with an astounding profusion. It could be understood that Kossovo had really been fertile, that it had once supported many fat villages. The two soldiers who were guarding the monument came down to the gate to meet us, two boys in their earliest twenties, short and sturdy and luminous with health, their skins rose under bronze, their black eyes shining deep and their black hair shining shallow.

When I admired the garden one of them fell back and picked some flowers for me from a bed, not in the main avenue, lest the general effect should be spoiled, and Constantine said to the other one, "You are a Serb from the North, aren't you?" He answered, smiling, "Yes, I am from the North, I am from the same town as you, I am from Shabats." "What!" exclaimed Constantine, looking like a baby that has seen its bottle. "Do you know me?" "Which of us in Shabats does not know the great poet who sprang from our town?" replied the soldier; and I liked the people of Shabats, for I could see from his face that they knew the best as well as the worst of Constantine, and revered him as well as mocked him. "But tell me," interrupted Dragutin, "is that other one not a Croat?" "Yes," he said, "he is from Karlovats." "Is it not hard to be here all day with a Croat?" "No, indeed," said the soldier, "it is most surprising how pleasant he is; he is my true friend, and he is a good soldier; I never would have believed it." "You don't say so!" said Dragutin. "I tell you," said Constantine, "there are many good Croats, and we Serbs must make friends with them." "So," said Dragutin.

We were silent for a time at the foot of the memorial which bore the appalling words, "To the heroes who fell for the honest cross, freedom, and the right of the people, 1389–1912, erected by the people of Prishtina." It made the head ache with its attempt to commemorate people who were utterly outside the scope of memory; slaves born of slaves, who made their gesture of revolt and died, isolated by their slavery from the weakest, furthest light and warmth of fame. When we turned our faces to the garden again, we found the other soldier standing beside us, holding out a bouquet that was like a bouquet on a fire-screen made for a court, that had form and a tune of colour. All Slavs, except those who become florists, have a natural genius for arranging flowers. After I had thanked him, Dragutin said, "Hey, Croat! You're a brave fellow. How do you like us Serbs?" "Very well, very well!" he answered, smiling. "Everybody is kind to me here, and I had thought you were my enemies." "Eyah!" said Dragutin, twisting the lobe of the boy's ear. "We'll kill you all some day." The boy wriggled and laughed, and they all talked till we turned to go, and Dragutin gave the boy a great smack on the back, saying, "Well, you two, if you come to Skoplje, you'll find me at the Ban's garage, and maybe there'll be some paprikasch for you. You're what Yugoslavia needs." On this little ledge they met and clung together, on this cross-wide space from which the dark grasses of Kossovo had been driven back, they who had been born under different flags and had to beat down a wall of lies before they could smile at each other.

If the battle of Kossovo was invisible to me it was because it had happened too completely. It was because the field of Kossovo had wholly swallowed up the men who had awaited destiny in their embroidered tents, because it had become sodden with their blood and now was a bog, and when things fell on it they were for ever lost. Constantine said, "Now I am taking you to the mausoleum of the Sultan Murad, who was commanding the Turkish forces and was killed the night before the battle by a Serb called Milosh Obilitch, who had been suspected of treachery by our people and wished to clear his name." The Sultan Murad, or Amurath, was the son of Orkhan the Victorious and a Greek girl raped from her bridegroom's arms, whom the Turks called Nilufer, the Lotus Flower, and his records suggest an immoral attempt to create the kind of character admired by morality, for an astounding cruelty seems to have been introduced as an alloy to harden the soft gold of his voluptuous delight in all exercises of the mind and body. "His mausoleum," said Constantine, "was built where he fell."

A track led from the road across the opaque and lustreless pasture-land characteristic of this place, to what looked like a deserted farm-house. As we came to the gate in the farm paddock it was as it had been at the tomb of Gazi Mestan: the bare countryside exhaled people. They came to meet us at the gate, they whipped round the corners of the paddock, men in Western clothes who had the look of Leicester Square or Place Pigalle touts, not that they knew much or perhaps anything of infamy. The resemblance lay in their terrible desire to sell what they had, which since they had nothing caused them to make piteous claims to the possession of special knowledge, the power to perform unusual services. Their bare feet, treading softly on rag-bound leather sandals, pattered before us, beside us, behind us, as we followed a stone path across a grassy quadrangle. A house looked down on us, its broken windows stuffed with newspaper, its wall eczematous where the plaster lacked.

Through another gateway we came on a poor and dusty garden where the mausoleum stood. A fountain splashed from a wall, and there was nothing else pleasant there. The door of the mausoleum was peculiarly hideous; it was of coarse wood, painted chocolate-colour, and panes of cheap glass, all the wrong shape. Public libraries and halls in small provincial towns in England sometimes have such

712

doors. Beyond was a rough lawn, cropped by a few miserable sheep, which was edged with some flowers and set with two or three Moslem graves which were of the handsome sort, having a slab as well as a column at the top and bottom, but were riven across by time and neglect. On the grass sat some veiled women picknicking among their pretty, sore-eyed children, with the infinitely touching sociability of Moslem women, which reticently reveals a brave and frustrated appetite for pleasure, doling itself out crumbs and making them do. On a fence made of small sticks, defending a young tree from the sheep, hung a line of many-coloured rags, just recognizably garments that had been washed very clean. At least one of these women lived in a cottage so far from all other water that it was worth her while to bring her washing to the fountain; yet on these bare downs it could be seen there was no cottage for a mile or two.

We drew near to the hideous door of the mausoleum, and it was opened by an old man whom we knew to be an *imam*, a priest, only from the twist of white cloth about his fez; not in his manner was there any sign of sacred authority. He greeted us blearily and without pride, and we followed him, our touts padding behind us, into the presence of the Sultan Murad. The walls of his last lodging were distempered in drab and ornamented with abstract designs in choco-late, grey, and bottle--green, such as Western plumbers and decorators loved to create in the latter half of the last century, and its windows were curtained with the intensely vulgar dark green printed velvet used in wagons-lits. In a sloping gabled coffin such as sheltered Gazi Mestan, but covered with velvet and votive offerings of stuffs by some halfpence costlier, lay Murad. His turban hung from a wooden pole at the head of the coffin, a dusty wisp. The priest turned blindish eyes on Constantine and told him something; after the telling his fishlike mouth forgot to close. "This old one is relating that only the Sultan's entrails are here," said Constantine, "the rest of him was taken away to Broussa in Turkey, but I do not know when." Even the most rational person might have expected that the priest would have shown some slight regret that this shrine held the entrails of the Sultan and not his heart or his head. But in the pale luminousness of his eyes and the void of his open mouth there was seated the most perfect indifference.

Two of the touts padded past us and sank mumbling into the prostration of a Moslem prayer, in the hope that we might gape and tip. It is impossible to have visited Sarajevo or Bitolj or even Skoplje, without learning that the Turks were in a real sense magnificent, that there was much of that in them which brings man off his four feet into erectness, that they knew well that running waters, the shade of trees, a white minaret the more in a town, brocade and fine manners, have a usefulness greater than use, even to the most soldierly of men. They were truly aristocratic, they had prised up the clamp of necessity that fixes man with his belly close to the earth. Therefore it was painful to see these Turks to whom two full meals in succession were more remote objects of lust than the most fantastic luxuries had been to their forefathers, to whom rags and a dusty compound represented a unique refreshment. These mock devotions were disgusting not because they were prostitutions of a gallant religion, since that represented an invincible tendency of mankind, but because they were inspired by the hope of dinars far too few for any purchase worth making. I turned away; and the tail of my eye caught the touts in a furtive movement betraying an absolute bankruptcy of the vital forces, an inability to make an effort except when financed by some expectation for that specific purpose. Once they saw they had not interested us they stopped their prostrations in mid-air, wearily straightened themselves, and shuffled after us into the paddock.

"It is silly to bring foreigners to see these old Turkish things," said Dragutin to Constantine. "Everything Turkish is now rotten and stinks like a dunghill. Look at these creatures that are more like rotten marrows than men, they ought to be in mausoleums themselves, their mothers must have been dead for years before they were born." His animal lack of pity was the more terrible because it was not even faintly malicious. We hurried out of the paddock, some of the touts gaining on us and pattering ahead, looking back at us with their terrible inexorbitant expectancy. One could easily have become cruel to them. Beyond the gate Constantine led us along the plasterless walls till he found the spot where, it is said, the man who murdered Murad was put to death, "His name," he said, "was Milosh Obilitch; but to tell you the truth it was not. It was Kobilitch, which means Brood-mare, for in those days our people, even in the nobility, did not have surnames but only Christian names and nicknames. But in the eighteenth century when all the world became refined it seemed to us that it was shameful to have a hero that was called Brood-mare, so we dropped the K, and poor Milosh was left with a name that meant nothing at all and was never his.

What he would have minded worse was that many people nowadays say we should not honour him at all, because he gained the Sultan's presence by a trick, by saying that he was a deserter and wished to join his enemies. He felt, and patriots still feel, that he had to clear his name in the eyes of his people from the suspicion of being a traitor, and that he had bought the right to play that trick on the Turks because he gave them his life in return."

"It is strange," I said, "that the Turks were not disorganized by the murder of their Sultan." "Nothing could have disorganized them," said Constantine, "they were superb, they had *superbia*, they were all as Mohammed would have had them, they were soldiers ready to submit to all discipline because they believed that they had been enlisted by God, who at the end of the world would be with them as their general." "Our Sir Charles Eliot," I said, "wrote of them that 'The Sultan may be a Roman Emperor, but every Turk is a Roman citizen with a profound self-respect and a sense not only of his duties, but what is due to him.'" As I spoke I noticed that my husband was no longer walking beside me, and, as wives do, I looked round to see what the creature might be doing. He was some paces behind us, giving some dinars to the touts, who were taking them with a gentle, measured thankfulness, unabject in spite of their suppliance, which proved that what Eliot had said of them had once been true, though the total situation showed it to be now false. They stopped following us after that, and remained staring mildly after us, boneless as flames, their pale faces and dusty clothes dingy in the sunlight. They stood wide, wide apart on the dark grass of Kossovo, for their flesh was too poor to feel the fleshy desire to draw together. A people that extends its empire too far from its base commits the sin of Onan and spills its seed upon the ground.

We had not been driving very long when the road ran through a grove, and Dragutin brought the automobile to a halt. "Here we will eat," he said, holding the door open. "What do you mean?" asked Constantine. "Well, did you people not bring bread and wine and eggs from Skoplje?" asked Dragutin. "This is the best place to eat them, and it is high time too, for it is very late and the English are accustomed to meals at regular hours. So get you out and eat." "No, no," said Constantine, taking out his watch and shaking his head, "we must push on to Kossovska Mitrovitsa, and it may be dark before we get there." "What are you talking about?" said Dragutin. "It is about three in the afternoon, this is May, and Kossovska

Mitrovitsa is not two hours away. Step quickly, you must get out."
He did not speak out of insolence, but in recognition that Constantine
had suffered some sort of disintegrating change during the last few
days, and that his judgement was not now to be trusted. Constantine
looked at him in unresentful curiosity, as if to say, "Am I as bad as
that?" and obeyed. Dragutin put out the rugs and the food on the
grass and said, "There now, you can have fifteen minutes," and
walked up and down the road in front of us, eating an apple. He
called to me, "You don't much like being here." "No," I said, "it's
too sad. And just now I have been thinking of the Vrdnik monastery
in the Frushka Gora, where I saw the body of the Prince Lazar and
touched his hand." "Ah, yes, the poor saint," said Dragutin, "they
cut off his head because our Milosh Obilitch had killed their Sultan,
though doubtless they would have done it anyway. They were
wolves, it was their nature to shed gentler blood. Well, it could not
be helped. We were not of one mind."

He took another mouthful of apple and munched himself down
the road, and I said to Constantine, "'It is strange, he does not
blame the nobles for quarrelling among themselves." Constantine
said thoughtfully, "No, but I do not think that is what he means."
"But he says, 'We were not of one mind,' he has said it twice today,
and in all the history books it is said that the Slavs were beaten at
Kossovo because the various princes quarrelled among themselves.
What else can he mean?" "It is true that our people always say that
we were beaten because we were not of one mind, and it is true that
there were many Slav princes before Kossovo, and that they all
quarrelled, but I do not think that the phrase has any connexion
with that fact," said Constantine. "I think the phrase means that
each individual Slav was divided in his attitude to the Turk, and it
makes an allusion to our famous poem about the grey falcon."
"I have never heard of it," I answered. Constantine stood up and
called to Dragutin, who was now munching his way back to us,
"Think of it, she had never heard of our poem about the grey falcon!"
"Shame!" cried Dragutin, spitting out some pips, and they began
chanting together:

> "Poletio soko titsa siva,
> Od svetinye, od Yerusalima,
> I on nosi titsu lastavitsu. . . ."

"I will translate it for you," said Constantine. "In your language

I cannot make it as beautiful as it is, but you will see that at any
rate it is not like any other poem, it is peculiar to us. . . .

There flies a grey bird, a falcon,
From Jerusalem the holy,
And in his beak he bears a swallow.

That is no falcon, no grey bird,
But it is the Saint Elijah.
He carries no swallow,
But a book from the Mother of God.
He comes to the Tsar at Kossovo,
He lays the book on the Tsar's knees.
This book without like told the Tsar:
'Tsar Lazar, of honourable stock,
Of what kind will you have your kingdom?
Do you want a heavenly kingdom?
Do you want an earthly kingdom?
If you want an earthly kingdom,
Saddle your horses, tighten your horses' girths,
Gird on your swords,
Then put an end to the Turkish attacks !
And drive out every Turkish soldier.
But if you want a heavenly kingdom
Build you a church on Kossovo;
Build it not with a floor of marble
But lay down silk and scarlet on the ground,
Give the Eucharist and battle orders to your soldiers,
For all your soldiers shall be destroyed,
And you, prince, you shall be destroyed with them.'

When the Tsar read the words,
The Tsar pondered, and he pondered thus :
'Dear God, where are these things, and how are they !
What kingdom shall I choose?
Shall I choose a heavenly kingdom?
Shall I choose an earthly kingdom?
If I choose an earthly kingdom,
An earthly kingdom lasts only a little time,
But a heavenly kingdom will last for eternity and its centuries.'

The Tsar chose a heavenly kingdom,
And not an earthly kingdom,
He built a church on Kossovo.
He built it not with floor of marble
But laid down silk and scarlet on the ground.

There he summoned the Serbian Patriarch
And twelve great bishops.
Then he gave his soldiers the Eucharist and their battle orders.
In the same hour as the Prince gave orders to his soldiers
The Turks attacked Kossovo.

"There follows," said Constantine, "a long passage, very muddled, about how gallantly the Tsar fought and how at the end it looked as if they were to win, but Vuk Brankovitch betrayed them, so they were beaten. And it goes on:

Then the Turks overwhelmed Lazar,
And the Tsar Lazar was destroyed,
And his army was destroyed with him,
Of seven and seventy thousand soldiers.

All was holy, all was honourable
And the goodness of God was fulfilled."

I said, "So that was what happened, Lazar was a member of the Peace Pledge Union." Through a long field of rye on the crest of a hill before me, a wind ran like the tremor that shuddered over my skin and through my blood. Peeling the shell from an egg, I walked away from the others, but I knew that the poem referred to something true and disagreeable in my own life. "Lazar was wrong," I said to myself, "he saved his soul and there followed five hundred years when no man on these plains, nor anywhere else in Europe for hundreds of miles in any direction, was allowed to keep his soul. He should have chosen damnation for their sake. No, what am I saying? I am putting the state above the individual, and I believe that there are certain ultimate human rights that must have precedence over all others. What I mean is rather that I do not believe in the thesis of the poem. I do not believe that any man can procure his own salvation by refusing to save millions of people from miserable slavery. That it was a question of fighting does not matter, because in actual fact fighting is not much more disgusting, though probably slightly so, than many things people have to do in order that the race may triumph over certain assaults. To protect us from germs many people have to perform exceedingly distasteful tasks in connexion with sewage, and to open to the community its full economic resources sailors and miners have to suffer great discomfort and danger. But indeed this poem shows that the pacifist attitude does not depend on the horrors of warfare, for it never mentions them. It goes straight to the heart of

718

the matter and betrays that what the pacifist really wants is to be defeated. Prince Lazar and his troops were to take the Eucharist and they were to be destroyed by the Turks and then they would be saved. There is not a word about avoiding bloodshed. On the contrary, it is taken for granted that he fought as well as he could, and killed every Turk within reach. The important thing is not that he should be innocent, but that he should be defeated."

I realized fully why this poem had stirred me. When I had stood by the tomb in the monastery at Vrdnik in the Frushka Gora and touched Prince Lazar's mummied hand, I had been well aware that he was of a pattern familiar to me, that he was one of that company loving honour and freedom and harmony, which in our day includes Herbert Fisher and Lord Cecil and Professor Gilbert Murray. Such people I have always followed, for I know that they are right, and my reason acknowledges that by their rule and by their rule only can a growing and incorrupt happiness be established on earth. But when all times have given birth to such good men and such as myself who follow them, why has this happiness not long been accomplished? Why is there still poverty, when we are ready for handsomeness? Why is there carelessness for the future of children? Why is there oppression of women by men? Why is there harshness of race towards race? I know the answer. I had known the answer for long, but it had taken this poem to make my mind admit that I knew it.

It is revealed at all meetings addressed or attended by the lesser of those who care for the freedom and the well-being of others, which often exhale a strange sense of danger. Meetings of the opposite party, of those who desire others to be enslaved for their benefit or to preserve iniquitous social institutions because of the profit they derive from them, offer the simple repulsiveness of greed and stupidity, but not this sense of danger. It is evoked in many ways: by the clothes worn by the women among the speakers and the audiences, which are of a sort not to be accounted for by poverty and by overwork, since they are not specially cheap and must indeed require a special effort to find, so far do they depart from the normal. They can serve no purpose save to alienate public opinion; and it is sad that they should not do all that they can to secure the respect of the community when they are trying to revise communal beliefs. It appears possible that they do not really want to succeed in that attempt; and that suspicion is often aroused by the quality of the speakers' voices and the response of their audiences. The speakers use all accents of sincerity and sweetness, and they continuously praise virtue; but they never speak as if power would be theirs tomorrow and they would use it for virtuous action. And their audiences also do not seem to regard themselves as predestined to rule; they clap as if in defiance, and laugh at their enemies behind their hands, with the shrill laughter of children. They want to be right, not to do right. They feel no obligation to be part of the main tide of life, and if that meant any degree of pollution they would prefer to divert themselves from it and form a standing pool of purity. In fact, they want to receive the Eucharist, be beaten by the Turks, and then go to Heaven.

By that they prove themselves inferior to their opponents, who do not want to separate themselves from the main channel of life, who believe quite simply that aggression and tyranny are the best methods of guaranteeing the future of man and therefore accept the responsibility of applying them. The friends of liberty have indeed no ground whatsoever for regarding themselves as in any way superior to their opponents, since they are in effect on their side in wishing defeat and not victory for their own principles. Not one of them, even the greatest, has ever been a Cæsar as well as his kind self; and until there is a kind Cæsar every child of woman is born in peril. I looked into my own heart and I knew that I was not innocent. Often I wonder whether I would be able to suffer for my principles if the need came, and it strikes me as a matter of the highest importance. That should not be so. I should ask myself with far greater urgency whether I have done everything possible to carry those principles into effect, and how I can attain power to make them absolutely victorious. But those questions I put only with my mind. They do not excite my guts, which wait anxiously while I ponder my gift for martyrdom.

"If this be so," I said to myself, "if it be a law that those who are born into the world with a preference for the agreeable over the disagreeable are born also with an impulse towards defeat, then the whole world is a vast Kossovo, an abominable blood-logged plain, where people who love go out to fight people who hate, and betray their cause to their enemies, so that loving is persecuted for immense tracts of history, far longer than its little periods of victory." I began to weep, for the left-wing people among whom I had lived all my life had in their attitude to foreign politics achieved such a betrayal. They were always right, they never imposed their rightness. "If this disposition to be at once Christ and Judas is inborn," I thought, "we might as well die, and the sooner the better, for the defeat is painful after the lovely promise." I turned my back on the plains, not to see the sodden grass, not to think of the woman stupid under her ploughshare in Prishtina, the weak-eyed loving brothers embracing feebly in the standard-bearer's mausoleum, the pale touts falsely and hungrily genuflecting about the Sultan's coffin, not to imagine the lost glory of the Christian Slavs, the glory, different but equal and equally lost, of the Ottoman Turks. Even when I saw none of these things with the eye of the body or the mind I felt despair, and I began to run, to be more quickly with my companions.

The party I had left had now been joined by a fourth, an old Albanian wearing the white skullcap which is as the fez to the Moslems of that people. He had been invited to share our food, and he was sitting on the ground with his back to me. When I drew nearer he turned about to greet me with the smiling social grace peculiar to Albanians, and I saw that in his arms there was lying a black lamb such as I had seen sacrificed at the rock of the Sheep's Field; and the meaning of Kossovo was plain.

The black lamb and the grey falcon had worked together here. In this crime, as in nearly all historic crimes and most personal crimes, they had been accomplices. This I had learned in Yugoslavia, which writes obscure things plain, which furnishes symbols for what the intellect has not yet formulated. On the Sheep's Field I had seen sacrifice in its filth and falsehood, and in its astonishing power over the imagination. There I had learned how infinitely disgusting in its practice was the belief that by shedding the blood of an animal one will be granted increase; that by making a gift to death one will receive a gift of life. There I had recognized that this belief was a vital part of me, because it was dear to the primitive mind, since it provided an easy answer to various perplexities, and the primitive mind is the foundation on which the modern mind is built. This belief is not only hideous in itself: it pollutes the works of love. It has laboured for annulment of the meaning of Christianity, by insinuating itself into the Church and putting forward, by loose cries and the drunkenness of ecstasy, a doctrine of the Atonement too absurd to be set down in writing. By that doctrine it is pretended that Christ came to earth to cook up a senseless and ugly magic rite, to buy with his pain an unrelated good, and it is concealed from us that his death convicted us of sin, that it proved our kind to be so cruel that when goodness itself appeared amongst us we could find nothing better to do with it than kill it. And I had felt, as I walked away from the rock with Militsa and Mehmed, that if I thought longer about the sacrifice I should learn something more, of a nature discreditable to myself.

Now that I saw the lamb thrusting out the forceless little black hammer of its muzzle from the flimsy haven of the old man's wasted arms, I could not push the realization away from me very much longer. None of us, my kind as little as any others, could resist the temptation of accepting this sacrifice as a valid symbol. We believed in our heart of hearts that life was simply this and nothing more, a man cutting the throat of a lamb on a rock to please God and obtain happiness; and when our intelligence told us that the man was performing a disgusting and meaningless act, our response was not to dismiss the idea as a nightmare, but to say, "Since it is wrong to be the priest and sacrifice the lamb, I will be the lamb and be sacrificed by the priest." We thereby set up a principle that doom was honourable for innocent things, and conceded that if we spoke of kindliness and recommended peace it was fitting that afterwards the knife should be passed across our throats. Therefore it happened again and again that when we fought well for a reasonable cause and were in sight of victory, we were filled with a sense that we were not acting according to the divine protocol, and turned away and sought defeat, thus betraying those who had trusted us to win them kindliness and peace.

Thus it was that the Slavs were defeated by the Turks on the field of Kossovo. They knew that Christianity was better for man than Islam, because it denounced the prime human fault, cruelty, which the military mind of Mohammed had not even identified, and they knew also that their essential achievements in conduct and art would be trodden down into the mud if they were vanquished. Therefore, because of the power of the rock over their minds, they could not go forward to victory. They knew that in this matter they were virtuous, therefore it was fitting that they should die. In that belief they betrayed all the virtuous who came after them, for five hundred years. And I had sinned in the same way, I and my kind, the liberals of Western Europe. We had regarded ourselves as far holier than our tory opponents because we had exchanged the role of priest for the role of lamb, and therefore we forgot that we were not performing the chief moral obligation of humanity, which is to protect the works of love. We have done nothing to save our people, who have some little freedom and therefore some power to make their souls, from the trampling hate of the other peoples that are without the faculty for freedom and desire to root out the soul like a weed. It is possible that we have betrayed life and love for more than five hundred years on a field wider than Kossovo, as wide as Europe. As I perceived it I felt again that imbecile anxiety concerning my own behaviour in such a crisis, which is a matter of only the slightest importance. What mattered was that I had not served life faithfully, that I had been too anxious for a fictitious personal salvation, and imbecile enough to conceive that I might secure it by hanging round a stinking rock where a man with dirty hands shed blood for no reason.

"Is this not a lovely old Albanian man?" asked Constantine. Indeed he was; and he was the lovelier because he was smiling, and the smile of an Albanian is cool and refreshing as a bite out of a watermelon, their light eyes shine, their white teeth gleam. Also this old man's skin was white and transparent, like a very thin cloud. "I think he is very good," said Constantine, "and he is certainly very pathetic, for he has guessed we are going to the Trepcha mines and he wants us to get a job for his grandson, who, he says, is a clever boy. I wonder if we could not do something about it." Constantine was always at his happiest when he was being kind, and this opportunity for benevolence made his eye shine brighter than we had seen it for many a day; but the cheek below was pouched and raddled like a weeping woman's. Perhaps he had been weeping. The grey falcon had visited him also. He had bared his throat to Gerda's knife, he had offered his loving heart to the service of hate, in order that he might be defeated and innocent.

"Naturally," said Dragutin, speaking broken German so that the old man should not understand, "this one must be something of a villian, since he is an Albanian. The Albanians, having the blood-feud and being brigands and renouncers of Christ, are great villains. But this one is poor and very old, and whatever harm he does he cannot do for much longer, so let us do what we can for him." He shuddered, then laid his open hand on his chest and breathed deeply, as if he had thought of old age and was restoring himself by savouring his own health and strength. It would have been possible to take him as an image of primitive simplicity had he not, only a little time before, recited this subtle and complicated poem about the grey falcon, and had not that poem survived simply because his people were able to appreciate it. This is the Slav mystery: that the Slav, who seems wholly a man of action, is aware of the interior life, of the springs of action, as only the intellectuals of other races are. It is possible that a Slav Cæsar might be moved in crises by a purity of metaphysical motive hardly to be conceived elsewhere, save among priests and philosophers. Perhaps Stephen Dushan was not only influenced by thoughts of innocence and guilt, as all great statesmen are, but was governed by them almost to the exclusion of simpler and more material considerations. Perhaps he died in his prime as many die, because he wished for death; because this image of bloody sacrifice which obsesses us all had made him see shame in the triumph which seemed his destiny. He stood at his doorway in the Balkan mountains and looked on the gold and ivory and marble of Constantinople, on its crosses and its domes and the ships in its harbours, and he knew that he was as God to these things, for they would cease to be, unless he retained them as clear thoughts in his mind. He feared to have that creative power, he stepped back from the light of his doorway, he retreated into the blameless world of the shadows; and Constantinople faded like a breath on a window-pane.

"Yugoslavia is always telling me about one death or another," I said to myself, "the death of Franz Ferdinand, the death of Alexander Obrenovitch and Draga, the death of Prince Michael, the death of Prince Lazar, the death of Stephen Dushan. Yet this country is full of life. I feel that we Westerners should come here to learn to live. But perhaps we are ignorant about life in the West because we avoid thinking about death. One could not study geography if one concentrated on the land and turned one's attention away from the sea." Then I cried out, for I had forgotten the black lamb, and it had stretched out its neck and laid its cold twitching muzzle against my bare forearm. All the men laughed at me, though the Albanian was careful to keep a central core of courtesy in his laughter. I returned their laughter, but I was frightened. I did not trust anybody in this group, least of all myself, to cast off this infatuation with sacrifice which had caused Kossovo, which, if it were not checked, would abort all human increase.

Montenegro

ROAD

I woke early.*◇◇ I had had to dine on sardines, dry bread, red wine, and black coffee, and the diet had not suited me. I crept out of my room and along the groaning, grumbling corridors and down into the street, and took a cab out to the Patriarchate, because I wanted to have another look at the huge Madonna and her tiny rebellious and athletic Christ-child. The Albanian cab-driver brought a friend with him on the box, who also, he said, wished to enjoy the opportunity of conversation with me, so I spread out my dictionary on my knee and did what I could for them. The cab-driver was a sombrely handsome young man of a type familiar in the Balkans; his friend was a natural comedian, a Robin Goodfellow, with straight red hair long about his shoulders, a crowing voice, and stiff, signalling hands. They were Roman Catholics, but I found they knew nothing of the sayings or doings of Pope Pius X, and most of their Western co-religionists would have found them not altogether congenial. The driver was single, but Robin Goodfellow had married a girl of fourteen seven years ago and had six children. They were resentful against the Government and expressed the desire and even an intention to murder as many of its officials as possible, but their chief grievance seemed nothing more than the price of sugar. This is indeed high, owing to the state monopoly, but not so high as to justify this extreme ferocity. They were very much interested in all sweet things, and had heard about the superiority of English and Swiss chocolate, so I had to talk with the pedantry of a wine connoisseur about Peters and Tobler and Nestlé, Cadbury and Rowntree and Fry. Jam and spices they wanted to learn about also; but I failed to surmount the difficulty of describing curry in an imperfectly mastered language. They asked me how old I was, what my husband did, and why he had not come out with me. When I said he was still asleep they suggested to each other, not facetiously, but as realists in a world of men, that he had as like as not been drunk the night before.

*[In Petch.]

The garden of the Patriarchate was golden-green in the slanting early sunlight, the church was honey-coloured and filled with the honey of the Abbot's voice. Among the chief glories of the Orthodox Church are the number of priests who can sing and speak as the mouthpieces of a god should do. I had come in for the end of a service which had been attended by two middle-aged men, who bore themselves like devotees of unusual fervour, some young women with their children, and a number of straight-backed old ladies in trousers whom I had noticed here before. When the service was over I had half an hour with the frescoes, which were now still lovelier than I had thought them. The morning light, striking the windows of the dome at right angles, was deflected into the softest possible radiance as it poured down into the church, and under it the paintings gave up their full gentleness, the elegance and springlike freshness that made them kin to much early Italian art. I looked not so long at the terrible Mother and Child as at the scenes which showed the Christian legend taking place in a country that I had thought to be ancient Tuscany, that I now knew to have wider frontiers. Then I went into the sunlight, warm enough now to draw the scent out of the walnut trees and the pines, and I took a last draught of the healing water from the fountain before I went to say good-bye to the priest, who was drinking his morning coffee at a table under the trees. I stood beside him for a minute before he noticed me, for his Albanian servant and an old labourer had laid down before him a plant with fleshy leaves and stem that had been trampled and broken, and he was staring at it, with his elbows on the table and his coffee-cup held in his hands. I think they were debating what animal had been that way. Their deliberation had an air of essential virtue. By such carefulness life survives.

On the way home the cab-driver and his friend inquired what countries I had visited, and which I liked best. I said I had been to the United States and every country in Europe except Russia, Roumania, Poland, and Portugal; and that I liked Yugoslavia, the United States, France, and Finland best of all. They cried out at the name of France. The French they could not abide. They had fought against them in the Great War, they said, and they were glad of it. They liked, they said, the Germans and the Bulgarians, and they hated the Serbs. They both agreed that they would thoroughly enjoy another war if only it would give them the chance of shooting a lot of Serbs. They held up their left arms and looked along them and twitched their right thumbs against their left elbows and said "Boom! Boom! A Serb is dead!" I said, "But what have you against the Serbs?" They said, "After the war they ill-treated us and took our land from us." There was some justification for this, I knew. The district of Petch was handed over to an old man who had been King Peter's Master of the Horse, and he appears, like our own followers of the Belvoir and the Quorn, to have offered conclusive proof of the power-fully degenerative effect of equine society on the intellect. "But now what do they do to you?" I asked. They shrugged and grumbled. "We live so poor," they said; "in Albania our brothers live far better than we do." It was as pathetic as the belief of the Bulgarian school-boy in Bitolj that Bulgaria was a richer country than Yugoslavia; for everybody who comes out of Albania into Yugoslavia is amazed at the difference, which is all in Yugoslavia's favour, of the standard of living.

When they left me at my hotel, I gave the driver a good tip, and he thanked me in a phrase so remarkable that I made him repeat it several times. But it was true; he had really said, "I am glad of this money, for tomorrow I am going to Paris to be married." It sounded such a *Sketch* and *Tatler* thing to do that, though by this time I was exhausted by the strain of picking a conversation piecemeal out of a dictionary, I made him explain it. The explanation gave me fresh evidence of the capacity of France to assimilate strange stuff and make it her own. "You must know," he said, "that I am not only the driver of this cab, I own it." "He is Rothschild!" shrieked Robin Goodfellow, poking him in the ribs, "he owns a dozen cabs." He owned in fact eight. They took the visitors to Dechani, and anyway no woman of property went about Petch on foot except to the market. When he had bought the eighth he had written to his aunt, who had married the Italian proprietor of a small hotel in Paris, and asked her to find him a wife. She had found him the photographs of several candidates in the Albanian colony of Paris, which was small but prosperous, and he had chosen one to whom he was to be married in five days' time. In a missionary spirit I said, "Is your aunt happy in Paris?" "Yes," he said, "she and her husband made a lot of money, and they say they are very free there." "And the Albanians who live there, are they happy?" "Yes," he answered, "they are all doing well." "But don't you think maybe that means the French are good enough people?" I said. But it was not a point that was likely to convince people who had been brought up to regard as normal a state where different races grew up in conditions decided by a distant ruler. To them the idea of a country being directly governed by its inhabitants is one of abnormal compactness, like a hermaphrodite.

I went up to our bedroom and found my husband locking his suit-case. On the middle of my bed there had been built with offensive ingenuity a little cairn of the things I had forgotten to pack in mine. "They are all things," I pointed out, "that I would not mind losing." "Packing," said my husband, "belongs to a different category from criticism." The little Hungarian chambermaid popped her head inside the door, and we tipped her fifty dinars, which is four and twopence, and she thought it so handsome that she kissed my hand furiously. "That is a good little one," said Constantine, as he went downstairs to breakfast; "this morning she helped me to pack and she said to me, 'I tell you, I would have liked to be with you, you are so charming, so very cultured, it might even have been that you would have quoted select passages of poetry to me. So I have been to you every night when I had finished my work, but each time you had fever, you were red as a lobster, so I saw it was not written in the stars that we should be together.' "

We had our breakfast outside the large restaurant, and presently Constantine left us to say good-bye to the Chief of Police, who was giving some advice to a man standing with two pack-horses in the middle of the road, and we were joined by the Danish seller of agri-cultural machinery,* who regarded us with a benevolence that was galling. We had the impression that he had just received information that we were completely harmless and unimportant, and that in any case even if we had some grain of significance we were leaving, so it did not matter. "You are going, *hein?*" he said. "Over the moun-tains to Kolashin and then to Tsetinye? And up the coast to Split, and then to Budapest, and home, very nice, very nice." "How kind of you to be so interested in our itinerary as to find out what it is," said my husband. "Oh, the people here talk, you know," said the alleged Dane. "I should think it more likely that they read," said my husband darkly. There fell a silence, which I weakly broke by saying to him, "Look, do you see that young man walking along carrying that black portfolio? Bow to him, he has greeted us. It is the clerk of the court, who so kindly offered to show us the sights of the town the first night we got here." The alleged Dane burst into

*[From an earlier encounter in which the "Dane" was clearly a German spying out the land.]

728

laughter. "That young *Lümmel*! He was fool enough to tell me what he earns. Think of it, he is a university graduate, and he makes each week twelve marks—one of your pounds! Here they're a starveling lot." "Yes, it's a pity they're so poor," said my husband. "For they are such nice people," said I. "You waste your pity," said the alleged Dane, in sudden and brutal passion; "these are Slavs, they have no right to anything, they are as sheep, as cattle, as swine."

The hotel tried to overcharge us, but its experience of the world was so small that its efforts were scarcely perceptible. However, Constantine and Dragutin were very indignant, and we did not get clear of the dispute until ten minutes past seven. Then we started off for the gorge, for Tserna Gora. "Now we will climb like eagles!" cried Dragutin. "And there," he said, as we passed a grassy patch under the willows on the river's bank on the way to the Patriarchate, "is where I have slept each night since we came to Petch. These accursed thieves at the hotel tried to charge me, a chauffeur, for my room at the same rate as you people, and though I knew you would have paid, I would not have it so, and I came out here and flung myself down, and it was no sacrifice, for I slept like a king."

We left the bosomy domes of the Patriarchate behind us, and we went into the Rugovo gorge, which would at any time be superb, and was now a pageant of the sterner beauties possible in nature and man. It was over the rocks at the mouth of this gorge that the retreating Serbian Army of 1915 pushed its guns lest the Austrians and Bulgarians should make use of them, and walked on into ice and famine; and the scenery is appropriate to that drama. Its sheer precipices and fretted peaks show the iron constitution our planet hides under its grass and flowers; and down the road there were swinging in majestic rhythm men and women who showed the core of hardness humanity keeps under its soft wrapping of flesh. They were going down to the market at Petch, and most were on foot; before nightfall they would return to their homes. And they were coming from villages five, ten, and even fifteen miles up the gorge. In fact, they were going to walk ten to thirty miles in the day, the latter half of the journey up a steep mountain road. It seemed so Herculean a trip that we got Constantine to question two typical wayfarers, an Albanian wearing a white turban with its ends brought across his throat, to hide one of the goitres which are so common in the mountains, and his wife, a raw-boned woman wearing a black dress which oddly broke into a flounce just above her knees, with something of a Cretan air. Yes, they came from that village up there, about a mile away on the hillside, and they would walk to Petch and back by nightfall. There was no question of riding their pack-pony for it was loaded now with what they were going to sell, which was wool, and on the return journey it would be loaded with what they were going to buy, which would probably be wood, if the price were right; in any case I doubt if it could have carried their pylonlike forms. Their leathery faces slowly split into enormous grins as they grasped our astonishment. All these people on the road were very deliberate and stiff and emphatic in their movements and their speech, like frescoes come to life. One woman, who was sitting in a cart with her young child under her blue mantle, resembled exactly one of the Madonnas of Dechani, twisted by the strain put upon her endurance by her love. Again it seemed that Byzantine art is not so much stylized as we believe, and that it may be a more or less naturalist representation of a highly stylized life.

The gorge widened to a valley where snow mountains looked down on beechwoods, widened and steepened to another Switzerland; and so it might be, and may yet become. The grass grows short and thick as gourmand cows would have it. Here there might be cheese and tinned milk and milk chocolate, if the population could but afford to buy good cows and knew how to keep them. In Stephen Dushan's time fat flocks and herds were driven up here every summer, but under the Turks such luxurious husbandry was forgotten among Christians, and only a few nomads cared for pastures in such a disputed district as the frontier between Montenegro and Albania. Even those had their movements circumscribed by the definition of the Yugoslavian frontier, for some of them had their winter pastures in territory that was assigned to Greece and to Albania, hence they could no longer pass from one to the other. Also there might be practised a moderate form of mountaineering, for there is some excellent rock-climbing and some eternal snow; but the tradition of guides and chalets has yet to be created. There are as good as Swiss flowers. Where the road mounted to the pass it hairpinned across a slope too high for trees, which was clouded purple with crocuses, golden with kingcups. On the razor-edge of the pass we looked, as one may often do in Switzerland, backward and forward at two worlds. Behind us the mountains stretched to a warm horizon, themselves not utterly cold, as if the low hills and plains beyond exhaled a rich, thawing breath from their fertility. Before us the mountains and valleys fused into a land cooler than all others, as a statue is cooler than a living body. It is not, as the school books have it, that Montenegro is barren: that is a delusion of those who see it only from the sea. Its inland half, if it has little for the plough, has many woods and pastures. But they are held in a cup of rock, they are insulated from the common tide of warmth that suffuses the rest of earth. What the cup holds is pure. In summer, they say, there is here pure heat; in autumn pure ripeness; in winter pure cold. Now, in this late springtime it was pure freshness, the undiluted essence of what that season brings the world to renew its youth.

"At this pass was the old Turkish frontier," said Constantine. "And is no more, and is no more, thank God," said Dragutin. Down below, at the end of a valley bright with the thin green flames of beechwoods and clouds of flowers, we came on a poorish village and halted at the inn. "Now I must ask the way to Lake Plav," said Constantine, "for you should certainly see Lake Plav. Did you ever hear of it?" I knew the name. An unfortunate *contretemps* occurred here during the Balkan War. When Montenegro captured the village of Plav from the Turks in 1912, they were greatly aided by a local Moslem priest, who joined the Orthodox Church and was appointed a major in the Montenegrin Army. His first action when left unsupervised was to hold a court-martial on his former congregation and to shoot all those who refused to be baptized. They numbered, it is said, five hundred. The incident has the terrible quality of juvenile crime. Little Willie was told to be a good boy and keep his baby from crying, and it was precisely because he wanted to be a good boy that he held a pillow over baby's face. I had thought of the place where this happened as a circle of mud huts in a hollow of gleaming stones below vertical mountains. But two or three miles over a bumpy road took us to a place that was a perfect and rounded image of pleasure. A circle of water lay in a square of emerald marshland, fringed with whitish reeds, and framed by hills patterned with green grass and crimson earth, with a sheer wall of snow mountains behind them. The glowing hills and the shining peaks were exactly mirrored in the lake, and received the embellishment of a heavenly bloom peculiar to its waters. We sat down on a stone dike, shaded by a thorn which the winds had whipped into the form of a modest Chinese lady. Below us a man was cutting turf at the lake edge, and loading it on a bright-blue cart drawn by a grey pony; he was as graceful as if he had never known fatigue in his life, and his white shirt, kilt, and trousers and black

731

bolero were white as snow and black as coal against the emerald marsh. This was as good a place as can be, if beauty is of any good. "Lake Plav," said Constantine, "means blue lake. *Plav* is a strange word. It means blue or fair-haired. All that is beautiful without being sombre."

Back at the inn, we had an early lunch in disasteful surroundings. A dog that had lost a paw limped about our feet; it was still, they said, wonderful at rabbiting, and it looked up at us with the cold eye and the snarl of one who lives in pain and by wile. As we ate, a motor bus which had left Tsetinye at dawn arrived and disgorged a load of pallid people, holding the battered yellow hemispheres of sucked lemons and making no effort to conceal that they had found the remedy against sickness not wholly satisfactory. One demonstrated that in her case it had been completely ineffectual. "There is everything here that Aldous Huxley could desire," said my husband; and it was true, for in the inn garden on the other side of the road was a little building like a summer-house, poised high on piles over a stream, which we were forced to believe was a sanitary installation of too simple a kind. But squalor is not a Montenegrin characteristic. If the country has a blatant fault, it is a chilling blankness. The typical house stands high-shouldered on a small base under a steeply raked roof tiled with what looks like slate but is pine; its face is singularly inexpressive. It is often isolated, for as this land was not occupied by the Turks there was not the same necessity to huddle together for protection from armed raiders; but even when such houses are gathered together in villages they never warm into welcoming sociability, Andriyevitsa, a village of fifteen hundred inhabitants, which we came to after ten miles' drive through olive groves and plum orchards, is well set on a ledge above a river with heaths and pinewoods about it, and has a handsome main street planted with great trees and lined with substantial stone houses, which are ornamented with fine balconies, an architectural feature which marks that one has crossed the cultural watershed and has come down on the side of Dalmatia and Venice and the West, for the Oriental cares little for them. In spite of these advantages its effect on the stranger is cold and dreary. It is as if the genius of the place lacked emotional and intellectual pigmentation. And that effect is intensified by the terrible purity of Montenegrin good looks. The beauty of both the men and the women is beyond what legend paints it; because legends desire to please, and this perfection demonstrates that there can be too much of a good thing. They are fabulous non-monsters. Such symmetry of feature and figure, such lustre of hair and eye and skin and teeth, such unerring grace, chokes the eye with cream.

Outside the village of Andriyevitsa, on a glassy plateau high above a river, was a kind of park which contained a new white church built in the Byzantine style and a war memorial consisting of a black marble needle marked in white letters with a prodigious number of names. We went to see what this might be, and a young man who had been asleep in the long grass beside the memorial rose up in such white immobile handsomeness as Disraeli would have ascribed to a duke, and told us that it commemorated the members of the Vasoyevitch tribe who had fallen in the wars. The Serbs who took refuge here after Kossovo split up into tribes, each with its own chief, very much after the order of our Scottish clans, and the Vasoyevitches were among the most powerful. All four sides of the needle were covered with names; there must have been seven or eight hundred of them. I exclaimed aloud when I saw that the inscription gave the dates of the war as 1912–21, but of course it is true that this country was continually under arms for nine years. First they joined with the Serbs in the Balkan wars, but when the Turks were beaten they had to continue a local war with the Albanians until the Great War came, and then the Austrians attacked them; and the peace brought them none, for they fought against the Serbs in protest against their incorporation in Yugoslavia. As we stood there we were joined by an elderly woman, poorly dressed but quite as aristocratic-looking as the young man; and they acted as our host and hostess in a tour of interesting graves. Two generals belonging to the tribe were buried in the park; and over the road, in the open heathland, lay two tribesmen who had been hanged on this spot by the Austrians, and not far off two other members of an earlier generation who had been imprudent enough to demand a liberal constitution from King Nicholas.

The air we breathed was pine-scented and rarefied by height; the moorland and mountain and waters about us enjoyed their elemental innocence; these marvellously beautiful people, placid as prize animals, showed us the tombs of their butchered kin. I remembered that this country, with greater certainty than any other country that I could think of, might attribute its survival to one single event, and that that event was loathsome in character. For three hundred years after Kossovo the Montenegrins fought against the Turks with unremitting courage, and vanquished them again and again. But when the Turks were outside Vienna in 1683 and then were driven out of Hungary they turned their full attention to this enemy who was weaker and nearer home. They marched through the mountains, guided by Montenegrins who had adopted the Islamic faith, and they occupied Tsetinye. Thereafter it seemed that the last Christian Slav stronghold must fall, largely because there were so many of the renegades. Two-thirds of the Albanian people had been converted during the seventeenth century, and it looked as if their example had corrupted their neighbours. In 1702 a bishop was kidnapped by the Turks when he was on his way home from the consecration of a new church and he was held to ransom. The ruler of Montenegro, Daniel Nyegosh, saw that his people must strike then or perish. It is told in one of the national ballads that he called a meeting of the tribes and bade them go forth on Christmas Eve and offer every Montenegrin Mohammedan the choice between baptism and death. Five brothers named Martinovitch alone obeyed him, and though the ballad assumes that they themselves executed the plan, it is obvious that they must have used the whole of their tribe. "The time fixed for the holy vigil is at hand; the brothers Martinovitch light their holy tapers, pray earnestly to the new-born God, drink each a cup of wine to the glory of Christ. Seizing their consecrated maces, they set out in the dark."

I am on the side of the brothers Martinovitch. Having seen what Turkish conquest meant to the Slav, it is certain they were justified in their crime. A man is not a man if he will not save his seed. But the destiny is abhorrent that compelled the brothers, who may be assumed to have been of flawless and inhuman beauty, like the Montenegrins of today, to go out into the night and murder the renegades, who also would be beautiful. "Please give me some brandy," I said to my husband, "I feel rather ill." But when he poured it out of his flask it was not what I wanted. I would have preferred a drink that was enormously strong, that would instantly have clouded my consciousness, that would have smelt of nothing, like vodka. The bouquet of brandy recalls the pageant of the earth, the lovely and logical process of flower and fruit that causes man, with his leaning towards argument by analogy, to harbour such excessive hopes concerning his own life. It is a subtlety, and up here subtleties seemed doomed. As we drove out of the heathland into greener country, where there were farms that were astonishingly trim, considering they had to stand on end, we passed churches that had neither with-

734

in nor without the faintest air of mysticism. They might have been town-halls, or even, in some cases, blockhouses.

That was natural enough, for in Montenegro church and state were till recently not merely welded but identical. In the sixteenth century the last king of the line of John Tserno, John the Outlaw, after whom the land was named Tserna Gora, abdicated and went to live in Venice; and before he left he called an assembly of the people and transferred his authority to the Bishop of Tsetinye, who was the head of the Montenegrin Church. Even so the Emperor Constantine the Great, on leaving Rome to found Constantinople, transferred his authority to the Pope, and thus gave the Papacy its claim to temporal power. Thus it happened that until 1851, when Danilo II fell in love with a pretty girl and changed the constitution so that he could marry her and transmit his royalty to their children, Montenegro was governed by a succession of prince-bishops who passed their power from uncle to nephew. The Church was, therefore, the Government, and its buildings were therefore adapted to the state's chief function, which was to resist the Turk: not here could goodness be adored and its indestructibility be recognized in ecstasy. The first and real need was an altar where the Martinovitch brothers could take a stirrup-cup before they set out on their pious errand, their truly pious errand, swinging their consecrated maces. Christianity was still an inspiration, and one that had proven its worth, but, like Montenegrin houses and good looks, it was too simple, too stark, so full of one perfect thing that it was as good as empty.

"Have the Montenegrins not made enormous sacrifices to preserve their independence?" I asked Constantine, and he answered, "Greater than you can believe. They have sacrificed almost everything except their heroism. They are nothing but heroes. If they eat or sleep it is so that they shall wake up heroes. If they marry it is so that they should beget little heroes, who would not trouble to come out of their mothers' wombs were they not certain that they would grow up in heroism. They are as like the people of Homer as any race now living: they are brave, and beautiful, and vainglorious. A soldier must be vainglorious. He must go into the battle believing that he is so wonderful a human being that God could not let it be that the lesser men in front of him should kill him. And since the men in front of them were Turks who were often really prodigious fighters, there was no end to the fairy-tales that the Montenegrins had to tell to themselves about themselves. You get it in the two classic stories that are always told about these people. One is really true; it was a thing noticed in the Balkan wars. You know that when soldiers drill they have to number off—'One, two, one, two.' In the Montenegrin Army it could not be done. No man was willing to be second, so the first man said, 'One,' and the second said, 'I-am-beside-him,' very quickly. The other may be true, but perhaps only in the spirit. It is said that a traveller said to a Montenegrin, 'How many of your people are there?' and he answered, 'With Russia, one hundred and eighty millions,' and the traveller, knowing there were not two hundred thousand of them, said, 'Yes, but how many without the Russians?' and the Montenegrin answered, 'We will never desert the Russians.' And it was not a joke, for the vainglory of these people was necessary to them lest they should be conquered in battle.

"This vainglory will not permit them to have any other characteristics, except a little cunning that is quite simple, like the cunning of the Homeric heroes, for to be perfectly and absolutely vainglorious you must hold back from all activity, because you dare not ever fail at anything. So the Montenegrins are not really interested in any kind of work, and that makes it very difficult to fit them into the modern state of Yugoslavia. For in earlier centuries they lived by fighting, which always included a lot of looting, and by foreign subsidies, which were freely given, as this state was an important strategic point on the Adriatic coast; and in the late nineteenth and twentieth centuries they lived very much on these subsidies, particularly from Russia. And now all that is over, and they must earn their livings, and they do not want to do anything at all, for even farming used to be done chiefly by their women, since they always were at war or resting between wars, and no work interests them. No child here says, 'I would like to be a builder, or a doctor, or a carpenter,' though some want to be chauffeurs because to them it is still a daring and romantic occupation. So they pester the Government with demands for posts as functionaries and for pensions, which are of a terrible simplicity, for there is no need for so many functionaries, and if there were these people could not perform their functions, and God Himself, if He had a knife at His throat, could not invent a reason why they should all have pensions. This is hard on a poor country like Yugoslavia, and this is not an easy matter to settle by patience and patriotism, as many things can be settled in Bosnia and Old Serbia and Macedonia, because the Montenegrins are empty-headed except for their wild and unthinking heroism, which is to say they

736

are often like madmen. I tell it you, this country is a sacrifice to itself of itself, and there is nothing left."

There is no way out of the soul's dilemma. Those displeased by the rite on the Sheep's Field, who would be neither the priest nor the black lamb, who would be neither converted to Islam nor defeated on Kossovo plain, are forced to fight the priest. Since we must live in the same world as those we fight, this means sharing this upland bleakness, furnished too simply with its bloodstained monolith. "Whoso liveth by the sword shall die by the sword" is only half the damnatory sentence passed on mankind by war; the other half reads, "Whoso refuseth to die by the sword shall live by the sword." Montenegro was something like a poison. Though it was airy as Heaven, instead of airless, like other prisons, it was stony like a cell, and it reeked of heroism as strongly as institutions reek of disinfectant; and the straitened inhabitants were sealed up in space with the ideas of slaughter and triumph as convicts are in their confinement with guilt and punishment. If one shut the eyes and thought of any pleasantness but the most elemental, any enjoyment that helped the mind further on its task of exploring the universe, one had to say on opening them, "It is not here, nothing but the root of it is here."

So it seemed. Then the road looped round the mountainside to a steeper mountain, and wound up to yet another pass, so high that as we rose the noontide sky showed pale above the distant peaks, though it was deeply blue above us. The country, which here is highly variable, changed its character again; it was Buckinghamshire on this cool northward slope, so tall the beeches, so dense the woods they drove to the skyline, so gardenish the grass. Up and up we drove until we had to stop, to cool the engine. We none of us regretted it, for there were many gentians on the banks beside the road, and below us the woods lay like bonfires of green flame on the mild rolling turf, and further the distant infinity of mountains was blue as wild hyacinths. We sat there so long that a woman we had passed on a lower curve of the road overtook us, halted in her trudging, came up to the car, and laid her arm along the frame of the open window, looking round at us all. Her face had once been perfect but was no longer so, and was the better for it. "Good morning," she said to Constantine, "who are you?" "I am Constantine," he said, "I am from Shabats and I am a poet." "And who are you?" she asked my husband and me. "They are English," said Constantine. "A very fine

737

people," she said. "Why do you think that?" said Constantine. "Because they are great fighters, and they love nature," she said. "How do you know they are like that?" asked Constantine. She lifted her arm from the window, took a ball of fine white wool and knitting-needles from her other hand, and set to work again, as if sensing from his question an indication that the conversation might not be of the first order and she might as well get on with her material duties. "Oh, everybody knows that," she answered absently. "And you," said Constantine, "who are you? Are you a native of this place?" "No," she said, "I live here now, but I was born by Durmitor." Durmitor is the great snow mountain, with a black lake at its foot, on the northern side of Montenegro. "Who brought you here?" asked Constantine.

She laughed a little, lifted her ball of wool to her mouth, sucked the thin thread between her lips, and stood rocking herself, her eyebrows arching in misery. "It is a long story. I am sixty now," she said. "Before the war I was married over there, by Durmitor. I had a husband whom I liked very much, and I had two children, a son and a daughter. In 1914 my husband was killed by the Austrians. Not in battle. They took him out of our house and shot him. My son went off and was a soldier and was killed, and my daughter and I were sent to a camp. There she died. In the camp it was terrible, many people died. At the end of the war I came out and I was alone. So I married a man twenty years older than myself. I did not like him as I liked my first husband, but he was very kind to me, and I had two children of his. But they both died, as was natural, for he was too old, and I was too old, and also I was weak from the camp. And now my husband is eighty, and he has lost his wits, and he is not kind to me any more. He is angry with everybody; he sits in his house and rages, and I cannot do anything right for him. So I have nothing." "Are you poor?" asked Constantine. "Not at all," she said. "My husband's son by his first wife is a judge in Old Serbia, and he sends me three hundred dinars a month to hire a man to work our land, so we want nothing. Oh, that is all right, but the rest is so wrong." "Oh, sister, sister," said Constantine, "this is very hard." "Yes, it's hard," she said. "And can we do nothing for you," asked Constantine, "for we feel very friendly towards you? Can we not give you a lift to where you are going?" "That you cannot do, though you mean so kindly," she said, "for I am not going anywhere. I am walking about to try to understand why all this has happened. If I had to live, why should my life have been like this? If I walk about up here where it is very high and grand it seems to me I am nearer to understanding it." She put the ball of wool to her forehead and rubbed it backwards and forwards, while her eyes filled with painful speculation. "Goodbye," she said, with distracted courtesy, as she moved away, "goodbye."

This woman was of no importance. It is doubtful whether, walk as she would on these heights, she would arrive at any conclusion that was of value even to herself. She was, however, the answer to my doubts. She took her destiny not as the beasts take it, nor as the plants and trees; she not only suffered it, she examined it. As the sword swept down on her through the darkness she threw out her hand and caught the blade as it fell, not caring if she cut her fingers so long as she could question its substance, where it had been forged, and who was the wielder. She wanted to understand the secret which Gerda denied, the mystery of process. I knew that art and science were the instruments of this desire, and this was their sole justification, though in the Western world where I lived I had seen art debauched to ornament and science prostituted to the multiplication of gadgets. I knew that they were descended from man's primitive necessities, that the cave man who had to hunt the aurochs drew him on the rock-face that he might better understand the aurochs and have fuller fortune in hunting and was the ancestor of all artists, that the nomad who had to watch the length of shadows to know when he should move his herd to the summer pasture was the ancestor of all scientists. But I did not know these things thoroughly with my bowels as well as my mind. I knew them now, when I saw the desire for understanding move this woman. It might have been far otherwise with her, for she had been confined by her people's past and present to a kind of destiny that might have stunned its victims into an inability to examine it. Nevertheless she desired neither peace nor gold, but simply knowledge of what her life might mean. The instrument used by the hunter and the nomad was not too blunt to turn to finer uses; it was not dismayed by complexity, and it could regard the more stupendous aurochs that range within the mind and measure the diffuse shadows cast by history. And what was more, the human will did not forget its appetite for using it.

I remembered what Denis Saurat had said about Militsa: "If there are but twenty people like her scattered between here and China, civilization will survive." If during the next million generations there is but one human being born in every generation who will not cease to inquire into the nature of his fate, even while it strips and bludgeons him, some day we shall read the riddle of our universe. We shall discover what work we have been called to do, and why we cannot do it. If a mine fails to profit by its riches and a church wastes the treasure of its altar, we shall know the cause: we shall find out why we draw the knife across the throat of the black lamb or take its place on the offensive rock, and why we let the grey falcon nest in our bosom, though it buries its beak in our veins. We shall put our own madness in irons. Then, having defeated our own enmity, we shall be able to face the destiny forced on us by nature, and war with that. And what does that mean? What name is behind nature, what name but one name? Then there will be the wrestling match that is worth the prize, then defeat will be eternal glory, then there can be no issue but magnificence. That contest may endure a million, million years, seeing the might of the combatants. And after that, what then? Could the mind twitch away the black curtain behind the stars, it might be dazzled by a brightness brighter than the stars, which might be the battlefield for another splendid conflict as yet not to be conceived. It was towards this splendour that the woman was leading, as we passed her later, leaving the road and treading a path over the turf among gentians which she did not see. "Good-bye!" Dragutin cried to her. "Good-bye, Mother!"

FROM Epilogue

That was the end of our Easter journey. We said good-bye to Constantine at Kotor and caught our great white shining boat, and before we slept laid eyes again on Dubrovnik, which was complete beyond the habit of real cities against the whitish darkness of the starry June night, complete as a city on a coin. In the morning the Dalmatian coast slid by us, naked as a quarry, until at dusk we came to Sushak, the port where we had started. The next day we travelled back towards Zagreb. ❖ ❖ ❖

In my sitting-room* I found a golden-haired girl, with a letter from a Viennese friend of mine who coaches university students in English, saying that this was one of his favourite pupils and that she had chosen my works as the subject of her thesis. I was naturally appalled. I explained that I was a writer wholly unsuitable for her purpose: that the bulk of my writing was scattered through American and English periodicals; that I had never used my writing to make a continuous disclosure of my own personality to others, but to discover for my own edification what I knew about various subjects which I found to be important to me; and that in consequence I had written a novel about London to find out why I loved it, a life of St Augustine to find out why every phrase I read of his sounds in my ears like the sentence of my doom and the doom of my age, and a novel about rich people to find out why they seemed to me as dangerous as wild boars and pythons, and that consideration of these might severally play a part in theses on London or St Augustine or the rich, but could not fuse to make a picture of a writer, since the interstices were too wide.

To my annoyance the golden-haired girl treated this explanation as a proof of modesty, which it was not, and I saw something inexorable in her intensity, which I could not regard as proof of my importance, in view of the determination of every German university student to find a subject for his thesis which nobody has treated before. I remembered how one such student had gained his doctorate by a thesis on

*[In Vienna, on the way home.]

Mealy Potatoes, a Drury Lane dancer, mentioned on one single occasion by Dickens, whose identity he had tracked through London parish registers, and how he had been surpassed by a successor whose effort was entitled "*Die Schwester von Mealy Potatoes*." The golden-haired girl belonged to this inexorable tradition, and my uneasiness did not prevent her from putting to me a long list of questions. But my answers soon made her even more uneasy than I was. She wanted to pigeon-hole me into a recognized school, and demanded to know what writers had influenced me. It disconcerted her when I reported that as a young person I had tried to write like Mark Twain, that he still seemed to me more fortunate than the princes of the earth in his invariably happy relations with his medium. "But is not Mark Twain an American?" she asked doubtfully. "And a humorous writer?" It was instantly clear to me, as it would have been to any writer, that literature was a closed territory to her and that she would never be able to read a single book. In spite of my glowering she continued, but we found no common ground in the discussion of any of my preferences, even when she accepted them as legitimate.

Presently she said, "I have enough about English writers now?" looking at her notes with some sullenness, as if she foresaw trouble before her in pushing my mind, which appeared to have lost its label, into the proper pigeon-hole. "Tell me," she asked, "about the European writers that have influenced you." "There was Dumas first of all," I said, "whose *Three Musketeers*, whose *Count of Monte Cristo*, taught one in the nursery what romance was, how adventure could prove that what looks to be the close-knit fabric of life is in fact elastic. Then in one's early teens there was Ibsen who corrected the chief flaw in English literature, which is a failure to recognize the dynamism of ideas. The intellectual world is largely of English creation, yet our authors write of ideas as if they were things to pick and choose, even though the choice might be pushed to the extremity of martyrdom, as if they could be left alone, as if they came into play only as they were picked and chosen. But that ideas are the symbols of relationships among real forces that make people late for breakfast, that take away their breakfast, that make them beat each other across the breakfast-table, is something which the English do not like to realize. Lazy, bone-lazy, they wish to believe that life is lived simply by living.

"Yes," I continued, glowing with interest in my theme, though my listener was not, "Ibsen converted me to the belief that it is ideas

742

which make the world go round. But as I grew older I began to realize that Ibsen cried out for ideas for the same reason that men call out for water, because he had not got any. He was a moralist of an extremely simple sort, who had heard, but only as a child might hear the murmur of a shell, the voice of the philosophical ocean. *Brand* is not a play about religion, it is a crude presentation of the ascetic impulse. A *Doll's House* is not a play about the emancipation of women—indeed none of the fundamental issues of that movement are touched—but a naïve and sturdy suggestion that in the scales of justice perhaps mean integrity may weigh less than loving fraud. But with my appetite for ideas whetted by Ibsen I turned back to the literature of my own country, which was then claiming to satisfy it. For this was the time of Galsworthy, Wells, Shaw—"

"Ah, Show, Show," cried the golden-haired girl, pronouncing it to rhyme with "cow." "'Shaw," I said irritably. "'Yes, Show, Show," she went on, "we have not talked of him. I suppose you admire him greatly." "Not very much," I said. "How is that possible?" she asked. "Here we think him your greatest writer, next to Shakespeare and Oscar Wilde." "Next to Oscar Wilde, perhaps, but not to Shakespeare," I snapped; "and now that I re-read him I cannot find traces of any ideas at all. Wells at least had an idea that people would have ideas if they were taught by other people who had some, and was also almost as sublime a controversialist as Voltaire when he met with an irrational fool, but Shaw stands for nothing but a socialism which has nothing to it except a belief that it would be a nicer world if everybody were all clean and well fed, which is based on no analysis of man and depends on no theory of the state, and an entirely platitudinous denunciation of hypocrisy, which nowhere rises to the level of *Tartuffe*. Of course our country has produced better than Shaw and I found them later, but they are not easy to find, for there is a lack of continuity about our literature. A man starts up in isolation, inspired by an idiosyncratic passion to write about a certain subject, but rarely inspired to read what other people have written about it. That is why French literature is of such service to the mind, since each writer is fully aware of his own culture, and knows when he takes part in an argument precisely to what stage his predecessors have brought it."

"But what is this you are saying about French literature?" interrupted the golden-haired girl. I repeated it, and she exclaimed in amazement, "French literature! But surely all French literature is

743

trivial and artificial?" "Trivial and artificial!" I echoed. "Abélard! Ronsard! Joachim du Bellay! Montaigne! Rabelais! Racine! Pascal! La Fontaine! Voltaire! La Rochefoucauld! Balzac! Baudelaire! Victor Hugo! Benjamin Constant! Proust! And Diderot—did you never read *Le Neveu de Rameau?*" "I do not read French," she said; "hardly any of us learn French. But surely all these people put together do not equal Goethe?" I grieved, for it seemed to me that any one of them had as much to say as Goethe, whose philosophy, indeed, boils down to the opinion, "Ain't Nature grand?" I said, "It is a pity you cannot read Montaigne; he also thought much about nature, though he thought of it not as grand, but as inevitable." She looked at me as if she thought that was no very great discovery to have made, and I looked back at her, wondering what words would convey to her the virtue that lies in the full acceptance of destiny, realizing that my words would convey it to her better than Montaigne's. For there was as yet nothing in her which could appreciate what he meant when he said that nothing in the life of Alexander the Great was so humble and mortal as his whimsical fancy for deification, and that it was no use thinking to leave our humanity behind, for if we walked on stilts we still had to walk on our legs, and there was no way of sitting on the most elevated throne save on the bottom. I found myself smiling as I remembered how he adds, inconsequently and yet with the most apposite wisdom, that for old people life need not be so realistically conceived, "Or, la vieillesse a un peu besoin d'être traitée plus tendrement."

Though I was completely preoccupied as I stared at her face, my eyes eventually pressed some information about it on my mind. I realized that her brows and her cheekbones were cast in a mould that had become very familiar to me in the past few months, and that she was fair not negatively, like a Nordic woman, but after the fashion of the golden exceptions to the dark races, as if she had been loaded with rich gold pigment. A suspicion made me look at her visiting-card, which I had been twisting between my fingers, and I exclaimed, "But you are not an Austrian! You have a Slav name!" She answered, "I have lived in Vienna nearly all my life," but I did not notice her tone and objected, "All the same you must be Slav by birth." Miserably, shifting in her chair, with the demeanour of a justly accused thief, she said, "Yes! Both my parents are Croats." I was embarrassed by her manner and said, "Well, I suppose you speak Serbo-Croat as well as German and English, and that is another

744

language for your studies." She answered passionately, "No, indeed, I speak not a word of Serbo-Croat. How should I? I am Viennese, I have lived here nearly all my life, I have not been to Croatia since I was grown up, except for a few days in Zagreb." "And did you not find the people there very clever?" I asked. "I did not speak to them," she cried scornfully. "I thought it a horrible little town, so provincial." "Are you not at all proud of having Slav blood in you?" I exclaimed. "Why should I be? What is there to be proud about in being a Slav?" she asked blankly.

Such is the influence that Central Europe exerts on its surroundings. It cut off this girl from pride in her own race, which would have been a pity had her race had much less to be proud of than the superb achievement of defending European civilization from extinction by the Turks. It cut her off from enlightenment by that French culture which has the advantage over all others of having begun earlier, branching straight from the Roman stem, and having developed most continuously. What it offered her instead was sparse, was recent. It might fairly be defined as Frederick the Great and Goethe. In music it might have offered enough to compensate for all its other lacks, but it had annulled the harmonies of Bach and Beethoven, Mozart and Haydn, by its preference for the false genius, Wagner. It had left this girl flimsy as a jerry-built house with no foundation deeper than the nineteenth century, when loyalty to her Slav blood and adherence to the main current of European culture would have made her heiress to the immense fortune left by the Western and Eastern Roman Empires. Not only Constantine, but this girl and her family, and many others like them, had made this curious choice. Nothing is less true than that men are greedy. Some prefer poverty to wealth, and some even go so far as to prefer death to life. That I was to learn when I returned to England.

This return meant, for me, going into retreat. Nothing in my life had affected me more deeply than this journey through Yugoslavia. This was in part because there is a coincidence between the natural forms and colours of the western and southern parts of Yugoslavia and the innate forms and colours of my imagination. Macedonia is the country I have always seen between sleeping and waking; from childhood, when I was weary of the place where I was, I wished it would turn into a town like Yaitse or Mostar, Bitolj or Ochrid. But my journey moved me also because it was like picking up a strand of wool that would lead me out of a labyrinth in which, to my surprise, I had found myself immured. It might be that when I followed the thread to its end I would find myself faced by locked gates, and that this labyrinth was my sole portion on this earth. But at least I now knew its twists and turns, and what corridor led into what vaulted chamber, and nothing in my life before I went to Yugoslavia had even made plain these mysteries. This experience made me say to myself, "If a Roman woman had, some years before the sack of Rome, realized why it was going to be sacked and what motives inspired the barbarians and what the Romans, and had written down all she knew and felt about it, the record would have been of value to historians. My situation, though probably not so fatal, is as interesting." Without doubt it was my duty to keep a record of it.

So I resolved to put on paper what a typical Englishwoman felt and thought in the late nineteen-thirties when, already convinced of the inevitability of the second Anglo-German war, she had been able to follow the dark waters of that event back to its source. That committed me to what was in effect some years of a retreat spent among fundamentals. I was obliged to write a long and complicated history, and to swell that with an account of myself and the people who went with me on my travels, since it was my aim to show the past side by side with the present it created. And while I grappled with the mass of my material during several years, it imposed certain ideas on me.

I became newly doubtful of empires. Since childhood I had been consciously and unconsciously debating their value, because I was born a citizen of one of the greatest empires the world has ever seen, and grew up as its exasperated critic. Never at any time was I fool enough to condemn man for conceiving the imperial theory, or to deny that it had often proved magnificent in practice. In the days when there were striking inequalities among the peoples of the earth, when some were still ignorant of agriculture and the complex process that lies behind the apparent simplicity of nomadism, and were therefore outrageously predatory in their hunger, when some were still candid in their enjoyment of murder, those further advanced must have found the necessity to protect their goods and their lives turn insensibly into a habit of conquest. In those times, also, it could well be that barbarians might possess a metal or a plant for which more cultured peoples had invented a beneficial use, and might refuse them access to it from sheer sullenness; and then, should one hold a communist theory of life and believe that all things are for all people, an attempt to break down that refusal must be approved. It is true that long ago it became untrue that peoples presented any serious damage because of backwardness; the threat of savagery has for long lain in technical achievement. For many centuries, too, a war waged by the civilized for access to materials unused by their primitive owners has failed to remain absolutely justifiable for long, since the inequality between the parties involved tempted the stronger to abuse. But if these moral sanctions for imperialism could not be claimed without hypocrisy in its later stages, they then acquired the value of all hypocritical pretences, which is to give a good example. The theory of the British Empire that it existed to bring order into the disordered parts of the earth was more than half humbug, but it inspired to action those in whose love of action there was nothing humbugging. These fought plagues and flood and drought and famine on behalf of the subject races, and instituted law courts where justice, if not actually blind when governors and governed came into conflict, was as a general rule blindfolded. These services might be conceived—though probably nothing could be more irritating to those who were its objects—as chivalrous acts, and those who performed them as *veray parfit gentil* knights. This had the wholly satisfactory result that the common people, proud of their empire and its builders, adopted the standpoint of chivalry. ◇ ◇ ◇

But I saw in British imperialism room for roguery and stupidity as well as magnificence. A conquered people is a helpless people; and if they are of different physical type and another culture from their conquerors they cannot avail themselves of anything like the protection which would otherwise be given them by the current conceptions of justice and humanity. ◇ ◇ ◇ *

So much I had read in books. But in Yugoslavia I saw with my own eyes the German hatred of the Slavs: as a scar on the Slav peoples, in the chattering distraction of Croatia, and the lacerated moral beauty of Bosnia; as an abscess on a German soul, when Gerda

*[The author's long and brilliant summary of the "disadvantages of Empire" ranges back to Rome's conquests of Africa (to which she refers in her *St. Augustine*, above) and of the long-dead Illyria. It continues through Byzantium, the Turks, and Venice to the Habsburgs in Austria and currently, in 1941, to the Germans under Hitler. Much of this has appeared in other contexts in earlier portions of her book.]

looked on the seven thousand French graves at Bitolj and wounded a husband who had treated her with infinite tenderness by saying sourly, "To think of all those people giving their lives for a lot of Slavs"; as a womb swollen with murder, in the German war memorial at Bitolj. For the first time I knew the quality of the parties to this feud. I saw the solemn and magnificent embroideries of the Slav peasant women and knew what degeneration of skill and taste was represented by the bright little flowers and hearts on the Austrian belts that the skiers like to bring back from St Anton. I saw the Serbs, who make more sombre expeditions than open-air meals at little restaurants in the Wienerwald, who go in pilgrimage to the Frushka Gora and see defeat itself in the person of the Tsar Lazar, laid in a golden shroud: it is headless, as defeat should be, since it is a frustration of personality, but its hands are preserved, as is fitting, for it is the hand that is the sign of humanity, that distinguishes man from all other animals, and it is conflict with defeat that divides human beings from the natural world. I saw the Serbs, to whom the subjects of the Habsburgs could certainly teach nothing. Twice the Serbs drove their would-be teachers out of Serbia, and being vanquished the third time, not so much by arms as by sickness and famine, fled through icy mountains to the sea, rested for a little space, then fought them a fourth time, and were victorious. Such is not the proper relationship between pupil and professor. I saw in Yugoslavia many people such as the mother of the idiot child at the tomb of Sveti Naum who said to us, "I don't know what to say to God about this, there's so much to say, I don't know where to begin, it's such a strange thing to have happened," and the old woman who walked on the mountain road in Montenegro, asking the skies, "If I had to live, why should my life have been like this?" There were others, such as Militsa, who is a poet and a scholar and a woman of the world, yet recognizably the sister of these women, to prove that they were not merely exhibiting a pristine excellence preserved by the lack of use, that their subtlety was no superficial bloom which would be brushed away by their first contact with modern civilization, that their stuff was of the sort that can achieve what is most cause for pride among human achievement. I knew that few Austrians had shown the degree of sensibility that would enable them to instruct such people, and that it would not have mattered if there had been few or many of them, for they would have recognized that people like these have no need to be instructed by other human beings, but can learn for themselves.

I said to myself quite often, as I wrestled with the material of this book, that now what was well would at last happen. For the old Turkey had gone and its successor had no interest in Empire, and Russia was a Union of Soviet Republics, and the Habsburgs were fallen; and the treaties of Versailles and Trianon and St Germain had set the small peoples free. Freedom was for these people an ecstasy. That I knew to be true, for I had seen it with my own eyes. Finland, Estonia, Latvia, Czechoslovakia, and Yugoslavia, they were all like young men stretching themselves at the open window in the early morning after long sleep. To eat in a public place in these countries, to walk in their public gardens, was to fill the nostrils with the smell of happiness. Nothing so fair has happened in all history as this liberation of peoples who, during centuries of oppression, had never forgotten their own souls, and by long brooding on their national lives had changed them from transitory experience to lasting and inspiring works of art. It is not even imaginable what they would have achieved, had they been given time to acquire the technique of self-government, for though there are free peoples, and these have contributed largely to civilization, they have been free because they were fortunate, and have not, like the Slavs and the Finns and the Balts, learned that wisdom which "is sold in the desolate market where none comes to buy, And in the withered fields where the farmer ploughs for bread in vain." ◇ ◇ ◇

◇ ◇ ◇ Only part of us is sane: only part of us loves pleasure and the longer day of happiness, wants to live to our nineties and die in peace, in a house that we built, that shall shelter those who come after us. The other half of us is nearly mad. It prefers the disagreeable to the agreeable, loves pain and its darker night despair, and wants to die in a catastrophe that will set back life to its beginnings and leave nothing of our house save its blackened foundations. Our bright natures fight in us with this yeasty darkness, and neither part is commonly quite victorious, for we are divided against ourselves and will not let either part be destroyed. This fight can be observed constantly in our personal lives. There is nothing rarer than a man who can be trusted never to throw away happiness, however eagerly he sometimes grasps it. In history we are as frequently interested in our own doom. Sometimes we search for peace, sometimes we make an effort to find convenient frontiers and a proper fulfilment for racial destinies; but sometimes we insist on war, sometimes we stamp into

749

the dust the only foundations on which we can support our national lives. We ignore this suicidal strain in history because we are consistently bad artists when we paint ourselves, we prettify our wills and pretend they are not parti-coloured before the Lord. We pretend that the Thirty Years' War disappointed the hope of those who engineered it because it brought famine to Central Europe, famine so extreme that whole villages were given over to silence and the spreading weed, so extreme that bands of desperate men waylaid travellers and ate their flesh. Yet perhaps these engineers of war did not like villages, and felt queasy at the thought of a society enjoying wholesome meals. It seems that, choked with our victory in the last war, we now have an appetite for defeat. The new states were full of of life, Yugoslavia shook its clenched fists and swore it meant to live. Therefore England and America and France turned away, for what lived disgusted them; they wanted a blanched world, without blood, given over to defeat. ◇ ◇ ◇

History, it appeared, could be like the delirium of a madman, at once meaningless and yet charged with a dreadful meaning; and there existed a new agent to face this character of our age and intensify it. The kind of urban population which Mussolini and Hitler represented had been drawn away from the countryside to work on the production and distribution of machinery and manufactured goods; and this mechanical effort had given us the aeroplane. It was the dictators' perfect tool. For by raining bombs on the great cities it could gratify the desire of the mass to murder the mass; and by that same act it would destroy the political and economic centres of ancient states with pasts that told a long continuous story, and thus make an assault on mind, tradition, and what makes the settled hearth. Such warfare must mean ruin for all, for mass was nearly balanced by mass, and because it would be beyond the power of the world to rebuild what it had taken centuries and unclouded faith in destiny to build, save in an equal number of centuries and by an equal poetical achievement of the soul. But experience of this would not avail to stop these wars, for this was the gibbering phase of our human cycle, and defeat and extinction would be as eagerly pursued as victory. This I could deduce from the facts I was working on, and it was confirmed by the newspapers every day I wrote. These recorded the advance of a state of universal and imbecile war and worse beside. For they recorded the rehearsal of such a conflict, carried on openly and unimpeded by

Germany and Italy on Spanish soil, while the powers it threatened, though still splendid with inherited strength, sat by in cataleptic quiet.

In the country it sometimes happens that the sleeper awakes to an unaccustomed stillness. It is as if silence stretched for miles above him, miles around him; and daybreak does not bring the usual sounds. He goes to his window and finds that the world is under snow. White the lawn, white the trees, white the fields beyond, black the frozen water on the path. No birds and beasts are abroad, and no labourer comes out to work. Nothing is heard but the singing of the blood in the ears, and in a pure light forms stand forth in their purity. The air, too, is cleansed by cold and is like absolution in the nostrils. Such sounds as there are, as the cry of a wild swan, such motions as there are, as the lope of a grey squirrel over the roadway, are more than they would be in a less lustrated world. That day, that week, the next week, the snowfall is an austere and invigorating delight, but if month passes month, and the snow still lies and the waters are still black, life is threatened. Such snows and ice are well on the heights which are frequented only for adventure, but ill on the lowlands where the human process is carried on. The cattle cannot drink when the springs are frozen at their sources, the sheep cannot find the hidden grass, seed cannot be sown in the adamantine earth, the fruit trees cannot put forth their buds. If the snow does not melt and the waters flow, beauty becomes a steely bondage and then a doom, by which all animals must die, and man among them. We tell ourselves, when the whiteness lasts too long, that all seasons have their term and that the spring has always come in time; and so it happened this year and last year. But it may not happen so next year. Winter has often made this visit that far outstays safety and consumes leaf and flower and fruit and loin. Snow has covered first threshold, then windows, then chimneys, of many an upland farm, enclosing at the last a silence that does not thaw in the spring sunshine. Sometimes fields and orchards that had not been thought to lie too high have been burned by cold as by fire, and those who tended them have gone down starving to the plain. And there was once an Ice Age.

In England there was such a stillness, such a white winter of the spirit, and such a prolongation of it that death was threatened. It would have been expected, with fascist Italy and Nazi Germany crying out to kill, and England being what they both needed to kill, that there would be much bustling to and fro on the building of defences, that there would be shouts of warning, proclamations, calls to arms, debates on strategy. But there was silence, and no movement. It was as though a pall of nullity covered all the land, as if the springs of the national will were locked fast in frost. Certainly some people cried out in fear and anger against the dictators, but they were drawn from those who had detached themselves from the main body of Englishmen, some because they were better, some because they were worse. But the main body itself lay in an inertia in which, at first, there was reason for hope. For before England could attain mastery over her time she had to suffer a profound alteration from her bustling polychrome Victorian self, which was infinitely credulous regarding her own wisdom, that would assume, at a moment's notice and without the slightest reflection, the responsibility of determining the destiny of the most remote and alien people, whose material and spiritual circumstances were completely unknown to her. She needed to learn that action is not everything, that contemplation is necessary for the discovery of the way and for the refinement of the will. She needed to be still for a time and surrender herself to the mystical knowledge which cannot give instruction while logic, with its louder voice, holds the floor. It was good that she should lie under quiescence as under snow, that there should be no coming and going, that the air should be cleansed by scepticism, and that only the simplest and most fundamental activities should be carried on, to reveal the essential qualities which had been forgotten in the more crowded days. There could have been no greater misfortune for England than that the period of inactivity which was superintended by Lord Baldwin should have so perfectly resembled in outward appearances that period which would have been a necessary preliminary to her regeneration. For it might have been that a party which belonged to the past was confessing its inability to cope with the present, and was waiting to yield stoically and without fruitless struggles to the new and appropriate forces.

But the quietness lasted too long. The new forces did not emerge. The obsolete party did not mean to yield power. On the contrary, it gripped the nation's throat with a tenacity that was terrifying, because it pertained to another realm than life. For the grip of a living man must relax if he grow tired; it is only ghostly hands that, without term, can continue to clench. But these were not honest ghosts, for had they been such they would have re-enacted the pomp of Elizabeth's power; even if the dust lay thick on the national stage, they would have repeated the imperturbable insolence of Victoria, even if the words came hollow from the fleshless thorax. They were, however, as much strangers to all tradition of English pride as though they were alien in blood. Mussolini and Hitler threw courtesy away and yelled at our statesmen as waiters in a cheap foreign restaurant might yell at kitchen boys. Their peoples accepted from them, almost without dissent, a gospel which was in essence a call to the destruction of the British Empire and its regeneration in a baser form, and that this word was to be made flesh, and that bleeding and lacerated flesh, was proved by the tearing up of treaties and the re-creation of forbidden armies. The prospect was unprecedented in its horror, because the mindless, traditionless, possessionless urban proletariat was delighted by the prospect of making airwarfare. In Germany and Italy the people as a whole licked their lips over the promise of air warfare that was held out to them by their leaders. But the governors of England hardly stirred. Their faces were bland bags. They gave no orders for our defence. Although not one sane man in the continent of Europe but knew that soon England would be bombed from the air, we built no planes.

The farmer's family, when the snow rises above the threshold and above the windows and still does not thaw, must have felt as we did. Violence is the more terrible when it comes softly, when there is no sound but the throbbing of the alarmed blood in the ears. But our woe was worse than would be known by the victims of a natural catastrophe, for it was not nature that was handing us over to death, but people of our own blood, people of a class whom we looked on with a filial trust. We knew that they would bully us out of claiming our full adult privileges when we came of age, we knew that they would make us pay them too much of our weekly wages as a return for providing us with a home, but we trusted them to act in any last resort as our loyal parents, who would fight to the death in the defence of their young. But here came death, and they did not defend us. Rather was it that they had taken away our weapons and bound our arms to our sides and opened the door to our enemies, saying, "Yes, we have them ready for you, we have trussed them up for killing, you will have no trouble with them."

Many of us thought then that our governors were consciously betraying us because they wished to establish a totalitarian system in this country, and were eager to co-operate with Nazi Germany and fascist Italy in the enslavement of Europe. Indeed thus alone could there be explained the British policy of "non-intervention" in the

Spanish Civil War, which was in fact a furtive discouragement of any action, however licit, that might have aided the survival of an independent and friendly Spain, and a furtive encouragement of all actions, however illegal, that enabled our natural enemies the Germans and Italians to establish themselves on both flanks of our natural allies the French. To some small degree the allegation of treachery was valid. The coarser kinds of rogue love money, and the City therefore must inevitably hold a high proportion of them; and these were solidly pro-Nazi and pro-fascist. Finance certainly threw some considerable influence on the side of complete surrender to Germany, on condition that the wealth of England be allowed to remain in the same hands as before. There were also certain influences in the Foreign Office which were against the defence of England. The British Minister to a certain Danubian country never ceased throughout his tenure of office to carry on fervent propaganda in favour of the Nazi plan for dismembering this country; and an attaché at a certain important Central European Legation made a point of intercepting visitors and urging on them the manifest superiority of the German people to all others, the wrongs it had suffered from the Peace Treaty, and the necessity for showing penitence by giving the Nazis all they demanded. But these were as much exceptions to the general mood as was a desire to arm against the dictators. The governors of England have proved beyond doubt their innocence of that particular crime. If they had wished to establish fascism they would certainly have attempted a *coup d'état* in the days of shame and bewilderment that followed Munich. But from that action, as indeed from all others, they refrained.

Now it was plain that it was not sleep which made the earth so still; it was death. As extreme cold can burn like fire, so an unmeasured peace was stamping out life after the fashion of war. Presently war itself would come, but it would destroy only what had already been destroyed. Our houses would fall on our broken bodies; but it was long since our hearthstones had been warm, and our bodies were as destitute of will as corpses. Under an empty sky lay an empty England. There is a pretence that this was not so, that Munich was not negative but positive, that Neville Chamberlain signed the treaty because he knew his country to be unprepared for war and therefore wanted to gain time for rearmament. If this were true it would still not acquit him of blame, since he had been a member of the Government which was responsible for the lack of arms; but it is a lie.

He and his colleagues made no use of the respite to defend their people. Here and there individuals who individually loved life worked frantically in the Army, in the Navy, in the Air Force, in the factories; but the mass of England was still inert. Our governors stood beside us as we lay bound and helpless at their feet, smiling drunkenly without the reasonable excuse of consumed alcohol, while the strange treacherous spirit which possessed them continued to issue invitations to our enemies, saying, "Come quickly and finish them now, they can do nothing against you."

I, like all my kind, who could read and write and had travelled, was astonished. But as I looked round on this desolate historical land-scape, which was desert beyond my gloomiest anticipation of where my ill fortune might bring me, it was not unfamiliar. "I have been here before," I said; and that was true, for I had stood on the plain of Kossovo. I had walked on the battle-field where Christian rulers, faced with those who desired to destroy their seed and their faith and their culture, resigned themselves without need to defeat, not from cowardice, not from treachery, but in obedience to some serene appetite of the soul, which felt fully sanctified in demanding its gratification. The difference between Kossovo in 1389 and England in 1939 lay in time and place and not in the events experienced, which resembled each other even in details of which we of the later catastrophe think as peculiar to our nightmare. There was in both the strange element of a gratuitous submission to a new menace of a technical sort. Even as the Nazis threatened us by their ardently prepared Air Force, so the Turks subdued the Balkan peoples by their ferocious and ingenious use of cavalry; and even as the English, though they made good guns and planes and were good artillerymen and aviators, built up no defences against attack from the air, so the Balkan peoples, though they had horses and a fine tradition of horse-manship and a long acquaintance with Turkish methods of warfare, gathered together no appropriate counter-forces. There was in both the same vertiginous spectacle of a steep gradient slanting from un-challenged supremacy down to abjection; the great Serbian Emperor Stephen Dushan, who was the most powerful monarch in the Europe of his time, died only thirty-four years before Kossovo, Munich was only thirty-seven years after the funeral of Queen Victoria.

Defeat, moreover, must mean to England the same squalor that it had meant to Serbia. Five centuries hence gentleness would be for-gotten by our people; loutish men would bind ploughshares to their women's backs and walk beside them unashamed, we would grow careless of our dung, ornament and the use of foreign tongues and the discoveries made by the past genius of our race would be phantoms that sometimes troubled the memory; and over the land would lie the foul jetsam left by the receding tide of a conquering race. In a *Denkmal* erected to a German aviator the descendant of his sergeant in the sixteenth generation, a wasted man called Hans with folds of skin instead of rolls of fat at the back of his neck, would show a coffin under a rotting swastika flag, and would praise the dead in a set, half-comprehended speech, and point at faded photographs on the peeling wall, naming the thin one Göring and the fat one Goebbels; and about the tomb of a murdered *Gauleiter* women wearing lank blonde plaits, listless with lack of possessions, would picnic among the long grasses in some last recollection of the Strength Through Joy movement, and their men would raise flimsy arms in the Hitler salute, should a tourist come by, otherwise saving the effort. In the towns homeless children, children of homeless children, themselves of like parentage, would slip into eating-houses and grovel on the dirty floor for cigarette-butts dropped by diners reared in a society for long ignorant of the nice. That is defeat, when a people's economy and culture is destroyed by an invader; that is conquest, that is what happens when a people travels too far from the base where it has struck its roots.

It seemed that there was no help for us; for the Government was contriving our defeat, was beyond reason and beyond pity, caught up in a painful, brooding exaltation, like the Tsar Lazar.

> There flies a grey bird, a falcon,
> From Jerusalem the holy,
> And in his beak he bears a swallow.

◇ ◇ ◇

> When the Tsar read the words,
> The Tsar pondered, and he pondered thus:
> "Dear God, where are these things, and how are they?
> What kingdom shall I choose?
> Shall I choose a heavenly kingdom?
> Shall I choose an earthly kingdom?
> If I choose an earthly kingdom,
> An earthly kingdom lasts only a little time,
> But a heavenly kingdom will last for eternity
>   and its centuries."

756

So the Tsar chose a heavenly kingdom and the ruin of all his people.

Then the Turks overwhelmed Lazar
And the Tsar Lazar was destroyed,
And his army was destroyed with him,
Of seven and seventy thousand soldiers.

All was holy and honourable,
And the goodness of God was fulfilled.

So it had been at Kossovo, and so it was in England now. . . .*

---

*[The closing pages cover the Yugoslav resistance and the Hitler take-over. The Dedication to the book, written in 1941, reads:]

TO MY FRIENDS IN YUGOSLAVIA,
WHO ARE NOW ALL DEAD OR ENSLAVED

Καὶ τὴν ποθεινὴν πατρίδα παράσχου αὐτοῖς,
Παραδείσου πάλιν ποιῶν πολίτας αὐτούς.

Grant to them the Fatherland of their desire,
and make them again citizens of Paradise.

APPENDIX
Biographical Note

Bibliography

INDEX

Biographical Note

Cicily Isabel Fairfield was born December 21, 1892, in London. Her father had come from County Kerry, Ireland; she acquired her early education in Edinburgh. She adopted her pen name, Rebecca West, from the strong-willed character of that name in Ibsen's social drama, *Rosmersholm*, in which she once acted in her late teens. She began to appear in print as a journalist and political writer in London as early as 1911, in *The Freewoman*, and was soon deeply involved in the causes of feminism and social reform. These interests were prominent in her journalism, and later were echoed in her fiction, her biographical writings, criticism, satire, travel, and history, which have alternated and supplemented each other throughout her long career.

Her first book, *Henry James*, was published in 1916, the year of James' death. An annotated list of her published books appears in the bibliography that follows. Her latest novel, incomplete and unpublished up to the time of appearance of a portion in this *Celebration*, is announced as *This Real Night*, a sequel to *The Fountain Overflows*.

Her only child, Anthony West (b. 1914), was the son of the novelist H. G. Wells. In 1930 she married Henry Maxwell Andrews, the banker, and began a lifelong companionship at their country house, Ibstone, in Buckinghamshire; with visits to London, and on many travels together, including the journey to Yugoslavia that inspired *Black Lamb and Grey Falcon*, her two-volume *magnum opus*. She was honoured as a D.B.E. (Dame Commander, Order of the British Empire) in 1959. After her husband's death in 1968 she moved to London, where she has continued to make her home, with intermittent travels to the United States, Mexico, and the Middle East. In official biographical entries she has chosen to list the following among her other awards and affiliations:

Member, Order of St. Sava. 1937.
Chevalier, Legion of Honour, 1957.
Fellow 1947, Benson Medallist 1967, and Companion of Literature 1968: Royal Society of Literature.
Honorary D. Litt., New York University, 1965.
Honorary Member, American Academy of Arts and Letters, 1972.
Dame Commander, Order of the British Empire (D.B.E.), 1959.

Bibliography

I. FICTION

The Return of the Soldier. New York: The Century Co., 1918; London: Nisbet & Co., 1918.

The Judge. London: Hutchinson & Co., 1922; New York: George H. Doran Company, 1922.

Harriet Hume: A London Fantasy. London: Hutchinson & Co., 1929; Garden City, New York: Doubleday, Doran & Company, Inc., 1929.

War Nurse: The True Story of a Woman Who Lived, Loved and Suffered on the Western Front. New York: Cosmopolitan Book Corporation, 1930. Anon.

The Harsh Voice: Four Short Novels. London: Jonathan Cape, 1935; Garden City, New York: Doubleday, Doran & Company, Inc., 1935. Life Sentence, There is No Conversation, The Salt of the Earth, The Abiding Vision.

The Thinking Reed. New York: The Viking Press, 1936; London: Hutchinson & Co., 1936; reissued by Macmillan & Co., London, 1966.

The Fountain Overflows. New York: The Viking Press, 1956; London: Macmillan & Co., 1957.

The Birds Fall Down. London: Macmillan & Co., 1966; New York: The Viking Press, 1966.

II. NON-FICTION

Henry James ("Writers of the Day Series," edited by Bertram Christian). London: Nisbet & Co., 1916; New York: Henry Holt and Company, 1916.

The Strange Necessity: Essays and Reviews. London: Jonathan Cape, 1928; Garden City, New York: Doubleday, Doran & Company, Inc., 1928. The Strange Necessity, Sinclair Lewis Introduces Elmer Gantry, Uncle Bennett, Sherwood Anderson, Poet, The Classic Artist.

Ending in Earnest: A Literary Log. New York: Doubleday, Doran & Co., 1931. Rescued from Excess, Concerning the Censorship, Another Kind of Censorship, Manibus Date Lilia Plenis, The Hardy Fleur-de-Lis, And Again, The Dead Hand, Feminist Revolt, Old and New, Journey's End, The Dutch Exhibition, Ravel, Toller, Notes on the Effect of Women Writers on Mr. Max Beerbohm, "Journey's End" Again, Rapt Out of Time, Prizes and Handicaps, Gosse, Mr. Smithers, Oranges to

Oranges, O. M., Ex Multis Unum, Pervigilium Veneris, Head of a Girl, Every Third Thought, Increase and Multiply, Striking Example of the Power of the Machine Age Over Thought, Miss Gye, Curious Idolatry, Formidable, Triumph or Error, Gide, Autumn and V. Woolf, Seeing Snakes, Evelyn Waugh, Elementary Considerations, Maurice and Constant Lambert, The Pitoëffs, Valentine Tessier, French Life and the French Stage, Le Monsieur aux Camélias, Elegy (D. H. Lawrence), Regretfully.

St. Augustine (a biography). London: Peter Davies Limited, 1933; New York: Appleton & Co., 1933.

Black Lamb and Grey Falcon: A Journey through Yugoslavia. New York: The Viking Press, 1941; (with subtitle, *The Record of a Journey through Yugoslavia in 1937*) London: Macmillan & Co., 1942.

The Meaning of Treason. New York: The Viking Press, 1947; London: Macmillan & Co., 1949. The Revolutionary, The Insane Root, The Children, The Epilogue. *The Meaning of Treason,* 2nd ed. London: Macmillan & Co., 1952. (Additional penultimate essay: The New Phase.)

The New Meaning of Treason. New York: The Viking Press, 1964; (with title, *The Meaning of Treason, revised edition*) London: Macmillan & Co., 1965. The Revolutionary, The New Phase, The Decline and Fall of Treason, Conclusion.

A Train of Powder. New York: The Viking Press, 1955; London: Macmillan & Co., 1955. Greenhouse with Cyclamens I (1946), II (1949), III (1954). Opera in Greenville (1947), Mr. Setty and Mr. Hume (1950), The Better Mousetrap (1953).

The Court and the Castle: some treatments of a recurrent theme. New Haven: Yale University Press, 1957; (with subtitle *A Study of the Interactions of Political and Religious Ideas in Imaginative Literature*) London: Macmillan & Co., 1958.

III. BOOKS WITH DAVID LOW

Lions and Lambs. 27 cartoons by Low with interpretations by "Lynx" (pseudonym). London: Jonathan Cape, 1928; New York: Harcourt, Brace & Company, 1929.

The Modern "Rake's Progress." 12 paintings by Low, words by Rebecca West. London: Hutchinson & Co., 1934.

IV. PUBLISHED LECTURES, PAMPHLETS, LIMITED EDITIONS, ETC.

D. H. Lawrence. London: Martin Secker, 1930; (with title, *Elegy*) New York: Phoenix Book Shop, 1930 (included in *Ending in Earnest,* 1931).

Arnold Bennett Himself ("John Day Pamphlets Series"). New York: The John Day Company, 1931.

A *Letter to a Grandfather* (an essay; "Hogarth Letters Series," no. 7). London: L. & V. Woolf at the Hogarth Press, 1933.

The Vassall Affair. London: The Sunday Telegraph, 1963.

McLuhan and the Future of Literature. Presidential Address. London: The English Association, 1969.

V. ANTHOLOGIES AND PUBLISHED SYMPOSIUMS TO WHICH REBECCA WEST CONTRIBUTED

(excluding those that have appeared in her own books)

"Women as Brainworkers." In *Women and the Labour Party*, edited and with an introduction by Dr. Marion Phillips. London: Headley Bros. Publishers, Ltd., 1918.

"The World's Worst Failure." In *The Woman Question*, edited by T. R. Smith. New York: Boni and Liveright, Inc., Publishers, 1919.

"My Religion." In Arnold Bennett et al., *My Religion*. London: Hutchinson & Co., 1925; New York: D. Appleton and Company, 1926.

"Tradition in Criticism." In *Tradition and Experiment in Present-Day Literature*. London: City Literary Institute, 1929; New York: Oxford University Press, 1929.

"Divorce Is a Necessity." In Bertrand Russell et al., *Divorce as I See It*. London: Noel Douglas, 1930; New York: The John Day Company, 1930.

"They that Sit in Darkness." In *The Fothergill Omnibus*, with introductions by John Fothergill, R. G. Collingwood, and G. Gould. London: Eyre and Spottiswoode, 1931; (with title *Mr. Fothergill's Plot: His Conspirators*) New York: Oxford University Press, 1931.

"Woman as Artist and Thinker." In *Woman's Coming of Age: A Symposium*, edited by S. D. Schmalhausen and V. F. Calverton. New York: Liveright, Inc., 1931.

"Charlotte Brontë." In *The Great Victorians*, edited by H. J. Massingham and Hugh Massingham. London: Ivor Nicholson & Watson, Ltd., 1932; New York: Doubleday, Doran & Company, Inc., 1932.

"Blessed Are the Pure in Heart." In *Ventures in Contemporary Reading*, edited by L. W. Smith, V. H. Ogburn, and H. F. Watson. New York, London, and Toronto: Longmans, Green and Co., 1932.

"Mrs. Pankhurst." In *The Post-Victorians*, with an introduction by W. R. Inge. London: Ivor Nicholson & Watson, Ltd., 1933.

"The Necessity and Grandeur of the International Ideal." In Philip Noel Baker et al., *Challenge to Death*. London: Constable & Co., Ltd., 1934, and New York, 1935.

"A Foreword on Lytton Strachey." In *The Woollcott Reader: Bypaths in the Realms of Gold*. New York: The Viking Press, 1935.

"Parody Party." In E. C. Bentley et al., *Parody Party*, edited by L. Russell. London: Hutchinson and Co., Ltd., 1936.

"The Woman in Industry." In *The New Republic: Anthology 1915-35*, edited by G. Conklin, with an introduction by B. Bliven. New York: Dodge Publishing Co., 1936.

"Mind and Materialism." In F. Swinnerton et al., *The University of Books*. London: Newnes, 1936.

"Elizabeth Montagu." In *From Anne to Victoria*, edited by Bonamy Dobrée. London: Cassell and Co., Ltd., 1937; New York: Charles Scribner's Sons, 1937.

"Snobbery." In W. R. Inge et al., *The English Genius: A Survey of the English Achievement and Character*, edited by H. Kingsmill. London: Eyre and Spottiswoode, 1938.

"The Duty of the Writer." In *Writers in Freedom: A Symposium*, edited by H. Ould. London: Hutchinson & Co., Ltd., 1942.

"I Believe." In W. H. Auden et al., *I Believe*. London: George Allen & Unwin Ltd., 1940.

"The Second Commandment." In Thomas Mann et al., *The Ten Commandments: Ten Short Novels of Hitler's War Against the Moral Code*, edited by A. L. Robinson, with a preface by Herman Rauschning. New York: Simon and Schuster, 1943; London: Cassell and Co., Ltd., 1945.

"A Day in Town." In *The New Yorker Book of War Pieces*. New York: Reynal & Hitchcock, 1947.

"The Englishman Abroad." In *The Character of England*, edited by Ernest Barker. Oxford: Clarendon Press, 1947.

"Goodness Doesn't Just Happen." In *This I Believe* [Vol I]: *The Living Philosophies of One Hundred Thoughtful Men and Women in All Walks of Life*, edited by E. P. Morgan, with a preface by Edward R. Murrow. New York: Simon and Schuster, 1925.

"Encounter." In *International Literary Annual No. 1*, edited by John Wain. London: John Calder, 1958.

"The Event and Its Image." In Royal Society of Literature, *Essays by Divers Hands*, edited by Peter Green. London: Oxford University Press, 1962.

VI. BOOKS BY OTHER AUTHORS WITH INTRODUCTIONS BY REBECCA WEST

Austen, Jane. *Northanger Abbey*, preface by Rebecca West ("Traveller's Library Series"). London: Jonathan Cape, 1932.

Causton, Bernard, and Young, G. Gordon. *Keeping It Dark or the Censor's Handbook*, preface by Rebecca West. London: Mandrake Press, 1930.

Chapman, Hester W., and Princess Romanovsky-Pavlovsky, eds. *Diversion*, introduction by Rebecca West. London: Collins, 1946.

Coyle, Kathleen. *Liv* (a novel), introduction by Rebecca West. London: Jonathan Cape, 1929.

Gissing, George R. *Workers in the Dawn*, introduction by Rebecca West. New York: The Bowling Green Press, 1930.

Jewett, Sarah Orne. *The Only Rose and Other Tales*, introduction by Rebecca West ("Traveller's Library Series"). London: Jonathan Cape, 1937.

Sandburg, Carl. *Selected Poems*. Edited by Rebecca West. New York: Harcourt Brace, 1926; London: Jonathan Cape, 1926.

VII. BOOKS ON REBECCA WEST

Hutchinson, G. Evelyn. *A Preliminary List of the Writings of Rebecca West: 1912–1951*. New Haven: Yale University Press, 1957.

Orlich, Mary Margarita, Sister. *The Novels of Rebecca West: A Complex Unity*. Ph.D. dissertation on microfilm, The University of Notre Dame, 1966.

Rubin, D. S. *The Recusant Myth in Modern Fiction*. Ph.D. dissertation, University of Toronto, 1968.

Wolfe, Peter. *Rebecca West: Artist and Thinker* (Crosscurrents/modern critiques). Carbondale, Illinois: Southern Illinois University Press, 1971.

Wolfer, Verena E. *Rebecca West: Kunsttheorie und Romanschaffen*. Bern: Francke Verlag, 1972.

VIII. SOME ARTICLES AND REVIEWS ON REBECCA WEST

Adcock, St. John. "Rebecca West and Her Contemporaries." *The Bookman*, September 1958.

Connell, Brian. "Dame Rebecca West: A Critic in Perpetual Motion." *The Times*, London, September 1, 1975.

Davies, A. Powell. "The Bewitchment of Rebecca West." *The New Republic*, June 8, 1953.

Davis, Herbert. "The New Writers—Rebecca West." *Canadian Forum*, June 1931.

Ellmann, Mary. "The Russians of Rebecca West." *Atlantic Monthly*, December 1966.

Enright, D. J. "Rebecca West's Novels." *New Statesman*, November 1966.

BIBLIOGRAPHY

Feld, Rose C. "Rebecca West Explains It All." *The New York Times Book Review*, November 11, 1923.

Halper, Nathan. "James Joyce and Rebecca West." *Partisan Review*, July 1949.

Kalb, Bernhard. "Biographical Note on Rebecca West." *Saturday Review of Literature*, March 19, 1955.

Kobler, Turner S. "The Eclecticism of Rebecca West." *Critique: Studies in Modern Fiction*.

Rainer, Dachine. "The Scope of Rebecca West." *The New Republic*, November 25, 1957.

——. "Rebecca West: Disturber of the Peace." *Commonweal*, May 10, 1968.

Thompson, C. Patrick. "The New Rebecca West." *New York Herald Tribune Magazine*, February 7, 1932.

Walpole, Hugh. "Some Younger English Novelists." *The Bookman*, May 1925.

Webster, Harvey Curtis. "A Visit with Rebecca West." *Saturday Review of Literature*, December 8, 1956.

IX. OTHER

Van Druten, J. *The Return of the Soldier*. A play in 3 acts adapted from Rebecca West's novel. London: Victor Gollancz, 1928.

INDEX

In this selective index, the principal characters from Rebecca West's own fiction are alphabetized by their first names if they commonly appear so in the stories. In the nonfiction, actual people and main events are listed in the normal way. Titles of Dame Rebecca's own books included in the text appear in the Table of Contents; her other titles are in the Bibliography. Names of other authors, artists, and composers mentioned are listed in full; titles of their works, listed separately, are usually identified only by the surname. All place-names are included for her travels in *Black Lamb and Grey Falcon*, but not for her other books.

Abélard, Peter, 744
Absent-minded Beggar, The (Kipling), 441
Adelphi (periodical), 394
Adeodatus (son of Augustine), 176, 189, 190, 196
Admiral, The (father of seven daughters named for ships in *Parthenope*, 469–96)
Adriatic (sea), 563, 589, 590, 598, 614, 674, 736
Africa, 747. *See also* Augustine, St, *passim*, 159–236. African place-names not itemized separately here.
Albania, 570, 588, 671, 697, 703, 721, 723, 725–27, 729–30, 733–734
Albina (Melania's mother), 225–27
Alexander the Great, 251, 744
Alexander I, Tsar (of Russia), 610
Alexander I, King (of Yugoslavia), 552, 564, 566–68, 571, 593, 651
Alice Darrell ("Aunt Alice" to "Uncle Arthur" in *Parthenope*, 469–96)
Alice Pemberton (wife of Jimmy in *The Salt of the Earth*, 69–111)
Alverstone, Viscount, 332
Alypius, Bishop of Thagaste, 166, 183, 186, 188, 189, 192, 193, 194, 195, 196, 197, 225–27, 232

Ambrose, St, Bishop of Milan, 184, 185–86, 187, 188, 191, 192, 195, 196–97, 201–202, 207–208, 225
Amerika (Kafka), 412, 420
Amurath. *See* Murad, Sultan
And Even Now (Beerbohm), 387
André de Verviers (a suitor of Isabelle in *The Thinking Reed*, 115–55)
Andrews, Henry Maxwell, 115; "my husband" (*Black Lamb and Grey Falcon*, *passim*, 551–757)
Andriyevitsa (Montenegro), 732–33
Androcles and the Lion (Shaw), 449
Andronnikov, Prince, 363–64
Andrus, Colonel, 252
Angelina, Duchess (daughter of Skanderbeg), 671, 672
Anna Karenina (Tolstoy), 436
Anthony, St, 193, 194; Confraternity of, 603
"Apis," of the "Black Hand" (Dragutin Dimitriyevitch), 654
Apuleius, Lucius, 173–74, 178, 219–20
Aquinas, St Thomas, 210, 390
Arethusa (a daughter of the Admiral in *Parthenope*, 469–96)
Arians, 620–21
Arran, Earl of, 351, 353